ALLE ZEIT WACH
1842

Cognitive Psychotherapy

Theory and Practice

Edited by

C. Perris, I.M. Blackburn, and H. Perris

With 15 Figures

Springer-Verlag
Berlin Heidelberg New York
London Paris Tokyo

Professor Carlo Perris
Department of Psychiatry & WHO Collaborating
Centre for Research and Training in Mental Health,
University of Umeå,
S-901 85 Umeå, Sweden

Dr. Ivy M. Blackburn
MRC Brain Metabolism Unit, Royal Edinburgh Hospital,
Edinburgh, Scotland, United Kingdom

Professor Hjördis Perris
Department of Psychiatry,
Mariedal Cognitive Treatment Centre,
University of Umeå,
S-901 85 Umeå, Sweden

ISBN-13: 978-3-642-73395-6 e-ISBN-13: 978-3-642-73393-2
DOI: 10.1007/978-3-642-73393-2

Library of Congress Cataloging-in-Publication Data. Cognitive psychotherapy: theory and practice/edited by C. Perris, I.M. Blackburn, and H. Perris. p. cm. Includes index. ISBN-13: 978-3-642-73395-6 1. Cognitive therapy. I. Perris, Carlo. II. Blackburn, I.M. (Ivy Marie), 1939– . III. Perris, H. (Hjördis), 1940– . RC489.C63C647 1988 616.89'14-dc 19 88-24790

Softcover reprint of the hardcover 1st edition 1988

Typesetting: Overseas Typographers, Inc., Makati, Philippines

2126/3130-543210 – Printed on acid-free paper

Preface

Developed in the early 1960s by Aaron Beck and Albert Ellis in the USA, mostly for the short-term treatment of patients suffering from emotional disorders, cognitive psychotherapy has rapidly expanded both in its scope and geographically.

In fact, when attending recent European conferences relating to psychotherapy, for example, those organized by the European Association of Behaviour Therapy and the European Branch of the Society for Psychotherapy Research, the 13th International Congress of Psychotherapy, and the two international conferences on cognitive psychotherapy which took place in Lisbon in 1980 and in Umeå in 1986, one could not but become aware of the active interest in cognitive theory and practice on the European continent. It is stimulating to find that cognitive approaches to the understanding of human emotion and behaviour, which find their origin in the writings of the ancients as well as in eighteenth-century philosophers, principally Kant, are no longer a strictly transatlantic movement.

As the chapters of this handbook demonstrate, researchers and clinicians from many different European countries have been developing the theoretical aspects of the cognitive theory of the emotional disorders and applying it in their practice. These chapters can of course represent but a sample of all the work being carried out, but we hope that they will be both informative and stimulating to researchers and therapists on both sides of the Atlantic.

The theoretical section develops current models in cognitive abnormal psychology – the systems approach, information processing and psychophysiology, constructivism and attachment theory. Although principally theoretical in orientation, the chapters in this section focus on clinical examples and experiments and, more importantly, suggest further experiments for empirical validation. The chapter on cognitive measures in the area of depression underscores the need for valid instruments to test theoretical propositions.

The bulk of the book describes practical applications of cognitive therapy, with special emphasis on new clinical areas which further expand the scope of cognitive therapy. The best-known and validated application of cognitive therapy is individual therapy with the adult depressed patient. Since this topic has been repeatedly treated in other books, we decided not to include such a chapter in this handbook, but to concentrate instead on how cognitive therapy can be used with other populations of psychiatric patients suffering from different psychopathological illnesses. However, comparative studies are still needed to test the relative efficacy of cognitive therapy for these problems. Such studies, we know, are under way, and this book may inspire others to carry out more studies. The controlled trials of cognitive therapy in depression, which are thoroughly reviewed, indicate the type of studies that can be carried out and still need to be carried out.

The development of more sensitive measures would improve our understanding of the process of therapy and the delineation of cognitive vulnerability factors. The chapters on depression underscore the fact that it is depression which has received the most attention to date, so that if much more research is desirable in this field, cognitive research in other areas of psychopathology can be said to be still in its infancy. Finally, since adequate training in cognitive therapy is of paramount importance for both clinical and research purposes, a whole chapter is devoted to factors relevant to the training of cognitive therapists.

Our main aim in this handbook has been to bring together up-to-date reviews and original papers in cognitive therapy by authors from both sides of the Atlantic. It is hoped that these contributions will be of help to clinicians and researchers already working in this area and perhaps stimulate others to develop an interest in an approach which promises fruitful clinical application.

Umeå and Edinburgh, May 1988

C. Perris
I. M. Blackburn
H. Perris

Contents

C. PERRIS
The Foundations of Cognitive Psychotherapy and Its Standing in Relation to Other Psychotherapies 1

L.-G. LUNDH
Cognitive Therapy and the Analysis of Meaning Structures . 44

G. LIOTTI
Attachment and Cognition: A Guideline for the Reconstruction of Early Pathogenic Experiences in Cognitive Psychotherapy . 62

M. KOUKKOU
A Psychophysiological Information-Processing Model of Cognitive Dysfunction and Cognitive Treatment in Depression (With 2 Figures) 80

I. M. BLACKBURN
Cognitive Measures of Depression 98

T. C. STILES and K. G. GÖTESTAM
The Role of Cognitive Vulnerability Factors in the Development of Depression: Theoretical and Methodological Considerations (With 1 Table) 120

B. F. SHAW and D. WILSON-SMITH
Training Therapists in Cognitive-Behaviour Therapy (With 1 Figure and 1 Table) 140

I. M. BLACKBURN
An Appraisal of Comparative Trials of Cognitive Therapy for Depression (With 4 Tables) 160

J. COTTRAUX and E. MOLLARD
Cognitive Therapy of Phobias (With 2 Figures) 179

L. COVI, D. M. ROTH, J. H. PATTISON, and R. S. LIPMAN
Group Cognitive-Behavioral Therapy of Depression: Two Parallel Treatment Manuals for a Controlled Study (With 5 Tables) 198

A. Freeman
Cognitive Therapy of Personality Disorders:
General Treatment Considerations (With 2 Figures) 223

R. B. Jarrett and A. J. Rush
Cognitive Therapy for Panic Disorder
and Generalized Anxiety Disorder 253

L. Joyce-Moniz
Self-Talk, Dramatic Expression, and Constructivism
(With 2 Figures and 1 Table) 276

F. M. Mc Pherson
Cognitive Therapy for Bulimia 306

C. Perris
Intensive Cognitive-Behavioural Psychotherapy with Patients
Suffering from Schizophrenic Psychotic or Post-Psychotic
Syndromes: Theoretical and Practical Aspects
(With 3 Figures and 2 Tables) 324

P. M. Salkovskis and H. M. C. Warwick
Cognitive Therapy of Obsessive-Compulsive Disorder
(With 2 Figures and 6 Tables) 376

T. C. R. Wilkes
Cognitive Therapy with Depressed Adolescents
(With 1 Figure and 2 Tables) 396

Author Index 411

Subject Index 419

The Foundations of Cognitive Psychotherapy and Its Standing in Relation to Other Psychotherapies

C. PERRIS

Introduction

Cognitive psychotherapy, as originally conceived and developed by Beck and his followers (Beck 1963, 1964, 1976, 1985), is a now well-estabished method of treatment in many countries, where active training and research centres contribute to its further refinement and diffusion. National societies of cognitive psychotherapy have been established, meetings and symposia occur frequently, and a number of specialized journals are regularly issued. During recent decades substantial evidence has been accumulating that lends support both to the theoretical basis of cognitive psychotherapy and to its therapeutic effectiveness in the treatment of various kinds of psychopathological disorders. Its place among the powerful methods of treatment is properly acknowledged in modern psychiatric textbooks.

However, resistance continues against the realization that the emergence of cognitive psychotherapy and the development of its theoretical foundations represent a paradigmatic shift, in Kuhn's sense (Kuhn 1962), not only in the field of psychotherapy, but, very likely, as argued by the present author elsewhere (Perris 1985a), also across the whole field of understanding the development of psychopathological phenomena.

One of the ironies of paradigm clashes, as Kuhn noted, is the inevitable demand by each paradigm to compete on its own terms. That such demands are currently heard has been recently pointed out by Beck and Mahoney (1979), while the debate continues as to whether the focus on cognitions signifies a revolution in psychological thinking (Dember 1974; Beck 1976; Mahoney 1977) or represents merely a passing phase (Wilson 1978). In the context of this debate, cognitive psychotherapy is often referred to either as a further development of behaviour therapy (Wilson 1978) or as a kind of therapy somewhere between psychoanalytically oriented psychotherapy and behaviour therapy – apparently without any full understanding of its unique characteristics (Liotti and Reda 1981). On the other hand, whereas cognitive psychotherapy is criticized by behaviourists and by dogmatic psychoanalysts with mutually antagonistic arguments, both behaviour therapy and psychoanalysis are themselves becoming increasingly cognitive. However auspicious this trend toward convergence may seem, the differentiation of cognitive psychotherapy from the other two major therapy systems,

Umeå University, Dept. of Psychiatry & WHO Collaborating Centre for Research and Training in Mental Health, S-90185 Umeå, Sweden

as already pointed out by Beck (1970, 1976) and Ryle (1984), must be further stressed in order to avoid theoretical and methodological confusion (Liotti and Reda 1981).

This chapter was conceived in the realization that misconceptions as to the true position of cognitive psychotherapy still occur and in attempts to dissipate some of the most common misunderstandings. Indeed, since the claim of being "cognitive" is increasingly frequent in various quarters, a clear demarcation of cognitive psychotherapy from other psychotherapeutic systems must be explicitly articulated. The scope of the present chapter will therefore be rather wide. First, a short review will consider historical sources of the guiding principles of cognitive psychotherapy. Secondly, a sketch of the system of cognitive psychotherapy in its various aspects will be presented. Finally, a comparison will be made between cognitive psychotherapy and the other major therapeutic systems.

Philosophical Foundations

Probably no other ancient philosopher has been quoted more frequently in the cognitive literature than the freed Roman slave, Epictetus (born 60 A.D.). The most widely used quotations have come from his *Handbook on the Art of Living* (*Encheiridion*), composed by his most productive pupil, Arrianus. In Chap. 5, for instance, Epictetus maintains that "men are not disturbed by things but by the opinions they make of them .... When we are impeded or disturbed or grieved let us never blame others, but ourselves, that is, our opinions." As we shall see below, this perspective lies at the very core of cognitive psychotherapy. In fact, even if sometimes phrased in the other terms, Epictetus' view has remained prominent in the thinking of major philosophers both in the West and the East from ancient times to the present day. The actual importance of Epictetus' perspective, however, lies in its reflecting the priority which the Stoics placed upon acknowledging the subjective side of reality and upon recognizing the value of introspection.[1]

In a similar vein to that in which Plato's famous passage on dreams in the *Republic* and his metaphor of the chariot in *Phaedrus* anticipated some of Freud's conceptions,[2] the insights of Cicero (born 106 B.C.), Seneca (born 3 B.C.), Marcus Aurelius (121–181 A.D.), and other Stoics of antiquity form a cornerstone for that perspective which has become the foundation for cognitive psychotheraphy. Ellis,

[1]It should be emphasized that the *Encheiridion* also contains what could probably be regarded as the very first suggestion of "cognitive rehearsal" (Chap. 4). Also repeatedly discussed are thought distortions of the type known in cognitive psychotherapy as "personalizing" and "misattribution" (e.g. 1984, chaps. 25, 44).

[2]The passage in "the *Republic*" reads: "In sleep the wild beast in us, full-fed with meat or drink, becomes rampant and shakes off sleep to go in quest of what will gratify its own instincts .... In phantasy it will not shrink from intercourse with a mother or anyone else, man, god, or brute." In the *Phaedrus* the soul is compared to the joint forces of chariot and driver: "First of all, it is a team of two horses that the driver within us has to rein; furthermore is one of the horses noble and good, and of good origin whereas the other is of the opposite kind and origin."

for example, the proponent of the type of cognitive therapy known as rational-emotive therapy (RET; Ellis 1962) derived from the Stoics his major tenet: "There are virtually no legitimate reasons why human beings need make themselves terribly upset, hysterical, or emotionally disturbed, no matter what kind of negative stimuli are impinging on them" (Mahoney 1974).

Stoicism was introduced to the Romans by Cicero, who is credited (Mora 1975) with having presented one of the earliest detailed description of emotional disorders ("passions" in his terminology), and whose psychotherapeutic insights are still of value today. He emphasized in his *Tusculanarum Disputationum* (45 B.C.) that "discomfort (*aegritudo*) does not depend upon the objective reality of the things but on a subjective judgement of the mind" (III, XXVIII:71). "Thus, while the equilibrium of mind consists of knowledge, its disorders are the product of erroneous evaluations" (IV, XXXVII:79).

Cicero's opinions were echoed at the beginning of the Christian era by Seneca, who in one of his letters to Lucilius wrote: "Everything depends on one's opinion.... We suffer according to our opinion. One is as miserable as one believes oneself to be" (1966, 78:13, 14). Later, one of the last great Stoics of Roman, the Emperor Marcus Aurelius, referred to Epictetus as having been his philosophical mentor. In his *Reflections* Aurelius insisted on the importance of subjective opinions as a source of discomfort: "If you are pained by any external thing, it is not this thing that disturbs you, but your own judgement about it. But it is in your power to wipe out this judgement" (1948, VIII:47; cf. IV:3 and V:16). As other Stoics before him, Aurelius emphasized the importance of introspection (e.g. 1948, VI:11; VII:26–28). He should also be credited with one of the first observations on the importance of empathy; he wrote: "Make it your habit to listen as attentively as possible to what another tells you; and try as far as possible to enter into the mind of who is speaking" (1948, VI:53).

It is not possible to leave the context of ancient philosophy without mentioning those philosophers, especially Socrates, from whom cognitive psychotherapy has borrowed its main methodological approach, the dialectical deductive technique in the dialogue between therapist and patient. This has its origins in the work of Anaximander (born 610 B.C.), was later developed by Zeno of Elea (born 490 B.C.) and became the most distinguishing characteristics of Socrates' teaching. Socrates' method was based on putting forth hypotheses aimed at stimulating the independent thinking of his disciples – assisting them through "intelligent questions" in their deductions until a conclusion was reached. This method can be referred to as "majeutics" (midwifery) since it is comparable to the work of a midwife. An example of Socrates' teaching which has particular relevance for the methodology of cognitive psychotherapy can be found in Plato's *Meno*. In this dialogue Socrates succeeds in guiding one of the Meno's completely unskilled young slaves to draw a square with a surface exactly double that of a previously given square.

That cognitive-pscyhotherapeutic concepts and practices can be traced back to ancient Eastern philosophies and religions has recently been pointed out by MacHovec (1984). MacHovec draws parallels between the assignment of homework in cognitive psychotherapy and behaviour therapy, on the one hand, and, on the other, the use of *yanas*, which are purposefully planned physical actions to facilitate *satori* (that is, "a flash of insight") in Zen Buddhism. MacHovec also quotes from the Buddhist *Dhammapada*: "All we are is the result of what we have thought, it is founded on and made up by our thoughts." This echoes the views of the Stoics reported above.

The notion that we actively distort our view of reality was reinforced by Francis Bacon in his *Novum Organum Scientiarum* (1621), at the dawn of the scientific revolution. Bacon observed that: "All perceptions, both of the senses and the mind bear reference to man and not to the universe; and the human mind resembles those uneven mirrors which impart their own properties to different objects. . . and distort and disfigure them." In the preface to his unfinished monumental work (that he expected to replace Aristotles' textbook of logic, the *Organon*) Bacon maintained that "when we want to gain new insight, it must be our first concern to make us free from old prejudiced opinions."[3] To achieve this goal Bacon proposed the use of the inductive method of scientific research.

Neu (1977) has recently presented a thorough analysis of Hume's and Spinoza's conceptions to trace the philosophical foundations of more recent theoretical developments in psychotherapy. Neu points out that both Hume and Spinoza, albeit to different degrees, acknowledge the importance of thought processes for the experience of emotions. Neu notes that for Hume not only are emotions "thought-dependent" but he affirms that "the contents of the relevant thoughts help determine what one's state of mind is" (Neu 1977, p. 38). To illustrate the importance of thought in the causation of emotions, Neu points out that "one may be afraid in circumstances which are not dangerous; what matters is that one believes them to be dangerous" (Neu 1977, p. 39).

Another important issue in Hume's system is the principle of association: "However changeable our thoughts may be, they are not entirely without rule and method in their changes. The rule by which they proceed, is to pass from one object to what is resembling, contiguous to or produced by it" (Hume 1898 Chap. II, p. 293). Elsewhere he writes: "It is evident that there is a principle of connexion between the different thoughts or ideas of the mind" (Hume 1977, Sect. III). As an example of the orderly association of emotions, Hume observes: "All resembling impressions are connected together, and no sooner one arises, than the rest immediately follow. Grief and disappointment give rise to anger, anger to envy, envy to malice, and malice to grief again, till the whole circle be completed" (1898, Chap. II, p. 83). Although Hume's conceptions require a great effort to become intelligible, his principle of association anticipates important theoretical tenets both in psychoanalysis and in behaviour therapy. In addition, Hume's scepticism toward everything that is not directly supported by experience, (that is,

[3]Such opinions Bacon referred to as "idols"; these he classified into four groups: *idola specus*, that is, the prejudice of looking at things from one's own perspective, limited by environmental and educational factors; *idola tribus*, that is, the prejudices implicit in human nature, with all its limitations; *idola fori*, that is, the prejudices shared by the community; and *idola theatri*, refering to the teachings of the various philosophical schools. It could be said that the concept of *idola specus* is a forerunner of the Piagetian concept of "egocentrism", whereas *idola fori* correspond in cognitive therapy to the type of thought distortions termed "oversocialization", which entail the unquestioning acceptance of culturally shared values.

"observable") makes him the most important forerunner of methodological behaviourism.[4]

More explicit in his conception of the relevance of thought for the experience of emotion was Spinoza, who emphasized that " to experience certain emotions, it is necessary to have certain beliefs", and that "a change of belief can lead to a transformation of the very character of the emotion" (1959, Chap. V, prop. 9; see also Neu 1977, p. 93). Elsewhere (1959, Chap. V, prop. 2; Chap. III, prop. 48) Spinoza maintained that in so far as an emotion is constituted by the thought of an external cause, the rejection of that thought as false leads to the destruction of the emotion. It is important to note that Spinoza was aware that the mind could be affected not only by ideas related to present events but also by ideas related to past or future events: "Since the mind conceives of things according to reason, it becomes equally affected both when the idea concerns a future or past thing, and a present one" (1959, Chap. IV, prop. 62).[5] Thus, whereas Hume regarded (mnemonic) ideas as "faded copies", hardly able to produce an impact comparable with present "impressions", Spinoza argued that "a man is affected by the image of a past or future thing with the same emotion as that with which he is affected by the image of a present thing" (1959, Chap. III; prop. 18). The relevance of Spinoza for psychoanalysis lies in his assertion that "the recognition of a thought as a memory, that is as referring to the past, weakens the hold of the emotion on us" (1959, Chap. IV, props. 9, 10).[6] On the other hand, Spinoza, as acknowledged by Neu, seems to be closer than Hume to the truth in maintaining that thoughts are of greater importance than feelings in the classification and discrimination of emotional states. If it is taken into account that Spinoza maintained that a new way of thinking can also be a new way of feeling, it is not going too far to maintain that Spinoza's views contribute to showing that cognitive psychotherapy makes philosophic sense.

One often encounters the name of Kant in the literature on cognitive therapy literature. Kant maintained that the only feature common to all mental disorders is the loss of "common sense" and the development of a unique "private sense" of reasoning (Kant 1917, vol. 7, p. 219; 1964). He also successfully applied the cognitive strategy of "attention-diversion" to himself when troubled by painful gout (Meichenbaum 1977, p. 171). "Private sense" is for Adler one of the basic characteristics of all failures in life. He maintained that in psychotherapy the patient must learn "to re-see the world and alter his old private view in order to bring it more into harmony with a common view" (Adler 1956, p. 254). The Piagetian concept of "egocentrism" can be see as nothing other than the Kantian "private sense". The influence of Kant on cognitive psychotherapy can thus be

[4]Rychlak (1969) observes the importance here of Locke's earlier position and points out that the series of associations taken into account in behaviour therapy is the modern counterpart of Locke's simple ideas, flowing in efficient cause-to-effect fashion.

[5]The conception that future things could be a cause of discomfort had been anticipated by Marcus Aurelius (1948, Chap. VII, p. 8).

[6]Other anticipations of psychoanalytic concepts in Spinoza's *Ethica* concern the psychoanalytic assumption of internal determinism (e.g. 1959, Chap. II, prop. 48) and the Freudian concept of transference (e.g. 1959, Chap. III, props. 16, 17).

traced through the Adlerian and the Piagetian influences on the theorizing of cognitive psychotherapy.

In *The Critique of the Pure Reason* Kant maintained that man's mind never senses reality directly, that is, it never deals directly with "things – in – themselves" ("noumena") but only with their sensory representations ("phenomena") as mediated by understanding. Crucial in the Kantian conception, as stressed by Rychlak (1969), is the view of mind as an active process, imposing meaning by organizing experience in a certain way (cf. the concept of "meaning structures" in Lundh, this volume). However it should not be forgotten that Kant opposed the extreme rationalism of his time, and that he saw as his mission the establishment of an equilibrium between cognitive science and romanticism (Yesavage 1980). Even the cognitive therapist Ellis (1962) divorces himself from the extreme rationalism of the eighteenth century, admitting that reason has inherent limits. However, Ellis argues that to be aware of the limits of reason is, ultimately, rational.

The ancient conceptions of the Stoics can be recognized in the writings of the neo-Kantian philosopher Hannah Arendt, who maintained that "what becomes manifest when we speak about psychic experiences is never the experience in itself, but whatever we think about it when we reflect upon it . . . . What appears in the outside world in addition to physical signs is only what we make of them (i.e. feelings, passions, emotions) through the operations of thought" (Arendt 1978, p. 31).

Having pointed out above the inspiration which cognitive psychotherapy has had from conceptions of Adler's "individual psychology", the relevance (mediated through Adler) of Vaihinger's (1911) philosophy of "as if" or "fictionalism" cannot be neglected. In fact, it is from Vaihinger that Adler received inspiration for his formulation of the "neurotic apperceptive schema" (Adler 1956) that has its counterpart in the cognitive distortions taken into account in cognitive psychotherapy.[7]

Although the philosophical excursus presented so far has made no pretence to exhaustiveness, we must by no means ignore the role of Bertrand Russell. In fact, R.A. Wessler and R.L. Wessler maintain in their recent textbook on rational-emotive therapy that "the core of RET might be characterized as the applied philosophy of Russell" (R.A. Wessler and R.L. Wessler 1980, p. 3). Most of Russell's views that are relevant to cognitive psychotherapy were formulated in his *The Conquest of Happiness* (1930). Here Russell makes a thorough analysis of the most common sources of human unhappiness and maintains that these can be traced to deprivation during childhood and youth. Thus, he suggests, the first step toward happiness consists of "the liberation from the tyranny of early beliefs" (Russell 1930, p. 16), that is, the liberation from that which in cognitive psychotherapy is

[7]"Fictions", according to Vaihinger, are ideas (including unconscious notions) which have no counterpart in reality and are to be regarded as mental structures. Adler's neurotic apperceptive schema, inspired by the work of Vaihinger, includes "perceptual selectivity", "dichotomous thinking" and "inappropriate evaluations of own behaviour" – all of which are concepts taken into account in cognitive psychotherapy.

known as "basic dysfunctional assumptions". After having discussed at some length the defeating effect of anxiety, Russell proposes that when some misfortune threatens, one should seriously consider what is the worst that could possibly happen as a result of it. Russell believes that when one has considered for some time the worst possible outcome and has said with genuine conviction to himself, "Well, after all, that would not matter so very much", one finds that his worries diminish to quite an extraordinary extent (Russell 1930, p. 59).

Russell seems to be aware that conscious, rational thinking may prove insufficient to free one from worries. On the other hand, he points out that there has been a great deal of study on the operation of the unconscious upon the conscious – but much less study on the operation of the conscious upon the unconscious. His contention is that conscious thought "can be planted into the unconscious if a sufficient amount of vigour and intensity is put into it" (Russell 1930, p. 58). He further suggests that a man "should make up his mind with emphasis as to what he rationally believes, and should never allow contrary irrational beliefs to pass unchallenged or obtain a hold over him, however brief" (Russell 1930, p. 83). Russell deals here also with the dislike of rationality by those who believe that rationality "if allowed free play, will kill all deeper emotions" (Russell 1930, p. 83). According to Russell, such a belief depends entirely on an erroneous conception of reason in human life. His contention is that it is a function of rational psychology to find ways of preventing such emotions that are an obstacle to well-being, but that this does not imply a minimizing of those passions which reason does not condemn.

The System of Cognitive Psychotherapy

An early analysis of the status of cognitive psychotherapy was presented some 10 years ago by Beck (1976). At that time Beck stressed that it is crucial to distinguish between a system of psychotherapy that represents genuine progress in the evolution of psychotherapy and a set simply of new techniques. Beck elaborated both a set of standards for evaluating theories of psychopathology and a set of standards specifically intended for evaluating systems of psychotherapy; he furthermore produced evidence to show that cognitive psychotherapy meets the basic requirements of a therapeutic system. In fact, cognitive psychotherapy is based on a comprehensive, cogent theory of psychopathology, and it also meets the specific requirements for a unified system of empirically based therapy.

However convincing and comprehensive Beck's analysis may be, it nevertheless fails to cover a number of aspects that may be regarded as necessary both for a basic description of the state of art in cognitive psychotherapy and for its direct comparison to other therapeutic systems. There are several reasons which justify an updating. First, Beck's systematic presentation of cognitive therapy was published more than 10 years ago. Since that time important developments have taken place, especially as concerns the structuring of data which constitute the theoretical bulk of cognitive psychotherapy (e.g. Mahoney 1980a,b, 1985; Guidano and Liotti 1983, 1985; Beck and Emery 1985). Secondly, Beck's main focus here was on emotional disorders, particularly those of a depressive type. However, evidence has since accumulated which indicates cognitive psychotherapy to be both feasible and effective in several other types of disorders as well. Thirdly, the publicity which the effectiveness of cognitive therapy in the treatment of depression has achieved has contributed to an impression that cognitive therapy is effective *only* for depression. Fourthly, the cognitive therapy of depression is correctly understood as a type of (in most cases) short-term psychotherapy; however, the opinion that cognitive psychotherapy is *only* a short-term form of treatment has unfortunately been generalized from the case of depression, with the consequence that some scepticism exists concerning its use in other morbid conditions that are hardly amenable to short-term treatment. This regards in particular the treatment of patients with personality disorders, which has become one major focus in psychoanalysis and psychoanalytically oriented psychotherapy.

Finally, the particular attention paid by behaviour therapists to mediating factors and the endorsement by these therapists of the label "cognitive-behavioural therapy" have contributed to a blurring of boundaries between cognitive therapy and behaviour therapy to a much larger extent than was the case when Beck published his work. Moreover, the emphasis on "structure" and that on the use of active techniques in cognitive psychotherapy has lead to a faulty understanding of its essence. This misunderstanding is in part due to the fact that cognitive psychotherapy, being based on the correction of faulty thinking, seems to be in too sharp a contrast to other therapies, based on the expression of emotion and on catharsis, which have become so popular during the last decade.

It is the purpose of this section to build on the foundations established by Beck and to expand his characterization of cognitive psychotherapy. We will, in part, follow here the approach proposed by Ford and Urban (1965) in their comparative analysis of various systems of psychotherapy (those of Freud, Jung, Adler, Wolpe, Rank, Rogers, Horney, Sullivan, etc.).This approach should also enable the reader to make his own comparisons to these additional systems. In addition, a comparison will be made also to systems which have been developed since the appearance of Ford and Urban's work.

Personal Background

Ford and Urban pointed out that all the theorists whom they had taken into account represented Western European and North American culture. They maintained that the systems which these theorists have developed could therefore be regarded as strongly influenced by the Graeco-Judaeo-Christian tradition and, thus, as culture-bound. On the whole, a similar generalization could apply to the original proponents of cognitive psychotherapy. However, as noted above, there are hints in the philosophies of the ancient East which suggest that the general themes of cognitive psychotherapy may, indeed, allow generalization to other cultures as well. For example, a close scrutiny of Morita therapy (Reynolds 1976), undoubtedly bound to the culture of the East (through its principles of Zen Buddhism), reveals some relationship with RET, as developed by Ellis (1962).

Whereas most of the theorists considered by Urban and Ford had been medically trained, many leading authors on cognitive psychotherapy are psychologists. It is important to recognize this difference in background training among proponents of cognitive psychotherapy as compared to those of other psychotherapies. This difference explains, in fact, some of the differences in emphasis on various themes, easily recognizable in the work of cognitive therapists. One such difference, for example, concerns the importance given to the therapist-patient relationship.

One of the first dissidents from psychoanalysis who emphasized a cognitive approach was Lungwitz (Becker 1985). However, his monumental textbook (*Lehrbuch der Psychobiologie*), published between 1933 and 1970 (the last volume postumously) has never been translated into English and is little known outside Germany. Lungwitz' cognitive approach, or *Erkenntnistherapie* (1955/1980) seems to be of an educative type and to be deeply rooted in biological concepts, thus rejecting any mind-body dualism (Lungwitz 1980, p. 239). It emphasizes, by using the metaphor of the mountain climber and his guide (Lungwitz 1980, pp. 202–203), the active work of the patient in correcting misconceptions through active learning (Lungwitz 1980, p. 224). It was conceived as a therapy of relatively short duration (12–16 weeks, 2–3 weekly sessions) and comprised both homework assignments (Lungwitz 1980, p. 223–224) and booster sessions (Lungwitz 1980, p. 231).

Later, a trend originated within psychoanalysis toward cognitive psychotherapy which culminated in the foundation of the "cognitive-volitional school" (Arieti 1974) and the approach of "cognitive psychoanalysis" (Bieber 1980). However, both Arieti and his followers and Bieber remained within the approach of psychoanalysis. The birth of genuine cognitive psychotherapy coincided with the departure in the 1960s of Beck and Ellis, both trained analysts, from the domain of psychoanalysis and their developing a new therapy system.

At the same time, another current developed within the area of psychology in the works of such authors as Davison, Goldfried, Meichenbaum and Mahoney, with backgrounds as psychologists trained in the behaviouristic and the social-learning tradition. The convergence here of different therapy forms led most behaviour therapists to define themselves as cognitive-behavioural therapists. More recently a second generation of cognitive psychotherapists, both physicians and psychologists, is maturing, without previous affiliations either to psychoanalysis or to behaviourism.

This difference in respective backgrounds becomes particularly evident not only in the terminology used by different authors – and in the emphasis on the use and the meaning of various techniques – but also with regard to the relative importance assigned to the patient's past history and to the relationship between therapist and patient.

Although "cognitions" are now increasingly taken into account in most therapeutic systems, including psychoanalysis, the position accorded them varies substantially (Schwartz 1982). In the cognitive-therapy systems developed by Beck and by Ellis it is assumed that it is cognition which influences behaviour rather than vice versa; nevertheless, however, a "cognition-emotion-behaviour loop" is generally acknowledge. Whereas the psychoanalytic theory of cognition is mentalistically associationistic, and stimulus-response mediational theories are behaviouristically-associative, the developmental theory at the basis of cognitive psychotherapy is constructivist and interactionist and is based on the postulate that cognitions are complex, organized internal structures that obey their own sets of laws.

Underlying View of Man

According to Ford and Urban, two general views of the nature of man appear to have been operative in most theories of psychotherapy: that of man as a "*pilot*"and that of man as a "*robot*". Implicit in the former is the conviction that a man can be responsible for his own behaviour, while implicit in the latter is the conviction that a man is not responsible for the direction of his ship as it "follows the currents in the sea of life" (Ford and Urban 1965, p. 597). The theories of Adler, Rank, Rogers, and the existentialists are built largely upon the "pilot" view of man, whereas those of Freud, Wolpe, Dollard and Miller, and the radical behaviourists exemplify the "robot" view.

Schafer (1976), Messer and Winokur (1980), and Murray (1983), among others have discussed different visions of life from the perspective of Frye's (1957) four mythic forms. They seem to agree that the psychoanalytic view is principally a "tragic" and "ironic" one, whereas the behavioural approach is associated particularly with a "comic" vision of life.[8] Messer and Winokur refer to Freud (Breuer and Freud 1893), who maintained that the patient can, at best, hope "to change neurotic misery for everyday suffering", as support for their thesis. Murray suggests that the difference between psychoanalytical and behaviouristic views may not be universal and consistent, and Schafer maintains that all four visions of reality (romantic, ironic, tragic and comic) all together constitute the implicit psychoanalytical world view.

The Freudian tragic view of life has been commented upon by Fromm (1962,1970). Fromm, acknowledging that Freud's model was constructed in the spirit of nineteenth-century materialistic thought, is critical of its conception of man as a machine, "driven by a relatively constant amount of sexual energy called libido" (Fromm 1962, p. 34). Later, however, Fromm (1970, pp. 46–47) pointed out that Freud was also a romantic who believed could gain control over the unconscious with the help of the analytic method. On the other hand, more recent developments within psychoanalysis (by Peterfreund and Kohut, among others) seem to suggest a less pessimistic view of man than that held by Freud.

The view of man prevalent in cognitive psychotherapy is more that of the "pilot" than that of the "robot" and is thus closer to that of Adler, Rank, Rogers and the existentialists than to that of Freud and the behaviourists. Cognitive psychotherapy does not subscribe indiscriminately to Adler's enthusiastic statement that "anyone can do anything" (Ford and Urban 1965, p. 597), but it also rejects the

[8]The term "comic" is used in this context in the sense of "following the typical structure of dramatic comedy", and does not implicate any pejorative value.

Freudian deterministic power of the unconscious, dominated by destructive instinctual drives. Cognitive psychotherapy acknowledges cultural and biological constraints to human development and sees man as born with certain response potentialities. However, it rejects any conception of man as a tabula rasa upon which each culture writes its respective text. Its view of human development is constructivist and interactionist and is based on the assumption that most of human behaviour is potentially modifiable. In this respect cognitive psychotherapy approaches the interpersonal theory of Sullivan, the holistic principle of Horney, and, to a less extent, the conceptions of ego analysts, object-relations theorists and self analysts. Which view of man underlies a psychotherapeutic system is not without consequences for its practice. In fact, underlying assumptions about the nature of man determine that which is regarded as important to study and ,therefore, the kinds of behaviours that are to be observed. According to the "pilot" view of man, the responses by which man appears to perform his piloting are emphasized. Less emphasis is placed here upon situational events because it is the person's response to these (that is, how he perceives and evaluates them) that is important. In this context a high degree of correspondence is assumed between that which the patient reports and that which has actually occurred; this applies not only to the patient's description of his present subjective experiences but also to his recall of the immediate and the remote past. However, cognitive psychotherapy is not unaware that all our memories are later reconstructions which may have been influenced (and, thus, distorted) by later events.

Normal Course of Behavioural Development

The important aspect of the theory dealing with normal behavioural development has been comprehensively treated by Guidano and Liotti (1983, 1985), Liotti (1987) and Reda (1986), and its most important features are dealt with in other contributions in the present volume (cf. Lundh; Liotti). Thus, no repetition is necessary here. At this juncture, however, we should underline that a major assumption of cognitive psychotherapy is that the infant enters the world with a basic set of genetically determined potentialities, or rudimentary structures, which allow his active seeking and processing of information, and which unfold throughout the life cycle. Crucial for such potentialities are the integrity of the central nervous system and its maturation. Thus, it is assumed that any damaging influences – hereditary, pre- and post-natal – on the nervous structures or the biochemical mechanisms responsible for the perception, processing and storage of information will result in a deviation from normal development. Although the importance of neuro-humoural transmitter systems for the processing and the transfering of information is fully acknowledged, cognitive psychotherapy is not reductionist. In fact, as clearly underlined in the accompanying chapter in this volume by the present author, one of its main tenets is the assumption of a continuous dialectical interaction between the structure of the organism and the structure of the environment. In this respect the conception of behavioural development in cognitive psychotherapy is close to that of Piaget, Kelly and Bowlby. Guidano and Liotti (1983, 1985) have used the analogy of Lakatos' (1970) "*research plans*" to conceptualize the growth of personal knowledge. Their use of Lakatos' concepts is particularly fruitful, for it also allows a conceptualization of the process of change following the principles of cognitive psychotherapy (see also Perris 1986).

Development of Behavioural Disorder

The topic of the development of behaviour disorder is also treated extensively in other contributions to this volume, both in general terms and in relation to specific disorders (cf. Liotti; Stiles and Götestam; C. Perris). A detailed theoretical framework for an integrating conception of the development of psychopathology is presented by C. Perris (chapter on schizophrenia). It may suffice here to repeat that the focus of cognitive psychotherapy is on the development of dysfunctional meaning structures (dysfunctional schemata, or dysfunctional working models). In addition to the biological constraints mentioned above, it is assumed that basic dysfunctional structures develop as a result of deleterious interactions between man and his environment. In this respect cognitive psychotherapy is, again, quite close to the conceptions of Sullivan, Horney, other culturalist psychoanalysts and object-relations theorists. In particular, a special importance is given to Bowlby's (1979) concept of "attachment" and to its successive development.

Although it is generally recognized that basic dysfunctional schemata typically develop during infancy and childhood, it is also assumed that these may develop later in life in relation to major crises. It is also widely acknowledged that basic dysfunctional working models or assumptions may remain "silent" for a long time, to be activated then by the impact of relevant external events. However, this latter point is generally approached from the view of neuropsychology, and no use is made of the concept of "unconscious" in a Freudian sense. Nor does cognitive psychotherapy subscribe to the psychoanalytic concept of "*phase specific*" fixation/regression. It is interesting to note in this context that even contemporary psychoanalysts are critical of the concept of "phases" and seem to prefer the more neutral concept of "*moments of experience*" (cf. Pine 1985, Chaps. 4, 5 in particular). Further details on the interactionist view of the development of psychopathology can be found in the accompanying contribution in this volume by the present author.

Goals of Therapy

Who Determines the Goals

Cognitive psychotherapy was originally conceived for the short-term treatment of manifest emotional disorders; Beck, nevertheless, also emphasized its feasibility with other types of patients (Beck 1952, 1963, 1964). As many of the contributions to this volume testify, however, its scope has since expanded to reach far beyond the aim of assisting the patient merely to achieve control over his disordered emotions. Applications also include a number outside the field of psychiatry, for example, in the classroom (Meichenbaum 1977; Meichenbaum and Asarnow

1979) and in the training of elite sportsmen (Mahoney 1979). Both preventive goals and the goal of personality restructuring are accessible to cognitive psychotherapy.

As concerns the treatment of manifest disorders goals are easily agreed upon in a collaborative atmosphere between therapist and patient, although the former also has the role of assisting the patient in recognizing and conceptualizing his problems. Regarding other spheres of application decisions about the goals rest mainly with the client. It should be unnecessary to stress that no therapist can ever promote changes beyond those that the client/patient wants to effect.

On the whole, the position of cognitive psychotherapy as concerns the determination of goals is quite close to that of Sullivan, who emphasized that the therapist and the patient must agree explicitly on certain goals towards which they can work together. The same applies to a comparison between cognitive psychotherapy and psychodynamic psychotherapy. Moreover, it should be pointed out that in both types of therapy the determination of goals clearly depends on which approach (i.e. short- or long-term therapy) is feasible with a given patient in a given situation.

Nature of Goals

In commenting on the relevance of the therapeutic setting of "classical psychoanalysis", the analyst Klein wrote that "we must justify ... retention (of the classical psychoanalytic setting) mainly as an indispensable resource for the study in depth of personality and pathology, without leaning upon claims of superior therapeutic effectiveness" (Klein 1976, p. 37). Implicit in this statement is that it is the analyst who determines goals. It is obvious however that this cannot be extended to all psychoanalytic work, particularly to psychoanalytically oriented dynamic psychotherapy, which is undoubtedly conceived as a method of treatment. However, judging from Peterfreund's (1983) criticism of that which he defines as the "stereotyped psychoanalytical approach" (echoing a similar opinion expressed 4 decades earlier by Rank 1945), there is reason to suspect that all too often it is the analyst who determines both the goals of therapy and their nature.

Since psychotherapy intends to be nothing but a method of treatment, it would seem a truism to emphasize that its major goal should be the alleviation of the patient's emotional distress. However, such an affirmation can easily be misunderstood and equated with the simple elimination of manifest symptoms, even when a patient is assumed to be "ill" not only symptomatologically but also in his functioning in social relations. However important such an elimination might be, it would be open to question as to whether elimination of symptoms could justify the investment in time and manpower that the practice of psychotherapy implies. On the other hand, if one takes at face value the statement by Klein above, one could also wonder whether his suggestion about the nature of the goals of psychoanalysis could really be defended in a psychiatric setting as taking care of those who seek help for their psychopathological problems.

Frank, a psychoanalyst who at a very early stage (Frank 1961) endorsed a cognitive standpoint, has since maintained repeatedly (Frank 1971, 1974, 1985) that one primary function of all psychotherapies is to combat demoralization by restoring the patient's sense of mastery. Few cognitive psychotherapists should have any difficulty defining their goals according to Frank's more recent opinion. However, since a closer conceptualization of the nature of therapeutic goals may be appropriate, it can be said that these consist of taking into account the patient's view of himself, his environment and his future in order (a) to assist him in pursuing with the therapist a collaborative empiricism; (b) to recognize his habits of perceiving, thinking, feeling, behaving, etc.; (c) to challenge the validity of his faulty assumptions; and (d) to make those changes which fit his personal goals. When these changes occur, it is assumed that the patient will also gain an understanding of his difficulties, lose his symptoms and become more effective in his personal relations.

Conditions for Producing Behavioural Change

Ford and Urban pointed out that therapy theorists have, as a group, specified very little in the way of principles and techniques for producing behavioural changes. Some openly reject "technical rules" (e.g. Rank 1945), others appear to consider the issue of techniques to be antitherapeutic (e.g. the existentialists) and still others seem to take the position that they are not doing anything pre-established to produced behavioural changes. Rogers (1951), for instance, asserted that the therapist's task is to create certain conditions which make it possible for the client to change himself. There has also been concern, especially among older Freudian psychoanalysis, that published techniques might become accessible to patients, thus making treatment more difficult.

A major characteristic of cognitive psychotherapy, one shared with social-learning theorists, has been that specific techniques to promote behavioural change as well as the principles on which these techniques are based be spelled out from the very beginning. As pointed out by Beck the system of cognitive therapeutic procedures is clearly described, and the general principles of treatment are well articulated, so that "different therapists dealing with the same problem among similar patients can be expected to use similar techniques" (Beck 1976, p. 308).

More recently Peterfreund (1983), a "classical" analyst, has presented a thorough analysis of the psychoanalytic therapeutic process based on a conception strikingly similar to that of cognitive psychotherapy. Peterfreund, in fact, has adopted the concept of "working models" introduced by Bowlby (closely corresponding to the concepts of basic cognitive structures and basic schemata used in cognitive psychotherapy) and stressed that the modification of dysfunctional working models by a heuristic psychoanalytic approach, which he describes at some length, is the goal of psychoanalysis.

Patient Behaviour that Must Occur in Therapy

In classical psychoanalysis the patient must follow the "basic rule" of free association without screening what is reported or discarding any observation and without attempting to organize his report logically. The patient's major task is to be introspective and to observe and report his subjective thoughts, memories and affect. He must be willing to make the necessary effort to follow the fundamental rule and must be able to form some kind of interpersonal relationship with the therapist, without which therapy cannot succeed. Other therapy theorists, for example, Sullivan and the existentialists, have been less explicit as concerns what the patient is supposed to do in therapy. However, general agreement seems to exist on the necessity for the patient to be introspective and to develop a therapeutic relationship with the therapist, although the emphasis on these aspects is less pronounced on the part of social-learning theorists.

The particular patient-therapist relationship that characterizes cognitive psychotherapy has been defined by Beck (1976) as one of "*collaborative empiricism*". Borrowing from Kelly (1955) the metaphor of man as "scientist", Beck pointed out that it is expected that patient and therapist will work together as two research workers who formulate hypotheses, challenge their validity and search for alternatives when these prove untenable. The patient is expected to become well trained in how to focus on dysfunctional automatic thoughts related to various emotional experiences and situations and to learn how to recognize and challenge dysfunctional basic assumptions. Within the treatment sessions themselves it is the patient's activity which determines the length and the outcome of therapy. Compliance with homework assignments is assumed to facilitate the therapeutic process.

The reliance of cognitive therapy on the activity of the patient is reminiscent of the view maintained by Horney (1942, p. 14) who relied on the patient's "constructive activity"; the use of homework assignments, which is also a characteristic of behaviour therapy, is related to Adler's suggestion of specific actions for the patient to perform outside of therapy (Adler 1956).

Therapist Behaviour that Must Occur in Therapy

There is, according to Ford and Urban, considerable disagreement among psychotherapy theorists as to what the therapist should know about the patient in order to initiate therapy (Ford and Urban 1965, p. 673). In classical psychoanalysis a short trial period is suggested to assess the patient's suitability for treatment. More recently however the situation has changed, and a thorough intake evaluation is considered a very important prerequisite for the beginning of any psychotherapy that is not to be merely supportive.

In cognitive psychotherapy a thorough initial assessment of each candidate for psychotherapy, usually complemented by the use of specific assessment instruments, has always been a rule. Ford and Urban emphasize that "effective therapy requires controlled and directional change, not mere change in itself". Thus, they add, "selection of steps to be taken to alter a given behaviour pattern follows directly from an analysis of the behaviour and the conditions under which it occurs" (Ford and Urban 1965, p. 674). Virtually every cognitive therapist could be expected to agree with this opinion.

In traditional psychoanalysis the behaviour expected from the therapist is that of maintaining a hovering, free-floating attention and to intervene timely with passing remarks and, above all, with interpretations. This behaviour is expected to foster the working-through in the later phase of analysis and thus foster the therapeutic process itself. However, modifications of the classical technique were introduced early which entail a more active participation of the therapist. Stekel (1950), for example, stated that his emphasis on his role as a therapist more than on that as a scientist was the factor which sharply distinguished his procedures from those of Freud. He saw the analyst as an active partner of the patient throughout therapy and insisted that he should take an active role in the therapeutic process; accordingly, he referred to his procedures as "active psychoanalytic psychotherapy". A similar standpoint was endorsed by Adler, who dispensed with the couch and substituted face-to-face sitting positions. Also Adler assumed an active teaching role and conceived the therapist's responsibility to be that of pointing out self-deceptive tendencies to the patient.

More recently psychoanalysts, especially those belonging to the object-relations school, have emphasized even more the important impact of the therapeutic relationship and have stressed the importance of "good enough mothering" (Winnicott 1960) as a prerequisite context of security in which the patient can develop insights and effect changes. A relatively high degree of activity by the therapist is permissible also in the context of psychoanalytically oriented psychotherapy.

Beck and his co-workers (Beck 1976; Beck et al. 1979; Beck and Emery 1985) have been very explicit both as concerns the desirable characteristics of the therapist and his behaviour in therapy. As regards the former emphasis is placed upon warmth, appropriate empathy, and genuineness. Regarding the latter stress is put particularly on the establishment of rapport, basic trust, and, most typically of all, the spirit of "collaborative empiricism", as mentioned above. The therapist is expected to be active and directive and to make explicit use of hypotheses proposed to the patient for verification rather than relying on interpretations. The therapist is also expected to make consistent use of the Socratic method when helping the patient to authenticate introspective data and investigate underlying assumptions. The therapist must be able to conceptualize the patient's difficulties in terms amenable to cognitive interventions, and, obviously, he must be skilled enough to know which intervention is most appropriate on which occasion.

Appraisal of Behavioural Change

Until very recently there has been very little concern among psychotherapy theorists in systematically assessing whether their envisaged changes have actually occurred. Most seem to have relied almost entirely on the patient's reports and on that which could be observed in the interview situations. One reason for this neglect may have been the difficulty in reaching universal agreement on the conceptualization of improvement and, even more, so on that of cure. The great length of many analytic treatments may be due to this difficulty. However, things have been changing, and several efforts are now being made to define and assess the effects of psychotherapy.

In this respect cognitive therapy resembles behaviour therapy. In fact, the behaviour therapist's emphasis on eliciting precise data from the patient and his refined methods for quantifying behavioural changes were incorporated very early into the practice of cognitive psychotherapy. Moreover, during therapy the patient is encouraged, along the lines of a technique already used by Sullivan, to evaluate the progress of therapy and to conceptualize what changes have occurred.

Several contributions in this volume are concerned with a direct documentation and systematic appraisal of behavioural change in various morbid conditions.

Transfer of the Effects of Behavioural Change

Most theorists seem to assume that changes accomplished in therapy will automatically generalize to situations outside of therapy, and that no explicit planning for the latter instance is necessary. One notable exception is represented by Sullivan (1954) who, in terminating an interview or therapy series, prescribed actions which the patient was encouraged to try. In cognitive psychotherapy the assigning of experiments to be carried out as homework is one of the techniques used for monitoring the application of insights gained during the therapy session to other occasions. In addition, the consistent use of booster sessions after the termination of therapy, proper, represents a way to obtain feedback from the patient concerning the transfer of change achieved in therapy to other situations.

Verification of Theory

One of the most distinguishing characteristics of cognitive psychotherapy has been the formulation of its underlying theoretical bases in such a way as to be amenable to empirical verification. As cognitive psychotherapy was originally conceived for the treatment of emotional disorders, especially depression, it is understandable that studies have been concerned principally with verifying the cognitive theory of depression (cf. contributions by Blackburn and by Stiles and Götestam in this volume; a chapter by Rush and Giles in Rush 1982). Obviously there are many facets of the theory which remain the focus of evaluative research and await verification, however, other evaluative results, besides those concerning depression, are available in the literature. (The interested reader is referred to the several issues of *Cognitive Therapy and Research*; Kendall and Hollon 1979; Kendall 1982–1985; detailed accounts of assessment procedures are available in Merluzzi et al. 1981.)

Summarizing Remarks

Constraints of space have unfortunately not allowed for more detail here on the distinguishing features of cognitive psychotherapy. Additional information, however, will be presented below. This characterization, however sketchy, has hopefully contributed to illustrating that cognitive psychotherapy meets, as Beck (1976) had already pointed out, both the basic requirements of a therapeutic system and those for a uniform, empirically based theory. Thus, this section should provide a basis on which to grasp the essence of cognitive psychotherapy and a description of the main characteristics that distinguish it from other psychotherapy systems.

Cognitive Psychotherapy Versus Psychoanalytic Psychotherapy

In the first two sections arguments have been presented to show that current cognitive psychotherapy has a philosophical grounding, and that it represents a consistent therapeutic system, both at the level of clinical theory and at that of higher level explanations. In delineating the distinguishing features of the cognitive psychotherapy system some of the similarities and the divergencies in relation to other major therapeutic systems have been pointed out. In the following sections these similarities and divergences will be examined in greater detail. Although the focus will be at the level of clinical applications, a number of more general issues will be noted as well. As Peterfreund (1975) has observed, it is important to distinguish fundamentally between phenomena of observation and levels of theory about these phenomena when considering a psychotherapeutic system. Whereas Peterfreund, however, seems to be of the opinion that awareness of a difference in levels of explanation may prevent contamination in the practice of therapy, our position is that adherence to a higher level theoretical model inevitably influences how the therapeutic approach is conceptualized in practice.

Theoretical Issues

The theoretical foundations of psychoanalysis, that is, its metapsychology, have recently been criticized concerning drive-discharge theory, ego psychology, object-relations theory and self psychology – from authors both inside and outside the psychoanalytic domain (e.g. Peterfreund 1971, 1975, 1983; Peterfreund and Franceschini 1973; Holt 1972, 1981, 1982; Bowlby 1969–1980; Grünbaum 1983a,b). In particular, Peterfreund in his criticism of the nature of the psychoanalytic metapsychology pointed out that since this is fundamentally divorced from biology and from evolution (1971, p. 77), it has had to rely on an "anthropocentric, vitalistic ego concept to explain the existence of order, organization, control, regulation and adaptation in the psychological phenomena that are observed" (1971, p. 59); obviously, such a position not only is no longer in keeping with modern scientific knowledge but also, he adds, "inherently limits understanding and prediction" (Peterfreund 1971, pp. 40–41). Moreover, this merely states the generally acknowledged fact that psychoanalysis has no general theory of structure formation and learning (Rapaport 1959; Peterfreund 1971). This should not be surprising; in fact, as Peterfreund pointed out, "it is difficult to see how any adequate theory of structure formation and learning can develop out of a hydrodynamic model which has no location in time and space and is conceptually divorced from biology" (Peterfreund 1971, p. 83).

From another perspective, Eagle (1980), Blight (1981) and Grünbaum (1983a) have convincingly argued against the retreat of psychoanalysis to hermeneutics, such as advocated by Habermas (1971), Ricoeur (1970, 1981) and (in part) Klein (1976). In fact, such a retreat would represent a sharp contrast both to Freud's consistently held position (from the 1895 *Project* to the 1938 *Outline*) that psychology belongs to the *natural* sciences and to Hartman's (Hartman 1927, cited in Hartman 1951) emphasis on the relationship of psychoanalysis to the natural sciences.

Grünbaum's thorough, critical analysis is of particular interest because it opposes Popper's (1962) pointed assertion of the non-verifiability of psychoanalysis, at the same time that it points out the lack of validity of what he had previously (Grünbaum 1979) labelled the "tally argument" in Freud's (1917) cardinal epistemological defence of the psychoanalytic method of clinical investigation.[9] Grünbaum (1983b) in a reply to a debate article by Flax (1981) pointed out that his criticism of psychoanalytic theory extends to the post-Freudian self-psychology of Kohut and to the object-relations theory that Flax endorsed, in so far as these claim sanction for the generic repression aetiology of neuroses and hold that "free association has the *epistemic capability* to identify the unconscious *causes* of all kinds of thought and behaviour" (Grünbaum 1983b, p. 87; emphasis in original).

It could be maintained that criticism focussed on the psychoanalytical attempt to develop a body of high-level abstract theory does not necessarily invalidate lower levels of theorizing (e.g. the level of clinical empirical generalization or that of clinical theory). In fact, scientific explanations progress to the more general and abstract; thus the highest level of explanation achieved can be replaced without damage to that of lower levels. Freud was aware of this when he wrote that high-level theories are "not the bottom but the top of the whole structure, and they can be replaced or discarded without damaging it" (Freud 1914, p. 77). Accordingly, a replacement of the psychoanalytic metapsychology should not imply, as Peterfreund (1971, 1975; Peterfreund and Franceschini 1973) correctly points out, that even "the valid clinical observations of psychoanalysis and the valid empirical generalizations of clinical theory" must be replaced (1973, p. 224).

Obviously, this opinion is completely in keeping with the accepted logic of scientific theory. However, one important corollary of the necessity of making distinctions between levels of explanations is that one must always keep in mind, as Peterfreund (1971) has emphasized, that each level has its appropriate language, and that these languages must not be confused. He illustrates the dangers in such confusion by quoting a passage from Jacobson to point out how the latter used not only in the same context but also in a single brief phrase three languages (that of persons, that of a hydrodynamic psychic apparatus and that of physiological

[9]In particular, the "tally argument" comprises the following five claims of Freud: (a) the denial of data contamination by suggestion; (b) the affirmation of a crucial difference between psychoanalysis and other therapies, operating by suggestion; (c) the claim that psychoanalysis is able to validate its causal assumptions by retrospective methods; (d) the contention that favourable therapeutic outcome can be attributed to psychoanalytic intervention without statistical comparisons; and (e) the avowal that patient's self-observations can be credited once repressed conflicts have been resolved.

energy, physiological channels and biological prepatterns) as if there were no differences between these.[10] Peterfreund (1971, p. 62) appropriately comments that Jacobson's confusion of languages is analogous to that of one who uses sentences comprised of French, English and German words as if they belonged to a single language.

Consideration of these points is important in the context of the present discussion for two main reasons. First, the distinction between various levels of explanation is, unfortunately, never as sharp as would be desirable – a fact which Peterfreund has properly acknowledged. Thus, the risk of contamination, as the examples quoted by Peterfreund (1983) clearly suggest, is very high. In fact, Klein has pointed out that "some analysts foster the impression that their major function is to develop links to metapsychological theory" (Klein 1976, p. 63). Peterfreund's (1983) report of fragments of analyses published by distinguished analysts lends emphasis to Klein's opinion. A criticism largely similar to that of Peterfreund had also been voiced a decade earlier by Bruch (1974). Klein's own solution is to dispense altogether with the metapsychological theory and without replacing it. However, he correctly acknowledges that if one rejects the metapsychology in favour of the clinical theory, one comes to realize that "the terms of the clinical theory are just as abstract as the terms of metapsychology" (Klein 1976, p. 49). Moreover, retention of the clinical theory hinges on whether the clinical theory is explicatively autonomous, that is, without recourse to exogenous causes (Grünbaum 1984). Rubinstein (1976) and Eagle (1980) have cogently argued that this is not the case. Moreover, Holt (1982) has emphasized that remaining encapsulated within the explanatory horizons of the clinical theory forecloses any wider vision of the explanation of clinical phenomena.

The second, and far more important, reason is that replacement of a high-level explanation which proves to be untenable by another that is more in keeping with modern knowledge automatically implies that even those concepts belonging to the discarded theory and inappropriately used at other levels must also be discarded. This opinion, of course, is not new; it was voiced by Bruch already in 1974. Bruch, in fact, was critical of the rigid adherence to tradition in psychoanalysis and of the abuse of a terminology that had not changed despite radical reformulations of the theoretical premises which had motivated its original introduction.

Peterfreund, however, does not hesitate to dispense with such concepts as ego, id, primary and secondary processes, repression and many others which are the hallmarks of psychoanalytic theory. At the same time, he proposes that the present anachronistic psychoanalytic metapsychology be replaced by an information-systems theoretical frame of reference (Peterfreund 1971, p. 148). Consistently with this suggestion, Peterfreund (Peterfreund 1971; Peterfreund and Franceschini 1973) has shown how most psychoanalytic concepts can be more parsimoniously understood within the context of information theory, a conception supported

[10]The phrase by Jacobson to which Peterfreund refers is as follows: "undifferentiated psychophysiological energy within the primal, structurally also undifferentiated self". (Jacobson 1954).

thereafter by Ryle (1978) and Wegman (1985). A further attempt at approaching psychoanalytic conceptions from the perspective of information theory has been made by Horowitz (Horowitz 1977; Horowitz et al. 1980). Later Peterfreund (1983) developed some preliminary thoughts anticipated in his 1971 monograph and has published a thoughtful analysis of the psychoanalytic therapeutic process based upon information-systems concepts.

It is worth pointing at this point that also Bowlby (1969–1980), as mentioned in the previous section, has adopted in his object-relations theory a position analogous to that of Peterfreund. Bowlby also rejects the Freudian metapsychology in favour of an evolutionary system theory that takes into account both biological structures and information theory. However, in contrast to Bowlby, Ryle and Wegman, Peterfreund has not noticed that in pursuing this approach, he in effect endorses the high-level explanation, proper, of cognitive psychotherapy; indeed, he suggests those changes in the understanding of psychoanalytic concepts which are taken into account in cognitive psychotherapy.

Following the path struck by Freud (1915, pp. 121–122), psychoanalysis assumes that the mind is separate from the body (Peterfreund 1971, p. 84; 1975, p. 544), and it must resort to a vitalistic and antropomorphic concept of the ego to cope with the concept of adaptation. Cognitive psychotherapy, on the other hand, is deeply rooted in an evolutionary theory of learning that comprises biological structures in an attempt to explain biological order, organization, control, regulation and adaptation – all of which concepts are at the forefront of scientific interest. It will be observed below to what extent Peterfreund's change of theoretical frame of reference has brought his approach to the psychoanalytic therapeutic process close to the therapeutic process of cognitive psychotherapy.

Lundh (this volume) also emphasizes that the endorsement of a higher level evolutionary theory focussed on biological structures does not make cognitive psychotherapy alien to the concept of *meaning*. (See also Peterfreund 1971; Peterfreund and Franceschini 1973; Butcher 1984 for a further discussion of motivation and meaning conceived in an information-processing theoretical framework.) Thus, cognitive psychotherapy is based neither on a mindless conception of man, as in the case of radical behaviourism, nor on a separation between mind and brain, as in the case of psychoanalysis, but overcomes such reductionist dualism. As Mahoney has put it, "it is a comprehensive approach that recognizes the intricate complexity of human experience" (Mahoney 1977, p. 12).

I can conclude this section with another important observation by Peterfreund. Moving away from the language used to describe human experience and towards that of a higher level theory, may sound dehumanizing to those who put value on emotions and meaning, but, Peterfreund points out, to feel and sense a patient's emotions is by no means "inconsistent or negated by information-processing systems, neurophysiological theories, or other high-level explanations of these phenomena" (Peterfreund 1975, p. 546). The setting of the present writing in northern Sweden suggests a way to paraphrase this: the fact that one tries to explain the aurora borealis by means of electromagnetic theories does not mean that one cannot enjoy the beauty of the spectacle as well.

Therapeutic Components Common to all Psychotherapies and the Issue of Suggestion

While Frank (1974, 1985) is probably the most frequently acknowledged scholar concerning common features in various psychotherapies, other valuable contributions to this subject are also available (Strupp 1970, 1973; Brady et al. 1982; Garfield 1982; Goldfried and Padawer 1982). Briefly, Frank starts from the premise that some important generalizations concerning the outcome of psychotherapy seem to be relatively firmly established. Among these are: (a) patients who receive any kind of psychotherapy do somewhat better than controls who have received no formal therapy; (b) when two therapies yield differences in outcome at the end of treatment, these differences disappear over time; and (c) determinants of outcome lie more in the personal qualities of therapist and in the nature of interaction between therapist and patient than in the particular method used. Frank then proceeds to the assumption that patients who seek psychotherapy must share a type of distress that responds to the components common to all schools of psychotherapy; according to Frank, this common factor can be conceptualized as "demoralization". Demoralization occurs when the individual experiences a state of mind characterized by subjective incompetence, loss of self-esteem, alienation, hopelessness and helplessness.

Frank's list of features common to all psychotherapies includes the following:

1. An emotionally charged, confiding relationship with an empathic person
2. A special ("healing") setting arousing and strengthening the patient's expectations of help
3. A plausible explanation of the patient's symptoms
4. A consistent treatment procedure that both therapist and patient believe to be an appropriate method to restore health

Frank's conception gives rise to several important issues. First, Frank himself has emphasized (1985, p. 73) that even if his "demoralization" hypothesis is accepted, and morale can be restored by different therapeutic approaches, this does not imply that psychotherapies are interchangeable, nor that the mastery of one or more forms of psychotherapy is unnecessary. Secondly, the issue of a "placebo effect" must be considered; this has been addressed at some length by various authors (e.g. Garfield 1982; Grünbaum 1981). Here we can note, briefly, that, as Garfield observed, the factors mentioned by Frank may include fundamental ingredients of psychotherapy which must always be taken into account, and that this does not imply a mere placebo effect of therapy. In other words, when comparing psychotherapies, one must be able to specify what the ingredients expected to promote change are, and to what extent ingredients assumed to be specifically pertinent to one method are able to induce an overall change which lies beyond that obtainable by means of the (non-specific) common factors.

Reference to a possible placebo effect, however, is important for raising the issue of "suggestion". This was of much concern to Freud, who discussed it on numerous occasions (e.g. 1917, 1926, 1937). Apparently Freud was ambivalent on this issue because of his dual conception of psychoanalysis as both a method of scientific inquiry and a therapy. In fact, while he strongly rebuked any accusation that his discoveries could be the self-fulfilling products of unintentional suggestion (1917, p. 448), he admitted that the therapist makes it possible for the patient to overcome resistance "with the help of suggestion operating in an educative sense" (1917, pp. 450–451). Two decades later Freud returned to the subject (Freud 1937) and maintained that "the danger of our leading a patient astray by suggestion . . . has certainly been enormously exaggerated" (1937, p. 262). In this context he stressed that a patient's acceptance of the analyst's interpretation is of no value unless followed by indirect confirmations. However, it seems that Freud (Freud 1918, quoted by Gershman 1976) was aware that "it is very probable that the large scale application of our therapy will compel us to alloy the pure gold of analysis freely with the copper of direct suggestion and hypnotic influence". Strupp (1973) later referred to the therapeutic situation as a power base for psychological influence, and Flax (1981) affirmed that suggestion is an essential part of the analytic process. Also Peterfreund (1983) reports many illustrative cases from the literature which blatantly contradict the analytical immunity against twisting the patient's affirmations.

The relevance of these views to a comparative analysis of cognitive psychotherapy can be appreciated if one considers that while in psychoanalysis (and, to a certain extent, in psychoanalytically oriented psychotherapy) interpretations are presented by the analyst to the patient in a particular setting (one which fosters suggestibility), in cognitive psychotherapy no use is made of interpretations. Rather, in the latter the therapist and the patient *together* put forward hypotheses on which they both then work to find out whether these are tenable. Since this "research work" may extend to outside the immediate therapeutic situation (for example, by means of homework assignments), the risk of a suggestive influence on the part of the therapist is considerably reduced. However, one difference here exists between cognitive therapy as conceived by Beck (the subject of the present analysis) and the rational-emotive therapy developed by Ellis: in the latter the suggestive power of the therapist is both acknowledged and explicitly exploited to a large extent.

Peterfreund (1983) severely criticizes the stereotyped approach to the analytic process, in part because of the risk of twisting the patient's reports, and suggests the use of a heuristic approach to circumvent this risk. He proposes that the analyst must always be attuned to the patient and aware of conceiving his interpretations as hypotheses, and that he must always require a confirmatory exploration before these are accepted as valid and presented to the patient as interpretations. In this respect he reveals a correct understanding of the heritage left by Freud (1937) in one of his latest papers. Also, the case reports reveal not only Peterfreund's (1983) apparent freedom from the constraints of theoretical clichés but also his exceptionally developed capacity for empathy and his deep respect for the patient's opinion. When long-term cognitive psychotherapy is compared to his psychoanalytic approach, the differences between the two systems appear considerably reduced.

We have thus far considered elements common to all therapies, particularly in reference to their practical application. At a higher conceptual level it could be maintained, as Raimy (1975) noted, that the ultimate goal of all successful therapy is to change beliefs or other cognitions which are relevant to the patient's psychological problems. Thus, in so far as this goal is pursued, the results obtained using different techniques must necessarily be similar. Accordingly, advantages or disadvantages of different therapeutic approaches should be seen in terms of parsimony of theoretical postulates and of economy (in a broad sense) in application.

Comparative Aspects

Preliminary comparisons between cognitive therapy and psychoanalysis and psychoanalytic psychotherapy have been published by Beck (1976) and by Altshuler and Rush (1984). However, both of these are limited in scope; the latter, in fact, focusses chiefly on the treatment of depression. A different approach has been followed by Ryle (1984) who suggested that the relationship between different therapy systems could be analysed by locating these systems in terms of a more general, cognitive theory. Using a procedural sequence model, Ryle pointed out that cognitive therapy, in analogy with psychoanalysis, is concerned with high-level, life-plan relationships and, in analogy with behaviour therapy, with low-level, discrete behaviour or symptoms, and that it is thus more comprehensive than either of the other systems in its scope.

Choice of comparisons here must necessarily be arbitrary, given the relative chaos in the field; this chaos was noted by Colby (1964), and it has probably grown even more extreme in the meantime. Both in the mainstream of psychoanalysis and in that of the psychoanalytically oriented psychotherapies and beyond there is such a proliferation of competing proposals, concerning both theory and practice, to justify the pessimism expressed by a columnist in the *Saturday Review* (Feb. 21, 1976, quoted by Martin 1976), who referred to the current chaotic situation as a "jungle of psychotherapy". In fact, in 1975 Parloff reported counting more than 140 forms of currently practised psychotherapy.

This state of affairs prompted Kovel (1976) to publish a guide to therapy for the "consumer" in need of help. However, when attempting to describe psychoanalytically oriented psychotherapy, he felt compelled to admit that he was in a "no-man's land", or, better, in an "any-man's land", because of the countless varieties of approach, "generally heavily influenced by the personality of the therapist". Apparently even today when we speak of "psychodynamic psychotherapy", we assume the position of Lewis Carroll's Humpty Dumpty: "When I use a word, it means just what I choose it to mean – neither more nor less". Unfortunately, in contrast to the uniqueness of Humpty Dumpty, there are now too many people taking this view.

Thus any attempt to make comparison between systems is a complex issue, laden with difficulties which impose severe constraints. I must therefore begin by making certain limitations and exclusions. First, the present, tentative approach will focus only on a comparison of cognitive psychotherapy with psychoanalytically oriented psychotherapy[11] and with behaviour therapy. Secondly, I will not

[11] Owing to the difficulty of finding generally accepted, unequivocal definitions of the different types of therapy, the terms "psychoanalytic psychotherapy", "psychoanalytically oriented psychotherapy", and "psychodynamic psychotherapy" will be used here interchangeably. The author is aware that different meanings have occasionally been given to the various terms.

deal with interpersonal psychotherapy, Adlerian psychotherapy or Horneyan psychotherapy because the points of convergence (and divergence) of these therapies with cognitive therapy have recently been discussed by authoritative representatives of the respective schools (Rendon 1985; Shulman 1985; Crowley 1985). I will also not touch upon the convergence of the psychoanalytic conceptions of Arieti or those of Bieber with cognitive psychotherapy because these have remained within the domain of psychoanalysis. And, finally, Jungian analysis must unfortunately be omitted, due simply to the lack of sufficient competence on the part of the present author.

A second line in this approach will be to focus on some central issues which are at the core of all dynamic psychotherapies, independently of idiosyncratic approaches. In doing so we must remain aware of the pitfalls entailed by the choice of factors to be compared. In fact, as pointed out by Goisman (1985), one should use categories which are equally applicable to the various perspectives to be compared and not, themselves, products of any one system.[12]

The following examination of selected comparative aspects will consider together both long- and short-term psychoanalytic psychotherapy, in a broad sense, without necessarily going into detail as concerns the numerous varieties of these therapies as currently used. However, reference will be made to the characteristics of a particular approach where this is deemed necessary for a correct understanding of the issue under discussion.

Selection of Patients

Great variation evidently occurs among various proponents of psychoanalytically oriented psychotherapy, independently of whether the therapy is expected to be short- or long-term. Horowitz et al. (1984) maintain that Davanloo (1980) seems to employ the broadest set of indications for short-term dynamic psychotherapy. To illustrate this, these authors point out that, whereas Sifneos would recommend his type of anxiety-provoking psychotherapy for some 5%–10% of psychiatric out-patients, Davanloo would be prepared to accept 30%–35%. However, comparison of such percentages of out-patient populations cannot, in our opinion, be useful in this regard. To be more indicative such data should supply a detailed description of the characteristics of the whole patient population attending a given out-patient clinic.

Offenkrantz and Tobin (1974) present a catalogue of indications for psychoanalytic psychotherapy comprising virtually all kinds of psychopathological disorders – from acute symptomatic reactions to schizophrenic and manic-depressive conditions. However, they do not specify time limits but point out, instead, that since the goal of psychoanalytic psychotherapy is primarily the alleviation or elimination of whatever distress the patient has when he comes for help, termination should be considered when this point is reached. Most authors, however, enumerate a set of guiding criteria for the selection of patients, especially for

[12]Inclusion in a comparison of elements crucial to one system but omitted in another introduces a bias in favour of the former. In addition, the attempt to make a direct translation of concepts used in one system to concepts used in another may contribute in blurring the differences between systems.

short-term psychotherapy. Such criteria generally include psychological mindedness by the patient with some capacity for introspection (Davanloo 1980, Sifneos 1972), willingness (i.e. motivation) to work in interpretative therapy (Alexander and French 1946; Malan 1976; Sifneos 1972; Davanloo 1980) and the possibility of identifying a circumscribed focus for intervention (Mann 1969; Sifneos 1972; Malan 1976; Balint et al. 1972). In addition, many authors include some measure of ego strength, for example, the history of at least one meaningful relationship in the past and some degree of flexibility (Alexander and French 1946; Sifneos 1972; Davanloo 1980). Somewhat more divergent opinions are found regarding clinical diagnosis and duration of the disorder. However, less severe disorders of shorter duration are, as a rule, considered suitable for short-term psychotherapy.

In general, patients accepted for short-term psychotherapy are evaluated before treatment in one or more intake interview sessions, on which occasions frequent use is made of various rating instruments (Horowitz et al. 1984).

One the whole, these selection criteria apply to cognitive psychotherapy as well. However, the selection of patients in short-term cognitive psychotherapy focusses more on the clinical characteristics of the patient than on any particular conflictual area. Also, no use is made of the concept of ego strength, although attention is paid to flexibility in thinking. The focus of intervention is determined by a conceptualization of the patient in terms of patterns of dysfunctional basic assumptions and faulty cognitions. Assessment is carried out in evaluative sessions in which a larger and more systematic use of assessment instruments is made. In this respect, the greatest similarity is with the short-term psychotherapy proposed by Wolberg (1980). Patient's expectations and goals of treatment are dealt with as in the various types of psychodynamic psychotherapy. When long-term therapy is considered, there is no difference in scope of indications between the two therapy systems.

Therapy Sessions

The number and duration of therapy sessions are quite similar in psychodynamic and in cognitive psychotherapy. When conceived in a short-term format, 15–20 sessions with a frequency of once or twice weekly are planned. In both therapies the frequency of sessions may occasionally be higher in the very initial phase. In psychoanalytic psychotherapy there is concern to keep the number of weekly sessions to a minimum to minimize the occurrence of strong transference (and countertransference) reactions (Offenkrantz and Tobin 1974). Offenkrantz and Tobin suggest that such subtleties as offering different appointment times each week or seeing the patient in different places can be ignored, assuming that a previous agreement on these matters has been reached between therapist and patient.

Therapist-Patient Relationship

Two related but different aspects of the therapist-patient relationship must be considered. The first concerns the establishment of a working alliance, the second, the occurrence of transference and countertransference reactions.

In both therapies emphasis is placed on such therapist characteristics as warmth, genuineness and empathic understanding. Both therapies take into account that some kind of working alliance is necessary. The working alliance in cognitive psychotherapy is more explicitly defined in terms of "collaborative empirism", as described above (see p. 15). Attention is paid to the fact that the patient must become familiar with this type of partnership during the socialization process that precedes the beginning of therapy.

The possible occurrence of transference and countertransference reactions is taken into account in both therapies, however to a larger extent in psychodynamic psychotherapy, where it can become the major focus of treatment. Although conceptualized in different ways (see, for example, Mallinger 1974, for a cognitive formulation of transference), these terms can be assumed to refer to the same process in both therapies. In both short-term dynamic psychotherapy and short-term cognitive therapy transference reactions are dealt with whenever these occur. Since transference reactions occupy a more important position in psychoanalytic psychotherapy, descriptions as to how to deal with different types of these are more frequent in the psychodynamic than in the cognitive psychotherapy literature. Obviously, no attempt is made in cognitive psychotherapy to foster regressive transference. If anything, the establishment of a positive transference is favoured, although always in awareness of the inherent risk of dependency reactions. As pointed out by the present author in the accompanying contribution to this volume, the approach in the case of severely disturbed patients consists of promoting in the therapeutic situation a "secure base" for the patient (Bowlby 1979).

Structure of Sessions

The structure of therapeutic sessions is undoubtedly one distinguishing characteristics of the two respective therapies. Although a considerable scope of therapist activity is permissible in dynamic psychotherapy, the cognitive therapist is much more active than his counterpart in the former approach. Cognitive therapy sessions always follow a pre-established pattern comprising: a checking of the patient's feelings since the previous session, a review of homework assignments, the agreement on an agenda for the session, the assignment of homework, and a short summing up of what has happened during the session. Those with only a superficial knowledge of cognitive psychotherapy can easily obtain the impression that the conduct of this therapy is rigid and mechanical. However, the true situation is different from this image. As in the case of the psychodynamic therapist, the cognitive therapist is aware of the significance of non-verbal cues (voice intensity, rate of speech, silent pauses, occasional changes in the expression of emotions, etc.; for a recent account see Marcus 1985). Whenever any such cue occurs, occasional deviations from the pre-established agenda are prescribed for dealing with that which is immediately taking place. No systematic use of free associations or analyses of dream reports are made in cognitive psychotherapy. However, occasional associations may be provoked to substantiate the patient's dysfunctional thoughts. Also strategies for dealing with reports of dreams have been made available (Freeman 1981; Perris 1986), but such reports are not explicitly requested.

On the whole, both therapist and patient are expected to be very active, at the same time that a consistent use is made of diffrent behavioural or semantic techniques.

Interpretations Versus Hypotheses

Another feature distinguishing the two therapies is the differential use of interpretations as opposed to that of hypotheses. In dynamic psychotherapy therapeutic work is based on the use of interpretations, timely proposed by the therapist to the patient. Interpretations may concern both aspects of transference and aspects of resistance, or they may be provoked by the content of the patient's report or by the occurrence of non-verbal cues. Since it is generally accepted that interpretations should only be made when the patient is adjudged as prepared to accept them, it is obviously impossible to describe beforehand when they are appropriate. One rule of short-term dynamic psychotherapy is that interpretations should not extend beyond the area chosen as the focus of treatment.

The technique of cognitive psychotherapy differs in this respect mainly because of the difference in the structure of the working partnership. In talking with the patient the cognitive therapist makes consistent use of the Socratic method, that is, he assists the patient in deducing conclusions from premises which have emerged in the interaction and which are regarded as hypotheses. Verification of such hypotheses may be reached through deductive questioning or, whenever feasible, by some kind of homework assignment to be carried out by the patient between sessions. In a sense one could maintain that an interpretation is also a hypothesis formulated by the therapist and submitted to the patient for confirmation. However, cognitive therapists maintain that a major difference both in nature and purpose between interpretations and hypotheses does, indeed, exist. The primary purpose of a hypothesis is to act as a tool and to suggest a test: it looks forward and raises questions which demand answering. An interpretation, on the other hand, looks backward: it represents a tentative explanation applied to something that the therapist assumes to have already been observed or discovered. Whereas a hypothesis allows for a test, an interpretation often does not involve testable consequences.

There are also other important differences between an approach based on the use of hypotheses and one based on that of interpretations. These concern basically the often debated risk of acquiescence from the patient. With patients possessing a very low self-esteem the use of interpretations made by the therapist could contribute to consolidating their view that they are not able to reach any understanding by themselves. Thirdly, an untimely or wrong interpretation given in the therapy situation (which always implies some degree of dependency) is much more risky than reaching together with the therapist the formulation of a wrong hypothesis to be rejected when tested and proven untenable. In fact, the interpretation could become reminiscent of dysfunctional communication with a significant figure of the past, experienced earlier in life. Finally, reaching together with the therapist a hypothesis that eventually can be rebutted produces less anxiety and elicits accordingly, less resistance than an interpretation received from the therapist as an "expert".

Activity Between Therapy Sessions

The two types of therapy also differ regarding the nature of the patient's activity between therapy sessions, with particular attention being paid to this in cognitive psychotherapy. One of the dynamic psychotherapies which makes use of activities between sessions is that proposed by Wolberg (1980). However, this particular therapy is considered to be on the periphery of "pure" psychodynamic psychotherapy and among its more eclectic forms. As in behaviour therapy, the assignment of homework to be carried out between sessions is a rule in cognitive psychotherapy. This homework may consist of the monitoring of dysfunctional thoughts on particular occasions, the collection of evidence in support of hypotheses put forward during the session, and the rehearsal of the therapy session that has been recorded on an audiocasette and in appropriate readings, etc. A particular type of special purpose homework is the keeping of experiential diaries. It may be noted that also the therapist may agree on some homework that he will carry out before the next session, for example, a review of the videotaped recording of the session.

Resistance

The concept of resistance, discussed by Freud in his early writings (1895, 1896), is a very important, if controversial aspect of the psychodynamic therapeutic process. In short, resistance refers to factors and forces in the patient which oppose the treatment process. Sandler et al. (1970) correctly point out that the concept is a clinical rather than a psychological one, and that it can easily be extended to other situations besides psychoanalytic treatment. Originally conceived as the patient's opposition to the recovery of traumatic memories (Freud 1895), its meaning has later been developed and refined, both by Freud himself (e.g. 1904, 1926) and by his followers (e.g. A. Freud 1936; Deutsch 1939; Hartmann 1951; Greenson 1967). Numerous classifications of the various types of resistance have been proposed (e.g. Deutsch 1939; Sandler et al. 1970; Devald 1982). That proposed by Sandler and his co-workers is one of the most detailed and consists of ten different categories. These range from the classical conceptions of resistance, those due to the threat posed by the analytic procedure or due to transference-resistance, to those related to the use of faulty or inappropriate technical procedures (Greenson 1967) and those deriving from secondary gain. However, the most important forms seem to include "id resistance", due to the resistance of instinctual impulses to any change in their expression, "superego resistance", deriving from the patient's sense of guilt or his need for punishment, and "repression resistance", conceived of as the individual's defence against the emergence of painful, unconscious memories and impulses.

The occurrence of resistance has, of course, also been both observed and taken into account in cognitive psychotherapy. However, while there is no difference between the psychoanalytic and the cognitive therapeutic conception of resistance deriving from secondary gain or due to the inappropriate use of technical procedures, a difference exists concerning other types of resistance, as recently pointed out by Liotti (1987, in press) in his thorough analysis of the phenomenon. This is not only because the concepts of "id", "superego" and "repression" have no place in the theory of cognitive psychotherapy but also because a more parsimonious explanation of the concept of resistance can be derived form cognitive theory. This difference is examined in more detail in an accompanying contribution in this volume.

Termination

Since the primary goal of psychotherapy, especially of the short-term type, is the alleviation or elimination of the patient's distress, when this goal is reached, the patient must be prepared for termination. In practice, this means that residual transference reactions must be solved, together with any aspects of dependency that may have occurred. The importance of the termination phase, with its possible reactivation of anxiety, is properly acknowledged by all proponents of both long- and short-term therapies. Especially for short-term therapy Hoyt (1979) emphasizes that the issue of termination is always present, indeed "*it is the issue*". Hoyt points out that mere termination can be used suitably to further mourning and working through. Termination is probably less difficult in cognitive psychotherapy because booster sessions at pre-established intervals after termination are generally agreed upon already at the time of the initial contract. Follow-up interviews have been planned also by most therapists with a dynamic orientation (e.g. Mann 1969; Davanloo 1980; Wolberg 1980), but these interviews are not a necessary component of the treatment programme.

Offenkrantz and Tobin (1974) emphasize the ethical aspects of termination. In particular, they stress the necessity for the therapist to make it easy for the patient to terminate, believing the therapist's door to be open for him to return without risking humiliation.

Cognitive Psychotherapy Versus Behaviour Therapy

Introduction

With regard to the relationship of cognitive psychotherapy to behaviour therapy some preliminary comparative data have been presented by Beck (1970, 1976) and by Ryle (1984). In his comparison Beck pointed out that the two therapies had much in common, but that they could be distinguished on both practical and theoretical grounds. Among the common features Beck emphasized: structure of sessions, activity of therapist, focus on overt symptoms or behavioural problems, minor emphasis on recollection of infantile memories, and concern for experimental research work. Among the divergencies, on the other hand, Beck noted the different purpose for the use of the same techniques (see below) and, most important of all, theoretical differences in explaining the dissolution of maladaptive responses following therapy. With reference to the technique of systematic desensitization developed by Wolpe (1969) Beck pointed out that, whereas Wolpe utilizes behavioural or neurophysiological explanations, such as counter-conditioning or reciprocal inhibition, to explain the dissolution of the symptoms, cognitive therapy, focusses on the modification of conceptual systems. Beck's opinion of the relationship between the two therapies is implicit in the section heading he used: "Behaviour Therapy: A Subset of Cognitive Therapy" (Beck 1976, p. 320). This assessment is not likely one easily accepted by behaviour therapists.

In retrospectively evaluating Beck's comparison of the two therapies one gains the immediate impression that Beck's interest lay more in underlining the difference between cognitive therapy and psychoanalysis than in clearly emphasizing the independence of cognitive psychotherapy from both psychoanalysis *and* behaviour therapy. Nevertheless, he concluded his comparison by pointing out that the cognitive model was more parsimonious in its explanation of various neurotic syndromes than the elaborate theories of psychoanalysis, at the same time that he highlighted the weakness of behaviour therapy both in explaining the development of neurotic syndromes and in achieving their clinical improvement.

Judge from a historical perspective it is evident that the focus on cognitive processes which Beck (1970) took still represented a revolutionary conception in behaviour therapy. In fact, the interest of behaviour therapists in cognitive mediating processes was very new at that time, and its much heated debate developed only in the following years (cf., for example, the first issue of *Behaviour Therapy*, 1970; Lewidge's 1978 critique of cognitve-behavioral modification; and the debate between Beck, Mahoney, Ellis and Wolpe in *American Psychologist* in 1978–1979).

However, as acknowledgement of the importance of cognitive variables rapidly increased among leading behaviour therapists in the early 1970s (Franks and Wilson 1973–1976), it is not surprising that the revolutionary conceptions of cognitive psychotherapy were eventually re-interpreted as being mere "extensions and clinically relevant applications consistent with an existing conceptual model and empirical basis" (Wilson 1978, p. 17). This opinion has been reinforced by two factors. First, leading authors (e.g. Mahoney, Meichenbaum, Lazarus, Goldfried) very early assumed what, at least in part, could be seen as an intermediate position which largely satisfied both behaviour therapists and cognitive therapists. Secondly, the emphasis on evaluation and experimental research, common to the two therapy systems, favoured the friendly interaction between cognitive therapists and behaviour therapists of various orientations, making use of the same journals and participating in the same congresses. Beck and Mahoney (1979) pointed out in this regard that almost half the current editorial board of *Cognitive Therapy and Research* were also members of the Association for the Advancement of Behavior Therapy. Thus it should not be surprising if, at a superficial glance, the boundaries between cognitive therapy and behaviour therapy appear blurred; they are, indeed, difficult to distinguish.

The purpose here is to contribute to a clearer understanding of the demarcation between these two therapy systems, following an approach similar to that used in the previous section comparing psychoanalytically oriented psychotherapy and cognitive psychotherapy. However, we can dispense with a repetition at each instance regarding the distinguishing characteristics of cognitive psychotherapy, as these have already been defined above.

Theoretical Issues

Conflicting views at the theoretical level occur in behaviour therapy as well as in psychoanalysis. Mahoney has aptly pointed out that "many psychologists fail to realize that just as there are many subvarieties of psychoanalysis, there are a host of behaviorisms" (Mahoney 1980, p. 96). We will therefore begin this comparison of behaviour therapy and cognitive psychotherapy with a broad summary of the main theoretical orientations endorsed in behaviour therapy.

Watson (1913), regarded by many as the father of American behaviourism, originally proposed two subtypes of behaviourism: (a) metaphysical (or radical) behaviourism and (b) methodological behaviourism. The former is concerned principally with the subject matter of psychological inquiry; the latter with the procedures and methods of psychological inquiry rather than with its subject matter.

Early behaviourism, as Schwartz (1982) has pointed out, rejected the existence of "mind" and "mental states" because of the contemporary appeal of logical positivism. To a certain extent the influence of this philosophical school can still be seen. Besides the complete denial of any form of mentalism, radical behaviourism postulates that almost all human behaviour is determined (through classically conceived conditioning) by environmental influences. Metaphysical behaviourism, in other words, postulates an "external" determinism in contrast to the "internal determinism assumed in psychoanalytic theory. Consequently, the view of man in radical behaviourism is that of a passive tabula rasa on which the environment imprints its distinguishing marks. This conception is best illustrated by Watson's famous statement that, were he to be given "a dozen healthy infants" and his own "specific world to bring them up", he guaranteed that he could take anyone of them at random and "train him to become any type of specialist" he might select (Watson 1924, p. 104).

Another of Watson's tenets was that all experience could be reduced to glandular secretions and muscular movements; conscious mental processes were beyond the realm of scientific inquiry. This latter point was further emphasized in methodological behaviourism, rejecting as non-scientific data obtained by introspective analysis and placing a strong emphasis on "observability". This position has its historical roots in the conceptions of Hume (see "Philosophical Foundations", above). Other distinguishing tenets of methodological behaviourism are: a strongly held assumption of determinism, an emphasis on operationalization and testability, and a stress on controlled experimentation and independent replication.

Although Watson's metaphysical behaviourism is hardly endorsed in its original form by contemporary bahaviourists, traces of it are still detectable in some of Skinner's (1974) recent conceptions. On the other hand, adherence to methodological behaviourism has survived as a distinguishing characteristic of most psychologists (Mahoney et al. 1974).

Whereas the learning theory of radical behaviourism relied almost exclusively on the principles of Pavlovian conditioning (termed "type S learning", because of its stress on the stimulus), a later development, generally associated with the work of Skinner but, in fact traceable to that of Thorndike (1898, cited in Mahoney 1980a), relies on what has become known as "operant conditioning" ("type R learning", because of the emphasis on the response). According to the basic postulate of operant conditioning, the response is no longer conceived as merely reflexive but as intrumental (operant) in producing a consequence. The shift of emphasis from type S to type R learning has contributed, in fact, to bringing into focus the processes by which a response is strengthened (via reinforcement) or weakened (via punishment). Both reinforcement and punishment may have either positive or negative valence. The four resulting categories of consequences (positive and negative reinforcement, positive and negative punishment), together with the concept of "contingency" (i.e. the relationship between a set of antecedents, behaviours and consequences) and that of "extinction", are seen as representing the most fundamental concepts for a correct understanding of both the learning process and the procedure used in traditional behavioural modification. To be noted, also, in the case of operant conditioning is the fact that no specific attention is paid to such concepts as "thought", "feeling" and the like.

Most of the therapeutic work (or behavioural modification) carried out by behaviour therapists (or behavioural "modifiers" as they prefer to define themselves) has been based on the principles sketched above (cf., for example, Eysenck 1959, 1960; Eysenck and Rachman 1965; Ullmann and Krasner 1965; Ulrich et al. 1966–1970; Wolpe 1958, 1969). In this context neuroses or neurotic symptoms are conceived as learned habits existing in the present (Eysenck 1959), that is, as involuntarily acquired, reinforced responses to specific stimuli in the environment. Consistently with this assumption, emphasis has been placed on the elimination of symptoms to eliminate the neurosis (Eysenck 1979).

Although there are differences between the Wolpe-Eysenck and the Skinnerian approaches to the conception of neurosis and behavioural modification, there are also striking similarities. Both approaches, for example, focus on overt response, rely on a conditioning model and make use of the concept of reinforcement. Criticism of both approaches (see below) became clearly manifest in the middle of the 1960s, almost simultaneously with the emergence of cognitive psychotherapy.

Three works, all appearing in 1965, seem to have contributed fundamentally to the movement which was to produce cognitive psychotherapy. The first, by Goldiamond (1965), pointed out that the client, as well as the therapist, can alter his environment; this was seminal for the development of Bandura's view of "reciprocal determinism" (Bandura 1974, p. 866–867). The second article, that by Homme (1965), a former pupil of Skinner, defended the scientific legitimacy of examining the client's thoughts. This paper was important for a series of experiments on "covert conditioning" soon to follow (e.g. Cautela 1966, 1967, 1971). Proponents of this new view argued that thought processes must be considered as sequences of stimuli and responses ("S-R mediators"), and that thoughts could be rewarded and punished like overt responses. The third paper, and the most critical of the "learning-theory" approach to neurosis, was published by Breger and McGaugh (1965). This harshly criticized not only the emphasis put on the peripheral response and the use of the concept of reinforcement but also the very core assumption that concepts derived from Pavlovian and operant conditioning could be used as explanatory principles. After presenting cogent arguments in support of their criticism, Breger and McGaugh proposed a reformulation of current learning theory, centered around the concepts of information storage and retrieval. In keeping with this perspective, they proposed that a conceptualization of the problem of neurosis should be founded on the basic idea that "what is learned in a neurosis is a set of central strategies which guide the individual's adaptation to his environment" (Breger and McGaugh 1965, p. 355).

In summarizing the state of the art of behaviour therapy at the beginning of the 1980s Davison (1980) pointed out that the real cognitive revolution in behaviour therapy could be identified in the proposals to adopt a truly cognitive view of maladaptive behaviour, to take seriously what cognitive psychology has to offer, and to attempt to integrate cognitive theories into behaviour therapy. In particular, Davison emphasized that a "little r" theory was not a cognitive theory in a true meaning (Davison 1980, p. 207).

In addition, criticism came from other sources, for example, in the emphasis put by Beck (1963/64), Ellis (1962) and Frank (1961) on the importance of cognitions in psychopathology and psychotherapy. From these there developed the third major theoretical wave in behaviour therapy: the cognitive-social learning theory (CSL). As in the case of views founded on classical and operant conditioning, CSL also bases its conception of human learning on associationism, however the learning process is interpreted here as involving cognitive mechanisms rather than conditioning. In fact, Bandura (1977) proposed that four basic forms of learning should be taken into account: direct associative experience, vicarious learning, symbolic instruction and symbolic logic. In the light of this new conception the importance of the individual's perception of the stimulus, perception of the response and perception of the contingency is fully acknowledged. However, this acknowledgement is far from unanimous (cf. Mahoney 1977, 1980a; Farkas 1980; Grossberg 1981; Schwartz 1982 for reviews of the most recent debate).

It is against the background of the growth of CSL that the boundaries between behaviour therapy and cognitive psychotherapy seem to have become blurred, especially if the observer's attention if focussed more on the overlap in the use of techniques than on the underlying theoretical issues. Actually, a crucial difference between the behavioural and the cognitive approach concerns the status assigned to cognitions in the two systems. In the former cognitions are more like the links in an S-R chain (S-R mediators) which are behaviours in their own right (Ullmann 1970). In the latter cognitions are regarded as organized and quasi-autonomous systems which obey different sets of laws than overt behaviour, and which influence behaviour in complex ways.

In concluding this short review of the different theoretical approaches to behaviour therapy, we must mention some major attempts at integrating behaviour therapy and psychoanalysis. The first, made by Dollard and Miller (1950), consists of a thoroughly systematic effort at incorporating both subjectively and objectively observable responses into a behaviouristic position. The second is the more recent attempt by Wachtel (1973). Indicative of the attitudinal change which had occurred in the intervening 2 decades is the fact that whereas the Dollard and Miller effort (representing an early attempt to account for cognitive variables within a behaviouristic framework) received a mixed reaction in the behaviouristic literature and is not quoted in recent textbooks written by leading behaviourists (e.g. Eysenck 1960; Ullmann and Krasner 1975; Mahoney 1980a), Wachtel's book has promoted both efforts among the representatives of the two therapeutic systems to discuss differences with each other (cf. Wachtel 1982; Goldfried 1982) and practical applications (e.g. Birk 1974; Feather and Rhoads 1972; Rhoads and Feather 1974). In the epilogue to his work Goldfried could point to the growing awareness among psychotherapists from different orientations as to the need for self-examination and for attempts toward rapprochement (e.g. Dewald 1976; Silverman 1974; Lazarus 1977; Davison 1980). However, the suggestion of a rapprochement has not passed without debate (e.g. Birk and Brinkley-Birk 1974; Messer and Winokur 1980).

Comparative Aspects

While it was difficult above to specify a particular type of psychoanalytically oriented psychotherapy for the purpose of comparison, it would be senseless to try to identify any particular behaviour therapy approach and to use this as representative. In fact, behaviour therapy, in accordance with its very premises, comprises a large number of particular techniques related to each other by reliance on certain common theoretical principles and by a strong emphasis on methodological aspects. Also it would not make sense to include in a comparison variables which are relevant to psychoanalytic psychotherapy and/or cognitive psychotherapy but which are not equally applicable to the behaviour therapy perspective. Goisman (1985), for example, points out that it would not be useful to ask how psychoanalytic psychotherapy and behaviour therapy each deal with transference, since the concept of transference itself depends on psychoanalytical constructs that have no place in behaviour therapy.

Selection of Patients

Since behaviour therapy is primarily concerned wih the modification of manifest behaviour, there is in principle no category of patients deemed unsuitable for this therapeutic approach. However, at the time when behaviour therapy was not yet recognized as an acceptable treatment method other than in a few mental health institutions, the only patients for whom this method was considered suitable were those regarded least likely to improve: chronic, severely impaired schizophrenics and retardates. Only much later, when the results of early trials showed some efficacy (at least within the limits of the institution), was the application of behaviour therapy extended to more complex problems.

One particular feature of behaviour therapy, shared at least in part with cognitive psychotherapy, is the concern with a thorough assessment of the behaviour which is to be modified. In this respect a difference exists between orthodox behavioural assessment and CSL assessment. In the latter greater attention is paid to cognitive and emotional factors. In both instances the information to be assessed has importance for the formulation of therapeutic goals and for the choice of appropriate treatment techniques.

Assessment in cognitive psychotherapy aims at identifying the various types of faulty cognitions on the patient's part and the basic dysfunctional assumptions which influence his view of himself, his environment and his future.

Number and Structure of Sessions

No clear-cut recommendation as to the number of sessions, generalizable to all approaches, is available in the literature. In general it can be said that the number of sessions is largely determined by the achievement of stipulated therapeutic goals. Usually, however, it is contained within limits comparable to those of short-term psychotherapy.

Therapy sessions are highly structured, probably with less flexibility for the therapist than in cognitive psychotherapy. A consistent use is, of course, made of various therapeutic techniques, related to the patient's particular problems. Differences in the purpose served by the same therapeutic techniques in behaviour therapy and in cognitive psychotherapy have been mentioned above.

Therapist-Patient Relationship

A common misunderstanding is that the therapist-patient relationship in behaviour therapy is mechanical. Behaviour therapists have, themselves, contributed to such misunderstanding. Krasner (1962), in fact, depicted the behavioural, modifier as a learning technician or a "social reinforcement machine". Behaviour therapists do not dwell on the issue of the therapist-patient relationship, but to the extent that it is seen to be important in securing the patient's cooperation (APA's Task Force on Behavior Therapy, 1973), the therapist's use of warmth and acceptance is commonly acknowledged (Karasu 1977). Hollender (1975) has characterized the therapist-patient relationship in behavioural therapies as an "educative, teacher-pupil relationship", and Karasu (1977) portrays it as a deliberately structured learning alliance. Goisman (1985) has pointed out that true neutrality is less likely to occur because of the patient's view of the therapist's remarks as either reinforcing, punishing or neutral.

Activity Between Therapy Sessions

Since cognitive psychotherapy has taken from behaviour therapy the practice of homework assignments, there is no difference in the formal use of this technique in the two therapy systems. However, once again it should be noted that the purpose of homework assignments differs in the respective therapies, the difference being of the same nature as that for the other techniques mentioned above.

Resistance

A volume on the issue of resistance has recently been edited by Wachtel (1982) in collaboration with distinguished representatives of both the psychoanalytic and the behaviour therapy schools. Although the aim here was to find points of contact, the result rather reinforced the impression of a gulf dividing the two therapy systems. Whereas the psychoanalytically trained contributors discussed the issue of resistance in terms of those perspectives mentioned above contributors representing the perspective of behaviour therapy viewed the problems of resistance principally in terms of the individual's difficulties in carrying out specific homework assignments. In his concluding contribution to this collection, Goldfried had to confess that he was unable to specify any common elements and could only point to the differences between the two therapy systems. In this respect, the attitude of cognitive psychotherapy is closer to that of psychoanalytically oriented psychotheraphy than to that of behaviour therapy, although an interpretation of resistance is approached at a different level of explanation (Liotti 1987).

Focus on Cognition and the Emergence of a New Integrating Paradigm

In concluding this description of cognitive psychotherapy we can return to a statement made in the introduction. The emergence and the rapid growth of cognitive psychotherapy, with its specific focus on cognitions, represents, it was suggested, the emergence of a much needed integrating paradigm (Beck 1976; Mahoney 1977). As argued by the present author elsewhere (Perris 1985a, b), this new, encompassing paradigm is by no means limited to the field of psychotherapy but extends to conceptions of psychopathology as well.

According to Kuhn (1962), the emergence of a new paradigm is always preceded by a state of crisis that develops when it is recognized that the existing paradigm is failing in the face of mounting "anomalies". In the case of psychotherapy, however, to speak of a paradigm "shift" may be rather inaccurate. The concept of a revolutionary shift usually implies that a generally shared paradigm previously existed and commanded consensus but has entered a state of crisis. Psychotherapy, on the other hand, is unequivocally in a critical pre-paradigmatic state, or, if one prefers, in a state of competing paradigms, each in crisis. This is witnessed by the several competing schools and the lack of consensus regarding the definition of basic concepts, theories and even facts within each leading school. Colby (1964) pointed out that in the psychoanalytic field no new therapeutic concepts or techniques had emerged for years, and that psychotherapeutic research had ceased to have an effect on the practice of therapy. Grünbaum (1983) emphasized the logical incompatibility of some formulations of neo-revisionist theory, exemplified by the mutally antagonist views of Kohut and Kernberg, based on a schism between Klein and Fairbairn (Robbins 1980). Peterfreund, (1983) underlined that those working psychoanalytically according to what he defined as a stereotyped fashion "all too often, to demonstrate a given thesis" add "one questionable, unsubstantiated assumption to other equally questionable and unsubstantiated assumptions" (Peterfreund 1983, p. 53). The crisis of behaviour therapy prior to the growth of interest in "mediating" cognitive variables has been analysed by Farkas (1980) who pointed out, among other problematic issues, the uncertainties in defining even the concept of "behaviour".

Other signs of crisis in the psychodomain are the expansion of the theoretical suprastructure without any whole-hearted relinguishing of old-fashioned concepts (Bruch 1974), the tendency to an infinite regress implicit in the modern concept of ego functions, and the steady increase in the length of both treatment and training, as if obsessed by the mirage of mythical perfection (Farber 1963). In the field of behaviour therapy the culmination of the crisis can be summarized by the conclusion reached by Farkas that "the behavior therapy community-at-large has the choice of maintaining or relinguishing a label that is more symbolic of its authors' ideals than representative of typical outpatient practice" (Farkas 1980, p. 372).

What are, then, the credentials of cognitive psychotherapy to represent an integrating paradigm? It has been the aim of this chapter to provide such a set of credentials; the following few points may represent a summary.

1. Cognitive psychotherapy has developed from dissatisfaction with existing high-level explanations in the existing theories of psychotherapy. This dissatisfaction is not a completely new phenomenon but can be traced to the early deviationists from the original Freudian psychoanalytic theory.
2. Cognitive psychotherapy does not subscribe to a vitalistic separation of the mind from the body or to a mindless reductionism.
3. Cognitive psychotherapy is based on an evolutionary theory of learning that takes into account biological structures in an attempt to explain biological order, organization, control, regulation and adaptation.
4. Explanations in cognitive psychotherapy are more parsimonious than those adopted in psychoanalysis and do not rely on metaphorical concepts of psychic energies or forces. Nor is there the regressive necessity to rely upon anthropomorphic concept of ego for dealing with the issue of adaptation.
5. The most relevant concepts used by current therapy systems can easily be incorporated into, and more parsimoniously defined within, a cognitive therapy framework.
6. Although cognitive psychotherapy makes philosophical sense, it does not need to resort to high-level explanations of a philosophical nature.
7. Modern revisionist attempts within the major therapy systems tend to converge in their incorporation of concepts and principles derived from cognitive theory.
8. There is hardly any change effected by a psychotherapeutic method relying on the achievement of insight that is not "cognitive".

References

Adler A (1956) The individual psychology of Alfred Adler. Harper, New York
Alexander F, French TM (1946) Psychoanalytic therapy. Ronald, New York
Altshuler KZ, Rush AJ (1984) Psychoanalytic and cognitive therapies: a comparison of theory and tactics. Am J Psychother 38:4–16
APA Task Force (1973) Behavior therapy in psychiatry. APA, Washington DC (Report 5)
Arendt H (1978) Thinking. Harcourt Brace Jovanovich, New York
Arieti S (1974) The cognitive-volitional school. In: Arieti S (ed) American handbook of psychiatry, 2nd edn, vol. 1. Basic Books, New York, pp 877–903
Bacon F (1621) Nonim organum. Oxford Univ Press, Oxford (1889)
Balint M, Ornstein PH, Balint E (1972) Focal psychotherapy. Lippincott, Philadelphia

Bandura A (1974) Behavior therapy and the models of man. Am Psychol 29:859–869
Bandura A (1977) Self-efficacy: toward a unifying theory of behavioral change. Psychol Rev 84: 191–215
Beck AT (1952) Successful outpatient psychotherapy of a chronic schizophrenic with a delusion of borrowed guilt. Psychiatry 15:305–312
Beck AT (1963) Thinking and depression. I. Arch Gen Psychiat 9:324–333
Beck AT (1964) Thinking and depression. II. Arch Gen Psychiatry 10:561–571
Beck AT (1970) Cognitive therapy: nature and relation to behavior therapy. Behav Ther 1:184–200
Beck AT (1976) Cognitive therapy and the emotional disorders. International Universities Press, New York
Beck AT (1985) Cognitive therapy, behavior therapy, psychoanalysis, and pharmacotherapy. A cognitive continuum. In: Mahoney MJ, Freeman A (eds) Cognition and psychotherapy. Plenum, New York, pp 325–347
Beck AT, Emery G (1985) Anxiety disorders and phobias. Basic Books, New York
Beck AT, Mahoney MJ (1979) Schools of thought. Am Psychol 34:93–98
Beck AT, Rush AJ, Shaw BF, Emery G (1979) Cognitive therapy of depression. Guilford, New York
Becker R (1985) Die kognitive Wende in der Verhaltenstherapie. Eine Bruecke zur Psychoanalyse? Nervenarzt (Berlin) 57:379
Bieber I (1980) Cognitive psychoanalysis. Aronson, New York
Birk L (1974) Intensive group-therapy: an effective behavioral-psychoanalytic method. Am J Psychiatry 131:17–20
Birk L, Brinkley-Birk AW (1974) Psychoanalysis and behavior therapy. Am J Psychiatry 131:449–510
Blight JG (1981) Must psychoanalysis retreat to hermeneutics? Psychoanal Contemp Thought 4:147-205
Bowlby J (1969–1980) Attachment and loss. Basic Books, New York, vols 1–3
Bowlby J (1979) Self-reliance and some conditions that promote it. In: Bowlby J (ed) The making and breaking of affectional bonds. Tavistock, London
Brady JP, Davison GC, Dewald PA et al. (1982) Some views on the effective principles of psychotherapy. In: Goldfried M (ed) Converging themes in psychotherapy. Springer, Berlin Heidelberg New York, pp 155–190
Breger A, McGaugh JL (1965) Critique and reformulation of 'learning theory' approaches to psychotherapy and neurosis. Psychol Bull 63:338–358
Breuer J, Freud S (1893) Studies on hysteria. Standard edition, vol 2. Hogarth, London
Bruch H (1974) Learning psychotherapy. Rationale and ground rules. Swedish Translation Att lära sig psykoterapi. Natur och Kultur, Stockholm
Butcher P (1984) Existential-behavior therapy: a possible paradigm? Br J Med Psychol 57:265–274
Cautela JR (1966) Treatment of compulsive behavior by covert sensitization. Psychol Rec 16:33–41
Cautela JR (1967) Covert sensitization. Psychol Rep 20:459–468
Cautela JR (1971) Covert extinction. Behav Ther 2:192–200
Cicero MT (1980) Tusculanarum disputationum. Zanichelli, Bologna (own translation)
Colby KM (1964) Psychotherapeutic process. AM Rev Psychol 15:347–370
Crowley RM (1985) Cognitions in interpersonal theory and practice. In: Mahoney MJ, Freeman A (eds) Cognition and psychotherapy. Plenum, New York, pp 291–312
Davanloo H (1980) Short-term dynamic psychotherapy. Aronson, New York
Davison GC (1980) And now for something different: cognitions and little 'r'. In: Mahoney MJ (ed) Psychotherapy process. Lyle Stuart-Citadel, New York
Dember WN (1974) Motivation and the cognitive revolution. Am Psychol 29:161–168
Deutsch H (1939) A discussion of certain forms of resistance. Int J Psychoanal 20:72–83
Dewald PA (1976) Toward a general concept of the therapeutic process. Int J Psychoanal Psychother 5:283–299
Dewald PA (1982) Psychoanalytic perspectives on resistance. In: Wachtel PL (ed) Resistance. Plenum, New York, pp 45–68
Dollard J, Miller NE (1950) Personality and psychotherapy. McGraw Hill, New York
Eagle M (1980) A critical examination of motivational explanation in psychoanalysis. Psychoanal Contemp Thought 3:329–380.
Ellis A (1962) Reason and emotion in psychotherapy. Lyle Stuart-Citadel, New York
Epictetus (1984) Handbook on the art of living. Encheiridion. Swedish transl by G Grunewald & SY Rudberg P Åström, Gothenburg

Eysenck HJ (1959) Learning theory and behaviour therapy. J Ment Sci 105:61–75
Eysenck HJ (1960) Behaviour therapy and the neuroses. Pergamon, New York
Eysenck HJ, Rachmann S (1965) The causes and cures of neurosis. Knapp, San Diego
Farber LH (1963) Perfectibility and the psychoanalytic candidate. J Existent 3:285–292
Farkas GM (1980) An ontological analysis of behavior therapy. Am Psychol 35:364–374
Feather BW, Rhodes JM (1972) Psychodynamic behavior therapy. Arch Gen Psychiatry 26:503–511
Flax J (1981) Psychoanalysis and the philosophy of science: critique or resistance? J Philosophy 78:561–569
Ford UB, Urban DH (1965) Systems of psychotherapy. Wiley, New York
Frank J (1961) Persuasion and healing. John Hopkins University Press, Baltimore
Frank J (1971) Therapeutic factors in psychotherapy. Am J Psychiatry 25:350–361
Frank J (1974) Therapeutic components of psychotherapy. J Nerv Ment Dis 159:325–342
Frank J (1985) Therapeutic components shared by all therapies. In: Mahoney MJ, Freeman A (eds) Cognition and psychotherapy. New York, Plenum, pp 49–80
Franks C, Wilson G (1973–1976) Annual review of behavior therapy: theory and practice. Brunner/Mazel, New York
Freeman A (1981) Dreams and images in cognitive therapy. In: Emery G, Hollon SD, Bedrosian R (eds) New directions in cognitive therapy. Guilford, New York
Freud A (1936) The Ego and the mechanisms of defence. Hogarth, London
Freud S (1904) Freud's psychoanalytic procedure. Standard edition, vol 7. Hogarth, London, pp 249–254
Freud S (1914) On narcissism. Standard edition, vol 14. Hogarth, London, pp 73–102
Freud S (1915) Instincts and their vicissitudes. Standard edition, vol 14. Hogarth, London, pp 109–140
Freud S (1917) Analytic therapy. Standard edition, vol 16. Hogarth, London
Freud S (1926) Inhibitions, symptoms and anxiety. Standard edition, vol 20. Hogarth, London, pp 87–172
Freud S (1937) Constructions in analysis. Hogarth, London, pp 257–269
Freud S (1976a) Studies on hysteria. Standard edition, vol 2. Hogarth, London
Freud S (1976b) Further remarks on the neuro-psychoses of defence. Hogarth, London, pp 162, 185
Fromm E (1962) Beyond the chains of illusion. Trident, New York
Fromm E (1970) The crisis of psychoanalysis. Penguin, Harmondsworth
Frye N (1957) Anatomy of criticism. Atheneum, New York
Garfield SL (1982) What are the therapeutic variables in psychotherapy? In: Goldfried M (ed) Converging themes in psychotherapy. Springer, Berlin Heidelberg New York, pp 135–142
Gersham H (1976) Old and new therapies: discussion. Am J Psychoanal 36:315–318
Goisman RM (1985) The psychodynamics of prescribing in behavior therapy. Am J Psychiatry, 142:675–679
Goldfried M (ed) (1982) Converging themes in psychotherapy. Springer, Berlin Heidelberg New York
Goldfried M, Padawer W (1982) Current status and future directions in psychotherapy. In: Goldfried M (ed) Converging themes in psychotherapy. Springer, Berlin Heidelberg New York
Goldiamond I (1965) Self-control procedures in personal behavior problems. Psychol Rep 17:851–868
Greenson R (1967) The technique and practice of psychoanalysis. International Universities Press, New York
Grossberg JM (1981) Comments about cognitive therapy and behavior therapy. J Behav Ther Exp Psychiatry 7:25–33
Grünbaum A (1979) Epistemologic liabilities of the clinical appraisal of psychoanalytic theory. Psychoanal Contemp Thought 21:451–526
Grünbaum A (1981) The placebo concept. Behav Res Ther 19:157–167
Grünbaum A (1983a) The foundations of psychoanalysis. University of California Press, Berkeley, CA
Grünbaum A (1983b) Is object relations theory better founded than orthodox psychoanalysis? J Philosophy 80:46–51
Guidano VF, Liotti G (1983) Cognitive processes and emotional disorders. Guilford, New York
Guidano VF, Liotti G (1985) A constructivistic foundation for cognitive therapy. In: Mahoney MJ, Freeman A (eds) Cognition and psychotherapy. Plenum, New York, pp 101–142
Habermas J (1971) Knowledge and human interests. Beacon, Boston
Hartmann H (1951) Technical implications of Ego psychology. In: Essays on ego psychology. International Universities Press, New York, pp 142–154

Hollander M (1975) Behavior therapy approach. In: Loew C, Grayson N, Loew N (eds) Three psychotherapies. A clinical comparison. Brunner/Mazel, New York
Holt RC (1972) Freud's mechanistic and humanistic images of man. Psychoanal Contemp Sci 1:3-24
Holt RC (1981) The death and transfiguration of metapsychology. Int Rev Psychoanal 8:129-143
Holt RC (1982) The manifest and latent meaning of metapsychology. Annual Psychoanal 10:233-255
Homme LE (1965) Control of coverants, the operants of the mind. Psychol Rec 15:501-511
Horney K (1942) Self analysis. Norton, New York
Horowitz M (1977) Cognitive and interactive aspects of splitting. Am J Psychiatry 134:549-553
Horowitz M, Wilner N, Marmar C, Krupnik J (1980) Pathological grief and the activation of latent self-image. Am J Psychiatry 137:1157-1162
Horowitz M, Marmar C, Krupnik J et al. (1984) Personality styles and brief psychotherapy. Basic Books, New York
Hoyt MF (1979) Aspects of termination in a time-limited brief psychotherapy. Psychiatry 42:208-218
Hume D (1898) A treatise on human nature. Longmans Green, London
Hume D (1977) An enquiry concerning human understanding. Hackett, Indianapolis
Jacobson E (1954) The self and the object world. International Universities Press, New York, pp 14-15
Kant I (1952) The critique of pure reason. In: Hutchins RM (ed) Great books of the western world. Encyclopedia Britannica, Chicago, vol 42, pp 1-250
Kant I (1917) Gesammelte Schriften. Berlin, Reimer.
Kant I (1964) The classification of mental disorders. Doylestown Foundation, Doylestown
Karasu TB (1977) Psychotherapies: an overview. Am J Psychiatry 134:851-863
Kelly G (1955) The psychology of personal constructs. Norton, New York
Kendall PC (1982-1985) Advances in cognitive-behavioral research and therapy. Academic, New York, 4 vol
Kendall PC, Hollon SD (1979) Assessment strategies for cognitive-behavioral interventions. Academic, New York
Klein GS (1976) Psychoanalytic theory. International Universities Press, New York
Kovel J (1976) A complete guide to therapy. Penguin, Harmondsworth, Middlesex
Krasner L (1962) The therapist as a social reinforcement machine. In: Strupp H, Luborsky L (eds) Research in psychotherapy, vol 2. American Psychological Association, Washington, DC, pp 61-94
Kuhn T (1962) The structure of scientific revolutions. University of Chicago Press, Chicago
Lakatos I (1970) Falsification and the methodology of scientific research programmes. In: Lakatos I, Musgrave A (eds) Criticism and the growth of knowledge. Cambridge University Press, Cambridge, pp 91-195
Lazarus AA (1977) Has behavior therapy outlived its usefulness? Am Psychol 32:550-554
Lewidge B (1978) Cognitive-behavior modification. A step in the wrong direction? Psychol Bull 85:353-375
Liotti G (1987) The resistance to change of cognitive structures. A counterproposal to psychoanalytic metapsychology. Int J Cog Psychother (in press)
Liotti G, Reda MA (1981) Some epistemological remarks on cognitive therapy, behavior therapy and psychoanalysis. Cog Ther Res 5:231-236
Lungwitz H (1955-1980) Lehrbuch der Psychobiologie. Hans Lungwitz Stiftung, Berlin, 8 vol
Lungwitz H (1980) Psychobiologie der Neurosen. Presented by R Becker. Rombach, Freiburg
MacHovec FJ (1984) Current therapies and the ancient East. Am J Psychother 38:87-96
Mahoney MJ (1974) Cognition and behavior modification. Ballinger, Cambridge
Mahoney MJ (1977) Reflections on the cognitive-learning trend in psychotherapy. Am Psychol 32:5-13
Mahoney MJ (1979) Cognitive skills and athletic performance. In: Kendall PC, Hollon SD (eds) Cognitive-behavioral interventions. Academic, New York, pp 423-443
Mahoney MJ (1980a) Abnormal psychology. Harper and Row, San Francisco
Mahoney MJ (1980b) Psychotherapy and the structure of personal revolutions. In: Mahoney MJ (ed) Psychotherapy process. Plenum, New York, pp 157-180
Mahoney MJ (1985) Psychotherapy and human change processes. In: Mahoney MJ, Freeman A (eds) Cognition and psychotherapy. Plenum, New York, pp 3-48
Mahoney MJ, Kazdin AE, Lesswing NJ (1974) Behavior modification: delusion or deliverance? In: Franks C, Wilson G (eds) Annual review of behavior therapy: theory and practice. Brunner/Mazel, New York
Malan D (1976) The frontier of brief psychotherapy. Plenum, New York

Mallinger A (1974) Transference: a cognitive approach. Am J Psychoanal 34:51–62
Mann J (1969) Time-limited psychotherapy. Harvard University Press, Cambridge
Marcus Aurelius (1948) Ricordi. Greek text and Ital translation by C Mazzantini. Chiantore, Turin (own translation)
Marcus N (1985) Utilization of nonverbal expressive bahavior in cognitive therapy. Am J Psychother 39:467–478
Martin AR (1976) Old and new psychotherapy: a heuristic approach. Am J Psychoanal 36:291–310
Meichenbaum D (1977) Cognitive-behavior modification. Plenum, New York
Meichenbaum D, Asarnow J (1979) Cognitive-bahavioral modification and metacognitive development: implications for the classroom. In: Kendall PC, Hollon SD (eds) Cognitive-behavioral interventions. Academic, New York
Merluzzi TV, Glass CR, Genest M (1981) Cognitive Assessment. Guilford, New York
Messer SB, Winokur M (1980) Some limits to the integration of psychoanalysis and behavior therapy. Am Psychol 35:818–827
Mora G (1975) Historical and theoretical trends in psychiatry. In: Freedman AM, Kaplan HI, Sadock BJ (eds) Comprehensive textbook of psychiatry, 2nd edn. Williams and Wilkins, Baltimore, pp 1–75
Murray EJ (1983) Beyond behavioural and dynamic therapy. Br J Clin Psychol 22:127–128
Neu J (1977) Emotion, thought and therapy. Routledge and Kegan Paul, London
Offenkrantz W, Tobin A (1974) Psychoanalytic psychotherapy. Arch Gen Psychiatry 30:593–606
Parloff M (1975) Twenty-five years of research in psychotherapy. Albert Einstein College of Medicine, New York
Perris C (1985a) Cognitive therapy: the emergence of a new paradigm in psychotherapy and in psychiatry. Read at the WPA int symp on affective disorders, 13–17 Oct 1985, Athens, Greece
Perris C (1985b) Towards an integrating theory of depression focusing on the concept of vulnerability. Read at the WPA int symp on affective disorders, 13–17 Oct 1985 Athens, Greece
Perris C (1986) Cognitive therapy: theory and practice (in Swedish). Natur och Kultur, Stockholm
Peterfreund E (1971) Information systems, and psychoanalysis. International Universities Press, New York
Peterfreund E (1975) The need for a new general theoretical frame of reference for psychoanalysis. Psychoanal 44:534–549
Peterfreund E (1983) The process of psychoanalytic therapy. Lawrence Erlbaum Associates, Hillsdale
Peterfreund E, Franceschini E (1973) On information, motivation, and meaning. In: Rubinstein BR (ed) Psychoanalysis and contemporary science. MacMillan, New York
Pine F (1985) Developmental theory and clinical process. Yale University Press, New Haven, Conn
Plato (1963) Dialogues (in Swedish). Forum, Uddevalla
Popper K (1962) Conjectures and refutations. Basic Books, New York
Raimy V (1975) Misunderstandings of the Self. Jossey-Bass, San Francisco
Rank O (1945) Will therapy and truth and reality. Knopf, New York
Rapaport D (1959) The structure of psychoanalytic theory. Psychol Issues 6
Reda AM (1986) Sistemi cognitivi complessi e psicoterapia. Nuova Italia Scientifica, Rome
Rendon M (1985) Cognitions and psychoanalysis. A Horneyan perspective. In: Mahoney MJ, Freeman A (eds) Cognition and psychotherapy. Plenum, New York, pp 277–290
Reynolds DK (1976) Morita psychotherapy. University of California Press, Berkeley
Rhoads JM, Feather BW (1974) Application of psychodynamics to behavior therapy. Am J Psychiatry 131:17–20
Ricoeur P (1970) Freud and philosophy. Yale University Press, New Haven
Ricoeur P (1981) Hermeneutics and the human sciences. Cambridge University Press, New York
Robbins M (1980) Current controversy in object relations theory as outgrowth of a schism between Klein and Fairbairn. Int J Psychoanal 61:477–492
Rogers C (1951) Client-centered therapy. Houghton Mifflin, Boston
Rubinstein BB (1976) On the possibility of a strictly clinical psychoanalytic theory: an essay in the philosophy of psychoanalysis. Psychol Issues 9:229–264
Rush AJ (1982) Short-term psychotherapies for depression. Wiley, New York
Russell B (1930) The conquest of happiness. Allen and Unwin Reprint, London (1975)
Rychlak JF (1969) Lockean vs Kantian theoretical models and the 'cause' pf therapeutic change. Psychother Theory Res Pract 6:214–222
Ryle A (1978) A common language for the psychotherapies? Br J Psychiatry 132:585–594

Ryle A (1984) How can we compare psychotherapies? Why are they all effective? Br J Med Psychol 57:261–264
Sandler J, Holder A, Dare C (1970) Basic psychoanalytic concepts: v. Resistance. Br J Psychiatry 117:215–221
Schafer R (1976) A new language for psychoanalysis. Yale University Press, New Haven
Schwartz RM (1982) Cognitive-behavior modification: a conceptual review. Clin Psychol Rev 2:267–293
Seneca LA (1966) Ad Lucilium Epistularum Moralium, Rizzoli, Milan (own translation)
Shulman BH (1985) Cognitive therapy and the individual psychology of Alfred Adler. In: Mahoney MJ, Freeman A (eds) Cognition and psychotherapy. Plenum, New York, pp 243–258
Sifneos PE (1972) Short-term psychotherapy and emotional crisis. Harvard University Press, Cambridge, MA
Silverman LH (1974) Some psychoanalytic considerations of non-psychoanalytic therapies. Psychother Theory Res Pract 11:298–305
Skinner BF (1974) About behaviorism. Knopf, New York
Spinoza B (1959) Ethica. Boringhieri, Turin (own translation)
Stekel W (1950) Technique of analytical psychotherapy. Liveright, New York
Strupp HH (1970) Specific vs non-specific factors in psychotherapy and the problem of control. Arch Gen Psychiatry 23:393–401
Strupp HH (1973) On the basic ingredients of psychotherapy. J Consult Clin Psychol 41:1–8
Sullivan HS (1954) The psychiatric interview. Norton, New York
Ullmann LP (1970) = n cognitions and behavior therapy. Behav Ther 1:201–204
Ullmann LP, Krasner L (1975) A psychological approach to abnormal behavior. Prentice Hall, Englewood Cliffs
Ulrich R, Stachnik T, Mabry J (1966, 1970) Control of human behavior. Foresman, Glenview
Vaihinger H (1911) The philosophy of 'as if'. Harcourt Brace, New York
Wachtel P (1973) Psychoanalysis and behavior therapy. Basic Books, New York
Wachtel P (1982) Resistance. Plenum, New York
Watson JB (1913) Psychology as a behaviorist views it. Psychol Rev 20:158–177
Watson JB (1924) Behaviorism. University of Chicago Press, Chicago
Wegman C (1985) Psychoanalysis and cognitive psychology: a formalization of Freud's earliest theory. Academic, New York
Wessler RA, Wessler RL (1980) The principles and practice of rational-emotive therapy. Jossey-Bass, San Francisco
Wilson GT (1978) Cognitive behavior therapy. In: Foreyt JP, Rathjen DP (eds) Cognitive behavior therapy. Plenum, New York, pp 7–32
Winnicott DW (1960) The theory of the parent-infant relationship. Int J Psychoanal 41:585–595
Wolberg IL (1980) Handbook of short-term psychotherapy. Thieme-Stratton, New York
Wolpe J (1958) Psychotherapy by reciprocal inhibition. Stanford Univeristy Press, Stanford
Wolpe J (1969) The practice of behavior therapy. Pergamon, New York
Yesavage JA (1980) A Kantian critique of cognitive therapy. Am J Psychother 34:99–106

Cognitive Therapy and the Analysis of Meaning Structures

L.-G. LUNDH

Introduction

Each person has his own way of experiencing the world. How a given situation is perceived and interpreted varies from one person to another, and may also vary from one occasion to another within the same person. Different psychological theories have tried to approach these basic facts in terms of various concepts. According to Piaget (1951), Neisser (1976) and others, each person has his own "schemata", in terms of which he or she assimilates the world. According to George Kelly (1955), we all have our "personal constructs" which channel our psychological processes. Other psychologists speak in this connection of "mental structures" (e.g. Mandler 1975), "semantic networks" (e.g. Anderson and Bower 1973), "memory structures" (Posner 1973), and "interassociated nodes in long-term memory" (Shiffrin and Schneider 1977).

Common to all these theoretical approaches seems to be the basic assumption that human beings, as a result of biological preconditions and learning, develop a set of cognitive structures which channel their way of experiencing the world, regardless of what these structures are called. In this paper these will be referred to as *meaning structures* (Lundh 1983). The reason for this is that, as outlined in the theoretical approach below, the concept of meaning is seen as the basic concept in psychology. What interests us in psychology is not a description of physical stimuli and responses but a description of the meaning (sense, significance) that various situations, events, behaviours, etc. have for a certain person. As Beck puts it, "Meaning provides the richness of life; it transforms a simple event into an experience. Yet, contemporary systems of psychology and psychiatry either completely disregard meaning or go to extremes in seeking esoteric meanings" (Beck 1976, p. 47). The former is largely true of behaviorism, whereas the latter characterises classical psychoanalysis. Cognitive psychology and therapy may be said to contribute to the reestablishment of meaning as the central concern of psychology and psychotherapy.

Department of Clinical Psychology, University of Uppsala, Box 1225, S-751 42 Uppsala, Sweden

The Concept of Meaning Structures

A person's meaning structures, as the term is used here, may be defined as inner, cognitive structures which (a) in some sense are located in the brain, (b) develop as a result of genetic preconditions and learning and (c) can be said to "define", or "constitute", the person's meaningful world, i.e. the world as it has meaning specifically for that person. The basic notion is that the human mind may be seen as a system of meaning structures, and that all mental phenomena involve the activation of these meaning structures. A meaning structure may, then, be either in a passive or in an active state; whereas terms such as "knowledge", "beliefs", "memory" and "personality" refer primarily to meaning structures as such, whether in active or passive state, terms such as "perception", "thought", "emotion", "intention" and "recall" refer primarily to the activation of structures.

On the basis of such a very general definition, a research programme (Lakatos 1970) may be formulated which includes questions of the following kind: Is it possible to identify basic principles of how such structures are organized, are activated in the course of ordinary mental functioning, and develop and change? To try to answer these questions is a task for basic research in general psychological theory, but the answers have essential implications also for clinical psychology and psychotherapy. To understand a patient and his problems we need to analyse his or her meaning structures, and in order to do so we need a general psychological theory that tells us how such structures are organized, the principles of their activation, etc. And in order to treat our patients in the best possible way we need to know about the principles according to which cognitive structures of this kind develop and change. In terms of this theoretical approach all forms of psychopathology may be said to involve the presence of dysfunctional meaning structures, and the purpose of psychotherapy is to contribute to the development of more functional meaning structures.

Three Dimensions of Meaning

As to the organization of a person's cognitive structures, the basic hypothesis to be proposed here is that such structures involve three dimensions of meaning: (a) extension (categorization of the world), (b) intension (beliefs/mental representations), and (c) value (affective meaning). According to the hypothesis, it should, in principle, be possible to give an exhaustive description of cognitive structures in terms of these three dimensions.

Extension

The extension of a person's meaning structures refers to his system for categorizing the world. We automatically perceive the world in terms of categories or classes or kinds of objects, events, behaviours, etc. What we refer to here is not a conscious, or verbal, classification but primarily an implicit, non-verbal, non-conscious categorization, which is seen simply in the fact that we tend to respond in a similar way to situations which are taken as similar in some respect. These situations may then be said to have the *same* meaning for the person. Behaviourists refer to this as "stimulus generalization" (after Pavlov 1927) or as "stimulus classes" (Skinner 1935). Other psychologists speak of "stimulus equivalence" (Klüwer 1933), "generalizing assimilation to a schema" (Piaget 1936), "categorization", or "classification" (Bruner 1957). According to George Kelly (1955), our personal constructs always involve a kind of "equivalence/difference patterns". The psychoanalytic concept of "transference" (Gill 1982) also refers partly to similar phenomena. Categorization or generalization in this sense simply means the absence of differentiation. A person may, of course, learn to make gradually finer discriminations, but this only leads to making *less gross* generalizations, never to an *abandonment* of generalization as such.

In fact, it could be argued that generalization/categorization is a basic characteristic of all mental life. It is difficult to see how an organism could learn anything at all if it did not generalize in this way. Imagine, as a thought experiment, an organism that did not exhibit stimulus generalization. Suppose it to be true that exactly the same situation never repeats itself in the life of an individual – a point which was given a classical formulation by the ancient philosopher Heraclitus when he stated that we "cannot step in the same river twice". To the extent that this is true, it follows that an organism that does not exhibit stimulus generalization would be unable to learn from experience. Lashley formulated a similar conclusion in neurophysiological terms when he stated that "There is some reason for believing that generalization is one of the primitive, basic functions of organic nervous tissue" (Lashley 1942, p. 236).

The same principle applies to behaviour as well. Although a certain behaviour is hardly ever carried out in exactly the same way twice, it may still be regarded as "the same" behaviour as long as it expresses the same intention, i.e. aims at the same result. This phenomenon has been referred to as "motor equivalence" (e.g. Lashley 1942), or "equifinality" (von Bertalanffy 1968). What matters psychologically is not the physical topography of a behaviour but its meaning – and this meaning must be formulated in terms of classes of objects or events, as they are categorized by a person's meaning structures.

It should be noted that similar principles apply to the relation between thought and language; the essential thing about a thought is its meaning, not its verbal formulation. Each thought can be formulated in a large number of ways, even within a given language; that which remains invariant is the meaning. Thoughts, therefore, cannot be reduced to verbal formulations, just as perceptual experiences cannot be reduced to sensory stimulation, and behaviours cannot be reduced to physical movements.

If perception can be said to refer to the "incoming" process from external world to psychological meaning and behaviour to the "outgoing" process from psychological meaning (intention) to influencing the world, thought can be seen as the set of processes which occur *within* the realm of meaning. Although thought cannot be reduced to verbal formulations, however, it may well be that the learning of language plays an important role in the *development* of a person's meaning structures and his ways of thinking. The child's acquisition of language seems partially to be a matter of labelling categories that already exist in the child's mind, as evidenced by his sensorimotor behaviour (e.g. Macnamara 1972; Nelson 1974; Flavell 1977); but verbal learning largely involves the development of new categories at a more differentiated and abstract level.

There are a number of ways in which a person's category system may be dysfunctional. (a) It may not be sufficiently discriminating for certain purposes; the person then needs to learn finer discriminations, which may involve the learning of new perceptual skills, but also new motor skills and finer verbal discriminations. (b) Certain phenomena may be habitually put in the "wrong" category. Cramer and Stern (1986), for example, mention a case of a mother who categorized certain aspects of her infant's behaviour as "aggressive", which had negative effects on their relationship; the relationship improved substantially, however, when she learned to reclassify the child's behaviour as an expression of curiosity and exploration. (c) Various categorizations may come into conflict with one another, thus leading to confusion. An example here is that of Pavlov's (1928) "experimental neurosis" in a dog. The dog was trained to discriminate between two stimuli. Once the discriminations had been learned, the task was made more difficult by making the two stimuli progressively more similar. The result was that a stage was eventually reached at which discrimination became impossible, and the dog started to show symptoms of severe disturbance. The dog not only showed obvious signs of fear and anxiety about the experimental situation, but the symptoms carried over to its total behaviour; the dog huddled in the corner of his cage, cowered at the sight of his familiar handler, refused to eat regularly and overreacted to the slightest sound or distraction.

Another example is the so-called double-bind situation described by Bateson et al. (1956). A double-bind situation is a situation in which the individual is involved in an important relationship, in which it is vitally significant that he be able to discriminate accurately between various messages communicated, but in which the other person in the relationship is expressing two orders of message, one of which contradicts the other, and the individual is unable to comment on this contradiction in order to arrive at an unambigous categorization. An instance of this is provided by the mother who wants her child to respond to her as a loving mother, but who at the same time becomes anxious and withdraws if the child approaches her, and who, when the child in turn responds to her hostile and withdrawing behaviour, tends to simulate love or approaching behaviour as a way of denying that she is withdrawing. The mother may be seen as trapped in a vicious circle of ambivalent behaviour: when she begins to feel affectionate and close to her child, she feels endangered and must withdraw from him; but she cannot accept this hostile act and must simulate affection and closeness in order to deny it. The child, as a result, becomes the victim of two contradictory messages and experiences great difficult finding an unambiguous interpretation of the situation. Moreover, he cannot openly comment on the confusing messages from his mother in order to clarify their meaning since she will not admit her ambivalence. According to Bateson et al. (1956), the repeated experiences of such double-bind situations may lead to the development of schizophrenic symptoms; we need not, however, subscribe wholeheartedly to this theory in order to admit the significance of double-bind situations and their possible pathogenic nature.

Intension

Whereas extension refers to categories of phenomena that have the *same* meaning for a person, "intension" refers to the *content* of this meaning, that is, all kinds of expectations, beliefs, etc, which connect the various categories referred to above. This may, for example, involve expectations that a certain kind of event will occur in a certain kind of situation (i.e. a connection between a category of situations and a category of events), or that a certain kind of consequences will follow if one behaves in a certain way in a certain kind of situation (i.e. a connection between a category of situations, a category of behaviours, and a category of consequences). Intension, in this sense, has been referred to in the psychological literatue variously as "cognitive maps" (Tolman 1932), inner "models" (e.g. Craik 1943; Sokolov 1958) and "mental representations" (Chomsky 1980; Fodor 1975). It may involve beliefs of varying complexity about oneself, about other people, about relationships and about the world at large. And, again, what is referred to here is not only conscious expectations that a person may be able to report verbally, but all kinds of habitual connections between situations, events, behaviours, consequences, etc. which can be inferred from observations of the person's behaviour and interviews with him.

In cognitive therapy intensional structures are often referred to as "rules" or "assumptions" (Beck 1976; Beck et al. 1979). A rule, or assumption, functions as an implicit major premise which, as Beck observes, is

> "applied as though in a syllogism.
> *Major premise:* 'If I don't have love, I am worthless.'
> *Special case:* 'Raymond doesn't love me.'
> *Conclusion:* 'I am worthless.'
> Of course, the patient does not report a sequence of thoughts in the form of a syllogism. The major premise (rule) is already part of his cognitive organization and is applied to the presenting circumstances. The patient may ruminate over the minor premise (the specific situation) and is certainly conscious of the conclusion" (Beck 1976, p. 100).

This particular rule may be said to specify a category of interpersonal situations by the label "not being loved", and to connect this kind of situation with a category of negative self-evaluations. The connection between self-worth and being loved may be more or less strong. The strongest connection would be when the person's self-worth is *wholly* contingent on being loved, i.e. when he or she has no other way of attaining a feeling of self-worth. We would then have a meaning structure of the following form: "I have self-worth, if and only if I am loved." It may be hypothesized that a person whose self-worth is so strongly equated with being loved will be more vulnerable to experiences of losing a person's love than an individual who also has other ways of producing a positive self-esteem, i.e. has a meaning structure of the following form: "I have self-worth, If I am loved or if I . . . ."

Depression-prone individuals seem to be particularly vulnerable to events that are perceived as instances of rejection, failure, sickness or loss (Beck et al. 1979). This vulnerability may be the result of various kinds of "depressogenic assumptions" that make self-worth strongly dependent on being accepted, liked or loved, or on accomplishing, succeeding and not making mistakes, on being healthy, etc. When such individuals are confronted with events that are perceived as failures, rejections, losses, etc. they will respond according to the meaning structures involved and as a result have an automatic tendency to produce negative self-evaluations.

A person's self-concept may be said to involve a wide set of meaning structures, an important subset of which specifies the external conditions for positive and negative self-evaluations. Another important subset involves beliefs about self-efficacy (Bandura 1977, 1982), i.e. beliefs about one's coping capabilities in various kinds of situations. Self-efficacy beliefs may play an important role in the maintenance of various emotional disorders; a person who believes himself inefficacious in certain kinds of situations will tend to focus on his coping deficiencies when confronted with such a situation, and the result may be a high level of cognitively generated distress.

Another kind of belief that has been postulated as important for mental health is that about causal relationships in everyday life. Such beliefs are referred to as causal attributions, and these play an essential role in such phenomena as self-blame, self-criticism, low self-esteem and feelings of guilt. Moreover, some theorists (Abramson et al. 1978) have hypothesized that a certain attributional style (in which the person tends to attribute negative events to internal, stable and global factors) may predispose him to depression. Janoff-Bulman (1979) similarly distinguishes between "characterological self-blame" (to blame one's character) and behavioural self-blame" (to blame one's behaviour), and argues that depression is related to characterological, but not to behavioural, self-blame. This is consistent with findings by Anderson (1983) which indicate that people who suffer from depression and loneliness tend to attribute their interpersonal failures more to unchangeable character defects (e.g. ability deficits or interferring personality traits) and less to changeable behavioural mistakes (e.g. lack of effort or use of the wrong strategy) than do non-depressed and non-lonely persons and that this attributional style helps to maintain the motivational and performance deficits of these persons.

Both cognitive and psychoanalytic therapy can be said to aim at a transformation of the patient's beliefs, i.e. both could be referred to as "insight" therapies. The focus of the two, however, is rather different, and psychoanalytic interpretations are often said to go "deeper" than cognitive techniques. This assumption, however, needs to be questioned. The dysfunctional rules or assumptions that are focused on in cognitive therapy are beliefs that are actively involved *in the very organization* of the patient's behaviour and emotional functioning, and the aim of cognitive therapy is to *modify* these beliefs. Psychoanalytic interpretations, on the other hand, generally aim at the acquisition of *new* beliefs at a more intellectual level of the cognitive organization, i.e. beliefs *about* one's behaviour and emotional functioning (beliefs about defenses, conflicts, etc.) and about causal relationships between past events and present functioning. It could be argued that, to the extent that psychoanalytic interpretations lead only to new beliefs at this level but do not alter beliefs that play an active role in the organization of the person's behaviour – by means of some such process as "working through" (Freud 1914), "corrective emotional experiences" (Alexander and French 1946) or "transmuting internalization" (Kohut 1984) – they will lead mainly to rather superficial psychological changes.

Value

A person's meaning structures cannot be reduced to "category systems" or "beliefs". Terms such as "category systems" focus primarily on the extensional dimension, whereas such terms as "beliefs" capture primarily the intensional dimension; both however tend to neglect the affective dimension. Concepts such as "attitudes" and "sentiments", on the other hand, are more complete in the sense that they also take into account the affective dimension. According to McDougall's definition, "a sentiment is a system in which a cognitive disposition is linked with one or more emotional or affective conative dispositions to form a structural unit that functions as one whole system" (McDougall 1936, p. 437). According to Sherif, an attitude is "a cognitive-affective-motivational structure" that relates the person to a domain of objects "through categorization of that domain, beliefs about them, and attributions to them that are selectively biased for or against, positively or negatively, toward or away from objects in the different categories" (Sherif 1980, p. 18).

This third, affective dimension of meaning has been variously referred to as "cathexis" (Freud 1900; Tolman 1949), "valences" (Lewin 1951) and "reinforcement" (Skinner 1953). To evaluate the strength of reinforcing events for a person is, according to Skinner (1953, p. 74), to "discover what someone 'is getting out of life' ". Another term often used in this context is "investment": we are said to invest emotionally in various persons, objects, activities, ideas, etc. And the same is true of the investigation of this dimension as of the two others: it must rely both on phenomenological data and on behavioural observations. To a certain extent we may obtain information by asking a person about his preferences and feelings, but such information must be completed by behavioural observations, since "a reinforcing connection need not be obvious to the individual reinforced" (Skinner 1953, p. 75).

We shall refer here to the affective dimension of meaning as "value". Whereas extension refers to that which has the *same* meaning, and intension to the *content* of this meaning, value may be said to refer to *how much* meaning something has for the person. Value, as used here, then, denotes a quantitative dimension of meaning. Various categories of behaviours, situations, events and ideas may be more or less valued by the person. This value dimension is of central importance for both motivation and emotion. A person for whom nothing has any value would have no preferences whatever, would feel indifferent to everything and would not be motivated to any activity – he or she would be in a state of literally total meaninglessness. This applies not only to acting but also to thinking. As Piaget puts it, "affective life and cognitive life are inseparable because all interaction with the environment involves both a structuration and a valuation. . . . Thus we could not reason, even in pure mathematics, without experiencing certain feelings, and conversely no affect can exist without a minimum of understanding and discrimination" (Piaget 1947, p. 6).

Emotional responses in general seem to arise in relation to something that is invested with value. As Beck (1976) argues, the nature of a person's emotional response depends on whether he perceives events as adding to, subtracting from, endangering or impinging upon the domain of objects that he has invested with value. Joy is felt when we experience or expect an addition of something that is of value, sadness is felt when we experience or anticipate a loss of something to which we attach value, and anxiety is felt when we perceive that danger is threatening something that is of value to us. If nothing were to have value for us, there would be nothing that could make us respond with joy, sadness, anger, guilt, shame, or any other emotion.

If the general principle is that emotions arise in relation to things that are invested with value, the interesting question for the analysis of a person's meaning structures is *what* it is to which he or she attaches value. This will, of course, vary from one person to another, but certain general formulations seem possible. Close relationships to significant others seem to be an example of what is generally highly valued in humans; the desired characteristics of such relationships may vary, but may often be described in terms of "loving", "trusting", etc. A positive self-image seems to be another universally held value. Health, knowledge, freedom and honesty are also central values to most people. We also generally have certain goals, ambitions, ideals, favourite activities, possessions, etc. that we value. Emotional responses may arise in relation to that which happens with all these things.

A person's values form a hierarchy, in which lower-level values are connected to higher-level ones via various mediating beliefs. At the top of the hierarchy there are a number of "absolute" or unconditional values, i.e. categories of phenomena the value of which are independent of beliefs. At lower levels of the hierarchy there are a large set of relative, conditional values which are connected to these absolute values via beliefs about means-ends relationships. A positive self-image, for example, may be regarded as an absolute value which may invest other categories of phenomena with various degrees of value as a function of various kinds of beliefs. To the extent that the person has such beliefs as, "If other people don't like me, it means that I am worthless", being liked by other people will be invested with more or less value. An extreme case is the person who has the belief that "If I am not liked by everybody, it means that I am worthless"; such a person will attach an extreme value to being liked by others. The value of being liked by others may, in turn, function as a higher-level value which, if combined with beliefs such as, "I must be perfect, otherwise no one will like me", will produce the lower-level value of perfectionism.

Perfectionism implies very high standards for self-acceptance. Each person has a number of standards (Bandura 1977) which he must live up to in order to maintain a positive self-image. When a person exceeds some standard for self-acceptance, the result is a gain in self-esteem which is felt as joy and self-satisfaction; when he does not manage to live up to a standard, on the other hand, the result is a loss of self-esteem which may be felt as sadness or depression. If a person has such high standards that these put a great strain on his capacities, he will be less likely to experience joy and self-satisfaction and more likely to experience sadness and depression. Moreover, various kinds of anxieties may result when a person doubts that he will be able to live up to his standards. An individual whose self-efficacy beliefs about social situations do not measure up to his standards for self-acceptance in these same situations may, for example, be expected to experience more social anxiety. Social phobia may be seen as a disorder which is the result of a relatively wide discrepancy between self-efficacy beliefs and standards for self-acceptance in social situations. This implies that social phobias may be successfully treated by strengthening the patient's self-efficacy beliefs (by training social skills and developing realistic beliefs about self-efficacy in social situations) and/or by helping the person to lower his standards for self-acceptance in such situations – the treatment strategy being chosen on the basis of an analysis of the meaning structures involved. Such an analysis would then also have to include an identification of the kind of beliefs that invest perfectionism with such strong value if the patient has high standards for self-acceptance in this regard.

This means that if a person's relative values are dysfunctional, as, for example, is often the case with perfectionism, it becomes important to identify beliefs that invest perfectionism with such strong value. That is, the therapeutic focus is not on the value as such, but on the meaning structures which produce the dysfunctional valuation. These meaning structures may be analyzed in terms of higher-level values concerning various categories of phenomena which, via various mediating beliefs, produce the exaggerated value of perfectionism.

Values, then, may be dysfunctional because they are founded on dysfunctional beliefs. These beliefs may have developed because they were functional at an earlier time in the person's life; they may be due, for example, to contingencies of reinforcement that were operating in the person's childhood. It should be remembered that meaning structures are functional or dysfunctional only *in relation to* a certain environment. It is a common occurrence that values become dysfunctional because of real-world changes. Another example is the person whose self-image is heavily contingent on being young and physically attractive. Such a person will be more vulnerable to the physical changes that occur as the result of aging, and the value of being young and attractive will become progressively more dysfunctional. If the person's value structures are not adapted to the changes that occur with aging, various kinds of life crises may ensue.

The same applies to so-called traumatic crises. If, for example, a person loses someone who plays a significant role in his life – a person, in other words, who is invested with strong value for him – through death or divorce, his meaning structures will become dysfunctional, in the sense that the actual reality no longer conforms to the cognitive structure of habitual expectations connected to the lost person. The result may be a psychological crisis which calls for a reorganization of the person's meaning structures. In order to regain his psychological equilibrium the person may need to undergo a period of mourning, which leads him to accept what has happened and makes him able to go on living with the new reality. The more of life's meaning that was attached to the lost person, the more encompassing the transformation of meaning structures will be required to re-establish psychological equilibrium. This process may also require the development of new values which can give the person a new sense of meaning in his life.

The Activation of Meaning Structures

A meaning structure is a structure of categories. One of these may be called *the prime category*, since it involves the category of situations or events that tend to activate the meaning structure in question. Consider, for example, a structure that connects elevators with danger cognitions of "getting stuck in the elevator" and "going insane", and therefore produces symptoms of claustrophobia. There are three categories mentioned here: "elevators", "getting stuck in the elevator", and "going insane", each of which should be specified as to their extension when analysing this meaning structure. The category of elevators, however, occupies a special position and may be referred to as the prime category of this structure, since it refers to the class of situations that tends to activate the entire structure.

The extension of a prime category can be specified only by means of empirical investigations. Consider, for example, the question of whether there is a definite kind of attributional style that predisposes people to depression, as hypothesized by Abramson et al. (1978). An alternative view, in keeping with Bower's (1981) argument that mood may have substantial effects on cognition, is that the attributional style shown by depressed persons is rather a *result* of the person's depressed mood. One way of exploring this is by means of attributional questionnaires (Seligman et al. 1979; Anderson et al. 1983), in which the person is asked how he thinks he would attribute certain kinds of events if he were confronted with them. Such questionnaires can be administered to persons who are not depressed; this makes it possible to study correlations between attributional style at one time and depressive response to negative events at a later time. Positive correlations in this regard would be evidence for the causal role of attributional style in producing depression. The lack of such correlations, however, cannot automatically be said to falsify the hypothesis of such a causal connection. If attributional style is analysed in terms of the theory of meaning structures, we would have to ask for the prime category that activates the attributional pattern. One possibility is that this prime category involves a certain class of strongly negative events (and not necessarily *all* kinds of such events) but *not* the reading about hypothetical events of the same kind (people are not always able to predict their responses to strongly negative events). Considerations of this kind make it difficult to falsify theories of the causal role of attributional patterns and other similar theories. This does not, however, mean that the theories are in principle non-falsifiable; the final test is in the way of responding to real-life events.

Mental States

According to the theory presented here, each person experiences the world in accordance with his or her meaning structures. This, however, needs further specification, since one need not always interpret the same situation in the same way. How a given situation is perceived and interpreted varies not only from one person to another, but also from one occasion to another for the same person. In terms of the theory, this is conceptualized in terms of the activation of meaning structures. But the interaction between person and environment is not only an interaction between external stimulus information and a static set of meaning structures, for the human mind is seen as a dynamic system, in which the activation of new structures does not only depend on external stimuli but also on the kind of structures that are already in an *active* state.

Activated meaning structures tend to remain in an active state for a certain time. This is sometimes referred to as "short-term memory" or "short-term store". Shiffrin and Schneider, for example, describe memory as "a large and permanent collection of nodes, which become complexly and increasingly interassociated and interrelated through learning", and they define the short-term store as "the set of currently activated nodes" (Shiffrin and Schneider 1977, p. 155). The set of currently activated meaning structures will be referred to here as a temporary *mental state*; the mental state is manifested not only in the phenomena of short-term memory but also in those referred to as "mental set" and "mood".

An implication of this is that, since this set of activated structures exerts an influence on the new structures that are continually activated, certain mental states may tend to be self-perpetuating. One of the mechanisms involved seems to be this: the beliefs that are active cause the person to attend selectively to information that confirms the validity of these beliefs (as evidenced, for example, by studies carried out by Snyder and Swann 1976, 1978). This mechanism may lead an anxious person to become more anxious, and a depressed person to become more depressed or at least to maintain the level of anxiety or depression. Consider, for example, a case of hypochondriasis, where a person's belief that he is seriously ill causes him to attend selectively to bodily signs and sensations that he would probably not have noticed otherwise and to attribute these to illness, which in turn strengthens his conviction that he is seriously ill. Such a negative cycle might be found not only in pure hypochondriasis but also in cases of actual physical illness, which may be aggravated by dysfunctional beliefs about the severity of the illness.

The placebo effect may also depend on a similar mechanism, although it works in the opposite direction (Lundh 1987). Illness always involves psychological components; a person not only senses the signs of physical illness but also interprets these signs and responds emotionally to this interpretation. A person who believes that he has a serious illness may experience depression at having lost his good health and anxiety for fear of dying. That which is therapeutic about placebo beliefs (i.e. beliefs of the form "This treatment is going to cure me") seems to be their ability to counteract those kinds of beliefs that tend to produce anxiety and depression and to produce emotional responses (hope, calm, etc.) that are antagonistic to depression and anxiety. Moreover, a positive cycle may be produced to the extent that the placebo belief makes the person selectively attentive to signs of improved health. Persons who believe that they are seriously ill may be expected to attend selectively to signs that will confirm this belief, whereas persons who believe that they are getting better will tend to focus their attention on signs that can be construed as evidence for such improvement. Patients who begin to attend primarily to signs that can be taken as evidence of improved health will naturally notice more such signs than before, even if their physical health is unchanged. These signs may then be taken as confirmation of the correctness of the placebo belief. In this way a positive cycle is produced, whereby the belief in the efficacy of the treatment is reinforced, and the patient experiences a continued improvement of his health.

Whereas hypochondriacal concerns involve a self-perpetuating mental state with negative emotional effects, the placebo effect seems to involve a self-perpetuating state with opposite, positive consequences. It might be hypothesized that the more a person's illness involves psychological components of anxiety and depression, the more susceptible he will be to the induction of placebo effects; this is consistent with evidence that placebo effects are reported most frequently in patients with anxiety and depression (Gallimore and Turner 1977). Placebo effects seem to involve essentially *a change of mental state* (from anxiety and depression to hope and calm) but do not require any more permanent change in the person's meaning structures. Anxiety and depression may be alleviated by placebo effects, but the structures that predispose the person to respond with anxiety and depression in certain kinds of situations are left intact.

In psychotherapeutic research various writers (e.g. Frank 1973; Prioleau et al. 1983; Shapiro and Morris 1978) have argued that the placebo effect may be an important component of and perhaps the entire basis for the effectiveness of different kinds of psychotherapy. The reason why placebo treatment in many cases may be as effective as psychotherapy is, according to Frank, that the placebo condition "contains the necessary, and possibly sufficient, ingredient for much of the beneficial effects of all forms of psychotherapy. This is a helping person who listens to the patient's complaints and offers a procedure to relieve them, thereby inspiring the patient's hopes and combating demoralization" (Frank 1983, p. 291). Against this it might be argued that to "inspire the patient's hopes and combat demoralization" is only to produce a change in the patient's temporary mental state, while it leaves his basic meaning structures unchanged. It should be noted, however, that although the generation of placebo beliefs may primarily have a temporary effect on the person's mental state, the possibility cannot be ruled out that the generation of such beliefs may also facilitate new kinds of learning and thereby contribute to more permanent structural changes. It remains a possibility, in other words, that placebo beliefs may function as catalysts for other therapeutic effects.

The cognitive treatment of depression may also be seen to involve two phases: first a change of mental state, and then an attempt to transform more permanent meaning structures. Depression may be regarded as a form of self-perpetuating mental state, which is maintained by several kinds of vicious circles. The depressive state involves negative beliefs about the self, the external world and the future (Beck 1967). The depressed person, therefore, is selectively attentive to events and information that may be construed as evidence of these negative beliefs and is apt to interpret even slightly negative events as strongly aversive, which only serves to maintain these negative beliefs and the depressive mood. Further, the depressive state is manifested in a number of symptoms, e.g. inactivity, irritability and indecisiveness, which are inherently aversive and leads the person to label himself as ineffective and inadequate; Teasdale (1985) refers to this as "depresssion about depression" and argues that it serves to maintain the depressive state.

When a person has entered a state of depression, the primary goal is naturally to help him or her out of this state, and this may be attempted by means of various cognitive and behavioural techniques. The negative bias in the patient's information processing may be counteracted by a systematic reality testing of his automatic thoughts, and the symptoms of inactivity may be treated by means of activity schedules and graded-task assignments (Beck et al. 1979). Such techniques may serve to break the vicious circles that maintain the depressive state. If the therapy only produces such a change of the person's mental state, however, the dysfunctional meaning structures that predispose the person to respond with depression to certain kinds of stressing life events will remain within the person, in a dormant state, and make him or her vulnerable to new depressive episodes when confronted with similar kinds of events in the future. In cognitive therapy as treatment progresses and the patient's symptoms lessen, the focus of therapy shifts to working with these depressogenic assumptions.

Automatic Activation, Creativity, and Conscious Control

According to the present theory mental functioning is the result of an activation of meaning structures that already exist within the person as a result of genetic preconditions and learning. All such theories are inevitably confronted with two major problems: (a) how to account for human creativity, if all experiences and behaviours are the result of an activation of already existent structures, and (b) how to account for the experience of free will, or conscious control over behaviour and mental processes? These are questions which, in one guise or another, have engaged many philosophers and psychologists. This last section of the present chapter devotes itself to a brief discussion of these issues, and an attempt will be made to point out the direction in which they may be pursued in terms of the theory of meaning structures.

How can the existence of certain structures, which are always given as a result of the past, result in ever new experiences and thoughts and in human creativity? The general form of the answer seems to be that, although the person's meaning structures are always given as a result of the past, they may at any moment be activated in ever new *constellations*. Although the structures are old, the constellation of activated structures is new.

This has many implications. One concerns the distinction made in the psychology of memory (Tulving 1972) between "episodic" and "semantic" memory. Whereas semantic memory refers to the person's meaning structures as such and primarily to structures at the verbal level, episodic memory refers to the ability to reactivate the same constellation of meaning structures that were activated at the time of an earlier event. As to episodic memory, a controversial question is whether events of experience are stored and can be re-experienced later as they originally happened, of if later recollections always tend to involve a certain amount of reconstruction and distortion. This question can be reformulated in the following way: to what extent can the original meaning constellation be reactivated? If a person's meaning structures have changed in a fundamental way since the original event, a reasonable conclusion would be that it must be difficult to recollect the original experience. This is consistent, for example, with the theory of Piaget and Inhelder (1968); From their results it seems that the child reconstructs the past in terms of his present "schemata". Other experimental work also point to the relative ease with which even memories of relatively recent events mey be distorted – "colored by succeeding events, increased understanding, a new context, suggestions by others, other people's recollections" (Loftus 1980 p. 169). It may be concluded that the recall of an event is dependent not only on changes in the person's meaning structures that have occurred since the original event but also on the kind of meaning structures that are in an active state at the time of recall. Hence, even ordinary remembering seems regularly to involve a component of creativity.

The more a person has elaborated his meaning structures within a particular area, the larger will be his potential for creating new meaning constellations within that area. The creative individual is one who (a) strives for the construction of new meaning constellations, and/or (b) is attentive to new meaning constellations that are formed spontaneously as a part of living. The latter exemplifies an intuitive kind of creativity, one that relies on the automatic activation of new meaning constellations, whereas the former represents a more disciplined kind of creativity and relies on our ability consciously to control our activities. This leads to our second question: how can we account for the phenomena of conscious control and free will within a theory of meaning structures?

A basic assumption of the present theory is that meaning structures are activated continuously and automatically at a pre-attentive, non-conscious level, as part of a person's interaction with his environment. There is substantial evidence from studies on subliminal perception, selective attention, etc. (for a review and analysis of some of the evidence, see Lundh 1979), which shows that we are able to register a great amount of information on a purely pre-attentive level without conscious awareness. This includes not only physical characteristics of sensory stimulation but also word meaning and other rather complex kinds of information. The present theory predicts that a person may be able to register anything at a pre-attentive level, for which he has well-consolidated meaning structures (Lundh 1983), and that what may be registered pre-attentively may therefore differ from one person to another, according to their respective specific meaning structures. Conscious attention and thinking is required primarily when the person is confronted with new situations with which he or she is not acquainted and which he cannot handle automatically by means of already existing meaning structures. In this situation the person needs to think, analyse, make inferences, etc. but still has nothing else to go on than his already existing structures – his thinking, inferences, and analyses are necessarily limited by the logical space defined by these structures. The difference is merely that he need not be at the mercy of whatever structures are *automatically* activated by the given situation and context; he may intervene by means of various cognitive operations and exert a certain degree of conscious control over this activation. The result is that new constellations of old structures are produced which, if they prove adaptive, may be consolidated in the form of more permanent structures by means of which the person may become able to deal with these kinds of situations automatically and without conscious operations in the future.

This distinction between automatic activation and an activation that occurs under conscious control has much in common with Posner's (1973) distinction between "effortless retrieval" and "effortful retrieval", and with Shiffrin and Schneider's (1977) distinction between "automatic information processing" and "controlled information processing". Effortless retrieval, in Posner's terms, implies an automatic activation of memory structures, in which "the spread of activation in the structure is effortless" (Posner 1973 p. 139), whereas effortful retrieval is a more difficult and time-consuming process. "Much of what we call thinking", Posner argues, "appears to be just this difficult sort of retrieval processes" (Posner 1973, p. 42). And automatic information processing, in Shiffrin and Schneider's terms, is said to be characterized by "a sequence of nodes that nearly always become active in response to a particular input configuration", and, they add, "The sequence is activated without the necessity of active control or attention by the subject" (Shiffrin and Schneider 1977, pp. 155–156). Controlled information processing, on the other hand, "utilizes a temporary sequence of nodes activated under control of, and through attention by, the subject" (Shiffrin and Schneider 1977, p. 156). Whereas automatic processes may go on in parallel, very quickly and without effort or attention, controlled processing is strongly capacity-limited and proceeds much more slowly. Although much of what we generally call "thinking" seems to involve a controlled activation of structures, thoughts may also occur to us as the result of a purely automatic activation – what Beck (1976) refers to as "automatic thoughts" illustrates the latter.

The distinction between automatic activation and conscious control seems to be necessary for a general psychological theory; there is no way of denying the existence of a "controlled information processing". At first glance, however, the notion of conscious control – or of processes occurring "under the control of the subject", to use Shiffrin and Schneider's phrase – may seem a bit troublesome for a causal, scientific account. Can we ask for the causes of this conscious control, or are we dealing with some kind of absolute control which lies beyond the world of cause and effect? One reason why Penfield (1975) and Eccles (Popper and Eccles 1977) have arrived at the conclusion that the mind is separate from the brain seems, in fact, to be the assumption that conscious control means absolute control. It is interesting to note that both Penfield and Eccles equate the mind with that which has been referred to here as "conscious control", whereas all kinds of automatic activation are attributed to "the brain". According to Eccles, for example, "the self-conscious mind can effectively act on the brain events. This is most overtly seen in voluntary action, but throughout our waking life we are deliberately evoking brain events when we try to recall a memory or to recapture a word or phrase or to express a thought or establish a memory" (Popper and Eccles 1977, p. 362). Moreover, this activity of a "self-conscious mind" is seen as not caused by anything else; the mind, Eccles says, "has the choice. It selects at will" (Eccles 1977, p. 474). Or, as Penfield (1975, p. 86) puts this, the mind "decides what is to be learned or recorded"; it "conditions the brain".

Concepts such as "will", "decision", "choice", etc. are often taken to imply some kind of absolute self-control. Against this, however, various writers have argued that there are always limits to such self-control. Frankl (1978, p. 45), for example, argues that "there are certain activities that cannot be demanded, commanded, or ordered. The reason lies in the fact that they cannot be established at will: I cannot 'will' to believe; I cannot 'will' to hope; I cannot 'will' to love; and least of all can I 'will' to will". According to Watts (1957, p. 141):

> Our actions are voluntary when they follow a decision, and involuntary when they happen without decision. But if decision itself were voluntary, every decision would have to be preceded by a decision to decide – an infinite regression which fortunately does not occur. Oddly enough, if we had to decide to decide, we would not be free to decide. We are free to decide because decision "happens". We just decide without having the faintest idea of how we do it.

Or, as Mandler (1975, p. 54) expresses it, "the mechanisms of choice . . . are not conscious. It is presumably the operation of these mechanisms on material in the conscious state that give the epiphenomenal experience of free choice, the appearance that someone (the agent) is doing the choosing."

A person's decisions and choices take place within the matrix of his meaning structures, according to principles of activation that remain to be formulated. Generally, it may be argued that we decide and choose in accordance with our values. Each constellation of activated meaning structures involves a set of beliefs and valuations, and the decision depends on the relative strength of these different values in combination with the content of the person's present beliefs.

Summary

This chapter has presented a theory of the human mind considered as a system of meaning structures. As to the organization of these meaning structures the theory proposes that there are three dimensions of meaning: *extension* (categorization of the world), *intension* (beliefs, or mental representations), and *value* (affective meaning). Further, a person's values are assumed to be hierarchically ordered in such a way that lower-level values are connected to higher-level ones via various mediating beliefs. Psychopathology is seen as the presence of dysfunctional meaning structures, which can be analysed in terms of these three dimensions of meaning.

It is suggested that mental functioning involves a continuous activation of such meaning structures. As to the activation of structures the theory formulates three basic principles: (a) Activated meaning structures tend to remain in an active state for a certain period of time. This produces a temporary *mental state*; a person will perceive the same situation differently, depending on the mental state that he is in. Some mental states (e.g. depression) tend to be self-perpetuating since they cause the person to attend selectively to aspects that serve to keep the activated structures in an active state. Psychotherapy may help a patient out of a negative mental state by activating more functional structures, but in order to ensure a more permanent change it should help the patient to transform dysfunctional structures into more functional ones. Otherwise the dysfunctional structures remain in a latent state, to be activated again when the person is confronted with certain kinds of situations. (b) Although a person's meaning structures are always given as a result of the past, i.e. genetic preconditions and learning, they may be activated in ever new *meaning constellations*; this is what makes human creativity possible. (c) Meaning structures are *activated automatically* at a pre-attentive, non-conscious level when the person is confronted with an event or situation that belongs to the *prime category* of that meaning structure. The mechanisms of conscious control are strongly selective and are elicited particularly when the person is confronted with situations that cannot be handled by means of an automatic activation of already existing structures. Cognitive operations performed in this state may produce new meaning constellations which, to the extent that they prove adaptive in the person's interaction with the environment, may become consolidated in the form of a new meaning structure and thus be activated automatically in similar situations in the future.

References

Abramson LY, Seligman MEP, Teasdale JD (1978) Learned helplessness in humans: critique and reformulation. J Abnorm Psychol 87:49–74

Alexander F, French TM (1946) Psychoanalytic therapy. Ronald, New York

Anderson CA (1983) Motivational and performance deficits in interpersonal settings: the effect of attributional style. J Pers Soc Psychol 45:1136–1147

Anderson CA, Horowitz LM, French R (1983) Attributional style of lonely and depressed people. J Pers Soc Psychol 45:127–136

Anderson JR, Bower GH (1973) Human associative memory. Winston, Washington, DC

Bandura A (1977) Social learning theory. Prentice-Hall, Englewood Cliffs

Bandura A (1982) Self-efficacy mechanism in human agency. Am Psychol 37:122–147

Bateson G, Jackson DD, Haley J, Weakland JH (1956) Towards a theory of schizophrenia. Behav Sci 1:251–264

Beck AT (1967) Depression. University of Pennsylvania Press, Philadelphia

Beck AT (1976) Cognitive therapy and the emotional disorders. International Universities Press, New York

Beck AT, Rush AJ, Shaw BF, Emery G (1979) Cognitive therapy of depression. Guilford, New York

Bower GH (1981) Mood and memory. Am Psychol 36:129–148

Bruner JS (1957) On perceptual readiness. Psychol Rev 64:123–152

Chomsky N (1980) Rules and representations. Columbia University Press, New York

Craik KJW (1943) The nature of explanation. Cambridge University Press, Cambridge

Cramer B, Stern D (1986) Mother-infant psychotherapy: objective and subjective changes. Paper presented at the third world congress on infant psychiatry and allied disciplines

Flavell JH (1977) Cognitive development. Prentice-Hall, Englewood Cliffs

Fodor JA (1975) The language of thought. Harvard University Press, Cambridge

Frank JD (1973) Persuasion and healing. John Hopkins University Press, Baltimore

Frank JD (1983) The placebo is psychotherapy. Behav Brain Sci 6:291–292

Frankl VE (1978) The unheard cry for meaning. Simon and Schuster, New York

Freud S (1900) The interpretation of dreams. Hogarth, London

Freud S (1914) Remembering, repeating and working-through, standard edn, vol XII. Hogarth, London, p 147

Gallimore RG, Turner JL (1977) Contemporary studies of placebo phenomena. In: Jarvik ME (ed) Psychopharmacology in the practice of medicine. Appleton-Century-Crofts, New York

Gill MM (1982) Analysis of transference, vol I. International Universities Press, New York

Janoff-Bulman R (1979) Characterological versus behavioral self-blame: inquiries into depression and rape. J Pers Soc Psychol 37:1798–1809

Kelly GA (1955) A theory of personality. The psychology of personal constructs. Morton, New York

Klüwer H (1933) Behavioral mechanisms in monkeys. University of Chicago Press, Chicago

Kohut H (1984) How does analysis cure? University of Chicago Press, Chicago

Lakatos I (1970) Falsification and the methodology of scientific research programmes. In: Lakatos I Musgrave A (ed) Criticism and the growth of knowledge. Cambridge University Press, Cambridge

Lashley KS (1942) The problem of cerebral organization in vision. In: Pribram K (ed) Brain and behavior. II. Perception and action. Penguin, Harmondsworth

Lewin K (1951) Field theory in social science. Harper, New York

Loftus EF (1980) Memory. Addison-Wesley, Reading

Lundh LG (1979) Introspection, consciousness and human information processing. Scand J Psychol 20:223–238

Lundh LG (1983) Mind and meaning. Towards a theory of the human mind considered as a system of meaning structures. Acta Univ Ups Stud Psychol Ups 10:

Lundh LG (1987) Placebo, belief and health. A cognitive-emotional model. Scand J Psychol 28:128–143

McDougall W (1936) An introduction to social psychology. Methuen, London

Macnamara J (1972) Cognitive basis of language learning in infants. Psychol Rev 79:1–13

Mandler G (1975) Mind and emotion. Wiley, New York

Neisser U (1976) Cognition and reality. Freeman, San Francisco

Nelson K (1974) Concept, word and sentence. Interrelations in acquisition and development. Psychol Rev 81:267–285
Pavlov IP (1927) Conditioned reflexes. Dover, New York
Pavlov IP (1928) Lectures on conditioned reflexes: the higher nervous activity (behaviour) of animals, vol I. Lawrence and Wishart, London
Penfield W (1975) The mystery of the mind. Princeton University Press, Princeton, New Jersey
Piaget J (1936) The origin of intelligence in the child. Penguin, Harmondsworth, Middlesex
Piaget J (1947) The psychology of intelligence. Routledge and Kegan Paul, London
Piaget J (1951) Play, dreams and imitation in childhood. Norton, New York
Piaget J, Inhelder B (1968) Memory and intelligence. Basic Books, New York
Popper KR, Eccles JC (1977) The self and its brain. Springer, Berlin Heidelberg New York
Posner MI (1973) Cognition: an introduction. Scott, Foresman Glenview
Prioleau L, Murdock M, Brody N (1983) An analysis of psychotherapy versus placebo studies. Behav Brain Sci 6:275–310
Seligman MEP, Abramson LY, Semmel A, von Baeyer C (1979) Depressive attributional style. J Abnorm Psychol 88:242–247
Shapiro AK, Morris LA (1978) The placebo effect in medical and psychological therapies. In. Garfield SL, Bergin AE (ed) Handbook of psychotherapy and behavior change: an empirical analysis. Wiley, New York
Sherif CW (1980) Social values, attitudes, and the involvement of the self. In: Howe HE (ed) Nebraska symposium on motivation. University of Nebraska Press, Lincoln
Shiffrin RM, Schneider W (1977) Controlled and automatic human information processing: II. Perceptual learning, automatic attending, and a general theory. Psychol Rev 84:129–190
Skinner BF (1935) The generic nature of the concepts of stimulus and response. J Gen Psychol 12:40–65
Skinner BF (1953) Science and human behavior. Free, New York
Snyder M, Swann W (1976) When actions reflect attitudes: the politics of impression management. J Pers Soc Psychol 34:1034–1042
Snyder M, Swann W (1978) Hypothesis-testing processes in social interaction. J Pers Soc Psychol 36:1202–1212
Sokolov EN (1958) Perception and the conditioned reflex. Macmillan, New York
Teasdale JD (1985) Psychological treatments for depression: how do they work? Behav Res Ther 23:157–165
Tolman EC (1932) Purposive behavior in animals and men. Appleton-Century-Crofts, New York
Tolman EC (1949) There is more than one kind of learning. Psychol Rev 56:144–155
Tulving E (1972) Episodic and semantic memory. In: Tulving E, Donaldson W (ed) Organization of memory. Academic, New York
von Bertalanffy L (1968) General system theory. Braziller, New York
Watts AW (1957) The way of zen. Penguin, Harmondsworth

Attachment and Cognition: A Guideline for the Reconstruction of Early Pathogenic Experiences in Cognitive Psychotherapy

G. Liotti

Is it useful in the course of a cognitively oriented psychotherapy to spend part of therapeutic time on the patient's memories of childhood experiences? Only a minority of cognitive therapists would answer this question in the affirmative. In a recently compiled book, collecting the outlines of 10 different cognitive approaches to psychotherapy (Dryden and Golden 1986) only two contributions underscored the importance of exploring and understanding the patient's developmental history (Liotti 1986; Wessler and Wessler 1986). Most cognitive therapists view their clinical work as aimed at assessing and then actively modifying the patient's dysfunctional cognitions. From this perspective exploring the origins of maladaptive cognitive structures within the framework of the patient's childhood memories seems a minor concern and of only academic interest.

There are, however, both practical and theoretical reasons which may justify the costs, in terms of time and money, of a careful examination of the patient's developmental history.

Practical Reasons for Exploring the Patient's Childhood Memories

The practical importance of considering childhood memories becomes especially evident if one considers cognitive psychotherapy as facilitating self-knowledge rather than solely as a correction of dysfunctional cognitions. Self-knowledge is obviously incomplete without an understanding of the historical dimension of one's life. There is a human need to understand one's experiences in terms of a meaningful historical sequence – a need to narrate one's story to oneself or to others (cf. Jaynes 1982, p. 63; Landau 1984; Wessler and Wessler 1986, p. 200). Indeed, most patients show the spontaneous tendency (tentatively) to relate their cognitions, as these are assessed and challenged in the process of cognitive psychotherapy, to past events and earlier interpersonal influences in their life. Encouraging this tendency fosters one of the most natural ways to improve self-knowledge and self-understanding.

It may also be argued that to acknowledge and actively to encourage the patient's ability to relate the present to the past when examining his or her cognitions may help preserve the patient's self-esteem in the face of the challenges frequently entailed in cognitive restructuring, especially in the forceful disputation

Centre for Cognitive Psychotherapy, Via degli Scipioni, 00192 Rome, Italy

of irrational beliefs. Understanding how an irrational belief was acquired in past interactions with parents, peers, and educators supports one's confidence in the basic rationality of one's mind: the belief that now appears irrational and detrimental might seem in this context quite plausible. It is a healthy accomplishment to acknowledge one's fallibility in developing causal attributions concerning one's own emotions and in constructing representational models of self and others. It is quite another, and undesirable, matter to come to consider one's mind an unreliable instrument, capable of constructing sheer nonsense without any stimulation from the outside.

As regards the therapeutic relationship, the fact that the therapist recognizes the plausibility of the patient's dysfunctional cognitions in their original context while pointing out their limitations and counterproductiveness for the present makes the patient feel accepted on a basis of equality. When the therapist makes explicit his or her belief that the patient's irrationalities were once plausible appraisals of environmental circumstances, the patient understands that the therapist sees him or her as possessing a basically reliable "personal intelligence" (intelligence as to self and the emotions; cf. Gardner 1984) rather than as an emotionally or intellectually inferior "neurotic." This type of relationship between patient and therapist, in which the partners acknowledge both the fallibility and the reliability of each other's cognitive skills, approaches the ideal of a truly cooperative and equal therapeutic relationship – an ideal that is shared by most cognitive therapists (Dryden and Golden 1986).

A cooperative climate in the therapeutic relationship such as may be promoted by exploring developmental history before attempting to revise the patient's basic representational models seems especially helpful when one encounters particularly strong resistance to change in the patient's cognitive structures (Liotti 1987). To explore the origins of a resistant structure in the patient's early relationship with parents and significant others is a powerful therapeutic device; it can be instrumental in helping the patient to distance or decenter cognitions about the nature of self or of interpersonal realities that have been tacitly held since childhood, as absolute certainties (Guidano and Liotti 1983; Liotti 1986, 1987; Wessler and Wessler 1986).

Theoretical Relevance of the Reconstruction of Early Pathogenic Experiences

It is strongly felt in many scientific circles that we must understand the developmental roots of adult emotional disorders in terms of a testable theory based on direct observations of human behavior and on controlled empirical studies rather than according to the – while ingenious and important, nevertheless retrospective and too subjective – theories advanced by clinicians such as S. Freud, M. Klein, H. S. Sullivan, or E. Erikson (see Bowlby 1986; Cicchetti 1984; Guidano and Liotti 1983; Liotti 1984, 1986; Sroufe 1986; Sroufe and Rutter 1984). Terms such as "developmental psychopathology" (Cicchetti 1984; Sroufe and Rutter 1984) and "developmental psychiatry" (Bowlby 1988) have been proposed to denote the emerging disciplines whose chief concerns are individual differences in adaptation throughout life and the developmental roots of adult psychiatric disorders – rather than childhood emotional disturbances.

Cognitive psychotherapy may furnish an ideal setting for relating the adult's basic assumptions, belief systems, and representational models of self and others to specific sorts of early interpersonal experiences (Liotti 1984). By carefully collecting such clinical observations cognitive psychotherapists may contribute greatly to the field of developmental psychopathology. In turn, developmental psychopathology may provide a conceptual, explanatory framework and a set of confirmatory evidence – drawn for instance from longitudinal and prospective studies – for the "soft" data which may emerge during the process of cognitive psychotherapy, for example that concerning the relationship between adult dysfunctional cognitions and the recollection of early adverse experiences. Such a promising exchange between developmental psychopathology and cognitive psychotherapy could perhaps lead to an etiological theory of the cognitive dysfunctions that accompany emotional disorders. Such an etiological-developmental theory, as elaborated below (see thinking, feeling, acting), may shed light on the central problem in the clinical theory of cognitive psychotherapy, namely, that of the reciprocal relationships between thinking, feeling, and acting.

There are, then, numerous theoretical and practical reasons for carefully exploring the origins of pathological meaning structures in the patient's developmental history. In order to relate present dysfunctional cognitions (as assessed during the therapy of an adult patient) to past adverse experiences (as recollected by the patient or, perhaps, reported by a relative during a family interview) it is, of course, necessary to use a sound conceptual framework. This framework would concern the development of interrelated patterns of cognitions, emotions, and behavior in interpersonal contexts in which human cognitive and emotional growth takes place. The remainder of this chapter devotes itself to outlining such a conceptual framework. Since the major part of this framework draws upon Bowlby's attachment theory and upon the findings of a growing body of empirical research on attachment behavior, the next section will present a very brief account of Bowlby's theory. For the empirical body of evidence that supports the theory, the reader is referred to Bowlby (1973, 1980, 1982), Bretherton and Waters (1985) and Parkes and Stevenson-Hinde (1982); on the psychobiology-neuropsychology of attachment, see Emde and Harmon (1982) and Reite and Field (1985).

Attachment Theory

The major postulate of attachment theory is that human beings (like other mammals) have a strong *innate* disposition to make social bonds with particular others. This disposition manifests itself already during the second half of the first year of extra-uterine life in an attachment to a discriminated care-giver. The goal of this attachment behavior is to establish and maintain proximity to a specific adult thereby indirectly affording the infant protection from environmental dangers.

Viewed in the context of evolutionary theory attachment behavior has an obvious survival value, for it keeps the helpless infant in the range of protective action of a competent and caring adult.

After infancy and for the rest of human life the disposition to establish affective bonds with selected others takes forms different from that of attachment – such as relationships whose focus is on play, teaching/learning, sex, and other kinds of transactions – but these other types of interpersonal bonds never completely supplant the need for attachment. Whenever, for instance, an adult is sick, fatigued, frightened, or otherwise seriously distressed, he or she will tend to search for a person perceived to be wiser or stronger, toward whom a more or less modified version of infantile attachment behavior will be reenacted.

The important aspect of this basic postulate of attachment theory is that the tendency to establish interpersonal relationships is regarded as a *primary* component of our behavioral repertoire rather than as a secondary derivative of satisfying supposedly more basic needs, such as those for food and sex. The main body of experimental evidence supporting this view comes from Harlow's classic studies of primate infants' behavior: under conditions of stress infant macaques showed clear preference for cloth surrogate "mothers" over wire-mesh "mothers," even though only the latter were sources of food (Harlow 1958). Since K. Lorentz's discovery of imprinting in birds contemporary ethological-evolutionary thinking has strongly supported the idea that attachment is a primary motivational-behavioral system and is not the expression of a secondary drive derived from the mother's association with food, or an aspect of sexuality (see, e.g., Hinde 1982). From the point of view of evolutionary neuropsychology imprinting in birds and attachment behavior in mammals make their appearance during vertebrate evolution together with the development of the limbic system. It may, then, be assumed that attachment behavior is related to the activity of the limbic system and therefore requires neuronal structures that are more complex than those of the "reptilian brain" (see, e.g., MacLean 1977, 1978) – those in the latter being sufficient to regulate feeding and sexual behavior in the lower vertebrates, which do not show signs of attachment – but less complex than those of the human brain cortex.[1]

Attachment behavior may therefore be seen as the result of a behavioral control system developed through zoological evolution and probably related to the limbic structures of the mammalian brain. The operations of this control system in humans may be examined on three different *psychological* levels:

1. On the *behavioral* level the attachment system coordinates every type of behavior (crying, calling, smiling, following, clinging, etc.) that may result in establishing and maintaining proximity to the attachment figure.

2. On the *emotional* level the operations of the attachment system are felt as affects in the area of security and confort (when proximity to the attachment figure

[1]This draws upon MacLean's theory of the triune brain. According to MacLean (1977, 1978) humans possess three different, albeit interconnected, brain systems. The "reptilian" brain is similar in structure and function to the brain of reptiles. The limbic system is similar to the neuronal structures that make their first appearance during animal evolution in mammals. The neocortex is typical, in its full development, of *homo sapiens.*

is achieved) or in that of fear and distress (when the attachment figure is not available). There is a typical sequence of fear–anger–sadness–defensive emotional detachment that takes place whenever separation from the attachment figure is prolonged over time. This sequence seems invariant across the infants' range of temperaments (Bowlby 1982).

3. On the *cognitive* level the beginning operations of the attachment system in infancy entail principally the discrimination of the attachment figure, the monitoring of her whereabouts, and the appraisal of discomforting or frightening interoceptions and exteroceptions. In other words, the involved cognitive structures are mainly sensory-motor schemata (see e.g., Inhelder 1962 for a description of sensory-motor schemata). Later on in life, as the child's knowledge of self and others progresses, increasingly sophisticated working models of self and the attachment figure become able to regulate the operations of the attachment system. Bowlby's concept of "internal working models" (of the self and the attachment figure) is quite compatible with the concepts of cognitive psychology such as representations, constructs, and schemata. As Bretherton (1985) has observed, the term "internal working model" has the advantage over these other terms of drawing attention to the dynamic aspects of representation. By "working," or operating, on mental models the child generates interpretations of the mother's behavior, takes into consideration her moods and interests as revealed by past transactions with her, and evaluates alternative courses of future, anticipated actions.

It is important to note that the original perceptual discrimination of *one* attachment figure among the individuals making up an infant's interpersonal environment implies that the cognitive level of the attachment system tends to operate according to a principle of monotropy (Bowlby 1982). Among the baby's working models of mother, father, and other care-givers a hierarchy is established with regard to attachment behavior. At the top of the hierarchy is the representation of the preferred attachment figure. Other care-givers are regarded as subsidiary attachment figures, although they may well be, for instance, the baby's preferred playmates.

Relationships Between Thinking, Feeling, and Acting

With respect to the interactions between emotion and cognition there are two major theoretical positions in contemporary general psychology. According to the one, affect is postcognitive, in the sense that processes of evaluation and symbolization (through comparison with memory schemata) of the sensory inflow precede and determine the emotional experience (see, e.g., Lazarus 1984). According to the other position, emotion is primary and causally independent from cognition: thinking and feeling are related in a reciprocally noncausal manner (Zajonc 1980, 1984). The differences between these positions are perhaps confused by the rather ill-defined terms "emotion" and "cognition" (see, e.g., Wessler 1986).

Rather than generalizing about the relationship between cognition and emotion and taking a position as to whether emotion is precognitive or postcognitive, it is perhaps judicious to limit oneself to the reciprocal interactions between thinking, feeling, and acting *within each distinct domain of experience* and to the modifications of these interactions during cognitive development. This is the position taken by Lundh (this volume) who views the mind as a system of distinct meaning structures, each of which involves three dimensions of meaning: extension (related to behavior), intension (related to representations and beliefs), and value (related to affective experience). In a similar vein, Greenberg and Safran (1984, 1987; see also Safran and Greenberg 1986) have proposed a model of the cognitive-emotional-behavioral systems in which emotion is considered as a primary form of meaning, related to the survival of the organism and inextricably intertwined with cognitive processing and motor activity.

The conceptual framework of attachment theory is compatible with the positions of Lundh and of Greenberg and Safran and at the same time allows the application of these theoretical principles to both developmental and clinical problems. Thus, within the domain of experience (or meaning structure) to which we refer with the term "attachment," the infant's emotion and behavior originally depend on very simple appraisals of environmental stimuli (e.g., the whereabouts of the mother) and organismic stimuli (e.g., fatigue, pain). With cognitive growth the child's emotion and behavior as related to attachment come to depend with increasing frequency on previously constructed internal working models of the self and the attachment figure; the internal working models of the self probably incorporate the emotions previously experienced during the interactions with the attachment figure in the form of emotional schemata (Leventhal 1979). These working models shape the increasingly idiosyncratic way of feeling and behaving toward the attachment figure; as a result of these models stable individual patterns of attachment behavior come into existence (e.g., secure attachment, anxious attachment, or even avoidance of the attachment figure; see Ainsworth 1982; Bretherton 1985). While internal models of self and others regulate attachment behavior and related affects in rather stable and idiosyncratic ways, there is, however, always the possibility that the ontogenetically older and simpler emotional dynamics, characterizing the original functioning of the attachment system, may be evoked by sufficiently powerful environmental conditions. Thus, for instance, after a major loss different adults are likely to experience in a similar way the emotional *sequence* of protest (fear, anger) and despair (sadness, hopelessness) that is typical in the child separated from its mother, irrespective of their idiosyncratic ways of thinking, feeling, and behaving in interpersonal relationships otherwise. Individual cognitive models undoubtedly shape the experience of grief, but the fundamental structure of the grieving process is remarkably similar across individuals and cultures (Bowlby 1980; Parkes 1972).

The study of the attachment system provides a model for considering (in a developmental-structural perspective) the interactions between thinking, feeling, and acting within each behavioral system and within each meaning structure. According to the ethological-evolutionary perspective adopted here, the human being is endowed from birth with anlagen (drafts, primordia) of various behavioral control systems, each entailing cognitive, emotional, and motoric aspects of functioning. Some of these systems are already fully operative at birth (e.g., that controlling eating behavior), others are activated gradually in the first months of life (e.g., the attachment system), while still others come to function fully only when the maturation and growth of the organism allows for their operations (e.g., the system controlling sexual behavior). The various behavioral systems that make up our behavioral repertoire[2] are each activated under a set of distinct environmental and/or organismic conditions. At the beginning of life the interplay between various behavioral systems is primarily related to environmental and behavioral contexts. The environmental context has to do with what systems are activated and at what intensity. Thus, for instance, absence of the attachment figure in the immediate surroundings activates the infant's attachment system, while novel (unthreatening) objects in the baby's environment activate the system controlling exploratory behavior.

Behavioral context refers to the relative intensity of activation of the relevant systems (Ainsworth 1982, pp 4–5). Thus, if mother is present and the attachment system is therefore inactive or activated at low intensity, novelty will prompt the baby to explore. If, however, the baby strays too far from its mother during this exploration, the attachment system will be activated again, exploration will cease, and it will tend to return to its mother (Ainsworth 1982). As cognitive growth proceeds the cognitive levels of different behavioral systems are shaped not only by experience and learning but also develop according to the phases of cognitive growth, from the sensory-motor stage up to the stage of formal operations (see, e.g., Inhelder 1962). The progressive disengagement of cognitions from the situational "here and now" of the operations of a given behavioral system allows, in all probability, for the progressive integration of various behavioral systems. In other words, as a result of cognitive growth the interplay between the different behavioral systems comes to be related not only to environmental and behavioral contexts but also to the developing internal working models of self and reality. The self-schemata (see, e.g., Goldfried and Robins 1983) are probably the main regulators of the integrated functioning of different behavioral systems.

According to this ethological-developmental perspective, emotions in adults are related not only to very general and superordinate cognitions (such as self-schemata) that have developed gradually during the life span but also to the functioning of distinct behavioral control systems that were originally operating and may still operate independently from the hierarchically higher cognitive structures.[3] In this perspective it is therefore important to distinguish between seemingly similar emotions when they pertain to different behavioral systems

[2]For the understanding of clinical problems it is useful, in my opinion, to take into consideration the behavioral systems controlling attachment, feeding, territoriality, exploration, play, affiliation, dominance, sex, and parenting. Because of its key position in early social and cognitive development, the attachment system is, among these, of the utmost importance.

[3]Safran and Greenberg (1986) have argued convincingly in favor of a view of the relationships between cognition, emotion, and behavior that seems quite compatible with the perspective adopted here. For a full consideration of their arguments, which combine Gibson's ecological theory of perception with the paradigm of information processing, see also Greenberg and Safran 1986.

before relating them to superordinate cognitions. Anger, for instance, has a particular meaning when it appears during the operations of the attachment system, and this meaning is different from that of anger pertaining to the other behavioral systems, e.g., that controlling territorial behaviour.[4] Territorial aggression is aimed at defending one's physical (and, by semantic generalization, perhaps also psychological-ideological) space against intruders, while anger directed toward the attachment figure is aimed at attracting her attention, protesting against her unresponsiveness, or discouraging her from deserting (Bowlby 1973). A clinical example will illustrate the importance of discriminating between different types of seemingly similar emotions, by attributing them to distinct behavioral systems.

A. considered himself unwilling to be cared for and unable to love others. A. was prone to outbursts of (verbal) aggression and alleged this proneness to be a reason for his belief of being unlovable and unable to love. Many should's and must's characterized his inner dialogues and belief systems and were obviously related to his proneness to experience and express anger, both toward himself and toward others (cf. Ellis 1962). Rather than limiting myself to this kind of assessment of the relationships between superordinate cognitions (e.g., "I am unlovable because I am aggressive" and "People deserve punishment for their superficiality") and anger, I noticed that A.'s schemata could not properly assimilate different types of aggression. A. did not, for instance, discriminate between anger in the form of a request for attention and emotional comfort from his rather unresponsive wife, on the one hand, and anger aimed at keeping at a distance his decidedly intrusive mother-in-law, on the other. Every episode of angry interactions fed into his self-schemata, conveying a description of the self as aggressive, unlovable, and unwilling to love others. When A. began to see that *some* expressions of anger were a derivative of his (until then ill-recognized) longing for love and reassurance, the pathway was open for a revision of his mistakenly construing himself as unlovable and unwilling to be loved. He began, in other words, to construct self-schemata which were better able to assimilate emotions pertaining to his attachment system.

Healthy Cognitive-Emotional-Behavioral Development

A brief account of healthy development, as envisaged in terms of attachment theory, will serve here as a first step in delineating a conceptual guideline for the cognitive psychotherapist interested in reconstructing patients' early pathogenic experiences.

Studies of attachment conducted both in home settings – through the direct, naturalistic observation of infant-mother dyads – and in the so-called "strange-situation" (Ainsworth 1982; Ainsworth et al. 1978) have identified a pattern of attachment behavior that has been termed "secure attachment" and various patterns of insecure, anxious attachment referred to as "resistant," "avoidant" (Ainsworth 1982; Ainsworth et al. 1978), and "disorganized-disoriented" (Main and Solomon 1986). Longitudinal studies strongly suggest that patterns of secure or insecure attachment, as assessed at the age of 1 year, are related to security with

[4]Territoriality is the tendency to defend one's space against invasion (see, e.g., Bates 1970; Hinde 1982) and makes its appearance very early during the evolution of animal life. The corresponding behavioral system should have more relations with the structures of the reptilian brain than to the evolutionarily more recent ones of the limbic system, to which attachment is probably related (MacLean 1978).

the attachment figure and to the general organization of social-emotional behavior up to at least 6 years of age (for reviews of these longitudinal studies, see Ainsworth 1982; Bowlby 1982; Bretherton 1985; Main et al. 1985).

Securely attached infants constitute the largest and normative group in the samples of infant-mother dyads that have been observed by the various researchers in various countries. In the presence of mothers and in an unfamiliar setting these 1-year-old actively explore the environment. They are only mildly upset during brief separations (of a few minutes) from the mother. When the mother returns, these infants greet her and often seek close bodily contact with her. The pattern of behavior by insecurely attached infants is strikingly different (see next section). The main determinant of the baby's pattern of attachment is, according to now abundant empirical evidence (Ainsworth 1982; Bowlby 1982, 1988; Bretherton 1985), the mother's degree of sensitivity in responding to infant signals and communications.[5]

The internal working models (meaning structures) that develop in a securely attached child likely imply the following: (a) the appraisal of other people as basically helpful and available should one need their presence; (b) a positive view of oneself with regard to one's ability to cope with the normal difficulties and nuisances of everyday life and with regard to one's own trustworthiness and lovableness in relationships with significant others; (c) the drafting of self-schemata that are able, with the proper attribution of cause and meaning, to assimilate emotional information (i.e., one's own and others' perceived emotions) pertaining to the functioning of the attachment system; and (d) a smooth cognitive regulation of the interplay between various behavioral systems, particularly those that entail mutually incompatible actions (e.g., moving away from the attachment figure during autonomous explorations and searching for the attachment figure when during exploration one feels hungry, tired, or frightened).

Developmentalists are accumulating much empirical evidence to the effect that these are, indeed, the pathways of cognitive-emotional development related to secure attachment. It has been demonstrated, for instance, that secure attachment in infancy is positively correlated with a confident and constructive attitude later in childhood toward the exploration of novel environments, to meetings with peers and friendly adults, and to understanding one's own and other's social emotions (Bretherton 1985; Bowlby 1982, 1988; Main et al. 1985).

Especially when cognitive growth after adolescence permits, such a confident exploratory attitude toward the environment will probably develop – into a confident exploratory attitude toward oneself, that is, toward the "inner world" of feelings and thoughts. When linguistic development and cognitive skills at the

[5]This observed continuity in the social-emotional development does not imply that early infant-mother transactions inevitably set the pattern of a child's interpersonal relationship for all time. Changes in the child-mother interaction linked, for instance, to stresses in the mother's life, have been observed to reflect themselves in the organization of the child's attachment behavior (Ainsworth 1982). The relationship between early patterns of attachment and later social-emotional development is probably due to the combined effects of: (a) stability of the care-giver's attitudes toward the child, and (b) intrinsic resistance to change in the early internal models of self and the attachment figure (Bowlby 1982, 1988; Bretherton 1985; Main et al. 1985).

stage of formal operations (see, e.g., Inhelder 1962) allow articulate and stable self-descriptions, a confident exploratory attitude toward oneself prevents self-descriptions acquiring a dogmatic, overgeneralized, absolutistic, and defensive character. Positive attitudes toward oneself and toward others have been shown to be related in early and late adolescence to a low degree of egocentrism – taking the term to mean a lack of differentiation between one's own point of view and that of others (Baron 1986). One may safely infer, then, that the once securely attached infant is likely to develop into an adolescent possessing both a well-differentiated self-conception and a belief system that remains open to change, readjustment, and learning in new social interactions.

It does not seem unwarranted to assume that young men and women capable of this kind of social-cognitive functioning will be more likely than others to preserve or, indeed, even enhance a positive view of themselves and others while confronting the problems and crises of adult life. One may also safely hypothesize that they will be more likely than others to select suitable persons as intimate friends or spouses. Recent studies in social psychiatry and psychiatric epidemiology provide support for these assumptions: young girls who received inadequate care in their families present negative views of themselves twice as frequently as do girls who received adequate care; furthermore, these inadequately cared-for girls are more likely to enter unhappy marriages (Bowlby 1988; Ingham et al. 1986). A positive view of self and others, together with a stable, happy affective bond, constitute a safeguard against the development of emotional disorders and provide the basis for further favorable evolution of self-knowledge during adult life.

Adverse Influences on Cognitive-Emotional Development

In the above section, studies were quoted showing that the major feature of maternal behavior that is related to infant patterns of insecure attachment (resistant, avoidant, and disorganized-disoriented) is insensitivity in responding to the infant's signals and communications. Ainsworth and associates (1978) have defined various aspects of such maternal insensitivity, such as rejection, ignoring (the infant's communications), interference (in the baby's spontaneous activities), and inconsistency (in responding to the infant's signals). A further pattern of care-givers' behavior that is related to abnormal development of the attachment system and is now beginning to be systematically studied (Bowlby 1984) is that characterized by the infant or child becoming the target for violent words and deeds of the parents.

The best studied of the various dimensions of maternal insensitivity is rejection; this is strongly related to the avoidant pattern of attachment behavior. Rejection is characterized by a deep aversion to close bodily contact with the baby and frequent negative or critical comments about its behavior. The child in this case is likely to meet with rebuff when attempting to approach the mother. Perhaps as a result of their effort to control angry feelings toward their children, such mothers' vitality and mobility of emotional expression are rather poor. In contrast to securely attached infants – those mildly distressed during brief separations from the attachment figure and happy on reunion – children of rejecting mothers show little or no distress when the mother leaves and avoid contact, proximity, or even interaction with the mother when she returns (on avoidance of the attachment figure, see Ainsworth et al. 1978).

Infants showing an anxious-resistant pattern of attachmenl are very anxious in a novel environment, even in the presence of their mothers, to whom they tend to cling. Therefore they explore the surroundings much less confidently than do securely attached infants. When the mother leaves the scene, these infants are severely upset, and when she returns, they show her a mixture of proximity-seeking behavior and resistance to her efforts to reestablish an interaction. Anxious-resistant infants are likely to be the children of mothers who frequently interfere in the baby's spontaneous activities (e.g., autonomous exploration) and are inconsistent in responding to its communications.

Main et al. (1985 p. 79) have described infants classified as disorganized-disoriented as follows:

Dazed behavior on reunion with the parent..., disordering of expected temporal sequences (e.g., strong avoidance following strong proximity seeking), simultaneous display of contradictory behavior patterns (approaching with head averted, gazing strongly away while in contact), incompleted movements and undirected expressions of affect appeared in these infants.

These infants typically have parents who themselves had suffered unusual trauma in their own attachment histories and seem to have difficulty in assuming a stable role of protection and guidance in interaction with their children. Data collected by Main and associates suggest that these parents may tend to invert the functional roles in the relationship between the care-giver and the cared-for baby, themselves indirectly asking their children for emotional comfort and reassurance (see Main et al. 1985, p. 86, p. 99). Children seem to be sensitive to their parents' tacit or explicit requests for an inverted protective relationship. Thus, at 6 years of age the once disorganized-disoriented infants are likely to be controlling and subtly care-giving toward the parent on reunion after brief separations – even if they appear depressed and intermittently irrational in other situations (Main et al. 1985).

The hidden expectation that the child should function as a source of emotional support and reassurance – being promplty available to the parent's requests in a relationship of inverted care-giving attachment – also seems to be present in some adults prone to violent behavior toward their offspring. Some abused children have been observed to show an unusual sensitivity to the emotional needs of their abusing parents while their reactions to peers and adults making friendly overtures were marked by extreme approach-avoidance behavior (Bowlby 1984).

In childhood and adolescence various untoward patterns of parenting, all exploiting the continuing operation of the attachment system after infancy, may have further adverse effects to a cognitive-behavioral development already set on an unfavourable course by one of these types of insecure attachment in infancy. These adverse influences are made possible by cognitive and linguistic development of the child which makes it vulnerable to verbal threats (used by parents as a method of discipline) and able to apprehend the meaning of dramatic family interactions which may be witnessed.

Threats to withdraw the parent's love from the child, to desert it, or to abandon the family may induce in the child not only to feel quilty (negative self-schemata may develop in this way) but also to imagine fearfully a future of loneliness and helplessness. A similar effect occurs if parents' induce their children to feel guilty by claiming that the child's behaviour will be responsible for the parent's illness or death. The representation of the self as threatened by abandonment, loneliness, and helplessness may also enter the child's cognitive organization through other experiences. For instance, the child may witness quarrels during which one or both parents threaten to desert or even kill the other or to commit suicide (Bowlby 1973). The relationship between parental conflict during childhood (especially but not only when the conflict directly regards the child) and poor adaptation as an adult has been demonstrated in longitudinal studies (Chess et al. 1983).

Actual – as opposed to threatened or imagined – experiences of loss of an attachment figure before adolescence (death of a parent, divorce, etc.) also tend to exert a detrimental effect on a child's cognitive-emotional development, unless the loss is compensated by substantial care, understanding, and emotional intimacy provided by other care-givers (Bowlby 1980; Brown and Harris 1978). Parents' prolonged illness (and especially chronic depression and other psychiatric or chronic psychosomatic ailments) are also likely to produce negative effects on the child's cognitive-emotional-social development (Hirsh et al. 1985; Hirsch and Reischl 1985).

Besides controlling the child's behavior through the improper exploitation of painful emotions related to the attachment system (fear of loneliness, impotent anger, and sadness at being rejected), parents may also hinder the proper development of other behavioral systems in their children. Clinicians working with adult psychiatric patients frequently encounter the effects of adverse parental influences on the developing behavioral systems which control eating, exploratory, sexual, and other types of interpersonal behavior. It is worth noting here that parents have the power to influence the development of these behavioral systems principally because the operations of the attachment system make the child vulnerable to the kinds of threats described above and to similar, albeit less dramatic and more indirect, threats. For instance, the notion of deserving to lose parental love sometimes causes children and adolescents to regard their own sexual wishes as somehow dangerous, and to start to have an overcontrolling attitude toward these wishes. It is unlikely that such notions relating sexual wishes to personal unworthiness would appear in a child's mind without the linkage being supplied by the parents. (For a discussion of the probable social origins of various sexual "complexes" that Freud attributed to the spontaneous intrapsychic activity of the child, see, e.g., Schatzman 1973, in particular Chap. 8).

It should also be noted that the interplay between various behavioral systems (see Thinking, feeling, acting) is such that when one of these is disturbed, the ground is prepared for an unfavorable development in other systems as well. For instance, feelings of loneliness experienced because the attachment figure is frequently unavailable may result in the search for compensatory or distracting activities (e.g., overeating, prolonged day-dreaming, masturbating, etc.), controlled by behavioral systems other than that of attachment. These other systems thus become activated under conditions that are not those of their proper functioning. Another example, one of considerable clinical importance, concerns the interplay between the systems controlling exploratory and attachment behavior. An overprotective, overcontrolling parent may unduly hamper the child's autonomous exploration of novel physical and social environments. In this situation it is not unlikely that the child may tend to inhibit the operations of the attachment system, in order to acquire a false sense of emotional freedom and try to fulfil its wishes for autonomy. Overprotective parental attitudes – similarly to the rejecting parent's critical, ridiculing, or otherwise negative comments – may convey the message that the child is considered basically unreliable, weak, or unable to cope with the difficulties of the extrafamilial world. The child will then develop self-schemata that reflect the view of him- or herself obtained from these seemingly opposite, overcritical, and overprotective parental attitudes (see Guidano and Liotti 1983, for a discussion of this looking-glass effect in the development of self-knowledge). Similar pathogenic effects from negative criticisms and overprotection are evidenced in recent research on "expressed emotion" in families (Leff and Vaughn 1985).

Another major class of adverse influences on cognitive-emotional development concerns parental styles of communication characterized by hypocrisy, frequent lies, and concealment or gross distortion of information regarding important aspects of family life. Bowlby (1979, 1985) has reviewed some studies on this type of potentially pathogenic parent-child relationship and argues convincingly that a particularly detrimental source of cognitive disturbance derives from parents' attempting to prevent their children from further conscious processing of information that the children already possess about events which their parents wish they had not observed. Sexual intercourse between parents, secret encounters with an extramarital paramour, incestuous approaches to the child itself, abuse of alcohol or drugs, and suicidal attempts are among the events that a parent may strongly wish the child to forget, not to report to others, and not to reflect upon further. A parent may insist that the child should construe various aspects of less dramatic family interactions or of the child's own emotional experiences differently than the way in which the child is (probably rather correctly) interpreting them. For instance, a father may insist that a daughter construe his rejecting attitude as a means of disciplining her and motivated by love, while the girl correctly interprets her father's behavior as a consequence of his perceiving her demands for attention as interfering with his interests and activities. A further example is that of a mother who may encourage her son to misinterpret his sadness over her unavailability by repeatedly describing his state as "listless" due to alleged constitutional "weakness" or supposed ill-health.

In all these cases, as Bowlby (1980, 1985) has suggested, the ground is prepared for a dissociation between semantic and episodic memory. When an adult with this kind of childhood experience begins psychotherapy, the therapist may notice gross inconsistencies between generalized descriptions of the parents as provided by the patient (semantic memory) and implications of some episodes of interaction with the parents that the patient may recall (episodic memory). Similar inconsistencies may be uncovered between the generalized judgements which the patient makes about himself, and his reports of how he felt, thought, or behaved on particular occasions. Such a dissociation between semantic and episodic memory may set serious limits to the efficiency of cognitive processes in the solution of personal and interpersonal problems.[6]

Patterns of Abnormal Cognitive-Emotional Development

The deleterious influences on human development that have been described here should not be regarded as producing pathological effects in a linear, mechanistic fashion. From the beginning of one's life one has the potential to function as an active problem solver and organizer of one's own experiences (see, e.g., Guidano and Liotti 1983). Pathogenic patterns of parenting pose problems that the child may solve in various ways. Some solutions to a particular social-developmental problem may prove better than others for the future mental health of the child. A given solution may be rather effective within the family's style of interaction but prove inappropriate in other interpersonal contexts. Self-schemata that are constructed upon the child's solutions of early interpersonal problems with care-givers may not permit the proper assimilation of the emotional meaning of important life events during adulthood; these events may then become the precipitating factors of an emotional disorder (cf. Guidano and Liotti 1983; Liotti 1986).

Examples of how childhood solutions of social-developmental problems may predispose one to cognitive-emotional dysfunctions in adult life are provided by the histories of many agoraphobic patients (Guidano and Liotti 1983; Liotti 1986). These patients were often forced in childhood to cope with problems arising out of the relationship with an inconsistent, interfering, overcontrolling, and/or overprotective attachment figure. The attachment relationship in infancy was very likely of the anxious-resistant type. The resultant working models of the self and the attachment figure convey the expectancy of some hindrance during the exploration of the environment and provide little confidence either in one's own abilities to cope with difficulties or in the willingness of others to provide help if required to do so. In this situation, the activities of the behavioral systems mediating attachment and exploration or play are likely to clash. In order to solve the problems posed by conflicting desires for protection and exploration and by the relationship to an inconsistently responding or overcontrolling parent, the child may develop an overcontrolling attitude toward itself and toward others. The growing child may learn to control its parents' behavior (in order to capture their attention, to obtain their help, or to gain their permission to go out to play with peers) and also to control its own fear of separation (in order to fulfill a wish to stay away from home playing

[6] Adults who show this kind of episodic-semantic dissociation while speaking of their attachment histories (for instance, providing idealized descriptions of their attachment to their parents and at the same time recalling evidently unpleasant episodes of their attachment history) are likely to be the parents of insecurely attached children. Parents with similarly unfavorable attachment histories, who openly acknowledge that they had been unhappy with their own parents, are much more able to help their children to become securely attached to them (Main et al. 1985).

with peers, etc.). Acquiring such an overcontrolling attitude toward other people and toward one's own feelings of vulnerability may appear a rather good solution, and having pursued this solution, incipient agoraphobics may emerge from childhood and adolescence as apparently healthy young men and women. However, the ability quickly to control personal emotions (e.g., shutting them off from further conscious processing) and the manipulation of interpersonal relationships is not the best way to develop articulate knowledge of these emotions. The urge to exert immediate control over a given phenomenon in order to suppress it or to modify its course is basically incompatible with the capacity for carefully exploring that phenomenon. This is particularly true of one's own unpleasant emotions (such as fear of separation from a parent to whom one is anxiously attached) which need to be endured for a time in order to understand their relationship to various aspects of one's mental and interpersonal life. Agoraphobics exercising frequent control over emotions pertaining to their attachment system behave like those who dismiss the messenger before he has presented the message.

The self-schemata of agoraphobics therefore do not allow careful descriptions of an important type of personal emotions and interpersonal realities. When these persons experience events that entail an increased risk of loneliness (or of reduced personal freedom as an alternative to loneliness), their self-schemata cannot properly assimilate the relevant emotional information. Rather than understanding these emotions they will strive to control them and, if it proves impossible to suppress them (e.g., because the event becomes protracted over time, such as in a marital crisis leading to a possible separation), they will develop inaccurate hypotheses concerning their nature. They will find it difficult to associate the ostensible outward meaning of a personal, emotional experience to that which they are feeling and will construe many emotions related to the attachment system as signs of an alleged illness. Typically such symptoms suggest an illness which threatens their ability to keep control over themselves; fears of losing control, madness, fainting, etc. are cardinal features of agoraphobia. This mistaken causal attribution will, of course, evoke further fear reactions, thereby setting into motion the vicious circle of the agoraphobic syndrome (cf. Guidano and Liotti 1983; Liotti 1986).

Various patterns of abnormal development have been described, leading from childhood insecure attachments to adult agoraphobia (Bowlby 1973; Guidano and Liotti 1983; Liotti 1986), depression (Bowlby 1980; Brown and Harris 1978; Guidano and Liotti 1983), multiple personality (Bowlby 1985), obsessive-compulsive syndromes, and eating disorders (Guidano and Liotti 1983). The study of these and other patterns of abnormal or of more favorable development should always be based on the awareness of a fundamental principle of developmental psychopathology, which Bowlby (1988) has expressed in the following way:

> (I)t is necessary to think of each personality as moving through life along some developmental pathway, with the particular pathway followed always being determined by the interaction of the personality as it has so far developed and the environment in which it is then finding itself.... So long as family conditions are favorable the pathway will start and continue within the bounds of healthy and resilient development; but should conditions become sufficiently unfavorable at any time, it may deviate to a lesser or greater extent towards some form of disturbed and vulnerable development.

Abnormal patterns of development are characterized by distinctive features for each nosologic syndrome and for each individual, but they also show certain very general features that distinguish them, as a group, from the healthy developmental pathway outlined above. Abnormal patterns of development entail meaning structures which convey, in one form or another, a negative view of the self and/or of meaningful others and self-schemata unsuitable to the proper assimilation of some important type of emotional information. They are also characterized by a relatively high degree of egocentrism (lack of differentiation between one's point of view and the point of view of others) in one or another domain of meaning. Egocentrism, in turn, makes more likely a haphazard selection of friends or spouses and leads to frequent misunderstandings and occasions for mutual rejection in meaningful relationships. The result is a vicious circle of interpersonal problems, emotional suffering, and cognitive distortions – as is sadly so familiar to psychotherapists.

The purpose of this chapter is to provide the clinician with a conceptual guideline for the reconstruction of early pathogenic experiences. It is therefore important, finally, to consider briefly the principal reasons that many patients experience difficulty when asked to provide the detailed memories needed for this reconstruction. The first involves a structural-formal problem. Abnormal patterns of attachment constitute deviation from a functional norm and consequently involve cognitive-emotional processes and memory structures that are more complex than those accompanying secure attachment. Thus, from a formal standpoint it is difficult to reflect straightforwardly upon experiences associated with insecure patterns of attachment and to report them in detail. A second impediment is the pain in replaying the unpleasant emotional experiences that led, for instance, to fear of one's attachment figure; the tendency to avoid dwelling on these painful memories is quite understandable. The third reason is related to the dissociation between episodic and semantic memory, as described in the preceding section. Parents can force their children to adopt views of their own character and of family life that are inconsistent with the children's first-hand experience. The adult patient recollecting the descriptions of family interactions that he has been forced to adopt during his childhood may find it almost impossible to believe the information conveyed by fragments of episodic memories that contradict these descriptions (see, e.g., Guidano and Liotti 1983, pp. 77–79; Bowlby 1985).

In the face of these difficulties the importance for the clinician to become familiar with the various types of adverse influences on the cognitive-emotional development from infancy to adolescence cannot be overestimated.

References

Ainsworth MDS (1982) Attachment: retrospect and prospect. In: Parkes CM, Stevenson-Hinde J (eds) The place of attachment in human behavior. Tavistock, London, pp 3–30

Ainsworth MDS, Blehar MC, Waters E, Wall S (1978) Patterns of attachment: a psychological study of the strange situation. Erlbaum, Hillsdale, NJ

Baron P (1986) The relation between egocentrism and dysfunctional attitudes in adolescents. Br J Cog Psychother 4 [2]:71–77
Bates BC (1970) Territorial behavior in primates. Primates 11:271–284
Bowlby J (1973) Separation. Hogarth, London (Attachment and loss, vol 2)
Bowlby J (1979) On knowing what you are not supposed to know and on feeling what you are not supposed to feel. Can J Psychiatry 24:403–408
Bowlby J (1980) Loss. Hogarth, London (Attachment and loss, vol 3)
Bowlby J (1982) Attachment. 2nd edn. Hogarth Press, London (Attachment and loss, vol 1)
Bowlby J (1984) Violence in the family as a disorder of the attachment and caregiving systems. Am J Psychoanal 44:9–27
Bowlby J (1985) The role of childhood experience in cognitive disturbance. In: Mahoney MJ, Freeman A (eds) Cognition and Psychotherapy. Plenum, New York pp 181–200
Bowlby J (1988) Developmental psychiatry comes of age. The 1986 Adolf Meyer lecture, delivered to the American Psychiatric Association, Washington D.C. Am J Psychiatry 145:1–10
Bretherton I (1985) Attachment theory: retrospect and prospect. In: Bretherton I, Waters E (eds) Growing points of attachment theory and research. University of Chicago Press, Chicago (Monographs of the Society for Research in Child Development, vol 50, Serial No. 209)
Bretherton I, Waters E (eds) (1985) Growing points of attachment theory and research. University of Chicago Press, Chicago (Monographs of the Society for Research in Child Development, vol 50, Serial No. 209)
Brown GW, Harris TO (1978) Social origins of depression. Tavistock, London
Chess S, Thomas A, Korn S, Mittelman M, Cohen J (1983) Early parental attitudes, divorce and separation, and young adult outcome. J Am Acad Child Psychiatry 22:47–51
Cicchetti D (1984) The emergence of developmental psychopathology. Child Dev 52:44–52
Dryden W, Golden W (eds) (1986) Cognitive-behavioral approaches to psychotherapy. Harper and Row, London
Ellis A (1962) Reason and emotion in psychotherapy. Lyle Stuart, New York
Emde RN, Harmon RJ (eds) (1982) The development of attachment and affiliative systems. Plenum, New York
Gardner H (1984) Frames of mind: the theory of multiple intelligences. Heinemann, London
Goldfried MR, Robins C (1983) Self-schema, cognitive bias, and the processing of therapeutic experiences. In: Kendall PC (ed) Advances in cognitive-behavioral research and therapy, vol 2. Academic, New York, pp 33–80
Greenberg LS, Safran JD (1984) Integrating affect and cognition: a prespective on therapeutic change. Cog Ther Res 8:559–578
Greenberg LS, Safran JD (1987) Emotion in psychotherapy. Guilford, New York
Guidano V, Liotti G (1983) Cognitive processes and emotional disorders. Guilford, New York
Harlow HF (1958) The nature of love. Am Psychol 13:673–685
Hinde RA (1982) Ethology. Oxford University Press, London
Hirsch BJ, Reischl TM (1985) Social networks and developmental psychology. J Abnorm Psychol 94:272–281
Hirsch BJ, Moos RH, Reischl TM (1985) Psycho-social adjustment of adolescent children of a depressed, arthritic or normal parent. J Abnorm Psychol 94:154–164
Ingham JG, Kreitman NB, Miller P, Ross H (1986) Self-esteem, vulnerability and psychiatric disorder in the community. Br J Psychiatry 148:375–385
Inhelder B (1962) Some aspects of Piaget's genetic approach to cognition. In: Kessen W, Kuhlman C (eds) Thought in the young child. University of Chicago Press, Chicago, pp 17–32
Jaynes J (1982) The origin of consciousness in the breakdown of the bicameral mind. Penguin, Harmondsworth
Landau M (1984) Human evolution as narrative. Am Sci 72:262–268
Lazarus RS (1984) On the primacy of cognition. Am Psychol 39:124–129
Leff J, Vaughn C (1985) Expressed emotion in families. Guilford, New York
Leventhal H (1979) A perceptual motor processing model of emotion. In: Pilner P, Blankstein K, Spigel I (eds) Perception of emotion in self and others. Plenum, New York, pp 121–156
Liotti G (1984) Cognitive therapy, attachment theory and psychiatric nosology: a clinical and theoretical inquiry into their interdependence. In: Reda MA, Mahoney MJ (eds) Cognitive psychotherapies. Ballinger, Cambridge, pp 211–232

Liotti G (1986) Structural cognitive therapy. In: Dryden W, Golden W (eds) Cognitive-behavioral approaches to psychotherapy. Harper and Row, London, pp 92–128
Liotti G (1987) The resistance to change of cognitive structures: a counterproposal to psychoanalytic metapsychology. J Cog Psychother 1: 87–104
MacLean PD (1977) On the evolution of three mentalities. In: Arieti S, Chrzanowski G (eds) New dimensions in psychiatry, vol 2 Wiley, New York, pp 309-320
MacLean PD (1978) A mind of three minds. In: The National Society for the Study of Education, Seventy-seventh Yearbook, Chicago
Main M, Solomon J (1986) Discovery of an insecure disorganized/disoriented attachment pattern. In: Yogman M, Brazelton T (eds) Affective development in infancy. Ablex, Norwood, pp 119–140
Main M, Kaplan N, Cassidy J (1985) Security in infancy, childhood and adulthood: a move to the level of representation. In: Bretherton I, Waters E (eds) Growing points of attachment theory and research. University of Chicago Press, Chicago, pp 66–104 (Monographs of the Society for Research in Child Development, vol 50, Serial No. 209)
Parkes CM (1972) Bereavement: studies of grief in adult life. Tavistock, London
Parkes CM, Stevenson-Hinde J (eds) (1982) The place of attachment in human behavior. Tavistock, London
Reite M, Field T (eds) (1985) The psychobiology of attachment and separation. Academic, London
Safran JD, Greenberg LS (1986) Hot cognition and psychotherapy process: an information processing/ecological perspective. In: Kendall PC (ed) Advances in cognitive-behavioral research and therapy, vol 5. Academic, New York, pp 143–177
Schatzman M (1973) Soul murder: persecution in the family. Random House, New York
Sroufe LA (1986) Appraisal: Bowlby's contribution to psychoanalytic theory and developmental psychology. J Child Psychol Psychiatry 27:841–849
Sroufe LA, Rutter (1984) The domain of developmental psychopathology. Child Dev. 55:17–29
Wessler RL (1986) Conceptualizing cognitions in the cognitive-behavioral therapies. In: Dryden W, Golden W (eds) Cognitive-behavioral approaches to psychotherapy. Harper and Row, London, pp 1–30
Wessler RL, Wessler SWR (1986) Cognitive-appraisal therapy. In: Dryden W, Golden W (eds) Cognitive-behavioral approaches to psychotherapy. Harper and Row, London, pp 196–223
Zajonc RB (1980) Feeling and thinking: preferences need no inferences. Am Psychol 35:151–175
Zajonc RB (1984) On the primacy of affect. Am Psychol 39:117–123

A Psychophysiological Information-Processing Model of Cognitive Dysfunction and Cognitive Treatment in Depression

M. Koukkou

Introduction

In this chapter we attempt to synthesize knowledge from disciplines concerned with human behavioural organization with the aim of developing a unified psychophysiological approach to the brain mechanisms underlying (a) the expression of depressive symptoms as defined by Beck's cognitive theory of depression and (b) the psychological and/or pharmacological treatment of these symptoms. This synthesis is based on a psychophysiological model of brain functioning which was originally developed to explain dream mentation, i.e. mental experiences by healthy adults which are distinctly different from wakeful thinking and feeling (Koukkou and Lehmann 1980, 1983a). The application of the model to schizophrenic symptomatology and treatment and to neurotic symptomatology and treatment is discussed elsewhere (Koukkou 1980, 1987; Koukkou and Lehmann 1980, 1983b).

The model uses brain mechanisms established in experimental psychology, behavioural research, psychopharmacology, electrophysiology and developmental studies. It follows the themes of information theory, and the arguments are based on paradigms and data which indicate "memory-driven" brain mechanisms for the organization of behaviour. It describes information processing in terms of "automatized" access to activated storages of memory (state-dependent information processing).

The model is based specifically on the concept of functional states of the brain which are reflected in the electrical (electroencephalographic) activity of the brain. These refer to a certain organization of neural activity which is continuously and dynamically adapted – within the limits of the system – to the demands made on the organism by incoming internal and external events. The characteristics of this adaptation are evaluated and effected by the mechanisms underlying the orienting response. In information processing the functional states of the brain are manifested as state dependency of cognitive strategies and retrieval mechanisms.

The model suggests that during states of depression brain information processes have access to memory storages where "depression-specific" cognitive strategies and memory contents (verbal, symbolic *and* emotional) are stored and which in healthy states are not accessible. It does not postulate depression-specific information-processing mechanisms. It views depressive symptoms as the result of information processes which use the "normal set" of information-processing

---

Research Department, University Hospital of Psychiatry, Postfach 68, CH-8029 Zürich, Switzerland

mechanisms but "inadequate" ("depressogenic") memory storages. It proposes that depressive symptoms are manifested when the accessible state-dependent context information and cognitive strategies called upon to evaluate incoming events are inadequate to estimate momentary age- and state-relevant significance of the events for the organism. The purpose of this chapter is to outline the sequence of psychophysiological mechanisms which come into play during these information processes.

A Model of Brain Functioning

State Dependency of Learning and Retrieval

The evidence of state-dependent learning and retrieval came originally from pharmacological studies with centrally active drugs. It was shown that behaviour learned in a drugged state of the brain can be retrieved when the brain is again in the same state. However, when retrieval takes place in a non-drugged state, there are distinct retrieval differences (Overton 1972). This implies that operationally for each functional state of the brain there is an associated long-term memory store; the various storages may, of course, be physically the same structure but treated with different tools. Storage of new information is optimal in the directly state-associated storage; read-out of stored material is asymmetrical (Overton 1972), i.e. for a given functional state read-out is also possible out of "higher" (non-drugged, or more vigilant, more developed, more complexly organized) but not out of "lower"-state storages.

Relevant for our considerations and for the application of the model in depressive mentation are the following observations:

1. All centrally active drugs which have been found to produce state-dependent learning and retrieval produce changes in the brain's electrical activity (EEG).
2. Retrieval difficulties are also known for physiological states. These are early childhood (childhood amnesia) and sleep (remembering of sleep mentation, dreams). There are distinct EEG differences between childhood and adulthood; the greatest differences exist between early childhood and adulthood. The earlier an event occurs in the life of an individual, the greater the retrieval difficulties of the event in the later years. Additionally, there are distinct EEG differences between wakefulness and the various sleep stages. Awaking from the REM-sleep stage, which has the greatest similarities with the EEG of wakefulness, allows better retrieval of sleep mentation (for review see Goodenough 1978; Webb and Cartwright 1978). Generally, the greater the EEG differences between the sleep stage from which we wake a subject to ask for sleep mentation and wakefulness, the greater the retrieval difficulties. It is conceptually important to mention the distinct differences in cognitive style (including emotional style) between adult wakeful thinking and sleep mentation or childish thinking.
3. Drugs influencing psychopathology and, for the arguments of this chapter, drugs influencing depressive symptoms are associated with EEG changes;

moreover, there are statistically significant EEG differences between responders and non-responders to drug treatment (e.g. Koukkou et al. 1979, 1983, 1986; Saletu et al. 1982), and there are significant relationships between EEG variables and degree or kind of symptomatology (e.g. Perris et al. 1978; Kemali et al. 1980; von Knorring et al. 1983). The relevance of such findings is clear regarding clinically significant drugs, such as the phenothiazines and tricyclic antidepressants, which have not been studied within the context of state-dependent information processing. Questions of state dependence may be of relevance both in the analysis of the underlying mechanisms of drug action and in the assessment of the therapeutic efficacy of the drug.

4. A mood state-dependent retrieval and general cognitive style have been proposed theoretically, based on psychological and clinical observations (Rapaport 1971), and have been experimentally shown, considering mood changes in healthy people (Bower et al. 1978; Mecklenbrauker and Hager 1984) and in manic-depressive episodes (Reus et al. 1979; for review see Bower 1981; Gilligan and Bower 1984).

Retrieval is highly dependent upon the coincidence of cues available at the time of learning with cues available at recall (for a recent review see Leventhal and Tomarken 1986). An extensive review of the literature on pharmacological state-dependent memory by Eich (1980) also shows the importance of retrieval cues in the demonstration of this phenomenon. A similar conclusion is proposed by Baddeley (1982) for state dependency of the environmental context. For our considerations also very relevant is the observation that retrieval cues may be features of the immediate environment but also of the internal state, i.e. endogenous changes of a natural kind such as vigilance, hormonal changes and the mood state (e.g. Eich 1980; Mecklenbrauker and Hager 1984). This would correspond to the suggestion that arousal levels associated with affective states may be the prime retrieval cues. The functional model of the brain which we use includes the mechanism of state-dependent learning and retrieval. All these findings have been summarized in the model to indicate that the functional state of the brain, as reflected in the EEG, permits and restricts access to certain parts of long-term memory (Koukkou and Lehmann 1983a) and thus to certain knowledge, i.e. stored events and stored cognitive strategies developed to deal with the events.

The Human Information-Processing System

From the perspective of information theory, humans are in a continuous and selective interaction with their external environment and with their organism, i.e. their internal environment (see e.g. Hebb 1961; for recent reviews see e.g. Johnston and Dark 1986; Parasuraman and Davies 1984). This interaction is organized by the functions of the central nervous system. Behaviour is the "measurable" manifestation of these interactions. In other words, behaviour is the end product of the mental operations (brain activity) with which humans receive, analyse, interpret and select the answers to the messages which reach them continuously. Cognitive psychologists (e.g. Neisser 1976) who conceptualized the human organism as an information processor, have identified several operations which are involved in this selective interaction with the environment, i.e. functions with which the human brain deals with external and internal events and with representations and semantic information in memory in order to organize its behavioural answers.

Basic elements of the human information-processing system are (a) reflexive stimulus-response relationships, i.e. inborn programmes (unconditioned reflexes) which, however, become modified through experiences (see e.g. Konorsky 1967; Neumann 1984) and (b) memory stores of information (i.e. multidimensional complex representations of past events and experiences), developed skills (particular responses to particular target stimuli), and cognitive strategies for the analysis of and the coping with incoming information and its cepresentation in memory.

The human memory system may be thought of as a very large capacity store which is organized in nodal structures (Bower 1975) which are arranged in levels and sometimes in hierarchical "tree" structures. Levels refer to a temporal directionality of processing such that certain nodes activate other nodes but not vice versa (Shiffrin and Schneider 1977). The nodes include control elements of stimulus representations that code various aspects of the events and experiences; they are associatively related to contexts, to strategies developed to cope with the events, to programmes for responses or actions and to response-evoking structures (Estes 1973; Mandler 1975; Shiffrin and Schneider 1977). These relationships develope slowly with experience and, when well established, are manifested with the automatic information-processing mode (see below).

The inclusion of the emotional aspects of events and experiences in the concepts and assumptions of cognitive theorists about the human information-processing system is not clear. An important assumption for our consideration is that the multidimensional, complex representations of events in human memory include both the physical characteristics of the events and experiences coded in the verbal or other symbolic languages of the brain *and* the emotional aspects of these events and experiences coded in the emotional languages of the brain (e.g. Bower 1981; Koukkou 1987; see also Leventhal and Thomarken 1986). The emotional aspects of the events and of their representation in memory influence the responses attached to the events and the cognitive strategies developed to cope with them (see also Mayer 1986). Thus, the human memory system can be defined as the sum of all stored information about the verbal, symbolic *and* emotional aspects of previous internal and external events and experiences, the context in which they occurred and the responses and cognitive strategies developed to cope with these experiences.

At any given moment in time only a part of the memory contents (multidimensional representations, responses and cognitive strategies) are activated and thus accessible as working memory for information processing (e.g. Bower 1975; Norman 1976; Shiffrin 1976). Which memory contents are activated in a given moment depends on the internally (thoughts, emotions, feelings) and externally incoming information in close relation with the functional state of the brain at that moment. The functional state of the brain in our model is reflected in the electroencephalogram (EEG; see below).

Stages of Human Information Processing

Theories of human information processing suggest in general that after sensory excitation and encoding of the physical characteristics of the information into the verbal, symbolic *and* emotional languages of the central nervous system, the thus moulded multidimensional information is compared with the content of the working memory, i.e. with the momentarily activated parts of the long-term memory. This subset of mental operations is known as pre-attentive processes (Neisser 1967), initial interpretation of the information (Norman 1968) or information-evaluation processes (Duncan-Johnson 1981; Hillyard and Kutas 1983). Thus, the pre-attentive processes interact closely with the working memory. Informational input to the working memory may be internally or externally generated; thoughts and memories also function as input to the working memory. These stimulus-processing operations work continuously and in parallel for all "input channels" to the brain, i.e. they use the automatic information-processing mode (see below). They lead to a very rapid (range of milliseconds) automatic and preliminary but relatively complete identification of two basic properties of the information: present familiarity and present significance.

The identification of the information by the pre-attentive processes results in selecting the information-processing mode (automatic versus control, see below) which is applied to cope with the event; this elicits (a) the information-response processes, i.e. a psychophysiological response (to which a "no change" also belongs) and (b) the processes of the further analysis and evaluation of the information, which take into account the context in which the information was embedded, the initial response to the information and its consequences for the organism.

The processes of further analysis of the events have been summarized as the full or cognitive interpretation of the information (Norman 1973; Craik 1979). The cognitive interpretation lasts considerably longer than the initial one and requires extended knowledge of the context in which the information was presented, the retrieval of more related information from memory and the consideration of the system's present functional priorities. The sum of all these processes may be viewed as cognitive style. These processes are summarized in Fig. 1. Deviations of one or more of these processes have been hypothesized to result in the different cognitive styles recognized as psychopathological disorders.

Modes of Human Information Processing

According to major developments in attention and in human information-processing theory, mental operations and thus human performance functions in two different modes, referred to as automatic and control (consciously controlled) processing (e.g. Shiffrin and Schneider 1977; see also Neumann 1984; Posner 1982).

Control processing is a capacity-limited, serial, slow, easily established, flexibly allocated and individually regulated information-processing mode. On the other hand, automatic processing is a fast, parallel process that is innate (reflexive

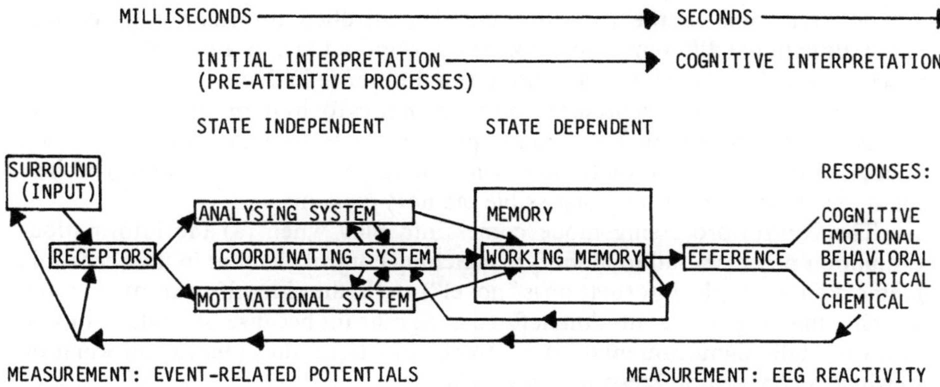

Fig. 1. Diagram summarizing the information-processing stages, their EEG concomitants and their relation to the momentary accessible working memory

stimulus-response relationships) or the result of practice and is responsible for performance of well-developed, skilled behaviour. For the level of complexity of human behavioural performance, automatic processing refers only to the results of practice. Thus it is clear that automatic processing reflects powerful long-term learning processes. That which becomes automatized as a result of practice is a coordination between an event and a complex response, a skill. Without automaticity these two (event and response) must be linked by a conscious act, which includes the appreciation of the event (cognitive interpretation) and of the choice and the execution of the action.

It is important to keep in mind that (a) to the same configuration of events different response categories can be attached and thus automatized depending on the context, and (b) it is not only overt responses but also complex mental operations such as "attention" and "strategy" which can be attached as responses to internal or environmental information inputs to the brain's information-processing system (Shiffrin and Schneider 1977).

As performance becomes with practice more automatic, the accuracy and speed of responding increase, but humans have difficulty controlling their ongoing automatic processing since responding occurs as a "passive" (automatic) consequence of the incoming event. Automatized event-response relationships once established are difficult to alter, to ignore or to suppress.

Automatic processing is "involuntary", that is, it can be triggered without a supporting intention and lacks conscious awareness (for an overview see e.g. Neumann 1984). The earliest possible conscious awareness of an automatic operation is the awareness of the selection of a response. Under normal circumstances, however, automatic processes inspite of lacking conscious awareness are not independent of the person's current general intentions – just the opposite: they facilitate accurate performance in the field of general intention and set free capacity of the control mode for the processing of information with which the individual is not familiar. Being automatic does not mean that these operations lack control, but that they are controlled below the level of conscious awareness, i.e.

without demands on the capacity-limited, controlled information-processing mode. Functional differences of automatic as opposed to non-automatic (control) processes are thus qualitative and not just a difference in degree.

The "choice" between these two different modes for human performance is the function of the information-evaluation processes (pre-attentive processes) which operate only with the automatic processing mode ("automatic detection") in close relation with the momentary accessible memory contents.

The control-processing mode comes into play when (a) the information-evaluation processes fail to identify a matching control element in the accessible memory contents (the information is "novel"), or (b) they identify information that matches memory representation defined as significant because of relationships to motivationally significant memory control elements, i.e. they identify information to which an "attention" response is attached.

The automatic processing mode comes into play when (a) the information-evaluation processes identify information to which an automatic (other than "attentional") adaptive response has been attached and (b) they identify a "to-be-ignored stimulus" (see also Öhmann 1979).

In summary, automatic detection and processing refers to the identification of an input and to the activation of a response by the information-evaluation operation that bypasses the serial (controlled) search through memory for adequate responding; therefore it bypasses attentional limitation but also attentional advantages. We have used these benefits and shortcomings resulting from the process of automatization in human performance to explain on the basis of our model so-called neurotic disturbances and their psychological treatment (Koukkou and Lehmann 1980, 1983a). In this chapter we suggest that the automatic information-processing mode may also play a role to the manifestation and maintenance of depressive thinking as defined by Beck's theory.

Electrophysiology of Information Processing and of the Orienting Response

Psychophysiologists who follow the theories and experimental designs of cognitive psychologists have used laboratory computers to examine the processing of sensory information in the human brain, i.e. to examine processes within the brain in the time between sensory inputs and behavioural outputs at a physiological level. The emerging field of cognitive psychophysiology uses mainly the technique of "event-related brain potentials" (ERPs) which requires computer averaging over many event presentations (e.g. Donchin 1984). This research has identified components of ERPs which vary as a function of physical stimulus parameters and components which only appear in conjunction with specific perceptual and cognitive processes. Thus, studies of ERPs have identified brain electrical manifestations which signify the temporal course of the human information-processing stages summarized as pre-attentive processes (e.g. Duncan-Johnson 1981; Hillyard and Kutas 1983) and electrical manifestations which are linked to the elicitation of the responses (e.g. Loveless 1983; Rohrbaugh 1984).

Cognitive psychophysiology has also used the "event-related EEG activity" (EEG reactivity), which permits the study of the EEG components of the orienting response and the study of the relationships between a complex event (external, e.g. short sentences, or internal, e.g. thoughts and feelings) and the brain's electrical state on single trials. This is the main topic of our research and is of particular interest for our considerations here.

Following the information-theory terms and an information-processing perspective of the orienting response (Öhman 1979), we have postulated (Koukkou and Lehmann 1980, 1983a, 1987; Koukkou-Lehmann 1987) that for each complex event which reaches the human information-processing system (i.e. the central nervous system) there is a psychophysiological response. This response is manifested as subjectively perceivable (cognitive and emotional) and objectively (electrically, chemically, behaviourally) measurable change or no-change at the level of functioning of the organism as compared to that just previously. The "characteristics" of this change or no-change are defined by the information-evaluation processes (automatic, pre-attentive processing) and reflect the necessary functional adaptation of the organism to the eliciting event. These are effected via the orienting response. The information-processing perspective of the mechanisms underlying the orienting response, as proposed by Öhman (1979), suggests clearly that it is elicited by the pre-attentive processes.

This orienting response incorporates a constellation of responses (components) which include changes in the central nervous system, the vegetative and somatic system and in behaviour, the adaptive significance of which has been emphasized by Sokolov (1975).

Considering event-induced EEG changes, this formulation indicates that the form, strength, topography and duration of the event-induced EEG changes manifest the functional adaptation of the brain to the demands made on the organism by the event as estimated by the pre-attentive processes. They introduce the brain's functional state during which the following cognitive interpretation of the event occurs.

A relationship of short-term brain states to different types or classes of cognitive and emotional processing of private experiences has been found in studies with spontaneous reports during EEG recording (Kuhlo and Lehmann 1964; Kamiya 1969; Koukkou and Lehmann 1976, 1980) and in studies with elicited reports (Lehmann et al. 1979; Machleidt et al. 1986). For instance, the EEG power spectra were significantly different in 36 subjects during 16-s periods immediately preceding reports of spontaneous reality-oriented abstract thinking, reality-remote non-visual fantasies and reality-remote visual fantasies (Lehmann et al. 1981); this was also found in 12 subjects during 20-s periods immediately preceding tetrahydrocannabinol-induced reports of visual hallucinations and body-image disturbances (Koukkou and Lehmann 1976). Similarly, other studies have reported EEG differences between periods when different cognitive activities were requested (Ehrlichman and Wiener 1980) and during various evoked emotions, such as intention, anxiety, aggression, sadness, and joy (Machleidt et al. 1986). Hypnagogic hallucinations are experienced during an EEG state (stage 1, non-REM), which is similar in spectral power distribution but very dissimilar in spectral coherence between scalp areas when compared with the state (stage 1, REM) in which dreams are most frequently recalled (Lehmann et al. 1979).

Our studies of event-induced EEG changes have shown that the form, strength and duration of these changes vary systematically as a function of increasing expectancy and familiarity and of decreasing complexity of the event (Koukkou 1985; Koukkou and Lehmann 1987 Koukkou and Manske 1985, 1986).

It is commonly observed that the changes of the various components of the orienting response during the course of so-called habituation proceed at different rates for the different components. There is a differential responsiveness among the various orienting-response components with repetition of an event; EEG and vasomotor responses appear to be virtually immune to complete habituation.

It has been argued that the orienting response as a unitary construct is valid only as an adaptive response to a sudden, unexpected and sufficiently intensive change in the environment. With repetition of such changes in the environment the different components of the orienting response become differentially "interchanged" with adaptive responses, which with further practice may become automatized. The nature of this automatized adaptation (of one or more components of the orienting response), i.e. the determination of which component will be interchanged with which adaptive response, depends on the functional significance of the component (and the organ of its expression) for the coping of the organism with the specific eliciting event, taking into consideration the momentary metabolic or homeostatic exigencies of the organism (e.g. Rohrbaugh 1984).

The debate continues concerning the functional significance of the orienting response generally or of its different components for human information processing and communication (compare e.g. Ohman 1979; Rohrbaugh 1984). Based on a non-unitary orienting-response construct and on the considerations described above, we propose that the functional significance of the orienting response be formulated as adaptation in the level of brain functioning and thereby of the whole organism to the demands made up on the organism by incoming events. The brain's functional adaptation is manifested in the EEG components of the orienting response and reflects the "width" of the working memory accessible for information processing.

EEG Functional States of the Brain and Information Processing

The functional model of the brain as shown in Fig. 2 integrates these findings and assumptions. This heuristic schema illustrates the principal interrelationships among the major determinants in the organization of the brain's functional states. The functional state of the brain in a healthy adult with his specific genetic constitution is determined at a given moment in time by the interacting convergences between (a) incoming information from the environment and the body (peripheral or central, e.g. thoughts, feelings, or memories), (b) past experiences (which include acquired motivations and cognitive strategies) as content of the working memory accessible for information processing, (c) metabolic and hormonal conditions (which correspond to drives), (d) circadian changes, and (e) before adulthood, the stage of brain's development. To these physiological factors must be added modifications by drugs and by physical or mental illness.

The basic proposal of the model is that the functional state of the brain is associated with specific electrical activity and with specific memory storages where

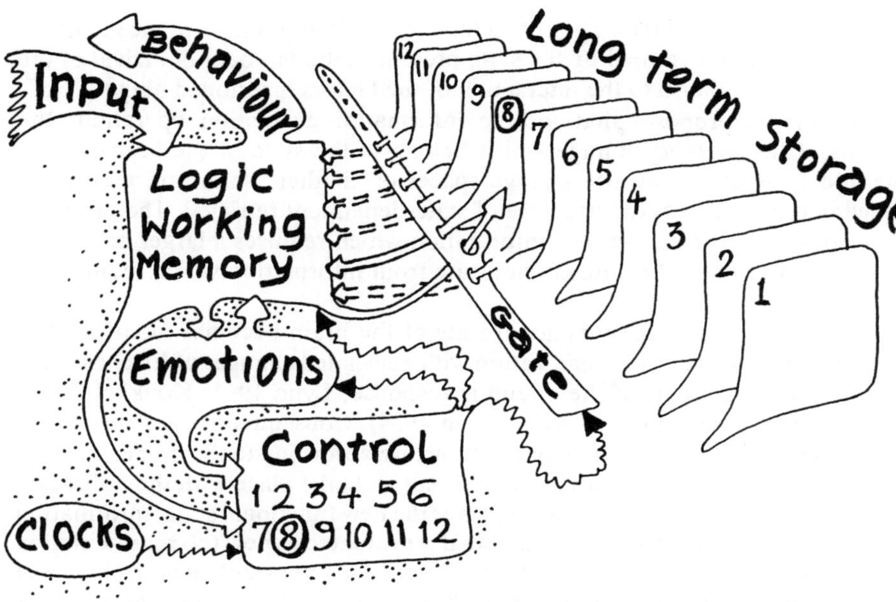

Fig. 2. Functional model of the brain. *Double lines,* open information channels; *dashed lines,* partially open information channels; *solid, thin lines with black arrow heads,* control channels. The functional state of the entire system (illustrated is state 8) is set by the control system according to "clock" input and to input received from the logic/processing (analysis) system with its short-term memory (working memory) from the motivation/emotion system and from the vegetative system. The control system in return adjusts the function of logic and motivation and vegetative system to the current functional state and opens the gate to the associated long-term memory space for deposit and recall (in the figure, space 8). Memory of higher arousal levels (9-10) can be partially recalled; for that of the lower levels only the next, neighbouring space 7 is partially open for recall. Shifts of the functional state put different memory spaces and processing strategies into use (Reprinted with permission of the publisher from Koukkou and Lehmann 1983a)

state-innate and state-acquired cognitive strategies as well as memory material are stored.

We have noted that there is psychophysiological evidence that the different states of the brain are manifested in the EEG and are associated with different cognitive strategies for dealing with the incoming information. Grossly different functional brain states are the circadian changes between wakefulness and sleep and the developmental changes between childhood and adulthood. Minor, short-lasting (range of seconds), induced or "spontaneous" fluctuations in the brain's functional states have also been found to be associated with changes in cognitive strategies, emotional patterns and EEG patterns.

The brain's functional states thus defined are governed by internal "clocks" similar to those influencing development and the circadian and hormonal cycles. Additionally, and important for our consideration, the state of the brain is being continuously and actively readapted during wakefulness and sleep according to the demands made on the organism by the continuously incoming internal and external events. These demands are estimated by the information-evaluation operation of the information-processing system in close interaction with the accessible memory storages. The characteristics of the adaptation to the incoming information are constrained by the state present at the moment of arrival of the information in addition to the interaction of the factors mentioned above.

The model proposes that for the information-evaluation operations the contents of the memory storage which belong to the state of the brain at that time and to some extent also storage spaces of "higher" states are accessible, following the asymmetrical structure of state-dependent retrieval. The information-evaluation process sorts out information which requires a larger or smaller readaptation of the brain's functional state from information which requires no such readaptation.

The adaptation of the functional state of the brain becomes manifested as modification in the level of organization with associated changes of EEG patterns (the central components of the orienting response; Lynn 1966; Koukkou 1980; Koukkou and Lehmann 1987 Rohrbaugh 1984). Consequently, a state change after the initial interpretation of an event means, according to the model, that the following cognitive interpretation of the event will take place with the utilization of stored material and cognitive strategies of the new functional state. Information which for the present state of the individual is evaluated as new (no representation is activated in the accessible memory contents) or as important elicits a change of state, i.e. an EEG change. On the other hand, if the initial interpretation of the information concludes either that it is safe to ignore the information, or that from previous experiences it is known how to cope with the demands of the information, no change of brain state occurs, although the behavioural response may appear (automatic processing).

In summary, the brain's functional states are not stable. They show changes over months, hours, minutes or seconds of clock time and in response to information from other structures of the organism (developmental phase, circadian rhythm, menstrual cycle, etc.) and over milliseconds as a function of the continuous adaptation to the internal and external reality of the organism by the mechanisms underlying the orienting reaction (pre-attentive processes). These long- and short-term adaptations permit and restrict access to certain parts of the memory and thereby to state-dependent knowledge (verbal, symbolic *and* emotional) and to state-innate and acquired cognitive strategies to cope with this knowledge (cue function of the state). The functional states influence behaviour.

Applying the Model to the Cognitive Theory of Depression

Cognitive Theory of Depression: An Overview

This short overview relies on the works of Beck and his followers on a cognitive theory of depression (Beck 1967, 1976; Kovacs and Beck 1979) and that by Rush and Giles (1982) on the theory and research of cognitive therapy of depression. It aims at a short description of the concepts of the theory for which the presented model proposes a psychobiological basis.

The cognitive model of depression postulates three concepts to explain the psychological substrate of depression:

1. Negative cognitive patterns that induce the patient to regard himself, his experiences, and his future in an idiosyncratic, negative (depressive) manner.
2. Schemata which are stable cognitive patterns developed early in life and define how an individual structures his experiences.
3. Faulty information processing.

The concept of schemata is fundamental for the cognitive theory of depression. It is used to explain why a patient maintains his negative (i.e. depressive) cognitive patterns about himself, his experiences and his future despite the presence of contradictory evidence.

According to Beck's model, schemata develope early in life from personal experiences. Once established, these are stable and form the "individual reality". They are the basis for screening, differentiating and categorizing the experiences that confront the individual and define his responses to them. Thus, schemata mould the adjustment of an individual to his internal and external reality, and as stable cognitive patterns they depict the basis for the regularity in interpretation of a particular set of situations by him. The similarity of the concept of schemata in Beck's theory with the concept schema of cognitive psychology (Neisser 1967) and that of control elements of human memory research is obvious.

Schemata, when not activated, remain without effect on behaviour. However, when a person faces a particular circumstance, a schema related to the circumstance is activated and used for the behavioural adjustment to the situation; particular schemata are activated by circumstances analogous to the experiences initially responsible for embedding the maladaptive schemata.

Activated schemata may be adaptive to reality and thus facilitate healthy behavioural adjustments, or they may be maladaptive and thus lead to faulty information processing and thereby to psychopathology.

According to Beck's cognitive theory, depression as mental disorder is the function of activated negative cognitive patterns and of major maladaptive schemata in the person's repertoire (individual reality) which lead to logical errors in drawing inferences about self, experiences and future from daily observations.

Depression as a mental disorder has cognitive, affective, motivational, behavioural and vegetative manifestations. Cognitive theory proposes that the maladaptive schemata and negative cognitive patterns account for all these manifestations of depression. Thus, the theory makes a causal relationship between these concepts and behavioural, affective and physiological manifestations of depression.

The cognitive treatment of depression aims at changing depressive manifestations by focusing on patient's misinterpretations, self-defeating behaviour and dysfunctional attitudes, i.e. by focusing on cognitive modification and reorganization of the negative cognitive patterns.

In summary, the theory proposes that negative cognitive patterns and maladaptive schemata are responsible for the manifestation and maintainance of depressive symptoms and are specifically implicated in vulnerability to depression and in relapses. Their modification and reorganization via cognitive therapy reduces symptoms and frequency of relapses.

The theory does not explain explicitly the relationships of emotions to cognitive processes. It does not address itself to the factors leading to the formation of the maladaptive schemata, i.e. their aetiology. It assumes that maladaptive schemata are not always activated and need a triggering event to activate them. However, there is no explicit proposal about the psychobiological mechanisms underlying the activation of the depressogenic schemata and the psychobiological mechanisms by which (a) the triggering events interact with the maladaptive schemata to induce and maintain an episode of illness and to produce the behavioural, affective and physiological manifestation of depression and (b) the cognitive reorganization is induced during therapy and influences the different manifestations of depression.

We propose that the psychophysiological model of electroencephalographically defined functional states of the brain with state-dependent information processing provides a framework to formulate hypotheses about the psychobiological basis of the cognitive theory of depression and about the underlying psychobiological mechanisms of action of cognitive as well as pharmacological treatment of depression, indicating their similarities and differences.

EEG-Functional States of the Brain and Manifestation of a Depressive Episode

Although not explicitly stated in the cognitive theory of depression, schemata (adaptive and non-adaptive) and cognitive patterns (positive and negative) become stored in memory. Thus, according to information theory, schemata affect behaviour by the role researches of human information processes and of human memory, and its physiological basis lies in the active and inactive memory storages.

We noted that memory contents are the basic elements of the human information-processing system; at any moment only a part of the memory contents are activated and thus accessible for the information-processing operations. Accessible memory storages define the operations summarized as information-evaluation and information-response processes. Thus, given that there be no structural dysfunction in one or more input channels and/or in response-execution channels of the human information processor, within- and between-subject differences in the information-evaluation processes as manifested in the characteristics of the responses to this information (psychophysiological response) indicate the usage of different or deviant memory storages with correspondingly different brain states.

Beck's theory of depression considers depressive symptoms as the result of activated maladaptive schemata and negative cognitive patterns which lead to faulty information processing. Accordingly, in the terminology of the information-processing approach to human behaviour Beck's cognitive theory of depression considers as decisive for the *manifestation* of depressive symptomatology the psychophysiological functions involved in (a) the activation and thus accessibility of previously stored memory contents and cognitive strategies (activation of the memory storages with the maladaptive schemata) and (b) the information-processing stages summarized as the information-evaluation processes; these lead to response manifestations which are recognized as depressive symptoms.

Which memory storages are accessible for information processing at a given moment is the function of the interaction between the brain's functional state (as defined by the convergence of its determinants) and the incoming events (state-dependent retrieval). As cues for retrieval function external (features of the environment) and internal (thoughts and feeling) information and internal states of the organism (drugged/not drugged, hormonal, wakeful, mood states). All these states of the organism are combined with particular EEG states.

Our model suggests that the electroencephalographically defined functional states of the brain are associated with specific memory storages. Thus, the EEG states of the brain define which memory storages – and thereby context information and cognitive strategies – will be called upon to evaluate incoming events and to define the behavioural (cognitive, somatic, emotional) response to these events at any given time, i.e. the information-evaluation and information-response processes.

We have seen that the electroencephalographically defined functional states of the brain reflect the interacting convergence of multiple factors; these are genetic constitution and internal clocks such as for developmental stage, vigilance level, metabolic and hormonal conditions. Additionally, the functional states of the brain adapt continuously and dynamically to the demands made on the organism by incoming information as evaluated by the pre-attentive processes which interact closely with the working memory. This adaptation is effected via the orienting response. Thus, the characteristics of the functional adaptation of the organism to the demands made by an event reflect the appraisal of the event based on the individual "knowledge" (working memory) and are manifested with behavioural, cognitive, affective and vegetative concomitants. They are determined and constrained by the state of the brain present at the moment of the arrival of the event in addition to the interaction of the factors mentioned above. Accordingly, in the line of the assumption of the model, all the possible combinations of the interactions among the factors which determine EEG-functional states of the brain and lead to the accessibility of the memory storages where the maladaptive schemata are stored, can be affected by "depressogenic" appraisals of the events and can thus trigger depressive symptoms. The symptoms will last as long as the storages with these "depressogenic cognitive strategies" are accessible for the brain's information-evaluation processes. The relationship of factors such as fluctuation in waking levels and metabolic or hormonal conditions to psychiatric illness and frequently to depression has been noted repeatedly (e.g. Bleuler 1964; Whybrow et al. 1984).

A number of studies have pointed to differences in electrical brain activity and in event-evoked brain potentials during episodes of affective illness (e.g. Kemali et al. 1980; von Knorring et al. 1983; Perris et al. 1978; Perris and Eisemann 1980; Prichep et al. 1986). Furthermore, as indicated above, drugs influencing depressive symptomatology change the brain's electrical activity differentially for responders and non-responders to the treatment.

According to our psychophysiological model of the brain's information processing and within the lines of cognitive theory we suggest that incoming events can trigger a depressive episode (affective, behavioural, cognitive and vegetative symptoms) in individuals who (for various, unspecified reasons) have developed maladaptive schemata, when the brain's functional state makes accessible for the information-evaluation processes the memory storages where these schemata have been stored. Thus, the psychobiological mechanisms underlying the activation of the depressogenic schemata are multiple and depend on the factors organizing the brain's functional states as an interacting convergence of its determinants. The triggering events produce the behavioural, affective and physiological manifestations of depression via the mechanisms underlying the orienting response.

The activated maladaptive schemata as stable results of experiences are automatized, i.e. induce their effects on behaviour (the psychophysiological responding) with the automatic information-processing mode. Thus, once activated they define the adjustments of the individual to his internal and external reality without his intention. The person is then confronted with his maladaptive adjustments.

Applying the Model to the Treatment of Depression

Pharmacological Treatment. We have noted that antidepressive medication influences the brain's electrical activity; furthermore, there are differences in the EEG effects of an antidepressive drug between responders and non-responders to the treatment. Thus, considering the mechanisms underlying the mode of action of antidepressives, the model suggests that they have an effect on the symptoms by changing the brain's electrical activity and thereby "closing" access to the memory storages with the "depressogenic" cognitive strategies and memory contents and facilitate access to memory storages with reality-including cognitive strategies. This enables the incorporation of the individual's stage- and age-reality in the brain's information-evaluation processes and thus reduces symptoms.

Cognitive Therapy. Considering the mechanisms underlying the mode of action of cognitive therapy of depression, the model suggests that this has an effect on symptoms primarily by changing the content of the "depressogenic" memory storages, i.e. by replacing the distorted and dysfunctional cognitive strategies with reality-including cues.

The change of behaviour – including physiological concomitants, emotional states and the internal behaviour of thinking – by stored, learnable and modifiable strategies and programmes has been shown repeatedly in the literature of human memory systems and their role for the modification of behaviour (e.g. Kahnemann 1973; Ursin 1978).

Concluding Remarks

According to the considerations described above as to the psychobiological mechanisms underlying the manifestation and treatment of depressive episodes, the model suggests that cognitive therapy acts by treating the "depressogenic" memory storages and pharmacotherapy by closing the access to these storages. The end effect is the same: the information-evaluation processes make no logic errors in drawing inference about the significance of the events for the individual since they no longer use "depressogenic" cognitive strategies for their operations. Thus, our model suggests common mechanisms for the mode of action of both pharmacotherapy and cognitive therapy in affecting depressive symptoms as concerns the role of the information-evaluation processes for the manifestation of the symptoms: they both change depressive symptoms by eliminating the effects of the dysfunctional beliefs on these processes. Findings of no differences in improvement rate between the two treatments support this assumption.

However, as concerns the role of the memory storages with the "depressogenic" cognitive strategies and context information for the predisposition to and the manifestation of the symptoms and for relapses, the model suggests different mechanisms of action for the two therapeutic approaches. Pharmacotherapy does not influence the memory storages with the "depressogenic" cognitive strategies; it thus acts symptomatically and cannot influence the aetiology of the manifestation of the episodes. Cognitive therapy, on the other hand, acts by changing the "depressogenic" storages, influencing the cause of depressive disorder. Recent findings of the comparison between the two therapies which indicate that cognitive-therapy patients have a lower risk for relapses and a longer maintenance of remission once drug treatment is discontinued (Simons et al. 1986) support this assumption.

References

Baddeley AD (1982) Domains of recollection. Psychol Rev 89:708–729

Beck AT (1967) Depression: clinical, experimental, and theoretical aspects. Hoeber, New York (Republished as Depression: causes and treatment. University of Pennsylvania Press, Philadelphia)

Beck AT (1976) Cognitive therapy and the emotional disorders. International Universities Press, New York

Blueler M (1964) Endokrinologische Psychiatrie. In: Gruhle HW, Jung R, Mayer-Gross W, Müller M (eds) Psychiatrie der Gegenwart, 1st edn, vol 1/lb. Springer, Berlin Heidelberg New York, pp 161–252

Bower GH (1975) Cognitive psychology: an introduction. In Estes WE (ed) Introduction to concepts and issues. Erlbaum, Hillsdale, pp 25–80 (Handbook of learning and cognitive processes, vol 1)

Bower GH (1981) Mood and memory. Am Psychol 36:129–148

Bower GH, Monteiro KP, Gilligan SG (1978) Emotional mood as a context for learning and recall. J Verb Learn Verb Behav 17:573–587

Craik FIM (1979) Human memory. Annu Rev Psychol 30:63–102

Donchin E (1984) Dissociation between electrophysiology and behavior – a disaster or a challenge? In: Donchin E (ed) Cognitive psychophysiology: event-related potentials and the study of cognition. The Carmel conferences, vol 1. Erlbaum, Hillsdale, pp 107–118

Duncan-Johnson CC (1981) P300 latency: a new metric of information processing. Psychophysiology 18:207–215

Ehrlichman H, Wiener MS (1980) EEG asymmetry during covert mental activity. Psychophysiology 17:228–235

Eich JE (1980) The cue-dependent nature of state-dependent retrieval. Mem Cog 8:157–173

Estes WK (1973) Memory and conditioning. In: McGuigan FJ, Lumsden DB (eds) Contemporary approaches to conditioning and learning. Winston, Washington, DC

Gilligan SG, Bower GH (1984) Cognitive consequences of emotional arousal. In: Izard CE, Kagan J, Zajonc RB (eds) Emotions, cognition, and behavior. Cambridge University Press, New York, pp 547–588

Goodenough DR (1978) Dream recall. In: Arkin AM, Antrobus JS, Ellman SI (eds) The mind in sleep. Erlbaum, Hillsdale, pp 113–142

Hebb DO (1961) Organization of behavior. Science Editions, New York

Hillyard SA, Kutas M (1983) Electrophysiology of cognitive processing. Annu Rev Psychol 34:33–61

Johnston WA, Dark VJ (1986) Selective attention. Annu Rev Psychol 37:43–76

Kahneman D (1973) Attention and effort. Prentice Hall, Englewood Cliffs, NJ

Kamiya J (1969) Operant control of the EEG alpha rhythm and some of its reported effects on consciousness. In: Tart CT (ed) Altered states of consciousness. Wiley, New York, pp 507–517
Kemali D, Vacca L, Nolfe G, Jorio G, De Carlo R (1980) Hemispheric EEG quantitative asymmetries in schizophrenics and depressed patients. Adv Biol Psychiatry 4:14–20
Konorsky J (1967) Integrative activity of the brain. University of Chicago Press, Chicago
Koukkou M (1980) EEG reactivity in acute schizophrenics reflects deviant (ectropic) state changes during information processing. In: Koukkou M, Lehmann D, Angst J (eds) Functional states of the brain: their determinants. Elsevier, Amsterdam, pp 265–290
Koukkou M (1985) EEG reactivity to stimuli as expression of orienting function: within and between session characteristics. Biol Psychol 20:201
Koukkou-Lehmann M (1987) Hirnmechanismen normalen und schizophrenen Denkens: eine Synthese von Theorien und Daten. Springer, Berlin Heidelberg wnew York
Koukkou M, Lehmann D (1976) Human EEG spectra before and during cannabis hallucinations. Biol Psychiatry 11:663–677
Koukkou M, Lehmann D (1980) Psychophysiologie des Träumens und der Neurosentherapie: das Zustands-Wechsel Modell. Fortschr Neurol Psychiatr 48:324–350
Koukkou M, Lehmann D (1983a) Dreaming: the functional state shift hypothesis: a neuropsychophysiological model. Br J Psychiatry 142:221–231
Koukkou M, Lehmann D (1983b) A psychophysiological model of dreaming with implications for the therapeutic effect of dream interpretation. In: Minsel WR, Herff W (eds) Research on psychotherapeutic approaches. Proc first eur conf of psychotherapy research, vol 2. Lang, Frankfurt, pp 27–34
Koukkou M, Lehmann D (1987) An information-processing perspective of psychophysiological measurements. J Psychophysiol 1:109–112
Koukkou M, Manske W (1985) Hemispheric EEG reactivity and information processing: within and between session characteristics. Electroencephalogr Clin Neurophysiol 61:S31
Koukkou M, Manske W (1986) Functional states of the brain and schizophrenic states of behavior. In: Shagass, Josiassen RC, Roemer RA (eds) Brain electrical potentials and psychopathology. Elsevier, Amsterdam, pp 91–114
Koukkou M, Angst J, Zimmer D (1979) Paroxysmal EEG activity and psychopathology during treatment with clozapine. Pharmakopsychiatry 12:173–183
Koukkou M, Zimmer-Höfler D, Lehmann D (1983) Lateralized aspects of forced EEG normalization and depressive symptoms in psychopathology. In Flor-Henry P, Gruzelier J (eds) Lateralization and psychopathology. Elsevier, Amsterdam, pp 301–313
Koukkou M, Woggon B, Angst J (1986) Longitudinal studies of EEG reactivity: a psychophysiological information-processing approach to psychopathology. In: Shagass C et al. (eds) Biological psychiatry 1985. Elsevier, New York, pp 419–420
Kovacs M, Beck AT (1979) Cognitive-affective processes in depression. In: Izard C (ed) Emotions in personality and psychopathology. Plenum, New York, pp 417–442
Kuhlo W, Lehmann D (1964) Das Einschlaferleben und seine neurophysiologischen Korrelate. Arch Psychiatr Nervenkr 205:687–716
Lehmann D, Koukkou M, Andreae A (1979) Daydreaming mentation and EEG patterns. Sleep Res 8:154
Lehmann D, Koukkou M, Andreae A (1981) Classes of day-dream mentation and EEG power spectra. Sleep Res 10:152
Leventhal H, Tomarken AJ (1986) Emotion: today's problems. Annu Rev Psychol 37:565–610
Loveless N (1983) The orienting response and evoked potentials in man. In: Siddle D (ed) Orienting and habituation: perspectives in human research. Wiley, New York, pp 71–108
Lynn R (1966) Attention, arousal, and the orienting reaction. Pergamon, New York (International series of monographs in experimental psychology, vol 8)
Machleidt W, Gutjahr L, Muegge A, Hinrichs H (1986) Differentiation of basic emotions by spectral EEG-analysis. In: Varbanova A (ed) Proceedings of the IVth international symposium school for young scientists "organization and adaptation of brain functions", Bulgarian Academy of Sciences, Varna
Mandler G (1975) Mind and emotion. Wiley, New York
Mayer JD (1986) How mood influences cognition. In: Sharkey NE (ed) Advances in cognitive science 1. Wiley, New York, pp 290–314

Mecklenbrauker S, Hager W (1984) Effects of mood on memory: experimental tests of a mood-state-dependency retrieval hypothesis and of a mood-congruity hypothesis. Psychol Res 46:355–376

Neisser U (1967) Cognitive psychology. Appleton-Century-jcrofts, New York

Neisser U (1976) Cognition and reality: principles and implications of cognitive psychology. Freeman, San Francisco

Neumann O (1984) Automatic processing: a review of recent findings and a plea for an old theory. In: Prinz W, Sanders AF (eds) Cognition and motor processes. Springer, Berlin Heidelberg New York

Norman DA (1968) Toward a theory of memory and attention. Psychol Rev 75:522–536

Norman DA (1973) What have the animal experiments taught us about human memory? In: Deutsch JA (ed) The physiological basis of memory. Academic, New York, pp 397–413

Norman DA (1976) Memory and attention. An introduction to human information processing. Wiley, New York

Öhman A (1979) The orienting response, attention, and learning: an information-processing perspective. In: Kimmel HD, van Olst EH, Orlebeke JF (eds) The orienting reflex in humans. Erlbaum, Hillsdale, pp 443–472

Overton DA (1972) State dependent retention of learned responses produced by drugs. In: Koella WP, Levine P (eds) Sleep. Karger, Basel, pp 48–53

Parasuraman R, Davies DR (eds) (1984) Varieties of attention. Academic, New York

Perris C, Eisemann M (1980) Further studies of averaged evoked potentials in depressed patients with special reference to possible interhemispheric asymmetries. Adv Biol Psychiatry 4:44–54

Perris C, Monakhov K, von Knorring L, Botskarev V, Nikiforov A (1978) Systemic structural analysis of the electroencephalogram of depressed patients. Neuropsychobiology 4:207–228

Posner MI (1982) Cumulative development of attentional theory. Am Psychol 37:168–179

Prichep LS, Lieber AL, John ER, Alper K, Gomez-Mont F, Essig-Peppard T, Flitter M (1986) Quantitative EEG in depressive disorders. In: Shagass C, Josiassen RC, Roemer RA (eds) Brain electrical potentials and psychopathology. Proceedings of the VII international symposium on clinical neurophysiological aspects of psychiatric conditions, 7–8 Sept 1985, Philadelphia, Pennsylvania. Elsevier, New York, pp 223–244

Rapaport D (1971) Emotions and memory. International Universities Press, New York

Reus VI, Weingartner H, Post RM (1979) Clinical implications of state-dependent learning. Am J Psychiatry 136:927–931

Rohrbaugh JW (1984) The orienting reflex: performance and central nervous system manifestations. In: Parasuraman R, Davies DR (eds) Varieties of attention. Academic, New York, pp 323–373

Rush AJ, Giles DE (1982) Cognitive therapy: theory and research. In: Rush AJ (ed) Short-term psychotherapies for depression. Guilford, New York, pp 143–174

Saletu B, Grger J, Linzmayer L, Taeuber K (1982) The pharmacokinetics of nomifensine. Comparison of pharmacokinetics and pharmacodynamics using computer pharmaco-EEG. Int Pharmacopsychiatr 17:43–72

Shiffrin RM (1976) Capacity limitations in information processing, attention and memory. In: Estes WK (ed) Attention and memory. Erlbaum, Hillsdale (Handbook of learning and cognitive processes, vol 4)

Shiffrin RM, Schneider W (1977) Controlled and automatic human information processing: II. Perceptual learning, automatic attending, and a general theory. Psychol Rev 84:127–190

Simons AD, Murphy GE, Levine JL, Wetzel RD (1986) Cognitive therapy and pharmacotherapy of depression: sustained improvement over one year. Arch Gen Psychiatry 43:43–48

Sokolov EN (1975) The neuronal mechanisms of the orienting reflex. In: Sokolov EN, Vinogradova OS (eds) Neuronal mechanisms of the orienting reflex. Wiley, New York, pp 217–235

Ursin H (1978) Activation, coping and psychosomatics. In: Ursin H, Baade E, Levine S (eds) Psychobiology of stress: a study of coping men. Academic, New York, pp 38–52

von Knorring L, Perris C, Goldstein L. Kemali D, Monakov K, Vacca L (1983) Intercorrelations between different computer-based measures of the EEG alpha amplitude and its variability over time and their validity in differentiating healthy volunteers from depressed patients. Adv Biol Psychiatry 13:172–181

Webb WB, Cartwright RD (1978) Sleep and dreams. Annu Rev Psychol 29:223–252

Whybrow PC, Akiskal HS, McKinney WT (1984) Mood disorders: towards a new psychobiology. Plenum, New York

Cognitive Measures of Depression

I.M. BLACKBURN

Introduction

The growing interest which has been shown recently in cognitive approaches to the understanding and treatment of various aspects of psychopathology has created a need for measures of cognition. It is, of course, recognised that reliable and valid methods of assessment are essential for both theoretical and practical advancement in a science. With regard to the role of cognition in depressive illness, such assessment fulfils several purposes:

1. To study the characteristics of depressive thinking which may distinguish it from those found in other disorders, that is, to study the specificity and generality of dysfunctional thoughts found in depressed patients.
2. To establish the role of certain types of thoughts in the maintenance or cause of depressive illness, that is, to investigate how depressed individuals differ when well and when recovered.
3. To determine whether certain characteristics of depressed thinking may act as vulnerability factors, or traits, which make some individuals more prone to depressive illness.
4. To test the comparative and specific effects of cognitive therapy and other treatments in the acute response to treatment and in the long term. For example, a researcher might be interested in finding out whether cognitive therapy, which is targetted on cognitions, changes cognitions before other symptoms, in contrast to, say, behaviour therapy, which may change behaviour before cognitions. In the assessment of the long-term effect of treatment cognitive measures may be able to determine possible cognitive factors which lead to recurrences of illness.
5. To study the relationship between the way in which stimuli are processed cognitively and the relationships between these cognitive processes, emotions and behaviour.

Thus, although measures of cognition need to be developed both to further cognitive theories and cognitive therapies of depression, research in this area has, on the whole, lagged behind experimental and therapeutic research. The general problem has been not a lack of awareness of the need for measures, but, often, a disregard for psychometric principles of objective assessment, a lack of careful

MRC Brain Metabolism Unit, Royal Edinburgh Hospital, Morningside Park, Edinburgh, EH10 5HF, United Kingdom analysis of different aspects of thinking and infrequent use of different methodologies. The past 20 years have witnessed a mushrooming of cognitive self-rating scales of various types, usually created for ad hoc purposes to fulfil the needs of particular studies, but there have also been some exemplary validation and cross-validation studies. Other assessment techniques, for example, thought sampling and assessment of imagery, as described by Kendall and Korgeski (1979), or think-aloud (Genest and Turk 1981) and thought listing (Cacioppo and Petty 1981), have scarcely received any notice.

The aim of this chapter is to present a critical review of the main cognitive measures of depression which have been described in the literature. Since these have usually been developed within particular theoretical frameworks, the plan will be to examine the measures as they relate to different cognitive theories, namely Beck's cognitive theory (1967), Seligman's attributional theory (1975), Ellis's rational-emotive theory (1962) and Rehm's self-control theory (1977).

Measures of Beck's Cognitive Theory

Because Beck's theory of depression is the cognitive theory which has been most widely studied in terms of its application to treatment, having led to a systematic method of treatment – cognitive therapy (Beck et al. 1979b) – it has inspired the development of the largest number of scales. Starting with the analysis of thought samples obtained from depressed patients during therapy, Beck (1963) has delineated three aspects of dysfunction in depressive thinking. Kovacs and Beck (1978) described these as disorders of (a) the *content of thought*, the general negative bias in thoughts relating to the self, the world and the future, labelled the negative cognitive triad; (b) the *process of thought*, that is, the processing errors which lead to the negative bias, for example, arbitrary inference, selective abstraction, magnification and minimisation, overgeneralisation and personalisation; and (c) the *structure of thought*, that is, the basic beliefs, attitudes or assumptions which integrate the various cognitive distortions and explain why some individuals, given certain internal or external cues, develop depression. Cognitive measures derived from the theory have, therefore, attempted to measure dysfunctions at each of these levels.

Content of Thought

Automatic Thoughts Questionnaire. A widely used general measure of negative content of thought is the Automatic Thoughts Questionnaire (ATQ), developed by Hollon and Kendall (1980). This is a 30-item self-rating questionnaire devised to measure the frequency of occurrence of automatic negative thoughts or negative self-statements. Each item is rated on 5 point scales rating frequency of occurrence over the past week. The original validation study was done on a sample of 312 undergraduate college students. Subjects were divided into depressed and non-depressed sub-groups on the basis of scores on two self-rated depression scales,

11+ on the Beck Depression Inventory (BDI; Beck et al. 1961) and 26+ on the Minnesota Multiphasic Personality Inventory, Depression Scale (MMPI-D; Hathaway and McKinley 1951). The validity of the ATQ was established in that it was found to discriminate significantly ($p < .01$) between the depressed and non-depressed samples and not to discriminate between males and females. It correlated highly significantly with the two depression scales and with an anxiety scale (STAI, Trait version; Spielberger et al. 1970), thus "precluding any interpretation of specificity to depression-related cognitions" according to the authors. Both split-half and alpha reliability coefficients proved highly satisfactory ($r = .97$ and .96, respectively; $p < .001$), showing that the scale was internally consistent.

The ATQ has since been used in a number of studies in both clinical and non-clinical populations and has been shown to be highly valid and reliable, despite the originally less than satisfactory validation study which used undergraduates diagnosed on self-rating scales. Eaves and Rush (1984) tested 31 depressed female patients meeting Research Diagnostic Criteria (RDC) for definite, unipolar, non-psychotic major depressive disorder (Spitzer et al. 1978) whom they sub-divided into endogenous and non-endogenous sub-groups. All patients were tested at time 1, when acutely symptomatic, and at time 2, when remitted. Treatment included antidepressant medication and/or psychotherapy but not cognitive therapy. The study included 17 non-depressed control subjects recruited from the community. The ATQ differentiated between depressed (means = 103.7 and 108.8, respectively, for endogenous and non-endogenous groups) and non-depressed, control subjects (mean = 39.7) and between depressed and remitted endogenous and non-endogenous patients (means = 55.5 and 46.7) but did not differentiate endogenous and non-endogenous depressed patients when ill or recovered. Number of previous episodes of illness or length of illness episode did not influence the score. Dobson and Breiter (1983) reported a validation study of the ATQ in 456 undergraduates. The ATQ showed high internal reliability ($r = .95$, $p < .001$), correlated significantly with the BDI ($r = .82$, $p < .001$) and differentiated male and female undergraduates ($p < .001$), which was in keeping with the finding that females had significantly higher BDI scores than males. Harrell and Ryon (1983) carried out a clinical validation of the ATQ on 21 clinic patients meeting criteria for depression (17+ on the BDI, 70T+ on the MMPI-D and 3+ on 5-point clinicians' ratings), 20 non-depressed clinic patients and 20 non-depressed medical patients. They found significantly higher mean scores for the depressed group (mean = 88.9) compared with the non-depressed psychiatric group (mean = 42.3) and the non-depressed medical group (mean = 38.3). The ATQ correlated highly significantly with severity measures of depression both within the depressed group and within the whole sample and both split-half and alpha coefficient were significant at $p < .001$. A discriminant function analysis showed that no non-depressed subjects were incorrectly classified as depressed.

Hollon et al. (1986) used the ATQ to test the specificity of depressed cognitions in clinical depression. They compared depressed patients with unipolar and bipolar symptoms, substance-abuse patients with secondary depression, non-depressed substance-abuse patients, general psychiatric non-depressed patients, medical controls, normal controls and remitted patients with unipolar and bipolar symptoms. The three depressed groups were highly differentiated from all other groups on the BDI and MMPI-D and in parallel they scored significantly higher on the ATQ (mean = 85) than the non-depressed or remitted groups (means = 41.2–60.2). The remitted groups did not differ either in level of depression or ATQ. The authors commented on the lack of specificity of the ATQ in that it did not discriminate between the different depressed groups and on its inability to pick up any cognitive vulnerability to depression in that it did not differentiate remitted groups from non-depressed controls. That the negative cognitions measured by the ATQ are state- rather than trait-dependent was noted by Simons et al. (1984) in the treatment trial of cognitive therapy versus antidepressant medication, each alone or in combination. All recovered patients, whether treated by drugs or cognitive therapy, showed a reduction to normal level in ATQ scores. Similarly, Blackburn et al. (1986) in a cross-sectional study, reported a significant difference between depressed (mean = 82.5) and recovered depressed subjects (mean = 42.4), the latter not differing from normal controls (mean = 34.9).

Correlations between the ATQ and other cognitive scales will be reported in later sections. The studies reviewed above indicate a consistency of results regarding the ATQ. It measures negative bias in the stream of thought, differentiates depressed from non-depressed subjects, but appears to co-vary with the depressed state rather than with any nosological group. With this proviso, it is a reliable and valid instrument, a score of about 80 being typical of the reports on various depressed clinical samples.

Crandell Cognitions Inventory. Very similar to the ATQ is the Crandell Cognitions Inventory (CCI), developed by Crandell and Chambless (1986). This consists of a self-report measure developed from 100 items measuring the frequency of occurrence of depressive automatic thought on a 5-point scale. Nineteen of the items are positive and are not included in the total score. In a comparison of 81 major depressed clinic patients, 51 non-depressed psychiatric controls and 80 normal controls, the authors found that 75 items discriminated among groups significantly, and in an effort to shorten the test further they excluded another 41 items which showed less discrimination. The final inventory now consists of 45 items, 34 highly discriminatory items and 11 buffer items. Age, sex, education and IQ were found not to be significantly correlated factors. Construct validity was established by correlation of the total score with the BDI ($r = .79, p < .001$) and the Dysfunctional Attitude Scale (DAS) ($r = .65, p < .001$). A discriminant analysis showed that 92.5% of the population could be accurately classified, thus establishing the predictive validity of the test. A factor analysis revealed two factors relating to a negative view of self and a negative view of the future and a third factor relating to helplessness or lack of control in a personal sphere, which partially supports Beck's postulated negative view of the world.

Hopelessness Scale. A more specialised measure of depressive content of thought is the Hopelessness Scale (HS; A.T. Beck et al. 1974), designed to measure only one element of the cognitive triad, namely a negative view of the future. This 20-item true/false self-rating scale has been well validated and used in a considerable number of studies. A.T. Beck et al. (1974) reported on a psychometric study of the HS in different patient samples: reliability was established in a population of 294 hospitalised patients who had made recent suicidal attempts; alpha coefficient yielded a reliability of .93 and item-total correlation coefficients ranged from .39 to .76. Concurrent validity was established by correlations with global clinical ratings of hopelessness in both general practice patients and hospitalised recent suicide attempters and by correlations with other measures of hopelessness in depressed hospital patients ($p <$ .001 for all correlations). The construct validity of the HS was established by testing various hypotheses relevant to the construct of hopelessness, as reported in various studies.

Minkoff et al. (1973) found that seriousness of suicidal intent is more highly correlated with negative expectations of the future than with depression. The statistical association between suicidal intent and depression is due to their joint relationship with a third variable, namely hopelessness. Beck (1974) reported that after success in a card-sorting task, depressed patients showed increased optimism regarding future success in similar tasks and a decrease of hopelessness, while failure on the task increased hopelessness. Depressed and non-depressed patients showed a significant decrease in hopelessness after successful completion of a graded hierarchy of verbal tasks. A principal-components factor analysis with orthogonal (varimax) rotation of the axes produced three clinically meaningful factors: feelings about the future (accounting for 41.7% of variance), loss of motivation (6.2% of variance) and future expectations (5.6% of variance).

Kovacs et al. (1975) replicated the finding of the predictive value of hopelessness for suicide attempts in a group of depressed and schizophrenic patients admitted to hospital after a suicidal attempt. They found that both hopelessness and depression (as measured by the BDI) correlated positively with a measure of suicidal risk, the Suicidal Intent Scale (SIS; Beck et al. 1973, 1979a) rated by experienced clinicians. However, hopelessness was more highly correlated with current suicidal risk than was depression and was significantly better in predicting patients' wish to die (self-rated on a Likert 8-point scale). Wetzel (1976) and Wetzel et al. (1980) reported essentially the same findings in both suicide attempters and suicide threateners. However, Pokorny et al. 1975 reported discordant findings in a study of 55 depressed suicide attempters admitted to hospital. They found that the correlation between depression and suicidal intent "was appreciably higher than that between suicidal intent and hopelessness" (.52 and .39, respectively, as compared with .44 and .64 in Minkoff et al. 1973). They attributed the discrepancy in the findings to demographic differences between the two samples: the sample of Minkoff et al. contained a higher proportion of women, racial or religious minorities and unmarried or separated individuals, whereas that of Pokorny et al. was primarily male, Caucasian, married and Protestant. Pokorny et al. comment that "These results suggest that against a background of depression, negative expectations about the future influence suicidal behaviour only in the presence of conditions which might have an effect on the suicidogenic potential of negative expectations about the future". Beck et al. (1985) followed up for 5–10 years 207 patients hospitalised because of suicidal ideation but not for suicidal attempts. Only the HS and the pessimism item of the BDI predicted the eventual suicides of 14 patients.

A normative study was carried out by Greene (1981) in a sample of 400 randomly selected adults in the general population. A wide distribution of scores was obtained, with a positively skewed curve and a mean of 4.45 (S.D. = 6.39). Nekanda-Trepka et al. (1983) established normative data in a sample of 88 depressed out-patients satisfying criteria for major depressive disorder, unipolar and non-psychotic (Spitzer et al. 1978). A mean score of 13.01 (S.D. = 5.17) was obtained, and it was noted that the distribution of scores was negatively skewed, with 12.5% of the sample obtaining scores of less than 6. Hopelessness was positively correlated with self-rated depression on the BDI ($r = 0.47, p < .001$) and with self-rated anxiety ($r = 0.28$, $p < .05$) as measured by the Irritability, Depression and Anxiety Scale (IDA; Snaith et al. 1978). There was no significant relationship with age, sex, social class, level of education, length of illness or severity of symptoms as rated by experienced observers on the Hamilton Rating Scale for Depression (HRSD; Hamilton 1960) or the Present State Examination (PSE; Wing et al. 1974). A subsidiary study of 20 patients satisfying the same criteria confirmed that hopelessness was more closely associated with suicidal wishes (measured by 10-point Likert scales) than with depression, and that the more hopeless patients tended to report more real-life problems, were more pessimistic about outcome and had less confidence in their ability to bring about an improvement.

Further validity data for the HS were obtained by Hamilton and Abramson (1983) and Blackburn et al. (1986). Hamilton and Abramson compared a group of depressed patients meeting RDC for unipolar major depressive disorder with a non-depressed psychiatric group and normal controls at admission into hospital and at discharge. The HS scores for the depressed group (mean = 10.2) at time 1 was significantly higher than for the two non-depressed groups (means = 2.1 and 2.3) and decreased significantly at discharge (mean = 4.1), whereas the scores for the two non-depressed groups were virtually identical at both testing times. Blackburn et al. (1986) in a cross-sectional design found that the HS discriminated significantly ($p < .001$) between depressed patients (mean = 11.4) on the one hand and anxious patients (mean = 5.9), recovered depressed patients (mean = 6) and normal controls (mean = 3.6) on the other.

Hopelessness and Social Desirability. The social desirability factor as a source of bias on the HS has also been investigated. Lineham and Nielsen (1981) sounded a note of caution about the use of the hopelessness scale in the study of suicidal behaviour when they reported that in a group of 196 male and female shoppers, the social desirability set, as measured by the Social Desirability Scale (SDS; Edwards 1970) was highly significantly and negatively correlated with hopelessness, current frequency of suicidal ideation, chance of future suicide and seriousness of past suicidal behaviour (rated on 9-point Likert scales). This relationship increased when examined only among those with past suicidal behaviour or ideation. Nevid (1983) criticised the above paper by arguing that the status of social desirability as a potential confounding factor in the interpretation of psychological tests should be re-examined. He questioned the validity of testing hurried shoppers, decried the lack of construct definition for social desirability and commented that it remained to be seen whether or not the structural relationships among the items in the HS and the SDS were factorially distinct. Lineham and Nielsen (1983) responded in the same journal with further findings from a clinical sample which supported their previous data from a shopping centre. They insisted that they had never called in question the validity of the HS, merely advised caution. It is likely that the high negative correlation between the HS and SDS scale is due to the fact that high SDS scorers are unwilling to divulge high hopelessness and suicidal ideation or behaviour rather than that low social desirability scores may be important for psychopathology, as argued by Nevid (1983). Petrie and Chamberlain (1983) in a sample of 54 attempted suicide patients found that social desirability (tested by the Crowne-Marlowe Social Desirability Scale; Crowne and Marlowe 1964) had no influence on hopelessness, as partialling out (i.e. controlling for) social desirability did not change the strength of the relationship between the suicide measures and hopelessness. This study was, in turn, criticised by Strosahl et al. (1984), mainly on the basis of the questionable validity of the Crowne-Marlowe Social Desirability Scale. Ellis (1985) also raised the question of the validity of the Crowne-Marlowe scale as a measure of social desirability as opposed to one of some aspect, or aspects, of psychological adjustment. It is felt that, so far, the debate is unresolved and that the need to measure social desirability remains for suicide prediction, at least in community studies, in an effort to decrease false negatives.

Suicidal Intent Scale. Many of the studies using the HS have also employed an observer-rated measure of suicidal intent developed by Beck et al. (1973), the Suicidal Intent Scale (SIS). R.W. Beck et al. (1974) reported on the inter-rater reliability of the first eight items which rate the objective circumstances of the attempt for suicide attempters and suicide completers ($r = .91$). Completed suicides had a significantly higher mean score than attempters on items 1–8 and patients who re-attempted suicide within 1 year of discharge had significantly higher scores on the complete scale than attempters who did not re-attempt suicide. Minkoff et al. (1973) found a correlation of .47 ($p < .001$) between SIS and HS in 68 suicide attempters admitted to hospital. The correlation between the observer-rated sub-scale (items 1–8) and the self-report sub-scale (items 9–15), was .43 ($p < .01$).

It can be generally concluded that a negative view of the future has been well established in depressed patients, though it is by no means universally present in all depressed patients. It is state-related and predicts suicidal ideation and suicidal behaviour, although it is possible that prediction may be less than adequate, yielding a number of false negatives, because of the confounding factor of social desirability.

Cognitive Style Test. A measure of the three elements of the negative cognitive triad is provided by the Cognitive Style Test (CST; Wilkinson and Blackburn 1981; Blackburn et al. 1986). It was specifically designed to assess the degree of negative interpretations for both pleasant and unpleasant situations. Thirty situations, ten each relating to the self, the world and the future are presented, with five pleasant and five unpleasant situations for each element of the triad. These are presented randomly, and four fixed-choice responses are available for each situation. An extremely negative response obtains a score of 4 and an extremely positive response a score of 1, with scores of 3 and 2 representing relatively negative and relatively positive reactions. Thus the bipolar range of optional responses allows for testing over-optimistic as well as over-pessimistic thinking. Apart from a total score of negative thinking, the CST provides a detailed analysis of different components of the triad and differentiates between interpretations of pleasant and unpleasant events.

Blackburn et al. (1986) reported on an improved version of the original CST (Wilkinson and Blackburn 1981), in which the situations and optional responses had been changed to increase its face validity for the "predominantly middle-aged target population of depressed patients". They compared a large group of depressed patients meeting RDC criteria for major depressive disorder ($N = 62$) or minor depressive disorder ($N = 10$) with anxious patients ($N = 21$), normal controls ($N = 31$), recovered depressed patients ($N = 29$) and recovered anxious patients ($N = 10$). The face validity of the scale was assessed by asking experienced colleagues to assign each item to a category and to grade the degree of negativity. Overall weighted kappa coefficients were significant beyond the .001 level (.92 for categories and .96 for ratings). Total CST score (CST-T) and five sub-scales were used in the comparison of groups, CST-P (pleasant events), CST-U (unpleasant events), CST-S (self), CST-W (world) and CST-F (future). Age was a significant co-variate on all the components (except CST-P), and an analysis of co-variance showed that the depressed group scored significantly higher on all the six sub-scales of the CST. The only scale which did not differentiate depressed and recovered depressed was CST-S, indicating that negative thinking relating to the self may be the more enduring component of depressive thinking. Anxious patients were differentiated from depressed subjects only on total score and on two sub-scales, CST-U and CST-W. In the depressed group, the CST scales correlated ($p < .01$) with the BDI but not with the HRSD or with the STAI. Within the anxious group, only one sub-scale, CST-U, correlated at ($p < .01$) with the STAI. All the sub-scales correlated highly significantly with each other and with the HS and the ATQ ($p < .001$).

Thus, the CST has been shown to be internally consistent and to have face and construct validity. Alagaratnam (1984) has also demonstrated the sensitivity of the test to depressed and elated mood in a mood-induction procedure in non-depressed and depressed subjects.

Process of Thought

The process of depressive thought, as described by Beck, has been tested less often, principally because process is more difficult to measure, but also because of lack of basic analysis of logical errors to support this aspect of Beck's theory. Weintraub et al. (1974) reported briefly on a story-completion test to measure logical errors in depressive thinking but they did not follow it up with validation studies. Moreover, they did not differentiate unrealistic depressive cognitions from unrealistic non-depressive cognitions.

Cognitive Response Test. Watkins and Rush (1983) have described a Cognitive Response Test (CRT) which they developed to assess process errors in thoughts elicited by specific situations. The scale is open-ended, consisting of 36 vignettes to which subjects write down their first response. The authors provide a manual and training programme for scorers to classify responses into four categories, rational (R), irrational-depressed (ID), irrational-other (IO) and non-scorable (NS). After four practice sessions 88% agreement was obtained between raters. Rational responses are related logically to the theme, do not contain characteristics of irrational responses, i.e. demandingness, attribution to luck, exaggeration and absolutism, and often are easily identified by the use of a qualifier or a question. ID responses are distinguished from IO responses in that they contain a negative bias regarding the self, the world or the future. Four groups of 15 subjects matched for sex, age and education were tested: depressed, normal controls, non-depressed psychiatric patients and non-depressed medical patients. Inter-rater reliability across four judges was .84. Validity was demonstrated by the highly significant discrimination between depressed subjects and other groups on the ID responses ($p < .0001$). The depressed group also gave fewer rational responses, while there were no significant differences on IO or NS responses.

Wilkinson and Blackburn (1981) used the CRT in the study reported above and found that CRT-ID correlated ($p < .001$) with the BDI, HS and CST-T, while CRT-R correlated negatively ($p < .01$) with the BDI and HS and ($p < .001$) with CST-T. Thus the CRT appears to be a reliable and valid measure of systematic errors in depressed thinking, but it does not differentiate between different types of errors.

Cognitive Bias Questionnaire. Krantz and Hammen (1979) developed the Cognitive Bias Questionnaire (CBQ) " as a research instrument for the investigation of mechanisms of depression" to measure Beck's hypothesised construct of depressive distortion. The questionnaire consists of six stories followed by four optional responses (three in one case) which can be either depressed or non-depressed in tone and distorted or non-distorted in terms of logical inference from the information provided in the story. Independent judges were unsuccessful in reliably separating the different types of error listed by Beck (arbitrary inference, selective abstraction, overgeneralisation, magnification and minimisation), but the distortions embedded in the optional responses are all examples of these errors. There was a high degree of inter-judge consensus (over 80%) on content validity for the scoring categories. Krantz and Hammen report a validation study on six samples, two large student samples, two experimental samples in which success and failure were manipulated in the one case and subjects engaged in different role plays to induce depression or elation in the other, and two clinical samples. In normal, generally non-depressed populations, depressive distortions were rare, whereas they were frequent in depressed clinical populations. There were no sex differences and no differences were attributed to the two main themes of the stories, achievement and interpersonal relationship. Coefficients of internal consistency were moderate as measured by alpha coefficient or item total correlations and possibly reflect the lack of homogeneity of the items.

Construct validity of the CBQ was obtained by significant discrimination between depressed and non-depressed subjects in degree of depressive-distorted responding and by correlations with the BDI. Depressive-distortion scores were stable over time, but varied with changes in mood in the normal student sample.

Clinically depressed patients who received treatment, as compared with a waiting-list control group, showed a decrease in depression paralleled by a decrease in depressive-distorted responses. The CBQ also appeared to have some specificity in that when the effects of other mood states, as measured by the Profile of Mood States (POMS; McNair et al. 1971), were held constant, the resulting partial correlations suggested that only depression ($r = .15, p < .01$) and vigor ($r = -.11$, $p < .05$) were related to depressive-distortion scores. The authors comment that not all depressed individuals showed biased thinking, and not all biased responding occurred in the presence of depression.

The CBQ has been used in some other studies, with mixed results. Blaney et al. (1980) reported a correlative stu in two large student samples: the depressive-distorted score correlated at a moderate level with BDI level ($r = .26$ and $.44, p < .001$) and the correlation with a measure of depressive attribution (Attribution Scale Questionnaire, ASQ; Seligman et al. 1979; see also below) was significant in one sample and not in another ($r = .26, p < .001$; $r = -.09$, NS). The authors concluded that the CBQ does not assess a characteristic that one must possess to be depressed, at least with respect to non-clinical depression. Norman et al. (1983) tested clinical samples of primary and secondary depressed patients and non-depressed psychiatric patients, using the CBQ, the BDI and the PSE. They found that the depressive-distortion score correlated significantly with the guilt factor from the BDI ($r = .50, p < .001$) and with the cognitive symptom ratings from the PSE ($r = .44, p < .001$). The two depressed groups were significantly differentiated from the non-depressed, but there was no difference between primary and secondary depression. Depressed subjects with high distortion scores also scored highly on cognitive symptoms on the BDI and the PSE but did not differ otherwise. Thus, the CBQ was not useful to identify sub-groups of depressive disorder.

Thought Sampling. The CBQ enables the researcher to obtain only a global score of depressive cognitive distortion. A recent study by Blackburn and Eunson (1986) employed a thought-sampling technique, as recommended by Kendall and Korgeski (1979), to analyse depressive distortions. From the thoughts collected from depressed patients during the course of cognitive therapy they were able to analyse the processing errors associated with different thoughts and emotions. They analysed 200 thoughts obtained from 50 patients and found that a thought typically contained more than one error, that errors could be reliably classified by two raters (with 95% consensus), and that the logical errors listed by Beck were sufficient to describe the whole sample of thoughts. Arbitrary inference was the most frequently occurring error (44%), followed by magnification (25%), overgeneralisation (19%), selective abstraction (8%) and personalisation (4%). Selective abstraction was preferentially associated with depressed mood, and arbitrary inference with anxious mood. Similarly, certain themes were disproportionately associated with certain errors, namely demandingness or "should" themes with selective abstraction and themes referring to illness with arbitrary inference. This methodology for the analysis of depressive thought processing lends itself to research into the specificity of cognitive distortions in depression by comparing data obtained from other diagnostic groups in the same way. It would also be useful to study change processes during treatment.

Repertory Grid Technique. Another technique for studying thought process is the repertory grid (Kelly 1955), which investigates formal thought disorder from the perspective of personal construct theory. Kelly proposed that two related processes, *constriction* and *pre-emption,* characterise depressed thinking. Constriction occurs when a person minimises apparent contradictions in his thinking by reducing the aspects of his environment to which he attends, and pre-emption occurs when a person limits the number of constructs which he applies to these aspects of his environment, thus dealing with events in an unvarying and stereotyped way. Thus, constriction and pre-emption are close to the concepts of selective abstraction, on the one hand, and overgeneralisation and magnification, on the other. Ashworth et al. (1982) administered repertory grids to groups of depressed, manic, schizophrenic, alcoholic, medical and recovered depressed patients. The grids consisted of ten role titles (including self, father, mother, spouse or opposite-sex friend, son or brother, daughter or sister, friend, disliked person, boss and ideal self) and 12 elicited constructs, with the construct "like myself" being provided. Principal-component analysis of each grid indicated that depressed patients were characterised by constrictive and pre-emptive thinking, a large perceived distance between self and others and low self-esteem. Ashworth et al. (1985) retested the depressed and manic patients on the same measures after clinical recovery and found that, for the most part, the cognitive abnormalities and features identified in the earlier study had disappeared. They concluded that the formal characteristics of thought found in depressed patients reflect clinical status rather than more permanent aspects of thinking. One other study using the repertory grid technique (Hewstone et al. 1981) reported that low self-esteem in depressed patients did not increase significantly from admission to discharge, but this may have been due to the shorter test-retest interval, 3.5 weeks compared with 17 weeks.

Structure of Thought

Dysfunctional Attitude Scale. The most widely used measure of the basic attitudes or beliefs which, according to Beck, underlie depressive thinking is the Dysfunctional Attitude Scale (DAS; Weissman and Beck 1978). The scale was developed from a list of items relating to the idiosyncratic beliefs which had been elicited from patients during treatment. They relate to themes of love, achievement, autonomy, demandingness, approval and perfectionism. Items are scored on a 7-point Likert scale measuring degree of agreement, and the score consists of the sum of scores received on each item. Two parallel forms (A and B) of 40 items were chosen from an original pool of 100 items after a factor analysis of the data obtained from 275 undergraduate students. The two forms appear to be equivalent, with a correlation of .79 obtained from a different student sample. Both forms proved internally consistent ($p < .001$) and reliable ($p < .001$) after retest at 8 weeks. Validity was established by correlations with the BDI ($r = .36, p < .001$), with the CBQ ($r = .52$, $p < .001$) and with the depression scale of the POMS ($r = .40, p < .001$). The DAS also appeared to have some specificity in this study in that when it was correlated with the six sub-scales of the POMS, depressed mood was the only significant correlation at retest.

Oliver and Baumgart (1985) investigated the psychometric properties of the DAS in 275 unselected normal adults. Test-retest reliability for the full DAS (DAS A and DAS B) was .73 ($p < .001$), and correlation with the BDI was .41 ($p < .001$). However, they found modest item-total correlations (.20 to .50), and a principal-components analysis of DAS A and DAS B revealed a different factorial composition for the two scales, DAS A being characterised by four factors (need for approval, perfectionism, avoidance of risks and a fourth, unnamed factor) while DAS B was characterised by four other factors (need for success, need to impress others, need for approval and need to control feelings). The authors concluded that the DAS was a valid measure of depressogenic attitudes, but that it would be more reliable used as a whole rather than in the two shortened versions. Nonetheless, most reported studies have used the DAS A version. Cane et al. (1986) in a large student population also found modest item to total correlations on DAS A, but an alpha coefficient of .87, indicating a high degree of internal consistency. In a principal-factors factor analysis with varimax rotation, they found two factors, one labelled performance evaluation (accounting for 47% of variance) and the other labelled approval by others (14% of variance). These are similar to the first two factors identified by Oliver and Baumgart (1985) in their four-factor solution. Another student population study was conducted by Dobson and Breiter (1983) who found a correlation of .36 ($p < .001$) with both the BDI and the ATQ.

Several studies have also been published using the DAS in clinical populations. Hamilton and Abramson (1983) in their test-retest study of depressed and non-depressed patients and normal controls found that the DAS decreased significantly in depressed patients from hospital admission to discharge (means = 148.5 and 116.6), whereas there was no change in the two non-depressed groups. Recovered depressed patients did not differ from the two control groups. They also found that a sub-group of depressed patients (50%) did not have abnormal DAS scores. They concluded that depressogenic attitudes were not a trait in depression-prone individuals and did not characterise all depressed patients. Silverman et al. (1984), in a similar test-retest study of 35 depressed patients fulfilling the same diagnostic criteria as the subjects of Hamilton and Abramson, found essentially the same results, that is, a decrease in mean score from 147.4 to 113.3 ($p < .001$). These results have been replicated by Simons et al. (1984) in their treatment trial of antidepressant medication and cognitive therapy, noting that parallel changes occurred in both treatments, and by Blackburn et al. (1986) in a cross-sectional comparison of depressed, anxious, recovered anxious, recovered depressed and normal controls. The latter study also demonstrated the specificity of depressogenic attitudes to depression by obtaining a significant difference ($p < .01$) between depressed and anxious subjects, the latter not differing from recovered patients and normal controls. Similarly, Hollon et al. (1986) in their comparison of unipolar and bipolar depressed patients with seven control groups, including recovered patients with unipolar and bipolar symptoms, found that the DAS was state-dependent, being within normal values for the two recovered groups. They found the DAS, however, to co-vary with syndrome depression rather than with nosologically defined groups, in that it did not differentiate unipolar and bipolar depression and schizophrenic patients. They also reported good concurrent validity, the DAS obtaining a correlation of .54 ($p <$ .01) with the BDI and a correlation of .83 ($p <$ .01) with the ATQ. Zimmerman and Coryell (1986) also found no significant difference in DAS scores between melancholics and non-melancholics, as defined by RDC.

There are at least two discrepant reports with regard to the stability of the DAS in depressed patients. Eaves and Rush (1984) tested endogenous and non-endogenous patients when ill and when recovered, as compared with non-depressed subjects also tested twice. Endogenous and non-endogenous patients, when ill, did not differ from one another but scored significantly higher than normal controls. After recovery endogenous and non-endogenous patients did not differ but still scored significantly higher than controls. Thus, in this study, the DAS appears to measure a depressogenic trait. The discrepant results may have been due to the time of testing on the second occasion. Patients were considered recovered when they scored 10 or less for two consecutive weeks on the HRSD. Reda et al. (1985) followed for 1 year 60 depressed patients treated with antidepressant medication. They found that although DAS scores decreased significantly, in parallel with the HRSD, from admission to discharge (reaching normal level) some beliefs had not changed. A year later, these same beliefs had remained stable, suggesting a depressogenic trait which was characterised by compulsive self-reliance.

Sociotropy-Autonomy. Beck et al. (1983) have proposed another possibly more stable characteristic of depressed patients which they describe as sociotropy and autonomy. They have developed a scale to measure this dimension, the Sociotrophy-Autonomy Scale (SAS), but the present author is unaware of any validation studies of the scale as yet. The scale is meant to measure basic personality types which create different vulnerabilities to depression. A person operating in an autonomous mode is expected to become depressed when the achievement of goals is thwarted by internal or external factors which are perceived as irreversible. On the other hand, the socially dependent person is expected to become depressed when factors that interrupt social relationships are perceived. Moreover, the authors suggest that from their clinical data autonomous and socially dependent depressions appear to have different sets of depressive symptoms and to respond to different types of therapeutic interventions.

From a different perspective Blatt et al. (1976, 1982) have developed a 66-item Depressive Experiences Questionnaire (DEQ) from which two independent types of experiences of depression have been reliably identified both in normal students and in a clinical population – dependency and self-criticism. These two different basic attitudes resemble the sociotropy-autonomy dimension identified by Beck et al. (1983), although no study has yet investigated the correlation between the two scales. Validity for these two schematic sub-types was provided by Hammen et al. (1985) in a prospective study of 93 college students. Two sub-groups of dependent and self-critical individuals were defined by a task of behavioural-example recall. The authors found that the dependent sub-group showed significantly stronger associations between depression and interpersonal events congruent with the dependent schema than between depression and negative achievement events which were not schema congruent. The opposite pattern was obtained for the self-critical schema sub-group.

Measures Related to Seligman's Learned Helplessness Model

The reformulated learned helplessness conception of depression (Abramson et al. 1978) proposed that the kind of causal attribution which people make for lack of control over events determines whether helplessness will result into depression. In particular, internal, global and stable attributions for negative outcomes and external, specific and unstable attributions for positive outcomes were proposed as characteristic of a depressive style of thinking. This attributional model of depression closely resembles Weiner's (1974) motivational model of depression.

Attributional Style Questionnaire. To assess various attributional styles the Attributional Style Questionnaire (ASQ) was developed (Seligman et al. 1979; Peterson et al. 1982). This consists of 12 hypothetical events, six describing good outcomes and six describing bad outcomes. Additionally, half the events are interpersonal/affiliative, while the other half are achievement-related. Subjects are asked to provide a cause for each event and then to rate the cause on 7-point scales corresponding to the internality, stability and globability dimensions. Seligman et al. (1979) administered the ASQ to 143 undergraduates who also completed the BDI and the Multiple Affective Adjective Check List (MAACL; Zuckerman and Lubin 1965). The results indicated that depressed students (scores > 9 on the short form of BDI; Beck 1967), as compared to non-depressed students, reported internal, stable and global attributions for bad outcomes and external, unstable attributions for good outcomes. All the correlations for bad outcomes and the BDI were significant, as were the correlations for good outcome except for globality. Only the internality and stability sub-scales for bad outcomes correlated significantly with the MAACL. Thus some support was obtained for a depressive attributional style. Peterson et al. (1982) reported on the psychometric properties of the ASQ in a study involving 130 undergraduate students. There were no sex differences and good events tended to be explained more internally, stably and globally ($p < .001$) than bad events, as would be expected in a predominantly non-depressed population. High internal consistency was obtained for the composite score for good and bad outcomes (alpha coefficients of .75 and .72) and the mean reliability coefficient for each attributional sub-scale was .54. The two goal areas, achievement and affiliation, were significantly correlated, but attribution score for bad outcomes was not correlated with attribution score for good outcomes ($r = .02$). The authors therefore advise users to examine their data separately. The three dimensions, internality, stability and globality were highly inter-correlated for good events, thus showing no distinctiveness; however, they were adequately distinctive for bad events. Test-retest with a time lapse of 5 weeks gave highly significant correlations ($p < .001$), indicating that the measures were stable over time for good and bad events.

In another student population study, Golin et al. (1981) administered the ASQ and the BDI on two occasions separated by a 1-month interval. The three dimensions of internality, stability and globality were found to be significantly but modestly correlated with self-rated depression. The possible causal role of attributions in mild depression was assessed through the use of cross-lagged panel correlations. Stability and globality for bad outcomes, but not internality, were identified as possible causes of depression. On the other hand, unstable attributions for good outcomes was identified as a possible cause of depression. O'Hara et al. (1985) found that female students coached in adaptive attributional style (according to the theory) changed their attributions in the expected direction. Subjects' views of adaptive causal attributions were congruent with predictions from the learned helplessness model.

Other studies of attributional style and depression in college populations have produced discordant results (Blaney et al. 1980; Hammen et al. 1981; Harvey 1981; Zuroff 1981; Zautra et al. 1985).

The ASQ has also been used in patient populations, usually with results only partially confirming the reformulated learned helplessness hypothesis. Raps et al. (1982) compared depressed patients with schizophrenic and medical patients. Relative to both comparison groups, depressed patients gave more internal, stable and global (in comparison with medical patients only) attributions for bad outcomes. Schizophrenic and depressed patients were not differentiated in attributions for good outcomes and only internality and stability differentiated depressed and medical patients. Hamilton and Abramson (1983), in their comparison of depressed patients with non-depressed patients and normal controls tested on two occasions, used only the composite score of the ASQ. The ASQ discriminated between depressed patients at admission to hospital and normal controls, but not between depressed and non-depressed psychiatric patients. There were no differences between groups at time 2 when the patients were recovered. Eaves and Rush (1984), in their study of depressed and recovered patients, found that the ASQ differentiated symptomatic depressed patients from normal controls, and after remission patients still scored higher than controls. Attributional style also correlated significantly with several measures of chronicity, suggesting that attributional biases may result from long-lasting depression or may lead to longer episodes of illness. Persons and Rao (1985) in a study of 49 psychiatric in-patients found that increased depression was accompanied by a decreased tendency to make internal attributions for positive life events. Contrary to prediction, depressed patients were found to make fewer stable attributions for negative events.

Coyne and Gottlib (1983) in a review of the literature on attributional style concluded that the evidence for a co-variation of depression and a specific attributional style is inconsistent. Peterson et al. (1985) have attempted to account for the inconsistent results in an analysis of 61 published tests of the reformulated learned helplessness theory. Their findings were that for stability, globality and the composite score, but not for internality, the theory is more likely to be supported when rated events are hypothetical rather than real, when many events are employed and when sample sizes are large. The results are more consistent when the ASQ is used to test attributional style rather than some other methodology, possibly because it is easily administered to large numbers of subjects, because it employs a large number of events and uses hypothetical events and thus functions as a projective test. The internal-external dimension still needs clarification. Finally, Peterson et al. (1985) found that the type of samples used – student populations or depressed patients – made no difference to the results.

Cognitions Questionnaire. A different measure pertaining to attributional style, the Cognitions Questionnaire (CQ), was developed by Fennell and Campbell (1984) to identify specific processing errors in response to negative, positive and neutral events. Five dimensions of response are measured: emotional impact, attribution of causality, generalisation across time, generalisation across situations and perceived uncontrollability. One important difference from the attributional model is that the dimensions, apart from attribution, apply to the consequences and not to the causes of the hypothetical situations. Eight situations are rated on five fixed-choice questions designed to measure the five dimensions of response. Fennell and Campbell applied the BDI and the CQ to hospital and community patients meeting research-diagnostic criteria for currently depressed (major depression), past depressed, depressed by other diagnosis (mostly anxious and phobic with BDI scores of 11 or greater) and not depressed. Sex and educational level did not influence scores. Total CQ scores ($p < .001$) were highly correlated with depression level and did not characterise all psychiatric groups, thus showing specificity to depressed mood. Negative events discriminated between non-depressed, mildly depressed, moderately depressed and severely depressed subjects, but positive and neutral events showed less discrimination. Although each response dimension differentiated depressed from never depressed subjects, generalisation was the most powerful discriminator. Only the interaction between generalisation and negative events discriminated between the recovered depressed and the never depressed groups, thus identifying perhaps a vulnerability factor to depression. Further, a discriminant function analysis revealed that the differentiating items between recovered depressed and never depressed related to the experience of depression itself.

In summary, attributional style has been shown, in general, to be an important aspect of depressive cognitive processing as assessed by the ASQ, the CQ and ad hoc measures devised for specific experiments. Of the three dimensions of attribution – stability, globality and internality – measures of the latter have received the least support. Brewin (1986) argued that low self-esteem in depression has not been shown to be related to internal attibution for negative outcomes. He suggested that non-causal cognitions, for example, negative self-evaluative judgements, provide a better alternative explanation of reduced self-esteem.

Measures of Ellis' Rational-Emotive Theory of Depression

Ellis (1962) proposed that certain irrational beliefs act as generalised predispositions by which events are interpreted and through which depression and anxiety are mediated. Two measures of irrational beliefs have been described, both of which have been used predominantly with non-clinical populations.

Irrational Beliefs Test. Cash (1984) found that in a group of female students, irrationality, as measured by the Irrational Beliefs Test (IBT; Jones 1968) was significantly related to externality, negative expectations of success, unassertiveness and BDI scores. Nelson (1977) found especially high correlations between BDI scores and some of the ten beliefs measured by the IBT, namely high self-expectations, reactivity to frustration, overconcern about possible misfortunes, helplessness and total IBT score. LaPointe and Crandell (1980), again in a student population, found that psychologically distressed individuals (high neuroticism score on the Maudsley Personality Inventory; Eysenck 1959), whether depressed or not, scored as more irrational overall than normal individuals. Moreover, depressed individuals scored as more irrational than equally distressed but non-depressed subjects. Newmark and Whit (1983), in the one clinical study which the present author has been able to find, reported that major depressed and schizophrenic patients scored significantly higher on the IBT than normal and manic groups. In a validation study in a large group of students Lohr and Bonge (1982) concluded that the reliability of the sub-scales of the IBT was not satisfactory and had to be improved by the addition of further items.

Rational Behavior Inventory. The second scale for measuring irrational beliefs is the Rational Behavior Inventory (RBI; Shorkey and Whiteman 1977). This is a 37-item questionnaire which provides a total score of irrationality and factors developed from a factor analysis of 119 items related to the irrational beliefs described by Ellis. All reliability and validity data appear to have been obtained from normal samples (Shorkey and Whiteman 1977; Ray and Bak 1980; Thyer and Papsdorf 1981; Thyer et al. 1983a, b; Himle et al. 1985).

Further studies in clinical populations are necessary before the usefulness of these two instruments can be assessed for theoretical or treatment research.

Measures of Rehm's Self-Control Model

Rehm's (1977) cognitive-behavioural model of depression is derived from Kanfer's (1970) self-regulation model. The self-control explanation of depression involves dysfunctions in three processes: (a) self-monitoring, whereby depressed patients attend selectively to immediate instead of delayed outcomes of their behaviour; (b) self-evaluation, depressed patients failing to make accurate internal attributions and setting themselves overly strict criteria; and (c) self-reinforcement, depressed patients having low rates of reward and high rates of self-punishment. This approach has not led directly to the development of measures aimed at testing the theory.

Self-Control Schedule. The only self-control measure, the Self-Control Schedule (SCS; Rosenbaum 1980) was not developed to measure depressive cognitions as such and was validated only on students. It consists of 36 items rated on 6-point Likert scales and taps the three processes elaborated by Rehm. Rosenbaum (1980) reported high reliability and internal consistency for the scale and, in addition, provided some evidence of concurrent validity in moderate correlations with externality on Rotter's (1966) I-E scale ($r = -.40, p < .01$) and with total score on the IBT ($r = -.48, p < .001$). Simons et al. (1985) found an interaction between SCS scores and response to treatment in their trial of the relative efficacy of cognitive therapy and tricyclic antidepressant medication. They reported that depressed patients with high SCS scores at the beginning of treatment did better than patients with low SCS scores in cognitive therapy, while the reverse pattern was true for responders to medication. They concluded that "learned resourcefulness" was a good predictor of response to cognitive therapy. There is further scope for testing the usefulness of this measure in depression, in particular, to establish whether it discriminates depressed patients from other psychopathological groups.

Attribution and Self-Reinforcement. Further measures which are relevant to test specific aspects of the self-control model are the ASQ (discussed above) and the Pleasant Events Schedule (PES; Brown and Lewinsohn 1984). The latter scale consists of 320 possible situations and activities from which an individual may derive pleasure, which are rated on the two dimensions of frequency of occurrence (3-point scale) and degree of enjoyability (3-point scale). Thus, a measure of the rate of reward that a person derives from his environment (the third process of the self-control model) can be obtained. Lewinsohn et al. (1979) have reported many studies showing low rates of self-reinforcement in depressed patients, but it is not clear whether this is a consequence rather than an antecedence of depression.

Conclusion

While this review does not aspire to be comprehensive, it has nonetheless shown that since Kendall and Korgeski (1979) expressed concern for the lack of research in cognitive assessment techniques, a great number of scales have, in fact, been developed within the respective frameworks of the various cognitive theories. These have, invariably, been self-report measures and usually of the forced-choice variety. It is difficult to envisage other methodologies than self-report when measuring thinking, because of the covert nature of the activity which is being measured. Moreover, when researchers have attempted to validate introspective reports by correlations with "objective" behavioural measures, the results have generally been disappointing (Tower and Singer 1981). However, forced choice techniques have the evident disadvantage of constraining the respondent to the dimensions and concepts of the theoretical bias of the researcher or clinician; more use of open-ended and naturalistic techniques must therefore be encouraged.

The assumptions underlying cognitive assessment are that people have access to their thinking processes and, moreover, that they are willing to report accurately that which they access. These assumptions have been called into question by several authors (Nisbett and Wilson 1977; Langer 1978). However, the high internal consistency which is generally found within scales, test-retest reliability data, evidence of concurrent and construct validity and replicability of results in different studies indicate that patients and people in general can report the products of their thought processes even if they cannot describe the process itself. More research is certainly necessary to establish the accuracy of such reports. For example, more elucidation of the social-desirability bias and of other factors which may have an adverse effect on accuracy is essential to improve methods of cognitive assessment.

References

Abramson LY, Seligman MEP, Teasdale J (1978) Learned helplessness in humans: critique and reformulation. J Abnorm Psychol 87:49–74

Alagaratnam WJ (1984) Depressive cognitive style: an enduring trait or an effect of mood state? Med Sci 12:606–607

Ashworth CM, Blackburn IM, McPherson FM (1982) The performance of depressed and manic patients on some repertory grid measures: a cross-sectional study. Br J Med Psychol 55:247–255

Ashworth CM, Blackburn IM, McPherson FM (1985) The performance of depressed and manic patients on some repertory grid measures: a longitudinal study. Br J Med Psychol 58:337–342

Beck AT (1963) Thinking and depression. I. Idiosyncratic content and cognitive distortions. Arch Gen Psychiatry 9:324–333

Beck AT (1967) Depression: clinical, experimental and theoretical aspects. Harper and Row, New York

Beck AT (1974) The development of depression: a cognitive model. In: Friedman R, Katz M (eds) Psychology of depression: contemporary theory and research. Winston, Washington, DC

Beck AT, Ward CH, Mendelson M, Mock J, Erbaugh J (1961) An inventory for measuring depression. Arch Gen Psychiatry 4:561–571

Beck AT, Herman I, Schuyler D (1973) Development of suicidal intent scales. In: Beck AT, Resnik HLP, Lettieri D (eds) Measurement of suicidal behaviors. Charles, New York

Beck AT, Weissman A, Lester D, Trexler L (1974) The measurement of pessimism: the hopelessness scale. J Consult Clin Psychol 42:861–865

Beck AV, Kovacs M, Weissman A (1979a) Assessment of suicidal intention: the scale for suicide ideation. J Consult Clin Psychol 47:343–352

Beck AT, Rush AJ, Shaw BF, Emery G (1979b) Cognitive therapy of depression. Wiley, New York

Beck AT, Epstein N, Harrison R (1983) Cognitions, attitudes and personality dimensions in depression. Br J Cog Psychother 1:1–11

Beck AT, Steer RA, Kovacs M, Garrison B (1985) Hopelessness and eventual suicide: a 10-year prospective study of patients hospitalized with suicidal ideation. Am J Psychiatry 142:559–563

Beck RW, Morris JB, Beck AT (1974) Cross-validation of the suicidal intent scale. Psychol Rep 34:445–446

Blackburn IM, Eunson KM (1986) A content analysis of thoughts and emotions elicited from depressed patients during cognitive therapy. Paper given at the II international conference on cognitive psychotherapy, Umea, Sweden

Blackburn IM, Jones S, Lewin RJP (1986) Cognitive style in depression. Br J Clin Psychol 25:241–251

Blaney PH, Behar V, Head R (1980) Two measures of depressive cognitions: their association with depression and with each other. J Abnorm Psychol 89:678–682

Blatt SJ, D'Afflitti JP, Quinlan DM (1976) Experiences of depression in normal young adults. J Abnorm Psychol 85:383–389

Blatt SJ, Quinlan DM, Chevron ES, McDonald C, Zuroff D (1982) Dependency and self-criticism: psychological dimensions of depression. J Consult Clin Psychol 50:113–124

Brewin CR (1986) Internal attribution and self-esteem in depression: a theoretical note. Cog Ther Res 10:469–475

Brown RA, Lewinsohn PM (1984) Participant workbook for the coping with depression course. Castalia, Eugene, Oregon

Cacioppo JT, Petly RE (1981) Social psychological procedures for cognitive response assessment: the thought-listing technique. In: Merluzzi TV, Glass CR, Genest M (Ed) Cognitive assessment. Guilford, New York, pp 309–342

Cane DB, Olinger LJ, Gotlib IH, Kuiper NA (1986) Factor structure of the dysfunctional attitude scale in a student population. J Clin Psychol 42:307–309
Cash TF (1984) The irrational beliefs test: its relationship with cognitive-behavioural traits and depression. J Clin Psychol 40:1399–1405
Coyne JC, Gottlib IH (1983) The role of cognition in depression: a critical appraisal. Psychol Bull 94:472–505
Crandell CJ, Chambless DL (1986) The validation of an inventory for measuring depressive thoughts: the Crandell cognitions inventory. Behav Res Ther 24:403–411
Crowne D, Marlow D (1964) The approval motive: studies in evaluative dependency. Wiley, New York
Dobson KS, Breiter HJ (1983) Cognitive assessment of depression: reliability and validity of three measures. J Abnorm Psychol 92:107–109
Eaves G, Rush AJ (1984) Cognitive patterns in symptomatic and remitted unipolar major depression. J Abnorm Psychol 93:31–40
Edwards AL (1970) The measurement of personality traits by scales and inventories. Holt, Rinehart and Winston, New York
Ellis A (1962) Reason and emotion in psychotherapy. Lyle Stuart-Citadel, New York
Ellis TE (1985) The hopelessness scale and social desirability: more data and a contribution from the irrational beliefs test. J Clin Psychol 41:634–639
Eysenck HJ (1959) The manual of the Maudsley personality inventory. London University Press, London
Fennell MJ, Campbell EA (1984) The cognitions questionnaire: specific thinking errors in depression. Br J Clin Psychol 23:81–92
Genest M, Turk DC (1981) Think-aloud approaches to cognitive assessment. In: Merluzzi TV, Glass CR, Genest M (Ed) Cognitive assessment. Guilford, New York, pp 233–269
Golin S, Sweeney PD, Shaeffer DE (1981) The causality of causal attributions in depression: a cross-lagged panel correlational analysis. J Abnorm Psychol 90:14–22
Greene SM (1981) Levels of measured hopelessness in the general population. Br J Clin Psychol 20:11–14
Hamilton EW, Abramson LY (1983) Cognitive patterns and major depressive disorder: a longitudinal study in a hospital setting. J Abnorm Psychol 92:173–184
Hamilton M (1960) A rating scale for depression. J Neurol Neurosurg Psychiatry 23:56–61
Hammen C, Krantz SE, Cochran SD (1981) Relationships between depression and causal attributions about stressful life events. Cog Ther Res 5:351–358
Hammen C, Marks T, Mayol A, de Mayo R (1985) Depressive self-schemas, life stress, and vulnerability to depression. J Abnorm Psychol 94:308–319
Harrell TH, Ryon NB (1983) Cognitive-behavioral assessment of depression: clinical validation of the automatic thoughts questionnaire. J Consult Clin Psychol 51:721–725
Harvey D (1981) Depression and attributional style: interpretation of important personal events. J Abnorm Psychol 90:134–142
Hathaway SR, McKinley JC (1951) Minnesota multiphasic personality inventory: manual. Psychological Corporation, New York
Hewstone M, Hooper D, Miller K (1981) Psychological changes in neurotic depression: a repertory grid and personal construct theory approach. Br J Psychiatry 139:47–51
Himle DP, Hnat S, Thyer B, Papsdorf J (1985) Factor structure of the rational behaviour inventory 41:368–371
Hollon SD, Kendall PC (1980) Cognitive self-statements in depression: development of an automatic thoughts questionnaire. Cog Ther Res 4:383–395
Hollon SD, Kendall PC, Lumry A (1986) Specificity of depressotypic cognitions in clinical depression. J Abnorm Psychol 95:52–59
Jones RG (1969) A factored measure of Ellis' irrational belief system. Diss Abstr 29:4379B–4380B (Ph D thesis, Texas Technical College, 1968)
Kanfer FH (1970) Self-regulation: research issues and speculations. In: Neuringer C, Michael JL (eds) Behaviour modification in clinical psychology. Appleton Century-Crofts, New York
Kelly G (1955) The psychology of personal constructs. Norton, New York
Kendall PC, Korgeski GP (1979) Assessment and cognitive-behavioural interventions. Cog Ther Res 3:1–21
Kovacs M, Beck AT (1978) Maladaptive cognitive structures in depression. Am J Psychiatry 135:525–535

Kovacs M, Beck AT, Weissman A (1975) Hopelessness: an indicator of suicidal risk. Suicide 5:98–103
Krantz S, Hammen C (1979) Assessment of cognitive bias in depression. J Abnorm Psychol 88:611–619
Langer EJ (1978) Rethinking the role of thought in social interaction. In: Harvey JH, Ickes W, Kidd RF (eds) New directions in attribution research, vol 2. Erlbaum, Hillsdale
LaPointe KA, Crandell CJ (1980) Relationship of irrational beliefs to self-reported depression. Cog Ther Res 4:247–250
Lewinsohn PM, Youngren MA, Grosscup SJ (1979) Reinforcement and depression. In: Depue RA (ed) The psychobiology of depressive disorders: implications for the effects of stress. Academic, New York
Linehan MM, Nielsen SL (1981) Assessment of suicide ideation and parasuicide: hopelessness and social desirability. J Consult Clin Psychol 49:773–775
Linehan MM, Nielsen SL (1983) Social desirability: its relevance to the measurement of hopelessness and suicidal behavior. J Consult Clin Psychol 51:141–143
Lohr JM, Bonge D (1982) The factorial validity of the irrational beliefs test: a psychometric investigation. Cog Ther Res 6:225–230
McNair D, Lorr M, Droppelman (1971) Profile and mood states. Educational and Industrial Testing Services, San Diego, CA
Minkoff K, Bergman E, Beck AT, Beck R (1973) Hopelessness, depression and attempted suicide. Am J Psychiatry 130:455–459
Nekanda-Trepka CJS, Bishop S, Blackburn IM (1983) Hopelessness and depression. Br J Clin Psychol 22:49–60
Nelson RE (1977) Irrational beliefs in depression. J Consult Clin Psychol 45:1190–1191
Nevid JS (1983) Hopelessness, social desirability, and construct validity. J Consult Clin Psychol 51:139–140
Newmark CS, Whitt JK (1983) Endorsements of Ellis' irrational beliefs as a function of DSM-III psychotic diagnoses. J Clin Psychol 39:820–823
Nisbett RE, Wilson TD (1977) Telling more than we know: verbal reports on mental processes. Psychol Rev 84:231–259
Norman WH, Miller IW, Klee SH (1983) Assessment of cognitive distortion in a clinically depressed population. Cog Ther Res 7:133–140
O'Hara MW, French CJ, Zekowski EM, Neunaber DJ, Schroeder GW (1985) Discriminating adaptive attributions: agreement between self-report and objective ratings. Cog Ther Res 9:267–275
Oliver JM, Baumgart EP (1985) The dysfunctional attitude scale: psychometric properties and relation to depression in an unselected adult population. Cog Ther Res 9:161–167
Persons JB, Rao PA (1985) Longitudinal study of cognitions, life events, and depression in psychiatric inpatients. J Abnorm Psychol 94:51–63
Peterson C, Semmel A, von Baeyer C, Abramson LY, Metalsky GI, Seligman MEP (1982) The attributional style questionnaire. Cog Ther Res 6:287–300
Peterson C, Raps CS, Villanova P (1985) Depression and attributions: factors responsible for inconsistent results in the published literature. J Abnorm Psychol 94:165–168
Petrie K, Chamberlain K (1983) Hopelessness and social desirability as moderator variables in predicting suicidal behavior. J Consult Clin Psychol 51:485–487
Pokorny AD, Kaplan HB, Tsai SY (1975) Hopelessness and attempted suicide: a reconsideration. Am J Psychiatry 132:954–956
Raps CS, Peterson C, Reinhard KE, Abramson LY, Seligman MEP (1982) Attributional style among depressed patients. J Abnorm Psychol 91:102–108
Ray JB, Bak JS (1980) Comparison and cross-validation of the irrational belief test and the rational behavior inventory. Psychol Rep 46:541–542
Reda MA, Carpinello B, Secchiaroli L, Blanco S (1985) Thinking, depression and antidepressants: modified and unmodified beliefs during treatment with amitriptyline. Cog Ther Res 9:135–143
Rehm LP (1977) A self-control model of depression. Behav Ther 8:787–804
Rosenbaum M (1980) A schedule for assessing self-control behaviors: preliminary findings. Behav Ther 11:109–121
Rotter JB (1966) Generalized expectancies for internal versus external control of reinforcement. Psychol Med [Monogr Suppl] 80:1
Seligman MEP (1975) Helplessness: on depression development and death. Freeman, San Francisco
Seligman MEP, Abramson LY, Semmel A, von Baeyer C (1979) Depressive attributional style. J Abnorm Psychol 88:242–247

Shorkey CT, Whiteman VL (1977) Development of the rational behavior inventory: initial validity and reliability. Educ Psychol Meas 37:527–534
Silverman JS, Silverman JA, Eardley DA (1984) Do maladaptive attitudes cause depression? Arch Gen Psychiatry 41:28–30
Simons AD, Garfield SL, Murphy GE (1984) The process of change in cognitive therapy and pharmacotherapy for depression. Changes in mood and cognition. Arch Gen Psychiatry 41:45–51
Simons AD, Lustman PJ, Wetzel RD, Murphy GE (1985) Predicting response to cognitive therapy of depression: the role of learned resourcefulness. Cog Ther Res 9:79–89
Snaith RP, Constantopoulos AA, Jardine MY, McGuffin P (1978) A clinical scale for the assessment of irritability. Br J Psychiatry 132:164–171
Spielberger CD, Gorsuch RL, Lushene RE (1970) Manual for the state-trait anxiety inventory. Consulting Psychologists, Palo Alto
Spitzer RL, Endicott J, Robins E (1978) Research diagnostic criteria for a selected group of functional disorder, 3rd edn. Biometric Research, New York State Psychiatric Institute, New York
Strosahl KD, Chiles JA, Linehan MM (1984) Will the real social desirability please stand up? Hopelessness, depression, social desirability, and the prediction of suicidal behavior. J Consult Clin Psychol 84:449–457
Thyer BA, Papsdorf JD (1981) Concurrent validity of the rational behaviour inventory. Psychol Rep 48:255–258
Thyer BA, Papsdorf JD, Kilgore SA (1983a) Relationships between irrational thinking psychiatric symptomatology. J Psychol 113:31–34
Thyer BA, Papsdorf JD, Neal L (1983b) Cognitive belief systems and their persistence: test-retest reliability of the rational behavior inventory. Psychol Rep 53:915–918
Tower RB, Singer JL (1981) The measurement of imagery: how can it be clinically useful? Kendall PC, Hollon SD (eds) Assessment strategies for cognitive behavioral interventions. Academic, New York
Watkins JT, Rush AJ (1983) Cognitive response test. Cog Ther Res 7:425–436
Weiner B (1974) Achievement motivation and attribution theory. General Learning, Morristown, NJ
Weintraub M, Segal RM, Beck AT (1974) An investigation of cognition and affect in the depressive experiences of normal men. J Consult Clin Psychol 42:911
Weissman AN, Beck AT (1978) Development and validation of the dysfunctional attitude scale. Paper presented at the annual meeting of the Association for Advancement of Behavior Therapy, Chicago
Wetzel RD (1976) Hopelessness, depression and suicide intent. Arch Gen Psychiatry 33:1069–1073
Wetzel RD, Margulies T, Davis R, Karam E (1980) Hopelessness, depression, and suicide intent. J Clin Psychiatry 41:159–160
Wilkinson IM, Blackburn IM (1981) Cognitive style in depressed and recovered depressed patients. Br J Clin Psychol 20:283–292
Wing JK, Cooper JE, Sartorius N (1974) The measurement and classification of psychiatric symptoms. Cambridge University Press, London
Zautra AJ, Guenther RT, Chartier GM (1985) Attributions for real and hypothetical events: their relation to self-esteem and depression. J Abnorm Psychol 4:530–540
Zimmerman M, Coryell W (1986) Dysfunctional attitudes in endogenous and nonendogenous depressed inpatients. Cog Ther Res 10:339–346
Zuckerman M, Lubin B (1965) Manual for the multiple affect adjective check list. Educational and Industrial Testing Service, San Diego
Zuroff DC (1981) Depression and attribution: some new data and a review of old data. Cog Ther Res 5:273–281

The Role of Cognitive Vulnerability Factors in the Development of Depression: Theoretical and Methodological Considerations*

T. C. STILES and K. G. GÖTESTAM

Introduction

Beck's cognitive theory of depression assumes that people who become depressed have relatively enduring cognitive processes and structures which rendered them vulnerable to depression (Beck 1976). This assumption stands in contrast to more traditional views (e.g. Silverman et al. 1984) which consider negative thinking as only a symptom of depression. There has also been considerable confusion and contradiction among researchers as to what is meant by Beck's assertion that cognitive factors play an aetiological role in the development of depression. Some authors also seem to equate the terms precipitation and vulnerability. This results in a failure to distinguish between (a) cognitions as causes of concurrent affective, motivational and behavioural symptoms of depression and (b) cognitions as enduring vulnerability factors (Coyne and Gotlib 1983).

Considerable research has tested the assumption that cognitive factors precipitate depression and have mostly provided results in the predicted direction (see Teasdale 1983, for a review). However, in this chapter cognitive processing as a long-standing vulnerability factor to the development of depression will be considered. First, Beck's model of depression with a special emphasis on his conceptualization of a cognitive vulnerability will be discussed. Three different hypotheses directly or partially predicted from his theory will be specified: (a) the schema-vulnerability hypothesis, (b) the schema-event specificity hypothesis, and (c) the differential activation hypothesis. Research studies designed to test at least one of these hypotheses will then be reviewed. Finally, theoretical and methodological issues as well as recommendations for future research will be considered.

Beck's Cognitive Model of Depression

The most striking feature of Beck's cognitive model is that it assigns cognition a major role in both the development and maintenance of depression. Cognition, however, is a broad term that refers both to the content and the processes involved in thinking (Kovacs and Beck 1978). One usually distinguishes

*This study was supported in part by the Medical Faculty of the University of Trondheim and by the Norwegian Research Board for Science and the Humanities.
University of Trondheim, Department of Psychiatry and Behavioural Medicine, Ostmarka Hospital, Trondheim, Norway

between three types of cogitions. First, cognition is used to describe thoughts and images occurring in the stream of consciousness; automatic thoughts are one example of such thoughts. These are mostly specific, discrete and extremely rapid events which may pass unnoticed unless the person focuses his or her attention on them.

A second usage of the term cognition refers to the transformation and processing of external stimuli; this is commonly referred to as "cognitive distortions", "cognitive appraisal", or "logical errors", whereby external events are necessarily interpreted in terms of their particular significance to the individual. But it also includes processes such as attention, retention, abstraction and encoding of information. Deficiencies in these processes are seen in the form of arbitrary inference (e.g. someone concludes that a friend has fallen out with him because he did not smile at him), selective abstraction (e.g. a person only notices the few bad things in a report about himself), overgeneralization (e.g. a person believes that failure on one exam means he will never pass other exams), magnification, personalization and dichotomous thinking.

The third usage of cognition occurs in the postulation of cognitive schemas. The schemas are the basic structural components of cognitive organization. When an event occurs, schemas which are relevant to the specific characteristics and context of the event are used to label, classify, interpret, evaluate and assign meaning to the event. The content of the specific schemas directly influences the content of a person's perceptions, interpretations, associations and memories at a given time and, in turn, triggers appropriate behavioural patterns. These schemas are sometimes referred to as "schemata", "structures", "assumptions", "concepts", "attitudes" or "beliefs". Kovacs and Beck (1978, p. 526) have variously defined such schemas as "relatively enduring aspects of a person's cognitive organization", "organized representations of prior experience" and "systems for classifying stimuli". Consequently, schemas are not found in the individual's moment-to-moment thinking, but are constructs used to account for more fundamental, long-standing cognitive characteristics.

According to Beck's model it is the existence of depressogenic schemas, primarily acquired during childhood, which renders people vulnerable to depression. The content of depressogenic schemas is related to some sort of loss in the personal domain. They can have a content such as "I must be loved in order to be happy" or "I must be a success in order to be worthwhile" (Beck 1987, p. 22). An active depressogenic schema is assumed to lead to a distorted screening and coding of information that causes systematic errors in thinking. Precisely *how* a depressogenic schema operates to distort experience and to mould data into depression-related automatic thoughts and images is, however, not specified. All the same, a depressogenic schema is assumed to exhibit three characteristics which it is important to consider. First, it is assumed to be an *enduring* dimension in the subject's cognitive organization. As Beck has put it, "These 'predisposing' attitudes are reflected in relatively stable schemas that reflect the individual's enduring orientations, rules, and behavioural inclinations" (Beck 1987, p. 14).

The second characteristic of a depressogenic schema is that it lies latent in a non-threatened, non-depressed individual and is not operative until it is activated by environmental events. Or, as Beck himself observed the vulnerability of the depression-prone person is:

"(It is) attributable to the constellation of enduring negative attitudes about himself, about the world and about his future. *Even though the attitudes (or concepts) may not be prominent or even discernable at a given time, they persist even in a latent state like an explosive charge ready to be detonated by an appropriate set of conditions.* Once activated, these concepts dominate the person's thinking and lead to the typical depressive symptomatology" (1967, p. 227; italics added).

The assertion that a depressogenic schema may be latent for a long period of time should sound a note of caution because a theory which includes such a variable is often hard to refute. If it is latent, how is it to be assessed? Is it, for example, possible to measure a latent schema by self-report instruments? Kihlstrom and Nasby (1981) have suggested the use of indirect techniques, such as measuring the accessibility of certain contents in memory to index the presence of a latent depressogenic schema. Recently, several researchers have applied such a schema-assessment approach (e.g. Hammen et al. 1985a, b; Dobson and Shaw 1987; Teasdale and Dent 1987). A different way of assessing latent schemas was proposed by Riskind and Rholes (1984), who suggested that researchers cognitively prime subjects' depressogenic schemas by exposing them to a stressful situation before assessment of negative cognitive processing occurs. Two studies have applied such an approach (Rholes et al. 1985; Stiles and Götestam 1988b). A third possibility, one which is more consistent with psychodynamic formulations (e.g. Arieti and Bemporad 1980), is that the depressogenic schemas have a more persistent effect on the depression-prone person's thoughts, feelings and behaviour, but that under most circumstances these operate automatically and without awareness. If so, the outcomes of cognitive processing may be inhibited from reaching consciousness (Power and Champion 1986).

The third characteristic of a depressogenic schema is that it initially is assumed to be activated by a limited range of stimuli, especially events that resemble the circumstances under which they developed.

For example, disruption of a marital situation may activate the concept of irreversible loss associated with death of a parent in childhood. Alternatively, depression may be triggered by a physical abnormality or disease that activates a person's latent belief that he is destined for a life of suffering. Unpleasant – even extremely adverse – life situations do not necessarily produce a depression unless the person is particularly sensitive to the specific type of situation because of the nature of his cognitive organization. (Beck et al. 1979, p. 16)

As the schema becomes more active, it can be evoked by a wider range of stimuli through the process of stimulus generalization (Beck 1967). Proponents of the model have emphasized different aspects of the schemas resulting in dissimilar predictions concerning cognitive vulnerability to depression.

The Schema-Vulnerability Hypothesis. Researchers emphasizing mainly the enduring aspect of the depressogenic schema have assumed that it is possible to identify a negative cognitive style in individuals not currently depressed which render them vulnerable to depression over time, especially in face of stress (e.g. Lewinsohn et al. 1981; Hammen et al. 1985a). This may be termed the schema-vulnerability hypothesis.

The Schema-Event Vulnerability Hypothesis. Some researchers who have also incorporated the latent and stimulus specific aspect of the schema have hypothesized that depression develops only when an individual's depressogenic schema is activated by a schema-congruent event (e.g. Riskind and Rholes 1984; Hammen et al. 1985b). This hypothesis may be labelled the schema-event specificity hypothesis. There are, however, two important predictions linked to the schema-event specificity hypothesis which are seldom recognized as different from one another. One concerns the accessibility of a depressogenic schema in a non-threatened, non-depressed individual. It predicts that depressogenic schemas lie latent and must be activated before adequate measurement can occur. The other predicts that depression develops in the presence of schema-congruent negative life events which match a depressogenic schema.

The Differential Activation Hypothesis. A third version of cognitive vulnerability has also recently emerged. Studies of the effects of mood on accessibility of memories, using both experimentally induced and naturally occurring moods, have shown that depressed mood increases the accessibility of negative cognitions and decreases the accessibility of positive cognitions (see Blaney 1986 for a review). Teasdale (1983), building on Bower's (1981) network account of state-dependent learning, has proposed that whether depression remains mild and transient or becomes severe and persistent depends on the type of cognitions that becomes accessible once the person is experiencing some depressed mood. This proposition, which has been termed the differential activation hypothesis (Teasdale and Dent 1987), is in contradiction to the schema-vulnerability hypothesis but in accordance with the first aspect of the schema-event specificity hypothesis, in that depressogenic cognitive processing is not accessible before adequate activation has occurred.

However, the differential activation hypothesis disagrees with the schema-event specificity hypothesis in the manner of activation. While the latter assumes that the cognitions are activated by schema-congruent life events, the former proposes that they are activated by depressed mood. According to Teasdale (1983), the type of events that ultimately leads to depression of clinical severity in a minority of people would initially produce at least mild depression in most people. Furthermore, the negative cognitions that are activated by depressed mood may have no relevance to the event initially producing the depression. Finally, the activation of negative cognitions will be the same regardless of whether the depression is produced by environmental or by biochemical events.

Thus the emphasis is not on the congruence between specific depressogenic schemas and specific life events, as the schema-event specificity hypothesis suggests, but rather on individual differences in the cognitions that have previously been associated with depressed mood. Elsewhere Beck et al. (1979) have also suggested that depressogenic schemas are activated by depression itself: "A set of dysfunctional 'cognitive structures' (schemas) formed at an earlier time becomes activated when the depression is precipitated (whether by psychological stress, biochemical imbalance, hypothalamic stimulation, or some other agent" (p. 20). This statement is quite consistent with the differential activation hypothesis, but contradicts the schema-event specificity hypothesis in specifying how depressogenic schemas are activated. Thus, the most fundamental theoretical question on which the schema-event specificity hypothesis and the differential activation hypothesis make different predictions is whether depressogenic schemas are activated by depressed mood or by schema-congruent events. In other words, the temporal sequence between cognition and affect in the development of depression becomes crucial. A recent study by Rholes et al. (1987) supports the view that an emotion-producing event can produce depression-related thoughts which influence memory retrieval independent of depressed mood. They suggested that both a cognitive priming and a state-dependent learning process can operate simultaneously.

A review of the empirical evidence is therefore needed regarding cognitive vulnerability with reference to the three different hypotheses derived from Beck's theoretical model. After a presentation of some additional relevant literature, not aimed at testing these hypotheses but useful elucidating some aspects of them, the three hypotheses will be discussed in the light of empirical studies specifically designed to study at least one of them.

Additional Relevant Research

A vast number of studies which have confirmed that depressed subjects display a negative cognitive style have been essentially correlational in form (see Coyne and Gotlib 1983, for a review). Although supportive of Beck's model, these fail to illuminate the temporal relationship between depressive cognitive processing and depressive affect in the development of depression. Other studies comparing subjects who have recovered from an episode of depression with control groups who have not experienced such episodes, have produced mixed results. Some studies (Eaves and Rush 1984; Dobson and Shaw 1986) have found significant differences on cognitive measures between recovered depressed subjects and controls, whereas most others have failed to find significant differences (Wilkinson and Blackburn 1981; Blackburn and Bishop 1983; Hamilton and Abramson 1983; Simons et al. 1984; Fennell and Campbell 1984; Silverman et al. 1984; Blackburn and Smyth 1985). Recently Simons et al. (1986) found that elevated scores on the Dysfunctional Attitude Scale (DAS; Weissman and Beck 1978) are predictive of relapse in remitted depressed subjects.

Finally, some studies addressing the relationship of cognitive vulnerability to depression have been designed within a learned-helplessness framework (Abramson et al. 1978). Although some have obtained supporting results (Golin et al. 1981; Metalsky et al. 1980), others have failed to predict future depression from current cognitions (Peterson et al. 1981; Danker-Brown and Baucom 1982; Manly et al. 1982).

Review of Empirical Evidence

A review of the literature reveals 12 recent studies in some way designed to test Beck's postulation of a cognitive vulnerability to depression. A descriptive summary of these studies is presented in Table 1.

Table 1. Summary of studies on cognitive vulnerability and depression

Study	N, sex	Sample source	Cognitive vulnerability measures	Conditions	Depression measures	Life-events assessment
Blackburn and Smyth (1985)	30, MF	Recovered depression patients, recovered anxiety patients, controls	ATQ-30, DAS, CST	Mood induction: MIP-D + MIP-N	Mood magnitude scale	None
Cash et al (1986)	54, F	College students	Irrational Beliefs Test	Mood induction: MIP-D, MIP-N or MIP-P	MAACL	None
Hammen et al. (1985a)	94, MF	College students	Self-schema task, psychopathological control	Longitudinal (4 months)	RDC interview, BDI	Self-report
Hammen et al. (1985b)	78, MF	College students	Self-schema task: self-critical subgroup, dependent subgroup	Longitudinal (4 months)	RDC interview, BDI	Self-report, interview
Lewinsohn et al. (1981)	998, MF	Community sample	Locus of control scale, expectancies of pos/neg outcome, irrational beliefs, perception of control, self-esteem	Longitudinal (8 months)	RDC-interview, CES-D	None
Olinger et al. (1987)						
Study 1	132, MF	College students	DAS	Correlational	BDI	Self-report,
Study 2	120, MF	College students	DAS	Correlational	BDI	Self-report
Persons and Rao (1985)	49, MF	Psychiatric in-patients	ASQ Irrational beliefs	Longitudinal (7 months)	BDI	Self-report
Rholes et al. (1985)						
Study 1	104, MF	College students	Cognition Checklist	Longitudinal (5 weeks)	BDI	None
Study 2	91, MF	College students	Cognition Checklist Hopelessness Scale	Longitudinal (5 weeks)	BDI	None
Stiles and Götestam (1988a)	68, F	College students	Factor II of ATQ-30	Mood induction: MIP-D or MIP-N	DACL	None
Stiles and Götestam (1988b)	81, M	Military recruits	DAS, ATQ-30, Impact of event	Longitudinal (3 months)	BDI	None
Teasdale and Dent (1987)	54, F	Recovered depressive, non-depressive students	Self-schema task, EPQ neuroticism	Mood induction: MIP-D	VAS	None
Zuroff and Mongrain (1987)	45, MF	College students	Depressive experiences quest: dependent, self-critical, control	Mood induction: Rejection and failure experience	Anaclitic, introjection, MAACL-modified adjective checklists	None

ATQ-30, Automatic Thoughts Questionnaire; DAS, Dysfunctional Attitude Scale; CST, Cognitive Style Test; ASQ, Attributional Style Questionnaire; EPQ, Eysenck Personality Questionnaire; MAACL, Multiple Affect Adjective Checklist; RDC, Research Diagnostic Criteria; BDI, Beck Depression Inventory; CES-D, Center for Epidemiologic Studies Depression Scale; DACL, Depression Adjective Checklist; VAS, Visual Analogue Scale.

Lewinsohn et al. (1981) conducted a large longitudinal study in the community, testing 998 individuals at two different occasions, separated by about 8 months. At time 1 subjects were given several cognitive-assessment questionnaires and were also tested for symptoms of depression. The cognitive measures included a locus of control measure, a measure of expectancies of positive and negative outcomes, an irrational belief inventory, a measure of perception of control and a measure of self-esteem. At time 2 subjects went through a complete diagnostic interview that assessed episodes of psychopathology at time 1 and time 2 and any history of prior depressive episodes. In addition, subjects completed a self-report depression scale on a tri-monthly basis.

These researchers found that the 85 subjects who became depressed during the course of the study did *not* exhibit different scores on any of the cognitive measures to those who had not experienced depression. Thus, the results indicated that people who are vulnerable to depression do not exhibit a stable pattern of negative thinking: instead, they support the more traditional view that people change their expectancies and subscribe to irrational beliefs as a result of being depressed. In addition, Lewinsohn and co-workers found that subjects with a history of depression but not depressed at time 1 did not exhibit a more negative thinking pattern than non-depressed subjects who had no history of depression. This finding, which relates to what these researchers called the "scar" hypothesis, suggests that cognitive changes during depression reverse themselves as the individual recovers.

Lewinsohn et al. (1981) did, however, find that those subjects who had more depression-related cognitions were less likely to recover. They thus concluded that depression-related cognitions make it more difficult to overcome depression. It is important to note that this study addressed the schema-vulnerability hypothesis that dysfunctional cognitions are traitlike and persist even in the non-depressed state. It did not address the assumption that dysfunctional cognitions are latent, to be activated if certain life events occur. The study has, however, two major methodological weaknesses in relation to testing Beck's cognitive model of depression. First, they did not assess stressful life events that may have occurred during the course of the study. Thus, it is uncertain how many of the 85 subjects who became depressed during the interval of the study were exposed to a provoking agent prior to becoming depressed. Nor do we know how many of the people who remained well did or did not suffer from a negative life event. It is possible that some subjects who were depression-prone did not develop depression because they did not experience a negative life event. Secondly, the cognitive-assessment questionnaires administered in this study were mostly either unstandardized or rather unrepresentative of Beck's cognitive model of depression.

The issue of cognitive vulnerability to future depression has also been addressed by Hammen et al. (1985a), who integrated hypotheses concerning cognitive vulnerability with developments in life-stress approaches. This is a very fruitful research strategy which has otherwise been virtually lacking, despite numerous calls for such efforts (e.g. Billings and Moos 1982; Brown and Harris 1978; Paykel 1979). It is well known that although life-stress research has become increasingly sophisticated in specifying the relationship between life events and depression, correlations between life stress and depressive measures have remained modest. The advantage of the approach which Hammen and co-workers utilize is that it opens the door to investigating how intra-individual cognitive mechanisms interact with stressful life events to produce depression.

Hammen et al. (1985a) explored in a longitudinal design the role of depressive self-schemas as vulnerability factors to depression. They identified five groups of subjects hypothesized to be at differential risk for depression on the basis of current mood and self-schema status; subjects were observed in four monthly follow-ups. Depressive self-schemas were assessed using an incidental learning procedure developed by Kuiper and colleagues (Derry and Kuiper 1981; Kuiper and Derry 1982) which is quite consistent with Beck's descriptive hypotheses. In addition, self-report and clinical interview measures of both depression and life events were conducted. Results showed that subjects who exhibited a relatively depressive self-schema but who were not initially depressed did not show an increased likelihood of depression over time. Initial depression status, on the other hand, was a strong predictor of subsequent depression. The design also tested the hypothesis that depressive self-schemas require activation by stressful events. However, the results indicated that the interaction of stressful life events and schemas did not contribute to the prediction of later depression. The study, however, did not test the proposition that only a limited range of events can activate depressogenic schemas. It is thus possible that Hammen and associates failed to find that an interaction between a depressive self-schema and stressfull life events could predict later occurrence of depression because they did not assess to what extent the impinging life events were congruent to the subjects' depressive self-schemas. Consequently the study tested only the schema-vulnerability hypothesis and not the schema-event specificity hypothesis.

In a separate experiment subjects were tested on a self-schema task adapted from Markus (1977) at 1 and 3 months after initial testing. The results indicated that self-schema status as assessed initially was not predictive of later self-schema processing. Responses of remitted depressed subjects resembled those of non-depressed subjects. Furthermore, current mood, but neither previous schema status nor schema status in interaction with negative life events, was capable of predicting depressive self-schema processing. A major question is whether the self-schema method used in Hammen et al.'s study is an accurate index of self-schema processing. A lack of stability in self-schema functioning independent of depressed mood level has also been found by Dobson and Shaw (1987), using a self-referent encoding task to assess the self-schema. The assessment methods perhaps relied here too heavily on adjectives that overlap with the symptoms of depression. Both Hammen et al. (1985a) and Dobson and Shaw's (1987) self-schema assessment methods involve the use of adjectives which refer more to aspects of the state of depression (e.g. downcast, "blue") rather than more enduring, global self-devaluative traits (e.g. inferior, worthless) (Teasdale and Dent 1987). Furthermore, self-schema assessment should not only include personal trait descriptions, but also propositions about what kinds of experiences are central to one's well-being or threatened well-being.

The hypothesized relationship of cognitive vulnerability to depression has also been assessed in a longitudinal study by Persons and Rao (1985). They tested a sample of psychiatric in-patients at three occasions: upon admission to hospital, upon discharge and at 7-month follow-up. At each testing subjects completed several self-report instruments: the Attributional Style Questionnaire (Peterson et al. 1982), a checklist of irrational beliefs, the Beck Depression Inventory (BDI; Beck et al. 1961) and a measure of life events. They found that attributional style but not irrational beliefs interacted with life events to produce depression. In this respect the results were more supportive of the reformulated learned-helplessness model of depression (Abramson et al. 1978) than they were of Beck's theoretical model. However, as in the case of the Lewinsohn et al. study (1981), the validity of the checklist of irrational beliefs here is uncertain. Furthermore, the study had two unexpected findings which limit generalization of results. First, they did not find the modest but significant relationship between depression and life events reported in a substantial number of other studies (e.g. Billings and Moos 1982; Paykel 1979). Secondly although they found a direct relationship between attributions and depression, the effect of one of the two significant variables was in the direction opposite to that predicted by the reformulated learned helplessness model.

Hammen et al. (1985b) performed a longitudinal study of the relation between depression and life events in dependent and self-critical college students. Subjects were assessed as dependent or self-critical on the basis of a stable, recall-based self-schema measure that primarily assessed thematic content. According to Beck (1982), dependent and self-critical individuals are depression-prone in response to different kinds of events. Subjects predominately exhibiting a dependent schema are expected to experience negative interpersonal events as relatively more depressing than negative achievement events, whereas predominately self-critical subjects are assumed to show the opposite pattern. Subjects were followed prospectively for four monthly assessments, using interview and self-report measures of both stressful life events and depression. As predicted, dependent subjects were found to be significantly more vulnerable to negative interpersonal life events than to negative achievement events. The opposite pattern for self-critical subjects was observed, but results were significant in only one out of six comparisons, thereby lending only some support to the schema-event specificity hypothesis.

Zuroff and Mongrain (1987) obtained results quite similar to those of Hammen et al. (1985b). In contrast to the naturalistic, longitudinal design of the latter, Zuroff and Mongrain employed a relatively well-controlled laboratory analogue experiment. Subjects were identified as dependent, self-critical or control according to their scores on the Depressive Experiences Questionnaire (Blatt et al. 1976). They listened to two audiotapes, one involving interpersonal rejection and the other achievement failure. Dependent variables were measures of anaclitic (dependent), introjective (self-critical) and global-state depression. The results indicated that both dependent and self-critical subjects displayed increased vulnerability to depression following both kinds of episodes. Furthermore, as predicted, they found that the interpersonal rejection episode activated more anaclitic depression in dependent than in self-critical or control subjects. This is consistent with the finding of Hammen et al. (1985b) that the correlation between interpersonal events and depression was higher for dependent than for self-critical subjects. Self-critical subjects, on the other hand, responded with introjective depression in response to both the achievement failure and interpersonal rejection episode. This response pattern is also quite consistent with the result in Hammen et al.'s (1985b) for self-critical subjects, who on five out of six comparisons were found not to be significantly more vulnerable to achievement than to interpersonal events.

According to Zuroff and Mongrain (1987), dependent subjects are more vulnerable to schema-congruent negative life events than are self-critical subjects, because dependent subjects' gradients of activation for anaclitic depression are steeper than self-critical subjects' gradients for introjective depression. They propose that it is unfruitful to assume that a depression-prone schema either is or is not activated by incongruent events. They assert that a less dichotomous conceptualization is needed. Specifically, they propose that the level of activation of a schema is a continuous function of the congruence of a given situation and the content of the schema.

Hammen et al. (1985b), on the other hand, have suggested two plausible explanations as to why fewer statistically significant associations between depression and achievement-related events were observed for self-critical subjects in their study. One is that the self-critical group being smaller resulted in a less sensitive test of hypotheses. Another possible explanation is that since the subjects participating in the study were college students, achievement events were more salient and were normative across both groups. They suggested that a non-student sample might be necessary in order to test adequately whether self-critical subjects are more sensitive to achievement events. Obviously, replication of these studies is called for.

It is also noteworthy that both schema-assessment methods applied in these two studies to identify dependent and self-critical subjects have been shown to have significant test-retest reliability (Hammen et al. 1985b; Zuroff et al. 1983). In addition, they make it possible to assess depression-prone schemas independent of current mood. Thus, both these schema-assessment methods offer promise for measuring relatively stable cognitive processing that have implications for impinging negative life events.

Another study which also supports the schema-event specificity hypothesis was reported by Olinger et al. (1987). In this study the Dysfunctional Attitude Scale (DAS; Weissman and Beck 1978) was used to assess schema vulnerability. The DAS is a self-report instrument designed to measure basic attitudes (schemas) associated with depression. In the first study they administered the DAS, the BDI and the Dysfunctional Attitude Scale-Contractual Conditions (DAS-CC) to a large sample of college students. The DAS-CC is a modified version of the DAS, designed to measure the presence or absence of life events that might impinge on a person's dysfunctional attitudes. Their findings were consistent with the schema-event specificity hypothesis in that depression arose in cognitively vulnerable individuals only when impinging life events were related to the individual's dysfunctional attitudes.

In a second study college students completed a different self-report measure of stressful life events, the Life Experiences Survey (Sarason et al. 1978), along with the DAS and the BDI. Again the interaction between stressful life events and high DAS scores significantly predicted high depression scores.

Although both studies reported by Olinger et al. (1987) support the schema-event specificity hypothesis, the generalizability of results may be limited by the nature of the design. Since it is a correlational study, it fails to demonstrate that dysfunctional attitudes temporally precede depressive symptomatology. In order to avoid circularity, a longitudinal study must be preferred.

In contrast to Olinger et al. (1988), Stiles and Götestam (1988b) conducted a longitudinal study which attempted to measure dysfunctional schemas in a stressful life situation assumed to have the capacity of activating latent depressogenic schemas. Young men enrolled in military service were tested on several self-report assessment instruments (e.g. Automatic Thoughts Questionnaire [ATQ-30](Hollon and Kendall 1980); DAS; BDI; impact of event), while they were waiting to be sent to northern Norway. This is known to be a very stressful life event for a significant number of young men. In order to test whether a high level of dysfunctional attitudes exhibited by non-depressed subjects render them vulnerable to depression following a stressful life event only subjects scoring 9 or lower on the BDI were included in the analysis. Their scores on the BDI, DAS and ATQ-30 were assessed again three months later while stationed in northern Norway. A hierarchical multiple regression analysis showed that higher levels of dysfunctional attitudes (entered in the computation after initial depression level and the impact of the event) significantly predicted depression level three months later.

This study has certain advantages compared to other studies. First, it is well known from clinical experience that many young men experience a depressive episode when sent to northern Norway; for some this is the first time they are separated from family and friends. Secondly, while several other studies have focussed on college students (e.g. Hammen et al. 1985a; 1985b; Zuroff and Mongrain 1987; Olinger et al. 1987), this study comprised subjects who were most typically working-class or unemployed prior to military service. In addition, their mean IQ level was lower than that usual in college populations. It is also possible that they completed the DAS more in accordance with their actual beliefs and thus were less influenced by intellectual awareness of the "desirable" response to each item of the DAS statements. A third advantage of using a sample of military recruits is that they live together and share common stressors which thereby limit extreme variability in life conditions.

Unfortunately, the occurrence of other significant life events was not assessed. It is thus impossible to know whether other positive or negative life events affected some of the subjects' depression level. In addition, the study did not specifically identify a dependent schema. It did, however, test subjects at two occasions, both involving separation. At the first assessment subjects were anticipating separation, at the second, separation had actually occurred. Beck's theory assumes, as do most other psychological theories of depression (e.g. Freud 1917/1957; Bowlby 1977; Horowitz 1979) that depression results from some sort of loss or separation. Consequently, although the study did not adequately show that depresssion occurs as a result of negative schema-congruent life events impinging on a depressive schema, it did support the view that subjects exhibiting a high frequency of activated dysfunctional attitudes are more vulnerable to experiencing depression in the future, especially in a life situation involving interpersonal separation.

Although the study assessed dysfunctional attitudes in a situation most likely to activate latent schemas, it did not experimentally test whether they actually resulted in making them more accessible. To our knowledge only one study has attempted to test the effect of cognitively priming subjects prior to assessment of cognitive vulnerability. Rholes et al. (1985) conducted two studies which tested college students on several self-report assessment instruments at two different times, separated from each other by 5 weeks. At the second study's first assessment half the subjects were exposed to a failure experience before they filled out the Cognition Checklist (Beck et al. 1986) and after they had completed the BDI and the Hopelessness Scale (Beck et al. 1974). The purpose of this procedure was to test the hypothesis that a failure experience would bring latent depressive cognitions to the surface. They found that the failure experience had no significant effects on the relationship between the Cognition Checklist and either the first-session or the second-session depression level.

Although they failed to support the hypothesis that depression-related cognitions need to be cognitively primed in order to become accessible, the results should be treated with caution. First, the capability of a mood-induction procedure such as a failure experience to activate depression-related cognitions may be questioned. Furthermore, they did not include any measure which could control that the failure experience actually had some effect on the subjects. The failure to find a difference in the Cognition Checklist could equally well indicate the ineffectiveness of the mood-induction procedure. In any case the difference between the mood-induction procedure used in Rholes et al's (1985) study and the in vivo anticipation of separation in the study of Stiles and Götestam (1988b) is substantial.

Secondly, it is puzzling why Rholes et al. (1985) did not have half the subjects complete the Hopelessness Scale after the failure experience. It is quite possible that a more or less hopeless view of the future might lie latent and become more accessible when appropriately primed. In any case it must remain for future research to test the validity of the first aspect of the schema-event specificity hypothesis, predicting that latent negative cognitive processing must be primed before adequate assessment can occur.

Despite the fact that Rholes et al. (1985) did not cognitively prime the subjects prior to assessment of hopelessness, they nevertheless found that hopelessness independently of current depression was a significant predictor of future depression, but that automatic negative thoughts were not. No attempt was made, however, to measure the occurrence of life events. The results consequently support the view that hopelessness represents a relatively stable vulnerability factor with respect to depression. More specifically, the study supports the schema-vulnerability hypothesis, but it was not designed adequately to test any aspects of the schema-event specificity hypothesis.

In contrast to Rholes et al. (1985), an analogue study by Stiles and Götestam (1988a) found that automatic negative thoughts can indicate cognitive vulnerability to depression. Prior to exposure to a mood-induction procedure college students were divided into two groups, hypothesized to be at differential risk for depression. Non-depressed subjects scoring above the median on factor II of the ATQ-30 (reflecting a negative view of the self and the future) were defined as a high-vulnerability group, and subjects scoring below the median were defined as a low-vulnerability group. Normative data were presented indicating that a score above the median (median = 10) was representative of high scorers. Stiles and

Götestam (1988a) found that subjects in the high-vulnerability group became significantly more depressed following a depression-induction procedure than did the low-vulnerability group. More specifically, the results suggest that it is possible to identify and measure the frequency of specific automatic negative thoughts concerning the self and the future which indicate that non-depressed subjects are vulnerable to depression, at least at the moment of testing. However no attempt was made either cognitively to prime latent negative processing prior to measuring depression-related automatic thoughts or to match the mood-induction procedure to the content of the thoughts of factor II of the ATQ-30.

In another study (Stiles and Götestam 1988b) the persistence of such thoughts was investigated. In contrast to other studies which have found the ATQ-30 to be state-dependent (Hollon et al. 1986; Eaves and Rush 1984), these researchers presented data which indicated that the ATQ-30 can display a fairly high test-retest reliability score ($r = 0.47$) at least over a 3-month period. How can this discrepancy in results be explained? The ATQ-30 has been shown to be state-depedent when one either compares depressed patients with non-depressed (Hollon et al. 1986) or tests depressed subjects on two different occasions – when they are symptomatic and when they are remitted (Eaves and Rush 1984; Simons et al. 1984). In the study by Stiles and Götestam (1988b), on the other hand, a normal sample of military recruits was studied over a 3-month period. Furthermore, on both test occasions the subjects were in a stressful life situation presumably capable of activating latent negative cognitions. Unfortunately, Rholes et al. (1985) did not report the test-retest reliability of loss cognitions in their study. More studies assessing the stability of depression-related thoughts in non-depressed samples, perhaps especially as reflected on the ATQ-30, is called for.

A mood-induction study by Cash et al. (1986) has also supported the schema-vulnerability hypothesis. They exposed subjects scoring extremely high or low on an irrational belief test to a positive, neutral or negative mood-induction procedure (MIP). The results were interactive, with "irrationals" showing affective susceptibility to the negative MIP but not to the positive MIP, and vice versa for "rationals".

Teasdale and Dent (1987) designed a mood-induction study aimed at testing two different but not mutually exclusive hypotheses. In addition to the differential activation hypothesis, they also intended to test a recently proposed hypothesis by Martin (1985) predicting that the personality dimension of neuroticism (Eysenck and Eysenck 1975) can act as a vulnerability factor to depression. Martin's (1985) hypothesis is in many ways consistent with the schema-vulnerability hypothesis in that both suggest depression-prone individuals to have persistent biases in cognitive processing which render them vulnerable to depression following a negative life event. This hypothesis, however, differs from the schema-event specificity hypothesis in that it does not require negative life events to be congruent with the content of the cognitive dysfunction.

The researchers tested the differential activation hypothesis by comparing recovered depressives with normal controls on a self-schema task after a depressed mood had been induced. The self-schema task was adopted from Derry and Kuiper (1981). However, state-dependent adjectives (e.g. downcast, "blue") had been replaced by more enduring negative traits (e.g. failure, unwanted). By comparing subjects in the two groups at similar level of induced depressed mood, they found, as predicted, that recovered depressed subjects recalled more negative adjectives previously rated as self-descriptive. According to Teasdale and Dent (1987) this supports the differential activation hypothesis in that those who become severely or persistently depressed differ from those with more transient depression in the type of cognitions activated in mildly depressed mood. The study also supported the hypothesis proposed by Martin (1985). Recovered depressed subjects scored higher on the personality dimension of neuroticism compared to normal controls, both when tested in the week following the experiment and when tested 3 years previously. This finding may also be interpreted as supportive of the schema-vulnerability hypothesis.

Finally, Blackburn and Smyth (1985) conducted a mood-induction study designed to test the hypothesis that a depressive cognitive style can more easily be triggered in depression-prone individuals. They compared recovered unipolar depressed patients with recovered anxious and non-psychiatric controls after exposing them both to a depression-induction and a neutral induction procedure. However, the hypothesis was not supported, presumably because the depression-induction procedure failed to produce significant mood changes in the recovered depressed group. If so, the experiment was an inadequate test of the hypothesis.

To summarize, although the empirical findings regarding the relationship of cognitive vulnerability to depression have been mixed, most studies have in some ways provided supportive results. Of the seven studies designed to test the schema-vulnerability hypothesis, five have supported it (Rholes et al. 1985; Cash et al. 1986; Stiles and Götestam 1988a, 1988b; Teasdale and Dent 1987), one has weakly supported it (Persons and Rao 1985) and two have failed to support it (Lewinsohn et al. 1981; Hammen et al. 1985a). Three studies specifically designed to test the schema-event specificity hypothesis have all produced at least some results in the predicted direction (Hammen et al. 1985b; Zuroff and Mongrain 1987; Olinger et al. 1987). Furthermore, the one study designed to test the differential activation hypothesis also produced results in the predicted direction (Teasdale and Dent 1987). Finally, Blackburn and Smyth (1985) failed to support any of the vulnerability hypotheses, probably because the MIP failed to affect the recovered depressives' mood level.

Methodological Limitations

Many of the studies designed to test the capacity of cognitive variables to predict future depression have made use of either college students or other non-psychiatric subjects. Generalization to a clinically depressed population should thus involve caution. The implicit proposition that mild depression in university students and other non-psychiatric populations serves as a valid analogue to clinical depression in psychiatric patients needs to be demonstrated rather than merely presumed.

Furthermore, these studies have mainly relied on the BDI to assess subjects' depression levels. Although it has been shown to be a reliable and valid measure of depression severity in a non-psychiatric population (Bumberry et al. 1978) at least on the day administered (Sacco 1981), it is not a diagnostic instrument. Another problem with the BDI as a dependent measure is that it is found to correlate strongly with self-report measures of anxiety both in college students (e.g. Hollon and Kendall 1980) and clinically depressed patients (e.g. Gotlib 1981). Other studies have also demonstrated a significant relationship between the BDI and other self-report measures of psychopathology (e.g. Blatt et al. 1982; Gotlib 1984).

Finally, the BDI is also strongly correlated with most cognitive assessment instruments. This has led Gotlib (1984) to suggest that the BDI, as with most other self-report instruments, measures only a unitary factor of general distress. If one follows Gotlib's (1985) line of reasoning, it is possible that the different cognitive assessment instruments used in the various studies could equally have been shown to be predictive of future anxiety.

To date only the study of Rholes et al. (1985) has tested this hypothesis. In contradiction to Gotlib's (1984) view, they found that depressogenic cognitive processing in the form of hopelessness was a significant predictor of future depression but not of anxiety. Nevertheless, since the BDI is not a diagnostic instrument and correlates significantly with self-report instruments of anxiety and other psychopathology, studies should ideally follow Hammen and colleagues' (Hammen et al. 1985a) example and include a non-depressed psychopathology control group and a self-report or interview based on a *diagnostic* instrument of depression.

Unresolved Theoretical Issues

Although most studies are supportive of at least one of the cognitive vulnerability hypotheses, it is at present not possible to ascertain which hypothesis leads to the most potent predictions for depression. The mere fact that three relatively dissimilar vulnerability hypotheses may be derived from the same theory suggests that Beck's model is too vaguely formulated, despite its adequacy for clinical purposes. Several questions need to be answered empirically before one can decide which of the hypotheses is theoretically most sound. It is still unclear to what extent it is possible to assess depressogenic cognitive processing in a non-depressed, non-threatened subject. If it turns out that a depressogenic schema needs to be triggered before adequate measurement can occur, the mechanism of action must be specified.

One possible mechanism of action is that the depressogenic schema is mood-state depedent, as the differential activation hypothesis proposes. The first link in the initiation chain would thus be a negative life event or a biochemical or neuroendochrinological agent that produces mildly depressed mood in most people. Depressed mood, in turn, would activate depressogenic negative cognitions or schemas through a state-dependent learning process. Whether or not the depression remains mild and transient or severe and persistent could be determined by the type of cognitions that become accessible once the person is depressed. According to the associative-network model (Bower 1981; Teasdale 1983; Ingram 1984) this would be strongly influenced by the cognitions activated in association with previous experiences of depression. If these cognitions are depressogenic, a reciprocal relationship between depression and cognitions may form the basis of a vicious circle which perpetuates and possibly leads to severe and persistent depression. It is also possible that when the depressogenic schema has become activated, it can gradually be used to label, classify, interprete and evaluate a wider range of events through the process of stimulus generalization.

Another possible mechanism of action is that the depressogenic schema is automatically activated to assign meaning to a negative event because its content is most relevant to the specific characteristics of the event. When a depressogenic schema is used to conceptualize an event, its depressogenic potency would then be expressed by interpreting it as representing a traumatic rather than as a minor loss. Once this has occurred, interpretation of other situations may be distorted to fit the prepotent depressogenic schema. Gradually, the depressogenic schema would thus prevent the matching of more appropriate schemas to situations. As they become even more active, they could be evoked by an expanding range of stimuli which are less logically related to them. In the end, the person's thinking may become completely dominated by the idiosyncratic schema and a severe depression could develop.

According to Beck (1967) schemas may vary both in complexity and in the range of stimuli to which they apply. Such individual differences between schemas directly affect the latency aspect of the schema and may thus represent an important vulnerability factor in the development of depression. This suggests that some people develop depressogenic schemas which can be activated by a wide range of events, probably due to more traumatic and prolonged losses in childhood. These people are at high risk for developing depression because quite a range of negative events have the potency to activate them. Others may be at lower risk for depression because the depressogenic schema is so stimulus-specific that it is only activated by a very limited range of events. Such individual differences in stimulus specificity between different types of depressogenic schemas suggest that dichotomizing schemas (e.g. either stimulus-specific or non-stimulus-specific) are artificial, and that grading them on a continuum may turn out more fruitful.

It may also be judicious to view the schema-vulnerability hypothesis and the schema-event specificity hypothesis not as contradictory but as corresponding to contrary extremes on a continuum of activation. This would permit empirical evidence to be more easily interpreted. This suggests that only some studies designed to test the schema-vulnerability hypothesis were supportive, while all studies designed to test the schema-vulnerability hypothesis were in some respect supportive simply because the latter studies were more sensitively designed. If so, in order to account for the stimulus specificity of depressogenic schemas, future studies should aim at assessing the occurrence of both schema-congruent and schema-incongruent life events, preferably on the basis of structured interviews.

Future Perspectives

Various diagnostic systems distinguish between different diagnostic categories despite claims for a more dimensional approach, viewing depressive disorders along a continuum (Perris 1987). For example, the DSM-III (American Psychiatric Association 1980) differentiates between five types of depression: bipolar disorder, major depression, dysthymic disorder, atypical depression and depressive adjustment disorder. Often clinically depressed patients are further divided into categories according to other dimensions, such as neurotic or psychotic, reactive or endogenous, primary or secondary, and single or recurrent episode. Is it to be assumed that cognitive factors play a major role in the development of all these types or categories of depressive disorders, or are they important in some but relatively insignificant in others?

Genetic studies have found that hereditary factors contribute to the development of bipolar disorder and major depression but may play no role in dysthymic disorder and depressive adjustment disorder (Torgersen 1984). Genetic factors, however, are insufficient to cause the disorder. That genetic factors may act as vulnerability factors for future depression does not therefore mean that cognitive factors and life events do not. Descriptive studies have shown that various life events, such as a poor marriage, can act as vulnerability factors for depressive disorder and even for endogenous depression (e.g. Roy 1987), which is presumed to be genetically linked. It is thus important that future studies designed to test cognitive vulnerability to depression make use of diagnostic types and subtypes so that the role of cognitive factors in the development of each can be assessed.

Furthermore, as pointed out by Depue et al. (1979), the predictive power of any single predisposing factor is likely to be relatively small. Thus it would be extremely useful to assess vulnerability factors within a multidimensional framework, in which psycho-social, cognitive and biological variables are explored simultaneously. This would make it possible to examine the relative contribution of each variable as well as how they may interact in the development of various types of depressive disorders. It might then be possible to decide to what extent cognitive factors play a major role in the development of depressive disorders. At present it is only possible to conclude that Beck's view of a cognitive vulnerability to depression represents a promising theoretical perspective, despite its need for refinement.

References

Abramson LY, Seligman MEP, Teasdale JD (1978) Learned helplessness in humans: critique and reformulation. J Abnorm Psychol 87:49–74

American Psychiatric Association (1980) Diagnostic and statistical manual of mental disorders, 3rd ed (DSM-III). Washington, DC

Arieti S, Bemporad JR (1980) The psychological organization of depression. Am J Psychiatry 137: 1360–1365

Beck AT (1967) Depression: clinical experimental, and theoretical aspects. Harper and Row, New York

Beck AT (1982) Cognitive therapy of depression: new perspectives. In: Clayton P, Barret J (eds) Treatment of depression: old controversies and new approaches. Raven, New York, pp 265–290

Beck AT (1987) Cognitive models of depression. J Cog Psychother 1:5–37
Beck AT, Brown G, Steer RA (1986) Development of the cognition checklist. Proc annual meeting of the Eastern Psychological Association, New York
Beck AT, Ward C, Mendelson M, Mock J, Erbaugh J (1961) An inventory for measuring depression. Arch Psychiatry 4:53–63
Beck AT, Weissman A, Lester D, Trexler L (1974) The measurement of pessimism: the hopelessness scale. J Consult Clin Psychol 42:861–865
Beck AT, Rush AJ, Shaw BF, Emery G (1979) Cognitive therapy of depression. Guilford, New York
Blackburn IM, Smyth P (1985) A test of cognitive vulnerability in individuals prone to depression. Br J Clin Psychol 24:61–62
Billings AG, Moos RH (1982) Psychosocial theory and research on depression: an integrative framework and review. Clin Psychol Rev 2:213–237
Blackburn IM, Bishop S (1983) Charges in cognition with pharmacotherapy and cognitive therapy. Br J Psychiatry 143:609–617
Blaney PH (1986) Affect and memory. A review. Psychol Bull 99:229–246
Blatt SJ, l'Affitti JP, Quinlan DM (1976) Experiences of depression in normal young adults. J Abnorm Psychol 85:383–389
Blatt SJ, Quinlan DM, Chevron ES, McDonald C, Zuroff D (1982) Dependency and self-criticism: psychological dimensions of depression. J Consult Clin Psychol 50:113–124
Bower GH (1981) Mood and memory. Am Psychol 36:129–148
Bowlby J (1977) The making and breaking of affectional bonds, I: aetiology and psychopathology in the light of attachment theory. Br J Psychiatry 130:201–210
Brown GWC, Harris T (1978) Social origins of depression. Tavistock, London
Bumberry W, Oliver JM, McClure J (1978) Validation of the Beck depression inventory in a university population using psychiatric estimates as a criterion. J Consult Clin Psychol 46:150–155
Cash TF, Rimm DC, MacKinnon R (1986) Rational-irrational beliefs and the effects of the Velten mood induction procedure. Cog Ther Res 10:461–467
Coyne JC, Gotlib IH (1983) The role of cognition in depression: a critical appraisal. Psychol Bull 94:472–505
Danker-Brown P, Baucom DH (1982) Cognitive influences on the development of learned helplessness. J Pers Soc Psychol 43:793–801
Depue RA, Monroe SM, Shackman SL (1979) The psychobiology of human disease: implication for conceptualizing the depressive disorders. In: Depue RA (ed) The psychobiology of depressive disorders: implications for the effects of stress. Academic, New York
Derry PA, Kuiper NNA (1981) Schematic processing and self-reference in clinical depression. J Abnorm Psychol 90:286–297
Dobson KS, Shaw BF (1986) Cognitive assessment with major depressive disorders. Cog Ther Res 10:13–29
Dobson KS, Shaw BF (1987) Specificity and stability of self-referent encoding in clinical depression. J Abnorm Psychol 96:34–40
Eaves G, Rush AJ (1984) Cognitive patterns in symptomatic and remitted unipolar major depression. J Abnorm Psychol 93:31–40
Eysenck HJ, Eysenck SBG (1975) Manual of the Eysenck personality questionnaire (junior and adult). Hodder and Stoughton, London
Fennell MJV, Campbell EA (1984) The cognitions questionnaire: specific thinking errors in depression. Br J Clin Psychol 23:81–92
Folkman S, Lazarus RS (1986) Stress process and depressive symptomatology. J Abnorm Psychol 95:107–113
Freud S (1957) Mourning and melancholia. In: Strachey J (ed) The standard edition of the complete psychological works of Sigmund Freud, vol 14. Hogarth, London, pp 243–288 (original work published 1917)
Golin S, Sweeney PD, Shaeffer DE (1981) The causality of causal attributions in depression: a crossed-lagged panel correlational analysis. J. Abnorm Psychol 90:14–22
Gotlib IH (1981) Self-reinforcement and recall: differential deficits in depressed and nondepressed psychiatric inpatients. J Abnorm Psychol 90:521–530
Gotlib IH (1984) Depression and general psychopathology in university students. J Abnorm Psychol 93:19–30

Hamilton EW, Abramson LY (1983) Cognitive patterns and major depressive disorders: a longitudinal study in a hospital setting. J Abnorm Psychol 92:173–184
Hammen CL, Marks T, de Mayo R, Mayol A (1985a) Self-schemas and risk for depression: a prospective study. J Pers Soc Psychol 49:1147–1159
Hammen CL, Marks T, Mayol A, de Mayo R (1985b) Depressive self-schemas, life stress, and vulnerability to depression. J Abnorm Psychol 94:308–319
Hollon SD, Kendall PC (1980) Cognitive self-statements in depression: development of an automatic thoughts questionnaire Cogn Ther Res 4:383–395
Hollon SD, Kendall PC, Lumry A (1986) Specificity of depressotypic cognitions in clinical depression. J Abnorm Psychol 95:52–59
Horowitz MJ (1979) Depressive disorders in response to loss. In: Sarason IG, Spielberger CD (eds) Stress and anxiety, vol 6. Halstead, New York, pp 235–255
Ingram RE (1984) Toward an information-processing analysis of depression. Cog Ther Res 8:443–478
Kihlstrom JF, Nasby W (1981) Cognitive tasks in clinical assessment: an exercise in applied psychology. In: Kendall PC, Hollon SD (eds) Assessment strategies for cognitive-behavioral interventions. Academic, New York, pp 278–317
Kovacs M, Beck AT (1978) Maladaptive cognitive structures in depression. Am J Psychiatry 135:525–533
Kuiper N, Derry P (1982) Depressed and nondepressed content self-reference in mild depressives. J Pers 50:62–74
Lewinsohn PM, Steinmetz JL, Larson DW, Franklin J (1981) Depression-related cognitions: antecedent or consequence? J Abnorm Psychol 90:213–219
Manly PC, McMahon RJ, Bradley CF, Davidson PO (1982) Depressive attributional style and depression following childbirth. J Abnorm Psychol 91:245–254
Markus H (1977) Self-schemata and processing information about the self. J Pers Soc Psychol 35:63–78
Martin M (1985) Neuroticism as predisposition toward depression: a cognitive mechanism. Pers Individual Differences 6:353–365
Metalsky GI, Abramson LY, Semmel A, Seligman MEP, Peterson D (1980) Attributional style and the emotional response to negative events: a test of the reformulated model of learned helplessness and depression. Unpublished manuscript, State University of New York at Stony Brook
Olinger LJ Kuiper NA, Shaw BF (1987) Dysfunctional attitudes and stressful life events: an interactive model depression. Cog Therapy and Research, 1, 25–40
Paykel ES (1979) Recent life events in the development of the depressive disorders: In: Depue RA (ed) The psychobiology of depressive disorders: implications for the effects of stress. Academic, New York, pp 245–262
Perris C (1987) Towards an integrating theory of depression focusing on the concept of vulnerability. Integrative Psychiatry 5:27–32
Persons JB, Rao PA (1985) Longitudinal study of cognitions, life events, and depression in psychiatric inpatients. J Abnorm Psychol 94:51–63
Peterson C, Schwartz SM, Seligman MEP (1981) Self-blame and depression symptoms. J Pers Soc Psychol 41:253–259
Peterson C, Semmel A, von Baeyer C, Abramson LY, Metalsky GI, Seligman MEP (1982) The attributional style questionnaire. Cog Ther Res 6:287–299
Power MJ, Champion LA (1986) Cognitive approaches to depression: a theoretical critique. Br J Clin Psychol 25:201–212
Rholes WS, Riskind JH, Neville B (1985) The relationship of cognitions and hopelessness to depression and anxiety. Soc Cog 3:36–50
Rholes WS, Riskind JH, Lane JW (1987) Emotional states and memory biases: effects of cognitive priming and mood. J Pers Soc Psychol 52:91–99
Riskind JH, Rholes WS (1984) Cognitive accessibility and the capacity of cognitions to predict future depression: a theoretical note. Cog Ther Res 8:1–12
Roy A (1987) Five risk factors for depression. Br J Psychiatry 150:536–541
Sacco WP (1981) Invalid use of the Beck depression inventory to identify depressed college-student subjects: a methodological comment. Cog Ther Res 5:143–147
Sarason IG, Johnson JH, Siegel JM (1978) Assessing the impact of life changes: development of the life experiences survey. J Consult Clin Psychol 46:932–946
Silverman JS, Silverman JA, Eardley DA (1984) Do maladaptive attitudes cause depression? Arch Gen Psychiatry 41:28–30

Simons AD, Garfield SL, Murphy GE (1984) The process of change in cognitive therapy and pharmacotherapy for depression. Arch Gen Psychiatry 41:45–51

Simons AD, Murphy GE, Levine JL, Wetzel RD (1986) Cognitive therapy and pharmacotherapy for depression. Sustained improvement over one year. Arch Gen Psychiatry 43:43–48

Stiles TC, Götestam KG (1988a) The role of automatic negative thoughts in the development of depression: an analogue study. Cog Ther Res in press

Stiles TC, Götestam KG (1988b) Cognitive vulnerability to depression: a lognitudinal study. Manuscript, University of Trondheim, Norway

Teasdale JD (1983) Negative thinking in depression: cause, effect, or reciprocal relationship. Adv Behav Res Ther 5:3–25

Teasdale JD, Dent J (1987) Cognitive vulnerability to depression: an investigation of two hypotheses. Br J Clin Psychol 26:113–126

Torgersen S (1984) Genetic factors in moderately severe and mild affective disorders. Arch Gen Psychiatry 43:222–226

Weissman AN, Beck AT (1978) Development and validation of the dysfunctional attitudes scale. Paper presented at the annual meeting of the Association for Advancement of Behavioral Therapy

Wilkinson IM, Blackburn IM (1981) Cognitive style in depressed and recovered depressed patients. Br J Clin Psychol 20:283–292

Zuroff DC, Mongrain M (1987) Dependency and self-criticism: vulnerability factors for depressive affective states. J Abnorm Psychol 96:14–22

Zuroff DC, Moskowitz DS, Wielgus MS, Powers TA, Franko DL (1983) Construct validation of the dependency and self-criticism scales of the depression experiences questionnaire. J Res Pers 17:226–241

Training Therapists in Cognitive-Behaviour Therapy

B.F. Shaw and D. Wilson-Smith

Therapy and Therapist Training

Despite considerable controversy in the field about the value of clinical trials research (cf. Strupp 1980; Parloff 1981) the public, government, insurance companies, and to a great extent the field itself have been increasingly concerned with the efficacy of psychotherapy. Clinicians and many psychotherapy researchers today agree that the answer to the question "Is psychotherapy effective?" is "yes" (Garfield 1983; Smith et al. 1980). Nevertheless we have made little advance in answering the question which Paul (1967, p. 111) posed: "What treatment, by whom, is most effective for this individual with that specific problem, and under which set of circumstances?" (see Stiles et al. 1986).

For many years the field of psychotherapy research has been beset by problems of differentiating specific from non-specific effects. Orne (1975, p. 140) pointed out that in the past, "psychotherapy based its legitimacy not on its outcome but rather on its scientific rationale." As a result elaborate conceptual frameworks were developed to account for symptom development and alleviation. It is difficult, however, to argue empirically that interventions unique to a particular system of psychotherapy effect change via the hypothesized mechanisms. In other words, the theory of behavioural change may be incorrect, yet the resultant interventions may be effective. Frank (1982) has cogently argued that the commonal feature across all psychotherapies is the engendering of hope within a framework that is believable to the patient and to the therapist. The proliferation of psychotherapies continues: Herink (1980) has estimated the number of "brand names" to exceed 250, and it has been described by Klerman as a billion-dollar industry. It has therefore become increasingly important to specify the therapeutic interventions under consideration.

Some clinical researchers remain convinced that most psychotherapy shares certain features with faith healing, namely the credibility and authority of the therapist and a believable rationale consistent with the cultural mores of the patient (e.g. Klein and Rabkin 1983). The issue of placebo response in this field was first considered by Shapiro in 1959 and has more recently been addressed by Wilkins (1986). A further challenge to the psychotherapy field was issued by Klein and Rabkin (1983) who commented on various types of psychotherapy, paraphrasing Bertrand Russell's dictum: "A difference that makes no difference is no

University of Toronto, Toronto General Hospital, 200 Elizabeth Street, Toronto, Ontario N5G 2C4, Canada

difference". Clearly the need is for researchers to demonstrate specific, replicable effects of therapists' interventions.

Past evaluations of the efficacy of psychotherapy have been of questionable value because the various psychotherapies under consideration were not well-defined. Kiesler (1966) referred to the uniformity myth, that is, the belief that all psychotherapies are the same. Any review of psychotherapy outcome studies (e.g. Waskow 1984) must avoid collapsing all sorts of psychotherapy under a common label, for it is simply not meaningful to speak of psychotherapy in general (Report of the Research Task Force of the National Institute of Mental Health 1976). The field needs to increase specificity in the independent variable in this research. Studying the efficacy of a treatment can be facilitated by clear descriptions of interventions, training programmes and quality-assurance observations in order to assure that the therapists, in fact, do what they say they are doing (Shaw 1984).

This chapter will not directly concern the question of efficacy and safety of psychotherapy, but any reader will readily acknowledge that without safety and efficacy our training programmes will not be based on firm foundation. The body of clinical knowledge related to psychotherapy is rich and descriptive. As we noted previously, there are many systems of psychotherapy and more than a thousand technical interventions.

In some forms of psychotherapy theoretical models are associated with specific interventions, for example, increasing positive reinforcers and social-skills training following Lewinsohn's (1974) behavioural approach. Other systems of psychotherapy are not as specific but do utilize standard methods of enquiry into the patient's psychological functioning (e.g. free association and collecting automatic thoughts), followed by a trial-and-error application of methods to promote change across a range of problems and disorders. The psychotherapy trainee is faced with an almost overwhelming choice of interventions and theories on which to base his/her psychotherapeutic work. The prevailing notion of students entering the field is that they will acquire specific methods that have specific effects on specific disorders. In reality, training frequently consists of acquiring valuable general skills, such as how to interview and to conceptualize complex problems, but little in the way of scientific evidence to facilitate rational choices amongst the various systems of therapy.

When faced with the multiplicity of systems of psychological therapy (Ford and Urban 1963) and modalities of therapy (e.g. individual, conjoint/marital, family, group), one soon recognizes the wide array of available therapeutic interventions. Furthermore, one must consider a variety of intervention methods within each of these systems and modalities. When one tries to consider the disorders for which these may be effective, the task becomes even more complex. Unlike the case of medicine, in which a physician acquires a general skill in prescribing a wide range of therapeutic agents, it may take years to become proficient in one system of psychotherapy. Given the limited range of therapeutic expertise on the part of individual therapists it is, in fact, surprising that there are not more frequent referrals between psychotherapists. The comparison of psychotherapists to special educators or to surgeons (Orne 1975) is reasonable in the sense that the key consideration in each of these fields should concern the questions of what procedures work with what type of patients with what type of problems.

The purpose of this chapter is to describe a training programme suitable for psychotherapy outcome research in one specific system of psychotherapy – cognitive-behavioural therapy (CBT) – and in the treatment of one major disorder or syndrome, i.e. major depressive disorder. This programme constitutes a response to the demand for greater specificity in training.

Before describing the training in this programme and its effects, however, we must consider a number of general points about the training of psychotherapists. One factor which is relevant to the training of therapists, for instance, is that of the type of patient selected. Unfortunately, because of the selection biases of some mental health systems inexperienced therapists are often asked to treat the *most difficult* patients: more experienced therapists may identify the "best bets" for change and decide to treat these patients themselves. While one could argue that given the shortage of therapists such selection criteria are warranted, there is a potential problem in assigning to *trainees* patients less suitable for psychotherapy. The inexperienced therapist is thereby burdened with a high probability of failure just when he/she is attempting to learn new skills. A training programme, regardless of its specific orientation, should attempt rather to provide graded success experiences for its trainees, for instance by selecting for them patients who are not particularly difficult (see Vallis and Shaw 1987, for a consideration of patient difficulty and therapist competency).

It is believed that therapists who are effective develop a habit of thinking that is based on a sound theoretical orientation, knowledge of the literature on behavioural changes and a set of technical interventions for specific therapeutic situations. The capacity for this is probably best acquired through systematic study, basic training and supervision in a single system of psychotherapy. In choosing a system of psychotherapy particular attention must be paid to which theory of behavioural change is utilized. At present we are limited by not having a coherent, unified theory of behavioural change. Nevertheless, we need not apologize for the plethora of theories; we must be willing simply to acknowledge that our own particular theory may be wrong, particularly as a guide to treating certain patients.

The therapist's theoretical orientation guides his/her interventions by providing a conceptualization or formulation of the patient's problems, disorders or symptoms. The applied theory may or may not facilitate a successful match between the therapist's expectations of change and those of the patient. Therapists typically attend selectively to the patient's behaviour (verbal and nonverbal) in order to conceptualize the patient's presented concerns or complaints within a particular framework associated with change. Patients only rarely come for assessment without at least a general idea of desired changes, although most have little or no understanding of how this change might occur. The therapist's initial problem is to decide whether the patient's desired changes are understandable and feasible within his/her particular theory and time commitment. Following this determination a judgement must be made as to whether the combination of the therapist's preferred system of psychotherapy and preferred modality (i.e. the set of technical variables) is likely to be effective in producing the desired changes.

When therapists consider whether their therapy will likely have the desired outcome, they might try to imagine their interventions as leading to their goal. Unfortunately they may assign their interventions an unduly high probability of success depending on the number of different scenarios thus constructed in which the intervention and the goal are linked. Once a successful therapeutic scenario is imagined, it is difficult to think of it leading to a negative outcome. The problem lies in the fact that therapists are prone to judgemental biases in selecting patients for treatment. In our training programme for cognitive-behavioural (CB) therapists we have considered these points, but in many ways our task was made easier by pre-determining the patient-selection criteria (primarily patients with major depressive disorder) and utilizing only one system of psychotherapy.

The present chapter describes a training programme suitable for clinical trials research in which the therapist's behaviour is brought under considerable scrutiny. The major questions here from a training perspective are the following: (a) How can skill acquisition in CBT be defined and measured? (b) Are the skills retained over a long period of time? and (c) Are the skills and interventions ultimately beneficial to the patient (Matarazzo 1978)? We will address these questions in terms of a specific training model of CBT developed for the Treatment of Depression Collaborative Research Program (TDCRP) of the National Institute of Mental Health.

Important criteria for the training of therapists include the following: (a) Individuals selected for training should possess good psychological adjustment, stability, open-mindedness and a positive attitude towards people and interpersonal skills (Matazzaro 1978). (b) Students of psychotherapy should be versed in the basics of interviewing with an emphasis on attentiveness, accurate reflection and summarization skills. The micro-training model of Ivey and Autheir (1978) and Evans et al. (1984) may be employed for this purpose. (c) On attainment of basic psychotherapeutic skills students should be able to make informed decisions about the usefulness of various therapeutic approaches and methods of intervention in regard to specific patient populations. (d) Training should be evaluated using well-defined criteria of competence. (e) Continuing education, including periodic monitoring or review of therapists' clinical work, should be mandatory.

It is on these latter points that controversy may develop. First, most students often lack the flexibility to choose training programmes consistent with their own knowledge of the literature. As a result they are trained in those methods that are endorsed by the training programme. Their belief systems thus tend to be moulded by the beliefs of their supervisors rather than by empirical work (although clearly these influences are not necessarily independent). Attention is sometimes given to identifying those patients likely to benefit from the "therapy of choice"; however rather than limiting the types of patients who are seen, the tendency is to accept a wide variety of patients. It could be an interesting exercise for the psychotherapy supervisor, given his/her knowledge of the patient, to predict the likelihood that the preferred psychotherapy will be effective.

Furthermore, it is desirable to define in the first few sessions the criteria for defining success (see, e.g. Newman and Ciarlo 1982, on mental health service evaluations; Rosen and Proctor 1981, on treatment evaluation). Rather than taking a graded-success approach supervisors tend to acknowledge simply that the first few cases may be problematic. As trainees may have little information regarding the causes of their success or failure, they may attribute the outcome to erroneous factors (for example, failure attributed to factors of patient difficulty rather than to limitations in the method employed or to a complex interaction of variables). Only through a knowledge of the multiple factors that may contribute to patient change is the possibility of rational analysis available to therapists. In general our field has not made great progress in predicting which patients will most benefit from the various systems of therapy.

There are two major models of patient-therapist matching. The first is typified by the short-term dynamic-therapy approaches by Malan (1976), Sifneos (1972) and others and emphasizes the qualities of patients that make them suitable for psychotherapy; positive patient predictors include here "problem-solving ability, verbal skills, emotional responsiveness, and the ability to establish rewarding relationships with others" (Frank et al. 1978, p. 72). The focal psychotherapeutic approach adds here the factors of patient's experience of intense affect and patient's ability to utilize interpretations within a psychodynamic framework.

The second model follows more traditional psychiatric-diagnostic schemes as exemplified in the *Diagnostic and Statistical Manual*, third edition (DSM-III). This approach in many ways follows a medical understanding in that it attempts to document the patient's symptomatology and to make decisions on the basis of this symptomatology. The best examples here are found in the literature on CBT such as presented in Beck et al. (1979), which utilizes symptoms of depression as a major point of departure for making decisions as to treatment. Other variables taken as predictors here include severity and chronicity of the disorder, presence or absence of melancholia and absence of psychosis. Some investigators consider the use of nosological schemes to be of dubious value (Strupp 1981). It is too early to make conclusive judgements about any patient-therapy matching procedures (see McLean 1981; Shaw 1981).

One trend in the field which is clear is the shift from the idealistic goal of complete cure towards an approach of effecting limited but significant changes in the ability of the individual to function (Balint 1964). It is generally accepted that the poorest candidates for psychotherapy are those individuals "least equipped to deal with life challenges" (Strupp 1981, p. 6). Garfield (1978) underscored this, noting that "patients who are initially better off are at higher levels (of functioning) at termination". Garfield added here, however, that if the actual amount of change is measured, this conclusion about predictive variables is not as evident. Furthermore, clinicians and researchers are concerned not only with clinical significance but also with statistical significance (see Cohen 1983), but the latter consideration is frequently not addressed when patient changes are reported.

Finally, we should note the caveat furnished by Matazzaro's (1978, p. 942) critique of knowledge on psychotherapy training:

> The slow rate of progress is partly due to the great complexity of this research area. That is, we are attempting to measure a combination of conceptual, experimental, and behavioural learning in a constantly shifting, never duplicated stimulus situation. We have poorly defined variables and inadequate measuring instruments that involve subjective judgement and whose use may not be comparable from one study to another. Because of the time-consuming nature of the measurements, the N in each study is likely to be small. Because of the complexity of the behaviour to be learned and the consequent complexity of the teaching programme, not all aspects of the programme are fully described, nor are their effects measured. None of the studies has been faithfully replicated.It is not surprising that a large aggregate effort has not resulted in a giant step forward. This research is further hampered by our fragmentary knowledge regarding what therapists do that leads to patient im-

provement along specific dimensions. Consequently, even if we define variables more clearly and increase the efficiency of teaching the defined behaviours, we are not sure that we are selecting the most relevant behaviours. Clearly, what we need is to study student acquisition of skill, which is then related to patient improvement.

Evaluation Programme for Training Cognitive-Behavioural Therapists

Cognitive-Behavioural Therapy

CBT is a system of psychotherapy which boasts a strong theoretical foundation, a body of empirical knowledge and a set of reasonably well-defined interventions. Cognitive theory places a major emphasis on the individual's phenomenology in the maintenance of a disorder. Most theoretical work in the area has concentrated on major depressive disorders (see Shaw and Segal, 1988), but its intervention strategies have more recently been extended to treating patients suffering from anxiety (Beck and Emery 1979) and anorexia nervosa (Garner and Bemis 1982). The training model presented in this chapter concerns the use of CBT for major unipolar depressive disorders. A number of outcome studies have shown CBT to have an effectiveness at least comparable to that of other treatments of depression (e.g. Rush et al. 1977; Blackburn et al. 1981). Furthermore, these benefits appear to be maintained for up to 2 years post-treatment (Blackburn et al. 1986; Simons et al. 1986; Hollon et al., in press).

Basically the cognitive pattern involved in depression is as follows: certain schemata (attitudes and/or self-constructs) predispose the individual, when faced with a loss from his/her personal domain, to adopt a rigid, dysfunctional set, as observed in the individual's self-report, with a distinct content (a negative self-evaluation) and a distinct process of thinking (as described by Beck et al. 1979, p. 15). Rather than promoting a reduction in stress through a problem-solving mode of thinking, the individual's cognitive set accentuates his/her coping inadequacy and sense of personal failure. This position does not imply any one single source of causality in depression but focusses rather on a specific aspect of the syndrome of depression while acknowledging that other major aspects involve affective, biochemical and behavioural systems.

The cognitive model of depression asserts that certain individuals are vulnerable to depressive episodes, and that risk factors are related to the individual's past experiences with loss and/or failure. The model asserts that if the individual persists in maintaining his/her dysfunctional attitudes or cognitive set, negative experiences accumulate, thereby deepening the depression. The types of attitudes observed in depression that are considered to be vulnerability factors deal with the individual's attempts to gain a positive self-concept and the respect of others via achievement or affiliation. For example, some individuals' sense of self-worth is contingent on achievements. When depressed, these people make negative predictions about the outcome of their actions – but persist in increasing personal demands to achieve, usually in the hope of neutralizing past failures. The stress engendered by such a strategy serves further to debilitate the individual, whereas a more functional approach would involve decreasing of demands by altering the link between self-worth and achievement and/or by adopting more readily achievable goals. Research continues on the importance of cognitive factors in the elicitation and the maintenance of major depressive disorders (for a more complete review of cognitive factors in depression, see Shaw and Segal, 1988).

Measuring Cognitive-Behavioural Therapist Competence

As noted above, it is essential to define the psychotherapeutic skills which are to be trained and to ascertain the degree to which these skills have been acquired. Our approach to this has been carefully to select and evaluate therapists using expert judges' ratings of the probability that (a) the applicant will become a competent CB therapist and (b) that he/she will be a good representative of CBT in an outcome trial. Upon their selection trainees attend a training programme involving didactic presentations and supervised experience towards the goal of meeting these evaluation criteria for CBT in clinical trials research. One should note that the skills and behaviour tested in research protocols have certain unique demands (see Weissman et al. 1982). In our case therapists were to be evaluated on two therapy protocols (each typically of 16–20 sessions). This evaluation involved unanimous agreement between two expert judges who evaluated four randomly selected tapes (two from each protocol). We measured therapist skilfulness, or competence, with an instrument developed specifically for this purpose. The Cognitive Therapy Scale (CTS; J. Young and A.T. Beck 1980 The Cognitive Therapy Scale: rating manual. Center for cognitive therapy, Philadelphia, unpublished manuscript; Vallis et al. 1986) is an 11-item scale which assesses both general psychotherapeutic skills (e.g. understanding and interpersonal effectiveness) and specific cognitive-therapy skills (e.g. focus on key cognitions and application of CB techniques). To achieve a high score (maximum 66) the therapist must identify the key cognitions relevant to the patient's problems or symptoms of depression and design a case-specific intervention strategy and set of homework assignments. Experts place the greatest weighting in their evaluation of therapist competence on the combination of specific and general skills in cognitive therapy (see Shaw 1984). Homework assignments designed to facilitate learning and generalization are also seen as particularly important (see Primakoff et al. 1986). In the present context competence refers to the capacity to function as a cognitive therapist within a research protocol. This definition is clearly restricted and may not allow generalization to clinicalcal practice per se. Competence evaluations furthermore include consideration of the therapist's adherence to the treatment manual, avoidance of techniques or methods that are not in the domain of the therapy system, provision of facilitative conditions for change and application of the technical interventions of CBT in a skilful manner. Therapist competence may be influenced by several patient factors, including degree of psychopathology, personality style and resistence to change.

It is generally recognized that the factors accounting for the greatest variance in outcome in psychotherapy are pre-existing patient variables (Bergin and Lambert 1978; Prochaska and Norcross 1982). Such patient predictors remain largely elusive, but some evidence suggests that these include attitude towards treatment, severity and chronicity of problems, and level of learned resourcefulness (Simons et al. 1983; Vallis and Shaw 1987).

Monitoring and Quality-Assurance Procedures

Once the therapists have been trained, the trainers' role shifts to that of monitoring their behaviour through monthly consultations. One of our evaluative responsibilities is to identify sessions in which therapist behaviour fell below a certain level, indicating that the independent variable in the research is being compromised. While variability in therapist behaviour is expected, we should not equate treatment protocols of therapist behaviour in our study with those in other studies or with the standards generally accepted by cognitive therapists. In the outcome trial the trainers' main function was to preserve the integrity of the independent variable, a secondary function being to provide consultations in order to help the therapists' work.

Monitoring of the therapists was relatively straight-forward. Rather than observing each therapy session as in the training phase 9 of the 20 sessions were monitored, according to a pre-selected schedule unknown to the therapists. The entire session was reviewed and rated using the CTS. This follows Matazzaro's (1978) advice that "there is no demonstrated, valid criterion measure of training benefit other than therapist behaviour in live interviews" (p. 962). Therapists conferred once a month with their trainers by means of a telephone conference call both in a group with their peers and individually with one trainer. In the group format each therapist presented one of his/her videotapes of a session for discussion in the group; this process was repeated the next month. The same therapist-patient pair was presented for two consecutive sessions to allow the group an opportunity to observe whether constructive change had occurred. The therapist was contacted immediately if trainers observed a major violation in the treatment protocol at any point during the monitoring. In addition, if the trainer observed two consecutive sessions in which the therapist's CTS score was more than one standard deviation below the group mean, individual contact with the therapist was increased to two individual consultations and one group consultation per month until three consecutive sessions were observed above this CTS value. (This point – below which the therapists are seen as being in danger – we refer to as the "the red line".) This measure serves the following functions:

1. It offers a quantitative method for measuring the overall level of performance or competence along a number of CBT dimensions.
2. It provides a means for detemining whether the therapist drifts from the protocol, i.e. whether he employes less adequate or tangential cognitive therapy or other modes of therapy.

3. It gives trainers a reliable, concise method of determining when and whether the therapist in question should be contacted for further consultation and/or questioning of the therapy being provided.
4. It provides a minimum quality assurance of each therapist's performance level to assure researchers as to the quality of CBT being provided.

To determine the red-line level more than 700 full-session videotapes were reviewed. The group mean was based on each therapist's final training case, a point at which it was assumed that his/her CB skills had stabilized. Means and standard deviations of CTS scores were calculated from the last case (based on at least 16 sessions) from each of eight therapists. (In all, ten therapists participated in the original training and eight were certified). An overall mean was then obtained, and the red-line level was set one standard deviation below this. For the TDCRP the red line was thus set at 39 (mean of 47.6 minus a standard deviation of 8.6, with all values rounded to the higher value).

An example of a therapist reaching the red-line point is illustrated in Fig. 1. Note that at sessions 10 and 11 his performance fell below the red line, as it did later at termination. This pattern indicated problems in consolidating the early work and in termination issues.

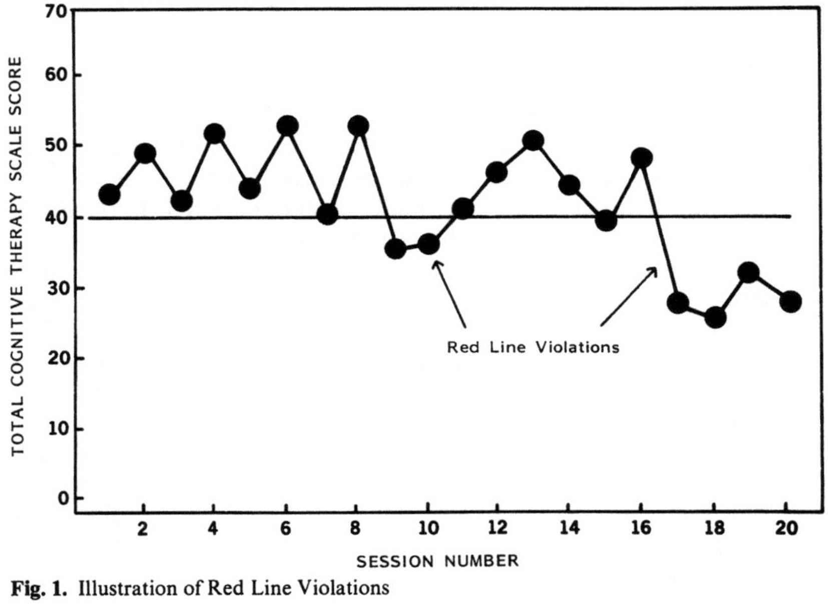

Fig. 1. Illustration of Red Line Violations

Implementation of the Programme

We now turn to the training programme employed in the TDCRP, paying specific attention to the details of selection, training and outcome in our training component of this outcome trial. The details of the study itself are presented by Elkin et al. (1985).

Selection of Trainees

Three research sites, representing a geographically distinct area of the United States, participated in the CB training programme. Each research site was responsible for soliciting therapists who had some experience in cognitive and/or behaviour therapy and who were interested in participating in the CBT component of the TDCRP. A total of 48 prospective therapists applied. The principal investigators for each research site interviewed applicants and judged their suitability for the research programme. This preliminary screening reduced the number of applicants to 21, seven at each of the three research sites.

These candidates were then introduced to the theory and application of CBT via various media. Beck et al. (1979) was used as the training manual, and videotapes of skilled CB therapists were observed. These materials allowed candidates to make more knowledgeable predictions about their probability of success and as to whether they felt they would benefit from CBT training. Each applicant was required to submit information that would expedite the final selection procedure, including a 50-min videotape of his "usual" interview behaviour, background information and references from past supervisors. Curricula vitae were examined and pertinent information noted. A self-selected example of each therapist's usual performance with a depressed patient was viewed and rated on scales measuring therapist performance, reflecting both general psychotherapeutic and CBT skills.

An appraisal report from a past supervisor or colleague familiar with the therapist's work was also considered in the selection process. Finally, each applicant completed a Therapy Preference Scale (TPS), a questionnaire designed to predict the likelihood that an applicant will be trained successfully. The TPS utilizes self-reports to assess candidates' commitment to involvement in a demanding and highly evaluative project lasting more than one year.

In October 1980 the principal investigators and independent experts in CBT at each research site made recommendations as to the nine most suitable trainees (three from each site). The three independent experts had considerable experience in teaching and evaluating CB therapists. Their involvement in the trainee-selection process was seen as the most valid procedure to identify the factors, including personal characteristics, associated with successful training. The three CB experts rated each applicant's self-selected videotaped therapy performance on two scales, the Pre-Practicum Appraisal Report (PAR) and the CTS. The PAR yielded a probability estimate that the trainee would become a successful CB therapist within the research protocol, while the CTS measured skilfullness in therapy in general and in tasks specific to CBT. (Reliability and validity data on the

CTS are presented in Vallis et al. 1986). An objective behavioural assessment was also employed to measure therapist's interactions; these included total number and length (in seconds) of therapist-patient interactions, length of total silences, average therapist reaction time in response to a patient, frequency of patient interruptions by the therapist and number of therapist errors, as measured by the Matarazzo Checklist of therapist behaviour (see Vallis et al., in press).

An applicant's ultimate suitability and acceptance for training was determined on the basis of a number of factors, including judges' evaluations of each applicant's overall psychotherapeutic skills and ability to conceptualize the patient's symptoms/problems in a form appropriate for intervention, in addition to other variables such as commitment to the CBT research programme. We found that the most highly rated applicants were those who (a) were most comfortable working in a short-term therapy framework, (b) able to adopt a goal/problem-oriented alliance with clients, and (c) reported a good conceptual fit between their usual work and the description of CBT methods in Beck et al. (1979). Less highly rated candidates were those observed to be either overly directive or non-directive in their therapeutic approach to therapy and uncertain about the utility of the cognitive theory of depression.

Ten of the 27 applicants were finally selected for the training programme, planned to last for 12–18 months, and eight of these ten were ultimately certified for participation in the trial.

Training Institute

The goal of the training programme was to determine whether consistently acceptable CBT performance could be achieved by experienced therapists in the relatively short training phase of 1 year. Each therapist had at least 2 years of clinical experience after obtaining a Ph D in clinical psychology or psychiatric residency and specific experience treating depressed patients, but they had not previously participated in an outcome trial using the Beck et al. (1979) protocol.

Training took place in two stages. First, the original nine trainees (one trainee went through the training at a later stage) attended an intensive, 2-week didactic workshop coordinated by Drs. J. Young and A. T. Beck at the Center For Cognitive Therapy in Philadelphia. Subsequently trainees began an intensive clinical practicum at their respective research sites. As described below, supervision of trainees utilized an experimental technique in which two videotapes and long-distance telephone calls were utilized.

The Institute training programme was designed to ensure that trainees acquired a firm grounding in the cognitive theory of depression, and the principles and techniques of CBT. A multi-faceted educational approach was utilized.

Beck et al. (1979) was used as the CBT manual; trainees were to use this as a guide rather than as a "cookbook". In time, as they gained experience, trainees were expected to improvise new "custom-designed" interventions based on CBT theory. Lectures augmented the descriptions found in the manual; demonstrations and role-playing gave trainees the opportunity to apply their newly acquired knowledge in a workshop in which difficulties were discussed, and deviations from protocol were identified. It was emphasized that while trainees' previous clinical experience was essential, they would be expected to follow the research protocol; there could thus be conflict between their "normal" judgement and behaviour, on the one hand, and that required by the protocol, on the other. Videotapes of experienced CB therapists lent a valuable component to the training process as trainees were able actually to observe the CB techniques applied skilfully in therapy sessions. It was hoped that the training would be successful if both theoretical and practical aspects of CBT were introduced together. As the conceptual basis of the approach is inseparable from the application of CB techniques, simply applying the usual techniques and methods of CBT without a conceptualization of their desired benefit was considered unacceptable.

The multi-faceted training approach was applied with the introduction of each CBT method, e.g. eliciting automatic thoughts, assessing hopelessness and suicidal ideation, evaluating underlying assumptions, assigning relevant homework and planning and implementing cognitive restructuring strategies. The focus of Institute training was on helping trainees conceptualize patient problems within a cognitive framework and employing cognitive and behavioural techniques to alter the targetted depressive symptoms. Frequently encountered therapy situations (e.g. suicidal symptoms and non-compliance with homework) were introduced and discussed. It was seen as imperative that trainees obtain this intensive introduction to CBT since their early performance in the practicum portion of training relied primarily on the acquisition of CBT skills in the workshop. Without such a solid foundation it seemed unlikely that the training goal of reaching consistently competent performance in approximately 1 year would be realized.

At the end of the 2-week workshop each trainee's knowledge and application of CBT was evaluated. Each trainee was required to take a written examination on the theory and practice of CBT. Questions focussed on a trainee's ability to conceptualize, plan and implement strategies, particularly in therapeutic situations. All trainees passed the written examination, and most obtained high scores. A trainee's actual skills in CBT were assessed in a more practical manner. Each trainee conducted a therapy session with an actress in the role of a depressed patient. To ensure that each therapist encountered essentially the same set of experiences in these mock sessions the actress followed a standard problem list. Each session was videotaped and evaluated on a number of dimensions by the Institute instructor most familiar with the trainee's work as well as by the principal investigator and project director of the CBT training programme. The PAR and CTS were employed to rate each trainee's performance and to determine specific areas of weakness that needed attention during the practicum phase. Overall evaluations were thus made on the basis of trainee's examination score and trainers' ratings of therapist behaviour. These data allowed *objective* judgements to be made regarding a trainee's readiness to proceed with the second stage, that of practicum training. Any reservations about an individual's ability to grasp CBT theory or apply its techniques were discussed with the principal investigator and the NIMH staff at the research site. At this stage all ten trainees were judged to be acceptable for further training.

Experience here showed that the acquisition of CBT theory and techniques was relatively straight-forward. The TDCRP provided for a 2-week training period; it was concluded, however, that this peiod was too long for trainees at this level, and that the content could be condensed into a 1-week period. Trainees' feedback was consistent with this observation; it was seen to be difficult to sustain the motivation to practise techniques and even to observe videotapes and demonstrations for an extended period. (In more recent training we have found it preferable to conduct a 3- to 5-day introductory workshop followed 6–8 months later with a second 2- 3-day "intermediate" workshop. It was crucial that trainees acquire a solid grasp of CBT theory and principles and at least a minimum mastery of its techniques to ensure that their performance with patients would be representative of acceptable CBT.

The comparison of trainee behaviour (as evaluated by the CTS) in the interview after this 2-week workshop (i.e. the session with the actress) to that in their previously submitted "usual" interview showed that therapists had, in fact, acquired CBT interviewing skills and structure. These changes were evident in the therapists' setting an agenda, obtaining feedback, interviewing in important areas of concern and assigning homework. The therapists' understanding, interpersonal effectiveness and pacing did not change significantly (Shaw et al. in preparation).

Although the acquisition of CB techniques was relatively rapid, the ability to apply appropriate conceptualizations and judgements about interventions usually developed somewhat more slowly. Novices tended to rely on one or two favoured techniques, applying them widely; when these interventions prove inappropriate or when confronted with non-compliance, inexperienced therapists frequently have difficulty adopting a different and perhaps more appropriate technique. The ability to develop alternative strategies was fostered in the practicum segment of the training programme and, amongst other issues, became a focus of supervision later. Interestingly, a trainee's knowledge of CBT theory and techniques, as measured by the written examination, did not predict his/her performance in the practicum training phase leading to certification. Evaluation of the trainees in their initial mock session performance at the Institute, on the other hand, was useful in predicting the outcome of training. This finding lends to a multi-dimensional *extensive* selection procedure.

Intensive Clinical Practicum

These ten therapists entered the clinical practicum portion of training at their respective sites. Each therapist was to receive intensive supervision on a minimum of four patients with unipolar depression over a 12-month period; two patients were seen for the complete 20-session protocol. Patients completing less than 12 therapy sessions were replaced. The purpose was to provide trainees with sufficient opportunity to acquire the requisite knowledge and skills in applying CBT within the research protocol and thereby enable them to perform CBT consistently and competently during the outcome study phase when therapist monitoring would be substantially reduced. Attempts were made to supply a range of depressed patients to each trainee-therapist in the training phase in order to provide experience over a variety of therapeutic situations. This became problematic however inasmuch as recruitment at the research sites proceeded more slowly than had been anticipated. Also problematic was patient attrition, for each patient with less than 12 sessions had to be replaced. Such difficulties caused the training phase to be extended for an additional 6–18 months. Although four therapists were certified after the originally planned 12-month training period, four others did not meet certification criteria until the 18-month evaluation. Eight of the ten trainees were certified for the outcome study. While all trainees saw at least four cases, some saw six before criteria were met.

The actual method of supervision was somewhat unique in that it utilized videotape review and long-distance telephone conferences. Each therapy session was videotaped and duplicated at the research site. A copy was sent to the trainer(s) at the training site who viewed the tape independently and rated therapist competence using the CTS. A time was subsequently determined for discussion of the session (via long-distance telephone). It was possible to view segments of the videotape simultaneously at two locations. Every session was viewed, critiqued and rated by the trainers; CBT evaluations were weighted at 2:1 to supervision. The 1-hour weekly supervision sessions focussed on both the therapist's behaviour (with an emphasis on identifying conceptual issues) and deviations from the protocol. Therapists and trainers reviewed pre-selected segments of sessions when either had questions. The therapist's thinking at the time of the intervention would then be explored to identify his/her conceptualization of the patient's situation; the supervisor could then suggest alternative conceptualizations. The supervisor would also explore alternative intervention strategies (via role-playing) based on the modified conceptualization. As in the case generally with psychotherapeutic supervision, these interactions provided support, positive feedback and suggestions to the trainees within a relatively short period of time after the session had occurred. Unlike more conventional supervision techniques this method offered optimal use of limited supervision personnel.

The distance between supervisors and trainees made extensive face to face supervision impossible; the only feasible alternative was long-distance supervision. The innovation of simultaneous videotape review clarified and expedited communication, enabling supervisors to give trainees specific, concrete feedback regarding their therapeutic behaviour. The only obvious disadvantage of the telephone/videotape method of supervision lies in the fact that rapport between trainee and supervisor may not be as well-developed as it might be in face-to-face supervision. Rapport between the trainers and trainees was nevertheless strong. Feedback, both verbal and in ratings, was generally excellent.

To strengthen trainees' CB skills and base of support group telephone calls with all trainees (at one site) and the trainers were conducted. These meetings were designed to teach new CBT methods that were of general interest. These bi-weekly (or monthly) group calls discussed critical incidents that had occurred in therapy, particularly those that threatened the research protocol (e.g. patients considering early termination, non-compliance issues). These meetings provided trainees with the opportunity to learn from colleagues' experiences and to discuss innovations in the CBT protocol in an informal situation. Trainees derived a sense of confidence from seeing that there were several shared problems in applying this method. Their feedback often confirmed that many methods were easy to learn but difficult to apply.

The goal of the training practicum was to produce therapists who acquired skills that allowed them to adapt their behaviour, while at the same time remaining within the CBT framework. It was essential to evaluate trainees' level of competence during and after the practicum training to determine whether they met criteria for inclusion in the study phase. The actual certification procedure was determined by supervisors and independent expert consultants in visits held at the training site. For these conferences a random sample of four full CBT sessions from each therapist was selected. Each expert and trainer observed and rated two sessions (using the CTS and PAR) from each of two patients as performed by the ten trainees.

The trainers' ratings were correlated with those of the independent experts. Correlations between ratings of experts and those of trainers were modest: for the CTS total score $r = .57$ ($n = 80, p < .01$) and for a global competence rating $r = .36$ ($n = 80, p < .05$); the overall competence rating was not reliable enough to be utilized. In general, trainers awarded significantly higher ratings of competence. It appears preferable that ratings from at least two judges be combined; this has the effect of increasing the reliability of CTS ratings.

There are several explanations for these findings (see K.S. Dobson and B.F. Shaw 1987, a comparison of the judgements of psychotherapy supervisors and experts on the competency of therapists in training. University of Toronto, submitted). One explanation notes the greater familiarity of trainers with the therapist's conceptualization of the cases. The results support the possibility of psychotherapy researchers and educators obtaining independent evaluation of therapist competence. Independent judges, as indicated, eventually certified eight of the ten trainees; there was thus complete agreement on each of the four tapes that the therapist in question could represent the CBT field in an outcome trial. Once he/she succeeded in fulfilling the criteria for certification, the therapist was scheduled to see patients in the outcome study phase of the project, in which consultation with trainers was greatly reduced.

Consultation and Videotape Reviews in the Outcome Study

The outcome study phase of the TDCRP was very similar to the training phase, with the exception of degree of supervision. In contrast to the training phase, in which trainees were monitored extensively, receiving up to 16 hours supervision per case, therapists during the outcome phase were provided as the norm with a maximum of 4 hours individual consultation per case. Additional contact was furnished only when the red line was reached (and then only until therapist behaviour returned to a level above the red line). Additional videotapes were requested for review when the therapist's performance dropped below the red line. During this phase only 9 of the 20 sessions in the CBT protocol were reviewed by trainers. A pre-determined schedule ensured, barring technical difficulties, a uniform data base. Telephone calls for individual supervision were made approximately once per month while the monthly group-consultation calls were continued unchanged. As might be expected by experienced psychotherapy supervisors it was found that therapists had difficulty with certain patients, some of whom, indeed, most therapists may have had trouble treating with short-term, "orthodox" CBT.

In general, the therapist training programme proved successful and we are confident that this system of monitoring therapist behaviour is useful for educational purposes. Determination of whether these competence ratings can predict treatment outcome must await further analysis. Many questions concerning the impact of these procedures also remain.

We must note, however, that two therapists were not certified. Neither their non-certification nor the certification of the remaining eight therapists should be interpreted as a judgement as to their respective psychotherapy skills in general. It is certainly not a reflection on the outcome with clients on the part of these two, as we carefully avoided disclosing this information to our external judges. Their non-certification does reflect their ability or inability to work within the structures of a specific CBT research protocol.

We wish, finally, to describe the results of the training. Table 1 presents data on the number of patients, total therapy time and total supervision time in the 13–18 months that the ten therapists spent in training. In addition to the time in direct supervision therapists frequently received individual homework assignments to review videotaped sections of their sessions. To evaluate training ratings of the therapists, treatment of four patients were examined. Training effects were evaluated by a two-way (therapist and patient) analyses of covariance. The replication factor was session CTS scores; patient difficulty was used as the covariate, as this variable has been shown to correlate significantly with the CTS (see T.M. Vallis and B.F. Shaw 1987, the relationship between patient difficulty and therapist competence in cognitive therapy for depression, submitted).

Table 1. Therapist time in training, total therapy time and total supervision time during the training phase

Therapist	Therapist time in training (months)	Total patient therapy time[a] (hours)	Supervision time with therapist (hours)
1	13	79	41
2	15	80	34
3	18	75	43
4	15	100	44
5	18	95	54
6[b]	18.5	100	62
7[b]	18	97	46
8	15	73	51
9	15	72	34
10	13	78	42

[a] Because of withdrawal and early termination, patient total therapy time varies across therapists
[b] Therapist not certified to enter the outcome phase

Before presenting the results of these analyses a number of methodological points must be made. First, rather than the rationally defined subscales of the CTS (general therapy skills and specific CBT skills), factor-derived subscales were used in the present analysis. Factor analysis (Shaw 1984) on a sample of cognitive therapists following a treatment protocol suggested that the division into general skills and CBT skills was not representative of this sample. Instead, the two factors that emerged reflected a broad, general CBT-skills factor (also including non-CBT general skills, such as understanding and interpersonal effectiveness) and a CBT-structuring skills factor (composed of agenda setting, pacing and homework). In other words, in this sample of more advanced trainees psychotherapy skills in general cannot be separated from more technical skills. The case is very different, however, when all therapists are not following the strict guidelines of the cognitive therapy protocol, in which good interpersonal skill is not synonymous with good cognitive therapy. For this reason factor-derived subscales were used to analyse training effects.

Second, it has been suggested that therapists' ability to conceptualize a case from a cognitive-therapy perspective is very important, yet most difficult to train (Shaw 1984). It might therefore, be expected that conceptualization skill lags behind skill in the use of interventions. For this reason we analysed data on the CTS conceptualization item and assessed conceptual ability (specifically, a narrative report on the therapist's choice of intervention strategy) separately. Analyses of covariance yielded significant independent effects across patients for the CB structuring subscale, the CTS conceptualization item and the CTS total score. A statistically non-significant trend was observed on the CBT-skills subscale. Mean scores increased over patients for all measures. Post hoc testing on the three variables that showed a significant independent effect for patients. On the CBT-structuring subscale and the CTS total score, means for patients 3 and 4 (numbered chronologically for the therapist) were significantly greater than those for patients 1 and 2; means did not differ significantly between patients 1 and 2 or between patients 3 and 4. On the CTS conceptualization item the mean score for patient 4 was significantly higher than that for patients 1, 2 and 3 (those in the latter set not differing significantly). Thus, significant training effects were found for the eight certified therapists.

The two therapists, on the other hand, who were not certified did not show such increase in competence over the course of the training phase. In fact, their competence scores *decreased*. Both therapists performed best on their *first* training case: the mean CTS total scores for the four patients treated were 43.31, 36.28, 36.52, 37.18, respectively. The CTS data thus support the independent decisions of the expert consultants not to certify these therapists.

Conclusion

Experience with the monitoring phase of the TDCRP leads us strongly to endorse the continuing-education goals of psychotherapists. Our CB therapists exposed themselves to intense training and monitoring. Each therapist's behaviour was reviewed critically, and, while there were certain satisfactions, the demands of providing "orthodox" CB therapy within a research protocol were high. In all, the therapists worked on the outcome trial for approximately 3 years; this clearly indicates their commitment to the field.

The professional has a responsibility to maintain his/her skills at an acceptable level of practice. As psychotherapists we recognize that our specific methods will not help everyone. In time we develop either implicit or explicit criteria for patient selection, and yet our selection criteria sometimes fail, and the outcome of therapy is poor; thankfully, however, at other times a positive result is obtained. Therapists tend to attribute these successes or failures to various factors, including patient difficulty and compliance, the adequacy of therapy methods and even personal errors in judgement. Future studies must attempt to relate such patient factors as well as those of the therapist and the patient-therapist interaction to treatment outcome. Future research on the data from our programme can address only the issue of whether training effects are maintained, not whether therapists' skill and technical interventions are beneficial to the patient.

C. G. Jung has observed that "It is in fact largely immaterial what sort of techniques he uses, for the point is not the technique .... The personality and attitude of the doctor are of supreme importance whether he appreciates this factor or not" (1934, pp. 159–160). As trainers in CBT, however, we have shown that we disagree with Jung. In our view, research studies on the outcome and process of psychotherapy offer the greatest promise in determining who is right. It is our hope that the field will be influenced by our work on training, and that clearly defined interventions by well-trained therapists with patients are the result.

Acknowledgements. We would like to acknowledge A. J. Rush, M. Kovacs, J. Young, G. Emery, M. Vallis and K. S. Dobson, who served as either trainers or judges/consultants in this study. We are also grateful to D. Wellsby for her assistance with manuscript preparation. This work was supported by NIMH grant MH35016 to Brian F. Shaw. Send all correspondence to Brian F. Shaw, Ph.D., Toronto General Hospital, Department of Psychology, 200 Elizabeth Street, Toronto, Ontario M5G 2C4.

The NIMH Treatment of Depression Collaborative Research Programme is a multi-site programme initiated and sponsored by the Psychosocial Treatments Research Branch, Division of Extramural Research Programmes, NIMH, and is funded by cooperative agreements to six participating sites (George Washington University MH33762; University of Pittsburgh MH33753; University of Oklahoma MH33760; Yale University MH33827; Clarke Institute of Psychiatry MH38231 and Rush Presbyterian, St. Luke's Medical Center MH35017). The principal NIMH collaborators are: Irene Elkin, Ph.D., coordinator; John P. Docherty, M.D., and Morris B. Parloff, former branch chiefs. Tracie Shea, Ph.D., George Washington University, is associate coordinator. The principal investigators and project coordinators at the three participating research sites are: at George Washington University, Stuart M. Sotsky, M.D. and David Glass, Ph.D.; at University of Pittsburgh, Stanley D. Imber, Ph.D. and Paul A. Pilkonis, Ph.D.; and at the University of Oklahoma, John T. Watkins, Ph.D. and William Leber, Ph.D. The principal investigators and project coordinators at the three sites responsible for training therapists are: at Yale University, Myrna Weissman, Ph.D., Eve Chevron, M.S. and Bruce J. Rounsaville, M.D.; at Clarke Institute of Psychiatry, Brian F. Shaw, Ph.D., T. Michael Vallis, Ph.D.; and at Rush Presbyterian, St. Luke's Medical Center, Jan A. Fawcett, M.D. and Phillip Epstein, M.D. Collaborators in data management and data analysis are C. James Klett, Ph.D., Joseph F. Collins, Sc.D. and Roderic Gillis of the Perry Point, Maryland VA Cooperative Studies Programme.

References

Balint M (1964) The doctor, his patient and the illness, 2nd edn. Pitman Medical, London

Beck AT, Emery G (1979) Cognitive therapy of anxiety and phobic disorders. Center for Cognitive Therapy, Philadelphia

Beck AT, Rush AJ, Shaw BF, Emery G (1979) Cognitive therapy of depression. Guilford, New York

Bergin AE, Lambert MJ (1978) The evaluation of therapeutic outcomes. In: Garfield SL, Bergin AE (eds) Handbook of psychotherapy and behavior change, 2nd edn. Wiley, New York

Blackburn IM, Bishop S, Glen AIM, Whalley LJ, Christie JE (1981) The efficacy of cognitive therapy in depression: a treatment trial using cognitive therapy and pharmacotherapy, each alone and in combination. Br J Psychiatry 139:181–189

Blackburn IM, Eunson KM, Bishop S (1986) A two year naturalistic follow-up of depressed patients treated with cognitive therapy, pharmacotherapy and a combination of both. Br J Psychiatry 139:181–189

Cohen J (1983) The benefits of meta-analysis. In: Williams JBW, Spitzer RL (eds) Psychotherapy research: where are we and where should we go? Guilford, New York pp 332–339

Elkin I, Parloff MB, Hadley SW, Autry JH (1985) NIMH treatment of depression collaborative research programme Arch Gen Psychiatry, 42:305–316

Evans DR, Hearn MT, Uhlemann MR, Ivey AE (1984) Essential interviewing: a programmed approach to effective communication 2nd edn. Brooks/Cole, Monterey, Ca

Ford DH, Urban HB (1963) Systems of psychotherapy. Wiley, gnew York

Frank JD (1982) Therapeutic components hared by all psychotherapies. In: Harvey JH, Parks MM (eds) Psychotherapy research and behaviour change. American Psychological Association, Washington D.C.

Frank JD, Hoehn-Saric R, Imber SD, Liberman BL, Stone AR (1978) Effective ingredients of successful psychotherapy. Brunner/Mazel, New York

Garfield SL (1978) Research on client variable in psychotherapy. In: Garfield SL, Bergin AE (eds) Handbook of psychotherapy and behaviour change: an empirical analysis. 2nd edn. Wiley, New York

Garfield SL (1983) Psychotherapy: efficacy, generality and specificity. In Williams JBW, Spitzer RL (eds) Psychotherapy research: Where are we and where should we go? Guilford, New York pp 295–304

Garner DM, Bemis KM (1982) A cognitive-behavioral approach to anorexia nervosa. Cog Ther Res 6:123–150

Herink R (ed) (1980) The psychotherapy handbook: the A to Z guide to more than different therapies in use today. New American Library, New York

Hollon SD, Evans MD, DeRubeis RJ (1987) Preventing relapse following treatment for depression: the cognitive-pharmacotherapy project. In: Schneiderman N, Fields T (eds) Stress and coping, vol 2. Lawrence Erlbaum, New York

Ivey AE, Authier J (1978) Microcounseling: innovation in interviewing, counseling, psychotherapy and psychoeducation, Thomas, Springfield

Jung CG (1934) The state of psychotherapy today. In: Civilization in transition. Princeton University Press, Princeton, pp 157–173 (Collected works, vol 10)

Kiesler DJ (1966) Some myths of psychotherapy research and the search for a paradigm. Psychol Bull 65 (2):110–136

Klein DF, Rabkin JG (1983) Specificity and strategy in psychotherapy research and practice. In: Williams JBW, Spitzer RL (eds) Psychotherapy research: Where are we and where should we go? Guilford, New York pp 306–329

Lewinsohn PM (1974) A behavior approach to depression. In: Friedman RJ, Katz MM (eds) The psychology of depression: contemporary theory and research. Wiley, New York

Malan DH (1976) The frontier of brief psychotherapy. Plenum, New York

Matarazzo RG (1978) Research on the teaching and learning of psychotherapies. In: Garfield SL, Bergin AE (eds) Handbook of psychotherapy and behavior change: an empirical analysis. Wiley, New York

McLean PD (1981) Matching treatment to patient characteristics in an outpatient setting. In: Rehm LP (ed) Behavior therapy for depression. Academic, New York

Newman FL, Ciarlo JA (1982) Outcome evaluation and quality assurance in mental health. QRB 8:27–31

Orne MT (1975) Psychotherapy in contemporary America: its development and context. In Friedman DX, Dyruch JE (eds) American handbook of psychiatry, vol 5, treatment. Basic, New York

Parloff M (1981) Psychotherapy evidence and reimbursement decisions: Bambi meets Godzilla. Paper presented at the 12th annual meeting of the Society for Psychotherapy Research, Aspen, Colorado, June 1981

Paul GL (1967) Strategy of outcome research in psychotherapy. J Consult Psychol 31:109–118

Primakoff L, Epstein N, Covi L (1986) Homework compliance: an uncontrolled variable in cognitive therapy outcome research. Behav Ther 17:433–446

Prochaska JO, Norcross JC (1982) The future of psychotherapy: a Delphi poll. Prof Psychol 13:620–627

Report of the Research Task Force of the National Institutes of Mental Health (1978). Submitted to President's Commission on Mental Health, vol IV, appendix, Washington DC

Rosen A, Proctor EK (1981) Distinctions between treatment outcomes and their implications for treatment evaluation. J Consult Clin Psychol 49:418–425

Rush A, Beck AT, Kovacs M, Hollon S (1977) Drugs comparative efficacy of cognitive therapy and pharmacotherapy in the treatment of depressed outpatients. Cog Ther Res (1):17–37

Shapiro AK (1959) The placebo effect in the history of medical treatment: implications for psychiatry. Am J Psychiatry 116:73–78

Shaw BF (1981) Cognitive therapy with an inpatient population. In: Emery G, Hollon SD, Bedrosian RC (eds) New directions in cognitive therapy. Guilford, New York

Shaw BF (1984) Specification of the training and evaluation of cognitive therapists for outcome studies. In: Williams JBW, Spitzer RL (eds) Psychotherapy research: where are we and where should we go? Guilford, New York

Shaw BF, Segal ZV (1988) Introduction to cognitive theory and therapy. In: Francis AJ, Hales RE (eds) Review of psychiatry, vol 7. American Psychiatric Press, Washington D.C.

Sifneos PE (1972) Short-term psychotherapy and emotional crisis. Harvard University Press, Cambridge

Simons A, Lustman P, Wetzel R, Murphy GE (1983) Predicting response to cognitive therapy of depression: the role of learned resourcefulness. Cog Ther Res 9:79–89

Simons AD, Murphy GE, Levine JL, Wetzel RD (1986) Cognitive therapy and pharmacotherapy for depression. Arch Gen Psychiatry 43:43–48

Smith ML, Glass GV, Miller TI (1980) The benefits of psychotherapy. Johns Hopkins University Press, Baltimore

Stiles WB, Shapiro DA, Elliott R (1986) "Are all psychotherapies equivalent?" Am Psychol 41:165–180

Strupp H (1980) Success and failure in time-limited psychotherapy: a systematic comparison of two cases (comparison 1). Arch Gen Psychiatry 37:595–603

Strupp H (1981) Some implications of psychotherapy research for training. Paper presented at the annual meeting of the American Psychological Association, Los Angeles, August, 1981

Vallis TM, Shaw BF, Dobson KS (1986) The Cognitive Therapy Scale: psychometric properties. J Consult Clin Psychol 54:381–385

Vallis TM, Shaw BF, McCabe SB (1988) The relationship between therapist competency in cognitive therapy and general therapy skill. J Cog Psychother (in press)

Waskow IE (1984) Specification of the technique variable in the NIMH treatment of depression collaborative research programme. In: Williams J, Spitzer R (eds) Psychotherapy research: where are we and where should we go? Guilford, New York

Weissmann MM, Rounsaville BJ, Chevron E (1982) Training psychotherapists to participate in psychotherapy outcome studies. Am J Psychiatry 139:1442–1446

Wilkins W (1986) Therapy-therapist confounds in psychotherapy research. Cog Ther Res 10:3–11

An Appraisal of Comparative Trials of Cognitive Therapy for Depression

I.M. BLACKBURN

Introduction

Cognitive treatment techniques are now applied to a whole range of psychological disorders and by an ever-growing number of clinicians, as clearly indicated by various chapters in this handbook and by earlier compendia (Foreyt and Rathjen 1978; Kendall and Hollon 1979; Emery et al. 1981). In addition to depression, general anxiety and panic disorders, phobias, eating disorders and obsessional disorders which are discussed in this volume, cognitive techniques have been used in the treatment of pain (Turk and Genest 1979), headaches (Holroyd et al. 1977), anger and stress (Novaco 1979), alcohol dependency (Emery and Fox 1981) and impulsivity in children (Meichenbaum and Asarnow 1979). However, there is no doubt that all of these applications of cognitive therapy depression has been the most systematically researched. It is the quality and promise of this research which has fostered interest in the wider application of cognitive therapy.

The early work of Beck (Beck 1961, 1967) and of Ellis (Ellis 1962) provides the historical reasons for the special place of depression in cognitive therapy research. Moreover, Beck et al. (1979) were among the first to provide a detailed treatment manual for the training of therapists. However, cognitive therapy has come to mean many different things to different people and is sometimes used as a generic term to describe quite divergent types of therapies which range from behaviour therapy with a cognitive component (Mclean and Hakstian 1979) to self-control therapies with equal stress on behavioural and cognitive components (Rehm 1977), cognitive therapy with behavioural components whose main aim is to modify maladaptive thoughts and beliefs (Beck et al. 1979), and cognitive therapies which focus on modifying maladaptive beliefs through primarily disputational techniques (rational-emotive therapy, RET; Ellis 1980). These various treatment approaches can be seen as falling along a continuum and reflect the various strands in the growth of the cognitive movement which were elegantly described by Mahoney and Arnkoff (1978). Although it is not appropriate to review again these various approaches here, it is particularly important to bear in mind the differences in the various treatment approaches when comparative trials of efficacy are considered. One of the weaknesses of early psychotherapy research has been the lack of

MRC Brain Metabolism Unit, Royal Edinburgh Hospital, Morningside Park, Edinburgh EH10 5HF, United Kingdom

definition of the treatment used and it is, therefore, essential that this mistake not be repeated. For the same reasons that drug trials would be less useful if great pain were not taken to define the dosages of the drug used and the method of administration, psychotherapy trials are meaningless unless the treatment method is well defined, and different treatment approaches must not be lumped together when they are being evaluated. Other methodological problems which are peculiar to psychotherapy trials are the importance of therapists' characteristics, such as their experience, involvement in the success of the treatment and personal attributes. These issues will be considered in this review chapter.

The term "cognitive therapy" (CT) will be reserved for treatment procedures described by Beck et al. (1979), and "cognitive behavioural therapy" (CBT) will be used for other treatment packages which include cognitive components but which differ from the CT format. The plan of this review is to appraise the efficacy of CT relative to pharmacotherapy and to other psychological treatments; to review trials of CBT; to evaluate the usefulness of CT in the prevention of relapse; to examine the findings on predictive factors of response; and to comment on the issues and criticisms which have been raised in previous reviews (Weissman 1979; Whitehead 1979; Williams 1984). Only published studies of a reasonable methodological standard will be considered.

Cognitive Therapy and Pharmacotherapy

General Characteristics

Seven studies to date have compared CT with pharmacotherapy, either alone or in combination, in the treatment of depressed patients. These are summarised in Table 1.

These treatment trials have three distinctive qualities: they explicitly apply CT as detailed by the manual (Beck et al. 1979); they deal with well-defined groups of patients, namely ambulatory patients satisfying Research Diagnostic Criteria (RDC; Spitzer et al. 1978) or Feighner's criteria (Feighner et al. 1972) for major or definite unipolar, non-psychotic depression, but including both endogenous and non-endogenous subtypes; they use, among others, the same outcome-dependent measures, the Beck Depression Inventory (BDI; Beck et al. 1961) and the Hamilton Rating Scale for Depression (HRSD; Hamilton 1960). Another important methodological point is that antidepressant medication, usually tricyclics, was prescribed in recognised therapeutic doses except in the case of the study by Teasdale et al. (1984) where general practitioners were free to treat patients as usual. However, even in this special case, 11 of the 17 patients in the CT group and 10 of the 17 patients in the usual-treatment group received antidepressant medication within recommended dose ranges.

Table 1 indicates that some studies have shown CT to be more effective than a standard tricyclic antidepressant (Rush et al. 1977; Blackburn et al. 1981, in the case of general-practice patients). Other studies have shown both treatments on

Table 1. Comparisons of cognitive therapy (CT) with pharmacotherapy

Study	Measures	Outcome
Rush et al. (1977) (*n* = 41; out-patients, unipolar non-psychotic)	BDI, HRSD	CT > imipramine
Beck et al. (1979) (*n* = 26; out-patients unipolar non-psychotic and schizo-affective)	BDI, HRSD	CT = CT + amitriptyline
Blackburn et al. (1981) (*n* = 64; hospital out-patients and general-practice patients, primary major unipolar depression, non-psychotic)	BDI, HRSD	Hospital clinic: Com > CT = ADM; General practice: CT = Com > ADM
Rush and Watkins (1981) (*n* = 38; diagnosed depressed out-patients, unipolar, non-psychotic)	BDI, HRSD	Individual CT = individual CT + ADM > group CT
Murphy et al. (1984) (*n* = 70; out-patients, primary major, unipolar, non-psychotic depression)	BDI, HRSD	CT = nortriptyline = CT + nortriptyline = CT + placebo
Teasdale et al. (1984) (*n* = 34; general-practice patients, primary major, unipolar, non-psychotic depression)	BDI, HRSD	CT + treatment as usual > treatment as usual
Beck et al. (1985) (*n* = 33; primary major depressed out-patients)	BDI, HRSD	CT = CT + amitriptyline

+, combined treatment; >, more effective than; = equivalent efficacy; BDI, Beck Depression Inventory (Beck et al. 1961); HRSD = Hamilton Rating Scale for Depression (Hamilton 1960); Com, combination of CT and antidepressant medication; ADM, antidepressant medication

their own to be of equivalent efficacy (Blackburn et al. 1981, in the case of hospital out-patients; Murphy et al. 1984). The combination of the two treatments has been shown to be equivalent to either treatment on its own (Murphy et al. 1984) or superior to either treatment on its own (Blackburn et al. 1981, in the case of hospital out-patients). Other studies have shown the combined treatment to be equivalent to CT alone (Beck et al. 1979; Rush and Watkins 1981; Beck et al. 1985), while Teasdale et al. (1984) found the combination of CT with treatment as usual to be superior to treatment as usual in general-practice patients.

Thus, the general conclusions from these studies are that CT is never less effective than antidepressant medication in the treatment of ambulatory patients with a diagnosis of major unipolar depression, non-psychotic subtype, and that the combination of the two treatments may or may not be an advantage.

Detailed Characteristics

The first comparative study of CT and pharmacotherapy by Rush et al. (1977) was criticised on several counts: medication was tapered off before outcome evaluation at 12 weeks, contrary to usual clinical practice; patients with a prior history of poor response to an adequate trial of tricyclic antidepressant were excluded; clinical ratings were not done by assessors blind to the treatment modality because they could detect side effects in patients on medication; the time spent with therapists varied in the two treatment modalities, so that an attention effect could not be ruled out; and finally the groups consisted predominantly of upper-middle class private patients. These issues have been addressed in part in later studies.

All the post-1977 studies from Table 1 (except possibly Rush and Watkins 1981, who do not specify when medication was stopped) reported final assessment at the end of treatment when patients were still on a full dose of medication. Thus, although Rush et al. (1977) may have given an unfair advantage to CT by stopping medication too early in their drug group, their results are not untypical relative to studies where this particular bias did not operate.

None of the other studies quoted excluded patients with a history of non-response to tricyclic antidepressants. In fact, Blackburn et al. (1981) tried to potentiate the likelihood of drug response by allowing prescribing psychiatrists and general practitioners to choose the medication best suited to the individual patient, taking into consideration past history and presenting symptoms, as long as adequate dosages were adhered to. Most of their patients, however, were prescribed amitriptyline or clomipramine. Rush and Watkins (1981) followed the same procedure, and Teasdale et al. (1984) also left the choice of medication to the discretion of the general practitioner.

Psychotherapy trials cannot, of course, be double-blind, as required in drug trials, but even single-blindness has proved quite problematical, as first noted by Rush et al. (1977). Only two of the studies listed in Table 1 have dealt adequately with this problem. Murphy et al. (1984) included a comparison group of CT and placebo in which the placebo tablets looked identical to the tricyclic antidepressant tablets and contained 0.05 mg atropine sulfate and 5 mg phenobarbital sodium to control for sedative and anticholinergic effects. Thus, although no special efforts were made to keep the independent assessors blind to treatment conditions, they were blind as to tricyclic antidepressant versus placebo in the combined-treatment conditions. The design of Teasdale et al. (1984) ensured that assessors remained blind to the treatment modalities because patients in both treatment groups were as likely to be receiving drugs. All other studies took at least minimal caution to avoid bias, in that the clinical assessors were independent, that is, not involved in the treatment itself; nevertheless bias cannot be ruled out. The elegant solution of Murphy et al. (1984) is, however, not perfect because it could not be applied to a straight comparison between drugs and CT, and in a comparison of combined CT and medication with combined CT and active placebo the latter treatment modality would not be representative of treatment with CT alone (Hollon and de Rubeis 1981; Shapiro and Morris 1978).

The attention effect or lack of specificity of CT has bedevilled the interpretation of comparative trials of CT and drugs. The argument is that, because patients treated with CT spend more time with their therapists, usually by a factor of 3 or 4, and invest more personal effort in their therapy, the therapeutic effect could be largely due to this non-specific factor. Typically, patients in the studies quoted in Table 1, have received 20 h of therapy, whereas drug patients see their therapists for 20 min every week for 12 weeks (Rush et al. 1977; Murphy et al. 1984) or for 20 min every 2 or 3 weeks (Blackburn et al. 1981). Williams (1984) stated that "despite the fact that few clinicians would wish to argue that therapist time alone is of therapeutic benefit for depressed patients, a design which does not control this variable ... is clearly deficient, whatever other strengths it may have." Pharmacotherapy and CT trials cannot adequately deal with this question. However, previous psychodynamically or insight-oriented psychotherapy studies (Whitehead 1979) with large groups of patients have shown no appreciable impact on depression, the main examples being the three National Institute of Mental Health collaborative studies (Covi et al. 1974; Klerman et al. 1974; Friedman 1975). The next section in this chapter will examine this issue further in comparative studies of CT and other psychological treatments.

The question raised by the Rush et al. (1977) study about the applicability of CT to less highly educated patients has been answered positively by later studies. Blackburn et al. (1981) found that although their general-practice patients were of significantly lower socio-economic level than the hospital out-patients, response to cognitive therapy was similar. Murphy et al. (1984) described their samples of hospital out-patients as of predominantly blue-collar socio-economic status, and the samples of Teasdale et al. (1984) were typically of socio-economic class III (non-professional, white-collar status).

Although all patients treated in these studies satisfied the same diagnostic criteria, the pattern of symptoms can differ in terms of the presence of endogenous symptoms (Spitzer et al. 1978). Blackburn et al. (1981) reported that there was no difference in the responses of patients with endogenous and non-endogenous symptoms to CT, drugs or the combined treatment. Most patients of Teasdale et al. (1984) had endogenous symptoms and Kovacs et al. (1981) also found that an "endogenomorphic" pattern of symptoms did not predict a worse outcome with CT. However, all patients studied so far have been non-psychotic, that is, without delusions and hallucinations, and no studies have yet been published for outcome in patients with bipolar depression. Although Rush et al. (1982) found that at the end of treatment CT resulted in significantly greater improvements in hopelessness and self-esteem than imipramine, Simons et al. (1984) found nearly identical improvement in cognitive measures at the end of treatment in their CT and pharmacotherapy groups. They concluded that their finding "has serious implications for the assumption that there is something unique about the cognitive change effected by cognitive therapy interventions. Cognitive processes do change, but these findings indicate it is more directly associated with clinical improvement than with a course of cognitive therapy." Blackburn and Bishop (1983) found essentially the same results, changes in views of the self, the world and the future being in parallel with the relative degree of improvement with CT, antidepressants or combined treatment. Only Rush et al. (1981) have so far reported on the order of change of different symptoms with cognitive therapy and pharmacotherapy using cross-lagged panel analyses. The results indicated that during CT improvements in hopelessness, views of self and mood generally preceded changes in vegetative and motivational symptoms, while no consistent pattern of change over time was observed during pharmacotherapy.

Finally, the combination of pharmacotherapy and CT has not been shown to be detrimental in any study, but results have been equivocal as to its advantage over either treatment alone. Rush and Watkins (1981), Murphy et al. (1984) and Beck et al. (1979, 1985) found no advantage in the combination. On the other hand, Blackburn et al. (1981) found the combined treatment superior to either treatment on its own in hospital out-patients, but in general-practice patients the combined treatment was equivalent to CT alone, both being superior to pharmacotherapy alone. Teasdale et al. (1984) also found that the combination of CT with treatment as asual in a general-practice setting was superior to treatment as usual at the end of the treatment period. The study of Murphy et al. is by far the best controlled one, as plasma levels of nortriptyline were monitored throughout the trial. Blackburn et al. (1981) expressed some doubt that their general-practice patients complied with their prescribed drug regimen, in view of the particularly poor response to drugs in this group (one out of seven). In a recent survey of 17 studies of combined psychotherapy and pharmacotherapy in the treatment of unipolar, non-psychotic affective disorders, Conte et al. (1986) concluded that the combined active treatments (drugs plus psychotherapy of various types) were considerably more effective than placebo, but only slightly superior to either treatment alone or to either treatment combined with a placebo.

Cognitive Therapy and Other Psychological Treatments

General Characteristics

Comparisons of the efficacy of CT and psychological treatments control not only for the time spent with the therapist (attention effect) but also for the non-specific effects of structure, credibility, effort invested and quality of relationship with the therapist. Table 2 lists the studies which have compared CT with other types of psychological treatments. Unfortunately, these studies are not up to the same methodological standard as the studies described above on three counts: the subjects were self-referred students or media-recruited depressed individuals who may differ considerably from clinic patients; the numbers involved were small; and the type of CT given, although derived from the same model, was somewhat different from the Beck et al. (1979) package adhered to in the pharmacotherapy trials.

Table 2. Comparisons of cognitive therapy (CT) with other psychological treatments

Study	Measures	Outcome
Shaw (1977) (n = 32; self-referred students)	BDI, HRSD	CT > BT = non-directive therapy > waiting list
Taylor and Marshall (1977) (n = 28 recruited depressed students)	BDI, VAS, D30	CT + BT > CT = BT > waiting lust
Zeiss et al. (1979) (n = 44; media-recruited depressed individuals)	MMPI-D	CT = social skills training = increasing pleasant activities > waiting list
Wilson et al. (1983) (n = 25; media-recruited depressed individuals)	BDI, HRSD, PFS	CT = BT > waiting list

BT, Behaviour therapy; VAS, visual analogue scale (Aitken 1969); D30 (Dempsey, 1964); PFS, Personal Feeling Scale (Weissman et al. 1960); HRSD, Hamilton Rating Scale for Depression; BDI, Beck Depression Inventory; MMPI-D, Minnesota Multiphasic Personality Inventory, Depression Scale; +, combined treatment; >, more effective than; =, equivalent efficacy

Detailed Characteristics

Shaw (1977) compared group treatments in a sample of students who had approached their university counselling centre for help with depression (n = 32). They had to score a minimum of 18 on the BDI and to have experienced depression for at least 3 weeks. They were randomly allocated to one of four groups: CT; behaviour therapy, using Lewinsohn's approach (Lewinsohn 1974); an attention/assessment, non-directive control condition; and a waiting-list control group. Treatments consisted of two 2-h sessions per week for 4 weeks. Assessments were conducted by blind assessors on the HRSD and self-ratings on the BDI were obtained. The results indicated that CT was significantly more effective than all other treatment modalities on both outcome measures, but at 1-month follow-up there was no longer a significant difference between the CT and the behaviour therapy group. Taylor and Marshall (1977) recruited by advertisement 28 depressed students on the university campus who had a BDI score of at least 12 and had been depressed for at least 2 weeks. Patients were given one of four forms of treatment: CT, behaviour therapy, combined cognitive and behaviour therapy and waiting-list control. The results indicated that the three treatment groups improved significantly more than the waiting-list controls on all dependent measures: BDI, a visual analogue scale (Aitken 1969), Dempsey D-30 (Dempsey 1964) and measures of self-acceptance and self-esteem. The CT group did not differ from the behaviour therapy group, but the combined treatment was more effective than either treatment alone.

Zeiss et al. (1979) assigned 44 media-recruited individuals, diagnosed as depressed according to the Minnesota Multiphasic Personality Inventory (MMPI) profile and score level and on a standard interview (Grinker et al. 1961), to CT, social skills training, increase in pleasant activities and a waiting-list control. They found no significant difference among active treatment groups on a vast array of dependent measures, including MMPI-D (depression) score. All active-treatment groups improved significantly more than the waiting-list controls. The version of CT used in this study, however, appears to differ considerably from that of Beck et al. (1979).

Wilson et al. (1983) allocated 25 media-recruited individuals, diagnosed on history, duration of episode and BDI scores (≥ 17), to behaviour therapy, CT and a waiting-list control. Behaviour therapy was based on Lewinsohn's conceptualization of depression, and the therapists ensured that no discussion of cognitive factors was included. CT followed Beck's conceptualization of depression, but the authors did not apply the full CT programme as described by Beck et al. (1979), in that they excluded the behavioural task assignments which are an important part of the package. Outcome results indicated that both active-treatment groups, in comparison to the waiting-list controls , showed greater improvement on the BDI, the HRSD and the rating of worst mood on the Personal Feeling Scale (Weissman et al. 1960), but there were no significant differences between the behavioural and cognitive treatments on any measure. At 5-month follow-up improvement was maintained on both treatments, again with no significant differences.

These comparisons of the relative efficacy of CT and behaviour therapy or non-directive supportive psychotherapy indicate that CT is equal or superior to behaviour therapy and always superior to no treatment. Thus, the studies discussed in this section do not provide evidence that the specific components of CT are responsible for the effectiveness of CT. It may be that, as Zeiss et al. (1979) and Kornblith et al. (1983) concluded, successful psychological treatments have three important non-specific characteristics in common: (a) they provide the therapist and the patient with a clear rationale which includes a vocabulary for defining problems and for describing mechanisms of change; (b) they are highly structured and thus provide clear plans for progress through treatment; and (c) they provide feed-back and support so that changes can be assessed realistically and become reinforcing.

However, the studies which are reviewed in this section do not provide a satisfactory test of these proposals because of their shortcomings, as specified earlier. These conclusions must, therefore, be considered as hypotheses which need further testing in well-controlled process studies.

Cognitive Therapy with the Elderly

The efficacy of CT with elderly patients has also been tested. Emery (1981) described CT with elderly patients as not different in structure from that with younger patients, although the length of sessions and the type of behavioural tasks must be tailored to the abilities and needs of the elderly. There are typical attitudes relating to old age, which become the focus of therapy. These are negative assumptions about age-related norms, dysfunctional beliefs as to own ability and capacities, unrealistic expectations of relatives and children and exaggeration of the invalidating effect of minor age-related ailments.

Gallagher and Thomson (1982) compared individual CT with behaviour therapy and brief psychodynamic psychotherapy in three groups of elderly patients. The results on the HRSD indicated that after 12 weeks of treatment all three treatments were equally effective, but improvement during the 1-year follow-up was maintained more effectively with CT and behaviour therapy than with psychodynamic psychotherapy. There was no difference between CT and behaviour therapy. Steuer et al. (1984) compared group CT with psychodynamic group therapy in four groups of elderly patients. The treatment lasted 9 months, and there was no difference between groups at the end of treatment on observer rating scales. However, on the BDI, groups receiving CT did significantly better.

Behaviour Therapy with Cognitive Components

As mentioned in the introductory section, the term "cognitive behaviour therapy" is used here to differentiate treatment methodologies which are explicitly different from the cognitive therapy of Beck et al. (1979), while including nonetheless a strong cognitive component. Table 3 summarises these comparative studies.

None of these studies, except those of McLean and Hakstian (1979) and Dunn (1979), used clinic patients. Shipley and Fazio (1973) describe their cognitive-behavioural approach as functional problem solving; this seems to consist of some of Beck's cognitive techniques and behavioural techniques such as assertiveness training. They obtained a significantly greater effect with CBT than with non-specific supportive psychotherapy. McLean and Hakstian (1979) in a well-controlled study assigned 178 patients satisfying the criteria of Feighner et al. (1972) for primary depression to four treatment groups: CBT, psychodynamic psychotherapy, relaxation training and drug therapy (150 mg amitriptyline per day). The targets of therapy in the behavioural-cognitive approach included cognitive self-control, level of activity, social interaction, assertiveness, decision making and problem solving. A multitude of dependent measures were used; on depression scales alone, the CBT group did better than all other groups, and the psychodynamic psychotherapy group did worst. Surprisingly, the drug group did not improve more than the relaxation group; the authors interpreted the relative success of relaxation training as the effect of non-specific factors in therapy.

The four studies from Rehm's group have attempted to tackle the question of which aspects of therapy are most effective by breaking down their self-control therapy into its three main components: self-monitoring, self-evaluation and self-reinforcement. Having demonstrated in the first two studies – Fuchs and Rehm (1977) and Rehm et al. (1979) – that self-control was more effective than group psychotherapy, assertiveness training or waiting-list control, they set themselves the task of identifying the active component in the self-control package by disassembling the programme. Two studies – Rehm et al. (1981) and Kornblith et al. (1983) – lead to the conclusion that all the components of self-control are equally effective for reducing depression as assessed by self-rating and clinicians' ratings. The improvements were equally maintained at 3-month follow-up. The

Table 3. Evidence of efficacy for cognitive-behavioural therapy (CBT)

Study	Measures	Results
Shipley and Fazio (1973) (*n* = 28; depressed undergraduates)	ZDS, MMPI-D	CBT > supportive psychotherapy
McLean and Hakstian (1979) (*n* = 178; depressed out-patients)	BDI	CBT > amitriptyline = relaxation training > insight therapy
Fuchs and Rehm (1977) (*n* = 36; media-recruited non-psychotics	BDI, MMPI-D	Self-control > group psychotherapy > waiting list
Rehm et al. (1979) (*n* = 25; media-recruited non-psychotic women)	BDI, MMPI-D	Self-control > assertive training
Rehm et al. (1981) (*n* = 56; media-recruited women, non-psychotic major affective disorder)	BDI, MMPI-D, HRS-D, RDS	Self-control = Self-monitoring = Self-monitoring + Self-evaluation = Self-monitoring + Self-reinforcement > waiting list
Kornblith et al. (1983) (*n* = 38; media-recruited women, non-psychotic major affective disorder)	BDI, MMPI-D, HRSD, global assessment scale	Self-control = Self-monitoring + Self-evaluation = Didactive principles of self-control minus behavioural assignments = psychodynamic group therapy
Dunn (1979) (*n* = 20; out-patients)	BDI, global observer measures of depression; count of non-depressive verbalisations	CBT + antidepressant > antidepressant + support

+, combined treatment; >, more effective than; =, equivalent efficacy; BDI, Beck Depression Inventory; HRSD, Hamilton Rating Scale for Depression; DACL, Depression Adjective Check List (Lubin 1967); MMPI-D, RDS; Raskin Depression Scale (Raskin et al. 1967); ZDS; Zung Depression Scale (Zung 1965)

exclusion of behavioural assignment did not make any difference to the efficacy of the programme.

The studies reviewed in this section tend to suffer from the same weaknesses as those discussed in the previous section, so that any conclusions drawn from them must be tentative. However, the McLean and Hakstian (1979) treatment trial stands out as the best controlled study in terms of number of patients per treatment cell, the use of diagnostic criteria, well-defined treatment modalities and outcome measures which included self-ratings and behavioural items. The three psychological treatment methods were made to seem credible to the patient and took equivalent therapist time. Moreover, one of the control treatments, relaxation, controlled for the use of home assignments in CBT by also including homework. The superiority of CBT over psychodynamically oriented psychotherapy and relaxation provides evidence of a specific effect for a therapy which includes a strong cognitive component; its superiority over amitriptyline supports results obtained in some CT studies (Rush et al. 1977) and confirms the effectiveness of cognqive restructuring in depression.

Follow-up Studies

The Problem of Relapse in Depression

The implicit promise of CT is that it may have a long-term or prophylactic effect on depression. In view of the recurring nature of depressive illness (Boyd and Weissman 1982) any treatment which could be shown to reduce the recurrence of the disorder, as well as effectively treating the acute condition, would be of indisputable importance. The prevention of relapse in depressive illness through the use of prophylactic medication has been widely studied, usually with pessimistic outcomes. Mindham et al. (1973) reported that 22% of patients on antidepressant medication had suffered a relapse at 6 months, compared with 59% of patients on placebo. Keller et al. (1982), in a naturalistic follow-up of 75 patients who had recovered from a major depressive disorder, found that the rate of relapse was higher in the first 8 weeks (20%) of the risk period (that is, after the patients had remained well for 8 weeks after recovery), declining to 4% by the 40th week of the risk period. Using life-table analysis (Fleiss et al. 1976) they established a cumulative rate of 38% relapse at 40 weeks. Since theirs was a naturalistic study, some patients would have been on medication and some not. Glen et al. (1984), in the multicentre MRC controlled trial of maintenance medication comparing amitriptyline with lithium, reported relapse rates of 45%, 59% and 70% on medication at 1, 2 and 3 years, respectively, for patients who had a history of more than one episode of depression in the 5 years prior to the index episode. For patients with a history of only one episode of depression within 5 years prior to the index episode there was a placebo group (only nine patients) and the relapse rates were 67%, 78% and 89% for 1, 2 and 3 years, respectively, while the corresponding rates on medication (amitriptyline or lithium) were 44%, 49% and 49%. Prien et al. (1973), in a 2-year follow-up study of the relative prophylactic efficacy of lithium and imipramine, found a 92% relapse rate in their placebo group.

Thus, although prophylactic medication reduces relapse rates, recurring morbidity remains disappointingly high. CT aims to treat depression not only by modifying the negative thoughts which maintain depressed affect and behaviour but also by modifying the basic attitudes and assumptions which are considered to be depressogenic. It would, therefore, lead to the prediction that patients who are successfully treated with CT not only learn new skills which they can apply to deal with future mood disturbances but also become less vulnerable to depression because they have developed more adaptive schemata. Has this optimistic expectation been borne out?

Long-term Effects of Cognitive Therapy and Pharmacotherapy

There are four published follow-up studies to date which deal with the long-term effects of CT and pharmacotherapy. These are summarised in Table 4. All four studies are naturalistic, in that patients were free to re-enter any treatment of their choice during the follow-up period. The one partial exception is the study by Blackburn et al. (1986), in which for the first 6 months of follow-up patients were maintained on the treatment they had received during the acute phase of treatment, that is, patients treated with antidepressant medication continued on medication, sometimes in reduced dosages; patients who had been treated with CT received booster sessions of CT every 6 weeks; and patients who had received the combined treatment continued taking medication and in addition, received 6-weekly booster sessions of CT.

Kovacs et al. (1981) reported on the clinical status after 1 year of the patients treated in the Rush et al. (1977) outcome study. According to self-ratings on the BDI and the Hopelessness Scale (HS; Beck et al. 1974), the 18 patients who completed CT and the 17 who completed pharmacotherapy maintained at 12 months the improvement they had shown at the end of treatment. However, patients treated with CT reported lower levels of depression on the BDI ($p < .03$) and less hopelessness on the HS ($p < .02$). The presence of endogenous symptoms of depression at pre-treatment assessment was not related to outcome. Looking at the clinical course over the whole year in terms of scores ≥ 16 on the monthly BDI, they found that twice as many patients from the drug group (35%) had been chronically symptomatic as compared with the CT group (17%), and, conversely, 56% in the CT group were in continuous remission, as compared with 35% in the drug group. However, the between-group differences were not statistically significant.

Beck et al. (1985) also found that both CT patients ($n = 13$) and patients who received the combination of CT and amitriptyline ($n = 11$) did not show any significant changes in BDI and HRSD scores at 6 and 12 months. Endogeneity at entry into treatment did not affect outcome at the two follow-up points. One-way analysis of covariance, using baseline BDI and HRSD scores as covariates, showed

Table 4. Naturalistic follow-up studies of cognitive therapy (CT) versus antidepressant medication (ADM)

Study	Period	Measures	Results
Kovacs et al. (1981)	1 year	BDI, HS	CT > ADM
Beck et al. (1985)	1 year	BDI, HS	CT = CT + ADM
Simons et al. (1986)	1 year	relapses	CT & CT + P > ADM & CT + ADM CT & CT + P & CT + ADM > ADM
Blackburn et al. (1986)	2 years	relapses	CT = CT + ADM > ADM

BDI, Beck Depression Inventory; HS, Hopelessness Scale ZBeck et al. 1974); relapses are defined in terms of BDI ≥ 16 or restart of treatment; &, collapsed treatment cells; +, combined treatment; >, more effective than; = , equivalent efficacy

no group differences on either measure. When they examined clinical status over the year in terms of BDI scores, they found that at 6 months 62% of the CT group were markedly improved (BDI scores of 0–9), 15% partially improved (scores of 10–15) and 23% not improved (scores $\geq$ 16). In comparison, 40% of the combined-treatment group were markedly improved, 20% partially improved and 40% not improved. At 12 months the combined-treatment group appeared to be doing better (82% markedly improved, 9% partially improved and 9% not improved) than the CT group (58% markedly improved, none partially improved and 42% not improved). However, group differences did not reach significance.

The group included in the outcome study by Murphy et al. (1984) were followed up for 1 year (Simons et al. 1986). One interesting finding here was that the large difference between responders and non-responders at termination of treatment had disappeared at 1 year, primarily because non-responders had continued to improve. Most of the 26 non-responders, 16 in all, had re-entered some sort of treatment, while five others who were symptomatic did not. Using the same criterion as in the two studies mentioned above (BDI score $\geq$ 16 or re-start of treatment), they found the following percentages of relapse in the various treatment groups at the end of 1 year: 20% in the CT group, 66% in the medication group, 18% in the CT plus placebo group and 43% in the CT plus medication group. These differences were not significant. However, when they collapsed their treatment cells into two cells based on whether the patients had received medication (drug alone or drug plus CT) or had not (CT or CT plus placebo), the proportion of relapses was significantly different (p = 0.2): 4/21 in the CT group and 12/23 in the drug group. When they grouped the patients according to whether they had received CT or not, 28% of patients from the collapsed groups (CT, CT plus placebo or CT plus drugs) relapsed as compared to 66% of the patients who had received drugs alone; this difference was also significant (p = .04). They concluded, therefore, that their results "suggest that patients who have responded to CT may be protected against the reappearance of depressive symptoms during one year following treatment."

In the study of Blackburn et al. (1986) patients who had responded to treatment, as reported by Blackburn et al. (1981), were assessed at 6, 12, 18 and 24 months after the end of treatment. As pointed out above, for the first 6 months the patients were on maintenance treatment, thus conforming to traditional medical practice. At 6 months relapse was defined as scores greater than 9 on the BDI and greater than 8 on the HRSD or re-entry into treatment, and thereafter recurrence of depression was defined by physicians' notes indicating the presence of depressive symptoms necessitating further prescription of antidepressant medication, re-entry into psychotherapy and/or admission to hospital.

There were no differences between the three treatment groups (CT, antidepressant medication, CT plus medication) at 6 months on the BDI, HRSD and HS, all mean scores being well within normal limits. However, Fisher's exact probability tests showed that at 6 months more patients in the medication group (3/10) had relapsed than in the combined treatment group (0/16) (p = .05). When the two groups who had received CT were combined, the proportion of relapses (1/31) was lower than the proportion in the medication group (p = .04). At 12,

18 and 24 months the trend was invariably for a higher proportion of relapses in the medication group than in the two CT groups, but the differences did not reach significance.

When the results were analysed in terms of the clinical status of each patient over the whole 2-year period, that is, in terms of the number of patients who had had a recurrence of illness at any point during that time, significantly different rates of relapse were obtained ($p < .02$). Of 13 CT patients 10 remained well (23% relapse), of the 9 patients in the medication group 2 remained well (78%), and of the 14 patients in the combined-treatment group 11 remained well (21% relapse). This analysis included both hospital and general-practice patients. The same results were obtained when hospital out-patients were examined separately.

The relapse rate at 6 months in the antidepressant medication group in this study is equivalent to that reported in drug maintenance studies over the same period (e.g. Mindham et al. 1973). The relapse rate at 2 years in the medication group (78%) is equal to that reported by Glen et al. (1984) for their placebo group but lower than that of 92% reported by Prien et al. (1973). The two CT groups, on the other hand, suffered less recurrence of illness than those on maintenance medication over the same period (59%, Glen et al. 1984).

There is, therefore, tentative evidence from the four studies described here that CT offers long-term protection against recurrence of depression. It is possible that this is due, as cognitive theories of depression would predict, to a weakening of depressogenic attitudes and to the application of coping skills learned during therapy. However, better controlled studies are needed to test the robustness and generalisability of these results. The numbers studied have been small so far, the methodology has been naturalistic and frequent follow-ups, including face-to-face interviews, are lacking.

Predictive Factors of Response

Very little is known to date about which depressed patients would benefit most from CT and which would not benefit. All the studies reviewed in this chapter have included only mildly to moderately depressed subjects, with minor or major depression, unipolar and non-psychotic subtype. There is, therefore, no indication that bipolar or psychotic depression would respond to CT. There is, however, evidence that the presence of an endogenous pattern of symptoms does not preclude response to CT (Kovacs et al. 1981; Blackburn et al. 1981; Beck et al. 1985).

The finding of Blackburn et al. (1981) of a different response pattern in general-practice patients and hospital patients leads to some practical inferences. Although both groups of patients satisfied the same diagnostic criteria and did not differ in levels of depression as assessed by the BDI and the HRSD, in the general-practice patients the combination of antidepressant medication and CT was not superior to CT alone, both being superior to medication alone. On the other hand, in hospital patients the combination of both treatments was superior to either treatment alone. There were some important differences between the two groups of patients in terms of both demographic variables and clinical features (Blackburn and Bishop 1981; Blackburn 1984). The general-practice patients were younger, less highly educated and from lower socio-economic groups than the hospital patients. A considerably higher proportion of general-practice patients (46%) had lost a spouse in comparison with hospital patients (16%). With regard to clinical features the general-practice patients were on the whole less severely ill (total score on the Present State examination, Wing et al. 1974). They had suffered less previous depressive episodes; their current episode of illness was of shorter duration; fewer had been previously hospitalised for a psychiatric illness; fewer had been previously treated with antidepressant medication; and fewer reported suicidal ideation or previous suicidal attempts. Symptoms which were endorsed significantly less often by general-practice patients were loss of libido, loss of energy, panic attacks, situational anxiety, social anxiety and loss of self-esteem. General-practice patients were also significantly less hopeless and less outwardly irritable.

Thus, the conclusion seems to be that for more chronic and severe depressions the combination of antidepressant medication and CT is indicated. However, such a typological approach to the understanding of differential response to treatment does not reveal a great deal about detailed characteristics of responders and non-responders. A stepwise multiple regression analysis was performed on both samples of patients combined, using percentage change in BDI score from pretreatment to end of treatment as the dependent variable. For response to combined treatment, two significant predictors emerged: long duration of illness was a negative predictor and higher educational level a positive predictor. For response to CT long duration of illness was again a significant negative predictor of response and a cognitive variable, negative view of the world or environment, was a positive predictor. The two significant predictors of response to pharmacotherapy were, as would be expected, being a hospital as opposed to a general-practice patient and the cognitive factor of high discrepancy between view of self and ideal self (poor self-esteem), which was a negative predictor. Fennel and Teasdale (1982), in a report on the effectiveness of CT in five chronic, drug refractory patients, obtained very modest results, which they attributed mainly to the chronicity and severity of the depression.

Simons et al. (1985) also applied stepwise multiple regression to the data obtained from the outcome study by Murphy et al. (1984) and used end-point BDI score as the dependent variable. They compared response to CT and to nortriptyline. Initial BDI scores contributed significantly to end-point BDI scores. After the effects of the initial BDI score was removed, they found that a cognitive variable termed 'learned resourcefulness', as measured by the self-control schedule (Rosenbaum 1980), predicted greater improvement with CT. Low learned resourcefulness tended to predict good response to pharmacotherapy ($p = .08$).

In short, both illness characteristics and the presence of certain cognitive factors appear to predict differential response to CT and to pharmacotherapy, but clearly a great deal more research is needed in this area.

Concluding Comments

The strengths and weaknesses in the research relating to the relative efficacy of CT in depression have been reviewed here. There are unpublished studies which are nearing completion or awaiting publication which will hopefully answer some of the pending questions which have been highlighted. However, a great deal has been learned since the pessimistic appraisal by Ledwidge (1978) and the various unanswered questions raised by Whitehead (1979). The most cogent practical questions which need further elucidation are the following:

1. How does a clinician decide whom to refer for CT? Goldberg (1982) concluded that in view of the complexity of CT and the scarcity of cognitive therapists pharmacotherapy will remain the treatment of choice, except in few instances. More predictive research is needed to help the clinician make a rational choice as to who would benefit from CT. If the promising results of pilot research in the prevention of relapse become established, CT will then be more economically viable and will, probably rightly, be demanded by more patients.
2. Can the training of cognitive therapists be made simpler? This is an aspect which has not as yet received any attention. It is possible that certain aspects of the treatment procedures have more impact than others and are more essential than others. If this is so, many more practitioners could be taught the more powerful techniques, which they may then be able to incorporate into their daily clinical practice without practising formal CT as such.
3. How does CT work? This question is linked to the previous one, but more detailed process research is needed before we can understand the mode of action of CT. It is possible that the key factor in the effectiveness of CT is not cognitive or behavioural change, but an increase in self-efficacy (Bandura 1977). More understanding of the process of change would certainly lead to better treatment delivery and possibly to a simpler version of CT.
4. Finally, the application of CT to different groups of depressed patients, in particular to patients with bipolar depression and severely depressed in-patients, needs investigating in order to set the limits of applicability on the basis of empirical findings.

References

Aitken RCB (1969) Measurement of feeling using visual analogue scales. Proc R Soc Med 62:989–993

Bandura A (1977) Self-efficacy: toward a unifying theory of behavioural change. Psychol Rev 84:191–215

Beck AT (1961) A systematic investigation of depression. Compr Psychiatry 2:163–170

Beck AT (1967) Depression: clinical, experimental and theoretical aspects. Harper and Row, New York

Beck AT, Ward CH, Mendelson M, Mock JE, Erbaugh JK (1961) An inventory for measuring depression. Arch Gen Psychiatry 4:561–571

Beck AT, Weissman A, Lester D, Trexler L (1974) The measurement of pessimism: the hopelessness scale. J Consult Clin Psychol 42:861–865

Beck AT, Rush AJ, Shaw BF, Emery G (1979) Cognitive therapy of depression: a treatment manual. Guilford, New York

Beck AT, Hollon SD, Young JE, Bedrosian RC, Budenz D (1985) Treatment of depression with cognitive therapy and amitriptyline. Arch Gen Psychiatry 42:142–148
Blackburn IM (1984) Setting relevant patient differences: a problem in Phase IV research. Pharmacopsychiatry 17:143–147
Blackburn IM, Bishop S (1981) Is there an alternative to drugs in the treatment of depressed ambulatory patients? Behav Psychother 9:96–104
Blackburn IM, Bishop S (1983) Changes in cognition with pharmacotherapy and cognitive therapy. Br J Psychiatry 143:609–617
Blackburn IM, Bishop S, Glen AIM, Whalley LJ, Christie JE (1981) The efficacy of cognitive therapy in depression: a treatment trial using cognitive therapy and pharmacotherapy, each alone and in combination. Br J Psychiatry 139:181–189
Blackburn IM, Eunson KM, Bishop S (1986) A two-year naturalistic follow-up of depressed patients treated with cognitive therapy, pharmacotherapy and a combination of both. J Affective Disord 10:67–75
Boyd JH, Weissman MM (1982) Epidemiology. In: Paykel ES (ed) Handbook of affective disorders. Guilford, New York, pp 110–125
Conte HR, Plutchik R, Wild KV, Karasu TB (1986) Combined psychotherapy and pharmacotherapy for depression. A systematic analysis of the evidence. Arch Gen Psychiatry 43:471–479
Covi L, Lipman RS, Derogatis LR, Smith JE, Pattison JH (1974) Drugs and group psychotherapy in neurotic depression. Am J Psychiatry 131:191–198
Dempsey P (1964) An undimensional depression scale for the MMPI. J Consult Psychol 28:364–370
Dunn RJ (1979) Cognitive modification with depression-prone psychiatric patients. Cogn Ther Res 3:307–317
Ellis A (1962) Reason and emotion in psychotherapy. Lyle Stuart, New York
Ellis A (1980) Rational-emotive therapy and cognitive behavior therapy: similarities and differences. Cogn Ther Res 4:325–340
Emery G (1981) Cognitive therapy with the elderly. In: Emery G, Mollon SD, Bedrosian SD (eds) New directions in cognitive therapy. Guilford, New York, pp 84–89
Emery G, Fox S (1981) Cognitive therapy of alcohol dependency. In: Emery G, Hollon SD, Bedrosian RC (eds) New directions in cognitive therapy. Guilford, New York, pp. 181–200
Emery G, Hollon SD, Bedrosian RC (eds) (1981) New directions in cognitive therapy. A casebook. Guilford, New York
Feighner JP, Robins E, Guze SB, Woodruff RW, Winokur G, Munoz R (1972) Diagnostic criteria for use in psychiatric research. Arch Gen Psychiatry 26:57–63
Fennel MJV, Teasdale JD (1982) Cognitive therapy with chronic, drug-refractory depressed outpatients: a note of caution. Cogn Ther Res 6:455–459
Fleiss JL, Dunner DL, Stallone F, Fieve RR (1976) The life table: a method for analysing longitudinal studies. Arch Gen Psychiatry 33:107–112
Foreyt JP, Rathjen DP (eds) (1978) Cognitive behaviour therapy: research and application. Plenum, New York
Friedman A (1975) Interaction of drug therapy with marital therapy in depressed patients. Arch Gen Psychiatry 32:619–637
Fuchs CZ, Rehm LP (1977) A self-control behaviour therapy program for depression. J Consult Clin Psychol 45:206–215
Gallagher DE, Thompson LW (1982) Treatment of major depressive affective disorder in older adult outpatients with brief psychotherapies. Psychother Theor Res Pract 19:482–490
Glen AIM, Johnson AL, Shepherd M (1984) Continuation therapy with lithium and amitriptyline in unipolar depressive illness: a randomised double-blind controlled trial. Psychol Med 14:37–50
Goldberg D (1982) Cognitive therapy for depression. Br Med J 284:143–144
Grinker RR, Miller J, Sabshin M, Nunn J, Nunnally JD (1961) The phenomena of depression. Hoeber, New York
Hamilton M (1960) A rating scale for depression. J Neurol Neurosurg Psychiatry 23:59–61
Hollon SD, de Rubeis RJ (1981) Placebo-psychotherapy combinations: inappropriate representations of psychotherapy in drug-psychotherapy comparative trials. Psychol Bull 9:467–477
Holroyd KA, Andrasik F, Westbrook T (1977) Cognitive control of tension headache. Cogn Ther Res 1:121–134

Keller MB, Shapiro RW, Lavori PW, Wolfe N (1982) Relapse in major depressive disorder. Analysis with the life table. Arch Gen Psychiatry 39:911–915

Kendall PC, Hollon SD (1979) Cognitive-behavioural intervention: theory, research and procedures. Academic, New York

Klerman GL, Di Mascio A, Weissman MM, Prusoff BA, Paykil ES (1974) Treatment of depression by drugs and psychotherapy. Am J Psychiatry 131:186–191

Kornblith SJ, Rehm LP, O'Hara MW, Lamparski DM (1983) The contribution of self-reinforcement training and behavioural assignments to the efficacy of self-control therapy for depression. Cogn Ther Res 7:499–528

Kovacs M, Rush AJ, Beck AT, Hollon SD (1981) Depressed out-patients treated with cognitive therapy and pharmacotherapy. A one-year follow-up. Arch Gen Psychiatry 38:33–39

Ledwidge B (1978) Cognitive behavior modification: a step in the wrong direction? Psychol Bull 85:353–375

Lewinsohn PM (1974) Clinical and theoretical aspects of depression. In: Calhoun KS, Adams HE, Mitchell KM (eds) Innovative treatment methods in psychopathology. Wiley, Chicester, pp 63–120

Lubin B (1967) Manual for depression adjective check lists. Educational and Industrial Testing Service, San Diego

Mahoney MJ, Arnkoff DB (1978) Cognitive and self-control therapies. In: Garfield SL, Bergin AE (eds) Handbook of psychotherapy and behaviour change. 2nd edn. Wiley, New York, pp 689–722

McLean PD, Hakstian AR (1979) Clinical depression: comparative efficacy of out-patient treatments. J Consult Clin Psychol 47:818–836

Meichenbaum D, Asarnow J (1979) Cognitive-behavioural modification and metacognitive development: implications for the classroom. In: Kendall PC, Hollon SD (eds) Cognitive-behavioural intervention: theory, research and procedure. Academic, New York, pp 11–35

Mindham RHS, Howland C, Shepherd M (1973) An evaluation of continuation therapy with tricyclic antidepressants in depressive illness. Psychol Med 3:5–17

Murphy GE, Simons AD, Wetzel RD, Lustman PJ (1984) Cognitive therapy and pharmacotherapy, singly and together in the treatment of depression. Arch Gen Psychiatry 41:33–41

Novaco RW (1979) The cognitive regulation of anger and stress. In: Kendall PC, Hollon SD (eds) Cognitive-behavioural intervention: theory, research and procedure. Academic, New York, pp 241–285

Prien RF, Klett J, Caffey EM (1973) Lithium carbonate and imipramine in prevention of affective episodes. Arch Gen Psychiatry 29:420–425

Raskin A, Schulterbrandt J, Reatig N (1967) Factors of psychopathology in interview, ward behavior and self-report ratings of hospitalized depressives. J Consult Clin Psychol 31:270–278

Rehm LP (1977) A self-control model of depression. Behav Ther 8:787–804

Rehm LP, Fuchs CZ, Roth DM, Kornblith SJ, Romano JM (1979) A comparison of self-control and assertion skills treatment of depression. Behav Ther 10:429–442

Rehm LP, Kornblith SJ, O'Hara MW, Lamparski DM, Romano JM, Volkin J (1981) An evaluation of major components in a self-control behaviour therapy program for depression. Behav Modif 5:459–489

Rosenbaum M (1980) A schedule for assessing self-control behaviors: preliminary findings. Behav Ther 11:109–121

Rush AJ, Watkins JT (1981) Group versus individual cognitive therapy: a pilot study. Cogn Ther Res 5:95–103

Rush AJ, Beck AT, Kovacs M, Hollon SD (1977) Comparative efficacy of cognitive therapy versus pharmacotherapy in out-patient depression. Cogn Ther Res 1:17–37

Rush AJ, Kovacs M, Beck AT, Weissenburger J, Hollon SD (1981) Differential effects of cognitive therapy and pharmacotherapy on depressive symptoms. J Affective Disord 3:221–229

Rush AJ, Beck AT, Kovacs M, Weissenburger MA, Hollon SD (1982) Comparison of the effects of cognitive therapy and pharmacotherapy on hopelessness and self-concept. Am J Psychiatry 139:862–866

Shapiro AK, Morris LA (1978) Placebo effects in medical and psychological therapies. In: Garfield SL, Bergin AE (eds) Handbook of psychotherapy and behavior change: an empirical analysis, 2nd edn. Wiley, New York, pp 369–410

Shaw BF (1977) Comparison of cognitive therapy and behaviour therapy in the treatment of depression. J Consult Clin Psychol 45:543–551
Shipley CR, Fazio AF (1973) Pilot study of a treatment for psychological depression. J Abnorm Psychol 82:372–376
Simons AD, Garfield SL, Murphy GE (1984) The process of change in cognitive therapy and pharmacotherapy for depression. Changes in mood and cognition. Arch Gen Psychiatry 41:45–51
Simons AD, Lustman PJ, Wetzel RD, Murphy GE (1985) Predicting response to cognitive therapy of depression: the role of learned resourcefulness. Cogn Ther Res 9:79–89
Simons AD, Murphy GE, Levine JE, Wetzel RD (1986) Cognitive therapy and pharmacotherapy for depression. Sustained improvement over one year. Arch Gen Psychiatry 43:43–48
Spitzer RL, Endicott J, Robins E (1978) Research Diagnostic Criteria (RDC) for a selected group of functional disorders. 3rd edn. Psychiatric Institute, Biometrics Research, New York State
Steuer JL, Mintz J, Mammen CL, Hill MA, Jarvik LF, McCarley T, Motoike P, Rosen R (1984) Cognitive-behavioural and psychodynamic group psychotherapy in treatment of geriatric depression. J Consult Clin Psychol 52:180–189
Taylor FG, Marshall WL (1977) Experimental analysis of cognitive-behavioural therapy for depression. Cogn Ther Res 1:59–72
Teasdale JD, Fennell MJV, Hibbert GA, Amies PL (1984) Cognitive therapy for major depressive disorder in primary care. Br J Psychiatry 144:400–406
Turk DC, Genest M (1979) Regulation of pain: the application of cognitive and behavioural techniques for prevention and remediation. In: Kendall PC, Hollon SD (eds) Cognitive-behavioural intervention: theory, research and procedure. Academic, New York, pp 287–318
Weissman AE, Ricks DF, Tyl MM (1960) Characteristics and concomitants of mood fluctuations in college women. J Abnorm Psychol 60:117–126
Weissman MM (1979) The psychological treatment of depression. Evidence for the efficacy of psychotherapy alone, in comparison with and in combination with pharmacotherapy. Arch Gen Psychiatry 36:1261–1269
Whitehead A (1979) Psychological treatment of depression. Behav Res Ther 17:495–509
Williams JMG (1984) Cognitive-behaviour therapy for depression: problems and perspectives. Br J Psychiatry 145:254–262
Wilson PH, Goldin JC, Charbonneau-Powis M (1983) Comparative efficacy of behavioural and cognitive treatments of depression. Cog Ther Res 7: 111–124
Wing JK, Cooper JE, Sartorius N (1974) The description and classification of psychiatric symptoms. Cambridge University Press, Cambridge
Zeiss AM, Lewinsohn PM, Munoz RF (1979) Non-specific improvement effects in depression using interpersonal, cognitive and pleasant events focussed treatments. J Consult Clin Psychol 47:427–439
Zung WW (1965) A self-rating depression scale. Arch Gen Psychiatry 12:63–70

Cognitive Therapy of Phobias

J. COTTRAUX and E. MOLLARD

Introduction

The cognitive approach to phobias (Beck and Emery 1985) emphasizes the mediating role of thought patterns and mental images that allow individual adaptation to internal and external stimuli. Cognitions themselves are not considered a cause of anxiety and avoidance behavior but represent an intervening information-processing system whose dysfunction may result from the interaction of an innate biological vulnerability with a faulty cognitive learning history. Therapeutic reduction of fear and avoidance is thought to result from the modification of maladaptive conscious or unconscious thought patterns.

Conditioning and Cognitive Models of Phobias

Conditioning models have been proposed since the late 1950s to explain the acquisition and maintainance of phobic behavior and to develop counterconditioning treatment (Wolpe 1975). Behavioral principles applied to phobias led to their succesful management by prolonged exposure in imagination and/or in vivo, presented under various labels and in numerous treatment packages (Marks 1981). The rationale for exposure in vivo is both the habituation of psychophysiological responses related to fear and the elimination of avoidance behavior. The patient unlearns phobic avoidance when he or she experiences the decline of anxiety and the lack of negative consequences resulting from prolonged and repeated confrontations with the phobic stimulus. Breger and McGaugh (1974) criticized behavior therapy for its emphasis on peripheral responses and its assumption that concepts taken from Pavlovian and operant conditioning can be utilized as explanatory principles. Breger and McGaugh reformulated learning theories with emphasis on central cognitive processes of acquisition and storage of information. However, conditioning explanations and cognitive theories are not mutually exclusive: exposure in imagination or in vivo to feared stimuli may activate latent cognitive schemata based on previous learning experiences stored in the long-term memory. This activation may increase emotional arousal and trigger avoidance and escape behaviors.

Psychiatre des hopitaux, charge de cours a l'Universite Lyon 1, Laboratoire de Psychologie Medicale, Hôpital Neurologique, 59 Boulevard Pinel, 69394 Lyon, France

Biological and Cognitive Models of Phobias

Recently biological theories of anxiety and phobias have witnessed an increasing popularity. D. Sheehan and K. Sheehan (1982) postulated that agoraphobia and social phobia could be part of an "endogenous anxiety syndrome," whose main feature is represented by "spontaneous" panic attacks, stemming from a biological disturbance of the central noradrenergic system. Experimentally induced panic attack response to lactate infusions was taken as a biological marker of endogenous anxiety. Conditioning, social, and cognitive factors are only secondary to panic attack which comes "out of the blue." Social phobia, in such a perspective, might occupy a position between isolated spontaneous panic attacks and the pervasive syndrome of agoraphobia. The purely unidirectional model of panic attacks proposed by D. Sheehan and K. Sheehan (1982) was criticized by Margraf et al. (1986). The latter did not deny the importance of biological factors, but they pointed out the lack of empirical evidence for such a model and proposed a bidirectional and psychophysiological one, taking into account the interactions between biological, environmental, and cognitive variables. Moreover, they suggested after a careful review of the 13 already published studies that the response to lactate infusions was not specific to panic anxiety. Van der Molen et al. (1986) showed in normal subjects receiving lactate infusion that anxiety was induced when they were instructed that they would experience anxiety while there was no anxious response when they were instructed that they would experience a state of pleasant excitement. Glucose perfusion did not induce anxiety responses in subjects regardless of verbal suggestion. Thus, the current status of research suggests that cognitive variables play a role in experimentally induced anxiety.

Classification of Phobias

The Diagnostic and Statistical Manual, third edition (DSM III; 1980), classifies phobias into agoraphobia with or without panic attacks, social phobias, and simple phobias. Sheehan's work on "endogenous" panic attack as well as DSM III were preceded by Goldstein and Chambless' agoraphobia reconceptualization (1978). They divided agoraphobia into two subtypes, simple and complex. Fear of being trapped, fear of the fear, and lack of assertiveness were the main symptoms of complex agoraphobias. The complex type of personality corresponded to "nonassertive, pervasively fearful individuals who perceive themselves to be incapable of functioning independently." The revised version of DSM III (DSM III-R; 1987), strongly influenced by biological psychiatry, accords a central position to the panic attack syndrome. The category of agoraphobia is replaced by panic disorder with extensive phobic avoidance, panic disorder with limited avoidance, panic disorder without phobic avoidance, and limited symptom attacks with phobic avoidance (agoraphobia without panic attacks). However, simple phobia and social phobia were not included in the growing body of panic disorders. Panic disorder is clearly differentiated from social phobia: panic disorder "should not be triggered by situations in which the individual was the focus of other's attention." Social phobia is "a persistent fear of one or more situations in which the individual is the focus of other's attention, and fears that he or she may behave in a way that will be humiliating or embarassing." Simple phobia is a residual category which corresponds to an avoidance and anxiety response to a situation "other than being alone or in public places away from home, or humiliation and embarassment in certain social situations" (e.g., animal phobias, blood and injury phobias). Despite the dimensional limitations of the categorical classification model represented by the DSM III (1980; pp 225–228) we will use it here to study the application of cognitive therapy to phobias.

Theoretical Problems

Cognitive Model: Information Processing

Cognitive models of phobias postulate that anxiety is associated with a bias in processing information related to danger. This bias constitutes a danger schema acquired during early experiences and activated under certain circumstances. The basic assumptions of the cognitive model derive from cognitive psychology (Hollon and Kriss 1984). Figure 1 represents the cognitive model of information processing.

According to cognitive psychology, the brain processes environmental events (stimuli) according to schemata, or knowledge structures, which contain information and theories about oneself and the external world, constructed from past information. Schemata are organized in stable constellations (cognitive sets) and stored in the long-term memory. Schemata which have been strengthened by information and repeated use are stable and quite difficult to modify. In phobias schemata are unconscious structures which select, filter, and interpret information according to silent, enduring hypotheses about danger. The schematic content determines affective and behavioral responses. They are stable and deep-seated cognitive structures, amenable to study through monitoring of cognitive events, which are superficial cognitive structures. Cognitive events are inner monologues, automatic thoughts, or mental images which can be observed by the subject when focusing his or her attention on the ongoing stream of consciousness. They can be elicited in therapeutic sessions when emotional outbursts appear during verbal reports of phobic situations. They can also be reproduced through mental imagery

Stimulus ⟶ Schema ⟷ Cognitive processes ⟷ Cognitive events ⟷ Behavior

Fig. 1. Cognitive model of information processing. The brain processes environmental events (stimuli) through deep seated, irrational, unconscious schemata of danger. Cognitive processes such as heuristics, assimilation, and accomodation – interrelated to schemata – transform the information into superficial cognitive events (inner monologues, thoughts, conscious mental images). Cognitive events interact with the behavioral response to environmental events. For instance, when an agoraphobic is confronted with a crowded place, constellations of danger schemata stored in the long-term memory are activated. Schemata of danger induce cognitive events such as negative anticipations, inner monologues centered on the inability to cope with the situation, and hypochondriacal mental images. These cognitive events trigger avoidance behavior which, in turn, perpetuate the negative cognitive set

techniques or instigated by role playing in social phobia or by exposure in vivo in agoraphobia and simple phobia. They can also be written down during self-monitoring homework on forms especially designed to record triggering internal or external events, emotions (fear, anger, sadness), and automatic thoughts (Beck et al. 1979).

Passage from deep structures (schemata) to superficial structures (cognitive events) is made possible by cognitive processes. Cognitive processes are rules of information transformation. Cognitive psychology describes some processes as assimilation, accomodation, and heuristics; these can be applied to the study of the ideational components of anxiets. Piaget (1964) traced the ontogeny of two cognitive processes, assimilation and accomodation, from innate neurological patterns of action to scientific knowledge. Assimilation selects information if it fits the silent hypotheses of the schemata or transforms information to make it compatible with these hypotheses if it does not. Conversely, accomodation modifies schemata to make them compatible with external reality. The dialectic of assimilation and accomodation explains the construction of reality and the development of logical thinking. Distortions of this two-sided process have been found in hysteria and obsessions (Tissot et al. 1980) and must yet be studied in phobias and depression. Primacy of assimilation could explain the self-perpetuation of cognitive schemata of danger. Enhancement of accomodation could be implied in the behavior therapy process, which is oriented toward reality testing through prolonged exposure in vivo to feared situations until anxiety subsides. Tversky and Kanehman (1974) explained the primacy of assimilation by heuristics, or shortcuts, which are quick judgements on events under conditions of uncertainty. Such a process, which can be innate, automatic, and unconscious, may confirm irrational danger schemata through a bypassing of logical inferences and hypothesis testing. Avoidance behavior and clinging dependency to contraphobic persons or objects retroactively confirm irrational beliefs of danger in reducing anxiety more quickly than prolonged exposure to feared situations.

Personal Danger Schemata

Hibbert (1984) and Beck and Emery (1985) suggested that subjects having generalized anxiety and/or panic attacks with agoraphobia showed a special ideational pattern. The main themes are the fear of physical illness, such as myocardial infarction or the fear of becoming crazy. Guidano and Liotti (1983) summarize agoraphobics' internal representations in three types: loss of control, serious threat to physical well-being, and inability to deal with external danger. Social phobics' fantasies usually revolve around the fear of others' negative evaluations. Subjects misinterpret environmental events, physical sensations, and others' social behavior, and they imagine scenes representing rejection and humiliation. Mental imagery is the consequence of illogical thoughts organized in clusters. Four main types of logical errors are found in phobias:

1. Arbitrary inference, which consists of drawing catastrophic conclusions without proof about the gravity of the physical symptoms of anxiety or about the potential danger of the phobic stimuli.

2. Overgeneralization to all possible situations from a unique experience of acute anxiety.
3. Maximization of dangers and minimization of safe situations.
4. Personalization of every event, recalling individual vulnerability and dependency and others' indifference and/or aggressivity.

According to Hibbert (1984), 50% of a group of subjects having agoraphobia with panic attacks started a panic attack with somatic symptoms different from those of anxiety. These symptoms were interpreted as the return of a deadly danger. Negative anticipations and self-fulfilling predictions of failure to cope with phobic situations are the consequences of this cognitive set.

The main criticism of the cognitive model has come from researchers who contend that there is a primacy of affective reactions over cognitions. Zajonc (1980) in a purely theoretical paper suggested that affective judgements were precognitive, nonverbal, automatic, and inescapable. In the course of evolution affects may have preceded "cold" and rational cognitions and remain independent of them. Affect and cognition belong to two systems which are separate although interrelated. Zajonc suggested that the change produced by cognitive-behavioral therapy was less related to a cognitive modification than to the reduction of emotional reactions and to the development of positive affects towards previously feared objects. Whatever the fate of the theoretical and experimental controversy on the primacy of affect, one should remark from a clinical point of view that even though therapeutic change is mediated by cognitions, there is no change at all if emotions or affects are not modified. Moreover, Beck and Emery (1985) contend that emotions are primarily related to the personal meaning of events and use besides cognitive interventions, specific techniques to modify affects and emotions in depression and anxiety disorders. Further basic research is needed to establish the hypothesis of the primacy of danger schemata in phobias.

Safety Signals: Ontogeny of Danger Schemata?

Gray (1971) added to the classical conditioning hypothesis of fears the notion of safety signals. One of the recurrent themes of agoraphobic patients is the fear of being trapped in a situation in which there is no access to safety signals, e.g., exit, hospital, doctor, significant person, or medication. They fear dying far from home in a place crowded with indifferent or hostile people. They try to control the environment in order to have access to a safe place which represents a safety signal. Fear is less an avoidance of danger than the search for immediate access to situations representing safety for the patient. Kandel (1983) suggested that simple phobic anticipatory anxiety was triggered by a signal, namely the phobic situation. This signal is a warning, meaning "beware, danger!" and, conversely, the absence of signal means safety. When a subject presents with generalized anxiety or a panic disorder, there is no signal to predict either danger or security. In agoraphobia with panic attacks the subject who has no internal safety signal tries at any moment to have access to external safety signals and accordingly monitors and controls his or her social and physical environment. Rachman (1984) suggested that death of a significant other, which is a frequent precipitating event in the onset of agoraphobia, may reduce the sense of safety and controllability of events in suppressing a safety signal. Some experimental works have studied the ontogeny of safety signals. Separation anxiety in childhood has been invoked as antecedent to adult agoraphobia with panic attacks. Klein (1981) suggested an analogy between panic attacks and protest-despair reaction observed by Bowlby (1975) in mother-infant separation in humans and other primates. However, Thyer et al. (1985) compared 44 agoraphobic patients with panic attacks to 83 simple phobics and found no difference between the two groups in the frequency of reported early separation. Timmermans et al. (1986) demonstrated that 1-year-old primates raised by surrogate mothers avoided a harmless unknown object containing food, while at the same age primates raised by their natural mother could approach this object without fear. This experiment suggests the necessity of a safety basis modeled by the mother in approaching foreign objects. It suggests also that safety signals and danger schemata could be internalized and stored at an early stage of development. Thorpe and Burns (1983) found in an epidemiological survey of an English sample of 963 agoraphobic subjects that 43% reported having had an overanxious mother. It could be hypothesized that such mothers were unable to insure a safe base for their children. However, further research on ontogeny of the developmental aspects of fear and safety representations is obviously needed.

Self-Efficacy, Positive Expectancies, and Therapeutic Change

Another explanation of the cognitive bases of phobic anxiety can be found in Bandura's self-efficacy theory. Bandura (1977) postulated a hypothetical construct, perceived self-efficacy, to explain sustained coping efforts in the face of aversive experiences, especially phobic situations. Self-efficacy represents "an integrative theoretical framework to explain and predict psychological changes achieved by different modes of treatment." Increasing the level of self-confidence results in a decrease of anxiety, instigates success expectancies, and facilitates prolonged and repeated exposure to fearful stimuli. However, Borkovec (1978) contended that although cognitive-behavioral therapy increases self-confidence and hence strengthens coping efforts with fearful situations, the most powerful agent of change was the modification of avoidance behavior. Self-efficacy could be a "potentially important reflection of behavioral change," rather tyan a mediator of change. To date, the methodological problems raised by self-efficacy theory have not been solved (Eastman and Marzillier 1984).

Internality and Externality: Misconceptions of Causality and Phobic Cognitions

Phobic patients' misconceptions of danger resulting from cognitive biases can be described in terms of altered patterns of causal inference. Rotter (1966) has shown the importance of conceptions and misconceptions of causality in normal and pathological subjects. Rotter isolated a psychological dimension related to the perception of the locus of control of reinforcement. The locus of control of reinforcement could be perceived as being inside or outside the subject. "Internal" subjects perceive events as being under their control while "external" subjects perceive events as being under the control of chance, destiny, or powerful persons. Internality-externality is a dimension which can be measured with rating scales. Emmelkamp (1982), in an experimental work, showed that subjects with panic attacks attributed anxiety symptoms to uncontrollable external factors; for instance, panic attacks were causally related to the crowd in a public place or were taken for a sudden cardiac illness or an acute psychotic episode. Therapeutic change in the locus of control perception has been demostrated by Adler and Price (1985); agoraphobic subjects, who had an external interpretation of causality in baseline conditions, became more "internal" after behavioral treatment.

Assessment of Cognitions

The cognitive model of phobias still needs empirical support regarding three theoretical issues. First, the production of maladaptive negative cognitions by phobic subjects in feared situations should be experimentally established. Second, the mediating role of such cognitions and their correspondence to fear responses should be assessed. Third, the significance of cognitive change for clinical outcomes should be demonstrated (Last 1984). Classical psychometric assessment with validated scales rating irrational belief systems have been used. Moreover, various methods have been proposed to rate cognitions in naturalistic conditions and establish their role in phobias. Thought-listing procedures immediately after exposure in vivo, "continuous thinking aloud" techniques during behavioral tests, and tape recordings of "thinking aloud" at fixed time intervals during exposure in vivo have been extensively used. Methodological problems have been found in monitoring phobics' negative cognitions. This type of measurement is very reactive: some subjects showed a marked cognitive improvement across assessments. Resistance to public elicitations of painful thoughts or the fear of criticism may prevent some subjects reporting all their thoughts. Thus, the reliability of phobics' cognitive assessment appears questionable.

Last's (1984) account of his own work and his review of experimental evidence suggest that phobics do have negative catastrophic thoughts when confronted with feared situations either in imagination or in real-life conditions. Negative thinking is positively related to patients' ratings of anxiety. In the same way phobics' psychophysiological fear responses are increased and intensified by maladaptive thoughts. Stefanek and Eisler (1983), reviewing the current status of cognitive variables in assertiveness training, concluded that even though some researchers have found that cognitions (e.g., irrational beliefs, facilitating or inhibiting self-statements) do play a role in assertiveness, treatments based on cognitive modification do not enhance the effectiveness of role rehearsal based on the social-skills model. More recently Monti et al. (1986) found a weak correlation between two subscales of an Irrational Belief Test and a Simulated Social Interaction Test in a miscellaneous sample of psychiatric inpatients. In an original vein, Schwartz and Garamoni (1984) suggested that positive and negative internal dialogues were interrelated and should be studied together. Three types of internal dialogue could be described: (a) positive internal dialogue, with 61.8% positive and

38.2% negative cognitions ("golden" section); (b) internal dialogue of conflict, with 50% negative and 50% positive cognitions, corresponding to mild anxiety and depression states; and (c) negative dialogue, with 61.8% negative cognitions, representing the inverse of the "golden" section and perhaps typical of severe anxiety and depression states. To date, the hypothesis of Schwartz and Garamoni rests on a meta-analysis of 32 cognitive process studies contrasting functional versus dysfunctional patients.

In the following we examine problems of the effectiveness of cognitive modification in studying successively the therapeutic methods as proposed by cognitive therapists and the outcome and process literature on cognitive therapy of phobias.

Therapeutic Methods

Ellis' Rational-Emotive Therapy

General Principles. Ellis (Ellis 1962; Ellis and Grieger 1977) proposes an A-B-C model for cognitive interventions on irrational belief systems in various psychological problems. This model has been used for agoraphobia in controlled studies (Emmelkamp et al. 1986). Typically the treatment is given in 15 1-h individual sessions or 6 2.5-h sessions in group. The A-B-C framework is presented in a didactic and persuasive way: "A" refers to an activating event or experience, "B" to the person's irrational beliefs about the activating event, which is assumed to lead to the irrational consequence "C."

Psychotherapeutic Tactics. In phobias an irrational belief system about danger (B) will lead the subject confronting a crowded situation far from home (A) to the irrational consequence of avoidance or escape behavior resulting from anxiety arousal (C). In the sessions patients must analyze their own emotional problems in A-B-C terms in a verbal way and on homework sheets. The patients also study a layman's booklet on Ellis' theories. Special emphasis is placed on challenging irrational beliefs by a rational confrontation on the part of the therapist or in a more Socratic way through dialogue and questioning. The use of confrontational or Socratic tactics depends on the therapist's charisma and on his conception of human relationships. Ellis (1979) stressed the importance of rationally disputing both discomfort anxiety and ego anxiety. Discomfort anxiety corresponds to an emotional tension resulting from irrational catastrophic thinking about comfort, survival, and obligation to avoid any anxiety feeling. Ego anxiety corresponds to emotional tension resulting from the patient's feeling that personal worth is threatened if he or she is phobic. Patients think they are obliged to follow the conformist imperative that they should perform well and be approved by others. Phobic subjects demand of themselves that they should approach feared situations and think that they are worthless individuals if they do not. Put in other words, Ellis makes a distinction between phobic cognitions related to anxiety (discomfort anxiety) and secondary depressive cognitions resulting from the incapacity to cope with phobic stimuli (ego anxiety).

Beck's Cognitive Therapy

General Principles. Cognitive therapy of phobias is a directive and didactic form of psychotherapy which aims at modifying erroneous basic assumptions concerning danger (Beck and Emery 1985). Therapy here is short-term and consists of 15–20 1-h sessions once or twice a week. In the first session the therapist provides an outline of general principles and basic hypotheses of cognitive therapy. Functional analysis emphasizes the interactions between thoughts, emotions, and behavior. During the first 5–10 sessions Socratic dialogue and real-life self-observation on daily recording forms elicit inner monologues, self-verbalizations, and dysfunctional ideas concerning danger and avoidance behavior. The links between anxiety, avoidance, and some recurrent involuntary and automatic thoughts are progressively pointed out. After 10 sessions it is generally possible to isolate logical errors through inductive reasoning and Socratic dialogue. Step by step the deeper basic schemata of danger are elicited and understood. Schemata are then progressively and tactfully disputed by the therapist, who confronts the negative expectancies of the patient with reality testing in the form of gradual, prolonged, and successful exposure in vivo to feared situations.

Psychotherapeutic Tactics. Three basic approaches are used to question the patient's catastrophic anticipations: (a) What is the evidence for and against such a feeling? (b) What are other ways of looking at the situation? (c) If the worst happens, so what; there is a way to cope with it. The questioning is maintained outside the sessions through a daily recording form which is discussed with the therapist at the next session. The links between cognitions, emotions, mental images, and behavior are constantly pointed out. The therapist follows the adage of "divide and conquer" and focuses first on the component most amenable to change; the therapist later focuses on more resistant components of phobic anxiety. Numerous techniques dealing with emotional, imaginal, cognitive, and behavioral components of phobias have been proposed by Beck and Emery (1985). Besides original cognitive techniques devised by Beck's group some techniques are borrowed from behavior therapy, multimodal behavior therapy (Lazarus 1976), Gestalt therapy, Ellis' rational-emotive therapy, and paradoxical-intention therapy.

One should note that homework exposure in vivo is constantly presented to the patient as the best way to test irrational hypotheses. Homework is recorded on forms checked by the therapist, discussed and readjusted in case of difficulties. Relaxation is also used to modify the affective component. The goal of relaxation is to increase self-awareness and to demonstrate to the patient a degree of self-mastery over the symptoms. In agoraphobias the therapist helps the hypochondriac patient, who thinks he has a heart attack or psychotic onset, to reattribute physical phenomena to anxiety. In social phobias negative social self-evaluations are elicited and disputed during Socratic dialogue, role playing, role reversal, therapist's corrective feedback, and cognitive and behavioral modification through homework assignments.

Therapeutic Relationship. In sum, the therapist teaches the patient to be aware of anxiety feelings, to accept these feelings, to challenge the basic belief that he or she is the central point of all events, and to develop coping plans. Cognitive therapy of phobias represents an eclectic and flexible package which can be used according to the need of each therapeutic situation. This must be tailored according to the specific problems of the patient. A positive alliance with the patient is a necessary condition for therapeutic effectiveness. Therapy is not a purely intellectual game which consists in persuading the irrational patient that he or she is wrong and the rational therapist right. It is a Socratic or "talmudic" dialogue which aims at uncovering irrational patterns of thoughts. The therapist should not "preach" the truth but rather suggest alternative ways to look at feelings of helplessness and at bodily sensations of the phobic's experience.

Clinical Case. To illustrate cognitive-behavioral therapy of phobias in its practical modalities we report here briefly on a case of agoraphobia with panic attacks and phobic dysphagia in a 23-year-old woman. The patient had suffered from dysphagia since she was a baby; her mother reported she had to pinch her nose to make her open her mouth and eat. When she was 10 years of age, she had a choking episode while eating in a restaurant, and people had to remove a piece of food from her mouth. Thereafter the patient could not eat unless she minced each piece of food. At 22 she had her first panic attack followed by a pervasive agoraphobic syndrome. The schema of danger was the same in agoraphobia and dysphagia: she constantly thought she was about to die from suffocation far distant from anyone who could help her. She was not able to attend university courses, she could not go shopping or drive away from home, and she avoided staying home alone. She had to mince her food and check with a mirror or her finger that there was no thick piece of food in her mouth.

A cognitive-behavioral functional analysis (Cottraux and Mollard 1986) was conducted, taking into account, besides emotional and behavioral components of her phobias, cognitive variables: negative anticipations, mental images, inner monologues, personal historical meaning, and the interaction with significant others. The patient was first trained in Schultz' relaxation and respiratory control and given exposure in imagination with cognitive restructuring. She was requested to imagine herself in a place she could not leave for a long while, with only a sandwich to eat; she was choking, but nobody was there to help her. She was instructed to cope with this hyperventilation-inducing representation through relaxation and respiratory control until anxiety subsided. After two sessions in imagination exposure, in vivo homework assignments were given: shopping alone, driving a car alone, etc. The patient completed the homework successfully and was able to give up the bottle of water which she had kept constantly with her in case of suffocation.

Dysphagia was the more resistant problem; this was treated with participant modeling and cognitive restructuring. The patient thought she had thick saliva in her mouth, and she wondered permanently whether this was saliva or a residual piece of food. The sensation led to the feeling of impending choking. The patient felt that the food in her mouth was as big as that on the plate. These interpretations of bodily sensations were discussed with the patient, and alternative sensations were sought. She remembered experiencing the same sensation when bursting into laughter. The dramatic interpretation was confronted by this more pleasant alternative. Then the cognitive distortion was explored. She chose the worst alternative because she thought she had never been lucky in her life. The trend to overgeneralize from a single choking episode was disputed, and the interest of being able to take a limited risk was stressed. Moreover, mental imagery was used to overcome the sensation. The therapist asked the patient to imagine the food as a tiny boat traveling in her mouth and her body as in a science fiction movie. She had then to eat in front of the therapist while imagining pleasant sensations, without checking her mouth. After 30 sessions the patient was able to stay home alone, had resumed university courses, did not mince food any more, and had considerably reduced her minor tranquillizer intake.

Meichenbaum's Self-Instructional Training

General Principles. Meichenbaum (1977) studied the role of negative self-talk in phobias and stress reactions and proposed to modify the dysfunctional internal dialogue, replacing negative self-talk by positive self-verbalizations. Such a cognitive restructuring method derived from the neurophysiological works by Luria (1961), who stressed the importance of the internal dialogue and its relation to complex behaviors.

Psychotherapeutic Tactics. Meichenbaum's cognitive restructuring therapy is presented to the patient in four successive stages:

1. Preparation consisting of explanations on anxiety management and the relations between internal dialogue and behavior.
2. In vitro confrontation of anxiety-provoking situations that are rehearsed in imagination.
3. Coping in imagination with phobic situations.
4. Reinforcement for any progress achieved by the patient in coping with imaginal situations.

During the four stages the patient is taught to ascertain how anxious he or she feels in order to become conscious of negative self-statements and to replace these by productive self-statements. For instance, the patient is instructed to notice negative self-talk, such as "I cannot go outside my home, I will die or become crazy in the crowd," and to replace this by a positive inner monologue, such as "I have already had this fear before, I did not die and had no heart attacks. Experiencing anxiety did not drive me crazy." It can be seen that this therapy is reminiscent of the popular method proposed by Coué (1956), which consists of "self-mastery through conscious self-suggestion."

Hyperventilation, Respiratory Control, and Reattribution Technique

General Principles. Chronic and acute hyperventilation is one of the clinical manifestations of agoraphobia and panic attacks. There is an overlap between hyperventilation syndromes, panic disorder, and agoraphobia, as shown in a study by Garssen et al. (1983). Clark et al. (1985) proposed a cognitive model to explain the interactions and the negative feedback loops between cognitions, hyperventilations, and external or internal triggering events (see Fig. 2). Control of hyperventilation was considered the key factor in the treatment of panic attacks and agoraphobia with panic attacks.

Methodological Problems. The first problem raised by this model is biological. Alkalosis results from the peripheral decrease of pCO_2 upon hyperventilation. However, Gorman et al. (1984) provoked panic attacks in subjects meeting DSM III criteria for panic disorder when breathing CO_2-enriched air. This finding was attributed to the central action of CO_2 on the brain stem noradrenergic structure locus ceruleus. Locus ceruleus electrical stimulation in animals and pharmacological stimulation in humans produces acute anxiety. Gorman concluded that peripheral alkalosis induced by hyperventilation was not in itself sufficient to trigger panic attacks. Alkalosis and the increase in pH could be more a consequence than a cause of panic attacks and might represent a state marker, which disappears after successful pharmacological or behavioral correction of panic attacks. However, the issue remains unresolved since there are great individual variations in ventilation and reactions to change in blood chemistry. Moreover, exposure to autonomic symptoms induced by CO_2 inhalation has been used successfully as a therapeutic agent and has been proven superior to propanolol in agoraphobia and panic attacks (Griez and van den Hout 1986).

The second problem raised by this model is to define the exact position of cognitions in the chain of events. Do cognitions precede hyperventilation, or are they secondary interpretations of physical sensations during hyperventilation? Is there a vicious circle between cognitions and physical phenomena, each rein-

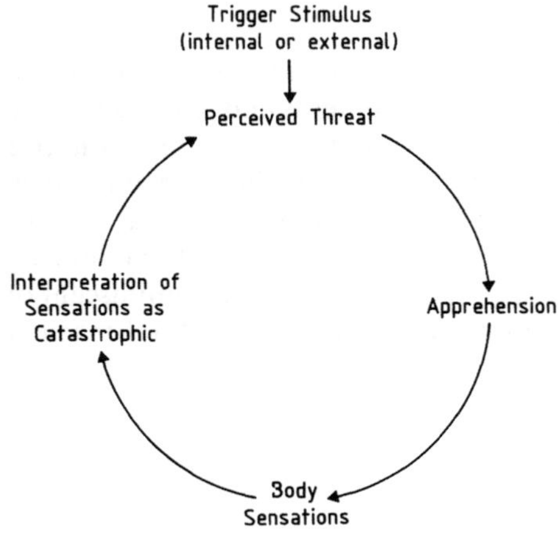

Fig. 2. Cognitive model of panic attacks (from Clark 1986)

forcing the other without any possibility of defining causal relationships? Ley (1985) produced some arguments in favor of a precedence of hyperventilation over cognitions, which then accelerate the hyperventilation-hypocapnia syndrome. The third problem is the fact that not all patients who develop panic attacks hyperventilate (Gelder 1986). Whatever the issue of these theoretical problems, therapeutic "cognitive-respiratory" techniques have been applied successfully in controlled and uncontrolled studies.

Psychotherapeutic Tactics. Therapeutic methods derive from the pioneering work by Lum (1976) who stressed the importance of respiratory control in anxiety and stress reactions. Treatment has two main strategies:

1. Teaching subjects to relabel their bodily sensations and to reattribute these sensations to hyperventilation induced by stressful stimuli. Instead of focusing on impending psychological or physical imaginal and "breathtaking" catastrophes, the subject becomes aware of the relationship between hyperventilation and panic attacks.
2. Teaching patients to avoid hyperventilation when they are under stress in order to control panic attacks at their inception (Clark et al. 1985).

Treatment requires about ten sessions and includes the following five stages:

1. Voluntary hyperventilation to make the patient aware of the similarity between panic attacks and hyperventilation.
2. Explanation of panic induction through hyperventilation.
3. Learning to slow down the breathing cycle to 8–10 respiratory cycles per minute.
4. Voluntary hyperventilation trials followed by voluntary, slow, controlled breathing.
5. This new pattern of breathing is used in real-life situations as a coping technique after identification of the panic-triggering events. Both spontaneous and situational panic attacks seem to respond to respiratory control. This can be used in agoraphobia where one of the main symptoms is the fear of the fear that precipitates hyperventilation (Clark 1986).

Results

Agoraphobia

Agoraphobia is the most disabling phobic disorder. To our knowledge, five controlled studies have been published. Emmelkamp et al. (1978) compared in agoraphobics prolonged exposure in vivo to a cognitive restructuring program inspired by Meichenbaum's work mentioned above. They used a cross-over design. At a 1-month follow-up exposure in vivo did better than cognitive restructuring for phobic anxiety and avoidance. No specific measure of intensity and frequency of panic attacks was reported.

In a later work Emmelkamp and Mersch (1982) compared three methods in which 27 agoraphobic patients received, in order of their application, (a) prolonged exposure in vivo; (b) cognitive restructuring of irrational beliefs, deriving from the work of Ellis and Grieger (1977); and (c) exposure in vivo combined with Meichenbaum's self-instructional training. At the end of the treatment phase exposure in vivo and the combined therapy showed a better outcome that did cognitive restructuring. However, at a 1-month follow-up only cognitive restructuring had a significant effect on depression, assertiveness, and perception of the locus of control. Agoraphobia improvement was comparable in the three groups at this 1-month follow-up.

Mavissakalian et al. (1983) examined 26 agoraphobics with panic attacks, randomized into two groups, and compared cognitive restructuring to paradoxical intention. In the cognitive-restructuring group as in the paradoxical-intention group the importance of prolonged exposure in vivo and habituation to feared situations was stressed. The first two sessions consisted of an outline of behavioral principles of phobia treatment. It was strongly suggested to the patients that once in the phobic situations they should remain until anxiety subsided. Ten sessions of either cognitive restructuring or paradoxical intention were then given in groups of five patients. Cognitive restructuring used Meichenbaum's format. In the paradoxical-intention sessions subjects were told to let go their anxiety instead of fighting it, a technique which is close to that of "flooding" in imagination. Both treatments were evaluated after 6 months, and they showed equivalent outcomes in the two groups. However, this study does not suggest a positive effect per se of cognitive restructuring or of paradoxical intention because the patients had exposure to in vivo instructions, which has clearly been shown to be effective in agoraphobia (Marks 1981; Lelliot et al. 1986).

Williams and Rappoport (1983) compared, in agoraphobics with panic attacks, exposure in vivo with a combination of exposure in vivo and a program of negative self-statement modification. Both groups showed improvement of subjective anxiety, but only the exposure in vivo group had a significant modification of agoraphobia.

Emmelkamp et al. (1986) compared three treatments of agoraphobics with panic attacks: (a) exposure in vivo, (b) cognitive restructuring presented according to Ellis' model of rational-emotive therapy, and (c) self-instructional training. After a posttest evaluation all patients had a treatment-free period followed by a reassessment. All patients were then treated by exposure in vivo. Statistical analysis showed that exposure in vivo was the method which produced the greatest changes in agoraphobic anxiety and avoidance. However, the two cognitive techniques produced significant intragroup changes, albeit of a lesser magnitude. No specific measure of panic attacks was reported. In sum, this study indicated that exposure in vivo was superior to cognitive treatment on the measures of agoraphobia, while there was no evidence of enhancement of exposure in vivo by priming agoraphobic patients with cognitive therapy.

Since panic attacks and agoraphobia are closely related, we will review studies dealing with panic attacks as the main problem.

Barlow et al. (1984) compared two groups of ten patients, each including five subjects with panic attacks and five subjects with generalized anxiety, according to strict DSM III criteria. One group was left on a waiting list while the other received relaxation, muscular biofeedback, and cognitive restructuring, as inspired by Beck.

At posttest and at a 3-month follow-up the treated group had better outcomes than those on waiting list for generalized anxiety and panic attacks. Contrary to DSM III classification, there were no clear differences in generalized anxiety level or frequency of panic attacks, nor were there differential therapeutic responses between patients diagnosed with panic disorder and those with generalized anxiety. The association of relaxation and biofeedback with cognitive therapy in this study precludes any conclusion about the effectiveness of cognitive therapy alone in panic attacks and generalized anxiety.

Bonn et al. (1984) compared two groups of agoraphobic patients with panic attacks. One group of seven subjects was treated successively by two sessions of respiratory control and seven sessions of exposure in vivo. In the second group five subjects were treated by exposure in vivo without preparation. At 6-month follow-up the group receiving the respiratory-control program was more improved on agoraphobia and panic-attack measures than the group treated with exposure in vivo only. Bonn concluded that if respiratory control was more effective for panic attacks and somatic symptoms, exposure in vivo was necessary to increase patients' autonomy.

Clark et al. (1985) treated eleven situational panics (agoraphobia) and seven nonsituational panics (panic disorder) in an A-B design which compared a baseline without intervention to an intervention phase in which subjects learned respiratory control according to the method described above. At a 2-year follow-up a statistically significant reduction of situational and nonsituational panic attacks appeared. Clark, who considers respiratory control as a cognitive modification technique, nevertheless suggests that this method may act through exposure and habituation to the sensations of the panic attacks.

Salkovskis et al. (1986) showed in a study on nine subjects treated by the same method a positive effect of respiratory training without exposure in vivo, both on panics and phobic avoidance.

Social Phobias and Social-Skills Problems

Evidence exists for the effectiveness in analogue populations of cognitive interventions in test anxiety, speech anxiety, and social anxiety (for a review see Beck and Emery 1985; Liebowitz et al. 1985). Social phobias, however represent a more enduring and stable condition, marked by a chronic social-skills deficit. There is a dearth of controlled studies of cognitive therapy in this important area of anxiety disorders.

Stravynski et al. (1982) compared in socially dysfunctional patients a social-skills training program, using role rehearsal, instructions, feedback, and homework assignments, with the same program associated with a cognitive restructuring method. A 6-month follow-up social-skills training had been followed by a significant improvement that was not enhanced by the addition of cognitive modification.

Jerrelman et al. (1986) classified social phobics into physiological and cognitive reactors on the basis of a psychometric and psychophysiological assessment. Patients were matched according to their reaction patterns either to applied relaxation or to self-instructional training. This classification did not predict differential outcomes with a physiologically or a cognitively focused method, respectively. Despite the present lack of evidence for its effectiveness, cognitive therapy should be studied more thoroughly in clinical samples of social phobics.

Simple Phobias

Two controlled studies have demonstrated negative outcomes on the effectiveness of Ellis' and Meichenbaum's cognitive therapy alone in simple phobias. Biran and Wilson (1981) compared two groups of patients suffering from phobias of darkness, elevators, or heights, treated either with guided exposure in vivo or a cognitive restructuring program derived from the work of both Ellis and Meichenbaum. At posttest and at 6-month follow-up exposure in vivo was superior to cognitive restructuring in enhancing approach behavior, reducing subjective fears, decreasing physiological reactivity to imaginal phobic scenes, and increasing strength of self-efficacy. Cognitive restructuring improved social functioning.

Ladouceur (1983) treated 36 individuals who were phobic of cats or dogs in four randomized groups: (a) participant modeling alone: the patient received exposure in vivo step-by-step, first modeled and then assisted by the therapist; (b) participant modeling with self-verbalization: the patient had to think aloud without the therapist's corrective feedback; (c) participant modeling associated with Meichenbaum's self-instructional training; and (d) placebo control group. At posttest the three groups who received participant modeling were improved on phobic and self-efficacy measures, while the placebo group was not. At follow-up the group combining participant modeling with self-instructional training showed more phobic behavior and lower self-efficacy than the other treated groups. The hypothesis that self-instructional training would enhance the effect of participant modeling was not confirmed.

Conclusion

The cognitive model of anxiety disorders enlarges the overly restrictive behavioral approach to phobias. If there is some clinical and experimental evidence for the role of cognitive variables in phobias, several issues must be explored. The most important of these is to define the status of emotions, affect, or feelings and their relationship to thoughts and behavior. Behavior therapy is said to be behavioristic because it stresses the importance of behavior modification, and cognitive therapy is said to be cognitive because it underlines the importance of thought-pattern modification. But despite their respective theoretical contentions close examination of behavior and cognitive therapeutic practice suggests that both deal with the emotional component of phobias. Behavior therapy through the various methods of exposure in imagination and in vivo is above all a means to instigate an emotional experience which is then used by the patient and the therapist to modify behavior and coping cognitions. Beck's cognitive therapy strongly emphasizes, besides cognitive modification, the importance of a working over of emotions and affects. The relative ineffectiveness of excessively intellectual forms of cognitive therapy, as exemplified by rational-emotive therapy and self-instructional training, may be explained by their exclusive focus on thought content and processes. In agoraphobia controlled studies have not, to date, shown compelling evidence in favor of the effectiveness of rational-emotive therapy or of self-instructional training alone, even though the management of negative cognitions appears to be an important component of any therapeutic intervention. Exposure in vivo remains the crucial ingredient in the treatment of agoraphobia with or without panic attacks. Relabeling of anxiety symptoms and respiratory control in agoraphobia with panic attacks should be evaluated alone in more controlled studies to establish their effectiveness independently of exposure in vivo. Preliminary evidence suggests that this emotion-centered cognitive therapy could be effective. In simple phobias, exposure in vivo remains the treatment of choice. Cognitive therapy has some effectiveness for the modification of test anxiety in analogue populations, but does not enhance the effects of social-skills training in socially dysfunctional patients. Beck's cognitive therapy, which has been recently applied to phobias, represents an eclectic and comprehensive "behavioral-emotional-cognitive therapy" which requires controlled research to establish its effectiveness and to understand its therapeutic process.

References

Adler D, Price J (1985) Relation of agoraphobics' health locus of control orientation to severity of agoraphobia. Psychol Rep 56:619–625

American Psychiatric Association (1980) Diagnostic and statistical manual, 3rd edn. APA, Washington, DC, pp 225–239

American Psychiatric Association (1987) Diagnostic and statistical manual of mental disorders, 3rd edn, revised version (DSM III-R). APA, Washington, DC

Bandura A (1977) Social learning theory. Prentice Hall, Englewood Cliffs, New Jersey, pp 84–85

Barlow D, Cohen A, Wadel MB, Vermilyea B, Klosko J, Blanchard E, Di Nardo R (1984) Panic and generalized anxiety disorders. Nature and treatment. Behav Ther 15:431–449

Beck AT, Emery G (1985) Anxiety disorders and phobias. A cognitive perspective. Basic, New York, pp 38–66

Beck AT, Rush AJ, Shaw BF, Emery G (1979) Cognitive therapy of depression. Guilford, New York, pp 142–164

Biran M, Wilson GT (1981) Treatment of phobic disorders using cognitive and exposure methods: a self-efficacy analysis. J Consult Clin Psychol 49(6):886–899

Bonn J, Readhead C, Timmons B (1984) Enhanced adaptative behavioural response in agoraphobic patients pretreated with breathing retraining. Lancet 2:665–669

Borkovec TD (1978) Self-efficacy: cause or reflexion of behavioural change? Adv Behav Res Ther 1:163–170

Bowlby J (1975) Attachment and loss, vol 2, Separation, anxiety and anger. Pelican, London, pp 334–355

Breger L, McGaugh JL (1965) Critique and reformulation of "learning-theory" approaches to psychotherapy and neurosis. Psychol Bull 63:338–358

Clark D (1986) A cognitive approach to panic. Behav Res Ther 4(24):461–470

Clark D, Salkovskis P, Chalkley A (1985) Respiratory control as a treatment for panic attacks. J Behav Ther Exp Psychiatry 16(1):23–30

Cottraux J, Mollard E (1986) Les phobies: perspectives nouvelles. Presses Universitaires de France, Paris, pp 60–65

Coué E (1956) La maitrise de soi-même par l'autosuggestion consciente. Oliven, Paris, pp 9–27

Eastman C, Marzillier JS (1984) Theoretical and methodological difficulties in Bandura's self-efficacy theory. Cog Ther Res 8(3):213–229
Ellis A (1962) Reason and emotion in psychotherapy. Lyle Stuart-Citadel, New York, pp 35–59
Ellis A (1979) A note on the treatment of agoraphobics with cognitive modification with prolonged exposure in vivo. Behav Res Ther 17(2):162–164
Ellis A, Grieger R (1977) RET handbook of rational emotive therapy. Springer, Berlin Heidelberg New York, pp 3–33
Emmelkamp P (1982) Phobic and obsessive-compulsive disorders. Theory, research, and practice. Plenum, New York, pp 40–41
Emmelkamp P, Kuipers A (1979) Agoraphobia: a follow-up study four years after treatment. Br J Psychiatry 134:352–355
Emmelkamp P, Mersch P (1982) Cognition and exposure in vivo in the treatment of agoraphobics. Short term and delayed effects. Cog Ther Res 6(1):77–88
Emmelkamp P, Kuipers A, Eggerraat J (1978) Cognitive modification versus prolonged exposure in vivo: a comparison with agoraphobics as subjects. Behav Res Ther 16:34–41
Emmelkamp P, Brilman E, Kuiper H, Mersch P (1986) The treatment of agoraphobia: a comparison of self instructional training, rational-emotive therapy, and exposure of vivo. Behav Modif (6):643–649
Garssen B, Veenendaal W, Bloeminck R (1983) Agoraphobia and the hyperventilation syndrome. Behav Res Ther 21(6):643–649
Gelder MG (1986) Panic attacks: new approaches to an old problem. Br J Psychiatry 149:346–352
Goldstein AJ, Chambless DJ (1978) A re-analysis of agoraphobia. Behav Ther 9:47–59
Gorman J, Liebowitz M, Klein OF (1984) Panic disorder and agoraphobia. Upjohn, Kalamazoo, pp 17–19
Gray J (1971) The psychology of fear and stress. McGraw Hill, New York, pp 196–218
Griez E, van den Hout A (1986) CO_2 inhalation in the treatment of panic attacks. Behav Res Ther 24(2):145–150
Guidano VF, Liotti G (1983) Cognitive processes and emotional disorders. Guilford, New York pp 204–242
Hibbert G (1984) Ideational components of anxiety: their origin and content. Br J Psychiatry 144:618–624
Hollon SD, Kriss MR (1984) Cognitive factors in clinical research and practice. Clin Psychol Rev 4:35–76
Jerrelman A, Jansson L, Ost LR (1986) Cognitive and physiological reactivity and the effects of different behavioral methods in the treatment of social phobias. Behav Res Ther 24(2):171–180
Kandel E (1983) From metapsychology to molecular biology: explorations into the nature of anxiety. Am J Psychiatry 140:1277–1293
Klein DF (1981) Anxiety reconceptualized. In: Klein DF, Rabkin JG (eds) Anxiety, new research and changing concepts. Raven, New York, pp 235–263
Ladouceur R (1983) Participant modeling with or without cognitive treatment for phobias. J Consult Clin Psychol 51(6):942–944
Last CL (1984) Cognitive treatment of phobias. Prog Behav Modif 16:65–82
Lazarus AA (1976) Multi-modal behavior therapy. Springer, Berlin Heidelberg New York, pp 9–19
Lelliot P, Marks I, Monteiro W, Tsakiris F, Noshirvani H (1986) Agoraphobics five years after imipramine and exposure: outcome and predictors. (in press)
Ley R (1985) Agoraphobia, the panic attack, and the hyperventilation syndrome. Behav Res Ther 23(1):79–81
Lum L (1976) The syndrome of habitual chronic hyperventilation. In: Hill OW (ed) Modern trends in psychosomatic medicine, 3rd edn. Butterworths, London
Luria A (1961) The role of speech in the regulation of normal and abnormal behaviors. Liveright, New York
Margraf J, Ehlers A, Roth WT (1986) Biological models of panic disorder and agoraphobia – a review. Behav Res Ther 24(5):553–557
Marks I (1981) Cure and care of neuroses. Theory and practice of behavioural psychotherapy. Wiley, New York, pp 45–66

Mavissakalian M, Michelson L, Greenwald D, Kornblith S, Greenwald M (1983) Cognitive-behavioural treatment of agoraphobia: paradoxical intention versus self-statement training. Behav Res Ther 21(1):75-86
Meichenbaum D (1977) Cognitive-behavior modification: an integrative approach. Plenum, New York, pp 17-54
Monti PR, Zwick WR, Warzak WJ (1986) Social skills and irrational beliefs: a preliminary report. Behav Ther Exp Psychiatry 17(1):11-14
Piaget J (1964) Six études de psychologie. Gonthier, Genève, pp 7-86
Rachman S (1984) Agoraphobia. A safety signal perspective. Behav Res Ther 22(1):59-70
Rotter JB (1966) Generalized expectancies for internal versus external control of reinforcement. Psychol Monogr 80:1-28
Salkovskis P, Jones D, Clark D (1986) Respiratory control in the treatment of panic attacks: replication and extension with concurrent measurement of behaviour and p CO_2. Br J Psychiatry 148:526-532
Schwartz RM, Garamoni GL (1984) The internal dialogue and anxiety: asymmetries between positive and negative coping thoughts. Paper presented at the annual convention of the Association for the Advancement of Behavior Therapy, Philadelphia, Pennsylvania
Sheehan D, Sheehan K (1982) The classification of phobic disorders. Int J Psychiatry Med 12(4):243-266
Stefanek ME, Eisler RM (1983) The current status of cognitive variables in assertiveness training. Prog Behav Modif 15:277-319
Stravinsky A, Marks I, Yule W (1982) Social skills problems in neurotic out-patients. Arch Gen Psychiatry, 39:1378-1385.
Thorpe RE, Burns LE (1983) The agoraphobic syndrome. Wiley, New York, pp 21-22
Thyer B, Nesse R, Cameron D, Curtis G (1985) Agoraphobia: a test of the separation anxiety hypothesis. Behav Res Ther 23(1):75-78
Timmermans P, Roder E, Hunting P (1986) The effects of the absence of the mother on the acquisition of phobic behaviour in cynomolgus monkeys (*Macaca fascicularis*). Behav Res Ther 24(1):67-72
Tissot R, Zutter A, Jorio G, Gaillard J, Burgmeister J (1980) Choix des symptomes dans les névroses: névroses hystériques et névroses phobico-obsessionnelles. Ann Med Psychol (Paris) 138(9):1037-1059
Tversky, Kahnemann (1974) Judgement under uncertainty: heuristics and biases. Science 185:1124-1131
van der Molen GM, van den Hout MA, Vroemen J, Lousberg H, Griez E (1986) Cognitive determinants of lactate induced anxiety. Behav Res Ther 24(6):677-680
Williams S, Rappoport A (1983) Cognitive treatment in the natural environment for agoraphobia. Behav Ther 14:299-313
Wolpe J (1975) La pratique de la therapie comportementale. Masson, Paris, pp 15-26
Zajonc R (1980) Feeling and thinking. Preferences need no inferences. Am Psychol 35:151-175

Group Cognitive-Behavioral Therapy of Depression: Two Parallel Treatment Manuals for a Controlled Study*

L. Covi[1], D.M. Roth[2], J.H. Pattison[2], and R.S. Lipman[3]

Introduction

A large measure of the development and validation of cognitive-behavioral models of depression have taken place within the past two decades. A variety of theoretical formulations have been proposed, but that originated by Beck (1967) is the most comprehensive and widely known and has attracted the interest of researchers, as well documented in this volume. A seminal study by Rush et al. (1977), reporting effectiveness of cognitive therapy in depression in a comparison with imipramine treatment, challenged clinical researchers to attempt replication. At about the same time, Shaw (1977) demonstrated effectiveness of cognitive group therapy in depression in a comparison with behavioral group therapy. In order to test the efficacy of group cognitive-behavioral therapy, a study was designed (Covi and Lipman 1987) in which group cognitive-behavioral therapy was compared with cognitive-behavioral therapy in combination with imipramine and with traditional interpersonal group therapy in outpatients with major depression. During the preparatory phases of this study numerous consultations were started with experts of both cognitive and traditional group therapy. Two manuals were drafted and later revised to guide the delivery of the two types of psychotherapy. In the hope to encourage further development of these techniques and to allow replication of this pilot study and the presently ongoing larger comparative trial, these manuals are presented here with some revisions.

It must be noted that while in the controlled pilot study cognitive-behavioral and traditional therapy were conducted in similar manner for number and length of sessions, traditional interpersonal group therapy is in present clinical practice a long-term therapy, usually practiced in diagnostically heterogenous groups. The traditional group-therapy manual therefore presents a model more suited to the study of basic group-curative factors common to all short-term groups rather than to that of the most specific advantages of interpersonal therapy.

---

*These manuals were developed with the support of USPHS Research Grant MH-33585 from the National Institute of Mental Health. Brian Shaw and Eduard Ascher were senior consultants on this project. T.A.R.U., Pikesville, MD 21208–3740, USA

[1]University of Maryland at Baltimore

[2]Sheppard Pratt Hospital, Towson, MD 21204, USA

[3]Friends Hospital, Philadelphia, PA 19124, USA

Manual for Group Cognitive-Behavioral Therapy of Depression

Role of the Group in a Cognitive-Behavioral Framework

Therapeutically beneficial change is the result of a multiplicity of factors. The therapist's style, group interaction variables, and particular treatment techniques are all significant facets of the therapeutic situation. Ensuring the maximum beneficial use of each of these parameters is perhaps the most difficult task of the cognitive-behavioral group psychotherapist. An apt description of the successful group psychotherapist is that of a conductor distributing his attention to the communication of all the members of the "orchestra" and harmoniously weaving together corrective group forces and effective cognitive techniques.

Because of the active interaction between patient and therapist typical of cognitive-behavioral therapy, the beginning cognitive-behavioral group therapist will tend to employ the same behavior with a group as with an individual patient, so that the session may be more individual therapy in a group than group therapy. When this occurs, members talk to the therapist but very little to one another: the group becomes the equivalent of a classroom or a seminar. While a psychoeducational approach is justified and widely used in cognitive treatment packages, therapeutic change can be enhanced by the promotion of group-curative factors. Yalom (1975) has enumerated 11 variables which he feels are responsible for the modification of dysfunctional patterns of behavior in group therapy. These variables are instillation of hope, universality,imparting of information, altruism, development of socializing techniques, imitative behavior, interpersonal learning, group cohesiveness, catharsis, corrective recapitulation of the primary family group, existential factors. These factors are of obvious relevance in group cognitive-behavioral therapy. In fact, Corsini and Rosenberg (1955) had previously identified a similar cluster of factors. These curative factors can be easily conceptualized in a cognitive-behavioral framework. Instillation of hope, for instance, can be viewed as representing the work being done in cognitive-behavioral therapy to change the negative view of the future. Some of the 11 factors can be related to skill learning, alternative techniques, or to cognitive work on depressogenic attitudes and on other basic beliefs.

Two important goals in the treatment of depressed patients may be realized by judiciously structuring the group interchange. First, it is characteristic of the depressed individual to be self-absorbed, believe that no one cares about him or her, think that he or she has problems which no one else may have, and so on. Such symptomatic features can be alleviated by systematically fostering group cohesiveness, exploring the universality of various concerns, and through the prompting and reinforcement of altruistic behavior. While it is being suggested that elements of the group process are eminently suitable for the treatment of depression, a caveat is in order. Catharsis is often an integral part of group therapy. A norm which encourages the free expression of dysphoric affect may further intensify hopelessness and pessimism and would, therefore, be antitherapeutic. One can circumvent this problem and demonstrate the utility of differing coping strategies by reinforcing solution-oriented cathartic exercises.

The efficacy of many cognitive-behavioral interventions can be enhanced by integrating them within the group interaction. In cognitive therapy great efforts are made to train patients to alter dysfunctional thoughts and beliefs through a process of entertaining alternative hypotheses. Rather than socratically questioning a single depressed individual, the therapist might address the entire group. As a social microcosm, the group is likely to produce a broader range in types of alternative cognitions than is the individual. The potency of the technique should thus be strengthened. Similarly, role-playing within the group is apt to have more beneficial effects than role-playing in the dyadic relationship. Here a patient is given the opportunity to practice communicating personal feelings, not just to a therapist but to a real-life peer. Hence, one would expect to find a heightened generalization effect. Analogous extrapolations are applicable to other cognitive interventions, such as reattribution therapy, assertiveness training, and so forth.

Role of the Individual in a Cognitive-Behavioral Group

While it is highly desirable to shape, prompt, and reinforce certain intermember transactions, there are times when it is necessary for a therapist to work quite closely with only one person. For example, patients often accept and feed upon each other's gloomy perceptions. When this happens, the therapist might socratically guide the client to endorse a more realistic and adaptive viewpoint. In general, the therapist endeavors to establish both a common language and conceptual framework during the first four to six therapy sessions. Often, this is best accomplished by working intensively with different patients. Therefore, one may find a disproportionately higher number of patient-therapist interactions during the early, as opposed to the later, therapy sessions.

A number of strategies are available for making patient-therapist interactions a valuable experience for the other participants. First, during the role-induction phase of treatment all clients should be told to expect occasions when they will not directly participate in an ongoing interaction. The "audience," so to speak, will be encouraged to assume an active-listener stance. By active listening, we mean that patients are informed that they could benefit by trying to identify the general therapeutic principles employed by the group leader and by determining whether these principles may be applied to their own similar problems. The therapist should make analogous efforts and, in so doing, will enhance vicarious learning opportunities. This latter point needs to be underlined as even the most reticent members of a group can realize therapeutic gains by modeling functional cognitive strategies. At the conclusion of a patient-therapist interchange, the group can be asked to comment upon what they have learned and to offer feedback. This procedure can be seen as reinforcing the audience's active-listening posture and ascertaining whether members have correctly identified meaningful intervention principles.

Another important factor to consider when conducting cognitive-behavioral group therapy involves the difference between common and individual treatment formats. There is a tendency among behaviorists to treat all patients within a given group almost identically, with each member essentially receiving the same intervention package.

For illustrative purposes, consider the problem of obesity. A number of researchers have hypothesized that obesity is functionally related to a positive energy balance (e.g., Mahoney and Mahoney 1976). As such, a group approach which demonstrates the use of a common treatment format would have all participants attempting to reduce caloric intake and increase their daily activity rate. An alternative strategy, typifying the individualized format, would have some members exercise more often, some members eat less, and some members doing both.

There are a variety of reasons which account for the use of a common treatment format. First, clinicians occasionally fall prey to the uniformity myth. It is often presupposed that a particular disorder is causally linked to one set of etiological factors, and that only a specific treatment can effectively modify a given symptomalogical pattern. Rather than applying the same techniques sequentially to a number of individuals as one would do in a dyadic relationship, the group may be seen as an efficient and economical use of the therapist's time. Analogously, many researchers find the group to be a convenient laboratory for studying the efficacy of a given treatment procedure (e.g., systematic desensitization). This setting allows one efficiently to boost the sample size. Perhaps more germane to the cognitive-behavioral treatment of depression is the dearth of sensitive psychological instruments. Although quite a few researchers have investigated the depressive's cognitive bases (Hammen and Krantz 1976), attributional style (Abramsen et al. 1978; Gong-Guy and Hammen 1980; D.M. Roth 1981, Relationship between depression and self-attribution, unpublished manuscript; Seligman et al. 1978), and pattern of attentional focus (Roth 1980), there are no validated tests which the clinician might use to individualize treatment efforts.

It is our contention that one can maximize the efficacy of group therapy by individualizing the treatment format. We clearly subscribe to the belief that the identification of patterns of maladaptive thought (i.e., automatic cognitions, cognitive mechanisms, and basic assumptions) is central to the treatment of depression. The introduction of certain treatment procedures and dyadic patient-therapist sessions throughout the course of treatment allows us to shape this therapeutic model to the unique needs of the individual treatment sessions. The first two occur at the beginning of therapy and are partially devoted to a collaborative assessment of the patient's problems. Pertinent for treatment are those problems which are symptomatic of depression (insomnia, concentrational difficulties, etc.) and causally related to depression (e.g., low baseline rate of daily mastery and pleasure experiences). Also, in order for a problem to be targeted for treatment a patient must be willing to discuss it within the group. During the ensuing time period, each patient is asked to review his or her problem list – adding, deleting, and modifying items whenever necessary.

A third individual session is held following the first two group sessions; in this third session the problem list is systematically reformulated. The advantages to a client of reformulating a problem list while alone with the therapist are twofold. First, greater attention can be directed to the identification of meaningful targets for intervention. For instance, a severely depressed person may benefit more by focusing his or her efforts upon a moderately important but easily achievable goal than by working upon a highly important goal which is more difficult to realize. The structure of an individual session provides the therapist an opportunity more fully to assess this situation. Second, given the operation of social forces and the tendency of certain depressed individuals to conform to the perceived desires of other people, initial problem reformulation in the group is not recommended. We have found that members influence each other's choice of personal problems. Hence, dyadically structured sessions are used to permit the selection of individualized intervention targets. The pragmatics of targeting personally relevent goals are as follows: the item felt to be most important to change at this stage in therapy is identified and restated as a long-term goal; long-term goal is broken down into a series of attainable short-term goals. In this manner individualized self-help exercises may be formulated, continuity of treatment is ensured, and members can assist one another in the development of new goals.

Occasionally patients run into problems when attempting to accomplish a particular long- or short-term goal. These difficulties are openly discussed within the group setting. Moreover, a formal review of the target symptom list is conducted at midcourse in the therapy program (i.e., group session 8). At this time, progress is reinforced and difficulties are dealt with in a problem-solving format.

Group Structure

The analogy has been made between the role of the therapist and that of the orchestra conductor. Therapists from all persuasions will, to varying degrees, shape the actions of their group members. This phenomenon is acutely highlighted in the case of cognitive-behavioral therapists because of their avowed directive and focused clinical style. Given this therapeutic stance, it is most important to pinpoint the structural elements of the group therapy experience. Only then can they be judiciously manipulated during the course of treatment. What follows will be an examination of various significant parameters.

One of the first questions which the therapist must answer concerns the nature of group composition. The two compositional models which have been discussed extensively within the group-therapy literature are those of patient homogeneity and heterogeneity. Essentially, it has been argued that the homogeneous group fosters cohesiveness and that the "social microcosmic" quality of the heterogeneous group facilitates interpersonal learning. However, as Yalom (1975) notes, this simple dichotomy breaks down when one looks at the group from multiple perspectives. Thus, the group which is homogeneous for sex is simultaneously heterogeneous for age.

With this in mind, one might conceptualize group composition within a functional framework. That is, membership must be consistent with, and follow from, an explication of the aims and goals of the group itself. Potential objectives are far-ranging and include: (a) determination of the efficacy of a given treatment strategy for either a multisymptomatic (Fairweather 1964; Flowers 1979; Rose 1977) or a monosymptomatic population (Rehm et al. 1979; Shaw 1977); (b) evaluation of the complex relationship between composition, group process, and treatment outcome (Cohen 1969; Flowers and Booraem 1980; Hand et al. 1974); and (c) co-development of cost-efficient therapeutic modalities for inpatient and outpatient clientele. It is important to note that these goals are by no means mutually exclusive or all-inclusive.

A second issue which must be addressed concerns the format of therapy sessions. This issue touches upon a number of related questions, one of which involves the scheduling of therapy sessions. Early in the course of treatment, when depressed individuals are most severely disturbed and in need of therapeutic counseling, it would be ideal if group sessions were held biweekly. In this manner the patient receives the greatest therapy contact at a time when it is most needed. Hence, group sessions 2 and 3 are held on successive days as are group sessions 4 and 5, with the same agendas discussed on consecutive days; we conceptualize these two 2-h sessions as being one 4-h therapy session.

A related question concerns the length of the entire treatment protocol. Do depressed patients benefit maximally from close-ended or from open-ended treatment? While there is a notable lack of studies addressing this issue, a number of prominent researchers have advocated the use of a time-limited, close-ended format (Beck et al. 1979; Lewisohn 1974). This recommendation is based upon the belief that therapy is most effective when it is problem-oriented, that depression can be readily treated within a period of 3–5 months, and that patients work harder when placed under time constraints. While we endorse these same principles and offer a 15-week trial of cognitive-behavioral group treatments, it is clear that a number of significant questions remain unanswered. For example, are clinically improved members of a group to be terminated before the final therapy session in nonresearch therapy programs? If not, how will their presence affect other members? If so, how will the group be affected, and is the vacancy to be filled? The latter questions bear upon the important issue of open-ended therapy groups. Community agencies, due to the nature of their mandates, must be able to offer treatment on request. Thus, it is imperative for the cognitive-behaviorist to develop and evaluate open-ended group models which are applicable to this setting. These issues have been addressed by our group in two related papers (Covi et al. 1982; Roth and Covi 1984).

Roles of the Therapist and Co-Therapist

Working with a group can prove to be both an emotionally and a physically draining experience. The sheer multitude of stimulation taxes the limited attentional and organizational capacities of even the best therapists. Potential consequences of attempting to balance the activities of all group members are the nonadherence to predetermined agenda items, frequent off-topic discussions, unchecked countertransference reactions, inefficient use of time, and so forth. Unfortunately, these problems are often magnified when working with a group of depressed patients. For instance, one occasionally meets the therapist who has caught the "blue" flu from his or her pessimistic groups.

This situation may be redressed by making use of a cotherapist team. Ideally, one member of the team assumes the position of the primary therapist. Functionally this person occupies a role which can be thought of as the "traffic director." It is the primary therapist who begins and ends the session, initiates and directs the discussion of various agenda items, summarizes the work of the session, handles the chalk, and so on. As traffic director, this same person must be familiar with the details of each case and, therefore, it is he or she who conducts the individual interviews.

While the primary therapist is actively engaged with the group, it is the cotherapist who reviews the homework assignments, monitors the group process, and tracks the primary therapist's transactional style. From this vantage point, important material which may have been otherwise overlooked can, instead, be introduced into the group discussion. For example, while the therapist is asking members to describe their personal agendas, the cotherapist will review and organize the collected homework assignments. By employing this system subsequent homework discussions can be systematically focused around common themes, significant events, or procedural misunderstandings. Alternatively, one relies more upon chance factors or prolonged explorative discussions to arrive at the same material.

Apart from the aforementioned role differentiation, it is important for both therapists to assume a collaborative posture. That is to say, both should have relatively equivalent access to a member or to the group. There is no a priori reason to assume that the primary therapist should make, initiate, and coordinate each intervention. Moreover, it often is therapeutically desirable for the patient to receive slightly different, albeit consistent, feedback from the two leaders. For example, consider the patient who evidences social-skill deficits. One therapist may legitimately address the patient's behavioral repertoire while the other therapist explores the cognitive constraints which this individual imposes upon himself.

In order for this relationship to work both therapists need to be cognizant of the direction the other is taking. Presession planning and postsession debriefing meetings are quite useful forums for coordinating cotherapist activity. Also, patients often benefit by observing the therapist team discuss their perceptions and spell out their assumptions. Finally, occasions will arise when a particular cotherapy issue goes unrecognized or is difficult to examine openly. As such, it is highly advantageous to make use of a consultant who has both the distance and the expertise necessary to bring such problems into focus and toward resolution.

Course of Treatment

The scientific merit of any given piece of research is partially related to the replicability of the study design and methodology. In order to meet this criterion the investigator who plans to conduct treatment-outcome research must develop and utilize a therapy manual which can be subsequently employed by other interested researchers. Extant treatment manuals typically conform to one of two formats. On the one hand, there are those manuals which specify, in detail, the procedures which will be implemented and the material that will be covered during each *session*. The work of Fuchs and Rehm (1977) and Rehm and Kornblith (1980, manual for self-control treatment of depression, unpublished manuscript) in the area of depression illustrates this orientation. On the other hand, an alternative manual design is one which delimits treatment principles and intervention techniques. Rather than strictly adhering to a standardized session structure, this type of manual outlines how pertinent procedures are to be used during different "phases" of the course of therapy. The manual for short-term, interpersonal psychotherapy of depression (Klerman et al. 1984) uses such a format.

There are clear advantages and disadvantages associated with each style of manual. Cross-study replicability is certainly heightened when using a manual which articulates the content of each and every session. However, there is one significant drawback with this genre of manuals. That is, in complying with the treatment structure, minimal allowance is made for the fact that all patients do not proceed at the same speed. Not only do groups progress at different rates, but so do individuals within a given group.

In taking this consideration into account, we have elected to design a phase-of-treatment-oriented manual. The therapeutic process may be subdivided into three major, overlapping stages. It is the therapist's task to structure his or her efforts so as to meet certain fundamental phase-relevant treatment objectives. When met, a foundation is established for the activities of the suceeding stage. Thus, the patient progresses smoothly into, through, and out of therapy. Each phase and its associated therapeutic goals will be described below. Interested readers are referred to an important article by Kanfer and Grimm (1980) for a more extensive discussion of the phases of therapy.

The clinical task of phase 1 is to facilitate the patient's entry into therapy. Treatment objectives include: (a) development of a working therapeutic alliance, (b) instillation of hope, (c) education of the patient regarding the principles of cognitive-behavior therapy and their relevance to depression, and (d) identification of significant problem areas. These treatment goals are expected to be reached by session 5.

Therapists have a wide variety of clinical strategies at their disposal for meeting stage 1 objectives. Foremost in their repertoire is the use of relationship-enhancement techniques such as empathy, genuineness, and warmth (Barrett-Lennard 1962). Acknowledging the importance of these transactional variables, Beck and his associates have developed a quite valuable therapist-competency checklist which can be used to monitor and provide feedback to therapists concerning their transactional style.

Patient education provides another means of achieving therapeutically oriented goals. For example, during the first two therapeutic contacts (individual sessions 1 and 2) a role-induction procedure is used to shape each participant's conception of the multidimensional nature of depression and its relationship to dysfunctional patterns of thought. Analogously, the therapist and patient collaboratively review the ground rules for participation in group psychotherapy. Thus, during the first assembled group session members are informed about the importance of confidentiality, participation, and so on.

What has been described up to this point is the use of "within-treatment" procedures. A fundamental premise of cognitive-behavior modification is that protherapeutic change takes place largely outside of the formal treatment environment. Self-help exercises are utilized to facilitate this process. Therefore, in meeting phase 1 objectives, "in" therapy experiences (e.g., reviewing *present symptoms*) are reinforced by the liberal use of "extra" therapy homework assignments (monitoring situation, thought, and mood, reading *Coping with depression*, etc.). A descriptive outline of stage 1 goals and associated clinical strategies can be found in Table 1.

If the tasks of phase 1 have been satisfactorily executed, the patient should be prepared to enter phase 2 of therapy. Clinical endeavors are now centered around the implementation of pertinent cognitive-behavioral modification techniques. Critical symptoms and negative automatic cognitions which have already been identified, as well as cognitive mechanisms and basic assumptions which will soon be pinpointed, are the targets of therapeutic efforts. Protherapeutic change is engendered by utilizing techniques which teach the client to test the accuracy of his or her cognitions, reattribute responsibility for his or her actions, rehearse alternative thoughts and behavior sequences, assert his or her rights, and so on (Beck et al. 1979). It is important to note that therapy is conducted on two levels. First, given our beliefs about the nature of depression, a number of techniques are applied to the group as a whole. For example, beginning in session 2 all members are trained to identify, recall, and initiate master/pleasure activities. Second, clinical regimes are individualized, matching procedures with personal goals. Thus, stimulus-control procedures might be recommended for weight-gain problems and distraction would be employed for ruminative difficulties.

Table 1. Phase 1 of therapy

Objectives	Techniques
1. Development of therapeutic alliance 2. Instillation of hope 3. Shape conceptualization of depression and treatment 4. Identification of significant problem areas	1. Establishment of collaborative relationship. Demonstration of warmth, empathy, genuineness. 2. Foster positive therapeutic expectancies. Patient informed about treatment efficacy (i.e., Beck and his associates). Differentiate between current and past therapies. 3. Symptom-oriented role-induction procedures. Help patient to identify dimensions of depression and expect symptomatic fluctuation. 4. Cognitive-behavior-therapy role induction. Point out the relationship between dysfunctional thought style and depression. Emphasize the importance of identifying and modifying maladaptive beliefs and cognitions. Read *Coping with Depression* (Beck and Greenberg 1974). 5. Treatment role induction. Emphasize the importance of regular attendance and completion of homework assignments. Patients are also asked to telephone if unable to attend a session and to participate in an exit interview if they are an early dropout. All individuals receive a schedule of group and individual meeting times. Confidentiality is stressed. The "go around" concept of noncoerced participation is described. The importance of constructive feedback is highlighted. Patients are encouraged to take notes during the session. 6. Significant problem areas contributing to depression are identified during individual sessions 1 and 2, reviewed at home, and reformulated during individualized session 3. Individualized long- and short-term goals are drawn up at this time.

The monitoring and evaluation of treatment efficacy is a common objective of phase 2. If therapy is to be effective, the clinician must know whether target symptoms are changing and whether patients are properly executing treatment strategies. To achieve this goal we regularly collect, inspect, and discuss BDI scores, completed homework assignments, and goal-orientation forms. Patients are also required to comment upon weekly self-help assignments. Information gained through these sources is openly discussed, with problems being resolved at each session.

Moreover, we conduct two review sessions during this phase of therapy. The first review concerns the basic cognitive skills that patients have been learning to use to cope with their depression. It is conducted after patients have discussed the following techniques: Master and Pleasure (M&P); Situation, Cognition, Mood (SCM); and Rational Thought Worksheet (RTW). The second review pertains to basic assumptions. It is held after all patients have begun to identify and evaluate their core depressogenic beliefs.

Phase 2 begins at individual session 2 with the introduction of a M&P assignment and ends at group session 13. Patients are faced with a bewildering array of therapeutic procedures, treatment objectives, etc. during the course of treatment. Confusion is minimized and learning is buttressed by reviewing basic techniques at group session 4 or 5 (i.e., M&P, SCM, RTW). As noted above, a similar review of the target-symptom list is conducted at midcourse in treatment. Table 2 contains an outline of phase 2 objectives and pertinent techniques.

The client's ability to utilize cognitive-behavioral techniques in order to prevent and remediate future depressive episodes is the hallmark of a successful clinical trial. The aim of the third phase of treatment is to maximize the likelihood that therapeutic gains will be continued after the patient formally terminates. In actuality, the seeds of this phase of therapy are sown in phase 2 of treatment. That is, the responsibility for developing homework assignments and deciding which technique to use is gradually shifted from therapist to client. In so doing, not only can the clinician pinpoint and correct mistakes, but the patient is provided with the opportunity to practice his or her newly acquired self-control skills.

Table 2. Phase 2 of therapy

Objectives	Techniques
1. Implementation of cognitive-behavior modification procedure	1. Pinpoint significant negative automatic cognitions, cognitive mechanisms, basic beliefs, symptomatic behaviors, and other factors which are causally related to depression.
2. Monitor and evaluate treatment efficacy	2. Implement pertinent techniques at both group and individual levels.
	3. Collect, and cotherapist reviews, BDI to spot critical areas and propose agenda items; goal orientation sheets and self-help exercises. Collaboratively discuss findings.
	4. Problem-solve with the group different means of resolving therapeutically relevant problems. Facilitate reinforcement or protherapeutic change.
	5. Review treatment strategies.
	6. Review progress upon target symptoms.

Table 3. Phase 3 of therapy

Objectives	Techniques
1. Examine and discuss termination issues 2. Maximize treatment generalization	1. Encourage patients to express fearsfully. Apply cognitive-behavioral techniques to negative predictions. 2. Review accurate post-treatment expectations. Acknowledge the possibility of future depressions. 3. Stress importance of continuing to use previously acquired self-control skills. Provide patients with package of relevant forms. 4. Foster, where appropriate, internal attributions for observed clinical improvement. 5. Review successful treatment strategies and progress on target symptoms.

Group sessions 14 and 15 are devoted to an examination of significant termination issues. During this time patients are encouraged to express and discuss their fears about leaving treatment. Common sources of anxiety center around the belief that they are not yet completely cured, or that they will experience future depressive episodes. In addition to questioning the accuracy of these negative predictions, members are reminded that it is human to become depressed, and that such experiences will enable them to develop continually and to refine their cognitive-behavioral skill repertoire. Members are provided with a packet of forms (e.g., RTW, M&P monitoring sheet, etc.) to use on these occasions. All participants are also asked to reflect upon the nature and degree of their clinical improvements. A formal review of each patient's progress upon target symptoms is conducted at the last session. Members identify procedures which were effective in remediating various problems. They are also encouraged to continue to design and implement self-help cognitive-therapy programs for any remaining areas of difficulty.

Finally, we have found that patients often attribute their protherapeutic change to the group. Efforts are therefore made to differentiate between externally relevant factors, such as group support, and internally meaningful attributions regarding their knowledge and successful use of self-help strategies. Table 3 outlines the objectives and techniques of phase 3.

Session Structure

Beck and his colleagues have emphasized the importance of structuring each therapy contact. We concur with this opinion for both research (e.g., internal validity) and clinical reasons. By structuring the therapy session one increases the likelihood that: (a) significant clinical material will not go unattended, (b) relevant concepts and techniques will be brought up for discussion, and (c) "in" therapy experiences are reinforced by "extra" therapy activities. The need to structure each session is further underscored when working the multitude of stimuli which are present in the group context. We have found that treatment flows smoothly and that clinically pertinent issues are addressed when the following format is employed:

1. Describe personal agenda items
2. Review "unfinished" agenda items of prior session
3. Review patients' responses to prior session(s)
4. Examine significant shifts in clinical status
5. Review homework assignments
6. Discuss personal agenda items and special topics
7. Assign homework
8. Summarize this session

The establishment of personal agenda items is a central point in the therapy session. Patients are asked to state briefly what they would like to focus on during the session. Pertinent for discussion are experiences related to depression and goal-oriented progress reports. In this manner continuity of treatment is ensured while not at the expense of overlooking crisis situations. Efforts are made by the cotherapist to integrate personal agenda items into the homework review. Otherwise, in the interest of efficiency, assignments will be reviewed which represent common experiences, illustrate a principle which is difficult to grasp, are worthy of social reinforcement, exemplify a topic which will be discussed that session, and so forth.

Significant shifts in clinical status are examined next. Patients are asked to report any changes. At this juncture the cotherapist is responsible for checking critical items of the BDI (i.e., suicidality) and determining whether this particular score significantly departs from past patterns of scores; the cotherapist deems it appropriate, he or she then proposes to discuss such critical areas.

It has been our experience that patients often enter a session with "unfinished business" from previous contacts. For instance, a patient may be angry with the clinician because of a faulty interpretation of a therapeutic directive, or the disclosure of a highly personal concern may have resulted in significant embarrassment. Until these feelings and associated cognitions are thoroughly examined and dealt with, a patient may get little out of a therapeutic encounter. We therefore ask patients to bring such problems to our attention at the beginning of each session. It is important to note that these reviews are aimed not only at the processing of negative experiences. Patients are also encouraged to describe the positive effects of group therapy (e.g., cohesion, interpersonal learning), the benefits of a particular technique, and so on.

The bulk of most treatment sessions involves the discussion of personal agenda items and special topics. Part of this time may be spent addressing a new technique or concept which has been introduced by the therapist. For instance, the alternative-thought technique may be brought up during one session, the importance of monitoring M&P experiences may be discussed during another session, and the notion of basic assumptions may be the focus of a third session. This time is also spent comprehensively examining patients' personal agenda items. Whenever possible, similar topics are "chunked" and reviewed conjointly. Efforts are made by both therapists to cover all agenda items. However, there will be occasions when a disproportionate amount of time must be devoted to one or more patients. Such inequitable distributions of time should be corrected at subsequent sessions.

Individualized self-help exercises are formulated at the end of each session. Ideally, homework assignments are directly related to material discussed during that same session. These "extra" therapy experiences are designed to aid patients in their endeavors at obtaining long- and short-term goals and to develop adaptive styles of thinking. Assignments should be realistically achievable given a person's behavioral repertoire and level of functioning. The responsibility for creating a particular self-help exercise should be shared between the patient, the therapist, and the group. As the course of therapy progresses, patients should assume an increasingly greater responsibility for designing their own assignments.

The session typically ends with a review of the day's highlights. To check upon the group's assimilation of important concepts, the therapist may ask members to summarize what they have learned. Patients are also requested to note which material had not been covered and therefore needs to be reviewed next week. Finally, group members may be polled about their response to the session. In this way, closure may be reached upon issues which might otherwise have had a disruptive effect upon the members' functioning.

Table 4. Pre-set agendas

Individual session 1

1. Set agenda (preset form)
2. Complete administrative activities
   A. Consent form
   B. Role of clinical evaluation
   C. Calendar of study
3. Develop therapeutic alliance
4. Determine therapeutic expectations
5. Review clinical history – complete clinical forms: GAS, CARD, target symptoms
6. Begin to identify significant problem areas
7. Implement cognitive-behavior modification role-induction procedure
   A. Central concepts
   B. Illustrate relevance of model by focusing on target symptoms
   C. Language
8. Foster positive therapeutic expectations
9. Review use and rationale of activity-mood worksheet
10. Explain importance of self-help assignments
11. Have patient monitor activity and mood
12. Ask patient to read *Coping with Depression*
13. Elicit feedback about session
14. Summarize the session

Individual session 2

1. Set agenda (preset form)
2. Scan BDI for critical areas
3. Elicit reactions to first session
4. Discuss current clinical status
   A. Complete clinical forms GAS, CARD, target symptoms
   B. Review possible new target symptoms
5. Review patient's response to *Coping with Depression*
6. Go over mood and activity homework
7. Discuss the influence of intervening cognitions
8. Point out the importance of monitoring and recalling mastery and pleasure experiences (M&P)

9. Continue to identify significant problem areas
10. Have patient monitor and review M&P experiences
11. Elicit feedback about the session
12. Summarize session

Group session 1

1. Set agenda (preset form)
2. Scan BDI for critical areas
3. Introduce patients to one another
4. Review ground rules
5. Discuss expectations about group therapy
6. Implement group-therapy role-induction procedure
7. Develop group cohesion by discussing reasons for attending therapy
8. Ask for feedback about individual session 2
9. Discuss current clinical status
10. Go over M&P assignment
11. Discuss personal agenda and the relationship between situation, cognition, and mood (SCM)
12. Assign M&P and SCM monitoring exercise
13. Elicit feedback about session
14. Summarize session

Group session 2

1. Set personal agenda
2. Scan BDI for critical areas
3. Elicit reactions to past session
4. Discuss current clinical status
5. Review SCM and M&P homework
6. Discuss personal agenda items
7. Reassign M&P and SCM monitoring exercise
8. Remind patients that problem areas will be reformulated in the next session
9. Elicit feedback about the session
10. Summarize the session

Individual session 3

1. Set personal agenda and explain purpose of session
2. Scan BDI for critical areas
3. Elicit reactions to past group session
4. Discuss issues which patient had difficulty addressing in the group
5. Discuss current clinical status
6. Review target symptoms and discuss any new symptoms
7. Review M&P and SCM assignment
8. Discuss personal agenda items and reformulate problem list
9. Reconceptualize most important problem in the form of short- and long-term goals
10. Reassign session 2 homework and an additional self-help exercise which pertains to target goal
11. Elicit feedback about the session
12. Summarize the session

Group sessions 3–13

1. Set personal agenda (allow for session to review cognitive skills and basic beliefs)
2. Scan BDI for critical areas
3. Elicit reactions to past group sessions
4. Discuss current clinical status
5. Review homework
6. Discuss personal agenda items and special topics
7. Assign homework
8. Elicit feedback about the session
9. Summarize session

Table 4 *(Continued)*

Group sessions 14 and 15
1. Set personal agenda
2. Scan BDI for critical areas
3. Elicit reactions to past session
4. Discuss clinical status and overall progress
5. Review homework assignments
6. Discuss personal agenda items and concerns about termination
7. Develop post-therapy goals and associated self-help exercises
8. Provide therapy forms to patients
9. Review progress on target symptoms and techniques utilized
10. Elicit feedback about the session
11. Summarize the session

Manual for Short-term Traditional Group Psychotherapy of Depression

General Principles

Short-term group psychotherapy for depressives is an experimental program designed to enlist the therapeutic modalities of dynamic-group psychotherapy in the service of short-term therapy for patients with moderately severe depressive illnesses treated in diagnostically homogeneous groups.

The techniques presented in this manual are based on a number of operational assumptions:

1. A group of depressed patients will share a variety of depressive themes. Facilitating identification with each other and, thereby, promoting the development of group cohesiveness will foster the therapeutic effects of universality (Yalom 1975).
2. The depressive's "problem with authority," compounded by difficulties expressing and exploring the ramifications of resentment, disappointment, and anger and by unacknowledged dependencies, can be dealt with better within a group setting, where this problem may be faced in its complexity in the company of peers, than it can be alone with the therapist.
3. Diagnostic clarity with respect to the peculiarities of the depressive psychodynamics in the individual patient will enable the therapist to be a more effective leader, while expediting the achievement of insight into his or her depressive predicament.
4. The expectation of a treatment course of predetermined and relatively brief duration will accelerate the processes of self-disclosure. This, in turn, will lead to greater interaction, while promoting group cohesiveness and the therapeutic dynamics of confrontation, clarification, and insight.
5. The group therapist is an experienced clinician who has been trained in dynamic-group psychotherapy.

Table 5. Outline of the course of short-term group psychotherapy for depressives

Phase 1:	Sessions 1–4 – Evocative-supportive phase The intent is to promote cohesion, universality, and altruism by way of the balanced sharing of symptomatology, aggravating circumstances, insights, and by the discussion of emergent themes. *Transitional question:* "How well do we understand each other's predicament?"
Phase 2:	Sessions 5–9 (10, 11) – Clarification by way of identifying self-defeating trends and resistances to change The intent is to impart an appreciation of how one's illness or dysphoria is determined or influenced by idiosyncracies of perceptions and response. Consideration is given to what is changeable and to what is unlikely to change. A typical question from the leader is, "How well does the group [sic] understand X's predicament?" *Transitional directive:* "I would like each of you to share with us what you have so far learned about how you make things worse for yourself."
Phase 3:	Sessions (10, 11) 12–15 – Assimilative-reorientation phase The intent is to utilize our understanding of self-defeating assumptions, trends, attitudes, and character traits in an ongoing endeavor to initiate a better way of life as defined by one's own aspirations and interests.

Formulation of the Group

Patient-selection criteria will vary according to the exigencies of clinical practice or the particularities of one's research interests. For the purposes of our current investigative work, patients selected will have the diagnosis of Major Depressive Episode as defined by DSM-III (1980). Patients with psychotic features, addictions, histories of manic episodes, or in need of hospitalization will be excluded. Intelligence and motivation will be judged adequate for a short-term course of psychotherapy. Prospective patients must be willing to enter a group which will include six to eight patients together with a therapist and an occasional observer.

The group will meet for 2 h, once weekly, for a total of 15 sessions. All patients will begin treatment at the same time; no patients will be introduced during the course of treatment.

Role Induction: Pre-Group Individual Sessions

Each patient will meet with the therapist twice, in individual sessions, in advance of the initial group meeting. There are three purposes to be served in these preparatory meetings. The first is to ascertain the nature of the depressive psychopathology in the individual patient. The second is to outline the process and purposes of group psychotherapy. The third purpose is to establish rapport and a therapeutic alliance, while being mindful that initially the patient's allegience to the group is mediated by the leader.

Depression may be viewed as a result of developmental deficits, traumatic events, and pathological-depressive assumptions (Frank 1961). Inevitably there is a degree of loss of self-esteem which is associated with assumptions of deficiency and inferiority, together with a pervasive sense of helplessness and vulnerability. Frequently, there is difficulty in expressing and managing emotions, particularly anger. Frequently, there is a history of object loss, or threatened loss, in association with pathological dependency and the assumption that without the significant other(s) "I am lost." It is important to be aware of the successes the individual has enjoyed, as well as the failures and the attendant demoralization. Inquiry will be made in reference to moral standards, issues of conformity, the super-ego, and ego-ideal; parallel issues are those of self-esteem, self-confidence, and feelings of worthlessness. The therapist should ascertain whether there is a conspicuous narcissistic orientation, with the corresponding assumptions of privilege, entitlement, and superiority, together with unrealistic expectations of others, and what they will supply. He or she will also determine whether the depressive psychopathology has been accentuated by loss of role status and/or reinforcements and incentives.

After the developmental and psychiatric histories have been reviewed with the patient's participation, an outline will be presented of what the upcoming group psychotherapy seeks to accomplish. The patient will be advised that group interactions should broaden his or her perspectives on the how's and why's of the depressive experience, and that the group should become an educational process in which the participants come to appreciate what can be done in order to escape the depressive predicament. The patient will be asked to scrutinize his or her thinking and behavior (within the group and outside of it) in order to discover for himself or herself how certain idiosyncratic assumptions about self and others maintain and perpetuate the depressive condition. The point will be made that group interactions can expose these enduring, but often preconscious, assumptions so that the patient can eliminate them or restrict the scope of their effects.

The fact that the group provides an opportunity for the depressed person to discover how his or her depressive demeanor affects others will also be illustrated.

Next, the patient is informed that group psychotherapy proceeds on the assumption that all participants agree on, and comply with, certain norms. The most important of these are: participation is essential and should be interactive and responsive; what is disclosed should be attended to in a thoughtful but nonjudgmental fashion; it is important to be aware of and to give expression to resentment, conflict, affection, and other feeling states; and, finally, the identity of or other information about the participants should not be revealed to outsiders. The importance of regular attendance, as well as of being on time for all meetings, is stressed. Patients will be advised that they may consider dropping out at some point during the group process; they should give careful attention to why they are thinking of leaving the group and should share their thoughts with the group. They are informed that dropping out can be damaging to beneficial changes which depend on completion of the therapeutic task. Manifest resistance to group psychotherapy should be dealt with in advance, and if the prospective patient is judged not suitable for a group approach, an alternative treatment should be recommended.

Group Process

Initial Phase

In the first group meeting the leader announces that the group will convene once weekly for a series of 15 sessions. He or she reminds the group that the sessions will last 2 h. He or she then invites the patients in turn to introduce themselves, to report what has been most troubling, to outline briefly the aggravating circumstances and what has been tried in an effort to overcome the depression, and, finally, to share with the group what insights they may have into how they themselves makes life more difficult or trying. The therapist then tells the group that anyone who wants to ask a question or add a comment may do so at anytime. Notice is thereby served that group therapy is relational, dynamic, interactive, and that the initiative belongs with the patient.

After the introductions the therapist proposes a topic for consideration by all members, again for the purpose of promoting interactions but also in order to focus on emergent themes. If anger or resentment has been conspicuous in the introductions, he or she will ask the group to reflect on the varieties of ways in which people manage anger and kindred emotions. Discussions of anger lead naturally to considerations of how we manage guilt, helplessness, failure, separation, disappointment, and loss. Other themes or topics which are especially significant for depressives include self-confidence, and the lack of it, and conflicts inherent in conformity and in dependency. Many of these issues will have been identified by the therapist in the pre-group role-induction sessions and will emerge in the group setting in the introductory comments.

The introduction of topics for discussion serves to involve the patient in the group process while respecting the patient's anxiety and defensive disinclination to expose him- or herself in the initial sessions.

It is incumbent upon the therapist to see to it that each member has an opportunity to comment on some aspect of his or her illness, on perceptions of self and others, in each meeting. If there is a manifest resistance to involvement, the therapist seeks an explanation from the patient – if one is not forthcoming in response to questioning by other group members. The passivity and isolation which are characteristic of the depressed patient are countered by the demand characteristics of the situation and by the arousal of a variety of emotions, whether by transference or by the inevitable conflicts of values and loyalties among the individual patients.

The therapist's primary responsibility in the first four meetings is the unification of the group. The unification of the group is expedited by the rule of sharing and responding. It is further expedited by identification (whether by virtue of age, sex, life circumstances, experiences, or common allegiances) and by the recognition, appreciation, and support deriving from this. The first stage is, by intent, evocative and supportive. In the first phase, which spans the first four sessions, the group is modeling interactive-introspective self-disclosure. The expectation is that we learn together to see ourselves as others see us. The collective insight enlarges our perspectives and inculcates an appreciation of the diversity of experiences and of actions and reactions. This in turn promotes a sense of freedom which invites self-determination while modifying the isolation and helplessness which are so frequently parts of depressive experiences.

In an effort to establish momentum the therapist terminates each of the first two meetings by asking the patients each to bring to the next session one or two items which they believe will add to our understanding of their depressive predicament and of their efforts to escape or to endure. The group members are further advised that if they find themselves resistive to our efforts to understand each other better, these resistances should also be revealed so that the group may comment on them.

Starting with the onset of the third session, the therapist looks for volunteers to open the meeting. He or she begins to discern patterns of activity and passivity, of initiative and retreat.

We find it expedient to break for 10 min midway in the 2-h sessions, not only for the purposes of a brief rest and refreshments but also because a break can introduce a change of focus. The therapist may elect to continue with the discussion which was interrupted for the sake of the break.

Our procedure provides for an individual interview for 1 h after the second group meeting. The primary purpose of the session is to anticipate resistance to group involvement and to deal with those which are apparent.

The patient is asked to reflect on whether the preceptions, judgments, attitudes, and behavior of group members are reminiscent of his or her experiences with family, peers, teachers, fellow workers, and marriage partners. Patients are apt to be very explicit in reporting how they identify with one or more of the group members. They may recognize the transferential aspects of their impressions of the others, including, of course, the leader. If, in the group a patient appears isolated, the therapist will call attention to common bonds, predicaments, and themes.

In this private session the therapist is asked to comment on those themes which have been of special interest to him or her in the group discussions, which will include anger, guilt, loss, dependency, and failure. We may discover that the patient is hesitant to divulge information or to ask questions. Usually, we reassure patients that it is right and proper to do so. We remind them that it is their group, their opportunity, and that their contribution is vital to the ongoing effectiveness of the group.

How may the introductory phase of short-term group psychotherapy modify the depressive's psychopathology? It offers the depressed patient supportive allies, who, like the patient, are conversant with the depressive experience; it also offers an expectant hopefulness by way of the group's availability and expressed interest in what the patient says about him- or herself and others. The presumed benefit is mainly preparatory. The depressed person may gain recognition and approval when he or she ventures an opinion or shares an observation. If the patient is called upon to elaborate on or to clarify what has been said, it is likely that the leader will communicate his or her interest and appreciation, verbally, or by gesture. If the patient is excessively dependent on one or more significant other (outside the group), the pathological dependency may be diluted or attenuated by involvement in the group, where the focus is on self-differentiation. If the patient does not find a measure of recognition and acceptance in the introductory-preparatory phase, the likelihood that he or she will drop out is increased.

Middle or Transitional Phase

The leader opens the fifth session by asking the group to respond to the question, "How well do we understand each other?" The intent of the question is twofold. First, it serves to bring summaries of each patient's current predicament to the attention of the group. The responses are measures of the clarity and openness of the members' self-disclosures and also of resistances and evasiveness. Each patient is given an opportunity to clarify his or her position and to ask for clarification from those whose remarks remain obscure. Secondly, the question introduces the group to the second stage, or process, in short-term psychotherapy, which is a concerted effort to expose and to identify self-defeating trends and assumptions (including persistent avoidance of changes and experimentation).

The middle phase is often characterized by disillusionment, ambivalence, and conflict, accentuated by the depressive's yearning for a nurturing, omnipotent, and infallible guide, or by his or her hidden competitiveness and envy, and by the knowledge that ours is a short-term venture.

The therapeutic aim in the second stage is to facilitate the acquisition of insights by balancing confrontations with supportive endeavors, a balance which is often provided by the group members with minimal involvement by the therapist. The therapist emphasizes the importance of a diversity of opinion, inclination, and emotionality, as the members evaluate each other's life experiences and adaptive responses. He or she invites the participants to expand the scope of alternative ways of thinking and acting by giving expression to their evaluations of each other's remarks and behavior. The overall intent is to expose latent conflicts both between members and within individuals, so as to prepare the way for adaptive and rewarding changes, which will be considered in the final stage. The therapist speaks favorably of conflict and diversity by indicating to the group that constructive-therapeutic changes presuppose a recognition of options as well as ideals and knowledge of one's strengths and weaknesses.

The group therapist prefers a less active role in the second (middle) stage. The tendency is to invite the group to respond to the individual patient's comments or behavior, while judging for him- or herself how well the patients' therapeutic needs are being met. The therapist does not assign "homework" or otherwise direct the members to consider specific questions or topics beyond the confines of the group meeting. Instead, he or she looks to the group to provide a diversity of appraisals, suggestions, comments, questions, challenges, and choices, in the expectation that with conflict and variety the likelihood of maturational changes is increased. If the leader succeeds in cultivating an increasingly interactional group, he or she will become aware of resentments and anger, whether expressed openly, or covertly in dreams or in nonparticipation. He or she will be reminded that changes are difficult, and that resignation or retreat may be more tolerable. Nevertheless, the individual patients within the group are not apt to be left alone. Others tend to exhort them to give consideration to their options and opportunities.

In the second stage the group ideally becomes the primary therapeutic agent. Ideally, no one person, whether leader or member, becomes the court of last resort. Presumably, the effect is to bring the individual patient to a more vivid realization of what can change and what cannot as a result of one's own efforts in the present life situation.

How may the confrontation and the exposure to conflict and to the diversities of opinion and feeling states which are emphasized in the second stage benefit the depressed patient? A patient may learn that the expression of anger can be a legitimate, appropriate, and effective communication to significant others, alerting them to what is vital to him- or herself, that the dominant other(s) in the past or present has other, more generous and accepting counterparts elsewhere in the world, and that more benign or permissive standards may offer incentives for less constricting self-appraisals. By intent, the second stage facilitates the acquisition of a more mature individuation by way of selective changes in goals, attitudes, evaluations, and behavior.

The therapist's involvement with the group continues beyond the period of the meeting. Immediately after each session the therapist devotes him- or herself to a period of review, and then prepares a written summary of the session to be distributed to the members. In doing this the therapist also reconsiders each patient's characteristic difficulties with self-esteem, anger, dependency, standards (whether external or internal), and with separations and losses. He or she reflects on whether the group is sufficiently coherent and supportive, on the one hand, and on the other, adequately devoted to the tasks of clarification and confrontation, if the second stage has been reached for all, or for most. The therapist prepares him- or herself for the next meeting by being alert to each patient's unfinished business, so that he or she can intervene at opportune moments (if the fellow patients are not doing it themselves) on behalf of patients who are resentful but whose anger is suppressed and on behalf of patients who are unduly dependent or submissive, whether within the group or without. The primary therapeutic task is to direct attention to what the patient is doing, or not doing, to perpetuate his or her depressive position.

Final Phase

In the last four to six meetings, the leader prepares the patients for the impending dissolution of the group. Whereas the leader was the dominant figure in the first stage, and the group was consulted preferentially in the middle period, in the last stage the individual patient is called to account for what he or she has assimilated from the group and discovered by reactive introspection. The therapist opens the final phase with the request, "I would like each one of you to share with us what you have so far learned about how you make things worse for yourself." This statement presupposes that the group in its development in the previous weeks has highlighted certain pathogenic attitudes and assumptions underlying tendencies to avoid making forthright statements to important others or to a persistent inability or unwillingness to permit exploitation (to specific typical depressive quandaries). The task at hand is to assist individual participants in coming to an awareness of what they themselves are doing to perpetuate the depressive illness.

When the responses are characterized by insightful self-awareness, they are then considered in conjunction with the question, "What can you do in order to escape from the depressive predicament?"

If a patient affirms that he or she has discovered nothing which will enable avoidance of a depressive illness or attenuation of its effects, the group must address the helplessness and/or defiance which is implied, together with considerations of levels of aspiration and resignation, and those "reality considerations" which are not likely to be modifiable.

Initial responses tend to be evasive, halting, and self-depreciatory because of the separation anxiety inherent in the situation; but we begin with the assumption that the patients have gained, or regained, a sense of what they can do in order to establish a degree of satisfying autonomy, while reviewing various options and respecting the diversity of opinions as to what they should do.

With termination, the loss of the group's support and the attendant mourning may enable patients to live tolerably well with imperfections as perceived in themselves and in others, which is a major achievement for the depressive with a substantial narcissistic orientation. But, although there is a place for resignation and acceptance, the therapist seeks to inculcate a degree of hopefulness in all parties throughout the course of therapy, in the expectation that in spite of defeats, failures, and losses, it is worthwhile to consider new careers, new roles, and new endeavors, always in response to the question, "What is truly important to me?"

Special Problems

The Late Comer. A patient who arrives late is admitted to the group upon arrival, but it is not our policy to comment on his tardiness, nor do we accomodate him by recapitulating what has transpired in his absence. The late comer is asked to fill out any rating scales due during the intermission or after the group session has ended.

The Absentee Therapist. In the event that the therapist anticipates his absence, he will advise the group in advance. An observer or other colleague will take his place. Concern has been expressed that if the group knows that the therapist will be absent, there is an added incentive for the patients to skip the session. But if the group is coherent and dedicated, this should not happen and, besides, the therapist expects the patients to notify him in advance if they expect to be absent.

The Suicidal Patient and Symptomatic Deterioration. Inevitably suicide becomes a focal point for discussion in a group of depressives. The potentially lethal sequence of despair and constriction, coupled with the realization that one can indeed put an end to one's present sufferings by suicide, can be neutralized by those in the group who can appreciate the ambivalence and conflict attending suicidal reflections. As a result, the impetus towards a suicidal act is weakened by contextualization with other psychological events and influences and by empathic involvement with others.

In the event that a patient's condition deteriorates to the point that alternative treatment is mandatory in the judgment of the therapist, the patient is discharged from the group and referred to a different treatment modality, mainly, of course, to provide optimal care for the patient but also to forestall the group's attention being disproportionately focused on a single patient. Symptomatic worsening can happen in response to the impending dissolution of the group, to a pervasive sense that once again one is failing to measure up to expectations, and as a result of unconscious resentments in response to the frustrations of infantile strivings for unconditional and everlasting acceptance.

The Returning Absentee. If the absentee has not given a cogent reason for absence, it is our policy to contact him or her and to advise that we are hopeful that he or she will return to the group for the next session. When the absentee returns, it is not the leader's practice to summarize the previous session. If the absentee has questions relating to what has transpired in his or her absence, the unannounced expectation is that the absentee will ask them on his or her own initiative. Absences are especially disruptive of the therapeutic process in short-term group psychotherapy.

The Drop-Out. Dropping out, as a resistance phenomenon or as a consequence of disillusionment, is dealt with initially by way of anticipation. In the role-induction sessions preceding the first meeting of the group the patients are each advised that they may consider leaving the group during the course of treatment because of intragroup stresses, disillusionment, or unanticipated inconveniences. They are informed that if they are considering dropping out, they should bring this matter into the group for discussion. We recognize that there are perceptual distortions in depressives which tend to mitigate against a therapeutic outcome in group psychotherapy: others are viewed as demanding or critical, and the depressive reacts with avoidance, a rising sense of failure, helplessness, resentment, and isolation. Some patients do not accept and/or assimilate the norms and tasks which belong to the group-therapeutic enterprise, whether because of the severity of their illnesses and/or because of substantial narcissistic traits. The dropping-out phenomenon suggests to the therapist that there has been a lack of balance between unduly stressful exposures and interactions within the group, on the one hand, and supportive measures, on the other, to which the patient has responded by a regressive avoidance of conflicts, or "flight into health."

The single most important factor in dropping out in the early stages is the patient's relationship to the leader. The three individual sessions held early in the treatment course should strengthen that tie and thereby reduce the likelihood that the patient will leave the group.

Final Assessment

Each patient is seen by the therapist and by an independent evaluator following the last group session. The purpose of this session is to assess improvement and indications for further treatment.

An auxiliary consideration in the final assessment is our ongoing interest in further defining the indications and contraindications for short-term group psychotherapy for depressives.

Afterword

These two manuals were elaborated through an extended period of pilot work on a controlled study of group cognitive-behavioral therapy, group cognitive-behavioral therapy combined with imipramine, and traditional interpersonal group psychotherapy, which has been presented elsewhere (Covi and Lipman 1987; Covi and Lipman in press). The concepts and techniques presented are the result of the experience of the authors, as well as the derivation of consultations with several experts of both cognitive and traditional therapies. These techniques and our application of them have further evolved in the past few years, and our manual has been somewhat modified and enriched in the ongoing, larger, controlled study which developed from the earlier pilot study. In addition to our research work we have also continued to conduct a clinical practice group in an open-ended format and the specific techniques used in this group have been reported elsewhere (Roth and Covi 1984; Covi and Primakress). We hope that by making available these manuals we will stimulate other clinicians and researchers to develop further the techniques of group psychotherapy and to systematize them in treatment manuals. We would also greatly welcome replication of our research work.

Acknowledgement. Mundi Winogrodski lent secretarial assistance to the preparation of this chapter.

References

Abramson LY, Seligman MEP, Teasdale JD (1978) Learned helplessness in humans: critique and reformulation. J Abnorm Psychol 87:49–74

Barrett-Lennard GT (1962) Dimensions of therapist response as causal factors in therapeutic change. Psychol Monogr 76(43):562

Beck AT (1967) Depression: clinical, experimental, and theoretical aspects. Harper and Rowe, New York

Beck AT, Greenberg RL (1974) Coping with depression. Institute for Rational Living, New York

Beck AT, Rush AJ, Shaw BF, Emery G (1979) Cognitive therapy of depression. Guilford, New York

Cohen R (1969) The effects of group interaction and progressive hierarchy presentation on desensitization of test anxiety. Behav Res Ther 7:15–26

Corsini R, Rosenberg B (1955) Mechanisms of group psychotherapy: processes and dynamics. J Abnorm Soc Psychol 51:406–411

Covi L, Lipman RS (1987) Cognitive behavioral group psychotherapy combined with imipramine in major depression. Psychopharmacol Bull 23:173–176

Covi L, Lipman RS (1988) A comparison of group cognitive therapy alone and in combination with imipramine and with traditional group therapy. In: Cognitive Psychotherapy. An Update Perris C. Eiseman M. (eds) Umea, Sweden, DOPUU Press

Covi L, Primakoff L (1988) Cognitive group therapy. APA Update (in press)

Covi L, Roth D, Lipman RS (1982) Cognitive group psychotherapy of depression: the close-ended group. Am J Psychother 36:459–469

Fairweather GW (ed) (1964) Social psychology in treating mental illness: an experimental approach. Wiley, New York

Flowers JV (1979). Behavioral analysis of group therapy and a model for behavioral group therapy. In: Upper D Ross SM (eds) Behavioral group therapy 1979: an annual review. Research Press Champaign, Illinois

Flowers JV, Booream CD (1980) Four studies toward a fuller understanding of behavioral group therapy: cohesion, client flexibility, and outcome generalizations. In Upper D Ross SM (eds) Behavioral group therapy, 1980. Research Press, Champaign, Illinois

Frank JD (1961) Persuasion and healing. Johns Hopkins, Baltimore

Fuchs CZ, Rehm LP (1977) A self-control behavior therapy program for depression. J Consult Clin Psychol 45:206–215

Gong-Guy E, Hammen C (1980) Causal perceptions of stressful events in depressed and non-depressed outpatients. J Abnorm Psychol 89:662–669

Hammen CL, Krantz S (1976) Effect of success and failure on depressive cognitions. J Abnorm Psychol 85:577–586

Hand I, Lamontagne Y, Marks IM (1974) Group exposure in vivo for agora-phobics. Br J Psychiatry 124:588–602

Kanfer FH, Grimm LG (1980) Managing clinical change: a process model of therapy. Behav Modif 4:419–444

Klerman GL, Weissman MM, Rounsaville B, Chevron ES (1984). Interpersonal psychotherapy of depression. Basic Books, New York

Lewisohn PM (1974). Clinical and theoretical aspects of depression. In: Calhoun KS, Adams HE, Mitchell IKM (eds) Innovative treatment methods in psychotherapy. Wiley, New York

Mahoney MJ, Mahoney K (1976) Permanent weight control. Norton, New York

Rehm LP, Fuchs CZ, Roth DM, Kornblith SH, Romano M (1979) A comparison of self-control and assertion skill treatment of depression. Behav Ther 10:429–442

Rose SD (1977) Group therapy: a behavioral approach. Prentice Hall, Englewood Cliffs, New Jersey

Roth DM (1980) Suggestions for behavioral group treatment of depression. In: Upper D, Ross S (eds) Behavioral group therapy, 1980. Research Press, Champaign, Illinois

Roth DM, Covi L (1984) Cognitive group psychotherapy of depression: the open-ended group. Int J Group Psychother 34:67–82

Rush AJ, Beck AT, Kovacs M, Hollon S (1977) Comparative efficacy of cognitive therapy and pharmacotherapy in the treatment of depressed outpatients. Cogn Ther Res 1:17–38

Seligman MEP, Abramson L, Semmel A, von Bayler C (1978) Depression attributional style. J Abnorm Psychol 88:242–247

Shaw BF (1977) Comparison of cognitive therapy and behavior therapy in the treatment of depression. J Consult Clin Psychol 45:543–551

Yalom ID (1975) Theory and practice of group psychotherapy. 2nd edn. Basic Books, New York

Cognitive Therapy of Personality Disorders: General Treatment Considerations

A. Freeman

Personality is generally defined as a group of relatively enduring traits that serve to influence behavior. The various combinations and permutations of these traits account for the myriad behavioral patterns observed in people. How personality forms, what maintains particular personality patterns, and what factors induce or encourage change in personality are and have been widely debated over the years. When Alfred Adler was asked by a student as to why he and Freud, both so creative and intelligent, could not come up with a unified theory of personality, Adler related the following story:

A rabbi was approached by a priest with the idea to combine their two congregations and thereby to achieve greater brotherhood and peace. The priest's idea was to arrange a joint celebration of Christmas and Chanukah (which occur at roughly the same time each year). The rabbi thought about the suggestion and responded, "I appreciate your idea, Father, but you see, Christmas has one meaning for you, and Chanukah has a very different meaning for us. By combining them we both lose what is important to us." The priest, undaunted, thought and came up with the idea to combine Easter and Passover, "After all, Rabbi, our Lord's Last Supper was a Passover Seder. Here is a clear connection." The rabbi thought and shook his head, "You are right, there is a connection, but to combine these two important celebrations would mean that we would both lose something important to us." The priest turned to the rabbi and asked, "Rabbi, what ideas do you have to bring our people closer?" The rabbi thought for a moment and replied, "First, this Jesus Christ story has got to go." (K. Adler 1968, personal communication).

Every theorist has his or her view of what personality is and what accounts for personality disorganization or disorder. Several collections of personality theories (Byrne and Kelley 1981; Corsini 1979; Hall and Lindsey 1978; Hjelle and Ziegler 1981; Schultz 1981; Sherman 1979) discuss the range of theoretical orientations. What causes difficulties in integrating these theories is the notion that the integration may cause each theory to lose something that is considered important or essential.

Understanding disorders of personality is similarly problematic since a disorder in personality can only be seen within a particular theory of personality. Moreover, for every personality theorist there is a theory of disorder, so that even within the range of a single theory, e.g., psychoanalytic theory, there is a range of ideas about personality disorders. Within the psychoanalytic framework there are several different positions representing different foci of treatment. Masterson (1987, p. 42) states, "It became clearer and clearer that (psychoanalytic thinking) as practiced by classical analysts . . . did not work with patients with personality

Center for Cognitive Therapy, University of Pennsylvania, 133 South 36 Street, Philadelphia, PA 19104, USA

disorders." Masterson goes on to advocate an object-relations focus as the most effective psychoanalytic approach.

Personality disorders have become an area of increasing interest for clinicians. The body of psychotherapeutic literature on treatment of personality disorders is growing rapidly. The principal theoretical orientation in the present literature is psychoanalytic. Some studies focus on the general area of personality disorder (Goldstein 1985; Gunderson 1984; Kernberg 1975; Lion 1981; Millon 1981; Saul and Warner 1982) and others on specific areas of disorder, such as borderline personality (Abend et al. 1983; Chatham 1985; Kernberg 1984; Masterson 1978), antisocial personality (Reid 1981), hysterical personality (Horowitz 1977), and adolescent borderlines (Masterson 1980, 1985). Millon (1981) is one of the few authors that offers a behavioral focus. The cognitive-behavioral literature on the treatment of patients with personality disorders is unfortunately almost nonexistent. The first volume to take a specifically cognitive-therapeutic approach to the treatment of personality disorders is presently in press (Beck and Freeman 1988).

Given the long-term nature of patients' characterological problems, their general avoidance of psychotherapy, their frequent referral through family pressure or legal remand, and their seeming reluctance or inability to change, these patients are often the most difficult patients in a clinician's caseload. They can, and often do, require more work within the session, a longer time for therapy, and more therapist energy than other patients – all of this without the same rate of change and satisfaction as is gained with other patients. Due to the lack of relevant data it is difficult to estimate the number of patients with personality disorders being seen in private practice.

Referral

Patients typically seek therapy for difficulties other than their axis II problems, often complaining, for instance, of depression and anxiety. With depression and anxiety superimposed on, or fueled by, the axis II personality, treatment is far more complicated than it is for the typical non-axis II patient with the same presenting complaints. Duration of treatment, frequency of treatment sessions, goals and expectations for both therapist and patient, and the techniques and available strategies need to be altered in the cognitive-therapeutic treatment of personality disorders. Despite the difficulties inherent in working with personality disorders they are not untreatable. The personality-disordered patient will often see the problems that he encounters in the world as not related immediately to him but rather as outside himself. Personality-disorder problems are most often self-consonant, and personality-disordered patients do not generally enter therapy to deal with characterological problems. These patients often have no idea of how they became as they are, or of how they might change. Other patients are referred by family members or significant others who recognize a dysfunctional pattern, or who have reached their personal limit in attempting to cope with the individual. Still other patients are remanded by the judicial system. This latter group are often given the choice of going to prison or going to therapy.

Diagnosis

While some personality disorders are diagnosed rather early in treatment, a clinician may not be aware of the characterological nature, chronicity, and severity of the patient's personality problems. The problems that the patient presently experiences may not have been obvious in the past. For example, Mary, a 23-year-old computer programmer, came to therapy because of "tremendous work pressure, inability to enjoy life, a perfectionistic approach to virtually all tasks, and a general isolation from others." She was working very hard at her job but getting very little satisfaction from the work. She was constantly late in getting her work completed, and her boss was constantly asking her for the finished programs: "He doesn't understand that I work very slowly and carefully; he just wants the work done quickly, and I have my standards of what I consider good enough to submit." She would have to take work home on weekends and stay in the office until 7 or 8 p.m. during the week to get the work done according to her "standards." Mary did very well in school, getting honors at graduation. Throughout her school experience she had little time for friends, leisure activities, or fun. "I was determined to do well. When I finished school, I figured that I could then relax and have fun." Her compulsive personality traits were rewarded in school and at home. Teachers always remarked on her neat, perfect work, and this resulted in her receiving many awards at graduation. After school ended, work took all of her time, but she was no longer rewarded for her perfectionism.

A personality disorder can, in fact, help some individuals become very successful, for example, in politics and the military. Those with a dependent personality may be ideal for service in the military because they are compliant toward orders. A 66-year-old man, diagnosed as both compulsive and avoidant personality, remarked that, "The best time in my life was in the army. I didn't have to worry about what to wear, what to do, where to go, or what to eat."

The Diagnostic and Statistical Manual – in both its first edition (DSM I; 1950) and its second (DSM II; 1968) – was an important contribution to the standardization of psychiatric nomenclature. But whereas both these editions were based on psychoanalytic theory, the publication of DSM III (1980) shifted the diagnostic focus more to behavioral descriptions. By setting out the guidelines of specific criteria for diagnosis and a multiaxial system of diagnosis, the clinician could now more easily make consistent diagnoses. This shift of emphasis has been extended to DSM III-R (revised third edition; 1987), which, although by no means perfect, has taken further steps toward identifying behaviors that are part of broad disorders or syndromes. Previously, the clinician was left to interpret the exact nature of the problem. One glaring example was the earlier conceptualization of "borderline" as a patient on the border between neurosis and psychosis who, at times, went "south of the border." The removal of neurosis as a diagnostic category in DSM III left the concept of "borderline" hanging in the space between psychosis and something else that no longer existed. Achieving a mastery of DSM III-R is essential in diagnosing personality disorders on axis II. By familiarizing oneself with the diagnostic criteria the clinician is able to further question symptom patterns or constellations. If a patient presents with several of the diagnostic criteria, the clinician can question as to whether other criteria in that symptom picture are present. The meeting of axis II criteria, for instance, would suggest an exploration of axis II issues.

Diagnostic signs that may point to the possibility of axis II problems include the following:

1. In doubting the existence of a problem a significant other may report, "Oh, he has always done that – since he was a little boy," or the patient himself may state, "I've always been this way."
2. The patient is not compliant with the therapeutic regimen. While this noncompliance (or resistance) is common in many problems and for many reasons, persistent noncompliance should be a signal for further exploration of axis II issues.
3. Therapy seems to have come to a sudden stop, with no apparent reason. The clinician working with such a patient can often help him reduce the referral problems of anxiety or depression, only to be stopped short in the therapeutic endeavor by the personality disorder.
4. The patient seems entirely unaware of the effect of his behavior on others. For example, a woman came into the waiting room at our Center and did not like the station to which the radio was tuned, so she turned it off. The radio was there for two reasons: first, to entertain the receptionist and, second, to muffle sound in the waiting room. The patient thought the radio irritating; it did not occur to her that other patients might like the radio station, that it was there to muffle sound, that she could ask whether it was alright to change the station, or that the receptionist working in that room had set the radio to a station that the receptionist enjoyed. The patient was not aware that her behavior had an effect on other people and did not understand why people were often hostile to her.
5. There is doubt as to the patient's motivation to change. This is especially true for patients who have "been sent" to therapy by family members or the courts.
6. The patient may give lip service to the therapy and to the importance of change but manages to avoid changing.
7. The patient's problems appear to be self-consonant. The problems that such a patient reports seem an inimical part of himself, as opposed to some problem outside of him. For example, a depressed patient without an axis II diagnosis may say, "I just want to get rid of this depression. I know what it is like to feel good, and I want to feel that way again." The axis II patient sees the problems as part of himself: "This is how I am", "This is who I am."
8. The axis II patient sees problems as "out there." In terms of Beck's cognitive triad (Beck 1979), they see their problems in terms of the world "doing to" them.

Cognitive-Therapeutic Conceptualization of Personality Disorders

In visualizing the personality we may liken it to a wheel of Swiss cheese. Different cheeses may be of differing size, and the wheel may be solid enough to support a person's weight, but when cut through the center, the cheese will be seen to have many holes. These holes may be many or few, they may be large or small. The larger the holes in essential areas, the greater the disorder. If the "hole" or area of deficit is one associated with affiliation, we find personality disorders of the avoidant or schizoid types; if with autonomy, the dependent type; if acceptance of social norms and strictures, the antisocial type; if impulse control, the borderline or histrionic type; if altruism, the narcissistic type; or if flexibility, the compulsive type. With many areas of deficit there will, of course, be several areas of disorder. Smaller "holes" may cause behavior labeled "eccentric" and may cause some minor psychic discomfort or life difficulty. Involvement in a particular environment or group may aliow acceptance of behaviors that in other quarters would be seen as unacceptable. In fact, personality-disordered behavior that is characterological may become the stuff of myth and legend. Early 18th century North American fur trappers and traders are an example; they spent most of the year alone in the forest, tending their traps, and came into civilization only to sell their furs, purchase supplies, and then retreat quickly to their isolation. This avoidant behavior became immortalized in song and story; today it might be seen as diagnosable on several axes.

Personality disorder is probably one of the most striking examples of Beck's notion of schema (Beck 1977; Beck et al. 1979; Freeman 1987; Perris 1986). Adler originally used the term "life schema" but changed it to "life-style" (Ansbacher and Anspacher 1963). Schemata are basic organizing factors, or rules, of life. Individuals have many different schemata, e.g., personal, cultural, religious, and gender related. These develop as we move through life. From birth to middle childhood these rules are in a state of constant evolution. Seen in terms of a Piagetian model, there is a constant need for adaptation to the requirements of life. These schemata, which allow us to organize and understand our world, change as a result of the interactive processes of assimilation and accomodation. If one were to ask a 2-month-old infant for its conceptualization of food seeking, it would probably answer that, "To obtain food you have to cry until the woman with the food comes; then you open your mouth, the food is presented, and you are allowed to take as much as you want – sometimes out of the one container and sometimes out of the other, matching container." As children mature, these schemata evolve. For many reasons some schemata do not mature but are maintained at an earlier level of development. This is the beginning of an axis II problem. Schemata that are basically functional in an earlier phase of life continue to be applied during later, more demanding times. Certain schemata are reinforced and/or modeled by parents.

Active schemata are those which govern everyday behavior. These have to do with where one chooses to sit after entering a room, how one chooses to dress, and how one relates to people and tasks. *Dormant schemata*, on the other hand, are essentially out of one's awareness. They are available however when the individual is stressed, and at this point they become active and begin to govern behavior. When the stressor is no longer present, these schemata recede to their previous state of dormancy. For example, if a person were asked his thoughts about killing, he might respond with the Biblical maxim, "Thou shalt not kill." Such beliefs about killing may or may not extend to eating meat, hunting, etc. If, however, this person were asked about his probable behavior should the life of his children be threatened, he might speak of the *need* to kill in order to protect one's children. Here, stress evokes the schema, "it is essential to protect one's children;" when stress is over, such a schema returns to dormancy.

Some schemata are noncompelling while others are very compelling. The compelling/noncompelling nature of a particular schema can be placed along a continuum. A noncompelling schema is one that the individual believes in but can relatively easily challenge and/or surrender. Compelling schemata are not easily challenged and are surrendered only with great difficulty, if at all. Examples are the religious and political martyrs who chose to die rather than surrender their compelling views. They adhered to rules that were very compelling and cannot be broken. The therapist dealing with axis II patients generally confronts very compelling schemata. The chronicity of the personality disorder derives from schemata in place since middle childhood or earlier; while most such early schemata were once functional, they have long since lost their functional value as a result of not having been modified by the individual to meet changing life/social circumstances.

For example, if a 1-year-old child wishes to be picked up, it conveys this message to its caretaker by lifting its arms and grunting or crying, and the caretaker responds by picking the child up. As the child matures its schemata alter. The schema "I can do for myself" develops, and the child no longer has the schematic world view that "I need others to take care of me and to meet my most basic needs." When a child at the age of 1 year demands attention and help, it is often seen as cute. When that same schema is manifested at age 31, it is not cute, but quite dysfunctional. A second example is that of a 2-year-old who acts in an impulsive manner and tells its parents, in effect, "No one should stop me from doing what I want to do." In dealing with a 2-year-old, such behavior is expected, although not enjoyed. If at age 32 there is a passive-aggressive view of the world or an antisocial attitude, the lack of impulse control is not welcome. With certain personality disorders the individual acquires schemata which find such expression as "I don't have to accept controls; I don't have to build controls, and I can do whatever I want to do." Axis II patients manifest behavior that has been reinforced by parents and other caretakers. They maintain these early developmental rules and do not seem to have developed alternative schemata or to have adapted the earlier schemata to the changing demands and circumstances of the world.

In view of the chronic nature of the problems one must question why these behaviors are maintained. They may cause difficulty at work, school, or in personal life. In some cases they are reinforced by society, for example, by the teachers who encourage a child deemed "a real worker," "a kid that doesn't fool around," "a kid who hasn't messed around while other kids were messing around," "a kid who really works hard and gets good grades." The axis II patient either does not see the problem or externalizes and sees it as outside himself. He sees others as too demanding or as picking on him: "It's not me, it's them." The very "me-ness" of the problem must be addressed.

An image recorded by Joel Chandler Harris (1984) can be invaluable for better understanding this problem. Chandler collected the stories of storytellers in slave camps of the American South prior to the American Civil War (1860–1865). He invented the archetypal storyteller and keeper of the oral tradition, named Uncle Remus, who relates the tale of "Br'er Rabbit," "Br'er Bear," and "Br'er Fox." (The Walt Disney film, "Song of the South," presents these stories; "Br'er" was a coloquial contraction of "Brother.")

Br'er Fox and Br'er Bear were always trying to catch Br'er Rabbit, but he always managed to outsmart them and escape. After many tries Br'er Fox came up with the idea to build a tar baby. This figure, made of tar and dressed in clothes, attracted Br'er Rabbit. Br'er Rabbit approached the tar baby, thinking it was a real person. When he greeted the tar baby, and the tar baby did not respond, Br'er Rabbit punched him to teach him a lesson in manners. By striking the tar baby, Br'er Rabbit became stuck fast to it and was easily captured by Br'er Fox and Br'er Bear. They threatened to tear Br'er Rabbit limb from limb. The cunning Br'er Rabbit, implored them, "You can tear me limb from limb, but whatever you do, please don't throw me in that there briar patch!" "We're going to make rabbit stew out of you," said Br'er Fox. "You can sure do that, Br'er Fox, but whatever you do, please, please, don't throw me in that briar patch!" "We are going to leave you out for the crows to eat," answered Br'er Fox. "That's okay, but don't, don't throw me into that there briar patch!" begged Br'er Rabbit. With that, Br'er Fox threw Br'er Rabbit into the briar patch. As Br'er Rabbit landed on the thorns and briars, he shouted in pain. Then, suddenly, there was laughter from the briar patch. Br'er Rabbit was laughing and shouting, "You fools! I was born and bred in this here briar patch. This is my home." Br'er Rabbit had escaped once again.

While the briar patch may be rather small, Br'er Rabbit is safe inside. He may go out at night to search for food but is vulnerable and at risk whenever he does. The personality disorder is like a briar patch; this rather restricted space is where the personality disorder "lives." The individual tries to find the safe walkways within it but may periodically get stuck by a briar. And although he does not like getting stuck, he also does not like being vulnerable. Vulnerability means experiencing high levels of anxiety, and he therefore seeks the safety of his "briar patch." One of the most important considerations in treating personality-disordered patients is to be aware of the "briar patch syndrome." Therapy evokes anxiety because it asks the individual to give up being who he is and to step out of his briar patch. It may be uncomfortable, limiting, and lonely in there, but leaving it spells anxiety and potential harm.

In discussing plans for therapy with one patient, she asked "Why are you trying to teach me to control my anxiety? I'm depressed, I'm not anxious at all." At that point the therapist told her the story about the briar patch. The patient responded "It's good to have that safety, and I don't understand why I should ever give it up." As the therapist starts to work on a patient's ability to step outside the briar patch, the patient needs to have ways of coping with the increased anxiety which this entails. Unless he is able to cope with the anxiety, he may leave therapy and jump right back into the briar patch. [Space limitations preclude a detailed discussion of anxiety treatment, cf. Beck and Emery (1985); Freeman and Simon (1988).]

Cognitive Therapy of Personality Disorders

The initial goals of therapy are to assess and conceptualize the patient's problems and to develop an appropriate treatment plan. Specific techniques for this are provided in Beck et al. (1979) and Freeman et al. (1988). The therapist must thereupon ensure the patient's socialization or education to the cognitive-therapeutic model. That which is involved in cognitive therapy, the goals and plans of the therapy, and the importance of therapeutic collaboration need to be stressed.

The initial therapeutic focus may be on relieving the presenting symptoms, e.g., anxiety or depression. In helping the patient deal with his anxiety or depression the therapist can teach the patient the basic cognitive-therapy skills that will be necessary in working with a difficult personality disorder. If the therapist can help the patient become less depressed or less anxious, the patient may accept that this therapy can perhaps be of some value after all, and that it may be worthwhile continuing to work in therapy. Having brought their anxiety and depression under control with fairly standard techniques, some axis II patients may wish to leave therapy. One technique that may be helpful with these patients is to differentiate between "symptom therapy" and "schema therapy;" having explained to him the importance of working on schemata, the patient may then choose to stay in therapy.

The essential nature of a therapeutic collaboration, as stressed by Beck et al. (1979), is nowhere more important than with the axis II patient. This relationship is one of the key ingredients in the therapy of personality disorder, for it furnishes a microcosm of the patient's responses to others in his environment. Due to the sensitive nature of this relationship the therapist must exercise great care in working with these patients. Being even 2 min late for a session with the dependent personality may produce anxiety over abandonment. The same 2 min can raise the spectre of being taken advantage of by the paranoid personality. Building and maintaining trust, essential to good therapy generally, is imperative here. Few patients test the patience and mettle of a therapist in this regard more than do those in the axis II group. Issues of the therapist's countertransference (his response to the patient's verbalizations and actions) must be acknowledged and addressed directly by the therapist. For example, a 42-year-old man was referred by a therapist who had told the patient "I think I have helped you all I can." In a conversation with the new therapist, the previous therapist said:

This is one of the most demanding guys I have worked with in 20 years of practice. I've really had it with him. He called me at 3 A.M. to tell me that a woman had stood him up for a date. When I asked what time the date was set for, the patient said 9 P.M. the previous evening. When I asked him why he didn't call then, he replied "I didn't want to bother you then." When I asked the patient if he was aware of the time, he replied "Of course, but that's why you're there."

The collaborative nature of therapy must be constantly stressed. The therapy of a personality disorder must include a strong supportive/expressive component. Without the therapist's active support the patient may quickly become frightened and disillusioned and leave therapy. The collaborative set involves establishing mutually acceptable goals for therapy. These goals must be reasonable and proximal. The patient who expects to become a totally different person as a result of therapy will invariably be disappointed. By making small steps toward the desired goals therapy can advance slowly but effectively.

The rate of treatment and the time frame involved must be discussed. The patient who has read of cognitive therapy and expects to be "cured" in 12–20 sessions must be apprised of the greater severity and chronicity of the problems and of the fact that these problems will take a longer time for treatment. A far more reasonable time frame for personality disorders is 12–20 months.

The patient's significant others can be invaluable allies in the therapeutic endeavor by helping the patient do homework and reality testing and by offering support in effecting desired changes. Significant others can also be important sources of data as to the patient's past behaviors. In a negative vein, meeting with significant others may enable the therapist to piece together a family history of problems and to understand that which keeps the patient behaving in a dysfunctional way. Finally, significant others may be brought into marital or family therapy with the patient.

Working with Schemata

The patient's cognitive distortions serve as signposts that point to his schemata. The goal of therapy is to help the patient identify the various rules that he lives by. The therapist has several options as to what may be done to work with the schemata.

The first option is *schematic restructuring*. This may be likened to urban renewal: having decided that a structure is unsound, the decision is made to tear down the old structure and build a new one in its place. (This has been a goal of therapy for many years, particularly in psychoanalysis.) Whether such restructuring is reasonable is very questionable. An example of successful schematic restructuring is enabling a paranoid personality to become a fully trusting individual.

A second possibility is *schematic modification*. This involves effecting smaller changes in the patient's basic manner of responding to the world. An example of this is enabling the paranoid personality to trust some people, in some situations. An alternative here is to help the paranoid personality self-instruct not to respond in his typical, undesirable manner.

The third possibility is *schematic reinterpretation*. This involves helping the patient understand and reinterpret his life-style and schemata in more functional ways. One can also work toward restructuring schemata, or rebuilding them if this is possible, but the most reasonable goal when working with an axis II patient lies in reinterpreting the schemata. In schematic reinterpretation the therapist explores ways for the patient to deal with his schemata rules in a more adaptive and functional manner. These rules are not necessarily good or bad in themselves; all depends on how these are interpreted. For example, if one has a great need to be loved or admired, one may choose to teach preschool children, who kiss and hug the teacher. If one needs to be looked up to and respected, earning or buying a title, e.g., Professor, Doctor, or Colonel, can meet this need for status. Many vocational choices are made because the career or occupation seems to offer an opportunity to meet a schematic need.

Dealing with Noncompliance

The noncompliance[1] often observed in the axis II patient is not simply a problem of the patient's not wanting to change or to make progress. It is overly simplistic to presume that if a patient makes good progress in therapy, it is because of superior therapy, and if he does not, it is because of resistance. There are, in fact, several

[1]I have chosen to use the term noncompliance rather than the more traditional term resistance inasmuch as the latter has specific psychoanalytic meaning.

reasons for patient noncompliance with therapeutic regimen. These apply to all noncompliance and not only that on the part of patients with personality disorders.

Lack of Motivation. The axis II patient often comes to therapy because of family pressure or the demand of a spouse or the courts. The reason for their not complying is the lack of intrinsic motivation to change.

Patient's Lack of Skill to Comply. A patient may never have learned certain things that are commonly taken for granted. For example, a 39-year-old attorney had recently been abandoned by his wife, who left him for another man after 6 years of marriage. He was her fifth husband. The patient had never dated during high school. He studied so that he could get into college, and in college he studied so that he could get into a good law school. He attended Harvard Law School, and throughout his time there he studied in order to get a good legal clerkship. Because of his work he never dated. At a Christmas party a woman came up to him and said "Hi!" He answered, "Hello," and within an hour she took him back to her apartment; there he had sex for the first time in his life. They married within 4 months. In his view dating was very simple: all he had to do was keep saying "Yes." He entered therapy severely depressed. His goal was to start dating. He had great difficulty telephoning any of the dozens of phone numbers that were given to him because he had never in his life telephoned a woman for a date. The first step of therapy in this case involved specific skill building. This was followed by dealing with the evident schemata.

Therapist's Lack of Requisite Skills. Therapists cannot be equally skilled in dealing with every patient problem or patient category. A patient may appear noncompliant with the therapeutic regimen because the therapist is not able to conceptualize the patient problem, to convert his conceptual understanding into a reasonable treatment program, or to utilize the various cognitive and behavioral techniques with equal facility.

Power Issues Between Patient and Therapist. For patients who experience very little control in their lives, therapy may provide the only setting in which they can take control. A 29-year-old man remarked "In my life everyone controls me. Well I'd like to not do anything. Make me do something." Very often such a patient may respond with "Yes, but . . ." throughout therapy.

Secondary Gain. Some patients may perceive great value in axis II behavior. It is worthwhile in some way for them to stay in their personal briar patch. The patient's significant others may, in fact, reinforce his dysfunctional behavior because they are afraid of the patient, or afraid of what may happen to him if anyone fails to yield to him. The patient may therefore gain great power or status through his pathology.

Patient Cognitions About the Chance of Failing in Therapy. When a patient addresses the issue of changing, the therapist may begin to hear such cognitions about changing as "If I change, it would be awful. I couldn't do it. I'll fall on my face."

Patient Cognitions About the Consequence of Change to Others. Often the content of the patient's concern is the effect that his change may have on the significant others in his life: "If I change, what will happen to them?" or "How will they be able to deal with me if I'm different?"

Patient Cognitions About Consequence to Self. It may be frightening to the patient to contemplate being different. He may be concerned that others will not like him as much, accept him, or even recognize him if he changes.

Environmental Stressors Maintaining Axis II Behavior. If the environment has reinforced axis II behavior until now, why should we expect this reinforcement to stop? This is a common problem in working with adolescents. As they start to do the restructuring and to change their behavior, they may be removed from therapy because the parents do not like what therapy is doing to them.

Therapist Cognitions Congruent with Patient Cognitions or Therapist Schemata Congruent with Patient Schemata. The therapist needs to be aware of his own belief systems. These should not interfere with his helping the patient meet the goals that the patient has set for himself. For example, a very perfectionistic therapist presented a patient in supervision. "This is a very perfectionistic patient and very demanding," he observed. When the supervisor asked "What are your goals in therapy?" The therapist answered "I think the goal is to get rid of all this perfectionism," in other words not to modify it but to eradicate it. The patient in this case might thereby be predestined for failure.

Poor Timing of Interventions. The patient must not be pushed too hard. We must recognize that axis II patients often have problems associated with low frustration tolerance. If they are frustrated, they will leave therapy and will leave very quickly. We must recognize the rigidity of the boundaries of the patient's briar patch.

Need for a Strong Working Alliance. Without a collaborative set and a strong relationship the therapist may not get much chance to do therapy or to work with the patient to practice skill building. It is essential to obtain the patient's acceptance of the goals of treatment and the rate of treatment and to set mutual, realistic, and proximal goals.

Patient Rigidity. The very nature of axis II problems may foil compliance. The patient, firmly entrenched in his briar patch, may be blocked through his own rigid personality style from leaving the briar patch. This will often be compounded by the patient's low frustration tolerance.

Poor Socialization to the Model. The patient who has not been well educated/socialized into the therapy model may not easily comply because he may not be sure as to what he is being asked to comply with. A clear statement of the goals, purposes, and techniques of therapy is important. These may need to be repeated often. One patient stated "I read you're supposed to start feeling good quickly. They say you can get rid of all of your problems in 12 weeks." It must be stressed that therapy will take place one step at a time. It is at this point that the therapist can differentiate between symptom therapy and schema therapy.

Intrapsychic Conflict. Conflict of an intrapsychic sort approaches the traditional concept of resistance. There may be conflicts that are out of awareness, and that preclude the patient's compliance with a therapeutic regimen for change. The range of schemata must be made manifest.

Countertransference. The therapist cannot always expect the patient to make good progress, steady progress, or to smell good. When the axis II patient acts in a way characteristic of axis II patients, the therapist's patience may be sorely tried. When the therapist begins asking "Why doesn't the patient appreciate what I am trying to do for him?" or "Why doesn't this patient change more quickly?" therapist frustration may interfere with effective therapy.

Cognitive and Behavioral Techniques

The cognitive therapy of personality disorders progresses in the same manner as cognitive therapy with other disorders. The patient is helped to gain the skills to deal with the more serious manifestations of his personality disorder by practicing on the relatively simpler axis I problems. Identifying the patient's pattern of distorted thinking is followed by testing the meaning, reality, and validity of his thoughts and perceptions. The techniques available here can be roughly divided into the cognitive and the behavioral. The particular combination of cognitive and behavioral techniques is, of course, determined by the needs of the patient. A general rule suggests that the more severe the pathology, the more behavioral the approach should be; conversely, the less severe the behavioral pathology, the more cognitive the approach should be (Fig. 1).

Schemata are held firmly in place by their behavioral, cognitive, and affective elements. Changing only one such factor will probably not be effective in changing the overall schema. The therapeutic approach must combine these three dimen-

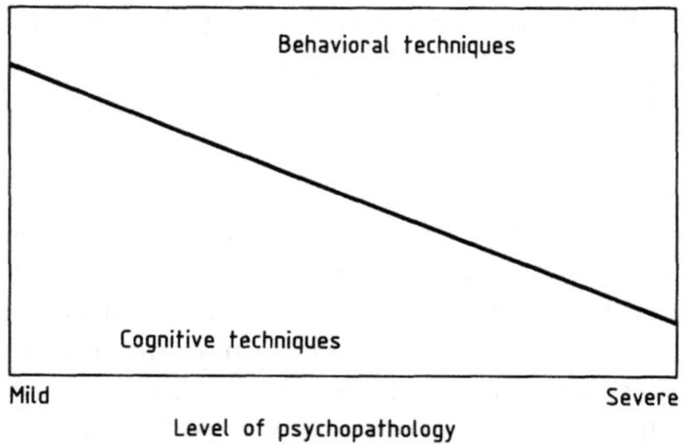

Fig. 1. Relationship between degree of pathology and type of treatment

sions. Ultimately ineffective are the purely cognitive approach of trying to argue the patient out of his distortions, structured behavioral approaches, and having the patient merely abreact within the session to fantasies or recollections. The therapeutic program must address each of these three areas; any one of them alone cannot succeed.

Cognitive Techniques

Understanding Idiosyncratic Meaning. Once a patient identifies or labels a feeling or thought, it is important for the therapist to help him understand the special meaning that this has for him. Therapists must not assume that they know intuitively what the patient's actual meanings are. The question "What do you mean by that?" is one that the therapist must constantly ask; the patient, on the other hand, must learn to ask himself "What do I mean by that?"

Questioning the Evidence. Everyone uses some sort of evidence to validate and maintain his own thoughts and beliefs. The therapist and patient need to identify clearly what evidence is being used to maintain the patient's belief system.

Reattribution. Examining the patient's attributions, the therapist can help reattribute responsibility for various actions and learnings as maintained by the patient.

Examining Options and Alternatives. While still caught in his briar patch, the axis II patient confronts a seemingly very limited set of the options for thought and behavior. The therapist can question him as to what other sorts of behavior could be added to his response repetoire.

Examining the Advantages/Disadvantages of Maintaining a Belief. What does maintaining a particular belief offer the patient (besides a relief from anxiety)? By having the patient examine in detail and in writing either side of an issue, the therapist can examine what additional gain the patient may obtain from maintaining a belief.

Scaling. Having the patient scale discrete experiences in his life can often serve to decatastrophize them for him. For example, one patient rated requesting a salary increase at 8 on an anxiety scale (10 maximum, 0 minimum). He was then asked to imagine the most anxious experience (receiving 10) and the most relaxing experience of his life (receiving 0). On this scale he could then rerate the experience of asking for a raise. By establishing life-perspective anchor points this experience may then be seen as deserving a lower anxiety rating.

Use of Replacement Imagery. The patient often entertains catastrophic images of future events; these catastrophic images contribute in large part to the formation and maintenance of his anxiety. By helping the patient to imagine scenes of coping or relaxing the anxiety cycle can be broken.

Labeling of Distortions. The patient can be helped to gain personal awareness of the very automatic behavior and thinking patterns which are typical of the axis II patient. Once the patient can be made aware of the fact that he does distort in some major areas of response, he can be helped to identify the particular style and content of his distortions.

Guided Association. This may be referred to as the "then what?" technique. By accepting the possibility that the patient's images are true the therapist can progress through the various levels of meaning. The following provides an example:

P: I'll fail.
T: Let's suppose you do, then what?
P: Well, I'll never be able to go there again.
T: And what if that's true, then what?
P: I'll lose opportunities to meet people.
T: If you cannot go there, you lose the opportunity to meet some people. Is that right?
P: Yes.
T: And if that's true, then what?
P: Well, I don't know. Now I'm confused.

Cognitive Distraction. Distraction is an excellent technique for helping the patient cope with anxiety. It is difficult to maintain two competing sets of thoughts, and the patient's use of imaginal distraction (relaxing scenes) can help distract him from the anxiety-producing thoughts. Examples include counting by some unusual number (e.g., 14) to 200 and counting people dressed in red or blue clothing. This has the effect of limiting the growth of an anxiety cycle and giving the patient a greater sense of control.

Self-Instruction.[2] The therapist can help the patient replace faulty or dysfunctional self-statements with more adaptive and effective self-instructions. For the patient with impulse-control problems the instruction might be, for example, "Count to 10 and walk away" or "Scan the environment and check my data."

Behavioral Techniques

There are three major facets of behavioral techniques: (a) the therapist may need to work very directly on altering self-defeating behaviors; (b) patients may be skill-deficient, and the therapy must include a skill-building component; and (c) behavioral assignments can be used as homework to help test cognitions.

Activity Scheduling. The activity schedule (Fig. 2) can be used retrospectively to assess the patient's use of time and prospectively to plan more effective time utilization.

---

[2]For further descriptions of self-instructional techniques, see Meichenbaum, (1977); Novaco (1975); Kendall and Braswell (1985).

Weekly activity schedule
Note: Grade activities M for Mastery and P for Pleasure 0-10

		M	T	W	Th	F	S	S
	6-7							
	7-8							
Morning	8-9							
	9-10							
	10-11							
	11-12							
	12-1							
	1-2							
Afternoon	2-3							
	3-4							
	4-5							
	5-6							

		M	T	W	Th	F	S	S
	6-7							
	7-8							
	8-9							
Evening	9-10							
	10-11							
	11-12							
	12-6							

Remarks:

Fig. 2. Weekly activity schedule

Mastery and Pleasure Ratings. The patient can be helped to plan activities that yield a greater sense of mastery (how well they see themselves in performing an activity) and a greater sense of pleasure (how much they enjoy the activity).

Graded Task Assignment. The therapist can work collaboratively with the patient to set behavioral assignments that are arranged in a series of small, sequential steps. By helping the patient master simpler tasks the ground work is set for more difficult and complex tasks.

Assertiveness Training. For the patient who is skill-deficient in assertiveness the therapist needs to consider including assertiveness training within the therapy.

Relaxation Training. In cases in which anxiety reduction is an essential component of therapy the patient must be taught to utilize the broad range of available relaxation techniques. These include meditation, large-muscle relaxation, and hatha yoga.

Behavioral Distraction. Techniques of behavioral distraction are equally as valuable in altering the anxiety cycle as those of cognitive distraction. Having the patient perform an engaging task (e.g., attending to and counting foot tapping) can help distract and shift the patient's focus from anxiety-producing images.

Behavioral Rehearsal/Role Playing. Role playing of various situations with the patient enables him to practice adaptive responding and behaving. By switching roles the patient can begin to gain a sense of how others may respond to him.

In Vivo Exposure. The patient's problems often cannot be effectively dealt with in the confines of the consulting room. The therapist can accompany the patient to feared situations and monitor the cognitions as they develop; can also offer support and modeling of adaptive responses – both cognitive and behavioral.

Case Material Illustrating the Cognitive Therapy of Personality Disorders

In this section each of the various personality disorders will be presented. Case material is used to illustrate how typical schemata underlying the disorder manifest themselves in the behavioral style of the patient; these schemata are presented along with treatment goals to indicate the direction of therapy. Examples are drawn from patients in whom the particular disorder is clearly primary. One must note, however, that axis II patients have mixed diagnoses; in DSM III-R more than one personality disorder can be diagnosed if the patient meets the corresponding criteria (p. 336).

Personality disorders are divided into three groups or clusters (DSM III-R, p. 337). Cluster A includes the paranoid, schizoid, and schizotypal personality disorders; these are labeled "odd or eccentric." Cluster B includes the antisocial, borderline, histrionic, and narcissistic personality disorders, labeled, "dramatic, emotional, or erratic." Finally, Cluster C encompasses avoidant, dependent, obsessive-compulsive and passive-aggressive disorders and are labeled, "anxious or fearful."

Paranoid Personality Disorder

Typical Schemata

People will eventually try to hurt me.
People cannot be trusted; they will always take advantage of me.
People will try to bother or annoy me.
Don't get mad, get even.
Any insult directed at me, no matter how slight, should be punished.
Stay on guard; always be prepared for the worst.
To compromise is to surrender.
Avoid intimacy; if I get close to people they can find out my weaknesses.
Keep alert for anyone who has power; they can hurt me.

Case Illustration

John was a 29-year-old engineer who entered therapy because of "difficulty at work." His supervisor had suggested that John "get help" and referred him to the company counseling center. Rather than visit company counselors who, John was sure, would not keep confidential what he said, he sought private therapy. He set as a precondition for therapy that while the fact of his being in therapy would be shared with his employer, nothing he said there would ever be shared with his employer. In John's view the reason for his referral was a personal vendetta against him by his supervisor. The problem at work was so severe, in fact, that John was threatened with dismissal if he did not change his attitude and behavior at work.

John was unmarried and did not date. He did not see his lack of social life as either unusual or problematic. When asked about his lack of dating, he replied "There are really few nice women out there. They're just out to get what they can from a guy – money, sex; you know what I mean?" John had never had many friends; he had two male friends since childhood, both of whom were also single. He said that he trusted both of these friends, but not totally: "You can never tell when someone will turn on you."

John had been employed by the company for 6 years and worked in an office with several other men. He refused to talk with them and insisted that they address him as "Mr. Smith", rather than as "John:" "We're not friends; why should I be so familiar with them?" His goal in therapy was simply to meet his employer's requirement. John intended to stay in therapy until the present crisis "blew over."

Recognizing the nature of John's difficulty as one involving axis II issues, the therapist chose to maintain the therapeutic relationship on a professional title basis; John was addressed as "Mr. Smith" and the therapist as "Dr. Freeman." By keeping the relationship "professional" the attempt was made to avoid exciting John's anxiety about closeness. The focus of the therapy was initially on helping John behave differently at work in order to maintain his job. Trust needed to be built very slowly. At one point the therapist was 5 min late for a session. This was taken as "evidence" for the therapist's lack of trustworthiness. When the therapist took a 1-week vacation, John said that he understood the therapist going on vacation, "But why at such an inconvenient time for me?"

With the focus being on changing John's work behavior other areas of concern could be brought in to the therapeutic collaboration, e.g., social interaction and seeking "safe" pleasure activities.

After 18 months of therapy on a weekly basis John agreed to enter a group. Here John was willing to self-disclose on a very limited basis and to experiment with the response of others in the group. He tried to predict the response of others but found himself incorrect much of the time. Since John was so very sure of what others were thinking or planning, he experienced cognitive dissonance and anxiety over this. He affiliated with a woman in the group, a very dependent 32-year-old, and they began dating. John was, of course, in the position of power, but this relationship represented the first long-term relationship he had ever had. He terminated therapy shortly after this relationship began. His job problems had been modified, and he was now able to talk with his coworkers. He was no longer in danger of being fired.

Schizoid Personality

Typical Schemata

Why should I be close to people?
Being close to others is of little importance.
I am my own best friend.
Stay calm; displays of emotion are unnecessary and embarrassing.
What others say is of little interest or importance to me.
Sex is okay, but just for release.

Case Illustration

Dan, a 66-year-old retired chemist, came for therapy because of anxiety. He had never married but was presently dating a woman whom he had dated for the past 8 years. He saw her once a week on Saturday night to go a movie and have sex, after which he would then go home: "Why stay over?" I did what I came for. That's pretty funny, what I 'came' for."

Dan had been in various therapies over the past 40 years. His first therapy experience was in Europe while attending medical school in Switzerland on the GI Bill. After a year there he began experiencing panic attacks and entered a Jungian analysis. He remained in analysis for only 6 months and left when he experienced a diminution in anxiety. He left medical school and returned to the United States, where he completed graduate school with a PhD in chemistry.

Dan portrayed himself as "low-keyed" and claimed "I never get angry." The therapeutic goals in Dan's case were, first, to lower his anxiety and then to explore his avoidance behavior – or lack of understanding as to why people spend time together. He came for weekly therapy sessions, which he seemed to enjoy. Dan reported that when he was 2 years old, his mother became quite ill with tuberculosis and was sent to a sanitarium for 2 years. She returned home for several months but then had to return to the sanitarium, where she died. During his mother's illness he lived with his maternal grandmother, where he remained until age 6. At that time his father remarried, and Dan had to return to live with his father and stepmother, although he did not want to leave his grandmother and barely knew his father. Dan's lack of a family feeling and his difficulty in seeing himself as related to others probably stemmed from these early unsuccessful affiliation experiences. Throughout childhood, adolescence, and young adulthood he avoided relationships. A major personal schema of his was "Getting attached to people is not a good idea; they'll probably leave me." Therapy focused on increasing Dan's interactions with others. He began to spend weekends with his girlfriend, attend family functions with her (weddings, Thanksgiving dinner, Christmas, and funerals), and went away on a 2-week vacation with her.

Dan was not in principle against spending time with another person; this was simply something that he had never really understood. While it was not his original preference, he did begin to spend time with his girlfriend; he needed to use self-instructional strategies to be with others. The self-instruction here was "When in doubt, don't be alone." In Dan's case, the behavior was altered, but not the underlying schema. With continued interpersonal contacts newer schemata were introduced which served to modify older schemata.

Schizotypal Personality Disorder

It is very difficult to isolate specific schema that are idiosyncratic to the schizotypal personality disorder. Patients with this disorder are usually seen by others as strange or peculiar. These eccentricities, while readily observable, are not severe enough to meet the criteria for schizophrenia (DSM III-R, p. 340). The major goals in working with these patients resemble those in working with schizophrenics, i.e., social-skills training (including grooming, interpersonal skill development, and generally appearing less peculiar), anxiety reduction, and self-instructional training.

Antisocial Personality Disorder

Typical Schemata

Rules are meant for others.
Only fools follow all the rules.
Rules are meant to be broken.
Look out for "number 1."
My pleasure comes first.
If others are hurt, offended, or inconvenienced by my behavior, that is their problem.
Do it now! I will not allow myself to be frustrated.
I will do whatever I must to get whatever I want.
I'm really smarter than almost everybody else.

Case Illustration

Joe was a 24-year-old male, referred to therapy by his probation officer. He had been in trouble with school and legal authorities since the age of 15. Although he was supposed to come to our Center for therapy on a twice-weekly basis, Joe came on the average of three times a month and always had a reason for having missed a session. His excuses, however, were often so simple as to be naive, for instance: "I had to go to another city to get a part for a truck that I am thinking of buying from some guy I just met, and it took 2 days to get the part." When asked as to why he had to buy the part for a truck he did not own, why it could not be obtained in his city, and why the part had to be gotten on days that sessions were scheduled, he would develop the story even further. When the therapist attempted to do reality testing with him, Joe became offended that he was not being believed: "If you don't trust me, how can you help me?"

Treatment with Joe focused on building prosocial behaviors – in effect, building a superego. The therapist was gentle but firm in not accepting Joe's constant excuses. Therapy sought to help Joe accept responsibility. By challenging cognitive distortions and alerting him to the dysfunctional nature of his schemata, Joe began to see how his behavior, viewed by himself as clever and complex, was in reality transparent and childlike. Joe became extremely anxious when his persona was threatened. His difficulty in changing lay in his not seeing his behavior as a mask but as the only way to behave. Once Joe accepted that he could get more from the world by becoming part of the system rather than trying always to fool it, he began to act more adaptively. In his goal of getting the most for himself, nevertheless, Joe did not waver; he now tried to get it in ways that got him into far less trouble. He returned to school to finish his high-school diploma and then continued on to a 2-year college program. On follow-up over 2 years Joe continued to stay out of legal problems.

Borderline Personality Disorder

Typical Schemata

I am not sure who I am.
I will eventually be abandoned.
My (psychic) pain is so intense that I cannot bear it.
My anger controls me; I cannot modulate my behavior.
My feelings overwhelm me; I cannot modulate my feelings.
He/she is so very, very good that I am lucky – (or alternatively and quickly) he/she is so very, very awful that I cannot bear him/her.
When I am overwhelmed, I must escape (by flight or suicide).

Case Illustration

Alice, a 34-year-old woman, was referred by a psychiatrist because of her ongoing depression; pharmacotherapy had been ineffective, as had a year of insight-oriented therapy. Alice was married to an accountant for 15 years. She had completed a master's degree in education and had worked as a teacher for 6 years. At the beginning of therapy she had not worked for 6 years: she stayed at home, "too depressed to do anything." When Alice was asked to make a list of her negative thoughts, she began her list with "I was bad before I was born, I was a bad fetus." She described her mother having harangued her for years about how bad she (Alice) had been in utero. (Her mother had had a difficult first trimester with a great deal of nausea, could not sleep because of chronic lower-back pain in the second trimester, and was bedridden for the last 4 months of pregnancy.)

Alice had few friends throughout childhood and adolescence. Her mother attempted to inoculate Alice against the "viciousness" of the world by slapping Alice across the face almost daily. If Alice cried, her mother kept hitting her to teach her to resist the pain of the world. Finally, Alice could accept the slaps without crying; at that point, however, Alice's mother would hit her to make Alice more emotionally responsive.

When Alice graduated from high school and discussed going to college, her mother became distraught. Her mother told Alice "I can't stand the thought of you going away. I'll die without you here. You are all I have to live for. Can't you forget college and get a job in town? Please don't leave me." Alice chose a college close to home for the first 2 years and commuted to school. Her second 2 years were spent on a campus at some distance from her home.

Therapy proceeded for 13 months before Alice felt she could *begin* to trust the therapist. Therapy was a stormy road. When the therapist told Alice about an impending vacation 1 month in advance, she withdrew from therapy. "What is the use of being in therapy when you are leaving ?" she asked. When told that the therapist did intend to return, Alice questioned "How do I know that?" Any separation was seen by Alice as irrevocable; the therapist's return was seen by Alice as anticlimactic. She feared the coming year and the separation of the next summer's vacation. Alice had few ideas as to how her mistrust and fear of separation (and abandonment) had come to be. After the second year of therapy, Alice told the therapist about an incident that had occurred when she was 7 years old. Her father was in the navy and stationed in Japan. Her mother had Alice spend a week in the beginning of summer with Alice's maternal grandmother. Alice was told that during that time Alice's father would return home, and that her mother and father would come to get her. Alice's grandmother worked as a matron at a state orphanage. For the first week Alice lived in her grandmother's room. When her mother and father did not call or come to get her, Alice was moved into the orphanage dormitory, where she remained for the rest of the summer. Plans were then made for Alice to attend school at the orphanage. Three days before school was to begin, she was brought to her grandmother's room where she was greeted by her parents. Her mother's only comment was "Your father was delayed." When questioned in therapy as to why she had not mentioned this experience earlier, Alice replied "I didn't think that it was all that important." Using this abandonment as a clue, the therapist inquired as to whether there were other incidents of her being left, abandoned, separated, or taken from her parents. Alice went on to describe several other instances of being emotionally abandoned (her mother would get angry at her and not speak to her for weeks at a time) or physically abandoned (being left for hours sitting on a bench in a shopping mall or store and told not to move). With these early experiences Alice's schemata about being abandoned were strongly established. When asked about her relationship with her husband, she said that she did not trust that he would stay with her for very long.

The first goal of therapy was to try carefully to challenge the idea that she would be abandoned. Alice was unwilling at first to risk that the therapist would return upon once having left – or that the therapist would leave, return, and still be willing to work with her. Her distortion in this regard was that the therapist would forget about her while he was away. A second goal was to work with Alice together with her husband in order to improve their marital relationship. Couple's sessions were begun to help her husband better understand Alice and her problems and to help Alice risk telling her husband of her dissatisfaction with many aspects of their relationship.

In the 3rd year of weekly therapy Alice was less depressed and less anxious than she had initially been. It is questionable as to whether Alice will ever work again. The therapeutic relationship, as a microcosm of her relationships with the world, continued to be the arena for Alice to understand her fear of abandonment and to frame experiments to test this early schema.

Histrionic Personality Disorder

Typical Schemata

Appearances are important.
People are judged on external appearances.
I must be noticed.
I must never be frustrated in life.
I must get everything I think that I want.
Emotions should be expressed quickly and directly.
Beauty is the most important consideration in judging someone.

Case Illustration

Marta was 30 years old and unmarried. She came for therapy because of depression; her Beck Depression Inventory (BDI) score was 47 (a score this high is not typical of depressed outpatients). She was beautifully dressed, her makeup was perfectly applied, and her affect appeared non-depressed. Her first statement to the therapist was "I'll bet that you don't think that I'm depressed. Just because I don't look or sound depressed doesn't mean a thing." Marta went on to describe her emotional outbursts, temper tantrums at home, the hours she spent each day on her appearance, and her sexual exploits. She would meet men in bars and, at times, have sex consecutively with two or three men in the course of an evening. When questioned about her sexual behavior, she said "If they find me attractive, it helps reduce my depression and negative thoughts about myself. What's wrong with that?"

The goals of therapy were to help Marta reduce her excessive behavior. Modulation was the watchword of treatment. When Marta was less emotionally or sexually expressive, she became "anxious," and this would lead once again to excessive behavior. By helping her deal with her anxiety, therapy enabled Marta to become more selective in her various expressions.

Narcissistic Personality Disorder

Typical Schemata

I must have my way in every interaction.
I must not be in any way foiled in seeking pleasure or status.
I am more special than anyone else.
I should only have to relate to special people like me.
I must be admired.
No one should have more of anything than I have.

Case Illustration

Sam was a 64-year-old professor of surgery at a medical school. He came to therapy with great reluctance and as part of marital therapy. He had been married to Anita for 42 years. She had suffered a "nervous breakdown" (major depressive episode) which required her being hospitalized. The hospital physician strongly recommended marital therapy. As part of the assessment Sam himself was to be seen for two sessions. He made it quite clear that he did not like being in the therapist's office, did not want to be part of the therapy, and did not think that anything wrong with his wife had anything to do with him. He was, at first, quite pleasant and charming, trying to convince the therapist that his (Sam's) involvement in therapy was unnecessary. Failing that, he became brusque, bordering on rudeness. "Why," he inquired, "am I seeing a therapist who is only an associate professor, when I am a full professor? If I have got to be part of this ridiculous business, I might as well have the best person."

The marital issue revolved around Sam's demanding that his wife wait on him hand and foot; she had a virtual servant status and was expected to provide for his every whim. In recent years his wife had become increasingly "down" until she finally ceased being able to function and entered the hospital. His view of Anita's problem was that she was simply "too moody, too weak, too spoiled, and too reluctant to do her job," her job being, in his eyes, to do his bidding. Sam considered his position in life as one that he well deserved. He described himself as a tyrant in the operating theater because "I'm damn good." He described with great relish how his residents and nurses jumped whenever he came into the room.

The goal of therapy within the context of the agreed marital work was to have Sam respond differently to his wife, thus enabling her to return to full functioning. It was pointed out to Sam that if he continued to create stress for her, his wife would continue to be depressed and would be unavailable to meet his needs. With this as a goal, he continued in therapy. Marital sessions were held weekly, and Sam was seen on alternate weeks. The therapy work with Sam was quite limited. Much of the therapy work consisted of direct instruction on more adaptive ways to behave with Anita. His more pervasive behavioral response was not dealt with in the therapy. He was able, in fact, to alter his response to Anita, not because he agreed with it, but because if he did not make this alteration, he would get even less of what he wanted. The focus of work with Anita was to have her be more assertive and try to refuse doing things that she did not want to do. If Sam wanted certain things done, they could hire someone and pay them to do it, or he could do it himself. After 6 months of therapy Sam and Anita terminated the therapy. She was less depressed and described Sam as more responsive. She also pointed out that any response on Sam's part was more response than she had gotten in the past.

Avoidant Personality Disorder

Typical Schemata

I must be liked.
I must not look foolish to myself or others at any time.
The world is a dangerous place.
I must depend on others to take care of me.
Isolation is better than being put at risk of being hurt.
All criticism is the same; the slightest criticism is the same as massive condemnation.
People must offer me unconditional guarantees of acceptance before I commit myself to relating to that person.

Case Illustration

Alan, a 20-year-old undergraduate, came to therapy self-referred because of "social anxiety." (While social anxiety was a major component of Alan's life, he met the criteria for avoidant disorder). He had decided that after 2 years at the university he needed finally to make friends. He had no contact with others in his dormitory, not even with his next-door neighbors. Because of his anxiety he spoke only infrequently to other students in his classes. Alan's mother called the therapist after the first session and reported that when at home, Alan was "funny and related well to all of his relatives." Alan's father had died when Alan was 6 years old. He was raised by his maternal grandmother while his mother worked. Being an only child, his grandmother was afraid to allow him to play with other children because he might get hurt. He was expected to return home directly after school so as to be safe. Clubs, scouting, and other extracurricular activities were discouraged because of the potential danger involved. Alan reported the following example of childhood overprotection: "I must have been about 8 or 9. It was during the summer and my mother and grandmother had rented a summer cottage. I was playing outdoors, and my grandmother was sitting on the porch watching me. I saw some kids playing two houses away and started walking towards them. My grandmother came off of the porch towards me. I was almost to the kids when my grandmother grabbed me by the arm. The other kids saw that and started making fun of me. They called me 'momma's boy,' 'sissy,' and 'fairy.' My grandmother yelled at them, and that made it even worse. I didn't want to go out of the house for fear of seeing those kids again."

Therapy was very problem-focused. It lasted for 20 months, excluding the summer months when Alan returned home. A series of graded task assignments (e.g., asking a student in class for an assignment), role play in the office with clinic staff acting as role-play assistants, and directly challenging Alan's distortions and their underlying schemata were the main tools here. When the new school year began, Alan started speaking to other students in class and began relating to others in his dormitory. He began spending time with a small group of students whom

Alan labeled as "nerds and losers, just like me." His self-esteem was still quite low, but he had effectively begun the process of trying to be more social. Anxiety-reduction techniques were essential in Alan's treatment. By the end of the 2nd year of therapy, Alan was involved with others in his dormitory and had begun dating.

Dependent Personality Disorder

Typical Schemata

I cannot function without the support of others.
Without the advice and reassurance of others I cannot exist.
In any situation I am probably wrong.
I cannot offend other people because they may become angry and abandon me.
If I am abandoned I will be destroyed.
I must keep people near to me.
If I am alone, I may be hurt.
Working with others is far better than working by myself.

Case Illustration

Sally was a 34-year-old, unmarried teacher. She had been teaching first grade for the past 12 years. Her previous therapist had referred her to her present therapist with the statement "I believe Sally to be untreatable; her great dependence precludes her ever changing." Sally was, indeed, dependent. She would not make decisions without consulting her mother, her therapist, her two best friends, and her father. She did not ask simply for opinions but rather for decisions. If the decisions that she obtained were at variance with one another, Sally would become very anxious. Her dating pattern involved becoming attached to a man after the first date; if he did not telephone her, she would become distraught. The following instance demonstrates the severity of her dependent personality disorder. A man took her out for a date and tried to rape her. When she fought him off and forced him to leave her apartment, he called her a "tease" and told her that he would never telephone her again. Sally became upset – not because of the attempted rape but because of his abandonment of her.

The goal of therapy with Sally was to have her attempt to make small decisions on her own. Almost any situation in her life could become a setting for this therapeutic purpose. An example is provided by her taking a vacation – her first in 10 years. Her rationale for not having gone on vacation was that she never had anyone to go with and could not decide where to go, when to go, how long to stay, how much to spend, etc. With the discrete goal of going on vacation small goals of gathering information and turning plans into action became the focus of therapy. Sally's choice of vacation locale was England, the same vacation that the therapist had taken the previous year. Inasmuch as the goal was *any* vacation rather than none, no interpretation of the continued dependence was made. Sally planned to go on a tour with a group of teachers; the trip was planned and taken with the help of a guide. The success experience of having gone on vacation was then used to demonstrate to Sally that she could do things on her own. Sally has subsequently taken two other vacations, developed a relationship with a man, and changed her school teaching assignment to another building and a new grade. She still experiences great anxiety in new situations but is now willing to take chances in these situations.

Obsessive-Compulsive Personality Disorder

Typical Schemata

There are strict rules in life.
By focusing on the details of a situation, one will reduce the chances of making errors.
A person is defined by what he does.
The better the job you do, the better the person you are.
Rules must be adhered to without alteration.
Never discard anything that may be of some value.
Emotions must be controlled.

Case Illustration

Phyllis was a 35-year-old executive working for a large corporation and earning a high salary. She had no social life, no friends, did not date, and had never had sexual intercourse. Her workday began at 6:30 A.M. and lasted until 9:00 P.M., and she also worked 5 hours Saturdays and Sundays. Her referral was due to a germ phobia for which she had sought treatment from several therapists over the past 25 years; in all her previous therapy her phobia had been the major focus of therapy work. In drafting a problem list at the outset of therapy the therapist tried to establish a hierarchy of problems to be worked on; Phyllis listed the germ phobia as being the most important. Since this was a chronic symptom and one that did not incapacitate her but only discomforted and inconvenienced her, the therapist questioned whether it might not be of value to begin with other problems. The agreed therapeutic goal was to gain some success with other symptoms rather than repeat past failures by focusing all the therapeutic energy on the phobia; the therapist recommended concentrating initially on developing social interactions. Therapy work in the 1st year was on skill building and experimenting with various types of social interactions. Phyllis' first dating situation ended after two dates when the man, a 40-year-old divorced attorney and far more experienced than she, wanted immediately to start a sexual relationship. Her choice of this man was made on the basis of his status as an attorney with a successful practice. Her second dating experience, with Henry, lasted for 1 year and did include a sexual experience. Although this man was unsatisfactory to Phyllis for many reasons, his occupational status was impressive to her. Throughout the therapy work Phyllis spoke of her germ phobia, which, although still a problem, was placed lower down on the list of therapy issues.

After 1 year Henry told Phyllis that he wanted to stop seeing her. Phyllis immediately focused on the catastrophe of this loss, sure that she would never meet another man. Shortly thereafter she met Bill, who seemed right for her in many ways except one: his job was essentially a lower status managerial one and with a lower salary than hers. Phyllis and Bill became intimate rather quickly and within several months began discussing living together and marrying. Her parents were concerned that this relationship should not interfere with her work. "After all," her mother said, "there are many fish in the ocean." When Phyllis discussed this in therapy, i.e., ending the relationship so that she would not be distracted from her work, the therapist pointed out that there were indeed many fish in the ocean, but that she had not caught very many. Therapy is continuing. Phyllis and Bill are getting married and have purchased a house together. Phyllis has modified her work hours and has slowly become part of Bill's social circle. Her parents would still like to see her concentrate on work, but she has resisted this. The germ phobia remains an irritant.

Passive-Aggressive Personality Disorder

Typical Schemata

I should only have to do what I want to do.
People should not make demands of me.
Others undervalue my work and worth.
People in authority are generally unfair.
I should not be asked to do so much work.
Deadlines and pressures are unfair and should be resisted.
Anger cannot be directly expressed.
Anger is dangerous and must be avoided.
Whatever can be put aside can be left for tomorrow.
Get away with whatever you can.

Case Illustration

Kevin was a 32-year-old, 3rd year medical resident. Mary, Kevin's fiancée had been seen for the treatment of depression, and this had been very successful. She had met Kevin and planned to marry him. She requested couple's therapy to help deal with "some tensions" that they were experiencing. Kevin was a chronic procrastinator and had gotten into significant difficulty with his residency director because Kevin was far behind in his reports and charts. Kevin expressed dissatisfaction with his residency because "They're all out to screw me; I just want to get out." He broke promises to Mary and always apologized, blaming his lack of follow-through on his work load, on-call assignments, poor schedule, and lack of motivation. Despite Mary's asking Kevin to tell her when he did not intend to do what he had promised, he did not comply. He was abjectly sorry when they lost a deposit on a house because he forgot to tell Mary that he had not obtained the proper signatures on a loan application.

Despite their difficulties they married. Kevin continued promising to turn over a new leaf. On their honeymoon they took a prepaid tour to the Bahamas. At their first dinner together as man and wife Mary ordered a glass of wine to celebrate. When the waiter brought the wine, Kevin asked if the wine was included in the prepaid meal. When the waiter informed them that the wine cost $2.00 extra, Kevin sent it back. "After all," he told Mary, "we've got to watch our money very carefully now." He found reasons to inspect the contents of her purse ("I was just looking for a pen."). He insisted that she could only purchase pizza from a particular restaurant which was farther from home because it was $1.00 less expensive, although they agreed that this pizza was inferior to that served at a restaurant closer to home (Mary had to do the travelling).

A crisis arose when Kevin was suspended from his residency with 2 months left to finish his training. He had told his residency director that he and Mary would be taking 2 weeks for a vacation in 3-days time. Although Kevin had earned the vacation time, his request was denied. He was informed that he knew the rule regarding vacation requests required these to be submitted 30 days in advance. When Kevin tried to explain to his director that he (Kevin) had arranged for coverage of his patient load, and that he was not needed, the director told Kevin that the issue was his having broken, bent, and generally ignored rules that other residents observed. Kevin asked whether his request would have been approved if he had asked 30 days earlier. The Director replied that it would most certainly have been approved. "Well then," Kevin responded, "if it would have been approved 30 days ago, why make a fuss now?" Kevin was nonetheless forbidden to absent himself. Kevin saw this as another instance of "they" being out to get him. He took the vacation and was suspended.

In therapy Kevin always saw himself as the wounded, victimized, assaulted, and picked-upon member of the relationship. Despite the very clear exposition of Kevin's schemata, he was determined to maintain what he saw as his "integrity." Mary eventually left Kevin. Kevin stayed in therapy for three sessions, during which time his purpose seemed to be merely to convince the therapist that his (Kevin's) position was correct. He then left therapy.

Summary

For every theory of personality there is an accompanying theory of causes for disorders of personality. Acquiring skills to treat personality disorders has become a major interest among therapists. This interest results from the apparent increase in the number of patients treated for psychological disorders that include axis II problems. While these patients do not generally come for therapy specifically for axis II problems, they often do come for axis I problems. These patients require a longer time in treatment and more energy and time from the therapist, and they do not show the same rate of gain as do patients whose problems are not complicated by personality disorders.

Axis II problems exemplify Beck's concept of the schema as a central issue in the formation of these disorders. Personality disorders basically result from undeveloped or unevolved schemata. Schematic representations that were once used effectively by the individual become a source of dysfunction. Because of the chronic nature of personality disorders cognitive therapy can be used successfully in their treatment. The arena for treatment is the therapeutic relationship. The patient is first taught the necessary skills for dealing with his personality disorder by dealing with axis I problems. Through such processes as schematic restructuring, schematic modification, or schematic reinterpretation the patient can be helped to deal with the long-standing life problems that are a part of the personality disorder.

The present chapter is meant as a very preliminary work. By setting out treatment ideas and sharing the author's clinical experience, clinicians will hopefully be encouraged to develop their own applications of cognitive therapy to this difficult but treatable group of patients.

References

Abend SM, Porder MS, Willick MS (1983) Borderline patients: psychoanalytic perspectives. International Universities Press, New York

Ansbacher H, Ansbacher R (1963) The individual psychology of Alfred Adler. Basic Books, New York

Beck AT (1977) Cognitive therapy and the emotional disorders. International Universities Press, New York

Beck AT, Emery G (1985) Treatment of anxiety and phobia. Basic Books, New York

Beck AT, Freeman A (in press) Cognitive therapy of personality disorders. Guilford, New York

Beck AT, Rush AJ, Shaw BF, Emery G (1979) Cognitive therapy of depression. Guilford, New York

Byrne D, Kelley K (1981) An introduction to personality, 3rd edn. Prentice Hall, Englewood Cliffs

Chatham PM (1985) Treatment of the borderline personality. Aaronson, New York

Corsini R (ed) (1979) Current personality theories. Peacock, Itasca

DSM I – Diagnostic and statistical manual, 1st edn. (1952) American Psychiatric Press, Washington DC

DSM II – Diagnostic and statistical manual, 2nd edn. (1968) American Psychiatric Press, Washington DC

DSM III – Diagnostic and statistical manual, 3rd edn. (1980) American Psychiatric Press, Washington DC

DSM III-R – Diagnostic and statistical manual, revised 3rd edn. (1987) American Psychiatric Press, Washington DC

Freeman A (1987) Understanding personal, cultural and religious schema in psychotherapy. In: Freeman A, Epstein N, Simon KM (eds) Depression in the family. Haworth, New York

Freeman A, Simon KM (1988) Cognitive therapy of anxiety. In: Freeman A, Simon KM, Arkowitz H, Beutler L (eds) Handbook of cognitive therapy. Plenum, New York (to be published)

Freeman A, Simon KM, Fleming B, Pretzer J (1988) Clinical applications of cognitive therapy. Plenum, New York (to be published)

Goldstein W (1985) An introduction to the borderline conditions. Aronson, Northvale

Gunderson JG (1984) Borderline personality disorders. American Psychiatric Press, Washington DC

Hall C, Lindzey G (1978) Theories of personality. Wiley, New York

Harris JC (1984) Tar baby and other rhymes of Uncle Remus. Cherokee Press, Marietta

Hjelle, Ziegler (1981) Personality theories. McGraw Hill, New York

Horowitz M (ed) (1977) Hysterical personality. Aronson, New York

Kendall P, Braswell L (1985) Cognitive behavior therapy with children. Guildford, New York

Kernberg OF (1975) Borderline conditions and pathological narcissism. Aronson, New York

Kernberg OF (1984) Severe personality disorders: psychotherapeutic strategies. Yale University Press, New Haven

Lion JR (ed) (1981) Personality disorders: diagnosis and management. Williams & Wilkens, Baltimore

Masterson JF (1978) New perspectives on psychotherapy of the borderline adult. Brunner/Mazel, New York

Masterson JF (1980) From borderline adolescent to functioning adult: the test of time. Brunner/Mazel, New York

Masterson JF (1985) Treatment of the borderline adolescent: a developmental approach. Brunner/Mazel, New York

Masterson JF (1987) The real self. Brunner/Mazel, New York

Meichenbaum D (1977) Cognitive behavior modification. Plenum, New York
Millon T (1981) Disorders of personality. Wiley, New York
Novaco R (1975) Anger control: the development and evaluation of an experimental treatment. Lexington Books, Lexington
Perris C (1986) Kognitiv terapi i teori och praktik. Natur och Kultur, Stockholm
Reid WH (ed) (1981) The treatment of the antisocial syndromes. van Nostrand, New York
Saul LJ, Warner S (1982) The psychotic personality. van Nostrand, New York
Searles HF (1978) Psychoanalytic therapy with the borderline adult. In: Masterson JF (ed) New perspectives on psychotherapy of the borderline adult. Brunner/Mazel, New York
Searles H (1986) My work with borderline patients. Aaronson, New York
Sherman M (1979) Personality: inquiry and applications. Pergamon, New York
Shultz O (1981) Theories of personality. Brooks/Cole, Monterey

Cognitive Therapy for Panic Disorder and Generalized Anxiety Disorder*

R.B. JARRETT and A.J. RUSH

Introduction

Research findings on behavior therapy for phobic disorders (Barlow and Wolfe 1981) and cognitive therapy for depression (Beck et al. 1979) suggest that these approaches significantly reduce the distress and symptoms of affected patients. Such progress, as well as the potentially addicting effects of treatment with benzodiazepines, has encouraged clinical researchers to ask the question "Can cognitive-behavioral approaches be used in the treatment of nonphobic anxiety disorders? In this chapter we will briefly describe the nonphobic disorders and entertain this question.

How Are Nonphobic Disorders Categorized?

The second edition of the Diagnostic and Statistical Manual of Mental Disorders (DSM-II) (American Psychiatric Association 1968) characterized chronic tension, excessive worry, frequent headaches, or recurrent panic attacks as "anxiety neurosis." In DSM-II generalized anxiety disorder (GAD) and panic disorder (PD) were viewed as a unitary anxiety disorder. Current diagnostic systems separate the symptoms of persistent, pervasive anxiety (GAD) from those of recurrent but isolated panic attacks. Outside of North America, GAD and PD continue to be conceptualized as a unitary phenomena (Tyrer 1984). The controversy is about whether there is only a quantitative, rather than qualitative, difference between the "two" disorders. The quantitative argument focuses on the shared symptom of anticipatory anxiety and stresses that PD is only a severe form of GAD.

Barlow (1988) has reviewed and evaluated the major types of evidence used to support the validity of these separate categories within DSM-III (American Psychiatric Association 1980). First to support such separation was Klein's (1981) finding that imipramine reduced agoraphobics' panic attacks but did not reduce chronic anticipatory anxiety. Conversely, Klein also found that sedatives and

*Research was supported in part by a grant from the National Institute of Mental Health to the authors (MH-38238) and by a Mental Health Clinical Research Center Grant (MH-41115) from the NIMH to the Department of Psychiatry, University of Texas Southwestern Medical Center, Dallas, Texas.
Department of Psychiatry and Mental Health Clinical Research Center, University of Texas Southwestern Medical Center at Dallas, 5323 Harry Hines Blvd., Dallas, Texas 752315, USA

alcohol reduced anticipatory anxiety but did not reduce panic attacks. Second, Barlow and Craske (1988) noted that GAD and PD differ on measures of phasic arousal, tonic arousal, and on some questionaire measures. Third, family studies have indicated that probands with PD are more likely to have first-degree relatives with anxiety disorders than are probands with GAD (Merikangas and Weissman 1986). Even with these findings the preceding data bases include difficulties and have not conclusively demonstrated that PD and GAD are qualitatively distinct (Barlow, 1988).

In this chapter, GAD and PD will be described separately, and cognitive therapy for excessive nonphobic anxiety will then be discussed.

What Is Generalized Anxiety Disorder?

The central characteristic of GAD is persistent anxiety that lasts for at least 1 month. According to DSM-III (American Psychiatric Association 1980), patients must endorse symptoms from at least three of the four categories: (a) motor tension (shakiness, trembling, inability to relax, and being easily startled); (b) autonomic hyperactivity (sweating, heart pounding, dry mouth, light-headedness, stomach upset, frequent urination, and diarrhea); (c) vigilance and scanning (difficulty concentrating, insomnia, irritability, and impatience); and (d) apprehensive expectation (anxiety, worry, fear, rumination, anticipation of misfortune). The diagnosis can only be made in persons who are at least 18 years of age, and whose symptoms cannot be attributed to other mental disorders, such as depression or schizophrenia.

The large epidemiological survey of Weissman et al. (1978) used structured interviewing to examine data on the incidence and prevalence of GAD and PD. In the 511 interviews of individuals living in the New Haven, Connecticut, area the prevalence of any anxiety disorder was 4.3%; that of GAD was 2.5%, and that of PD was 0.4%. Fewer epidemiological and descriptive data are available on GAD than on PD. According to Gorman and Liebowitz (1986), the age of onset, natural history, and prognosis of GAD are not presently available.

What Is Panic Disorder?

Although the phenomenon of panic attacks was recognized and described by Benedikt as early as 1870 (Katerndahl 1984), it was not until 1980 that the diagnostic category of PD was used in DSM-III (American Psychiatric Association 1980). According to DSM-III, PD is characterized by episodes of unpredictable, sudden, and intense fear associated with at least four of the following symptoms: dyspnea, palpitations, chest pain, choking or smothering sensations, unsteady feelings, dizziness, vertigo, feelings of unreality, tingling in hand or feet, sweating, hot or cold flashes, trembling and shaking, faintness, and fear of collapsing, insanity, or loss of control. To receive a diagnosis of PD the patient must experience at least three panic attacks in nonthreatening situations within a three week period.

DSM-III-R (American Psychiatric Association 1987) adds the requirement that the worst point in the panic attack should occur within 10 min of the onset of symptoms to differentiate it from the gradual exacerbation of anxiety symptoms seen in GAD patients exposed to noxious situations. Norton et al. (1986) and Norton et al. (1985) have shown, however, that many of the symptoms of PD occur within nonclinical populations but simply do not occur at the frequency specified by DSM-III. Barlow and Craske's (in press) clinical sample of patients with PD reported an average of 1.31 panic attacks weekly. In diagnosing PD the clinician must rule out other physical disorders (e.g., hypoglycemia, hyperthyroidism, paraoxysmal tachycardias, phaechromocytoma, and drug withdrawal symptoms) (Judd and Burrows 1986) and mental disorders (e.g., major depression, somatization disorders, schizophrenia, or agoraphobia).

To rule out other psychiatric disorders such structured interviews as the Structured Clinical Interview for DSM-III, Upjohn Version (SCID-UP; Spitzer and Williams 1983), the Schedule for Affective Disorders and Schizophrenia, Lifetime Version (modified for the study of anxiety disorders; Mannuzza et al. 1985), or the Anxiety Disorders Interview Schedule (ADIS; DiNardo et al. 1983) are useful. To rule out the presence of medical disease all patients evaluated for GAD and PD should undergo standard laboratory tests. When evaluating PD, consultation with medical colleagues should be liberally used, as the diagnosis is in large part made by exclusion.

The onset of PD typically occurs before the age of 30 and occurs more often in women than in men (Weissman et al. 1978). It is estimated that PD affects approximately 4% of the population (Crowe and Noyes 1986) and results in more than $100 million in disability benefits and health care costs each year (Sheehan 1982). Typical complications of PD include alcohol and drug abuse, depression, and increased physical morbidity and mortality. In addition, the risk of hypertension and peptic ulcer in patients with panic disorder is twice that of the general population (Judd and Burrows 1986).

Family studies indicate that the risk of developing PD increases if one or both parents have PD (Klerman 1986). Although the cause of PD is unknown at present, the disorder can be precipitated by neuroendocrine changes (e.g., birth, pregnancy) and by psychosocial events (e.g., interpersonal conflict loss of a significant other). Panic attacks can be experimentally induced in vulnerable individuals by such physiological challenges as sodium lactate and glucose infusion (Pitts and McClure 1967), CO_2 (van den Hout and Griez 1984), hyperventilation (Clark et al. 1985), yohimbine (Charney et al. 1984), isoproterenol (Rainey et al. 1984), and oral administration of caffeine (Charney et al. 1985).

The DSM-III (American Psychiatric Association 1980) criteria distinguish PD from agoraphobia with panic attacks and from agoraphobia without panic attacks. DSM-III-R (American Psychiatric Association 1987) uses the extent of avoidance to aid in determining which of the following diagnostic categories should be used: uncomplicated PD, PD with limited phobic avoidance, PD with extensive phobic avoidance, and agoraphobia without panic attacks. This chapter will focus on the use of cognitive therapy to treat uncomplicated PD or PD with limited phobic avoidance because in vivo exposure therapy has been demonstrated to be a very effective psychosocial treatment for anxiety disorders involving extensive phobic avoidance (Barlow and Wolfe 1981). The proposed categories, PD with extensive phobic avoidance and agoraphobia without panic attacks, include the previously used category, agoraphobia. The rationale for the change in terms is that at present, agoraphobia is considered a severe type of PD (Noyes et al. 1986). The few studies available (Emmelkamp et al. 1978; Emmelkamp and Mersch 1982; Williams and Rappoport 1983) that compare the relative efficacy of exposure therapy to cognitive restructuring or to the combined treatment for agoraphobia suggest that graded in vivo exposure is a necessary treatment component to reduce avoidance. By definition, however, neither uncomplicated PD nor GAD involve avoidance of specific external stimuli. Therefore, a treatment other than in vivo exposure is necessary.

Why Treat Generalized Anxiety and Panic Disorders with Cognitive Therapy?

The thesis of this chapter is that the efficacy of cognitive therapy in the treatment of GAD and uncomplicated PD deserves a controlled, empirical evaluation. The rationale for treating these nonphobic anxiety disorders with cognitive therapy follows.

Beck and Rush (1975) described the "phobic-anxiety neurosis continuum." They maintained that "the stimuli in anxiety neuroses are broader, less specific, more frequently 'internal,' less easily avoided, and less directly related to the content of cognitions as compared with phobias." That is, phobic anxiety disorders involve easily identified, external phobic stimuli and avoidance, and they appear to respond well to in vivo exposure therapy. On the other hand, GAD and uncomplicated PD (the nonphobic disorders) involve stimuli that are more difficult to identify. We hypothesize that both GAD and PD involve internal and external stimuli, which can be eventually identified, as well as avoidance of such stimuli.

Barlow (1986) provided similar arguments in conceptualizing PD. He noted that initial unexpected panic attacks typically are associated with marked life stresses. Barlow (1986, p. 804) argued that patients with panic attacks have developed a "phobia of internal physical sensations that may represent the beginning of another panic attack." Barlow noted that this process, called "interoceptive conditioning", was recorded by Breggin (1964) as an explanation for panic attacks provoked with laboratory administration of epinephrine. While attempting to identify the stimuli associated with panic Barlow (in press) categorizes panic attacks as expected versus unexpected and cued versus uncued. Furthermore, Barlow maintained that the goal in treating panic is to expose the patient to the feared "interoceptive" cues (see Griez and van den Hout 1986 for initial, but promising support for this notion).

The hypothesis here is that GAD and PD involve internal stimuli, cognitions (as emphasized by Beck), and "interoceptive cues" or sensations (as emphasized by Barlow). These internal stimuli, which are also responses, are associated with the array of symptoms labeled anxiety and may or may not be associated with the same external stimuli across time. Cognitive therapy may be useful in treating GAD and PD because the functional analysis conducted during cognitive therapy forms the basis for identifying both the overt and covert stimuli associated with persistent anxiety or isolated panic attacks, and because it promotes eventual exposure to these stimuli. Cognitive theory provides a framework for clinicians to conceptualize and identify covert (i.e., cognitions, sensations) and overt stimuli associated with generalized anxiety and panic disorders. Successful treatment will involve exposure to external stimuli, interoceptive cues, and cognitions.

How Are Panic Disorder and Generalized Anxiety Disorder Conceptualized in the Cognitive Model?

Premise

The premise of the cognitive model is that cognitions (thoughts and images) influence emotion and other behaviors. This premise is founded in phenomenological psychology, which assumes that behavior is influenced by the individual's perception of the self and the world. Simply put, in this model it is the perception of the event rather than the event itself which influences emotion. The cognitive model includes elements (e.g., automatic thoughts, logical errors, assumptions) that are applied across disorders. Yet, the cognitive model for emotional disorders (Beck 1967, 1976) specifies that the *content* of cognition is highly related to the type of psychopathological disorder (e.g., depression, anxiety) which is present. Thus, Beck has argued that within each disorder there are characteristic cognitive themes.

According to the theory, the central themes of cognitions elicited from the anxious patient are those of anticipated or visualized danger and extreme vulnerability. Beck and Emery (1985) have traced the development of anxiety disorders from the naturally selected survival mechanism used by organisms to avoid objectifiable threats and dangers. They argued that anxiety cues the organism to take defensive action in order to avoid harm. When the organism perceives anxiety, there is automatic arousal, ongoing behavior becomes inhibited, and the organism selectively scans the environment for threatening stimuli (Clark and Beck, in press). It is assumed that these physiological, behavioral, and cognitive functions have been naturally selected. Their survival value in dangerous historic or contemporary environments is obvious. Anxiety disorders, however, develop when the physiological arousal, behavioral inhibition, and cognitive focus generated do not match the stimuli objectively present. Beck (1976) asserted that anxious patients overestimate the probability and severity of the feared event and underestimate the chance that they can cope independently or will receive assistance.

Elements

The elements within the cognitive model can be organized according to the amount of inference associated with each. The basic and least inferential element is the *negative automatic thought*. Negative automatic thoughts are what individuals think or imagine when they experience emotion (e.g., anxiety). Negative automatic thoughts involve inference because they are based on self-report and cannot be directly observed. Patients with GAD may report such negative automatic thoughts as "I can't function well enough and I can't count on anyone to help me." Patients with PD may report such negative automatic thoughts as "I'm feeling dizziness and I'm about to lose control."

Beck has distinguished between socially accepted or objective definitions of particular events and their private meaning (i.e., the significance of an event to an individual). He emphasized that the private interpretation of the event is that which is critical to the emotional response. The emphasis on the private meanings of events reflects the phenomenological conceptualization of psychopathology. Yet, the disparity between private and public meanings of events results in the discrimination between distorted and realistic thoughts.

The second element of the model is the *dysfunctional assumption* or rule. These are unarticulated beliefs about the self and the world which increase the probability that the individual will misinterpret events or situations. The dysfunctional assumption is a completely *inferred* construct and may not be reported directly by the patient. Dysfunctional assumptions are typically inferred by examining the situations, emotions, and themes associated with the array of negative automatic thoughts.

According to the cognitive model, when a person is anxious, these dysfunctional assumptions are activated more frequently and more easily than the more adaptive alternative assumptions. Second, it is assumed that as the anxiety becomes more severe, the individual's thinking in an ever widening variety of situations becomes more disparate from logical or objective evidence. Third, the cognitive model posits that negative automatic thoughts contain various logical errors indicative of the thinking process. Logical errors are identified by examining the relationship or lack thereof, between actual, specific events, objectively described, and the associated negative automatic thinking. Examples of logical errors include arbitrary inference, selective attention, overgeneralization, magnification or minimization, and personalization. Arbitrary inference occurs when the anxious person draws conclusions that are not supported by logic or environmental data. Selective attention refers to emphasizing certain details while ignoring others. Overgeneralization includes drawing conclusions about one's ability, performance, or worth based on a single incident. Magnification or minimization refers to exaggerating or diminishing the importance of an event. Personalization involves associating events with oneself when logic or data would prohibit such associations (Beck and Emery 1985).

According to Beck's model, it is the existence of rigidly held silent assumptions that increases an individual's vulnerability or predisposition to anxiety disorders. Theoretically, dysfunctional assumptions or beliefs develop during past learning periods and are activated when the patient currently experiences stimuli analogous to those present when the assumption developed. Thus, the assumption remains latent until there is an activating stimulus. Once activated, these assumptions are applied to an ever widening array of stimulus situations and thereby lead to more and more negative automatic thinking.

Beck and Emery (1985) have also maintained that dysfunctional assumptions with similar or related content are organized together in memory to form schemata. Schemata that are very situationally specific are called *cognitive sets* and those that are global or general are called *modes*. Activation of a schema increases the chance that consistent information is processed and decreases the chance that inconsistent information is processed. These constructs, schemata, cognitive sets, and cognitive modes are the most inferential constructs used in the cognitive model.

Content

Beck maintains that automatic thoughts, logical errors, dysfunctional assumptions, and schemata will involve content with perceptual themes characteristic of a given disorder. In the case of GAD Beck and Emery (1985) asserted that patients typically have distorted perceptions of their relations with others (i.e., sociality) or of their identity, mastery, autonomy, and health (i.e., individuality). They argued that these patients fear losing their caretakers and are thus vulnerable to the thoughts of death or injury, fear inadequate mastery, and thus think that they will be ridiculed or rejected. They argued that fears of incompetence may persist even in the face of demonstrated competence. They maintained that GAD can be distinguished from social phobia in that self-confidence is diminished in GAD, while in social phobia confidence may not have developed at all. Beck also asserts that patients with GAD have both "anticipatory" and "retrospective" anxiety and thus experience anxiety much of the time.

Beck (1988) and Clark and Beck (1988) outline the basic hypotheses in a cognitive conceptualization of PD. From a cognitive perspective, patients vulnerable to panic attacks are especially sensitive to internal sensations that they perceive as abnormal. They pay excessive attention to such sensations when they cannot find a benign explanation, or if the sensation could indicate severe biological or psychological disaster (e.g., dying, going crazy). Beck argued that this excessive attention is part of an "automatic reflexive processing." The consequence of such focusing increases the interpretation of impending danger, which further activates the autonomic nervous system. A vicious cycle develops between catastrophic interpretations of physiological arousal and increases in physiological arousal. One consequence of the vicious cycle is that the patients' ability to objectively evaluate their symptoms is impaired. In other words, the "automatic reflexive processing" (of impending disaster) interferes with "directive thinking" (e.g., evaluation of physical sensations).

Beck and Emery (1985) further hypothesized that as panic attacks continue, the individuals see their symptoms as cueing *immediate* danger, thus help-seeking behavior is initiated. Clark and Beck (1988) note that the concern of immediate danger and immediate help is characteristic of PD, in contrast to patients with hypochrondriasis who instead focus on the long-term danger associated with their bodily sensations.

Beck (1988) notes that the cognitive model describes PD but does not explain its etiology. He argues that the benefits of such a descriptive model are clinical (e.g., to facilitate diagnosis and pharmacological or psychological treatment) and conceptual (e.g., to understand the psychological effects of neurochemical events).

What Are the Testable Hypotheses?

The premise of the cognitive model, that the *perception* of the event rather than the event itself, influences emotion and other behaviors, has proved difficult to test. This premise is embedded in the mediational-nonmediational controversy in psychology (Beck and Mahoney 1979; Wolpe 1978; Coyne and Gotlieb 1983, 1986; Segal and Shaw 1986a,b). This controversy revolves around the issue of which variables in the causal chain of behavior receive the most weight. Nonmediationalists typically identify the precipitants of responses as environmental events (i.e., behavior is a function of the environment). In contrast, mediationalists include in their analysis other responses, which are often covert. As a complete discussion of these alternative perspectives is beyond the scope of this chapter, here the premise is identified as important, and is labeled as both controversial and historically difficult to test.

There are, however, testable hypotheses derived from the cognitive conceptualization of generalized anxiety and panic disorders. Some of these follow.

The Cognitive Content of Patients with Generalized Anxiety Disorder and Panic Disorder Differs from that of Normals

According to Beck, the content of cognitions of individuals with and without psychiatric diagnoses should differ. In particular, compared to normals it is predicted that depressed people view themselves, their world, and their future in a negative, distorted, and unrealistic manner and report cognitions involving loss. The predicted differences between normals and the depressed have been found, for example, in expectations of success (Norman et al. 1983; Lunghi 1977). At the same time, unpredicted differences have been found when normals evidenced a self-protecting bias (Gotlib 1983). Beck's model suggests that, given the same environmental or physiological precipitants, patients with GAD or PD should conceptualize the stimuli as more dangerous than normals.

It is noteworthy that the cognitive model has had difficulty accounting for findings which suggest that normals overestimate their social skills while depressives produce ratings that agree with those of trained observers (Gotlib 1983). Because these data have been associated mostly with social functioning of depressed people, it would be interesting to learn how the data compare to the interpersonal functioning of patients with GAD. If parallel, perhaps comparable findings will suggest that normals actually *underestimate* objective threats involved in social situations, while patients with both GAD and PD are more accurate, compared to an objective standard.

The Cognitive Content of Patients with Distinct Psychiatric Disorders Will Differ

Beck predicted that the cognitions of anxious patients will involve themes of danger. Butler and Mathews (1983) found that anxious patients overestimate the probability of future, negative hypothetical events. Beck (1988) has studied the cognitions of patients with "free-floating anxiety" and found that their cognitions generally involve danger. Such a prediction and finding can be contrasted with the prediction/finding that the cognitions of depressed patients involve loss (Thorpe et al. 1983).

In comparing GAD with PD, Beck (1988) predicts that the cognitions of patients with panic attacks should focus on mental or physical fears of catastrophy, while those of patients with GAD should focus on psychosocial fears. The data from anxious patients reported by Beck et al. (1974) show these characteristic themes. Hibbert (1984) reported that patients with panic attacks feared physical danger, while those with GAD feared the inability to cope with others. Similarly, Rapee (1985) reported that panic patients were preoccupied with heart attacks, fainting, dying, or going crazy, while patients with GAD reported that they are unreasonably anxious. Barlow et al. (1984) noted that subjects with PD reported more somatic symptoms than subjects with GAD. In addition, subjects with PD showed higher physiological responses (as measured by electromyograph, EMG) than did subjects with GAD. Thus, the modest data available to date support this hypothesis.

Panic Attacks Will only Occur when there Is a Physiological Change that Is Perceived as Catastrophic

Beck (1988) asserts that the variables which increase the probability of the occurrence of a panic attack are (a) a change in physiology and (b) a catastrophic interpretation. Several studies that have attempted to induce panic attacks and manipulate cognitive factors are relevant to this prediction. For example, Clark and Hemsley (1982) examined individual differences among normal subjects' response to hyperventilation. They found that whether subjects labeled hyperventilation as pleasant or aversive depended in part on what memories were associated with overbreathing. If subjects were reminded of sex or a drug-induced high, overbreathing was pleasant; if subjects were reminded of being about to faint, overbreathing was aversive. Van den Hout and Griez (1982) actually manipulated subjects' expectancy following CO_2 inhalation. One group of subjects was instructed to expect that CO_2 inhalation would produce a calm, relaxed state while the other group was told to expect a mildly aversive state. Only the subjects who were told that they would feel relaxed reported that CO_2 inhalation was pleasant. The aversive expectation, however, was not associated with significant effects.

Disruption of the Capacity to Appraise Symptoms Is the Central Feature of Panic Disorder

Beck (1988) asserts that during panic attacks, patients loose their ability to independently process information that could minimize or abort the attack. Beck termed this the dissociation between "reflective directive thinking" and "automatic reflexive processing." At present, we have found no published studies relevant to this prediction.

A Cognitive Vulnerability Factor Exists in the Form of Assumptions, Schemata, Modes, and Sets

These highly inferential cognitive variables (assumptions, schemata, modes, and sets), hypothesized to increase the probability of the initial occurrence of, recurrence of, and relapse in depressive and anxiety disorders, have proved difficult to test. Research in this area has been limited by difficulties in measuring constructs that use such theoretical concepts as latency and must be elicited by events that will, by definition, differ across individuals.

At what Stage of Development Is Cognitive Therapy for Generalized Anxiety Disorder and Panic Disorder?

Beck and Emery (1985) have provided a starting point for those interested in testing the efficacy of cognitive therapy with GAD and PD. While describing the conceptual framework for a cognitive theory and therapy of anxiety disorders, they noted that cognitive therapy is an integrated approach to psychotherapy rather than a collection of techniques.

In using the label "cognitive therapy" to refer to an integrated approach to psychotherapy it is also important to acknowledge that the terms cognitive therapy, behavior therapy, and cognitive-behavioral therapy have been inconsistently applied. Technically, the "cognitive therapy" described below overlaps with behavior therapy for anxiety disorders. The techniques associated with each label overlap, and the choice of label appears to be associated with the background of individual proponents or laboratories. To avoid confusion associated with these labels, explicit operationalization of the treatment approach used within a readily available treatment manual is ideal.

At present, no controlled tests of an integrated, complete cognitive therapy for PD or GAD have been published. There have, however, been tests of the efficacy of various cognitive strategies or techniques used within cognitive therapy with anxiety disorders involving phobic avoidance (see Last 1984). When the literature is reviewed to find studies of cognitive techniques with patients diagnosed as having PD, primarily case studies or reports surface.

For example, in the United Kingdom Clark (1986) has used "respiratory therapy" to treat patients with panic attacks. The basis for respiratory therapy was the observation that the symptoms of panic are similar to those experienced during hyperventilation (Lum 1976). Respiratory therapy involves teaching patients to (a) identify their catastrophic interpretations of bodily sensations, (b) apply alternative explanations for the sensations, (c) test the validity of the catastrophic interpretations, and (d) use controlled breathing as a coping skill to decrease the frequency and intensity of panic attacks. First, patients are asked to engage in a "diagnostic test" to learn more about their symptoms, in which they hyperventilate for 2 min. Following hyperventilation the therapist elicits thoughts and sensations and asks the patient to rate the degree of similarity between the hyperventilation and a panic attack. Second, the therapist describes the physiological effects of hyperventilation (i.e., blood chemistry changes, in that there is a decrease in the partial pressure of carbon dioxide and an increase in pH) as an alternative to the catastrophic interpretation of sensations. Next, as a response incompatible with overbreathing, the patient is taught to breath through the nose with mouth closed, taking in small amounts of air.

Three AB single case designs have been published to date on respiratory therapy. Clark et al. (1985) treated 11 patients with situational panic attacks and 7 patients with nonsituational panic attacks with two sessions of respiratory therapy. These patients all rated the hyperventilation as similar to their panic attacks and showed statistically significant reductions in the frequency of panic attacks with respiratory therapy. Patients were instructed not to increase their exposure to feared stimuli, and they reported no increases. Following respiratory therapy patients were treated with graded exposure (to avoided stimuli) and were treated with cognitive therapy for other difficulties. After a mean of 9.7 sessions the reduction in number of attacks was maintained through 6-month and 24-month follow-ups.

Salkovskis et al. (1986) replicated these effects with nine patients complaining of panic attacks. This study suggested that not only the frequency but also the severity of attacks and the generalized anxiety between attacks were less after treatment than before. Although patients were instructed not to increase exposure to feared stimuli, study patients reported reductions in the avoidance, unlike in the initial case (Clark et al. 1985).

Rapee (1985) reported the case of a patient treated with respiratory therapy who noted reductions in the frequency and intensity of panic attacks after treatment and throughout a 6-month follow-up. For each 3-week monitoring interval the frequency of attacks decreased from 22 to 2. For the same interval, the duration actually increased from 83.2 to 90, and the intensity decreased from 7.3 to 3.0. At follow-up the patient reported no attacks.

Although each of these studies suggests that this approach may be promising, it is noteworthy that none of them controlled for the nonspecific effects of treatment. In the Clark studies it is difficult to evaluate the clinical significance of the effects because one cannot judge what percentage of subjects continued to meet criteria for PD (individual data were not reported).

Waddell et al. (1984) reported on a multiple baseline design across three adult males diagnosed, according to structured interview, as suffering from PD. Following baseline, treatment consisted of cognitive restructuring alone, followed by cognitive restructuring plus progressive muscle relaxation. The cognitive restructuring component consisted of replacing negative, anxiety-producing thoughts with coping, adaptive thoughts (Meichenbaum and Turk 1973) and replacing the focus on somatic symptoms with attention to the ongoing tasks (Beck and Emery 1985). The three subjects reported decreases in the frequency and duration of intense anxiety, which was maintained at a 3-month follow-up. Only one subject reported a decrease in residual or "background" anxiety, and the other two subjects actually reported an increase. These effects were analogous to Klein's (1981) finding that imipramine will only reduce panic and will not reduce the anticipatory anxiety associated with panic attacks, according to Barlow and associates.

Taylor et al. (1982) compared the effect of diazepam, relaxation, placebo and a no-treatment control on 23 randomly assigned subjects with PD. They found that relaxation was associated with significantly greater pre- to post-treatment changes on the State-Trait Anxiety Inventory (STAI; Spielberger et al. 1970) than was placebo or diazepam treatment. On the Profile of Mood States (POMS; McNair et al. 1971) scale relaxation was associated with significantly greater changes than either placebo or the control. Diazepam was associated with significantly greater changes in baseline heart rate than was the control. Since none of the treatments were associated with a decrease in anxiety or depression by patient ratings recorded in daily diaries, the clinical significance of these findings is in question. The study is noteworthy in that it included 23 subjects and provided an exploratory, yet controlled, comparison of a pharmacological intervention (a benzodiazepine) and a psychological intervention in patients with a DSM-III (APA American Psychiatric Association 1980) diagnosis of PD.

The literature is even more barren when one searches for examples of published studies on the use of cognitive strategies with GAD. Woodward and Jones (1980) compared 22 randomly assigned patients with GAD to cognitive restructuring, modified systematic desensitization using coping imagery, a combined treatment (cognitive restructuring plus systematic desensitization) and a no-treatment control. The combination treatment reduced Fear Survey Schedule-Intensity (FSS-I; Wolpe and Lang 1964) scores more than no treatment or either treatment alone and reduced diary anxiety scores more than cognitive restructuring. No difference between treatments was found for Fear Survey Schedule-Severity (FSS-S; Wolpe and Lang 1964) scores, time spent worrying, the Zung self-rated anxiety scale (Zung 1971), fear thermometer, internal/external locus of control, and a behavioral assessment of anxiety. Systematic desensitization and the combined treatment reduced daily anxiety scores significantly more than cognitive restructuring. Interestingly, they found that subjects who reported that they spent large amounts of time worrying also reported the most anxiety.

Barlow et al. (1984) randomly assigned 11 patients with PD and 9 patients with GAD to a combined treatment frontal EMG biofeedback, relaxation, a cognitive treatment, or a waiting list control. The cognitive component consisted of Meichenbaum and Turk's (1973) stress inoculation training and cognitive restructuring of thoughts (Beck and Emery 1985). Treatment, as compared to the control condition, was associated with significantly greater anxiety reduction according to clinical ratings, psychophysiological measures, self-monitored daily anxiety, and questionaire measures of anxiety. Gains were maintained at a follow-up of at least 3 months.

In order to subject cognitive therapy for GAD or PD to an empirical test a treatment manual that illustrates the process of cognitive therapy using a session-by-session format would facilitate training therapists, evaluating their competence, assuring compliance with research protocols, and promoting the integrity of treatment. It is noteworthy, however, that Cerny et al. (1985), Jarrett (1986), and Andrews (1986) have drafted unpublished treatment manuals for use in research on PD. Michelson et al. (1987a,b) have drafted cognitive-behavioral treatment manuals for research on both disorders. Barlow and Cerny (1988) have published a treatment manual entitled *Psychological Treatment of Panic*, which should facilitate tests of the efficacy of psychological treatment.

What Does Cognitive Therapy of Panic Disorder Involve?

Hints from the Literature on Anxiety Disorders

In considering what components should be included in cognitive therapy for nonphobic disorders one is well advised to consult the psychological treatment literature on anxiety disorders to assess the general trends. As noted previously, in vivo exposure appears effective in the treatment of phobic disorders (Barlow and Wolfe 1981). Both cognitive restructuring and systematic desensitization also appear effective in the treatment of phobic disorders. In their review D.A. Shapiro and D. Shapiro (1982) concluded that cognitive restructuring was more effective than systematic desensitization, while Berman et al. (1985) suggested that this conclusion might have resulted from the fact that most studies reviewed were conducted by researchers who may have preferred cognitive strategies. They also noted that researchers preferring cognitive interventions tended to study test anxiety and animal phobias while those preferring desensitization tended to study agoraphobia. Thus, the conclusions may have been influenced not only by researcher bias for type of treatment but also by type of disorder treated. In contrast to D.A. Shapiro and D. Shapiro (1982) Berman and associates (1985) concluded that the effects of both cognitive restructuring and systematic desensitization were greater than no-treatment controls and were equal to each other. The effect of the combination did not exceed the effect of either treatment alone.

Additional complexities arise in this literature when one examines whether cognitive techniques have an effect equal to exposure or an additive effect to exposure in reducing fear and avoidance. For example, in vivo exposure was superior to cognitive restructuring in reducing fear and avoidance in agoraphobics and in social phobics (Biran et al. 1981).

The combination of cognitive restructuring plus in vivo exposure or in vivo exposure alone was superior to cognitive restructuring alone in reducing anxiety and avoidance in agoraphobics (Emmelkamp and Mersch 1982). In contrast, in reducing the driving fears of agoraphobics Williams and Rappoport (1983) found no advantage for the combination of cognitive restructuring plus in vivo exposure over in vivo exposure alone. In summary, it is uncertain that cognitive techniques add to the efficacy of in vivo exposure with phobic disorders.

On the other hand, the literature on phobic disorders as well as Beck's model of psychopathology provide some starting points for designing treatment on GAD and PD. If exposure is an essential ingredient in the treatment of phobics, exposure might also be essential for the treatment of GAD and PD if the "phobic stimuli" can be identified. Beck suggested that phobic stimuli in PD includes catastrophic interpretations of sensations. In GAD the phobic stimuli may include distorted interpretations of mastery and of social relationships. Thus, cognitive therapy for GAD and PD would require the identification of the feared stimuli and exposure of the patient to these stimuli without the experience of objective negative consequences. Because at the beginning of treatment the associated cognitions are the easiest stimuli to identify, such exposure first involves a response (cognitions), which serves a dual function as a stimulus. The cognitive model offers hypotheses regarding the *type* of stimuli that should be assessed in each disorder and offers techniques to promote exposure and compliance, with few, if any, side effects.

In 1986 our interest in the efficacy of cognitive therapy with PD increased when Beck, in collaboration with Sokol-Kessler and Greenberg, reported an uncontrolled, but promising pilot study of 28 patients suffering from PD (Beck 1986; Beck, personal communication). At baseline their mean number of panic attacks per week was 4.5 (range: 1–24). After 6 weeks of treatment subjects reported a mean of 1 panic attack per week (range: 0–2); after 12 weeks they reported a mean of 0.25 attacks per week (range: 0–1); and after 16 weeks of treatment (i.e., at termination) and at 3-month follow-up no patients reported panic attacks.

These data inspired a visit to the Center for Cognitive Therapy in Philadelphia (by R.B. Jarrett) to observe the clinical treatment of patients with PD. Much of the description of techniques used in cognitive therapy that follows is based on these observations, on conversations with Dr. Aaron T. Beck and his associates, and on our initial, but limited, use of the research treatment manual (Jarrett 1986).

Therapeutic Targets: General and Intermediate

In treating GAD and PD the general targets or goals are to (a) reduce the frequency, intensity, and duration of autonomic arousal and panic attacks (in PD), (b) reduce avoidance, and (c) facilitate the acquisition and use of skills that may have prophylactic value. In PD or GAD a liberal definition of avoidance is used in that patients may be avoiding covert responses (e.g., sensations, emotions, or cognitions) which can function as stimuli themselves. These general targets can be accomplished, presumably, by eliciting overt and/or covert stimuli and by exposing patients to them without their experiencing objective, negative consequences. These goals are accomplished by teaching the patient to identify the cognitions associated with his excessive arousal and/or avoidance and to test or analyze the validity of these cognitions. Because cognitive therapy is a process rather than a collection of techniques, intermediate therapeutic targets or goals will be identified, and *some* of the potential techniques for achieving the goals will be illustrated.

Socializing Patients to Treatment

Cognitive therapy for GAD and PD shares many of the features described in cognitive therapy for depression (Beck et al. 1979). Clark and Beck (in press) define the features of cognitive therapy as (a) being based on the cognitive model of emotional disorders, (b) being based on an educational model, (c) being brief and time-limited, (d) involving a collaborative endeavor between patient and therapist, (e) employing a Socratic rather than persuasive method, (f) including a solid therapeutic alliance as a necessary but not sufficient foundation for change, (g) being structured and problem-oriented, and (h) including homework in the natural environment. Socializing patients to cognitive therapy begins during the first session and consists of familiarizing patients with these defining features of cognitive therapy. Patients need to understand the structure of therapy (i.e., short-term and problem-oriented; including homework for building skills) and to experience the therapist as empathetic, competent, questioning, and interested. Furthermore, patients need to understand the cognitive model and how it applies to their problems.

Eliciting Automatic Thoughts and Sensations

To promote the cognitive model as the rationale for treatment and to encourage patients to apply the model to their problems it is useful to focus on the first or most troublesome panic attack (in PD) or the "worst" episode/period of anxiety in the past week (in GAD). The therapist elicits a detailed description of the sensations experienced and teaches the patient to record these in a diary used for self-monitoring. Our clinical experience suggests that cognitions can be more easily elicited from anxious patients by focusing on sensations rather than on emotions. In contrast to depressed patients, anxious patients seem to focus on their bodily sensations with limited use of the labels for such emotions. Situations in which sensations occur are identified, and any accompanying thoughts or images are recorded.

This part of therapy can be viewed as discrimination training. In particular, patients are taught to monitor, discriminate, and label sensations, situations, and cognitions. They learn to use their bodily sensations to cue answers to the questions: (a) What are these sensations? (b) What situations preceded or occurred with these sensations? and (c) What thoughts preceded or occurred with these sensations?

It is possible to identify the "private meaning" of these sensations by examining the array of thoughts associated with periods/episodes of anxiety that have (a) occurred in the past, (b) been recorded in the diary, and (c) been simulated or reproduced during therapy sessions. Beck and Greenberg (1988) called this process identifying "symptom equations." The following clinical excerpt [from a pilot case using Jarrett's (1986) treatment manual] illustrates the initial stages of identifying a panic patient's symptom equation "dizziness = going crazy or begin out of control."

It was out of the blue. Sort of, I think, it was out of the blue. Well, you know. My symptoms were completely different. I didn't have a pounding heart and my legs weren't shaking or anything. It was at a meeting for all of us. We had a new telephone system installed in the building, and we were all going up to the 16-floor conference room. It was kind of a rainy, hazy day out. The way the building is set up, it's like all glass on one side, and its got kind of a little patio that you can't go out on. I really couldn't see the ground. I had this horrible feeling that I was going to fall. It took everything I had to stay there for about half an hour and I keep having this . . . . I am embarrassed to tell you, but I really thought that I was going crazy, feeling like, I guess, there was a magnet that was just going to draw me to this window, and I was just going to come crashing through, or else something inside was going to make me get up and just run and jump out the window. I knew that I wouldn't do something like that, but in my mind, I kept saying, "Yes, you're going to do this. Yes, you're going to do this." You know, like in a horror film or something. I kept trying . . . . I couldn't get rid of the thoughts. I tried and I would distract myself for a little bit, and then they'd come back. It happened about four or five times, and I thought, "Well, I am going to have to get up and leave the scene." I don't even remember the words the instructor was saying.

Evaluating the Validity of Cognitions Associated with Sensations

Once these dysfunctional thoughts or private meanings are identified, patients can begin to develop methods to evaluate the validity of the automatic thoughts, and if needed, to restructure the thoughts. The general methods for accomplishing these goals involve teaching patients to use (a) experiments to test their validity, (b) logical analysis to examine the validity, and (c) experiments plus logical analysis. This cognitive restructuring is described in detail in Beck et al. (1979) and in Beck and Emery (1985). The process of cognitive restructuring is the same across disorders, but the content, focus, and most useful technique varies. The general process inherent in hypothesis testing is to teach the patient to view a thought as a hypothesis that can be tested. The patient then learns to (a) state the thought in a testable form (i.e., make a prediction), (b) arrange and implement a test of the prediction, (c) record the results, (d) compare the results to the prediction, and (e) query whether additional experiments are needed to test the validity of the thought.

In applying this process to PD Beck and Greenberg (1988) suggest that replication experiments are a useful technology for demonstrating that symptom equations are invalid and need revision. They describe methods of replicating symptoms in the sessions which include Clark's overbreathing technique, drinking caffeine, exposure to grid designs that produce the illusion of blurred movement, and running up stairs. The general process is to simulate the symptoms or to elicit the cognitions. If cognitions involve catastrophic interpretations, alternative explanations are offered. If the cognitions match the simulation (e.g., "My heart's racing because you just instructed me to run up the steps."), the sensations and interpretations are compared to those experienced during panic/anxiety. If the simulated sensations are similar to panic or anxiety, the patient and therapist try to determine why the cognitions differ in the face of experiencing similar symptoms. If the sensations are dissimilar, the experiment can be used to review the basic rationale for treatment (i.e., "You attributed your palpitations to running up the stairs rather than having a heart attack, so is it surprising that you feel calm? I wonder what keeps you from looking for alternative explanations for your palpitations when during your daily life you have the thought, 'My heart's beating fast, I could be about to have a heart attack'?").

Beck (1976) and Beck and Emery (1985) maintained that patients with anxiety disorders believe that they are extremely vulnerable to internal and external threats. In addition to feeling vulnerable they believe that their symptoms, once present, will escalate, and that they will be unable to cope. Once cognitions with the themes of "vulnerability," "escalation," and "copelessness" (Beck and Greenberg 1988) have been identified, patients are asked to implement experiments that test notions such as "I am very vulnerable; my anxiety will worsen, and there is nothing I can do." One method for testing such notions is to teach the patient anxiety-reduction skills that can be used during episodes of intense anxiety or panic. Such coping skills include relaxation, controlled breathing (Clark 1986), distraction, and logical analysis. Relaxation training has several variants (e.g., Jacobsonian, hypnotic induction, and guided imagery; see Goldfried and Davison 1976 for examples). Independent of the techniques used, the goals include teaching patients the relaxation skill in the session, having patients practice and acquire the skill outside the session, and encouraging patients to generalize the use of the skill to high-anxiety periods in an effort to test the validity of their predictions of vulnerability, escalation, and copelessness.

The same process is used with distraction. The goal, however, for distraction is to teach the patient to move the focus of attention away from sensations to an incompatible, alternative focus. Clinical experience suggests that distraction is most useful when it is planned in advance. That is, if the patient and therapist have identified situations or cognitions most frequently associated with anxiety, and alternative targets of attention have been planned and written on an easily accessible card, distraction can be used when needed. For example, a patient who often panicked when driving over bridges planned to focus on the view of the horizon outside her windshield rather than on her symptoms.

Logical analysis can be used in association with testing the validity of a cognition, or it can be used alone. When used in conjunction with an experiment it is viewed as a coping skill, and it is the independent variable in experiments that test predictions such as "I'm anxious/panicked, thus, I'm helpless." The basic process involved in logical analysis is to teach patients to examine their automatic thoughts and to pose and answer questions such as: "What evidence supports/refutes my thoughts?" "What part of this situation is fact and what part is belief?" "How would I look at this if I weren't anxious/panicked?" "How would someone else look at this situation?" "What would I say about this if it were happening to a friend or acquaintance?" In addition, patients are taught to discriminate and label "logical errors" (e.g., overgeneralization, personalization, jumping to conclusions, catastrophization, all-or-none thinking, emotional reasoning, etc.). Patients learn to use the presence of a logical error as a cue for implementing a logical skill used in restructuring thinking. For example, when catastrophizing the patient can calculate the probability that the worst will happen and then examine the evidence that the worst will/will not happen. When emotional reasoning occurs, the patient can separate objective facts from emotional beliefs.

Identifying Assumptions and Examining Their Validity

After the frequency, duration, and intensity of episodes of anxiety or panic have been reduced, it is possible to begin to identify associated dysfunctional assumptions. Patients are told that assumptions are general rules, ideas, or beliefs which they may have about themselves, the world, and the future, and which increase the probability that their symptoms may return. Assumptions are identified by examining all sources of data available (typically, diaries, in-session reports, and retrospective reports) and asking the question "What themes do these data have in common?" Clinical experience suggests that it is useful to identify themes that have recurred during the session and then to instruct patients to identify other themes from their diaries. Once the themes have been identified, it is possible to list *if-then* contingency statements that can be evaluated and restructured. For example, a PD patient identified the recurring theme of "being out of control." Her evidence for being out of control was her dizziness. She completed the statement: "If I'm dizzy, it means I'm out of control. If I'm out of control, it means I might be psychotic. If I'm psychotic then, I'll lose my daughter." Thus, she concluded that her assumption was "If I'm dizzy, then I'm psychotic, and I could lose my daughter." Once identified, this assumption could be evaluated using experimentation, logical analysis, or the combination thereof.

Exposure

The final stage of treatment involves exposing patients to the overt and covert stimuli associated with anxiety. In its final stage this involves exposing patients to the anxiety itself at its most intense level. To start, exposure is graduated and the pace is controlled by the patient. In general, exposure involves two stages: (a) exposure plus the use of coping strategies (e.g., relaxation, controlled breathing, distraction, cognitive restructuring) and (b) exposure with very limited use of coping strategies. The fact that anxiety-reduction skills have been taught prior to exposure may increase the probability that patients will comply with the instruction, even when the therapist cannot directly monitor compliance (in contrast to guided participation or therapist-assisted exposure). In addition, these coping skills may serve as a "psychological anesthetic" in that they may reduce the unpleasant emotional side effects that occur during in vivo exposure, flooding, or implosion. If side effects can be reduced, perhaps the drop-out rate associated with exposure can also be reduced.

Exposure to symptoms of anxiety/panic and their associated overt stimuli is implied in the use of experimentation throughout treatment. The final stage, however, consists of instructing patients to expose themselves to whatever situations have been avoided, to refrain from using any coping skills, and to observe the outcome. Such exposure tests the basic core assumption of vulnerability assumed to be inherent in anxiety, but it also functions to generalize acquired reductions in arousal and in avoidance to the natural environment.

Research Questions

Treatment Efficacy

The main purpose of this chapter has been to summarize data and logic that support the claim that cognitive therapy for the nonphobic anxiety disorders, GAD and PD, deserves a controlled test. Presently, the most important research question is: Will an integrated cognitive therapy (not isolated cognitive techniques) reduce arousal, avoidance, and panic more than a nonspecific (placebo) control group? In addition, it would be useful to compare the efficacy of cognitive therapy to pharmacotherapy (e.g., benzodiazepines or MAO inhibitors). It is important to note that arousal, panic, and avoidance must all be assessed. Ideally, tripartite assessment (i.e., cognitive, physiological, and overt responding) would be used. The use of such multiple dependent measures will allow discovery as to whether psychotherapy and phamacotherapy influence the same or different targets. Within the physiological realm it would be interesting to examine the relationship between biological variables and psychological treatment. For example, it would be interesting to use a Solomon-four group design (Campbell and Stanley 1963) to evaluate the extent to which vulnerable individuals panic under lactate infusion before and after exposure to cognitive therapy.

Mechanisms of Change

The preceding description of cognitive therapy for GAD and PD has identified intermediate therapeutic targets (e.g., discrimination training via daily self-monitoring; evaluation of the validity of cognitions through logical analysis, hypothesis testing, or their combination; increasing compliance with exposure by first teaching coping skills; and then reducing the sense of vulnerability through the learning of coping skills and exposure). The implicit hypothesis is that these targets must be achieved (not necessarily through the identified techniques) before the long-range therapeutic goals of reducing arousal, panic, and avoidance can be met. Although these intermediate targets were conceptually derived, they may be helpful in (a) evaluating the integrity of the cognitive therapy provided in research protocols, (b) identifying the active ingredients in therapy, (c) determining an appropriate pace for therapy (e.g., discrimination of automatic thoughts and emotions must be acquired before cognitive restructuring skills can be taught), and (d) training cognitive therapists and evaluating their competence. One of the first steps in empirically demonstrating the usefulness of this approach would be to develop dependent measures of these or other intermediate targets.

The Multiple Functions Served by the Cognitive Model

Research on cognitive therapy for nonphobic disorders (and other disorders) will progress further and faster if investigators separate the multiple functions which have been served by the cognitive model in the literature to date. The cognitive model has functioned to (a) describe psychopathology, (b) provide a rationale for treatment, and (c) provide an organization and framework for the therapist's case conceptualization and intervention. In addition, the cognitive model has been used to describe (a) the development and maintenance of disorders, (b) the mechanisms of change when treatment is effective, and (c) the mechanisms capable of reducing the probability of recurrence or relapse.

These functions of the cognitive model used in the literature on cognitive therapy must be viewed as independent until there are data to demonstrate an existing overlap. In addition, the functions served by the cognitive model and the efficacy of cognitive therapy with any disorder (e.g., nonphobic anxiety or depression) are also separate questions. For example, it is possible for the therapy to be effective, for the model to describe some features of psychopathology, and for the mechanisms of change all to function independently of each other and of the treatment rationale.

When applying the cognitive model and cognitive therapy to nonphobic disorders, researchers have a new opportunity to (a) evaluate separately the functions served by the cognitive model, (b) reduce the confusion in the terms cognitive, behavioral, and cognitive-behavioral by referring in the "methods" sections of manuscripts to explicit, available treatment manuals, and (c) work with a group of individuals whose prognosis looks promising when adequate treatment is offered.

Acknowledgements. The authors wish to express their appreciation to Aaron Beck, M.D., David Barlow, Ph.D., and David Clark, D. Phil. for sharing preprints of their work. Thanks are also expressed to Rodger Kobes, M.D., Ph.D. for his clinical involvement and careful reading of an earlier draft of this chapter, to Mr. David Savage for secretarial assistance and to Kenneth Z. Altshuler, M.D., Stanton Sharp Professor and Chairman for his administrative support.

References

American Psychiatric Association (1968) Diagnostic and statistical manual of mental disorders, 2nd edn. Washington, DC

American Psychiatric Association (1980) Diagnostic and statistical manual of mental disorders, 3rd edn. Washington, DC

American Psychiatric Association (1987) Diagnostic and statistical manual of mental disorders, revised 3rd edn. Washington, DC

Andrews G (1986) The panic disorder treatment program. Treatment manual. Unpublished manuscript, St. Vincent's Hospital, Darlinghurst, Australia

Barlow DH (1986) Behavioral conception and treatment of panic. Psychopharmacol Bull 22:802–806

Barlow DH (1988) Panic and the future of anxiety disorders. In: Last CG, Hersen M (eds) Handbook of anxiety disorders. Pergamon, New York

Barlow CH, Cerny JA (1988) Psychological treatment of panic. Guilford, New York

Barlow DH, Craske MG (1988) The phenomenology of panic. In: Rachman S, Maser JD (eds) Panic: psychological perspectives. Erlbaum, Hillsdale

Barlow DH, Wolfe BE (1981) Behavioral approaches to anxiety disorders. A report on the NIMH-SUNY, Albany, research conference. J Consult Clin Psychol 49:448–454

Barlow DH, Cohen AS, Waddell MT, Vermilyea BB, Klosko JS, Blanchard EB, Di Nardo PA (1984) Panic and generalized anxiety disorders: nature and treatment. Behav Ther 15:431–449

Beck AT (1967) Depression: clinical, experimental and theoretical aspects. Harper and Row, New York

Beck AT (1976) Cognitive therapy and the emotional disorders. International Universities Press, New York

Beck AT (1986) Cognitive approaches to panic disorder: theory and therapy. Presented at the NIMH conference on cognitive aspects of panic disorder, 2–3 June 1986. Bethesda

Beck AT (1988) Cognitive approaches to panic disorder: theory and therapy. In: Rachman S, Maser JD (eds) Panic: psychological perspectives. Erlbaum, Hillsdale

Beck AT, Emery G (1985) Anxiety disorders and phobias. A cognitive perspective. Basic Books, New York

Beck AT, Greenberg RL (1988) Cognitive therapy of panic disorders. In: Frances AJ, Hales RE (eds) American psychiatric press review of psychiatry, vol 7. American Psychiatric, Washington, DC, pp 569–581

Beck AT, Mahoney MJ (1979) School of thought. Am Psychol 34:93–98

Beck AT, Rush AJ (1975) A cognitive model of anxiety formation and anxiety resolution. In: Sarsason ID, Spielberger CC (eds) Stress and anxiety. Hemisphere, Washington, DC, pp 69–80

Beck AT, Laude R, Bohnert M (1974) Ideational components of anxiety neurosis. Arch Gen Psychiatry 31:319–325
Beck AT, Rush AJ, Shaw BF, Emery G (1979) Cognitive therapy of depression. Guilford, New York
Berman JS, Miller RC, Massman PJ (1985) Cognitive therapy versus systematic desensitization: is one treatment superior? Psychol Bull 97:451–461
Biran M, Augusto F, Wilson GT (1981) *In vivo* exposure vs. cognitive restructuring in the treatment of scriptophobia. Behav Res Ther 19:525–532
Breggin PR (1964) The psychophysiology of anxiety with a review of the literature concerning adrenaline. J Nerv Ment Dis 139:558–568
Butler G, Mathews A (1983) Cognitive processes in anxiety. Adv Behav Res Ther 5:51–62
Campbell DT, Stanley JC (1963) Experimental and quasi-experimental designs for research. Rand McNally, Chicago
Cerny JA, Klosko J, Barlow DH (1985) Anxiety treatment project: combined relaxation and cognitive therapy treatment manual. Unpublished manuscript, the phobia and anxiety disorders clinic, State University of New York, Albany, New York
Charney DS, Beninger GR, Breier A (1984) Noradrenergic function in panic anxiety: effects of yohimbine in healthy subjects and patients with agoraphobia and panic disorder. Arch Gen Psychiatry 41:751–763
Charney DS, Beninger GR, Jatlow PI (1985) Increased anxiogenic effects of caffeine in panic disorders. Arch Gen Psychiatry 42:233–243
Clark DM (1986) A cognitive approach to panic. Behav Res Ther 24:461–470
Clark DM, Beck AT (1988) Cognitive approaches. In: Last C, Hersen M (eds) Handbook of anxiety disorders. Pergamon, New York
Clark DM, Hemsley DR (1982) The effects of hyperventilation: individual variability and its relation to personality. J Behav Ther Exp Psychiatry 13:41–47
Clark DM, Salkovskis PM, Chalkley AJ (1985) Respiratory control as a treatment for panic attacks. J Behav Ther Exp Psychiatry 16:23–30
Coyne JC, Gotlib IH (1983) The role of cognition in depression: a critical appraisal. Psychol Bull 94:472–505
Coyne JC, Gotlib IH (1986) Studying the role of cognition in depression: Well-trodden paths and *cul-de-sacs.* Cog Ther Res 10:695–705
Crowe R, Noyes R (1986) Panic disorder and agoraphobia. DM 32:392–444
DiNardo PA, O'Brian GT, Barlow DH, Waddell MT, Blanchard EB (1983). Reliability of DSM-III anxiety disorder categories using a new structured interview. Arch Gen Psychiatry 40:1070–1078
Emmelkamp PMG, Mersch PP (1982) Cognition and exposure *in vivo* in the treatment of agoraphobia: short term and delayed effects. Cog Ther Res 6:77–88
Emmelkamp PMG, Kuipers ACM, Eggeraat JB (1978) Cognitive modification versus prolonged exposure *in vivo*. A comparison with agoraphobics as subjects. Behav Res Ther 16:33–41
Goldfried MR, Davidson GC (1976) Clinical behavior therapy. Holt, Rinehart and Winston, New York
Gorman JM, Liebowitz MR (1986) Panic and anxiety disorders. In: Cavenar JO (ed) Psychiatry, vol 1. Basic Books New York, pp 1–13
Gotlib IH (1983) Perception and recall of interpersonal feedback: negative bias in depression. Cog Ther Res 5:399–412
Griez E, van den Hout MA (1986) CO_2 inhalation in the treatment of panic attacks. Behav Res Ther 24:145–150
Hibbert GA (1984) Ideational components of anxiety: their origin and content. Br J Psychiatry 144:618–624
Jarrett RB (1986) Cognitive-behavior therapy for panic disorder. Treatment manual. Unpublished manuscript, University of Texas Southwestern Medical Center, Dallas, Texas
Judd FK, Burrows GD (1986) Panic and phobic disorders. Aust Fam Physician 15:150–154
Katerndahl DA (1984) Panic attacks. Psychologic response or medical illness? Postgrad Med 75:261–268
Klein DF (1981) Anxiety reconceptualized. In: Klein DF, Rabkin J (eds) Anxiety: new research and changing concepts. Raven, New York
Klerman GL (1986) Current trends in clinical research on panic attacks, agoraphobia, and related anxiety disorders. J Clin Psychiatry 47 (Suppl 6):37–39

Last CG (1984) Cognitive treatment of phobia. Prog Behav Modif 16:65–82
Lum LC (1976) The syndrome of habitual chronic hyperventilation. In: Hill OW (ed) Modern trends in psychosomatic medicine, vol 3. Butterworths, London
Lunghi ME (1977) The stability of mood and social perception measure in a sample of depressed inpatients. Br J Psychiatry 130:598–604
Mannuzza S, Fyer AJ, Klein DF (1985) Schedule for affective disorders and schizophrenia – lifetime version (SADS-LA). New York State Psychiatric Institute, New York
McNair DM, Lorr M, Droppleman LF (1971) Manual for the profile of mood states (POMS). Educational and Industrial Testing Service, San Diego
Meichenbaum DH, Turk D (1973) Stress inoculation: a skills training approach to anxiety management. Unpublished manuscript, University of Waterloo, Ontario, Canada
Merikangas KR, Weissman MM (1986) Epidemiology of anxiety disorders in adulthood. In: Cavenar JO (ed) Psychiatry, vol 3. Basic Books, New York, pp 1–12
Michelson L, Marchione K, Greenwald M, Glanz L (1987a) Panic disorder treatment manual. Unpublished manuscript, University of Pittsburgh, Western Psychiatric Institute and Clinic, Pittsburgh, Pennsylvania
Michelson L, Marchione K, Greenwald M, Glanz L (1987b) Generalized anxiety disorder treatment manual. Unpublished manuscript, University of Pittsburgh, Western Psychiatric Institute and Clinic, Pittsburgh, Pennsylvania
Norman WH, Miller IW III, Klee SH (1983) Assessment of cognitive distortion in a clinically depressed population. Cog Ther Res 7:133–140
Norton GR, Harrison B, Hauch J, Rhodes L (1985) Characteristics of people with infrequent panic attacks. J Abnorm Psychol 94:216–221
Norton GR, Dorward J, Cox BJ (1986) Factors associated with panic attacks in nonclinical subjects. Behav Ther 17:239–252
Noyes R, Crow RR, Harris EL, Hamra BJ, McChesney CM, Chaudhry DR (1986) Relationship between panic disorder and agoraphobia. A family study. Arch Gen Psychiatry 43:227–232
Pitts FN, McClure JN (1967) Lactate metabolism in anxiety neurosis. N Engl J Med 277:1329–1336
Rainey JM, Pohl RB, Williams M, Knitter E, Freedman RR, Ettedgui E (1984) A comparison of lactate and isoproterenol anxiety states. Psychopathology 17 (Suppl 1):74–82
Rapee RM (1985) Distinctions between panic disorder and generalized anxiety disorder: clinical presentation. Aust NZ J Psychiatry 19:227–232
Salkovskis PM, Jones DO, Clark DM (1986) Respiratory control in the treatment of panic attacks: replication and extension with concurrent measurement of behavior and pCO_2. Br J Psychiatry 148:526–532
Segal ZV, Shaw BF (1986a) Cognition in depression: a reappraisal of Coyne and Gotlib's critique. Cog Ther Res 10:671–694
Segal ZV, Shaw BF (1986b) When *cul-de sacs* are more mentality than reality: a rejoinder to Coyne and Gotlib. Cog Ther Res 10:707–714
Shapiro DA, Shapiro D (1982) Meta-analysis of comparative therapy outcome studies. A replication and refinement. Psychol Bull 92:581–604
Sheehan DV (1982) Current concepts in psychiatry: panic attacks and phobias. N Engl J Med 307:156–158
Speilberger CD, Gorsuch RL, Lushene RE (1970) Manual for the state-trait anxiety inventory (STAI). Consulting Psychologists, Palo Alto
Spitzer RL, Williams JBW (1983) Structured clinical interview for DSM-III – Upjohn version (SCID-UP). New York State Psychiatric Institute, New York
Taylor CB, Kenigsberg ML, Robinson JM (1982) A controlled comparison of relaxation and diazepam in panic disorder. J Clin Psychiatry 43:423–425
Thorpe G, Barnes G, Hunter J, Hines D (1983) Thoughts and feelings: correlations in two clinical and two nonclinical samples. Cog Ther Res 7:565–574
Tyrer P (1984) Classification of anxiety. Br J Psychiatry 144:78–83
van den Hout MA, Griez E (1982) Cognitive factors in carbon dioxide therapy. J Psychosom Res 26:209–214
van den Hout MA, Griez E (1984) Panic symptoms after inhalation of carbon dioxide. Br J Psychiatry 144:503–507

Waddell MT, Barlow DH, O'Brian GT (1984) A preliminary investigation of cognitive and relaxation treatment of panic disorder: effects on intense anxiety vs "background" anxiety. Behav Res Ther 22:393–402

Weissman MM, Myers JK, Harding PS (1978) Psychiatric disorders in a US urban community. Am J Psychiatry 135:459–462

Williams SL, Rappoport A (1983) Cognitive treatment in the natural environment for agoraphobics. Behav Ther 4:299–313

Wolpe J (1978) Cognition and causation in human behavior and its therapy. Am Psychol 33:437–446

Wolpe J, Lang PJ (1964) A fear survey schedule for use in behaviour therapy. Behav Res Ther 2:27–30

Woodward R, Jones RB (1980) Cognitive restructuring treatment: a controlled trial with anxious patients. Behav Res Ther 18:401-407

Zung WWK (1971) A self-rating scale for anxiety. Psychosomatics 12:371–384

Self-Talk, Dramatic Expression, and Constructivism

L. JOYCE-MONIZ

Regulating Self-Talk in Cognitive Psychotherapy

Does self-talk have overall regulating functions? If so, do cognitive therapists, explicitly or implicitly, believe that meaningful self-talk, internal dialogue, inner speech or self-statements can be used systematically for achieving self-control? How should self-instructions be structured in therapy in order to facilitate the client's acquisition of better coping skills, rational beliefs, problem-solving strategies, functional rules for reasoning or (inner) dialectical operations?

Cognitive therapists have, of course, an old, unresolved yet constructive affair with the presumed power of self-talk. But there have been even older affairs of this sort. Since the beginning of time philosophers, religious men, poets and politicians have questioned this power and have attempted to utilise it in their personal development. It is also relevant to recall that the objective use of self-referent speech has an important tradition in psychology (e.g. James 1890; Wundt 1886). Watson (1924), for example, made wide use of subjects' words as conveyors of meaning, while postulating that thinking and its verbal expression were only the result of measurable muscular contractions and glandular secretions. In the 1950s and 1960s cognitive developmental psychology was plunged into uneasy controversies over the relationship between thought and regulating self-talk (Luria 1961; Piaget and Inhelder 1955, 1963; Vygotsky 1962). Curiously enough, psychotherapy has traditionally considered that dialogue with the self reveals that which cannot be verbally controlled. The most radical expression of this distrust may be found in the replacement of literal self-talk by "body talk" as a primal dialectical route to self-discovery (Birdwhistell 1970; Fast 1971; Monroe 1971). Only the so-called "school of positive thinking" (Baudoin 1920; Coué 1922; Peale 1960) and, much later, cognitive-behavioural techniques of cognitive modelling and self-instructional training (Kazdin 1973a,b; Mahoney and Mahoney 1976; Meichenbaum 1977; Novaco 1975) have freed the practice of meaningful self-talk from epistemological and methodological suspicions and exorcisms.

In spite of this rebirth of interest cognitive psychotherapists continue to show mixed feelings about the use of self-talk and, in particular, its indiscriminate misuse. Mahoney (1980, p. 169) has observed that: "Words are crude and inadequate labels for some of the neural processes we refer to as 'thoughts'. They are the imperfect reflection of processes that they, in turn, influence, and we can never hope to observe that process in the richness of its complexity." In effect, the

---

University of Lisbon, Faculdade de Psicologia, Rua Pinheiro Chagas 17, 1000 Lisbon, Portugal

simultaneously *structuring* and *structured* features of self-talk may lead cognitivists to a common dilemma: should self-talk be emphasised in cognitive change because of its self-regulating functions or because of its camouflage function for something more meaningful?

It appears that dynamic theories still have an important influence on cognitive therapists. Private dialogue is said to reflect the emergence of irrational beliefs (Ellis 1973), cognitive distortions (Beck et al. 1979), deep structures (Arnkoff 1980), tacit meaning systems (Mahoney 1985), metaphysical hard-core and representational models (Guidano and Liotti 1983), and structural self-schemata (Turk and Speers 1983). From the dynamic viewpoint, evaluative thoughts are merely response mechanisms which, for instance, may block or divert a "natural" energetic discharge (Freud 1959), avoid an increase in anxiety (A. Freud 1946) or reduce fear (Rapaport 1951). Moreover, the very fact that both cognitivists and psychodynamic analysts rely heavily on procedures directly involving self-talk could reinforce the view of a theoretical convergence.

Nevertheless, there is a crucial difference between these approaches. Only cognitivists attempt explicitly to deal with the metacognition of self-talk, that is, they believe that their clients may utilise the structuring and structured features of self-talk for enhancing the acquisition of more adaptive knowledge or meanings about the self and the world, while considering it a necessary but not sufficient means to knowledge development. Guidano and Liotti (1983, p. 149) note in this regard that:

> Many cognitive therapy techniques involve giving instructions to patients to make them cognitively rehearse fear-sadness, or anger-causing situations.... Whenever patients actively substitute, according to such instructions, appropriate monologues or adaptive self-statements to the previous negative ones, not only are the superficial cognitions somehow changed, but the deeper rules governing them are usually brought a little more into the open.

Cognitive therapists have thus been promoting various ingenious procedures for helping clients substitute mere imitative, action-anticipatory, action-descriptive or emotional expressive self-talk with "self-reflective self-talk". This search for the metacognitive basis of our words probably also ensures the substitution of the camouflage function by the self-regulating function.

Cognitive modelling and *direct instruction of self-statements* (e.g. self-instruction training, assertiveness training, coaching, stress-inoculation) offer explicit examples not only of "how to think" but also of "what to say" in our inner speech. Often a model expresses in an audible voice a complete repertoire of rational self-referent thoughts for preventing the occurrence of or for coping with stressful, dysphoric, compulsive or other symptomatic episodes and for enhancing concrete action, sensory-motor capability, coping style, rational attitude and expectations of self-efficacy. The model represents an epistemological authority which requires a more or less strict adherence to one's principles and directions. There is little room for the client's metacognitive exploration when the self-instructions concern the correction of an emerged conflict (feedback) but much room when they promote creative processes (feedforward). Usually the therapist does not entirely assume his/her authority but rather relegates it to an abstract "majority" whose status and influence may seem much more impressive. Thus, the therapist may lead the client not only to suspect that confrontation or enhancement can succeed but also to realise a *social need* for it. Modelled self-instructions represent an almost always stable and predictable reality.

Reality-testing procedures also rely on direct contact with an objective reality. Clinicians programme concrete activities, organise experiences for successful (or unsuccessful) coping, model an instrumental approach to the situation of conflict or focus on the rationalisation of social stereotypes. They undoubtedly believe that clients may profit from such a *thoughtful* relationship with concrete reality, with or without self-talk. That is to say that self-instructional strategies, while not required, are probably welcome since they reflect the person's attempts at confirming and disconfirming performance expectations. Regulating features of self-talk are rarely made explicit. Eventually the required tasks do not demand meta-cognitive analysis. However, proponents of reality-testing believe that only thereby can the client achieve a conceptual and paradigmatic, existential shift. Self-talk is a by-product of intense, dialectical interaction with the environment.

Rational-emotive therapy (R.ET.; Ellis 1973) and Beck's cognitive therapy (Beck et al. 1979) are much more centered on irrational or dysfunctional self-talk than on adaptive self-instructions. Nevertheless, when clients finally localise irrational self-statements and invalid automatic thoughts, they are encouraged to fill a *normative gap* with a precise repertoire of new meanings. In other words, an ideal inner speech is promoted in every instance of rationalisation. A common strategy is to have the client consider problematic actions, ideas, feelings and values which have been successfully confronted in the past, or which are successfully solved by more rational people, since adaptive self-talk should emerge also from a predictable authority. In these models the emphasis on conflict with modes of normal reasoning helps the client adopt a regulating and metacognitive self-talk. Not surprisingly, this often reflects the therapist's own implicit views about "appropriate" contents of thought.

Scenarios such as these serve to illustrate the predominance of an epistemological conviction in cognitive psychotherapy. This conviction is that there exists "out there" a stable physical and social universe where a skilful individual may obtain solid and reliable knowledge which is then translated into rational self-talk. However, we still do not know much about such a putatively stable universe, and each time we place an active and creative individual in it, the universe begins to look less coherent and predictable. As the person actively and creatively talks to himself or herself, the universe "grows" since its meanings are questioned, destroyed, reconstructed, renewed and amplified. Self-talk integrates thought and represents its regulating and construing structures and processes.

In this chapter two main constructive convictions will guide speculations about the role of regulating self-talk in cognitive psychotherapy:

1. The first assertion states that self-talk may be seen as an expression of individual dialectical regulations, or compensations (Piaget 1975), for restructuring or rebalancing a perceived disturbance or disequilibrium. This has structured a series of studies conducted in Lisbon concerning endorsed or attributed self-instructions.
2. The second assertion translates a therapeutic objective: *training in dramatic expression* is an appropriate procedure for maximising the constructive functions of coping and exploring self-talk in individual therapy.

The second part of this chapter includes some guidelines for implementing this training (setting, accessories, improvisation, warming up, acting out and acting as if). Such progressive dramatisation enables the construction of elaborated meaning systems (in terms of increasing flexibility, reversibility and integration).

Self-Instruction and Compensatory Regulations

The following examples are from the Meichenbaum's (1977) masterful work on regulatory self-talk.

Cognitive modelling of covert assertion for obesity control (Mahoney and Mahoney 1976)

– Negative monologue about the difficulty of losing weight is followed by coping self-statements:

1. Pounds don't count.
2. Have patience – those pounds took a long time to get there. As long as they stay off permanently, I'll settle for any progress.

– Idem involving the lack of capabilities and coping:

3. There's no such thing as "will power" – just poor planning.
4. It's going to be nice to be permanently rid of all this extra baggage.

– Idem involving excuses for absence of control and coping:

5. Eating doesn't satisfy psychological problems – it creates them.
6. What I need to do is be a bit more creative in how to improve my eating.

– Idem concerning food compulsions and coping:

7. Fantastic – I had a small piece of cake and it didn't blow the day.
8. Whenever I find myself thinking about food, I quickly change the topic to some other pleasant experience.

Cognitive coping in stress-inoculation training (Meichenbaum 1974)

– Preparing for a stressor:

9. What is it you have to do?
10. No negative self-statements; just think rationally.

– Confronting and handling a stressor:

11. Just "psych" yourself up – you can meet this challenge.
12. This tenseness can be an ally – a cue to cope.

– Coping with the feeling of being overwhelmed:

13. When fear comes, just pause.
14. Don't try to eliminate fear totally; just keep it manageable.

– Reinforcing self-statements:

15. It worked; you did it!
16. It wasn't as bad as you expected.

Self-statements used in creativity training (Meichenbaum 1975)

– Set-inducing self-statements (attitudinal conceptualisation of creativity):

17. Think of something no one else will think of.
18. Get rid of internal blocks. Defer judgements.

— Problem analysis and task execution (mental abilities conceptualisation):

19. You have to put the elements together differently.
20. You're in a rut — okay, try something new.
21. Take a rest now; who knows when the ideas will visit again.
22. Good, you're getting it.

— Set-inducing self-statements (psychoanalytic conceptualisation):

23. Release controls; let your mind wander.
24. Refer to your experience; just view it differently.

These self-instructions are very direct. The imperative style predominates over the reflective, and the person invites himself to act immediately in accordance with logical certitudes. For easing this self-compliance self-statements are grouped here according to models of compelling inner dialectic: (a) directions about how to correct concretely perceived (emerged) problematic or disturbing meanings, systematised into four classes of symptoms;[1] (b) directions about how to anticipate concretely the emerging conflict and directions about how to correct it after its emergence, systematised in a sequence with four coping steps; and (c) directions about how to enhance generically the "conflict" (creative acts), systematised in three modes of warming up. This emphasis on concreteness (versus abstractness) and correction (versus anticipation) seems to be relevant for defining how new knowledge/meanings may spring from such an *inner* and an *outer* dialectic (Riegel 1975, 1976). As mentioned above, proponents of reality-testing favour the primacy of concreteness and retroactive processing of information: "Individuals' expectations about personal efficacy are believed to stem from information they receive about their ability to respond in certain situations ... According to Bandura, *performance accomplishments* (such as those resulting from in vivo desensitisation, direct exposure, participant modelling, etc.) are the most dependable and, therefore, the most heavily weighted sources of efficacy information" (Goldfried and Robins 1983, p. 37). On the other hand, theorists of the "motor theory of the mind" (e.g. Arnkoff 1980; Hayek 1952; Mahoney 1980, 1985; Weimer 1980, 1982) defend the primacy of abstractness and of anticipating information constructively.

As Leibniz indicated in the *Monadology*, all of what we call knowledge is a priori — it consists in our gradual realisation of information which is already present in the unconscious processes constituting our tacit mind. If therapy is ever to be effective, it must constitute procedures capable of tapping the abstract rules which literally are the client's mind, and redirecting their activity so that a better attunement between the client and his environment results (Weimer 1980, p. 383).

Nevertheless, the therapist may choose a compromise between these priorities. From a constructivist and psychogenetic viewpoint (Ivey 1986; Joyce-Moniz 1985; Piaget 1975), concreteness (versus abstractness) and feedback (versus feedforward) are essentially relative notions. For instance, sensory-motor structures are forms in relation to the simple repetitive reflexes and contents regarding the interiorised actions of the following representational level; concrete operations are forms in relation to the latter actions and contents relatively to formal operations. In addition, pre-operational structures tend to coordinate the whole and its parts and the successive and the simultaneous, but its regulations and compensations are only approximate, non-reversible and unfolding in time. Only operatory regula-

[1] Five classes of self-statements in the original work (Mahoney and Mahoney 1976).

tions, at concrete and abstract levels, allow for a balanced coordination between anticipations and retro-actions for preventing the emergence of the conflict instead of merely correcting it after it has emerged (Piaget 1968, 1970).

From the view of this developmental constructivism, the resolution of perceived conflicts depends upon the opening to, or the possibility of, more and new abstract conflicts. This suggests an active, dialectical, creative process involving balance/equilibrium and imbalance/disequilibrium for acquiring new knowledge/meanings. Piaget (1975) calls this "majoring equilibration". It does not represent a transition to a phenomenological state of harmony and final coherence but an epistemological evolution through the dialectics of concreteness versus abstractness, feedback versus feedforward, continuity versus discontinuity, destructuring versus restructuring, etc.

The metaphor of increasing equilibration permits an approximation between therapeutic process and "natural" development. The latter "should" guide the former (Ivey 1986; Joyce-Moniz 1985). Thus, cognitive-dialectical development of meanings about the self and the world becomes a model for clinical change of beliefs, values, norms, rules and so forth. Sequences of natural acquisition of progressively more adaptive meanings are substitutes for treatment sequences derived from positivist rationalisations. Dialectics in therapy is structured according to dialectics in cognitive development. Therefore, instead of falling into the dilemma of a choice between procedures favouring comprehension/insight and those favouring performance/coping the therapist recognises that both orientations can be ontogenetically integrated into active inner dialectics.

For Jung and Piaget, man grows through conflict and thereby creates new conflicts; both authors have characterised the *compensatory* dialectics of human development. Accordingly, most of us think that our clients deserve the same kind of development. We may be striving for self-talk procedures which help clients acquire and systematise regulating and meta-cognitive strategies for listening and speaking to themselves. Even though dialectic operations involving compensatory regulations may occur without self-talk, the latter is an adequate representation of the former. But since not all self-talk is involved in restructuring conflicts, it is important to specify which kind of inner dialogue is generally promoted in therapy.

Self instructions are the most direct and explicit compensations (i.e. compensatory regulations). These promote the movement of restructuring or re-equilibrium by suggesting what to say to ourselves when we perceive or understand the conflict. Self-instructions *anticipate* what to say before and not after the conflictual occurrence. The person must be ready to self-verbalise concrete and abstract directives for coping or enhancing purposes. For example, self-instructions for creating a problem-solving orientation (Gagné 1964; McKinney 1973), "appraisals" and "plans" (Janis 1965), a "cognitive ecology" (Mahoney and Mahoney 1976), stress (Meichenbaum 1974) and a meta-creative orientation (Meichenbaum 1975) are precisely what Kelly (1955) calls "replications" of events, that is to say, conceptual anticipations which are triggered for replicating the event.

The anticipatory nature of self-instructions has suggested (Joyce-Moniz, 1981, 1985) a Piagetian reading of their compensatory features.

Compensation by inversion anticipates annulment of the conflict and involves the complete negation of the disturbing meanings. For instance, the person perceives a compelling impulse, an anxiety-provoking image, dysphoric feelings or thoughts of doubt, and he self-verbalises: "I get upset with myself if I don't confront it", "This is absurd", or "Thinking about this is needless and makes me feel worse". Self-statements 1, 3, 4, 5, 10 and 18 (above) are also examples of dialectic by opposition. This form, however, can probably not be considered a simple negation of the negation. It is, rather, a compensatory regulation at a different conceptual level since it inverts the personal and social implications of the attributed meaning, thus allowing the transformation of the disturbing negativism. The negation of negativism is clearly not an affirmation (negation of the negation).

Compensation by reciprocity anticipates integration of the conflict into a system and presumably involves an equilibrium between incomplete negation and incomplete affirmation, leading to a better assimilation of the disturbing meanings: "Once this impulse vanishes, I am going to feel better", "When I think people are annoying me, I try to think of those moments when they have interested me", or "I have already carried out other projects as difficult as this". Self-statements 2, 8, 12, 13, 19 and 24 are also examples of this balanced compromising.

Re-equilibration may be achieved through a decentering process. When compensation establishes a spatial reciprocity, the person makes an explicit relation between meanings that are positively valued and disturbing meanings: "If I find it difficult to enact a given alternative, I try another, just as appealing as the first". The compensation can equally involve a distinct class (system) of meanings: "If I can't get what I want and become upset, I try to think about the pleasant things that I have been able to get". In this case, intra-systemic restructuring is postponed, but inter-systemic reciprocity occurs "emotionally". This may be considered a kind of "lesser evil" strategy. When compensation establishes a temporal reciprocity, the person balances positively valued meanings of the past or the future with disturbing meanings, while keeping this relation inside the system: "If I have trouble putting an alternative into practice, I wait until I'm able to do it for as long as necessary".

Partial reciprocity anticipates the integration of conflict into the system, but without a presumable equilibrium between an incomplete negation and an incomplete affirmation. These are more pronounced forms of lesser evil, compared to the one mentioned above: "It's preferable to have this feeling than another even worse", "I know that my pride always gets me into trouble, but I can try not to take this aggravation too seriously" (Novaco 1975), "When I have problems implementing the choice made previously, I choose a second alternative even though it is not as adequate as the first". Self-statements 7, 14, 16 and 21 constitute other examples of lesser evil reciprocity. In addition, this is a process of *inner* and *outer* confrontation largely used in R.E.T. for disputing irrational beliefs:

Question: "Why is it 'awful' to date men who mainly look upon me as a piece of ass, and who are not really interested in me as a person?"
Anwser: "It isn't! It's highly inconvenient and sometimes obnoxious. But it is not totally bad – and therefore not 'awful' " (Ellis 1981, p. 159).
Therapist: "Let's suppose your wife dies, and that you never do find another woman to live with. Why should you then have to be utterly miserable? Even if you *never* found a suitable woman to love again, couldn't you do other enjoyable things – tennis, for example, or listening to music or being absorbed in your work?" (Ellis 1981, p. 163).

This compensation may include a temporal compromising: "I prefer to worry about my score in the exam now than to worry about it after I get the exam back".

Compromising may also be spatial: "It's preferable to be sad about the exam score – and happy about other things". Combinations involving both conditions of frequency and extension are also possible.

Compensation by identity anticipates annulment of the conflict and involves the complete affirmation of an imperative with personal or social-moral connotations: "I'm unable to see things that way, since I am essentially optimistic", or "I want to feel good about it". This is, of course, the kind of compensation that the school of positive thinking favoured: "Tous les jours, a tous les points de vue, je vais de mieux en mieux."[2] There is no transformation of the disturbing meanings, which is to say that this form may be considered as reflecting the traditional negation of a negation: "A person like myself never considers suicide". This is different from compensation by inversion: "A person like myself thinks that suicide is ridiculous". Nevertheless, self-reinforcing statements such as "It's getting better each time you use the procedures" (Meichenbaum 1974) and numbers 15 and 22 (above) represent both regulating forms. The person is sensitive to the specific coping evaluation while making a general attribution of efficacy.

Most self-talk involved in cognitive modelling, self-instructional training, reality-training procedures and, eventually, in disputing beliefs, *represents coping by response systematisation.* There is, of course, another coping style which involves inter-systemic compensations leading to conflict resolution via conflict creation. The person changes the meaning of the conflict by inserting it in a different system, thus automatically creating a higher system which includes the previous ones as sub-systems. Most self-talk involved in problem-solving procedures (D'Zurilla and Goldfried 1971; Goldfried 1980) as well as that in *motoric* approaches (Guidano and Liotti 1983, 1985; Mahoney 1980, 1985) has these uncovering and creative functions. One could say that there is *coping by exploring* or *coping by systematising exploration.* This kind of coping appears that which structures primarily *insight* processes.

Compensation by exploration of possibilities anticipates all possible ways of transforming the conflict and involves its integration in different systems of meanings or references. This probabilistic anticipation concerns not only all possible transformations within the system but also all possible ways to transcend it. There is no regulatory construct which may structure such a creative process. Nevertheless, an exploratory action may be conceptualised in terms of a *natural* logic of hypotheses and propositions (Piaget 1975; Piaget and Inhelder 1955).

There are self-instructions which hardly resemble common self-talk, but which could integrate training in enhancing statements following a conflict in decision making. For reaching a balanced decision, the person may say:

(v) "I follow a good idea that spontaneously comes to my mind."
(w) "I let my mind wander and, trusting my intuition, retain the first idea which seems to be good."
(x) "I have an idea and try to get the opinion or advice of someone with similar interests and/or more experience."
(y) "I let the ideas flow and choose the one which seems to be the best, after considering the advantages and the disadvantages of each."

---

[2]Citation selected in Meichenbaum's work (1977, p. 160).

(z) "I try to have as many ideas as possible and analyse the advantages and the disadvantages of each, systematically comparing them to the advantages and the disadvantages of all the others."

Statements (v) and (w) resemble the kind of enhancing explorations used in self-instructional training for creativity: 6, 9, 11, 17, 20 and 23 (above). In all of these there is an unstructured way of structuring, which means that the processes for generating hypotheses and propositions are never made explicit. Methodological solipsism leads to epistemic intuition. And this is the stigma of creativity. It displays the most abstract incentive for producing insight and/or meanings. The person is invited literally to discover alternative meanings and meta-meanings (systems) from whatever inner source or structural coordination. In its common meaning, intuition is like brain-storming, since quantity prevails over quality. From a less superficial viewpoint, intuition may be considered as a promising exploration, including both productive and evaluative functions. Sometimes evaluation is not left in the dark since there is a vicarious authority to sanction the new meanings and meta-meanings: statement (x).

Statements (y) and (z) resemble the kind of enhancing explorations used in problem solving (D'Zurilla and Goldfried 1971; D'Zurilla and Nezu 1982). There is a structured way of structuring, and there are explicit processes for evaluating emerging hypotheses and propositions. For instance, strategy (z) involves an ordination or sequence of all possible ways of combining two-by-two alternatives. And each alternative also presents a dual or alternative *valorisation* in terms of advantages and disadvantages. This means that the person may attribute both a positive and a negative value/importance/belief to knowledge contained in each alternative. Considering an alternative A and an alternative B with respective advantages (A+, B+) and disadvantages (A–, B–), we may conceive 16 binary combinations derived from four basic propositions: A+B+, A+B–, A–B+, A–B–. Reasoning is thus operating in a systematic way upon all the possible conjunctions and disjunctions among the four valorisations. Piaget calls this formal operation *combinatory* (Piaget 1975; Piaget and Inhelder 1955).

This process allows for an evaluation of each alternative in coordination with all other evaluations but does not ensure a final choice or decision. Nevertheless, compensations by identity, inversion and reciprocity may be introduced into the combinatory. The resulting quaternary, or *Vierergruppe* for Klein (Piaget and Inhelder 1963), Piaget (1975) refers to as the INRC group, for the four possible operations within it: identity (I) or null operation; inversion (N); reciprocity (R); and correlative operation (C), which is the inverse of reciprocity. The four basic propositions undergo four possible transformations: NR = C, NC = R, RC = N and NRC = I. The INRC combinations allow for the control of the combinatory. Advantages and disadvantages may be exhaustively combined and transformed through the synthesis of inversions and reciprocities at a *meta-compensatory* level. It is virtually impossible to establish a direct representation of these transformations in terms of self-statements. However, in the following sections some INRC verbal coordinations will be illustrated.

A further possibility would be that everything, or almost everything, may be used to translate exploration of possibilities and creativity, including the construction of metaphorical self-instructions.

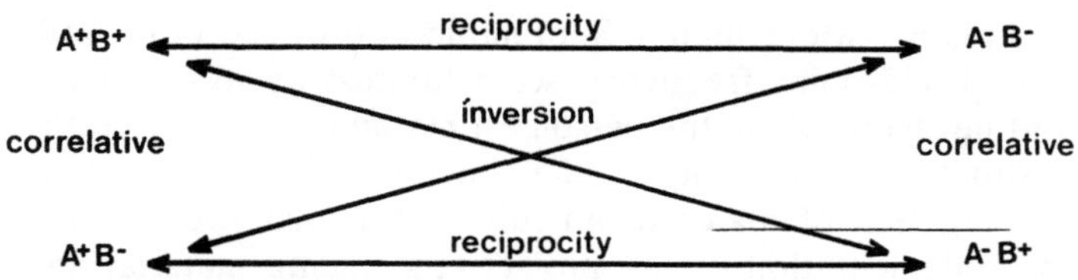

Fig. 1. INRC Control of combinatory

Endorsed Self-Statements and the Dialectic of Compromise: Specific Studies

What are the best compensatory regulations (or coping styles) for restructuring disturbing conflicts and frustrated coping attempts?

It is virtually impossible to provide a definite answer to this question since we do not have a reliable method for studying the person's idiosyncrasies in coping and meta-coping. But we can use *compensation by exploration* in an attempt to provide partial answers which will, in turn, raise other questions. In the studies described here a traditional method of employing self-statements is adopted for schematising coping styles or compensations of (a) scientific and artistic researchers, (b) undergraduate students taking a course in educational psychology, (c) depressives involved in cognitive therapy, and (d) recently divorced women involved in affirmative training.

During the past decade cognitive therapists have provided interesting conjectures about the way in which scientists function cognitively as problem solvers, self-controllers or decision makers (e.g. Arnkoff 1980; Guidano and Liotti 1983; Mahoney 1974, 1976, 1979, 1983, 1986; Mahoney and DeMonbreun 1977; Mahoney and Kimper 1976; Meichenbaum 1977). Unfortunately, there is little systematic investigation on this topic. The question of whether it is possible or worthwhile to train clients to cope with their difficulties in ways similar to those of scientists remains open. The following study does not fully answer this question but provides conjectures about which compensatory regulations researchers employ when they reflect upon common research/creativity problems and upon everyday symptoms of disturbance.

A survey was conducted at Arizona State University involving 35 professors with experience in scientific research andsartistic creation and 44 PhD and MFA candidates involved in research projects and artistic production.[3] Subjects were from departments of social sciences (education, history, philosophy and sociology), natural sciences (biology, botany, engineering and microbiology) and arts (dance, fine arts, printing and theatre).

Each subject was requested to respond to two questionnaires about regulating self-statements (compensations) in processes of research/creation and coping with disturbing thoughts. In addition, he/she was asked to engage in self-monitoring for

[3]The research project was partly supported by the Senior Scientist Programme of the NATO Scientific Affairs Division.

a week and to respond again. (More than 75% of subjects dropped out.) Both questionnaires comprised a 5-point frequency scale (almost always, usually, sometimes, seldom and never) in which the person estimated the relative occurrence of problematic situations concerning (a) the conception of a project (e.g. definition of topic, anticipation of material difficulties, personal strength and negative results); (b) implementation of the project (e.g. facing material and personal limitations, temptation for facilitating matters, verification of adequacy of the method); and (c) termination and analysis of results (e.g. strategies for analysis, confrontation with disappointment and guilt, use of less desirable results). Questionnaires also included items related to depressive, indecisive, obsessive and phobic thoughts. In addition, the subject had to choose or endorse the commonly used compensatory regulation adopted in these situations and thoughts from a list with three statements of compensation by inversion, four by reciprocity (including lesser evil), three by identity, five by exploration (two of intuition, one vicarious, and two combinatory) and four compensation attempts. Table 1 shows the frequency of occurrence above chance of first and second choices.

It is relevant first to note the great homogeneity among those from the three areas of discipline and the fact that students chose the same coping/meta-coping styles as did professors. Overall inter-group and process-related intra-group differences are nevertheless worth considering, if only briefly. (a) Corroborating common stereotypes, artists seem to rely on intuition more than do scientists during the conception and implementation phases of the project. (b) Scientists tend to abandon the combinatory in the last phase of termination and, much like the artists, rely then more on intuition (including vicarious intuition). (c) The relative frequency of disappointments, negative anticipations and self-criticism during both research/creation and decision-making processes suggests that most groups entrust their coping efforts to reciprocity. (d) The relative absence of depressive, phobic and obsessive thoughts (including compulsive impulses) possibly explains the fact that subjects rely on less sophisticated compensations, such as identity and inversion (Joyce-Moniz 1986; Fradique and Joyce-Moniz 1986). These findings may be clinically relevant, since they suggest that a more systematic confrontation with complex conflict situations involves the preferential use of compromise by reciprocity between positives and negatives.

This is also revealed in a more ambitious project conducted by Peixoto (1986) at the University of Azores. Using a survey similar to that above, he compared pre- and post-treatment compensatory self-instructions of 106 undergraduates enrolled in a course on educational-scientific measurement. These students were taught statistics by four different methods of instruction and were tested at the end of the course by means of a final examination involving two different levels of content complexity. The methods used were mastery learning (e.g. Bloom 1974; Block 1971), traditional lecture/discussion and two modified versions of these methods. Both mastery learning, based on behaviourist principles of reinforcement and corrective feedback, and the traditional lecture/discussion approach seem to require of students little more than the identification, retention and reproduction of content presented by the instructor. A constructivist attempt was made in the two modified versions. These two methods were considerably modified in order to accommodate a problem-solving orientation (Ellis and Hunt 1983), involving

Table 1. Employed compensatory regulations in research/creation and general coping

Subjects		Response Wave	Conception	Implementation	Termination	Decision making	Depression	Phobic	Obsessive-complusive
			explor. coping	explor. coping	explor. coping	explor. coping	coping	coping	coping
Social Sciences	Profes-sors	1st	comb. recip.	comb. rec/inv	vicar. recip.	comb. recip.	inver.	inver.	inver.
		2nd	comb. inver.	comb. recip.	com/int inver.	int/vic inver.	ident.	ident.	ident.
	PhD Cand.	1st	comb. recip.	comb. recip.	vicar. recip.	comb. recip.	ident.	inver.	inver.
		2nd	intui. inver.	comb. inver.	intui. inver.	int/vic inver.	recip.	ident.	ident.
Natural Sciences	Profes-sors	1st	comb. recip.	comb. recip.	comb. rec/t.c.	comb. recip.	t.c.	inver.	ident.
		2nd	comb. t.c.	comb. inver.	int/vic inver.	int/vic inver.	ident.	t.c.	inv/t.c.
	PhD Cand	1st	vicar. recip.	comb. recip.	comb. recip.	comb. recip.	inver.	inver.	ident.
		2nd	comb. ide/inv	comb. inver.	int/vic inver.	int/vic inver.	ident.	ident.	inv/t.c.
Arts	Profes-sors	1st	intui. recip.	comb. recip.	intui. recip.	comb. recip.	inver.	ident.	inver.
		2nd	vicar. inver.	intui. inver.	comb. inver.	int/vic inver.	ident.	inver.	ident.
	PhD Cand	1st	comb. recip.	comb. recip.	intui. rec/inv	comb. recip.	inver.	inver.	inver.
		2nd	intui. inver.	intui. inver.	comb. inv/rec	int/vic inver.	ident.	ident.	ident.

inv, inversion; recip, reciprocity; ident, identity; int, intuition; vic, vicarious; comb, combinatory; t.c., compensation attempts
Source: Fradique and Joyce-Moniz (1986)

strategies for the elaboration and analysis of alternatives and other processes of exploration.

Regarding compensatory regulations results showed that: (a) In all four groups the pre-treatment preference for compensations by inversion appears more closely tied to success in the final exam than preference for compensations by identity and frustrated attempts (mainly rationalisations about presumed conflict determinants). (b) Self-endorsement of compensations is also a better predictor of (higher) examination scores than self-assessment of efficacy, anxiety and locus of control. (c) Comparisons of pre- to post-treatment responses reveal in all groups a tendency for the conservation or maintenance of the more sophisticated compensations by combinatory and inversion/reciprocity (versus intuition and identity/non-compensatory attempts). On the other hand, the more significant *progressive* transitions or changes between pre- and post-treatment choices – from intuition to combinatory and from identity/attempts to inversion/reciprocity – are made by the problem-solving groups. And, curiously, these groups also obtained high scores in the more complex items of the examination.

It has been suggested elsewhere by the present author (Joyce-Moniz, *in press*) that research efforts in educational psychology should be aimed at determining whether teachers are adequately using their compensatory style in teaching practice in order to help students construe more adaptive knowledge – including adopting a better compensatory style for an inner dialectic. The same doubts could, of course, be raised concerning the therapist. The following study corroborates the importance of this question.

Fradique (1984) has investigated the choice/endorsement of compensations made weekly by 15 patients with unipolar depression who were given a therapeutic package including R.E.T. beliefs structuring (Ellis 1962), reality-testing procedures utilised in cognitive therapy (Beck et al. 1979) and relaxation training (Bernstein and Borkovec 1973). Comparison of successive choices of compensations and attempts/refusals at compensating, as recorded by a similar questionnaire, but with depressive thoughts selected on the Beck Depression Inventory (BDI; Beck et al. 1979) and excluding compensations by exploration, allowed the definition of three groups: (A) clients who benefit the most from treatment choose mainly compensation by reversibility at the beginning of the process and stay with it throughout treatment; (B) those who benefit from treatment only partially either make some transitions from non-compensatory (i.e. acceptance of symptoms and frustrated compensating attempts) to compensatory strategies (mostly inversion) or maintain the latter compensations throughout treatment; (C) those who do not profit from treatment – although improving their control of intense chronic pain – keep a single non-compensatory self-statement, that is, frustrated searching for symptomatic determinants.

This pattern confirms to a great extent previous observations (Joyce-Moniz 1985) suggesting a connection, on the one hand, between the prevalent use of non-compensating regulations and the manifestation of attributes of dissatisfaction, submission and passivity, negative and depressive thoughts, problems of gaining or losing interest in activities, persons and things and, on the other, frustrated attempts at regulation and magical-phenomenological attributes, Manichean and other obsessive thoughts and aggressive and/or compulsive behaviour.

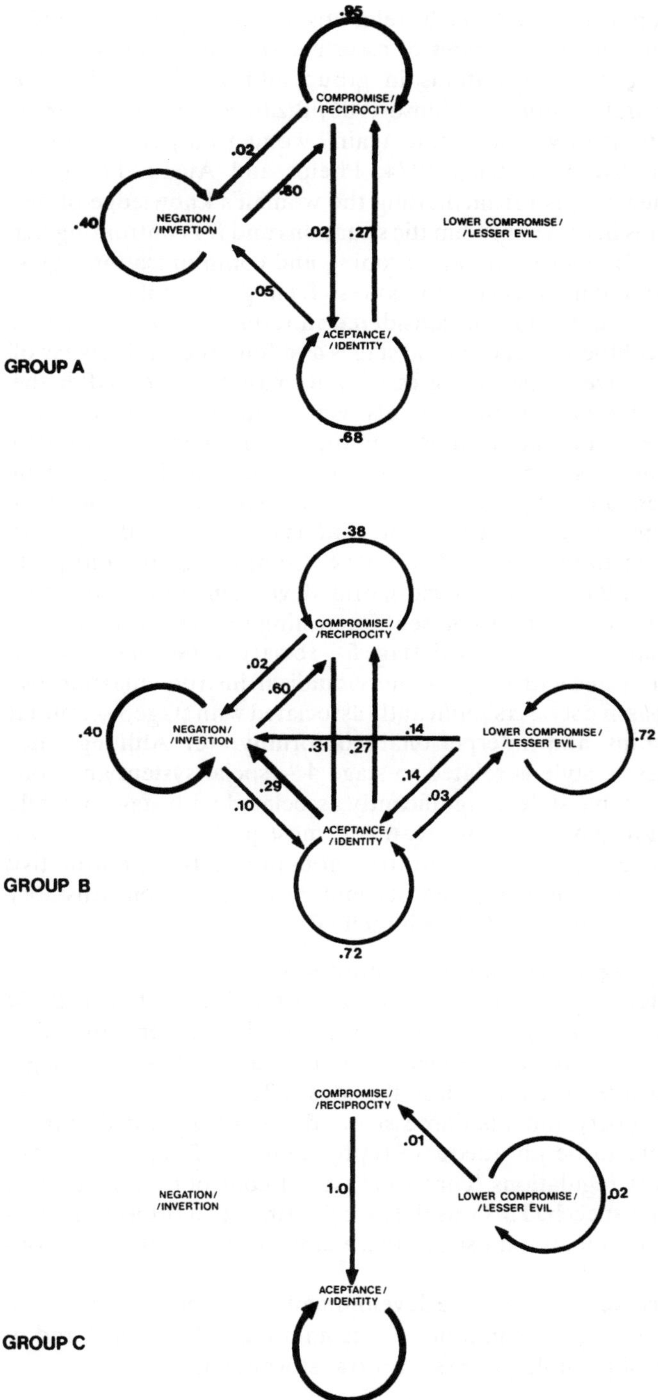

Fig. 2. State transition diagrams for groups A, B and C with correlation coefficients (Fradique, 1984)

Finally, it is worth reporting a study on the relationships among "socio-moral" levels of reasoning (Kohlberg 1976), styles of assertive and non-assertive communication and compensatory regulations in group affirmative training for recently divorced or separated women (Afonso 1986; Bizarro and Afonso 1986). Concentrating on situations in which "single-again" women may show lack of self-affirmation and assertiveness (Bach 1974; Phelps and Austin 1975), researchers presented video-scripts for facilitating the woman's knowledge of her common meaning systems in these problematic situations and for confronting her with more elaborate levels of socio-moral reasoning and communication styles. Each topic included three demands (i.e. to express feelings, to make requests, to answer criticisms); each demand was considered in terms of four alternative thoughts representing Kohlberg's socio-moral stages and four alternative ways of communicating (i.e. assertive, passive, aggressive and manipulative). After the presentation of the three situations participants were requested to choose one socio-moral self-statement and one form of communication in accordance with personal viewpoints. A broad group discussion was then promoted. In addition, in the first and the last sessions subjects had to endorse compensatory and non-compensatory self-statements related to the right of affirmation and to disposition in a questionnaire similar to those described above. Comparing pre- and post-treatment choices, the authors found socio-moral developmental patterns of reasoning and communicative styles to present interesting relationships. (a) The assertive style is significantly associated with stage 5 – social contract or utility and individual rights – and rejected with stage 2 – individualism, instrumental purpose and exchange. (b) The passive style is significantly associated with stage 3 – mutual expectations, relationships and interpersonal conformity. (c) Although not significantly, the aggressive style is related to stage 4 – social system and conscience. (d) The manipulative style is significantly associated with stage 5, while rejected with stage 4. Moreover, during treatment most participants showed a progression from lower to higher stages and from non-affirmative to affirmative styles, while changing from non-compensatory endorsements to compensatory ones, especially compensation by partial reciprocity (lesser evil).

These four studies suggest the following conjectures:

1. The most psychogenetically advanced compensatory regulations, that is, those by *reciprocity* and *exploration of possibilities,* seem to be the most effective. This means that the compensations acquired *later* in dialectical development (Piaget 1975) are those which were endorsed as the most effective by scientific researchers, artists, university students, depressive and recently separated women.
2. Self-instructions seem to be an adequate representation of coping and enhancing compensatory regulations. That is to say, self-control may be reached via restructuring inner speech. This was the case for almost all subjects, having illustrated their endorsements with suggestive examples of effective and non-effective self-talk.
3. The therapeutic process could aim at the development of dialectical *compromise* between positives and negatives in order to accommodate the conflict and of dialectical *exploring* of possible processes for transforming it.

In an epistemologically based therapy (Joyce-Moniz 1981, 1985) self-instructions may create appropriate dialectical conditions for the exploration of deeper, more tacit or unstructured meaning systems. They can provide the regulating monologue/dialogue for coping with the conflict, thus "freeing" the reasoning for exploring incentives and compensations, thus leading to new knowledge and/or meanings which transcend the original conflict. Therefore, the traditional utilisation of self-talk for uncovering hidden meanings is replaced by a structured and structuring inner dialectic for constructing more complex meaning systems (i.e. increasingly open, flexible, reversible, integrated, etc). It is not a task of *decamouflaging* but, indeed, of construction. It is not an epistemological "going back" but a "going forward". In the following section it will be suggested that *dramatic expression* is an appropriate method for processing that construction.

Training in Dramatic Expression in Epistemological Therapy

Drama is a widely used form in psychotherapy for representing human dialectics (Axline 1969; Haley 1976; Kelly 1955; Mead 1934; Minuchin and Fishman 1981; Moreno 1923; Scheff 1981; Wolpe and Lazarus 1966). For instance, in gestalt therapy "acting out" is a powerful means for restructuring:

> In gestalt therapy when we talk about "acting out" we do not mean living out but 'Be an actor'. We have a script in the form of a dream or a fantasy. We see that the dream or fantasy is a story, a drama, and we act it out again in therapy to make us more aware of what we are, of what is available. (Perls and Clements 1977, p. 16).

Drama therapists must be sensitive constructivists. Traditionally, they set the stage for a collective construction of personal conflicts. Each actor plays roles both for himself and for the other actors. Sometimes, he also plays for an audience (Moreno 1923). Interactions between the audience and the actor are as important as the dramatic action among actors. An *outer dialectic* is constantly stimulated since each actor constructs his roles while interacting with the other actors. In turn, these actively construe their own roles. If there is a "cast", casting problems over role acceptance and distribution are added to the dramatic action. Patients try to become *truly* spontaneous during the acting out of their hidden conflicts. It is generally believed that persistent intuition leads to personal creativity.

The participants of a psychodramatic therapeutic process are also reconstructing the world on a stage. They generate representations of reality, and they act upon them. They re-enact past, present and future conflicts, placing these in different systems of meanings and references. They relive experiences to understand underlying motivations, tacit meanings or unconscious forces. They are, as it were, involved in the Greek rite of acting out their realities. Nevertheless, drama therapy is not only "acting out" but also "acting as if". That is to say, the client knows that he is construing a fake reality. As a matter of fact, the main rule of this game is "construing as if". Re-enacted metaphors, encounters, climaxes, episodic roles or complex characters are conscious approximations of reality. As such, they provide dramatised contents for a *distanced* construction. The client plays destructurings and restructurings for testing his interpretations of the reality. Beliefs, values, norms, rules, anticipations, etc. are safely conceptualised and concretely re-enacted from different perspectives and with different emotional overtones. Since the client is both actor and spectator, he alternates between *centering* on the dramatic action and *decentering* from it. In other words, there are active periods of construction and reflective ones of reconstruction. Landy (1983, pp. 175–176) expressed this dramatic integration of inner and outer dialectics as follows:

> Distancing is relevant to drama therapy in that the therapist bases much of his work in examining the dialectics of actor and observer, self and role, one role and another role; and it is in exploring the degree of separation and closeness within these relationships that the therapist realizes his therapeutic goals. These goals might include enhancing the client's ability to differentiate between roles, to gain further mastery of a single role, or to expand his repertory of roles. More specifically, the drama therapist might aim toward helping clients distinguish between behaviour appropriate to themselves and behaviour appropriate to characters who are not themselves. A most important therapeutic goal might also be to help clients find the proper balance between participation in a dramatic action and observation of that action, that is, a balance between self as subject and self as object.

In the theatre itself dramatised reality offers all the elements for the dialectical emergence of meaningful conflicts, leading the spectator to subtle centerings and decenterings from action. For example, taking an overdistancing perspective the so-called "theatre of the absurd" (e.g. works by Adamov, Arrabal, Beckett, Ionesco and Jarry) and the "epic" methodology of Brecht aim at distancing the spectators from the emotional screens and biases of acting and at directing the audience's rationalisations toward the meaning systems of the characters.

Decentering and construing are at the heart of our own rationalisations about the dialectics between client and actor or client and character. The training in dramatic expression referred to here concerns individual therapy but not the whole process of individual therapy. This kind of dramatic training may have limited functions, sharing an instance of intervention with other procedures. However, it may also become the exclusive procedure during an entire session or a series of sessions. In addition, it cannot be applied to all problems and clients normally faced by a cognitive therapist. The main characteristics of this training can be outlined as follows:

1. The training in dramatic expression involves only an actor (the client) and a director (the therapist); it is a one-person performance. Johnson (1981) calls it an interpersonal relationship between the actor and his role.
2. Since acting to oneself is not the same as acting to other people, the construction of metaphors, encounters, roles or characters is expressed by self-talk – not colourless mumbling but resonant, articulated, sensitive self-talk (i.e. dialogues with self, monologues or soliloquies).
3. The client plays to himself and not to the therapist. But this omnipresent director is not passive. As suggested below, he is involved in cueing, modelling, guiding and correcting the performances.
4. Conscious improvisation is the name of the game. The client may be involved in "streaming" (verbalising whatever comes to mind) or in "acting out" an imitation of self, or "acting as if" another character could play self.
5. Restructuring or coping self-talk facilitates the improvising of roles and characters. In other words, dramatic construction can be enhanced through training in coping by compromising and exploring. Of special interest, if the client qua actor comes to cope with his acting difficulties (e.g. negative acting anticipations,

depressive performance evaluations, unreasonable acting fears and pervasive anxiety, sudden memory lapses, excessive reliance on the director's help, lack of comprehension of the characters' beliefs, values or norms), the client qua character comes to explore new meanings better and express different interpretations.

6. Themes for improvisation are based on cognitive-developmental theory and are introduced in dramatisation in accordance with socio-cogcitive sequences of "natural" development.

Setting and Accessories

Training in dramatic expression takes place in the therapist's consulting room; special arrangements are nevertheless required to transform this office into a small stage. There are, of course, many options here, as each therapist has a particular idea of the relationship that should be established between the client and the space around him. The best arrangements are probably those which stimulate the imagination of the therapist since he must, in turn, stimulate the imagination of the actors who perform on that stage. Yet in all cases a rather empty and open space is absolutely necessary because the actor should feel free whenever he wants to move around.

A functional stage is the one in which the actor finds what he needs for improvising: (a) no problems of entrances and exits, that is, the actor is always on the stage, whether for performing, following instructions, warming up, observing the director's modelling or watching videos of himself acting; (b) a floor for moving easily; (c) lighting appropriate for symbolic purposes (theatrical devices are not necessary), a setting with a minimum structure (e.g. an empty white wall for multiple purposes) and minimal furniture (e.g. couch, table, large box); and (d) video equipment for recording and reproducing at any time.

The client should be carefully instructed about the use of stage space. Any space in the room not used as stage should be identified, although this can remain available for acting, if necessary. In general, the whole consulting room and, sometimes, the waiting room must be adapted flexibly to the requirements of improvisation.

Accessories are the objects appearing on stage that are not part of the furniture. Ornamental or "dressing" pieces such as pictures, plants, porcelains, etc. should not interfere with the open space and, particularly, the construction of meanings. All accessories may be either integrated in the overall setting for not disturbing the performance or, rather, made salient for helping the actor improvise on specific themes. For instance, a telephone allows for an easy change from self-talk to talk with others; a videotape portraying one or more characters may introduce a convenient modification of action; instructions and/or questions can also be presented via tape recording. However, one should emphasise the importance of particular accessories for facilitating decentration.

The *mirror* fits popular methapors in psychology, e.g. Cooley's "looking-glass self" (1902). We can also ask clients to use this device for constructing a metaphoric self. In effect, when a client starts to look at and talk to his reflected image, he creates an interlocutor who looks exactly like self, talks just like self, but somehow acts differently. Some clients react to this minimal decentering or distancing by saying that they are feeling or becoming "unnatural". Yet most clients experience more or less long dialogues with their reflected images. There are "confidential mirrors" in fairy tales as well as in private and public washrooms.

The mirror can be placed on a table or hung on the wall. At the beginning of improvisation with this device, the client sits in front of the mirror, so that his face is fully reflected in it. The person must feel comfortable (he can lean back, lean on the table, etc.) since there is a more or less long period of concentration. The therapist sits behind the client, in such a way that he can also see the client's face in the mirror. This position does not mean that the therapist must play *auxiliary* or *alter egos*, but simply that he must occupy a strategic place on the stage for cueing and correcting the performance.

Masks and *make-up* are useful decentering devices that are being re-introduced into drama therapy (Breitenbach 1979; Landy 1983). These permit an easy change of roles and characters. The movement of decentering is done under emotional protection since *another* face represents self. In our training we use different masks for portraying different characters and different expressions of the same character (although these are never explicit in terms of emotional stereotypes such as tragic, comic, etc.). The client himself can fashion a mask out of paper and paste and paint on it the most common expression of the character or the expression that he likes or dislikes the most about that character.

Masks allow a quick step of decentering whereas make-up entails a progressive construction of the character's face. In addition, make-up is applied directly onto the face and may become a "second skin". A mask is an object which hides the face but provides the character with a frozen expression. The client should be informed about the different functions that these devices can play. For example, with greater or lesser cultural sophistication, the therapist explains that in theatre and in religion masks and make-up have always been used to give a different identity to the actor or celebrant, turning him into a character more easily identified with a known symbol or stereotype. The client has the opportunity to manipulate and try several masks, greasepaints, bases and theatrical make-up prior to improvisation. Everything must be planned for facilitating a good choice in and composition of the decentering device.

The client may, of course, utilise a mask or make-up merely for playing himself, that is, without the purpose of creating a distinct character. As such, the device serves both for masking the face and "unmasking" the soul (i.e. significations that client would not express otherwise).

Costumes and other objects may also be utilised as decentering devices or for emphasising the functions attributed above to masks and make-up. Normally, these are not provided by the therapist but by the client, who brings them to the training. For practical reasons the number and volume of costumes should be kept at a minimum; between sessions these accessories should remain in the room, while during sessions they can be available in a large and open box. Clients should not be encouraged to select particularly meaningful objects, related to his traumatic experiences, however the therapist should abstain from formulating any suggestions concerning these options. Clients should feel free to bring whatever costumes and small objects (including pets) they favour for their dramatic fantasies.

Posters may be designed, painted and affixed to the empty wall by the actor. Depicting the general characteristics of a character or the general lines of a script, these accessories may decrease anxiety over memory lapses and role deviations.

Phases and Techniques of Drama Therapy

Improvisation

Improvising is an active construction with sufficient cognitive, emotional and behavioural ingredients for producing a dialectical explosion. The client may become totally absorbed by this playful task of inventing self; he may, in fact overdo the game and instead of controlling the acting end up being completely controlled by it. Thus, training in improvisation should be structured in accordance with the characteristics of the actor and with the interpretative demands. Dramatic training should not be offered indiscriminately to everybody. Besides, the client qua actor is required to respect and please the client qua spectator. This is to say that although bad performances are permitted, the client should strive for improving his acting. As the actor learns to control his acting, his dramatic expression usually becomes more incisive and suggestive. Nevertheless, the quality of performance cannot be evaluated by the aesthetic criteria of traditional theatre; physical, vocal and emotional requirements of the stage are not applied to clients. Only the actor or actress and the therapist's evaluations should guide the progressive improvement of the quality of improvising. To facilitate this process we have chosen a sequential involvement in free self-talk, roles and characters. *Streaming, acting out* and *acting as if* represent three increasingly complex levels of improvisation, developing from a minimal to a maximal experience of decentration.

Streaming can be done anywhere on stage. The most common positions for verbalising "whatever comes to mind" are lying on a couch, sitting facing a mirror and standing in front of a wall. This so-called "free association" has evidently been engraved in many parchments of psychotherapy. We utilise this technique for warming up purposes and for generating unstructured self-talk in acting. In both cases the movement of distancing is restricted to disconnected meanings and meaning systems. As a procedure of warming up it does not demand a great effort of imagination. Its emotional overtones are neutralised by the lack of structure, although some clients may immediately take streaming for "releasing" purposes.

Acting out or *as if* allows a regulating exploration of underlying meaning systems. In this case emotional expressions of understanding are welcome since they enhance higher or more complex styles of improvisation. In general, the client is invited to play his *usual* roles and characters and to reflect upon coping and non-coping self-talk and underlying meanings. However, the performance may be restricted to improvising only one particularly meaningful role or character. Facing the mirror, in front of the wall or at the centre of the stage, the person takes the opportunity to experience minor and major distancings from himself while talking to self about self. For example, the client may choose acting out regular symptoms of anxiety and dysphoria, without any attempt whatever to cope with them, or the usual ways of interrogating self about self at home, or how one rehearses future confrontations with others. Above all the client is informed that he is free not no express embarassing or painful contents and that he may hold them back until feeling prepared to share them.

Acting as if another character is playing self naturally involves a higher level of improvising. The client qua actor approaches theatrical standards here since he must create a distinct character. Nevertheless, the characzer portrays (and meta-represents) the actor, which is rare in traditional theatre. In this sense, the character is the metaphor of the actor, and he the metaphor of the client; the character's role becomes the client's representation of his *possible* roles. In effect, one could say that creating a character is inventing a new self. In our training, the construction of a character portraying the actor is guided by a particular script. As such, the client is requested to create a character who goes through a series of developmental changes of meanings and meaning systems. The creative act is limited by external suggestions and controlled by restructuring and coping self-talk. We believe that these apparent restrictions help the actor reach a more effective level of improvising change.

Improvisation includes both verbal and non-verbal expressions of inner dialogue. Facial expressions, posture, gestures, relaxation, dancing and so forth are important stage activities for enhancing coping and creativity. Often in this training the person has the opportunity of re-experiencing a lost or forgotten body talk; he adopts children's movements to play adult games. In acting out and acting as if, body expression facilitates mental expression and vice versa. Dramatisation of meaningful events frees individual movements from social restrictions imposed by everyday roles and characters.

Although we recommend specific stage postures to help the emergence of improvisation (e.g. lying on a couch, sitting facing a mirror, or standing in front of a wall), once this begins, the actor should feel free to move. However, the therapist may interrupt and suggest specific positions or movements for the introduction or the development of a particular topic or theme.

Releasing

Aristotle formulated a concept that has been controversial both in theatre and in psychotherapy. In his view dramatic action produces a purification, or *catharsis*, of passions, thus freeing the spectator from himself. In other words, the delusions and excesses of the character may become so personally meaningful that the entire audience acts empathically as if the emotions of the character should be expressed by everyone.

However, in drama therapy as in distancing theatre (e.g. with Brecht and "theatre of the absurd") empathy may vary from identification, or complete acceptance of the character's significations, to compromising between what belongs to self and to the character and extend to antipathy and the denying of all dramatised meanings. Striking a balance between empathising and non-empathising resembles Scheff's (1979, 1981) concept of a dialectics between overdistancing, or remembering past memories, and underdistancing, or reliving/re-experiencing past events. From this perspective, the client reaches catharsis when he releases or acts out strong emotions but is not overwhelmed by them.

In our view, any expression of emotion during acting out and as if also represents an equilibration between destructuring and restructuring excessive and painful meanings. As an expression of individual holism the process of acting constantly balances cognitions, emotions and attitudes. Catharsis involves going through total experiences much more than driving out old evils. For example, the releasing of strong emotions during "playing symptoms" often indicates that the person is theatrically ready for trying new levels of improvisation and deeper understanding of his acting. And the acting out of normal complains, self-criticism and self-indulgence prepares the acting "as if somebody else is using *my* sweat, blood and tears".

It is important to inform the client that he should feel free to express strong emotions anytime during the training, but also that he is not obliged to do so. We do not force the person to become emotionally involved in dramatic action by shouting, shedding tears or heavy sighs. "Cold" acting may be as emotional as a "hot" acting. Besides, releasing oneself is not an unchanging compulsion. The therapist must consider three types of releasing: streaming, that is the client uses catharsis for warming up; accompanying the representation of symptoms during acting out and reflecting the distance between the person and the model of self; integrating the roles of the character who experiences different emotions for portraying the transformation of the client.

Warming up

The well-known psychodramatic principle that warming up and spontaneity are both cause and effect guides our conceptualisations. Moreno (1946, 1959, 1962) has often emphasised that warming up promotes spontaneity and this, in turn, shortens warming up; the two are thus dialectically entwined. In our training we use warming up for enhancing acting and acting for warming up the construction process. That is, the actor needs to activate the creative process constantly, using self-talk and stage movement. Curiously, words and gestures have the structuring and structured functions of integrating the warming up and the improvisation. As the actor becomes more creative he begins to improvise more easily. As he shortens the period of warming up, he improves the quality of improvisation. In the past we have told our clients that warming up is both the ignition key and the engine, but also that improvising provides the gas.

In its restrictive sense warming up corresponds to two distinct periods in our training: exercises for enhancing all levels of improvisation and streaming for experiencing a first level of improvisation.

Progressive relaxation by muscle tensing and releasing (Bernstein and Borkovec 1973), Schultz' (1935) autogenic training, or almost anything can be utilised in the initial warm-up (e.g. aerobics, aikido, biofeedback, dancing, drugs, hypnosis, massage, t'ai chi ch'uan, transcendental meditation). Our clients do not have a choice, since we always use some simple exercises of physical activation, in which the client begins to use self-talk to instruct himself, as well as speechless imagery before improvising. Activation involves unsophisticated exercises on the floor, standing in front of a wall or moving around while the person describes to himself what he intends to do or is actually doing. If the client finds this dialogue too dull, he has the alternative of verbalising what he intends to do during the following improvisation. About 5 min physical exercise seems to be enough for almost everyone. The client should not feel tense but only slightly tired. Speechless imagery allows for a verbal pause prior to the actual talk of improvising. In this sense our clients use some of the tricks utilised by professional actors for *avant-scene* "psyching" or concentrating without words. A detailed explanation of our procedures exceeds the purpose of the present outline. In general, the method of *streaming images* connected with acting while lying down with the eyes closed seems accessible to most clients. On the other hand, self-induced imagery with a minimum of verbal instructions, increasingly suggestive and hypnotic (Gibbons 1979), seems to require a careful preparation, which limits its applicability.

Streaming self-talk facing a mirror constitutes the first level of improvisation. Usually, the therapist asks the client *to look at the mirror and say whatever comes to mind, without worrying about the sequence of words or about whether these make sense or not.* The client is also told that he or she (a) is free not to mention painful or embarrassing things, (b) can look anywhere in the mirror, (c) can moan, cry, play the clown, etc. and (d) should not worry about time. The therapist gives the client 10 min in order that he or she may begin to talk. If this does not happen, the therapist starts *cueing: "Well, I'll give you a cue as in theatre rehearsals, so that you may improvise on the basis of what it may suggest to you."* A *cue* is self-talk for a dramatic entrance. As such, the therapist models part of the client's self-talk, mainly introductory sentences, and directs his or her attention towards meaningful stimuli for improvising (e.g., imperatives, expectations of success, attributions, past episodes, metaphors, rationalisations, etc.).

Acting out

The client qua incipient actor tries to pursue an imitation of self when he acts out symptoms and other personal dispositions underlying the conflict. This second level of improvisation thus involves higher forms of decentering than streaming. The actor or actress tries to produce his or her common meanings in the most natural way, and yet something sounds false – even the self does not look exactly like the self in the mirror. It is believed that this perception of distance facilitates the understanding of more abstract meanings of conflicts and restructurings at higher levels of coordination (and compensatory regulation).

Normally, acting out regular symptoms is chosen as the initial decentering step. The actor is asked to act current conflicts in common self-talk. He is free to utilise any place on the stage, accessories, lighting and body movement; he therefore makes important stage decisions traditionally reserved to the director. Most clients choose not only the same space and objects used in streaming but also

common symptoms (e.g. of anxiety and dysphoria). In addition, the same instructions given for streaming about freedom of improvisation and of content apply to this level. The actor should also benefit from warming up and concentration before acting. If this does not take place within scheduled time, the therapist begins modelling or acting out his own imitation of self and of the symptoms fictitiously attributed to self, and not an imitation of the client. As such, the therapist should place himself beside or in front of the client and not behind him, as in streaming. The therapist qua director fashions a technique of improvising self and nothing else. The modelling, of course, should be meaningful for the client, that is, therapist's symptoms must be in some way identical to client's. A number of therapists, however, recommend the opposite, that is, a *distance model.* Examples of initial sentences for helping the acting out of self include the following: "Should I feel sorry?", "Everything seems to happen without me", "I deserve what I have", "I feel anxiety spreading all over me", "I'm no good", "This is ridiculous – I feel like crying", "I have to check again", "I can't live without love", "She is going to be mad at me", "I don't believe in easy cures", "I feel like giving up". Taking Meichenbaum's viewpoint (1977), while there exists a modelled expression of dysphoria, anxiety, anger, pessimism, doubt, etc., the client is told that he should verbalise his own self-talk and not try to imitate the therapist.

In addition, acting difficulties may serve as a metaphor for common symptoms. For example, negative acting anticipations, depressive performance evaluation, unreasonable acting fears and pervasive anxiety, sudden memory lapses, and excessive reliance on the director's help may replace the acting out of usual symptoms or be combined with them. Paradoxically, the client can be informed that if he is ever to move beyond acting problems and start to imitate self, he should stop trying to play self as "naturally" as possible.

Acting out with a mask (and/or make-up) seems to be an appropriate method for attenuating acting difficulties since some actors improvise better with a strong but "protected" distancing or decentering technique, such as behind a screen, than with a small but "exposed" one, for instance facing the mirror and/or the therapist. In effect, decentering devices applied to the face somewhat neutralise fears of exposing to self or therapist uncomfortable or undesirable facial expressions of emotional self-talk. These devices may additionally facilitate the actor's concentration on body talk, that is, on a better representation of meaningful physical symptoms.

Play symptoms are not only for verbalising descriptions of disturbance but also coping self-talk, that is, restructuring utterances which may precede, accompany and follow symptomatic self-talk. Nevertheless, here the actor is not required to select a particular system of compensations for coping with the acted symptoms. He or she plays the *usual* restructuring self-talk and frustrated attempts at coping.

Acting as if

The third level of improvisation demands the highest decentering effort: to act as if another character could play self. That is, the person is requested to act role-reversal with self. This is therefore a "different" self than in streaming and acting out, since the client is asked first *to choose a mask for creating a character on the mirror and to engage a dialogue with this character.* The option of not using a decentering device or make-up should also be available. This invented interlocutor who looks like self models a construction of self while playing with self (or a reflected ego who plays alter ego with dramatic overtimes).

The client may create a character only somewhat different from self or one that is very much different (the therapist does not specify how different), or he may construct a "model", an ideal character that is more/less able, efficient, depressive, assertive, anxious, "ill", etc. At this point the client is free to improvise any type of character. Nevertheless, the actor should be told to avoid playing his normal self again. If the actor decides to remove the mask during the improvisation, the therapist should not interfere but must note all changes which occur after this transition: Does the actor still face the mirror? Does the actor replace dialogue by monologue? Does the actor keep the same emotional style? Does the actor begin to move around? Make-up should always be available, for the actor may choose to remove the mask and apply make-up. In addition, the character's face may be gradually developed and painted. There is no need to rush the composition of a character.

For warming up the creative process the client may be asked first to think about the character and try to describe the psychological (and sometimes physical) characteristics which he intends to attribute to the "other" self. The therapist takes note of all meaningful differences between the actual composition of the character and the composition of self during acting out. The client may also relate a story or episode in which the character is directly involved. He can use the telephone for establishing a first contact with the character who supposedly talks from the other end of the line; he may also do the opposite, placing the character on this end of the line, talking to self on the other, playing role-reversal with self. He may write down the main traits of the character – *never* a script at this time – in large script on a poster affixed to the empty wall. This scenic environment may facilitate improvising since the actor always has the possibility of avoiding the anxiety of deviations from role or of memory lapses about important features of the character.

In this training, the actor uses coping self-talk, self-instructions, personal imperatives, etc., for enhancing dramatic construction. The main rule of this particular game is to experience all forms of compensation. For example, the therapist replays some cues already utilised in streaming, and the client translates them in inverse, identical, reciprocal and exploratory *I statements* in front of the mirror.

General Themes

In our training we do not currently follow a specific set of themes for improvising, nor do we have specific scripts formalised a priori for particular disturbances. The therapist has the difficult task of relying on his own knowledge of socio-cognitive conceptualisations for defining and implementing a sequential script or specific theme. The following are general guidelines for facilitating this task:

1. The best scripts are those which combine several formalisations. For instance, Selman's (1980) levels for the acquisition of social roles and perspectives

and Kohlberg's (1976, 1981, 1983) levels for the understanding of rights and prescription of moral justice may both define the main characteristics of a character who goes through a series of existential conflicts and episodes of anxiety and dysphoria.

2. Looking for connections or co-ordinations is the principal goal of the therapist and the client. The latter provides the specific themes for improvising (e.g. contents for self-talk, gestures, facial expressions, movements on the stage) and the specific characteristics of the character (e.g. symptoms). The former sketches out the main characteristics of the character (e.g. general metaphysical beliefs, norms and values) and gives specific instructions during the actor's *semi-structured* improvisation. Both partners co-operate fully in defining the conceptual universe of the character; this involves a continuous interaction of ideas about the transformation, evolution and co-ordination of perceived meanings and meaning systems.

3. At all times the therapist must have a clear understanding of the metaphysical and epistemological characteristics of the character. He should be able to explain these features clearly, without alienating the actor's own ideas of how the character is developing his more basic meaning systems about reality and the relationship between knowledge and reality. Kitchener and King (1981) have established a sequence for the acquisition of metaphysical assumptions which may be used in enhancing the therapist's ideas. For example, in *stage 1* there is a conception of objective reality that exists as the individual sees it; beliefs simply exist and need not be explained. In *stage 3* there is also an objective reality but it can never be known without uncertainty; beliefs are justified with idiosyncratic knowledge claims and on idiosyncratic evaluations of data. In *stage 5* an objective understanding of reality is not possible since objective knowledge does not exist; beliefs are justified with appropriate decision rules for a particular perspective or context. In *stage 7* there is an objective reality against which ideas and assumptions must ultimately be tested; beliefs reflect solutions that can be justified as most reasonably using general rules of enquiry and evaluation.

4. The therapist becomes an active director who translates socio-cognitive developmental concepts into acting instructions. He wants the actor to experience new meanings and coordinations of meanings, to transform dramatised sequences for exploring evolution in the character and to be aware of the dialectics between the character and the actor. He gives specific instructions, for example, "Come on, give the character greater flexibility", "Think about *his* way of seeing reality", "Why don't you see if *he* can connect *his* beliefs with *his* professional attitudes?"

5. Symptoms themselves should be conceptualised in developmental terms, that is, the subjective experience of symptoms becomes a step-by-step progression of transformations of symptomatic meanings. This is a very difficult task, and many cognitive therapists are only now beginning to look at a developmental framework instead of the traditional psychopathology. Nevertheless, there are already good indications of a developmental ideology in the characterisation of common symptoms. For example, Kegan et al. (1981) have defined three levels of experiencing the usual symptoms of unipolar depression: *self-sacrificing* depression (e.g. dysphoria and discontent are described in terms of being unable to satisfy one's own wishes or in those of the increasing cost of doing so); *dependent* depression (dysphoria and discontent are described in terms of feelings about the

connections and disconnections with others: lonely, unloved, abandoned, betrayed, unworthy of others' attention and regard); and *self-evaluative* depression (dysphoria and discontent are described in terms of the failure to live up to one's own hopes for oneself, falling short of one's standard, negative self-evaluation). These three types of depression are based upon stages 2, 3 and 4 of Kohlberg's sequence of socio-moral development (Kohlberg, 1976, 1981, 1983).

Summary and Conclusions

In this chapter we have attempted to translate coping self-talk, regulating self-instructions, balanced personal imperatives and restructuring inner speech training into cognitive psychotherapy terms. More specifically, the client may utilise the structuring and structured features of self-talk for enhancing the acquisition of more adaptive knowledge or meanings about self. The dialectic of verbalised self-control is connected with that of self-understanding, better coping facilities, better exploration and vice versa. A Piagetian constructivist ideology has guided our position on the active, dialectical, creative process of equilibration (balancing) in psychotherapy. Cognitive-dialectical development of structures and meanings about self and the world becomes a model for the clinical change of the client's meaning systems. Self-instructions can provide the regulating inner speech for freeing reasoning and exploring incentives and compensatiocs which promote knowledge. Compensatory self-talk anticipates what to say before the occurrence of the conflict. Several studies conducted in Lisbon seem to suggest that the therapeutic process could aim at the development of a dialectic reciprocity between positives and negatives for accommodating conflict and of a dialectic exploring of *all* possible ways of transforming it.

The second part of this chapter attempted to introduce training in dramatic expression as part of the constructive process in individual therapy. Drama facilitates the emergence of a distanced or decentered construction since the client plays destructurings and restructurings on a stage for testing his interpretations of reality. In this training conscious improvisation guides the construction of metaphors, encounters, roles and characters. The actor is first involved in streaming – verbalising whatever comes to mind – secondly in acting out an imitation of self, and finally in acting as if another character could play self. In addition, restructuring or coping self-talk facilitates improvisation, that is, the dramatic construction is enhanced through dialectics of compromising and exploring, on the one hand, and, on the other, the themes for improvisation are suggested in accordance with socio-cognitive sequences of natural development.

References

Afonso H (1986) Desenvolvimento sociomoral e auto-afirmação em mulheres recém divorciadas/separadas. Thesis, University of Lisbon, Lisbon
Arnkoff D (1980) Psychotherapy from the perspective of cognitive therapy. In: Mahoney M (ed) Psychotherapy process. Plenum, New York
Axline VM (1969) Play therapy. Ballantine, New York
Bach GR (1974) Creative exists: fight-therapy for divorcees. In: Franks V, Burtle V (eds) Women in therapy: new psychotherapies for a changing. Brunner and Mazel, New York
Baudoin C (1920) Suggestion and autosuggestion. Allen and Unwin, London
Beck A, Rush A, Shaw B, Emery G (1979) Cognitive therapy of depression. Guilford, New York
Berstein DA, Borkovec TD (1973) Progressive relaxation training. Research Press, Champaign, Illinois
Birdwhistell R (1970) Kinesics and context. University of Pennsylvania Press, Philadelphia
Bizarro L, Afonso H (1986) Dialectic development and divorced women: affirmative training. 2nd international conference on cognitive psychotherapy, Sept. 1986, Umea, Sweden
Block JH (1971) Mastery learning: theory and practice. Holt, Rinehart, and Winston, New York
Blomm BS (1974) An introduction to mastery learning theory. In: Block JH (ed) Schools, society and mastery learning. Holt, Rinehart, and Winston, New York
Breitenbach R (1979) Secret faces. Dramatherapy 2:18–23
Cooley CH (1902) Human nature and the social order. Scribner, New York
Coué E (1922) The practice of autosuggestion. Doubleday, New York
D'Zurilla T, Goldfried M (1971) Problem solving and behavior modification. J Abnorm Psychol 78:107–126
D'Zurilla T, Nezu A (1982) Social problem solving in adults. In: Kendall PC (ed) Advances in cognitive-behavioral research and therapy, vol. 1. Academic, New York
Ellis A (1962) Reason and emotion in psychotherapy. Lyle Stuart and Citadel, New Jersey
Ellis A (1973) Humanistic psychotherapy: the rational-emotive approach. Julian, New York
Ellis A (1981) The rational-emotive approach to thanatology. In: Sobel H (ed) Behavior therapy in terminal care: a humanistic approach. Ballinger, New York
Ellis HC, Hunt R (1983) Fundamentals of human memory and cognition, 3rd edn. Brown, Dubuque
Fast J (1971) Body language. Pocket Books, New York
Fradique F (1984) Self-evaluation, reactivity and therapeutic confrontation. Thesis, University of Lisbon, Lisbon, Portugal
Fradique F, Joyce-Moniz L (1986) Dialectic and metacognitive processes in scientific and depressive patterns. 2nd international conference on cognitive psychotherapy, Sept 1986. Umeå, Sweden
Freud A (1946) The ego and mechanisms of defense. International Universities Press, New York
Freud S (1959) Inhibitions, symptoms and anxiety. In: Strachey J (ed) Standard edition, vol 20. Hogarth, London
Gagné RM (1964) Problem solving. In Melton A (ed) Categories of human learning. Academic, New York
Gibbons DE (1979) Applied hypnosis and hyperempiria. Plenum, New York
Goldfried M (1980) Psychotherapy as coping skills training. In: Mahoney M (ed) Psychotherapy process. Plenum, New York
Goldfried M, Robins C (1983) Self-schema, cognitive bias, and the process of therapeutic experiences. In: Kendall P (ed) Advances in cognitive-behavioral research and therapy, vol 2. Academic, New York
Guidano V, Liotti G (1983) Cognitive processes and emotional disorders. Guildford, New York
Guidano V, Liotti G (1985) A constructivist foundation for cognitive therapy. In: Mahoney M, Freeman A (eds) Cognition and psychotherapy. Plenum, New York
Haley J (1976) Problem-solving therapy. Harper and Row, New York
Hayek F (1952) The sensory order. University of Chicago Press, Chicago
Ivey AE (1986) Developmental therapy. Jossey-Bass, San Francisco
James W (1890) Principles of psychology, vol 1. Holt, New York
Janis I (1965) Psychodynamic aspects of stress tolerance. In: Klausner S (ed) The quest for self-control. Free Press, New York
Johnson D (1982) Principles and techniques of drama therapy. The Arts in Psychotherapy 9:83–90

Joyce-Moniz L (1981) From decentration to compensation: toward a cognitive-constructivist therapy. 1st european meeting on cognitive-behaviour therapies, Sept 19, 1981. Lisbon, Portugal
Joyce-Moniz L (1985) Epistemological therapy and constructivism. In: Mahoney M, Freeman A (eds) Cognition and psychotherapy. Plenum, New York
Joyce-Moniz L (1986) Perspectivas desenvolvimentistas em terapias cognitivas. Psiquiatria Clínica 7:117–125
Joyce-Moniz L (1988) Teacher's training: dialectic development and teaching dialectics. Proc 1st international meeting on psychological teacher education, May 1986, University of Braga, Portugal (to be published)
Kazdin AE (1973a) Covert modeling and the reduction of avoidance behavior. J Abnorm Psychol 81:87–95
Kazdin AE (1973b) The effects of suggestion and pretesting on avoidance reduction in fearful subjects. J Behav Ther Exp Psychiatry 4:213–221
Kegan R, Rogers L, Quinlan D (1981) The developmental organization of depression. APA symposium on new approaches to depression, Los Angeles, California
Kelly G (1955) The psychology of personal constructs. Norton, New York
Kitchener K, King P (1981) Reflective judgment: concepts of justification and their relationship to age and education. J Appl Devel Psych 2:89–116
Kohlberg L (1969) Stage and sequence: the cognitive-developmental approach to socialization. In: Goslin D (ed) Handbook of socialization theory and research. Rand McNally, Chicago
Kohlberg L (1976) Moral stages and moralization: the cognitive-developmental approach. In: Lickona T (ed) Moral development and behavior. Holt, Rinehart, and Winston, New York
Kohlberg L (1981, 1983) Essays in moral development, vols 1 and 2. Harper and Row, New York
Landy R (1983) The use of distancing in drama therapy. The Arts in Psychotherapy 10:175–185
Luria A (1961) The role of speech in the regulation of normal and abnormal behaviors. Liveright, New York
Mahoney MJ (1974) Cognition and behavior modification. Ballinger, Cambridge
Mahoney MJ (1976) Scientist as subject: the psychological imperative. Ballinger, Cambridge
Mahoney MJ (1979) Psychology of the scientist: an evaluative review. Social Studies Sci 9:349–375
Mahoney MJ (1980) Psychotherapy and the structure of personal revolutions. In: Mahoney M (ed) Psychotherapy process. Plenum, New York
Mahoney MJ (1983) Knowledge and power, privilege and privacy. Newsletter of the Society for the Advancement of Social Psychology 9:16–22
Mahoney MJ (1985) Psychotherapy and human change processes. In: Mahoney M, Freeman A (eds) Cognition and psychotherapy. Plenum, New York
Mahoney MJ (1986) Participatory epistemology and psychology of science. 1st american conference on psychology of science, April 1986, Memphis, Tennessee
Mahoney MJ, DeMonbreun BG (1977) Psychology of the scientist: an analysis of problem solving bias. Cognitive Therapy and Research 1:229–238
Mahoney MJ, Kimper TP (1976) From ethics to logic: a survey of scientists. In: Mahoney M (ed) Scientist as subject: the psychological imperative. Ballinger, Cambridge
Mahoney MJ, Mahoney K (1976) Permanent weight control. Norton, New York
McKinney J (1973) Problem solving strategies in impulsive and reflective second graders. Devel Psych 8:145
Mead GH (1934) Mind, self and society. University of Chicago Press, Chicago
Meichenbaum D (1974) Cognitive behavior modification. General Learning Press, Morristown
Meichenbaum D (1975) Enhancing creativity by modifying what subjects say to themselves. American Educational Research Journal 12:129–145
Meichenbaum (1977) Cognitive-behavior modification: an integrative approach. Plenum, New York
Minuchin S, Fishman C (1981) Family therapy techniques. Harvard University Press, Cambridge
Monroe RA (1971) Journeys out of the body. Doubleday, New York
Moreno J (1923) Das Stegreiftheater. Kiepenheuer, Berlin
Moreno J (1946, 1959, 1962) Psychodrama, vols 1, 2 and 3. Beacon House, New York
Novaco R (1975) Anger control: the development and evaluation of an experimental treatment. Heath, Lexington
Peale NV (1960) The power of positive thinking. Prentice-Hall, Englewood Cliffs

Peixoto E (1986) Problem solving strategies and dialectic self-monitoring in mastery learning and conventional instruction. Thesis, University of the Azores, Portugal
Perls F, Clements C (1977) Acting out vs. acting through. In: Stevens J (ed) Gestalt is. Bantam, New York
Phelps S, Austin N (1975) The assertive woman. Impact, San Luis Obispo
Piaget J (1968) Le structuralisme. Presses Universitaires de France, Paris
Piaget J (1970) L'épistémologie génétique. Presses Universitaires de France, Paris
Piaget J (1975) L'equilibration des structures cognitives: problème central du développement. Presses Universitaires de France, Paris
Piaget J, Inhelder B (1955) De la logique de l'enfant à la logique de l'adolescent. Presses Universitaires de France, Paris
Piaget J, Inhelder B (1963) Les opérations intellectuelles et leur développement. Traité de Psychologie Expérimentale, vol 7. Presses Universitaires de France, Paris
Rapaport D (1951) The organization and pathology of thought. Columbia University Press, New York
Riegel K (1975) The development of dialectical operations. Karger, Basel
Riegel K (1976) The dialectics of human development. Am Psychologist 31:689–700
Scheff TJ (1979) Catharsis in healing, ritual and drama. University of California Press, Berkeley
Scheff TJ (1981) The distancing of emotion in psychotherapy. Psychotherapy: Theory, Research and Practice 18:46–53
Schultz JH (1935) Uebungsheft fur das Autogene Training. Thieme, Leipzig
Selman R (1980) The growth of interpersonal understanding. Academic, New York
Turk D, Speers M (1983) Cognitive schemata and cognitive processes in cognitive-behavioral interventions: going beyond the information given. In: Kendall P (ed) Advances in cognitive-behavioral research and therapy, vol 2. Academic New York
Vygotsky LS (1962) Thought and language. MIT Press, Cambridge
Watson J (1924) Behaviorism. University of Chicago Press, Chicago
Weimer WB (1980) Psychotherapy and philosophy of science: examples of a two-way street in search of traffic. In: Mahoney M (ed) Psychotherapy process. Plenum, New York
Weimer WB (1982) Hayek's approach to complex phenomena. In: Weimer W, Palermo D (eds) Cognition and the symbolic processes, vol 2. Erlbaum, Hillsdale
Wolpe J, Lazarus AA (1966) Behavior therapy techniques. Pergamon, New York
Wundt W (1886) Éléments de psychologie physiologique, vol 2. Alcan, Paris

Cognitive Therapy for Bulimia

F.M. McPherson

Introduction

The behaviour of binge eating, or compulsive eating, i.e. consuming large quantities of food in short periods and beyond the point of subjective hunger, has been reported in obese individuals (e.g. Stunkard 1959; Marcus et al. 1985), in anorexic patients (e.g. Beumont et al. 1976; Garfinkel and Garner 1982) and in people of normal weight (e.g. Wardle 1980; Edelman 1981). Various operational definitions have been proposed which specify, for example, the amount eaten (Katzman et al. 1984) or the length of the episode (American Psychiatric Association 1980). However, the crucial feature which distinguishes binge eating from normal excessive eating is that the episode is experienced as being outside the control of the eater (Abraham and Beumont 1982; Fairburn 1983).

Although binge eating can occur as a relatively isolated phenomenon (e.g. Wardle 1980), it may also occur as a central feature of a constellation of behaviours which, when occurring in normal-weight individuals, is variously termed bulimarexia (Boskind-Lodahl 1976), the dietary chaos syndrome (Palmer 1979), bulimia nervosa (Russell 1979) and bulimia (American Psychiatric Association 1980). These terms are not used identically, but the constellation denoted usually involves, in addition to binge eating, self-induced vomiting or the abuse of purgatives and preoccupation with body weight and shape.

As yet there is no general agreement about the definition or labelling of this constellation. This chapter will therefore use the term 'bulimia', unless indicated otherwise, to refer to any constellation of eating and weight-related behaviours occurring in normal-weight individuals which has binge eating as a central feature. 'Binge eating' will refer to the behaviour of compulsive eating, however defined. The bulimic individual will be referred to as female, but both sexes will be implied unless stated otherwise.

Since bulimia has only relatively recently begun to be described and studied, this chapter will start with an account of the main features of the constellation.

Tayside Area Clinical Psychology Department, Royal Dundee Liff Hospital, Dundee DD2 5 NF, Scotland. United Kingdom

Features of Bulimia

Information about bulimia is available not only from descriptions of patients attending psychiatric hospitals (e.g. Russell 1979; Fairburn and Cooper 1984a) but also from interviews with, and questionnaire responses of, individuals who have approached clinics for help (e.g. Johnson et al. 1983; Cullari and Redmon 1984). Additional information has been provided by women who have responded to television or newspaper invitations in the United Kingdom (Fairburn and Cooper 1984b), Australia (Huon 1985) and France (Aimez and Michant 1986). Bulimics and binge eaters have also been identified in surveys of students (e.g. Halmi et al. 1981; Katzman et al. 1984; Leon et al. 1985) and in community samples such as among those attending family planning clinics (Cooper and Fairburn 1983; Cooper et al. 1984), at a general practice (Yeap et al. 1987) and among suburban shoppers (Pope et al. 1984).

These studies tend to support the following generalisations:

Personal Characteristics. The great majority of bulimics are *female*. *Age* of onset of binge eating is in the late teens and that of self-induced vomiting – if this occurs – about one year later. Those so far identified tend to be from *middle- or upper-class* backgrounds. Although their *weight* may currently be within normal limits, many have a previous history of extreme weight loss or of being overweight, and many are also attempting to attain a weight below the recommended ideal for their height and build. Of those who regard themselves as having an eating disorder a large proportion do not seek *professional help,* and those who do typically wait for 5 or more years after the onset of the condition.

Eating Behaviour. Most *restrict* their food intake, either in general by eating small amounts or by missing meals or avoiding a range of foods regarded as 'fattening'. The *binges* which are interspersed throughout these periods of restraint may be planned but often are precipitated by the breaking of dietary rules or by dysphoric feelings. These may last for only 15–30 min or for several hours. The modal frequency is about once per day, although instances of six or more discrete episodes per day have been reported. The binges mostly occur in late afternoon or early evening; although usually taking place at home, binge eating is almost invariably carried out in secret. The *caloric intake* during a binge varies considerably, with 5 000–10 000 cal per episode being common; the food consumed is often highly caloric, of a sort normally avoided, and is easily prepared and of a texture that makes swallowing easy. Binge eating is seldom *terminated* voluntarily and usually ends because of physical exhaustion or discomfort, social interruption, absence of food or self-induced vomiting.

Compensatory Behaviour. Whether or not all bulimic individuals also purge themselves depends upon the definition of bulimia; certainly not all those who binge eat also induce *vomiting,* although a high proportion do so. In most cases vomiting is used as a weight-control method, but in others it serves to alleviate the unpleasant physical sensations consequent upon a binge; many binge eaters discover these uses of vomiting for themselves although others obtain the idea from the mass media or from friends. The most commonly reported frequency of vomiting is once daily. Although less common than vomiting, *laxatives* are also often used, either on their own or together with vomiting, usually in excess of the recommended dose and frequency; *diuretics* are also used by some binge eaters.

Concomitants. Depressive symptoms are frequently reported by bulimic individuals, as is *anxiety,* in particular in connection with eating. *Physical* disorders are common, the most serious being due to potassium loss caused by vomiting and laxative abuse; the subsequent hypokalaemia in some cases causes cardiac arrhythmias, renal damage or epileptic seizures. Some bulimic women, on the other hand, show few or no signs of physical damage. *Social relationships* are often reported to be poor, as is *work performance.* A high proportion of bulimic individuals admit to *stealing* food and other items. As will be discussed in more detail below, characteristic *cognitions* are reported – in particular, preoccupation with, and extreme sensitivity to, changes in body weight and shape.

Categorisation of Bulimia

The two main psychiatric approaches to the categorisation of these factors are those of Russell (1979), modified by Fairburn (1983), and of DSM-III (American Psychiatric Association 1980). Important differences exist between these sets of diagnostic criteria, in particular the greater emphasis placed by Russell upon preoccupation with fatness – reflecting his hypothesis that bulimia is a variant of anorexia nervosa. More generally, the relationship between bulimia and anorexia – in particular the 'bulimic anorexia' subcategory (Beumont et al. 1976) – remains the subject of debate (e.g. Garfinkel and Kaplan 1986) as does the association of bulimia, depressive illness and depressed mood (Cooper and Fairburn 1986; Katz 1987).

Psychiatrically derived categories are often of limited relevance to cognitive, or other psychological, models (Hallam 1983), and as yet there have been no systematic attempts to devise a classificatory system for bulimia derived from psychological principles and processes.

Prevalence

Disagreements about definitions have led to difficulties in establishing the incidence and prevalence of bulimia, as also have the reliance of most investigators on self-report measures and ad hoc samples.

The proportion of young women who report ever having *binged* has been reported as very high in some female student groups, e.g. 64.6% (Touyz and Ivison 1985), and quite high among non-students. Thus, 20.9% of women attending a family-planning clinic reported having binged during the previous 2 months, while recent *self-induced vomiting* and *laxative abuse* was reported by 2.9% and 4.9%, respectively (Cooper et al. 1984).

The point prevalence of bulimia as defined by Russell (1979) or DSM-III is usually reported to be between 1.4 and 1.9% in young female populations (e.g. Yeap et al. 1988; Pyle et al. 1983; Cooper et al. 1984) although much higher figures have been reported (e.g. Pope et al. 1984) especially in female student samples (e.g. Touyz and Iveson 1985).

Cognitive Aspects of Bulimia

A cognitive model of bulimia has been outlined by Garner (1986), and features involved in the maintenance of the condition have been described in more detail by Fairburn et al. (1986). Many of the factors relevant to anorexia nervosa, discussed by Garner and Bemis (1982, 1985), Slade (1982) and others, are possibly also relevant.

It seems unlikely that a wholly cognitive explanation will prove adequate. After reviewing various theories, Agras and Kirkley (1986) conclude that both biological and sociobehavioural conditions are implicated, a conclusion suggested also by Wardle's (1987b) comparison of compulsive eating and addiction. Further, by analogy with other conditions such as depression, it is probable that bulimia is a final common pathway which can be reached in a variety of ways, each involving a different combination of biological and sociobehavioural variables. However, an account of some of the cognitive processes implicated in bulimia might prove useful, both in the building of a comprehensive model of the condition and also in identifying targets for therapeutic intervention.

The Basic Premise. Central to the cognitive model is the assumption that bulimics have dysfunctional beliefs and values about their shape and weight, and that these are of primary importance in the development and maintenance of the condition. "Thus, the extreme dieting, the vomiting and laxative abuse, the preoccupation with food and eating, the sensitivity to shape and weight . . . , even the apparently paradoxical binge eating can be understood in cognitive terms" (Fairburn 1985a, pp. 160–161).

Some elements of this model will now be discussed in greater detail.

Cultural Value of Slimness. It has been widely documented that Western society has been structured such that "Power, prestige, deferrence and attention are granted to 'beautiful' women" (S.C. Woolley and O.W. Woolley 1985, p. 391), and that beauty tends to be equated with slim body shapes (Furnham and Alibhai 1983). The mass media, which play an important part in moulding and perpetrating societal preferences (Faust 1983), have increasingly valued thin, light female bodies while the actual average size and weight of young women has been increasing (Garner et al. 1980).

Possibly as a consequence of these societal influences, many young women set for themselves target, or 'ideal', body weights which are unrealistically low for their height and build (e.g. Huon and Brown 1984) and many express a dissatisfaction with their bodies which increases between the ages of 12 and 18 years (Davies and Furnham 1986a). Many girls and young women regard themselves as fat even when within normal weight limits (Wardle and Beales 1986; Davies and Furnham 1986b). Slim body build, in addition to being regarded as physically attractive, is associated with a wide range of desirable personality characteristics (e.g. Brenver and Hinsdale 1978).

There is some slight empirical evidence relating body dissatisfaction and bulimia. College women with 'DSM-III bulimia' have a poorer body image than controls (Katzman and Wolchik 1984). The best predictors of bulimia were found in one study to be 'extent of satisfaction with body image' (Wolf and Crowther 1983), while in another the best indicators were 'self-body evaluation' and the bulimic woman's belief that her mother was critical of her (the daughter's) body (Debs et al. 1983, reported in Woolley and Woolley 1985). In a third study, scores on the Body Dissatisfaction scale of the Eating Disorders Inventory (Garner et al. 1983) correlated significantly with scores on the Eating Attitudes Test (Garner and Garfinkel 1979), an index of the symptoms of anorexia nervosa (Cooper et al. 1985).

The direct link between body dissatisfaction and bulimia may be dieting, which often begins as a consequence of such dissatisfaction (Huenemann et al. 1966) and is now very widespread among young women (Schleimer 1983; Wardle and Beales 1986). Thus, in one study, 22.5% of 14-year-old girls were dieting when questioned, and 55% had considered doing so (Davies and Furnham 1986b).

Need for Self-Control. Dieting is encouraged also by the need for self-control, which is frequently described in the clinical literature as being characteristic of both anorexic and bulimic women (e.g. Garner and Bemis 1982). Slade (1982) has proposed that personal dissatisfaction, e.g. due to interpersonal problems or failure at college, interacting with her perfectionistic tendencies (Halmi et al. 1977), cause the woman to attempt to achieve success by controlling one aspect of her life – what Kelly (1955) describes as the 'constriction' of the construct system. Her body is one of the few aspects over which she can achieve absolute control; hence, she diets.

Cognitive Assumptions and Distortions. Reflecting the cultural value placed upon slimness, the woman develops a coherent body of beliefs centred round the fundamental, underlying assumption that "weight, shape and thinness can serve as the sole or predominant referant for inferring personal value or self-worth" (Garner and Bemis 1982, p. 142). She can therefore maintain her self-worth only by ensuring that her weight and shape remain strictly under control. Regular weighing is thus a means by which the woman can immediately assess her self-value, and the extreme happiness or gloom which follows – even upon slight fluctuations in weight – are explicable in terms of their great implications for her self-evaluation.

This fundamental assumption, that value is assessed only or mainly by weight, is protected by *cognitive distortions* of the type described by Beck et al. (1979) but with weight-related content. Garner and Bemis (1982) and Garner (1986) give examples of reasoning errors which are typical of anorexic patients and which are likely to be similar to those of bulimic women. *Superstitious thinking,* reflecting belief in cause-effect relationships of non-contingent events, is illustrated by their assumption that even very small amounts of food will result in greatly increased deposits of body fat ("If I eat a sweet, I will put on pounds") and their persistence with vomiting and laxative abuse in the face of evidence of their ineffectiveness as fat-avoiding techniques. *Dichotomous reasoning,* involving thinking in extreme, all-or-none terms, is typically applied to food, eating and weight. Days are divided into 'good' and 'bad' according to whether a strict diet was adhered to, and food is similarly dichotomised into 'fattening' (to be avoided) and 'non-fattening'. No middle ground is seen to exist between thinness and gross obesity or between rigid restraint and uncontrolled gluttony, so that "If I gain one pound I will go on to gain 100". *Personalisation,* the egocentric interpretation of events, is often illustrated by the woman's conviction that other people are as sensitive as she is herself to minor fluctuations in her weight. *Selective abstraction,* the focusing on isolated details while ignoring more salient, contradictory evidence, is illustrated when the woman judges her success or effectiveness solely in terms of her weight or dietary restraint, taking no account of her performance socially, educationally and in other aspects of her life.

Although there is some evidence that bulimic women *over-estimate the size* of their own bodies (Freeman et al. 1984), possibly more important than how they actually see themselves is how they *think* they look (Whitehouse et al. 1986). Clinical accounts emphasise that many bulimic women misconstrue what they see and experience, e.g. by interpreting feelings of 'fullness', or slight temporary increases in the protrusion of the stomach, as evidence of significant weight gain.

In addition to these dysfunctional assumptions and values concerning body weight and shape, many bulimic women also appear to show similar thinking in relation to *self-evaluation in general.* Self-esteem is often evaluated exclusively against idealised, external standards and by comparison with others and almost never against self-defined goals and the experience of pleasure. Self-control is over-valued and underlying assumptions such as "My parents and family are inevitably better than me" are common (Garner 1986).

Binge Eating and Dietary Restraint. Binge eating and purging frequently begin after a weight-reduction diet (e.g. Cullari and Redmon 1984). Normal-weight binge eaters also tend to report high levels of dietary restraint (e.g. Pyle et al. 1981) while bulimic patients often practise severe restraint before and after binges (Garner et al. 1983).

The relationship between dietary restraint and binge eating has been the focus of many surveys and laboratory experiments and of two recent theoretical reviews (Polivy and Herman 1985; Wardle 1987b). Various studies have illustrated a counter-regulation, or disinhibition, effect of restrained eating upon clinically normal dieters. After a small, forced preload they eat little or no food ad lib and so maintain their diet; after being forced to eat a large preload of high-calorie food, they typically eat large quantities of food ad lib. Non-dieters typically behave more logically by eating less after the large preload (Herman and Polivy 1980). The behaviour of restrained eaters is similar to that reported by many bulimics (Abraham and Beumont 1982).

Herman and Polivy (1984) argue that just as dieting is a cognitively mediated activity, undertaken for personal reasons and often at variance with physiological well-being (Polivy and Herman 1985), so this disinhibitory effect is influenced more by cognitive than by physiological factors. Their boundary model of the regulation of food intake proposes that restrained dieters have learned to regulate their intake according to cognitive rules rather than the hunger cues which influence normal eaters. While they believe their diets to be intact, with themselves in control, they eat little; however, when they believe their diets have been violated, or that they cannot control their intake, these cognitive restraints are relaxed and they eat to a satiety boundary which has been elevated above normal by the psychobiological effects of chronic restraint.

Clinical research tends to support this postulated relationship between restraint and binge eating. Thus, Hawkins and Clement (1980), employing a self-report measure, reported a positive association between degree of dietary restraint and the severity of binge-eating.

Binge Eating and Stress. Clinical and research evidence suggests that amongst people who severely restrict their food intake dysphoric mood states lead to overeating (Cooper and Bowskill 1986). This may be because negative mood states reduce the woman's control over her eating. Women with poor coping skills might also use binge eating as a means of stress reduction. However, this distraction from anxiety causes additional stress because the women then tend to regard their eating habits as abnormal and their ability to cope as inadequate. Their self-esteem is thus lowered and their depression and anxiety increased. This in turn reduces their capacity to cope with stress and leads to further binges (Hawkins and Clement 1984; Johnson and Larson 1982; Weiss et al. 1985).

Development of Self-Induced Vomiting. Fairburn (1981) and Rosen and Leitenberg (1982) suggest that self-induced vomiting is initially a response to extreme anxiety about possible weight gain and the feelings of subjective discomfort which follow binge eating; laxative abuse can be regarded similarly. One possibility is that purging serves to return the individual to a state of hunger and deprivation which increases the probability of further binge eating, but which temporarily allows the woman to believe that once more she is in control of her eating. Rosen and Leitenburg emphasise the role of vomiting as "an escape response that is reinforced by the subsequent reduction in anxiety about weight.... Binge-eating usually only occurs in anticipation of vomiting ...." (Rosen and Leitenburg 1985, p. 196).

Targets of Treatment

From this outline model, several treatment targets can be identified.

Development of Realistic Attitudes to Body Weight and Shape. The cognitive approach assumes that the dysfunctional beliefs and values about body weight and shape which are described in bulimic women are not merely symptomatic but are of primary importance in the development and maintenance of the condition. Major targets of treatment are therefore to identify and modify the *underlying assumptions* about weight and shape which can be inferred from the woman's thinking and behaviour, including those which reflect the general cultural value placed upon slimness. *Reasoning errors* such as dichotomous thinking and selective abstraction also require correction. Assumptions to do with *body shape* and *bodily sensations* are particularly important targets.

Establishment of Normal Pattern of Eating. Following from the hypothesis that binge eating is associated with dietary restraint, another major target is to reduce restraint in its two forms, i.e. to establish a regular pattern of eating and to reduce adherence to a highly selective diet of 'non-fattening' foods.

Reduction of Binge Eating, Vomiting and Laxative Abuse. Treatment of bulimia is often evaluated according to its success in reducing the frequency with which the woman engages in episodes of binge eating, vomiting and laxative abuse. However, opinions differ as to whether these behaviours need to be the target of specific interventions, or whether, as implied by Fairburn (1985a), they will disappear after the introduction of a normal pattern of eating.

Improvement of Personal Functioning. According to the model certain long-standing aspects of *personality* predispose women to develop maladaptive methods of weight control when confronted by the ideal of thinness, e.g. the tendency to evaluate self-esteem against idealised, external standards and the high value placed upon self-control. In addition, the absence of effective means of *coping* with stress or negative feelings may result in eating being used for stress reduction. Finally, binge eating and vomiting may well precipitate *depression, anxiety* and *social withdrawal.* Treatment may therefore be required in some or all of these areas.

Establishment of Motivation for Treatment. The importance of encouraging the patient's motivation for treatment has been acknowledged in cognitive therapy (e.g. Beck et al. 1979) as in most other psychological treatments. It has been emphasised particularly in connection with the cognitive therapy of anorexia nervosa because of the tendency of anorexic patients to deny the abnormality, and even existence, of their weight loss and because of the positive reinforcement which they are assumed to receive from this loss (Garner 1986). The need to establish motivation is less obvious with bulimic women who often welcome treatment as a means of alleviating the stress caused to them by the physical and social consequences of bingeing and purging and by their feelings of loss of control. Although many postpone the decision to seek treatment, this is due to the guilt and shame accompanying the disorder rather than because of low motivation. On the other hand, the woman may well regard the reduction of bingeing and vomiting as the only treatment goal. She may be reluctant initially to regard the examination of her underlying assumptions and values as relevant, or if they are so regarded, she may be anxious about the prospect of change. One explicit goal of the early stages of treatment must therefore be to establish in the woman a wish to bring about change in her cognitions.

Relapse Prevention. Many of the cognitive and behavioural skills which the women acquire during treatment will serve a protective function and will reduce chances of subsequent stress leading to the re-establishment of disordered eating. However, the work by Marlatt (1982) in the field of addiction suggests the importance of including as an explicit target for treatment the training of the women to use self control procedures at times of likely relapse (Fairburn 1981).

Assessment in Cognitive Therapy

The assessment of bulimic women has been discussed by Johnson (1985) and Johnson and Pure (1986) and in connection with cognitive psychotherapy by Fairburn (1985a).

Usually, self-recorded diaries are kept of normal and binge eating, vomiting and laxative use and of the emotional, social and physical antecedents and consequences (Wardle 1987c). Various objective techniques exist for measuring 'body image' (McCrea et al. 1982), and there are several questionnaire measures of eating attitudes and style, e.g. the Eating Attitudes Test (Garner and Garfinkel 1979), the Restraint Scale (Herman and Mack 1975; Blanchard and Frost 1983), the Three-Factor Eating Questionnaire (Stunkard and Messick 1985) and the Dutch Eating Behaviour Questionnaire (Van Strien et al. 1986; Wardle 1987a) and of the tendency to binge eat (Hawkins and Clement 1980). Only one inventory, however, specifically addresses itself to the cognitive distortions present in anorexia and bulimia, the Eating Disorder Inventory (Garner et al. 1983). Some evidence for its validity is reported by Cooper et al. (1985).

Therapeutic Approaches

Fairburns Cognitive-Behavioural Therapy. The first, and most detailed, account of cognitive-behavioural treatment of bulimia was by Fairburn (1981, 1985a). This is an individual, outpatient programme of approximately 20 sessions. It illustrates the 'two-track' approach advocated by Garner in connection with anorexia nervosa, with one track aimed at the normalisation of the woman's eating and physical condition and the other, parallel, track concerned with "the more complex task of assessing and modifying misconceptions reflected in self-concept deficiencies, perfectionism, separation or autonomy fears, and disturbed relationships" (Garner 1986, p. 304).

The first phase of treatment, of about eight twice-weekly sessions, has the following aims: to establish a sound therapeutic relationship; to provide information about the physical dangers of binge eating, self-induced vomiting and laxative abuse and about the ineffectiveness of these last two as means of weight control; to enlist the co-operation of friends and relatives; to establish regular weekly weighings; to examine the 'function' of binge eating and self-induced vomiting; to disrupt the habitual pattern of binge eating, self-induced vomiting and laxative abuse; and to introduce a pattern of regular eating.

During the second phase, of approximately eight weekly sessions, the aims are: to establish and maintain a pattern of regular eating; to reduce dietary restraint; to identify the circumstances that tend to result in binge eating and to help the patient to cope more effectively with such circumstances and reduce the frequency of their occurrence; to identify and challenge thoughts, beliefs, and values that are perpetuating the eating problem; to help the patient deal with body image misperception and body image disparagement and to raise the issue of termination.

The third phase, of approximately three fortnightly sessions, aims to ensure that progress is maintained and to prepare for future difficulties.

Fairburn describes a variety of cognitive, behavioural and educational techniques. To identify and modify dysfunctional thoughts and beliefs, methods similar to those of Beck et al. (1979) are employed. The final phase of treatment employs cognitive-behavioural methods which are similar to those used for 'relapse prevention' in the treatment of addictive behaviour (Marlett 1982).

Behavioural methods are frequently used to bring about cognitive changes. Dietary restraint is reduced by the gradual establishment of a regular pattern in eating, with three or four meals plus planned snacks daily, and the gradual introduction into the women's diet of previously 'forbidden' foods. Exposure is used to deal with 'body image disparagement'.

Perhaps the most controversial aspect of this approach is that bulimia is conceptualised as a disorder of eating control, so that "vomiting per se does not need to be tackled, since in the great majority of cases it ceases once the patient has stopped overeating" (Fairburn 1985a, p. 174).

Other Cognitive Approaches. A modification of Fairburn's method, for use in groups, was reported by Schneider and Agras (1985). The cognitive therapy approach to anorexia nervosa described by Garner and Bemis (1982, 1985) can, with some alterations, be used also with bulimic patients. In these accounts, the authors describe in some detail the cognitive methods employed, which are largely adaptations of those of Beck et al. (1979), for example: articulation of beliefs, decentring, decatastrophising, challenging the 'should's' and reattribution techniques. Emphasis is also placed upon challenging cultural values regarding shape and weight. Cognitive methods for improving self-esteem and self-awareness are also described. In addition, various behavioural and educational methods are used.

It is difficult to compare the approach of Garner and Bemis (1982, 1985) with that of Fairburn (1981, 1985a). From the written accounts, the former appears to be somewhat less didactic and also to place the various techniques more firmly within the cognitive model. For example, weight gain and modification of eating patterns are construed as experiments through which the woman can test particular beliefs and assumptions.

The 'cognitive restructuring' used by Wilson et al. (1986) was similar to Beck's (1976) cognitive therapy but from which specific behavioural assignments were excluded. A method of identifying and changing incorrect and self-defeating attitudes, derived from the Goldfried and Davison (1976) model of rational restructuring, itself developed from the work of Ellis (1962), was used by Yates and Sambrailo (1984). Covert modelling, covert assertion and thought-management exercises, adapted from M.J. Mahoney and K. Mahoney's (1976) 'cognitive ecology' procedures, were used by Long and Cordle (1982). Women were encouraged to recognise and evaluate their maladaptive thoughts and feelings and to use behaviour-altering skills.

Exposure and Response Prevention. The anxiety model of bulimia which holds that vomiting is similar to the compulsive behaviour of obsessionals in that it is anxiety-reducing and hence maintains the binge eating (Rosen and Leitenberg 1982) has led to the use of exposure and vomit prevention. Thus, the woman binge eats in the presence of the therapist who encourages her not to vomit and discusses her thoughts and feelings about not having done so (Wilson et al. 1986). It is included here because Wilson (1986), following Beck et al. (1979), notes that exposure can produce cognitive changes by providing evidence that 'should's' can be ignored without dire consequences.

Other Methods. The wide range of behavioural, pharmacological, group, psychodynamic, self-help and other non-cognitive methods which have been employed in the treatment of bulimia have been reviewed recently by Griffiths et al. (1987), Fairburn (1985b) and Wilson (1986).

Outcome Studies of Therapy

Many psychological approaches to the treatment of bulimia involve some element of what is usually termed 'cognitive restructuring'. This section, however, will concern mainly those approaches whose central focus is the identification and modification of dysfunctional cognitions.

Uncontrolled Studies. Several uncontrolled evaluations report good results. Fairburn (1981) reported the effectiveness of the cognitive-behavioural approach described above. Of 11 patients who had binged and induced vomiting for a mean of 3.9 years and who vomited about three times daily, nine reduced their frequency of binge eating and vomiting to less than once per month; improvements were also reported in anxiety and depression and in the intensity of their dysfunctional attitudes to body weight and shape. Seven patients who were followed up for an average of almost 10 months had maintained their improvement. Fairburn adds that: "Subsequent experience with over 50 patients has confirmed that the majority of patients do indeed benefit from this cognitive-behavioural approach, with most remaining well and requiring no further treatment" (Fairburn 1985a, p. 161).

Encouraging results using this approach were also reported by Abraham et al. (1983) who reviewed 43 patients between 1 and 5 years after treatment. Assessed by interview, 40% were judged to be 'cured', in that body weight was stable, binge eating occurred less often than once monthly and no self-induced vomiting, laxative abuse or dieting were reported. A further 31%, who reported vomiting and laxative abuse less than once monthly and who employed 'suitable' methods of dieting, were judged to be 'improved'. Schneider and Agras (1985) adapted Fairburn's method for use in groups and reported that 13 women, treated in two groups, decreased their mean number of vomiting episodes from 24 to 2.2 weekly, with concomitant improvements in eating attitudes, depression and assertiveness; follow-up at 6 months showed only slight evidence of relapse. That these results were less good than those of Fairburn (1981) was attributed by Schneider and Agras to the greater severity of the disorder in their patients, to the shorter treatment (16 as opposed to 28 sessions) and to their failure to employ specific relapse-prevention strategies.

The 'cognitive ecology' procedures of M.J. Mahoney and K. Mahoney (1976) were among several techniques used by Long and Cordle (1982) in their successful treatment of two patients.

Controlled Studies. In a well-designed study, Fairburn et al. (1986b) contrasted the effects of the Fairburn (1981) approach with those of a form of structured psychotherapy which focussed on difficulties hypothesised to "underlie" eating problems. Both groups showed significant improvement, maintained over a 12-month follow-up period, in specific psychopathology such as attitudes to eating and frequency of self-induced vomiting, in general psychopathology including depression and in social adjustment. However, the 12 patients receiving the cognitive-behavioural treatment appeared to have done better than the 12 psychotherapy patients on several measures and indeed improved almost as dramatically as those reported by Fairburn (1981). Kirkley et al. (1985) compared the Schneider and Agras (1985) group method with a non-directive group procedure in which relevant problems, such as disordered eating, vomiting and stress, were discussed without specific interventions being proposed. At the end of treatment, only the cognitive-behavioural group showed reductions in the self-recorded frequency of binge eating and vomiting. However, at 3-month follow-up this advantage had disappeared.

Modest results were obtained in three other studies, although methodological limitations reduce their value. A treatment package which included cognitive restructuring along with other psychotherapeutic and behavioural interventions produced greater change than a waiting-list control group (Ordman and Kirschenbaum 1985). A 12-session cognitive-behavioural treatment was associated with improvement in bingeing and vomiting, maintained over 3–4 months, while a waiting-list control group showed no change (Lee and Rush, quoted in Wilson 1986). These authors note that "irrational attitudes towards body weight and shape were very difficult to alter", which is not surprising since apparently group discussion was the only method employed to identify and modify dysfunctional thoughts. Freeman et al. (1985) reported cognitive-behavioural therapy, individual behaviour therapy and educational group therapy to be equally effective.

Cognitive and Behavioural Methods. Three studies are relevant to the question of whether the *addition* of specific behavioural interventions enhances the effectiveness of cognitive therapy. Yates and Sambrailo (1984) compared a group which received cognitive therapy with one whose members in addition were given instruction in stimulus control, response delay and prevention, and other behavioural methods. Members of both groups showed some improvement after only six sessions, but the small number of patients precludes comparison of the two approaches.

Rossiter and Wilson (1985) used single-subject methodology with four patients and reported that relatively brief cognitive restructuring which was based wholly on verbal methods appeared to have minimal effects on binge eating and vomiting. However, the addition of exposure and vomit prevention appeared to produce significant improvement, maintained over 1 year, in binge eating, vomiting and attitudes to food and weight. These results were confirmed by Wilson et al. (1986) in a similar study of 17 patients. Verbal cognitive restructuring plus exposure and vomit prevention was significantly more effective than the former alone. Patients treated by the combined approach were totally free of binge eating and vomiting at 1-year follow-up and showed major changes in cognitions and feelings concerning food, as well as in their eating habits.

One study of a single case compared directly the effects of six sessions of exposure and response prevention and 10 sessions of cognitive intervention which included thought stopping/switching, covert sensitization and cognitive restructuring which involved the identification, evaluation and alteration of self-statements about the women's weight, eating and appearance. These cognitive interventions had no effect on the frequency of binging and vomiting urges and episodes, while exposure and response prevention was associated with significant improvement (Morin et al. 1987).

Methodological Aspects. These studies illustrate several methodological problems in the study of the outcome of treatments for bulimia. Because bulimia is a secretive condition, not amenable to observation, most studies are forced to rely on self-report measures. Standard definitions of "binges" are necessary since the amount of food consumed often decreases during treatment although the episodes continue to be labelled "binges" by the patient. There is no general agreement about what constitutes improvement and, for example, the extent to which changes in attitudes and values should be included along with reductions in frequency of binge eating, self-induced vomiting and laxative abuse. As the condition is episodic, with some women having lengthy spells of apparently spontaneous remission, long follow-up of outcome is required.

Process of Therapy

Components of Therapy. In most studies a mixture of cognitive, behavioural, educational and supportive techniques was employed. However, apart from those referred to above ("Cognitive and Behavioural Methods"), in none is it possible to identify the contribution of specific interventions.

Timing of Interventions. In treatment packages which include cognitive and behavioural methods, the timing of the various interventions is clearly important. Thus, Fairburn introduces cognitive methods only during the second phase of treatment because, in his experience, the women "are so demoralised by their loss of control and so preoccupied with food and eating that they are inaccessible to complex interventions" (Fairburn 1981, p. 710). Rossiter and Wilson (1984), on the other hand, note the reluctance of many women to undertake exposure and response prevention and recommend prior, intensive cognitive restructuring. No empirical evidence is available to guide decisions about timing.

Response to Treatment. Bulimic women form a heterogeneous group, and wide differences in response to treatment have been reported. However, there is no evidence which helps to identify the individuals who respond best to any cognitive treatment. Body weight, previous history of anorexia or obesity, abnormality of attitudes towards weight and shape, and available coping skills are factors which may be relevant, in addition to those found more generally to influence response to psychological treatment.

Conclusions

Cognitive Model. The above discussion suggests that while cognitive interpretations are possible of most of the major features and processes of bulimia, there is as yet almost no supporting empirical evidence. The cognitions of bulimic individuals have hardly at all been investigated systematically and never in ways which would enable any aetiological influence to be identified. The 'counter-regulation' explanation of binge eating relies mainly upon laboratory studies of unknown relevance, some of which are weakened by unsatisfactory measures (Fairburn et al. 1986a). The bulimic women's alleged need for self-control and adoption of cultural values concerning weight is confirmed for the most part only by uncontrolled, clinical observation.

Nevertheless, various 'cognitive' accounts of bulimia have gained a remarkable degree of acceptance, possibly because they appear credible to clinicians (Fairburn et al. 1986a), and because they allow some of the goals of therapeutic intervention to be identified.

Therapeutic Studies. The methodological limitations of most of the few, controlled outcome studies – few subjects, short periods of intervention, short follow-up, reliance on subjective measures of change – preclude confident conclusions about the effectiveness of cognitive methods in the treatment of bulimia. There is some evidence that distorted attitudes towards shape and weight can be altered more effectively by behavioural methods, such as exposure and response prevention, than by verbal methods alone. It is not clear whether a combination of verbal and behavioural methods is more effective than the latter alone; if so, there is little to guide the timing of the various interventions. Research is required on these topics and on questions relating to the measurement of outcome and the selection of women for treatment.

Until the necessary research in these areas is undertaken, cognitive methods of treating bulimia, and the cognitive model in general, can be regarded as no more than promising and as potentially of value.

Acknowledgement. I am grateful to Mrs. Margaret Ferrier for her expert and efficient secretarial assistance.

References

Abraham SF, Beumont PJV (1982) How patients describe bulimia or binge eating. Psychol Med 12:625–635
Abraham SF, Mira M, Llewellyn-Jones D (1983) Bulimia: a study of outcome. Int J Eating Disord 2:175–180
Agras WS, Kirkley BG (1986) Bulimia: theories of etiology. In: Brownell KD, Foreyt JP (eds) Handbook of eating disorders. Basic Books, New York, pp 367–378
Aimez P, Michant S (1986) Bulimia nervosa in France. In: Lacey JH, Sturgeon DA (eds) Proceedings of the 15th European Conference on Psychosomatic Research. John Libbey
American Psychiatric Association (1980) Diagnostic and statistical manual of mental disorders, 3rd edn. APA, Washington DC
Beck AT (1976) Cognitive therapy and the emotional disorders. International University Press, New York
Beck AT, Rush AJ, Shaw BF, Emery G (1979) Cognitive therapy for depression: a treatment manual. Guilford, New York
Beumont PJV, George GCW, Smart DE (1976) 'Dieters' and 'vomiters and purgers' in anorexia nervosa. Psychol Med 6:617–622
Blanchard FA, Frost RO (1983) Two factors of restraint: concern for dieting and weight fluctuation. Behav Res Ther 21:259–267
Boskind-Lodahl M (1976) Cinderella's step-sisters: a feminist perspective on anorexia nervosa and bulimia. Signs: J Woman Cult 2:342–356
Brenver D, Hinsdale G (1978) Body build stereotypes and self-identification in three age group of females. Adolescence 13:551–561
Cooper PJ, Bowskill (1986) Dysphoric mood and overeating. Br J Clin Psychol 25:155–156
Cooper PJ, Fairburn CG (1983) Binge eating and self-induced vomiting in the community: a preliminary study. Br J Psychiatry 142:139–144
Cooper PJ, Fairburn CG (1984) Cognitive behaviour therapy for anorexia nervosa: some preliminary findings. J Psychosom Res 28:493–499
Cooper PJ, Fairburn CG (1986) The depressive features of bulimia nervosa. Br J Psychiatry 148:268–274
Cooper PJ, Waterman GC, Fairburn CG (1984) Women with eating problems: a community survey. Br J Clin Psychol 23:45–52
Cooper Z, Cooper PJ, Fairburn CG (1985) The specificity of the Eating Disorder Inventory. Br J Clin Psychol 24:129–130
Cullari S, Redmon WK (1984) Questionnaire responses from self-identified binge eaters and purgers. Psychol Rep 54:232–234
Davies E, Furnham A (1986a) Body satisfaction in adolescent girls. Br J Med Psychol 59:279–287
Davies E, Furnham A (1986b) The dieting and body shape concerns of adolescent females. J Child Psychol Psychiatry 27:417–428
Edelman B (1981) Binge eating in normal weight and overweight individuals. Psychol Rep 49:739–746
Ellis A (1962) Reason and emotion in psychotherapy. Lyle Stuart-Citadel, New York
Fairburn CG (1981) A cognitive behavioural approach to the treatment of bulimia. Psychol Med 11:707–711
Fairburn CG (1983) Bulimia nervosa. Br J Hosp Med June: 537–542
Fairburn CG (1985a) Cognitive-behavioural treatment for bulimia. In: Garner DM, Garfinkel PE (eds) Handbook of psychotherapy for anorexia nervosa and bulimia. Guilford, New York, pp 160–192
Fairburn CG (1985b) Review: the management of bulimia nervosa. J Psychiatr Res 19:465–472
Fairburn CG, Cooper PJ (1984a) The clinical features of bulimia nervosa. Br J Psychiatry 144:238–246
Fairburn CG, Cooper PJ (1984b) Binge-eating, self-induced vomiting and laxative abuse: a community study. Psychol Med 14:401–410

Fairburn CG, Cooper Z, Cooper PJ (1986a) The clinical features and maintenance of bulimia nervosa. In: Brownell KD, Foreyt JP (eds) Handbook of eating disorders. Basic Books, New York, pp 389–404
Fairburn CG, Kirk J, O'Connor M, Cooper PJ (1986b) A comparison of two psychological treatments for bulimia nervosa. Behav Res Ther 24:629–463
Faust MS (1983) Alternative constructions of adolescent growth. In: Brooks-Gunn J, Peterson AC (eds) Girls at puberty: biological and psychosocial perspectives. Plenum, New York
Freeman C, Sinclair F, Turnbull J, Annandale A (1985) Psychotherapy for bulimia: a controlled study. J Psychiatr Res 19:373–378
Freeman R, Thomas C, Solyown L, Hunter MA (1984) A modified video camera for measuring body image distortion: a technical description and reliability. Psychol Med 14:411–416
Furnham A, Alibhai N (1983) Cross-cultural differences in the perception of female body shapes. Psychol Med 13:829–837
Garfield PE, Kaplan AS (1986) Anorexia nervosa: diagnostic conceptualisations. In: Brownell KD, Foreyt JP (eds) Handbook of eating disorders. Basic Books, New York, pp 266–282
Garfinkel PE, Garner DM (1982) Anorexia nervosa. A multidimensional perspective. Brunner/Mazel, New York
Garner DM (1986) Cognitive therapy for anorexia nervosa. In: Brownell KD, Foreyt TJP (eds) Handbook of eating disorders. Basic Books, New York, pp 301–327
Garner DM, Bemis KM (1982) A cognitive-behavioural approach to anorexia nervosa. Cog Ther Res 6:123–150
Garner DM, Bemis KM (1985) Cognitive therapy for anorexia nervosa. In: Garner DM, Garfinkel PE (eds) Handbook of psychotherapy for anorexia nervosa and bulimia. Guilford, New York, 107–146
Garner DM, Garfinkel PE (1979) The Eating Attitudes Test: an index of the symptoms of anorexia nervosa. Psychol Med 9:273–279
Garner DM, Garfinkel PE, Schwartz D, Thompson M (1980) Cultural expectations of thinness in women. Psychol Rep 47:483–491
Garner DM, Olmsted MP, Polivy J (1983) Development and validation of a multi-dimensional eating disorder inventory for anorexia nervosa and bulimia. Int J Eating Disord 2:15–34
Goldfried MR, Davison CR (1976) Clinical behavior therapy. Holt, Reinhart and Wilson, New York
Griffiths RA, Touyz SW, Mitchell PB, Bacon W (1987) The treatment of bulimia nervosa. Aust NZ J Psychiatry 21:5–15
Hallam RS (1983) Agoraphobia: deconstructing a clinical syndrome. Bull Br Psychol Soc 36:337–340
Halmi KA, Goldberg SC, Eckert E, Casper R, Davis JM (1977) Pretreatment evaluation in anorexia nervosa. In: Vigersky RA (ed) Anorexia nervosa. Raven, New York
Halmi KA, Falk JR, Schwartz E (1981) Binge eating and vomiting: a survey of a college population. Psychol Med 11:697–706
Hawkins RC, Clement PF (1980) Development and construct validation of a self-report measure of binge eating tendencies. Addict Behav 5:219–226
Hawkins II RC, Clement PF (1984) Binge eating: measurement problems and a conceptual model. In: Hawkins RC II, Fremouw WJ, Clement PF (eds) The binge-purge syndrome. Springer, Berlin Heidelberg New York, pp 229–251
Herman CP, Mack D (1975) Restrained and unrestrained eating. J Pers 43:657–660
Herman CP, Polivy J (1980) Restrained eating. In: Stunkard AJ (ed) Obesity. Saunders, Philadelphia, pp 208–225
Herman CP, Polivy J (1984) A boundary model for the regulation of eating. In: Stunkard AJ, Elliot E (eds) Eating and its disorders. Raven, New York
Huenemann RL, Shapiro LR, Hampton MC, Mitchell BW (1966) A longitudinal study of gross body composition and body conformation and their association with food and activity in a teenage population. Am J Clin Nutr 18:325–338
Huon GF (1985) Bulimia: therapy at a distance. In: Touyz SW, Beumont PJV (eds) Eating disorders: prevalence and treatment. Williams and Wilkins, Sydney, pp 62–73
Huon G, Brown LB (1984) Psychological correlates of weight control among anorexia nervosa patients and normal girls. Br J Med Psychol 57:61–66
Johnson C (1985) Initial consultation for patients with bulimia and anorexia nervosa. In: Garner DM, Garfinkel PE (eds) Handbook of psychotherapy for anorexia nervosa and bulimia. Guilford, New York, pp 19–51

Johnson C, Larson R (1982) Bulimia: an analysis of moods and behaviour. Psychosom Med 44:341-351
Johnson C, Pure DL (1986) Assessment of bulimia: a multidimensional model. In: Brownell KD, Foreyt JP (eds) Handbook of eating disorders. Basic Books, New York, pp 405-449
Johnson C, Stuckey M, Lewis LD, Schwartz D (1983) Bulimia: a descriptive study of 509 cases. In: Darby PL, Garfinkel PE, Garner DM, Coscina DV (eds) Anorexia nervosa: recent developments. Liss, New York, pp 159-172
Katz JL (1987) Eating disorder and affective disorder: relatives or merely chance acquaintances? Compr Psychiatry 28:220-228
Katzman MA, Wolchik SA (1984) Bulimia and binge eating in college women: a comparison of personality and behavioural characteristics. J Consult Clin Psychol 52:423-428
Katzman MA, Wolchik SA, Braver SL (1984) The prevalence of frequent binge eating and bulimia in a nonclinical college population. Int J Eating Disord 3:53-62
Kelly GA (1955) The psychology of personal constructs. Norton, New York
Kirkley BG, Schneider JA, Agras WS, Bachman JA (1985) Comparison of two group treatments for bulimia. J Consult Clin Psychol 53:43-48
Leon GR, Carroll K, Chenyk B, Finn B (1985) Binge eating and associated habit patterns within college student and identified bulimic populations. Int J Eating Disord 4:43-47
Long CG, Cordle CJ (1982) Psychological treatment of binge eating and self-induced vomiting. Br J Med Psychol 55:139-145
Mahoney MJ, Mahoney K (1976) Permanent weight control. Norton, New York
Marcus MD, Wing RR, Lamparski DM (1985) Binge eating and dietary restraint in obese patients. Addict Behav 10:163-168
Marlatt GA (1982) Relapse prevention: a self control programme for the treatment of addictive behaviors. In: Stuart RB (ed) Adherence, compliance and generalisation in behavioural medicine. Brunner/Mazel, New York
McCrea CW, Summerfield AB, Rosen B (1982) Body image: a selective review of existing measurement techniques. Br J Med Psychol 55:225-233
Morin CM, Winter B, Besalel VA, Azrim NH (1987) Bulimia: a case illustration of the superiority of behavioral over cognitive treatment. J Behav Ther Exp Psychiatry 18:165-169
Ordman AM, Kirschenbaum DS (1985) Cognitive-behavioral therapy for bulimia: an initial outcome study. J Consult Clin Psychol 53:305-313
Palmer RL (1979) The dietary chaos syndrome: a useful new term? Br J Med Psychol 52:187-190
Polivy J, Herman CP (1985) Dieting and binging. Am Psychol 40:193-201
Pope HG, Hundson JI, Yurgelun-Todd D (1984) Anorexia nervosa and bulimia among 300 surburban women shoppers. Am J Psychiatry 141:292-294
Pyle R, Mitchell JE, Eckert ED (1981) Bulimia: a report of 34 cases. J Clin Psychol 42:60-64
Pyle R, Mitchell JE, Eckert ED (1983) The incidence of bulimia in freshmen college students. Int J Eating Disord 2:75-85
Rosen JC, Leitenberg H (1982) Bulimia nervosa: treatment with exposure and response prevention. Behav Ther 13:117-124
Rosen JC, Leitenberg H (1985) Exposure plus response prevention treatment of bulimia. In: Garner DM, Garfinkel PE (eds) Handbook of psychotherapy for anorexia nervosa and bulimia. Guilford, New York, pp 193-209
Rossiter EM, Wilson GT (1985) Cognitive restructuring and response prevention in the treatment of bulimia nervosa. Behav Res Ther 23:349-359
Russell G (1979) Bulimia nervosa: an ominous variant of anorexia nervosa. Psychol Med 9:429-448
Schleimer K (1983) Dieting in teenage schoolgirls. Acta Paediatr Scand [Suppl] 312
Schneider JA, Agras WS (1985) A cognitive behavioural group treatment of bulimia. Br J Psychiatry 146:66-69
Slade P (1982) Towards a functional analysis of anorexia nervosa and bulimia nervosa. Br J Clin Psychol 21:167-179
Stunkard AJ (1959) Eating patterns and obesity. Psychiatr Q 33:284-295
Stunkard AJ, Messick S (1985) The three factors eating questionnaire to measure dietary restraint, distribution and hunger. J Psychosom Res 29:71-84
Touyz SW, Ivison DJ (1985) The prevalence of bulimia in an Australian university sample. In: Touyz SW, Beumont PJV (eds) Eating disorders: prevalence and treatment. Williams and Wilkins, Sydney, pp 52-61

Van Strien T, Fritjers JER, Bergers GPA, Defares PB (1986) Dutch Eating Behaviour Questionnaire for assessment of restrained, emotional and external eating behaviour. Int J Eating Disord 5:295–315
Wardle J (1980) Dietary restraint and binge eating. Behav Analysis Modification 4:201–209
Wardle J (1987a) Eating style: a validation study of the Dutch Eating Behaviour Questionnaire in subjects and women with eating disorders. J Psychosom Res 31:161–169
Wardle J (1987b) Compulsive eating and dietary restraint. Br J Clin Psychol 26:47–55
Wardle J (1987c) Disorders of eating and weight. Investigation. In: Lindsay SJE, Powell GE (eds) A handbook of clinical adult psychology. Gower, Aldershot, pp 467–487
Wardle J, Beales S (1986) Restraint, body image and food attitudes in children from 12–18 years. Appetite 7:209–217
Weiss L, Katzman M, Wolchik S (1985) Treating bulimia. Pergamon, New York
Whitehouse AM, Freeman CL, Annandale A (1986) Body size estimation in bulimia. Br J Psychiatry 149:98–103
Wilson GT (1986) Cognitive-behavioural and pharmacological therapies for bulimia. In: Brownell KD, Foreyt JP (eds) Handbook of eating disorders. Basic Books, New York, pp 450–475
Wilson GT, Rossiter E, Kleifield EI, Lindholm L (1986) Cognitive-behavioural treatment of bulimia nervosa: a controlled evaluation. Behav Res Ther 24:277–288
Wolf EM, Crowther JH (1983) Personality and eating habit variables as predictors of severity of binge eating and weight. Addict Behav 8:335–344
Woolley SC, Woolley OW (1985) Intensive outpatient and residential treatment for bulimia. In: Garner DM, Garfinkel PE (eds) Handbook of psychotherapy for anorexia nervosa and bulimia. Guilford, New York, pp 391–430
Yates AJ, Sambrailo F (1984) Bulimia nervosa: a descriptive and therapeutic study. Behav Res Ther 22:503–517
Yeap SS, Gamsu CV, McPherson FM (1988) DSM-III bulimia among women attending their general practitioners. Med Sci Res (to be published)

Intensive Cognitive-Behavioural Psychotherapy with Patients Suffering from Schizophrenic Psychotic or Post-Psychotic Syndromes: Theoretical and Practical Aspects

C. PERRIS

Introduction

The most widely known application of cognitive psychotherapy is that originally conceived and developed by Beck and his pupils (Beck 1976; Beck et al. 1979; Beck and Emery 1985) specifically for use in the short-term treatment of emotional disorders, especially of a depressive type. A comprehensive literature now exists, however, documenting its feasibility in a wide range of severe psychopathological conditions, both in individual and group formats (Freeman 1983) and in psychiatric and medical settings (Freeman and Greenwood 1986). Nevertheless, publications concerned with the use of this psychotherapeutic method with patients suffering from schizophrenic disorders are still limited in number and scope (Beck 1952; Meichenbaum and Cameron 1973; Hole et al. 1979; Adams et al. 1981; Jacobs 1980, 1982; Greenwood 1983; A. Palm 1985; U. Palm 1985; C. Perris 1986a,b). Thus, a thorough description of the feasibility of cognitive psychotherapy with patients suffering from schizophrenic, psychotic or post-psychotic syndromes is still warranted.

This chapter is concerned with the rationale for, and the use of, intensive cognitive-behavioural psychotherapy with patients suffering from schizophrenic syndromes. It is based both on data available in the literature and on personal experience gained in the treatment of schizophrenic patients – both as out-patients in an individual format and as in-patients in a particular setting developed at the Department of Psychiatry of Umea University. Although a short overview of our in-patient treatment programme will be also presented, the focus will be on individual treatment.

There should be little doubt that the therapeutic approach which one adopts towards patients suffering from mental disorders, in general, and with schizophrenic syndromes, in particular, depends largely not only on the immediate goals of treatment, but also, and perhaps to a much larger extent, upon which conceptual view of the origins and development of such disorders one endorses. For example, one ambiguous conceptualization frequent in psychoanalytic literature is implicit in the titles of books and articles devoted to the psychotherapy of "schizophrenia"; this is the case also in those written by authors who in practice have shown a deep understanding of the schizophrenic patient. In fact, what is erroneously conveyed by these titles is that treatment concerns itself with a circumscribed disease: unitary

Department of Psychiatry III and WHO Collaborating Centre for Research and Training in Mental Health, Umeå University, Umeå, Sweden.

in its origins, manifestations and course, whereas in reality those who are treated are individual patients, each of whom has his own personal background and his own potential outcome.

We should therefore begin by introducing the comprehensive model of psychopathology that has formed the basis of our research work for several years. This summarizes our view of mental disorders and may represent an initial rationale for the treatment method that will be considered here.

An Heuristic Interactional Model of Psychopathology

For several years we have suggested, in line with a general trend, that the most suitable approach to the understanding of mental disorders and to their effective treatment should be based on a complex model that takes into account the interaction of biological, psychological and social variables in the development of an individual's susceptibility to psychopathological manifestations and the interplay of the vulnerable individual with his environment (C. Perris 1981, 1985b; H. Perris 1982; Eisemann 1985). This basic approach is illustrated in its most rudimentary form in Fig. 1. This figure clearly indicates that the emphasis in our scheme is no longer on the clinical syndrome itself but on the more crucial concept of "individual vulnerability" since we regard this as the very core of all psychopathology. The arrows in the Fig. 1 signify that an interaction is assumed to occur between the variables on the left and on the right the scheme. We regard such an interaction of paramount importance, both for the occurrence and the treatment of every kind of mental disorder.

As concerns possible etiological factors, for example, it is important to emphasize the concept of interaction as distinct from that of a simple addition of

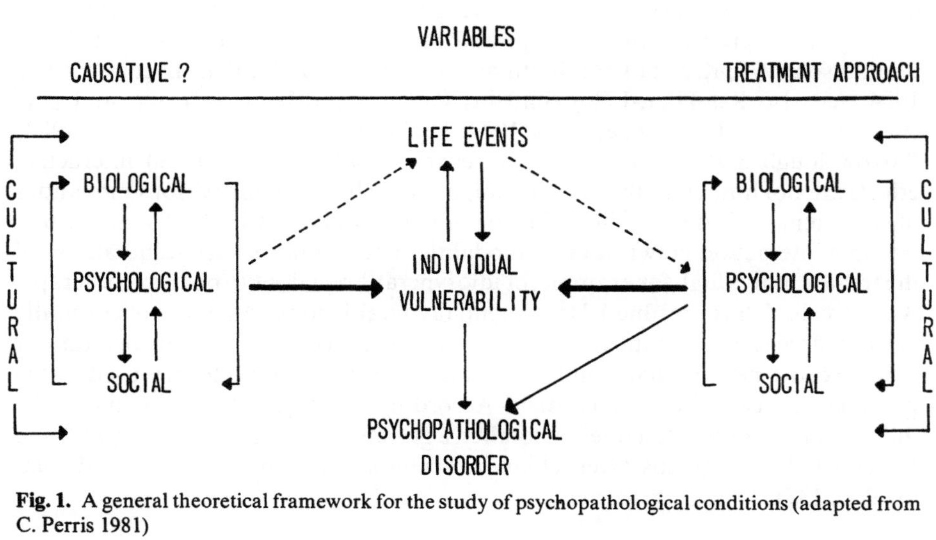

Fig. 1. A general theoretical framework for the study of psychopathological conditions (adapted from C. Perris 1981)

potential causal events. It is well known from other fields of research that interactive effects of two or more factors may result in something quite different from the mere addition of the effects of each factor, e.g. either potentiation or neutralization of single effects. However, interaction is not limited to the interplay among possible causative factors belonging to different domains but extends also to the continuous, dialectical interplay between the (vulnerable) subject and his environment. Because of this dialectical process vulnerability is not conceived as a static, enduring condition. Such variability has been emphasized by Erlenmeyer-Kimling (1979) with reference to gene-environment interaction in the development of depression; she suggested that vulnerability at any given moment in the life span, reflects a "cumulative feedback relationship that has taken place between one's genetic predisposition and one's entire history" (p. 393). Brody (1981) views vulnerability in schizophrenic patients "as epigenetically evolving via individual-environment transactions throughout life (although with major impacts from conception through adolescence)".

Another important assumption concerning interactive processes and vulnerability is that relevant interactions may have occurred a very long time before the immediate triggering of a disorder, so that they do not appear closely related to the debut of the clinical manifestation and are therefore difficult to detect. Thus, as Rutter (1985) has emphasized, interactive processes need to be considered over time as part of development. Finally, the concept of interaction, together with that of individual vulnerability, allows for framing the possible relevance of "life events" in a proper context. In fact, it can easily be hypothesized that many stressful events do not occur by chance but are a result of the interplay of an individual with his particular environment. Again, to quote Erlenmeyer-Kimling (1979), we believe that "life-events are obviously handled or mishandled in different ways by different people".

Also in the field of treatment interactions are of a paramount importance, not limited to the possible consequences of a simultaneous combination of different drugs. Evidence has accumulated showing the occurrence of both positive and negative interactions between drugs and psychotherapy (Docherty et al. 1977; Gunderson 1979; Karasu 1982; Beitman and Klerman 1984; Feinsilver and Yates 1984; see also Koukkou-Lehmann, this volume) and between drugs and psychosocial events (Brown et al. 1962, 1972; Leff and Vaughn 1981; Leff et al. 1982; Barrowclough and Tarrier 1984). Moreover, (positive or negative) interactive effects are not limited to those which might occur between the various modalities of treatment indicated on the right side of the model (see Fig. 1). There is also a possible interaction between these modalities and the particular vulnerability of the treated individual, for example, of idiosyncratic reactions to pharmacotherapy. An individual "preparedness" to respond favourably to certain types of culturally approved treatments could also be considered in this context. In many regards our scheme could be regarded as holistic, in the sense in which this term is used by the psychoanalytical school of Horney. According to the holistic principle, "The individual is viewed as an integral totality, a gestalt, acting on, interacting with and being acted upon by his external environment and internal processes" (Rubins 1969, p. 137).

We can now return to the concept of "individual vulnerability" and work towards its definition. Obviously this concept is not new in psychiatric literature; it may be regarded as a modern equivalent of the concept of diathesis. This concept has been known in psychoanalytic theory since Freud (1905) spoke of *Ergänzungsreihe* to explain the relation between constitutional and accidental factors in the development of neuroses. It has also been employed in modern biological psychiatry with reference, for example, to the studies of high-risk populations being carried out in many quarters.

In a sense our concept of "vulnerability" relates to that of *Anlage* as used by Jaspers (1913/1963), who maintained that, "All (psychopathological) phenomena are a result of the hereditary *Anlage* and the environment" (p. 514). Two important consequences derive from Jaspers' position. First, "Even illnesses which depend most definitely on hereditary factors require environmental conditions for their manifestation, and all environmental effects also require the *Anlage* if they are to come about." And, secondly, "In hereditary illness, the hereditary *Anlage* only manifests itself with certainty inside limits that have to be determined in every case, and it is by no means an absolute, inescapable doom" (p. 514). However Jaspers focussed on heredity in his description of the individual predisposition, and psychoanalytical authors who followed in the footsteps of Freud define vulnerability in exclusively psychological terms. Our scheme, on the other hand, explicitly assumes the continuous interaction between several factors and the individual in the determination of "individual vulnerability".

To the extent that genetic factors are important for the occurrence of a certain disorder, our interpretation of "vulnerability" resembles that of Cancro (1979) in a recent review of genetic studies of the schizophrenic syndrome. Cancro critically points out that such a complex disorder as the schizophrenic syndrome cannot be transmitted directly. What is assumed to be transmitted, rather, is a vulnerability or weakness, consisting at least implicitly of an abnormal trait. Cancro,however, suggests that an alternative formulation of vulnerability can be taken into account, according to which the transmitted trait would be seen as nothing more than a capacity for specifically schizophrenic illness if the individual were to become ill. Cancro's discussion of vulnerability is particularly important for the consequences that can be drawn from it. He concluded his review by suggesting that "the very fact that different gene-environment combinations can produce the phenotype, or phenotypes, which are necessary but not sufficient for the schizophrenic syndrome, means that there are multiple etiologic pathways through which this syndrome can develop" (p. 148). If this argument is accepted, "the search for a single etiology is unlikely to be productive, and... there is neither a single environment nor a particular genetic constellation which is schizophrenogenic" (p. 149). We believe that a similar conclusion can be generalized also to other mental disorders, for example, to the depressive type, for which the participation of genetic factors in causation is deemed relevant.

Since our early conception of vulnerability we have continued to develop the model in an attempt to identify various aetiological hypotheses concerning depressive disorders and to show how various factors may interact with each other (Perris and Perris 1985; C. Perris et al. 1986). Eventually our efforts resulted in a further elaboration of the basic scheme (C. Perris 1985b). This suggests the criteria particularly for a general integrative theory of depression, but these can easily be applied to other morbid conditions as well. This more comprehensive framework is depicted in Fig. 2. Here we have made an attempt to define more precisely the concept of vulnerability by giving emphasis to cognitive processes. Thus, we assume that cognitive processes, in general, and the taking in and the processing of information, in particular, represent a very crucial link in a chain of events which eventually leads to the occurrence of psychopathological manifestations. It should be emphasized that while our cognitive model overcomes the body-mind dualism and is not reductionistic (in contrast to psychoanalytic theory, which clearly separates mind from body: Freud 1915; Peterfreund 1971), it represents nothing but a conceptual framework for the study of possible factors that may contribute both to the occurrence of mental disorders and to their treatment.

It should also be observed that our emphasis on cognitive processes again brings us close to the conception of Cancro (1979). Cancro underlined the importance of attention regulation in the processing of information and assumed that this activity, of particular importance for the susceptibility to develop a schizophrenic syndrome, could be under genetic control.

Our model was thus originalpy conceived as a comprehensive framework for studying depressive syndromes and was only later generalized to studies of other mental disorders. We should point our that two other models, strikingly similar to our own, have recently been proposed by authors primarily concerned with studies of schizophrenic syndromes. The first of these has been presented by Ciompi (1985). Ciompi takes into account, as do we, both genetic and somatic influences (constitution, pre- and perinatal defects, etc.) and psychosocial influences (early childhood traumata, family communication style, acquired coping mechanisms, etc.) in the determination of "pre-morbid vulnerability". Such vulnerability, characterized, according to Ciompi, by a diminished capacity to cope adequately with complex emotional and cognitive stimuli (i.e. a disorder in information

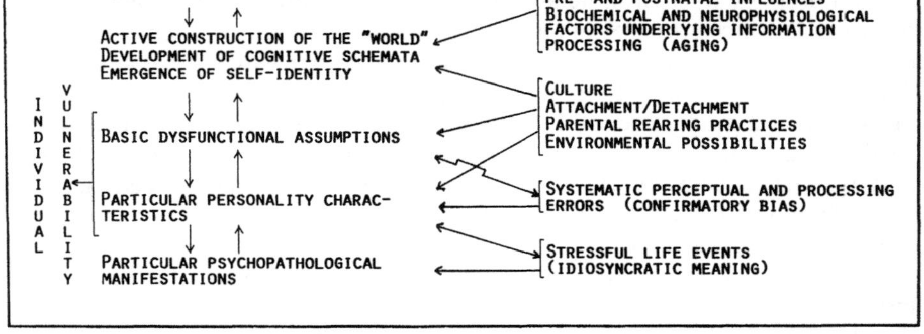

Fig. 2. A more detailed indication of factors which are assumed to contribute to the development of individual vulnerability (adapted from C. Perris 1985a)

processing) leads, when interacting with non-specific stress (i.e. life events), to acute psychotic decompensations and later contributes to the further course of the syndrome.

A second interactive vulnerability/stress model for the development of schizophrenic psychotic episodes has been presented by Nuechterlein and Dawson (1984a). Also these authors take into account enduring vulnerability characteristics which interact with stressful external environmental stimuli. These enduring characteristics are conceptualized in terms of reduced processing capacity, automatic hyperreactivity to aversive stimuli, and social competence and coping deficits. These three components are assumed to be products of specific and non-specific genetic factors interacting with early physical and social environmental influences. In addition, a previous, thorough analysis of the literature by Nuechterlein and Dawson (1984b) indicated several attentional and information-processing deficits to be associated with schizophrenic disorders, with great similarity across populations and for both actively symptomatic and non-symptomatic schizophrenic patients; this suggests that it is not merely a consequence of schizophrenic psychotic episodes. It is important to note that Nuechterlein and Dawson acknowledge "certain vulnerability factors" to be relatively specific to schizophrenic disorders, whereas others "may be associated with increased risk for a fairly wide range of disorders" (1984a, p. 305). A similar reflection also applies to our scheme.

While a critical discussion of these models lies outside the scope of this chapter, it is of interest to point out the degree of convergence among them. This points to the relevance of disorders of cognitive processes as a common denominator for a definition of "individual vulnerability" in subjects potentially at risk of developing a schizophrenic syndrome. There is now a vast body of observations, experimental data and related theory in support of this approach. This provides a justification to therapeutic interventions directly aimed at restructuring dysfunctional cognitive processes. In this context it is of interest to note that George and Neufeld (1985) concluded their recent review of cognition and symptomatology in schizophrenia by stating that "the cognitive perspective on schizophrenic symptomatology holds promise of providing an integrated, empirically anchored view of the schizophrenic process.... Such view could someday serve as a basis for cognitively oriented attempts to facilitate the treatment of schizophrenia" (p. 281).

Interest in the role of cognitive processes, however, has not been limited to attempts at identifying factors which could contribute to the development of psychopathology, as George and Neufeld seem to believe. On the contrary, a comprehensive therapeutic system focussed on cognitions has been developing in recent decades (as described in detail in a previous chapter by C. Perris in this volume) that has already proven to be particularly effective in the treatment of various kinds of psychopathological disorders, including those which may require long-term treatment (see Freeman and Simon, this volume). In the following sections we will examine the feasibility of cognitive psychotherapy with schizophrenic patients as well. First, however, we shall make a few more general comments on the state of art of the psychotherapeutic treatment of patients presenting schizophrenic syndromes.

Psychotherapy and Schizophrenic Syndromes

In recent years several surveys have been published on the use of individual psychotherapy in the treatment of "schizophrenia" (e.g. Rubins 1972; Arieti 1974a,b; Will 1975; Matussek 1976; Day and Semrad 1978; Gunderson 1979); these provide details concerning the feasibility of psychoanalysis and of psychoanalytically oriented psychotherapy in this field. The following general remarks are based largely on a conservative interpretation of these and other relevant works on the subject.

A first point of agreement among the various authors with the (possible exception of those belonging to the school of Klein) seems to be that the traditional psychoanalytic technique cannot be applied directly to the treatment of schizophrenic patients. Freud's pessimistic opinion of the schizophrenic's ability to develop a true transference (Freud 1924) very soon proved to be exaggerated (Sullivan 1931; Fromm-Reichmann 1948, 1954; Federn 1952). Since Freud most authors involved in the treatment of schizophrenic patients have agreed that modifications of the traditional psychoanalytic technique are necessary. It was precisely in the context of treating schizophrenic patients that the concept of "psychoanalytically oriented psychotherapy" was first introduced by Fromm-Reichmann (1958) to stress her departure from the classic psychoanalytic procedure. One of the psychoanalysts whose approach is closest to that discussed in this chapter is Arieti (1962–1974), who made distorted cognitions a major focus of his interventions in the treatment of schizophrenic patients. Another is the Adlerian Shulman (1968), who emphasized the changing of mistaken assumptions in his treatment approach.

A second point of common agreement concerns the importance given by most authors to the therapist-patient relationship, one complemented in the case of a few by the use of an "assistant therapist" (Federn 1952; Rosen 1962; Arieti and Lorraine 1972; Arieti 1974a; Day and Semrad 1978). The therapist-patient relationship has been conceptualized by Arieti (1962) as one of "relatedness", in the sense understood by the interpersonal school of psychiatry. In this context, relatedness includes not only the establishment of rapport or contact with the patient but also the classic psychoanalytic concepts of transference and countertransference (with emphasis on the latter) and, to a certain extent, that of object-relation. The emphasis is put on "empathy", defined by Searles as a kind of "mutual intuition" (Searles 1958; see also Fromm-Reichmann 1955 and Szalita-Pemow 1955) or understood in terms of an "I-Thou" relationship in Buber's sense: "a contact of the entire being with the one in whom one trusts" (Buber 1954/1959). Sullivan (1931) and Federn (1952) stressed the importance of "positive transference", and Racamier (1959) emphasized that the analyst must constantly be a "real presence" – warm, living and tangible. Thus, the main characteristics of the relationship must aim at emphasizing an atmosphere of "basic trust" (Erikson 1953; Arieti 1962a).

It is important, however, that relatedness not be considered just a part of supportive therapy. It is, according to Arieti (1962a), more nutritional than supportive, its aim being to offer the patient what he has previously lacked. Here one could also compare the concept of "corrective ego experience" by A. Freud

(1951), that of "facilitating environment" by Winnicott (1965) and the particular technique adopted by Sechehaye (1951). Also Eissler (1943) and Wexler (1951) emphasized that the love and patience we would shower upon the psychotic is connected developmentally with earlier phases of contempt and enmity. Later Rosen (1962) came to view the therapist's role as one of "foster parent": the context in which the patient lives during treatment is a foster home where the patient finds compensation for inadequacies in the early maternal environment (p. 631). Within the framework of the object-relations therapy of Azima et al. (1958; Azima 1963), on the other hand, the "mothering" principle is carried to an extreme, encouraging infantilization of the patient.

A further point of agreement (Rosen 1947, representing a notable exception) is the emphasis by most authors on addressing the healthy part of the patient's ego in a firmly task-oriented approach to individual psychotherapy (Fromm-Reichmann 1948, 1954; Federn 1952; Rosenfeld 1965; Arieti 1966; Rubins 1972). Arieti (1962a) gives particular importance to the therapist's being active in his interventions and suggests involvement in the life of the patient outside the ordinary therapeutic situation; it is in this context that he made frequent use of an assistant therapist (cf. Arieti and Lorraine 1972). Further, Arieti (1962a) maintained that especially at a late stage of treatment the schizophrenic patient wants tasks to be given to him; by fulfilling tasks of graded difficulty the patient will eventually gain self-esteem.

Finally, the controversy concerning the use of psychotropic drugs in connection with psychotherapy seems to have abated. The more sober attitude now seems to prevail that an appropriate and strictly individualized use of psychotropic drugs may at times be a necessary prerequisite to implement an effective psychotherapeutic approach, rather than their representing merely a disturbing factor (Havens 1963; Rubins 1972; Rubins and Rucker 1974; Arieti 1974a; Gunderson 1979; Matussek and Triebel 1974; Hymowitz and Spohn 1980; Matussek 1981). In particular Matussek (1981) emphasizes that the physician interested in psychotherapy should administer the necessary drugs himself and should identify himself with his measure instead of leaving this task to another person.

Cognitive-Behavioural Psychotherapy with Schizophrenic Patients

General Premises

To grasp the scope of cognitive-behavioural psychotherapy with schizophrenic patients, two general premises should be emphasized. First, it should be observed that the disability of the schizophrenic patient has been defined as the result of the concomitant effect of various types of handicaps (Wing 1974); this is illustrated in Table 1. Wing included in his definition an element that may exist independently of any illness, namely a lack of occupational or social skills, or lack of "coping ability", as an important component of the total disability. More recently Wallace (1984) has comprehensively reviewed the literature, documenting the poor interpersonal functioning of schizophrenic patients. He concluded that some forms

Table 1. Components of schizophrenic "morbidity"

Primary Impairments	e.g. thought disorders
Secondary Handicaps	e.g. maladaptive behavioural reactions
Social Handicaps	e.g. pre-existing lack of social skills or coping ability

of disturbed social behaviours often predate the onset of schizophrenic psychotic symptoms and are potential indicators of vulnerability.

On the other hand, it should be kept in mind for the implications that it has for treatment that poor interpersonal functioning is by no means a necessary characteristic of all schizophrenic patients or of any particular patient at all times. However, whenever there is an indication of pre-morbid, poor interpersonal functioning or lack of coping skills, a comprehensive treatment programme should also be directed toward the correction of these deficiencies. A large body of therapeutic strategies has been developed to this end (Bellack and Hersen 1979; Trower 1984). It should be observed, however, that the training of social skills and coping ability carried out in the context of a cognitive psychotherapeutic programme always implies, first and foremost, the correction of the dysfunctional cognitions behind these deficits and not the mere learning of appropriate behavioural responses in various social situations (cf. also Dow and Craighead 1984; Shepherd 1984; Dryden 1984).

Secondly, it is important to observe that Beck, originally a trained analyst, at a very early stage incorporated behavioural techniques into his therapeutic approach for patients suffering from emotional disorders at the same time that he emphasized the importance of the therapist-patient relationship. Thus, it should not be surprising to realize that widespread use of these techniques is suggested also in the treatment of schizophrenic patients. However, it must be clearly pointed out that in cognitive psychotherapy behavioural techniques are always used as a means to help the patient in identifying, challenging and eventually correcting the distorted cognitions (and more basic dysfunctional assumptions) which are assumed to be very important pathogenetic factors in the occurrence and maintenance of psychopathological disorders. Thus, whereas role-play, for example, is used in behavioural therapy to promote the learning of a particular skill in a particular situation, the same role-play in a cognitive-behavioural context is primarily used to elicit the patient's dysfunctional cognitions and related feelings in order to bring them to the patient's awareness and take a first step towards their correction. This important difference, stressed very early by Beck (1970), must be taken into account for a better understanding of the treatment programme described here. Thus, a comprehensive cognitive-behavioural treatment programme encompasses the use of strategies aimed at the restructuration of distorted cognitive processes and at a reparation of social and coping skills by incorporating techniques which belong to apparently different domains.

In practice various cognitive-behavioural strategies can be used in treating schizophrenic patients; the most common of these are enumerated in Table 2. Obviously various strategies can be combined in a single treatment programme,

Table 2. Levels of cognitive-behavioural interventions

Restructuring of "reality"
Training of appropriate self-instructions
Restructuring of the "internal dialogue"
Training of social skills and coping ability
Challenge and modification of cognitive distortions and of basic maladaptive assumptions

depending on the particular needs of the patient. One characteristic of cognitive psychotherapy is its flexibility (Beck 1976; Arnkoff 1981); this allows for the use of different techniques with different patients. However, the use of less common strategies should not occur haphazardly but always within the frame of the guiding principle of cognitive therapy.

Establishing a special therapist-patient relationship is not mentioned in Table 2 as a separate strategy. This is because the establishment of a situation of relatedness is an indispensable prerequisite for any kind of psychotherapeutic approach to severely disturbed patients, independently of the therapeutic orientation of the therapist (Perris 1986a). In particular, the establishment of basic trust is an essential prior condition to develop the atmosphere of collaborative empiricism that is one of the major characteristics of cognitive psychotherapy (Beck et al. 1979; Beck and Emery 1985). Further details about the particular characteristics of the therapeutic relationship with schizophrenic patients are considered below.

In the treatment programme that we have implemented at our Centre all the strategies mentioned in Table 2; also the family-like characteristics of the particular setting are exploited therapeutically.

A detailed account of all these strategies as they are currently used in our daily work is beyond the scope of the present chapter. Here we will highlight only certain general principles in the treatment of our patients. These principles can be generalized to the use of cognitive psychotherapy with similar patients in other in-patient settings. We will also describe more in depth the treatment in an individual format. First, however, we will consider a number of details about the Centre where our treatment programme is carried out.

Treatment Centre

Our Cognitive-Behavioural Treatment Centre Ersboda is a community-based unit located in a terraced-house of a newly built residential area. It can accomodate six patients of both sexes, who live in a family-like atmosphere where they perform daily chores, including shopping and the preparation of meals. There are two single bedrooms, two double rooms and appropriate space for daytime activities. A good relationship to the neighbours was established from the beginning, and frequent interactions occur between them and the patients at the Centre. Community-service facilities are within walking distance, and public transportation connects the area with the rest of the town.

The Centre is staffed by six mental-health nurses trained in cognitive psychotherapy who act as the main therapists. These work full-time on a rotation scheme and two additional full-time nurses share night duty on rotation. Part-time staff comprises one occupational therapist, one physiotherapist and one senior psychiatrist. The latter (the present author) acts also as the supervisor of the therapeutic programme in general and of the individual therapy sessions (once weekly). To each patient are assigned two therapists who are responsible for the individual therapy sessions.

Selection of Patients

Patients of both sexes, aged 18–35, are referred to the Centre from the associated out- and in-patient units within our district (Perris et al. 1985). This generally occurs after having been admitted to one of the acute wards or after having had repeated contacts on an out-patient basis. Although priority is given to patients who meet a DSM-III diagnosis of schizophrenic disorder, patients suffering from severe personality disorder are occasionally also accepted. The occurrence of evident psychotic manifestations does not represent a contra-indication for being accepted at the Centre. Excluded are patients with verified brain damage, a past history of prolonged drug or alcohol abuse or with recurrent syndromes of a schizo-affective type. Since participation in the treatment programme is voluntary, the patient must be prepared to spend the period of treatment at the Centre stipulated in the initial contact and to accept the general conditions of the programme.

Setting of Goals

Every admission is preceded by at least one interview, in which two of the therapists at the Centre, the patient and the patient's contact person at the referring unit participate. After a preliminary assessment of his patient's status and motivation for treatment has been made, a therapeutic contract is stipulated with each patient accepted at the Centre.

An agreement is first reached about the preliminary duration of the treatment; initially this is usually predicted to last about 5 months. Time limits, however, are flexible, and the possibility of a longer period of treatment is taken into account. Secondly, a preliminary agreement on the immediate goals of treatment is made. This agreement is based on an inventory of problem areas as indicated independently both by the patient himself and by his contact person at the referring unit. This first step in goal setting contributes to evaluating reality orientation by the patient. It also allows the beginning of reality restructuring, should gross distortions become evident in the setting of goals.

Although we speak of treatment, it should be evident that the simple control of psychopathological symptoms is not the primary goal of our programme. In fact, such a control can easily be achieved in a fairly large proportion of patients by the appropriate use of drugs. However, should productive symptoms still be present despite adequate medication, we would expect our treatment programme to influence even these. In practice, one of our major aims is to promote an increase in the patient's self-esteem and feeling of competence and thus to enhance his ability to live as comfortably and as independently as possible in a social context. Only with a few highly motivated patients is a more ambitious aim attempted: the working through, within a cognitive-therapy framework, of previous traumatic experiences which may have contributed to the occurrence and development of the disorder. Such reconstruction, as pointed out by Liotti (this volume), eventually implies the identification of more basic dysfunctional schemata and their successive transformation into more adaptive ones.

The following cases typify our patients.

J. was a 27-year-old previously unskilled male who still lived with his parents. He had been hospitalized on three occasions over the previous 5 years for periods of varying length. His main symptomatology, present also at the referral to the Centre, consisted of pronounced passivity, almost total social withdrawal, reduced and sometimes incoherent speech, lack of emotional expression and indecision. On previous occasions delusions of reference were also present, but these seemed at the time of referral to be well-controlled by medication. The main goals agreed upon with this patient were: to increase his level of activity in social contacts and to reduce his dependency upon his parents by helping him acquire skills which would enable him to participate in some kind of sheltered work.

A.-M. was a 30-year-old former school teacher who had been unable to work for several years because of an almost persistent hallucinatory-delusional syndrome that only occasionally responded to medication. She was dominated by an overinvolved mother who actively contributed to keeping her self-esteem at a very low level. When out of the hospital, she occasionally lived in a group home, but this experience had been negative. She lacked her own accomodation. A.-M. was referred from one of the acute wards where she had been admitted because recurrence of her hallucinatory symptomatology, disrupted thoughts and disordered behaviour. The preliminary goals agreed upon were: the working through of her relation to her mother, the possibility of getting her own small apartment and gradually returning to work. Additionally, this patient was highly motivated to try to reconstruct a series of traumatic early experiences which had frequently troubled her thoughts.

It should be evident that our primary goals, agreed upon at the time of the therapeutic contract, are essentially pragmatic. They aim, in the first place, at helping the patient achieve a more satisfactory life situation through increased comfort, effectiveness and self-awareness, as defined by Parloff et al. (1954). To better understand why the apparently limited goals described in the case illustrations above justify the effort of an intensive psychotherapeutic approach it must be pointed out that almost all patients referred to the Centre have already gone through conventional rehabilitation programmes, and that these have apparently failed. We should stress again that, in agreement with Arieti (1974a), we consider ending of treatment not simply when the patient loses his symptoms, but only when he succeeds in modifying his self-image, his vision of his environment and his future and no longer experiences a sense of passivity. In this context the patient's integration of the psychotic experience into his life history must also be considered.

Therapeutic Socialization

An important element in conducting cognitive psychotherapy is the socialization of the patient to the nature and rationale of cognitive treatment (Beck et al. 1979, p. 74). In the individual, short-term out-patient treatment of those suffering from emotional disorders this socialization occurs already at the first interview. With our particular patients, on the other hand, most of the 1st month of their stay at the Centre is devoted to socialization and the development of an atmosphere of basic trust, which we regard as the most important prerequisite for a successful therapeutic approach. Although particular attention is paid to establishing a good therapeutic relationship between the patient and the two main therapists assigned to him, one aim of the socialization period is to familiarize the patient also with the other members of the staff. As a rule, all six patients are admitted at the same time; thus the socialization process also involves becoming acquainted with the other patients and learning to live in a social group. It is during the 1st month that a closer definition of the immediate goals of treatment is agreed upon, and a preliminary treatment programme, individually tailored to reach these goals, is designed.

Outline of Treatment Programme

Although some recurring weekly activities are scheduled in which all patients are expected to participate, there is a large margin for individually tailored therapeutic activities according to the particular needs of each patient. The scheduled programme of recurring activities comprises training in the chores of daily life and includes the taking of responsibility by the patient for shopping and preparation of meals on a rotation basis. At the beginning of each week a programme for the week is agreed upon, and the patients are prompted to make their suggestions, also regarding the planning of leisure time. The occupational therapist assists patients in the planning of meals for the whole week without, however, interfering in their initiative in making suggestions and in reaching decisions. Already on these occasions patients may express negative views about themselves, which are then cognitively challenged. For the training of collaboration more talented patients are encouraged to assist the less talented in the completion of daily tasks.

Other joint activities comprise physical training sessions led by the physiotherapist, music listening, creative painting, and one supervised and one non-supervised group session each week. The occupational therapist leads the session devoted to creative painting that has been adapted to fit the cognitive therapeutic model, as described by Larsson (1986). Paintings created by the patients, either on a given theme or spontaneously, are used to analyse the patient's view of himself, his environment and the future, as expressed non-verbally in these drawings. In the discussion then, in which all patients participate, distorted opinions are challenged and eventually corrected.

One weekly group session is devoted to the training of communication skills (both verbal and non-verbal) according to a specially developed training manual. Negative self-evaluations are elicited, their validity questioned and the development of alternative views promoted. The other group session is not supervised; patients meet by themselves to discuss matters of common interest and learn to interact with each other without the structures of supervision. At the end of each week a joint summing-up session is held, in which both the patients and those among the staff who are on duty participate. This session aims at making the patients aware of their progress during the past week and counteracting the negative impact of failures which may have occurred.

Each patient also participates in individual therapy sessions, with a frequency ranging from twice a week to daily. The attempt is made to keep individual therapy limited to these sessions, but since patients and therapists often interact, a constant therapeutic orientation and a preparedness to make appropriate therapeutic interventions are consistently kept by the staff. Formal aspects of individual therapy sessions are discussed below.

Homework of graded difficulty is routinely assigned to each patient. This may consist of readings, writings or other small tasks to be performed at the Centre usually in the evenings or of small tasks to be accomplished outside the Centre in the community. When homework assignments involve a more complex task to be performed outside the Centre, cognitive rehearsal, role-play and problem-solving techniques are used in the supervised group session to prepare the patient for the task. On those occasions the other patients are encouraged to participate in the challenging of possible negative opinions that the patient performing the task may reveal. Particular issues related to the assignment of homework to schizophrenic patients will be discussed in a following section.

Principles of Individual Cognitive Psychotherapy with Schizophrenic Patients

The guiding principles of cognitive psychotherapy with schizophrenic patients in an individual format need to be described in some detail because these principles also apply independently of this setting. When different strategies are appropriate for in-patients and for out-patients, these differences will be high-lighted. The principles of individual therapy are derived from the cognitive model described by Beck and his colleagues (Beck 1976; Beck et al. 1979; Beck and Emery 1985) for the treatment of emotional disorders. However, while the general structure and specific procedures closely conform to the guidelines outlined by Beck, strategic modifications are sometimes necessary to deal with the particular cognitive disorders presented by schizophrenic patients.

Basic Assumptions

A short discussion of the development of dysfunctional assumptions at various levels in schizophrenic patients will provide the rationale for the various therapeutic strategies described below. However, the constraints of the present context allow only a rudimentary sketch of the many complex issues involved; unfortunately, consequent omissions may easily give rise to misunderstandings.

To conceptualize at least some of the clinical manifestations of schizophrenic patients in terms amenable to cognitive psychotherapy it is necessary to return to the theoretical frameworks described above ("Heuristic Interaction Model") into account certain relevant hypotheses which can be derived from them.

Man enters the world with genetically determined structures and with inborn neural patterns and related information-processing systems, which unfold later according to a genetically determined maturational programme. These programmes allow for handling adaptively all the stimulation that continuously impinges on the organism. Peterfreund (1971) has emphasized a result of this stimulation:

The organism may be under constant stress, with accompanying nonspecific biological reactions which include alarm and anxiety manifestations.... To minimize or eliminate stress and accompanying alarm and anxiety, the organism must respond in a specific adapted manner, exerting biological control and maintaining homeostasis and biological order (p. 169).

As pointed out by Singer (1986), both clinical evidence and results from experimental research indicate that cognitive functions must be learned. The structures of the brain serving these functions require sensory experience for their maturation; neuronal activity thus becomes an important shaping factor of these structures. To the extent that this neuronal activity is modulated by sensory signals, environmental factors can influence the development of neuronal networks. Importantly, Singer suggested in his article that "experience-dependent self-organization should be considered as an active dialogue between the brain and his environment."

From the scheme in Fig. 2 we may derive an hypothesis as to a possible disturbance in the taking in and/or processing of information already at an early stage of development in the person who will later develop a schizophrenic symptomatology. According to Nuechterlein and Dawson (1984b), the pattern of pre-morbid deficits in schizophrenic patients as reported in the literature is consistent with a reduction in the processing capacity that is available for task-relevant cognitive operations. These authors have suggested elsewhere (1984a) that various causes may be taken into account to explain this difference in available processing capacity. In Nuechterlein and Dawson's formulation, as well as in our own, it is generally assumed that these deficits are likely to be products of specific and non-specific genetic factors interacting with early physical and social environmental variables. It is of interest in this context to recall that Cancro (1975) assumes that "attention regulation" could be a factor under genetic control, contributing to the vulnerability for at least some form of schizophrenic syndrome. Cancro furthermore maintains that "attention regulation certainly could explain the basic disturbances of cognition and object relations which characterize the group of schizophrenias" (p 148). Besides the fact that Cancro's hypothesis approaches the identification of a possible genetic factor, his latter point here is especially interesting, for allows the introduction of another important variable from our scheme: attachment, both as originally conceived by Bowlby (1969/1980) and with reference to more recent studies (Reite and Field 1985). This variable is specifically relevant in the present context because a cross-fertilization between attachment theory and cognitive psychotherapy is already clear in the literature (Bowlby 1980, 1981; Guidano and Liotti 1983; Beck 1985; Liotti 1986; Perris 1986; Reda 1986).

Although a scholarly discussion of the relevance of attachment theory for cognitive therapy is available in Guidano and Liotti (1983) and in Reda (1986), it may be valuable to summarize why we have included attachment as a prominent variable in our theoretical framework. First, Bowlby's attachment theory is an evolutionary object-relations theory that takes into account biological structures in its attempt to explain the existence of biological order, organization, control, regulation and adaptation – all of which are concepts at the forefront of scientific interest. Thus, it meets the ordinary requirements of a scientific theory. In addition, it dispenses with the obsolete psychoanalytic concept of "drive-discharge" and with the vitalistic, anthropomorphic concept of ego (the pre-Darwinian "intelligent designer", according to Peterfreund 1971, p. 57), both of which burden other current object-relations theories and limit their power of explanation.

Secondly, attachment, in the sense used by Bowlby, refers to the "person who mothers a child" (Bowlby 1969, p. 29); although for most children this person is also the natural mother, this need not be so. Ethological studies (e.g. Jolly 1972), for example, have documented that male non-human primates have the capacity to be effective care-givers and socializers of the young. As concerns humans, Guidano and Liotti (1983) have aptly pointed out that if an empathic and available father is associated with an emotionally detached mother, he assumes priority in the hierarchy of attachment objects. (cf. also Ainsworth 1972; Hetherington 1972; Santrock 1972; Crumley and Blumenthal 1973; Biller 1974, for the importance of the father for the cognitive and emotional development of the child). Biller (1974) suggests that among humans and other primates there may be biological predispositions involved in father-child attachment. An important analysis of the importance of the father has been presented by Forrest (1967), who stressed that a negative influence on the development of the infant can occur at a very early age as a consequence of the father's attitude to the mother-child relationship. Recognizing the importance of attachment figures other than the mother is particularly important because it allows one to avoid an unconditional acceptance of the concept of the "schizophrenogenic mother", as postulated by Fromm-Reichmann (1948). Furthermore, an anecdotal report by A. Freud and Dann (1951), quoted both by Bowlby (1981) and by Field (1985), suggests that even peer attachment may occur very early in life. In a comparison of primary care-giving mothers and primary and secondary care-giving fathers, Field (1978) found that while fathers as a group differed from the primary caregiver mothers in providing more arousing stimulation, the primary caregiver fathers were similar to the primary caregiver mothers; that is, they engaged in less arousing but more comforting behaviours with their infants. From her further studies Field (1985) concluded that "different attachment figures may serve different needs of the infant, with mothers perhaps serving arousal-modulation needs, and fathers and peers serving stimulation needs" (p. 435).

Thirdly, attachment is not understood here as exclusively confined to early infancy – as other theories assume – but is conceived to be present and active throughout the whole life cycle (Bowlby 1980, p. 39). In this context it is important to note that although attachment behaviour, as conceived by Bowlby, seems to develop towards the end of the first 6 months of life, a vast body of evidence now suggests attachments to mother, father and peers to develop already in the very early months of life (Field 1985); this implies very important and complex pyschobiological interactive processes (Fox 1985; Reite and Capitanio 1985).

Fourthly, attachment theory postulates inheritance of a potential to develop certain sorts of behavioural systems, or a "cognitive map" (in practice corresponding to the information-processing programmes mentioned above), which, rudimentary at birth, becomes more and more complex with the growth of the child. In particular, Bell (1970) demonstrated an interaction between quality of attachment and cognitive development, "mother permanence" developmentally anticipating "object permanence" (see also Sroufe and Waters 1977). Since it is acknowledged that the development of more complex cognitive constructs ("working models" in Bowlby's terminology) is an active process by the child, it is possible to integrate the concepts of attachment theory both with those of Piagetian developmental psychology and with those of another theory of relevance for cognitive therapy, Kelly's "personal construct theory" (Kelly 1955). Personal-construct theorists (e.g. Shotter 1970; Salmon 1970, and more recently O'Reilly 1977) have addressed the origins of personal constructs and have emphasized the child's interpersonal relationships, in general, and the relationship between the child and a significant adult, in particular. Salmon (1970, p. 206) suggests that the mother, at least in the early stages, "helps to define the relevancies of situational contexts for the child, offering him a construction in terms of which he can act towards the situation". O'Reilly summarizes his view by stating that "a child born into a human community gains access to this system through his relationship with a caring adult (1977, p. 217). It is interesting to note that Bowlby's concept of "working models" (which corresponds to the concept of schemata used in cognitive psychotherapy literature) has recently been incorporated by the psychoanalyst Peterfreund (1983) in his scholarly study of the psychoanalytic process.

Furthermore, attachment theory utilizes concepts such as "defensive exclusion" (a concept related to that of "selective inattention" used by Sullivan 1954) which are of paramount importance for the understanding of information-processing disturbances in pathological subjects.

And, finally, psychopathology is regarded here as the result of a person's psychological development having followed a deviant pathway and not as due to his suffering a fixation at, or a regression to, some early stage of development (Bowlby 1980, p. 41).

In the case of schizophrenic development concepts derived from attachment theory become particularly important for an understanding of the schizophrenic's ambivalence towards relationships which can be interpreted by him as having self-contradictory characteristics. Such ambivalence, probably sustained by deviant communication, may result in the patient's double view of himself and reality and become the basis for the development of highly dysfunctional basic assumptions (described below).

The emphasis that we lend to the concepts of attachment and communication are intimately related to the importance that we assign to parental rearing attitudes. Despite some degree of inconsistency in the literature (Heilbrun 1960; Garmezy et al. 1961; Frank 1965; Piety 1967; Hirsch and Leff 1975; Liem 1980; Parker 1983) the findings that have most frequently emerged point to the perception by schizophrenics of their mothers as having been rejecting (Lane and Singer 1959), dominant and demanding (Heilbrun 1960; Garmezy et al. 1961; Lu 1961). In contrast, the role of the father has most often been regarded as more peripheral (Cheek 1965). However, the boy who is paternally deprived (through absence or inadequacy of the father) is likely to develop insecurity in his peer relationships as well as in his relationships with authority figures and may become even more tied to the mother (Biller 1974). More recently Parker (1983) reported that schizophrenic patients scored both parents as less caring than did controls.

Obviously there are many shortcomings in studies which attempt to relate parental rearing attitudes to pathology later in life. Methodological weaknesses include small sample sizes, selective inclusion of subjects, poor definition of criteria for parental disturbance and use of instruments with low discriminating power (Frank 1965; Parker 1983). Further limitations derive from schizophrenic patients having been regarded in most studies as belonging to a homogeneous group and the assumption of a linear relationship between deviant parental rearing and a specific disease. More relevant, in our opinion, is the importance that parental rearing attitudes may have on mediating variables which can add to individual vulnerability. Relevant here are studies which attempt to relate perceived parental behaviour to adult personality characteristics (for a recent review see Perris et al. 1985). One such study has been reported by Willenson (1960), who contrasted the personality organization of subjects who perceived themselves to have been either parentally accepted and intrinsically valued ("satellizers") or parentally rejected ("non-satellizers"). The results of this study clearly support the assumption that non-satellizers lack self-esteem and are less accepting and more self-critical than satellizers. These findings are compatible with the results of another investigation by Watson (1957), who found that permissive discipline was associated with better socialization and more effective cooperation with others. Other studies suggest that discrepant verbal ability is fostered by a close relationship to a demanding and intrusive mother (Bing 1963), and that excessive parental control inhibits the development of flexible thinking (Busse 1969). No study has yet examined possible relationships between deviant patterns of parental education and the development of dysfunctional assumptions in schizophrenic patients. However, a pilot study of healthy subjects conducted by our Department (Ollinen 1986) showed the endorsement of more dysfunctional assumptions on Weissman's Dysfunctional Attitudes Scale (Weissman and Beck 1978; Weissman 1980) in subjects who perceived their parents as rejecting.

The study of parental characteristics has received a new impetus since the early study by Brown et al. (1962) showed that deterioration in the behaviour of schizophrenic patients discharged from hospital was positively associated with the degree of emotion and of hostility expressed by the patient's key relative. Brown's original findings have been validated later in several other studies (Brown et al. 1972; Leff and Vaugn 1981). Parker (1983) reported a higher rate of re-admission in schizophrenic patients who had scored the rearing behaviour of their parents low in care and protection.

Establishing the Therapeutic Relationship

The quality of the therapist-patient relationship is important in all forms of psychotherapy and with all kinds of patients; it becomes crucial in the psychotherapy of patients suffering from schizophrenic syndromes. This relationship begins in the initial interviews. We use the plural here to emphasize that working with schizophrenic patients may require more than one session before a purposeful therapeutic relationship can begin to develop. The relationship continues to unfold during the entire therapeutic process, but its basis is clearly laid at the first contact with the patient. In fact, the therapist's approach to the patient sets the tone for the way in which the therapeutic work will unfold. Nicholi (1978) has aptly conceptualized the therapist's attitude toward the patient as follows:

> Whether the patient is young or old, neatly groomed or disheveled, outgoing or withdrawn, articulate or inarticulate, highly integrated or totally disintegrated, of high or low socioeconomic status, the skilled clinician realizes that the patient, as a fellow human being, is considerably more like himself than he is different and that even if he understands only a fraction of a patient's mental functioning, that patient will contribute significantly to the therapist's understanding of himself and of every other patient. (p.4)

Although the competence of the schizophrenic as a sender and receiver of consensual (particularly verbal) communication is often limited, the patient is nonetheless extremely sensitive to affects, emotions and personality qualities in those about him. This is one of the reasons why Fromm-Reichmann (1950) and her associates (e.g. Searles 1958) have made countertransference one of their major concerns.

One characteristic which schizophrenics share with other difficult patients is that they generally do not voluntarily seek treatment. Consequently the first responsibility of the therapist treating a schizophrenic is to clarify the nature of the presenting problem to break through the patient's barrier of diffidence. One must agree with Arieti (1974a) that it is advisable for the therapist to take the initiative with initially uncooperative patients and attempt to convey the feeling that a sincere effort is being made to establish contact. As Greenwood (1983) points out, in such cases it is better to err on the side of ensuring that the patient feels understood rather than articulating beliefs that are beyond his awareness. If the patient is very disturbed, incoherent or speaks about his delusions and hallucinations one should not pretend to understand him or to accept his symptoms but reply in a manner such as "I sense that you are trying to communicate something to me, but unfortunately I am not able at the moment to understand your message." Experience shows that even the most incoherently verbose patient is able to break through his incoherence and answer adequately if his attention is patiently diverted towards straightforwardly neutral subjects.

Once a good relationship has developed, the answer to delusional statements or questions may be formulated according to cognitive-therapy principles. A patient, for example, with whom a good relationship had developed over many years telephoned to say that she was afraid her bedroom ceiling might fall on her because she had stored a few things in a room above. To the question as to why she thought this, she related that once when at hospital, part of the toilet ceiling had fallen on her. However, she was able to acknowledge a difference between the two situations and to reach the conclusion that her fear was unfounded. On further probing as to whether there could be reason for telephoning other than to check the validity of her fear, she admitted that what she actually wanted was advice on how to behave toward a neighbour who felt disturbed by her getting up very early in the morning for work. This second, more rational request could, of course, also be handled easily by prompting her own possible solutions to the problem.

Between therapist and patient there must develop a situation of "relatedness": an exchange based upon trust, warmth and a desire to share and help. The concept of empathy (in the etymological sense of "Feel into") has become common usage to characterize a good therapeutic relationship, and substantial literature has been accumulating on this (e.g. Beres and Arlow 1974; Greenson 1967; Kohut 1959; Schafer 1959). The basic aim of cognitive psychotherapy is to help the patient identify attitudes and self-perceptions and to assist him in developing new, more adaptive cognitive structures. That which can be learned through empathy is how the patient organizes his wishes, thoughts, feelings and representations of self and of personal relationships. Schafer (1959) has defined empathy as "the inner experience of sharing and comprehending the momentary psychological state of another person". The most important clues to this inner experience emerge through the patient's non-verbal behaviour; this is as important in cognitive psychotherapy as in other forms of psychotherapy. In practice, it is this comprehension of the momentary state of the patient that guides the content and timing of therapist interventions.

If the relationship progresses as expected, basic trust eventually develops. This offers the patient a "secure base", as conceived by Bowlby (1973), that is, the confidence that standing behind him is a trustworthy person who provides him with a secure basis from which to operate and deploy his talents to best advantage.

Development of Collaborative Empiricism

Socialization refers to the process by which the individual learns what is expected of him in a variety of situations, and what he may legitimately expect of the individuals with whom he interacts in these situations. In the context of psychotherapy socialization refers to the patient's learning what his and the therapist's roles are to be during the therapeutic work. A patient who does not understand what is expected of him is almost certain to encounter difficulties. Some evidence suggests that role preparation enhances compliance with psychotherapy and may favourably influence outcome. A series of investigations carried out at the Johns Hopkins Psychotherapy Research Unit in Baltimore under the directorship of Frank in the mid-1960s (Frank et al. 1978; Frank 1985) documented that instilling suitable expectations in patients through systematic preparation before psychotherapy improves therapy behaviour, attendance and outcome. An attempt at replication, however, by Sloane and his group (Sloane et al. 1970) led to less impressive results.

The importance of preparing the patient for cognitive psychotherapy has also been emphasized by Beck and his co-workers (Beck et al. 1979, pp. 72–75), who underlined that the patient should understand the nature and rationale of cognitive treatment. This preparation is particularly relevant in cognitive psychotherapy because of the special characteristics of the activities it requires from both patient and therapist (Beck et al. 1979; Bedrosian and Beck 1980; Jansson 1986; Perris 1986). One might add in this context that the process of socialization should be carried out a slower pace with schizophrenics than with other types of patients, for example, those who are depressed.

With patients suffering from schizophrenic syndromes socialization may require more than one session and thus often become combined with substantive therapeutic work. In such sessions the therapist must assume the role of a teacher, however without pretending to convey to the patient – as the mullah in the Persian tale – everything that can be known about cognitive therapy. In particular, it is advisable at this stage to keep examples for explaining the relationship between thoughts, feelings and behaviour at a very general level and not to refer to the patient's present psychotic symptomatology. Greenwood (1983) suggests that self-disclosure may facilitate the establishment of contact with the schizophrenic patient. Self-disclosure has also shown itself useful in constructing initial examples of the relationship between feelings and automatic thoughts.

The explanation of fundamental concepts, such as schemata and cognitive distortions, must also be made in a language appropriate to the patient's present readiness to understand. There is no necessity to use any particular terminology during the socialization phase. Important is that the patient learn a rational basis for the work that he is expected to engage in, and that he be made aware of the common vicissitudes of every therapeutic process. Later, however, when the patient has become more confident in his role, the labels for various cognitive distortions must be taught to him so that he can identify and report on them when required.

Borrowing Kelly's (1955) metaphor, cognitive therapy regards the therapist and the patient as "personal scientists": both put forward hypotheses, try to verify them and accept or reject them in accordance with the results. Such collaborative empiricism implies that therapy is a joint trial-and-error endeavour which aims at the discovery, challenging and eventually modification of the dysfunctional cognitive rules that govern the behaviour of the patient and contribute to his disability. These concepts can easily be explained to the patient in plain words. What is most important for the patient to learn at this stage are the first rudimentary principles of how to behave in therapy. Similarly as the therapist cannot learn everything about the patient in the initial interviews, the patient cannot be expected immediately to learn all the terminology of cognitive psychotherapy. However, as it will become clear in descriptions of cognitive distortions below, it is unadvisable to make an explicit use of the term "scientist", because the patient may be unable to grasp its rather metaphorical meaning here.

It is important that the goals and some indication of the expected time required to reach them (however approximate) be discussed in the initial interviews. The therapist should assist the patient in formulating his own goals and begin with these in the following search for agreement. By no means should unrealistic goals be accepted. Striking the proper balance between agreeing on goals that cannot realistically be reached and the risk of giving a blow to the patient's self-esteem can be a very delicate matter. When confronted with unrealistic or very inflated goals, one may suggest a preliminary, more proximal goal in order to have an opportunity to experience the therapeutic process. This agreement also provides the therapist an opportunity to learn more about the patient's potential capacities. Not infrequently the patient asks whether the therapy will result in his being cured. In responding to such a question one can try, first, to elicit what "cure" means to the patient and then tell him that a likely result would be that he will feel more comfortable, less dependent on others and more able to enjoy life. Experience has shown that to speak of increased self-awareness or enhanced self-esteem does not make much sense to most patients at this stage.

Already in establishing a time schedule it is vital that the therapist inform the patient of possible interruptions in treatment which may occur because of vacations, traveling, etc. to prevent possible feelings of dejection should such interruption occur.

Psychotherapy with schizophrenic patients generally cannot be confined to the stipulated sessions. The schizophrenic patient, especially in the phase in which he makes a guarded effort to establish a relationship, needs to test again and again that he will not be disappointed. It is in this context that the availability of an assistant therapist is invaluable to supply the patient with at least two persons upon whom he can rely. If a co-therapist is to participate in some way in the treatment, he should also participate in the socialization interviews and in the stipulation of the preliminary therapeutic contract.

The therapist must always clearly define when and under what circumstances the patient can get in touch with him outside the scheduled therapy sessions. Most patients do telephone, some frequently. However, it is not difficult to make them accept that their call may sometimes be untimely. If possible, one should spend a few minutes speaking with them to discover the true reason for their call and to make some improvised therapeutic intervention. Such contacts are of a paramount importance because, correctly handled, they can contribute to the process of assisting the patient adapt to minor frustrations and accept reality.

Two additional points need to be emphasized. First, some minor therapeutic intervention can be attempted towards the end of the session to provide the patient with the opportunity of experiencing the flavour of the therapeutic work. One can ask the patient, for instance, what he felt before coming to the appointment, and what his thoughts had been – then, what he thinks now as the interview is coming to an end, and what his present feelings are. Another possibility is to ask the patient what he knew about cognitive psychotherapy before the interview, and what he knows now; this helps make him aware of the possibility of learning. The second point concerns the preparation for homework assignments. One can ask the patient whether he himself would like to propose something that could be relevant for the common work. If this does not succeed in eliciting a proposal, one can ask the patient whether writing down a few simple notes on his present problems or on any other life experience that he deems important would be a suitable task. However one should not insist at this stage of the treatment if the patient is not prepared to comply. On the other hand, very few patients refuse to cooperate in preparing a short list of their present problems to be used as a basis for the coming therapy session.

A special case is presented by patients who are so disturbed that even an elementary lecture on the principles of cognitive psychotherapy would be beyond their readiness to understand. While one must begin here with less attention devoted to the general guidelines of cognitive therapy, one should try as soon as possible to introduce at least the principal concepts.

Medication

Patients on medication may show either of two antithetical attitudes. They may fear that the beginning of therapy means they must stop the medication on which they feel protected from pathological experiences, or they may expect participation in therapy to mean that they can dispense with all medication. It is not advisable to make a radical change in medication in the very initial phase of therapy unless present dosages seem manifestly inappropriate. Drug therapy establishes a certain distance between the patient and his most distressing symptoms, whereas the experiencing of these symptoms may be an important prerequisite for the beginning of psychotherapeutic work. One should inform the patient as to the relationship between drug-based therapy and psychotherapy and propose that any decision about medication be jointly agreed upon after the treatment has been in progress for some time. Our own preference is to keep the patient at the minimum dosage of neuroleptic drugs necessary to preclude unwanted exacerbations of psychotic symptomatology, while assisting those not able to do this to learn to take the responsibility for their own medication.

Patient's Relatives

Schizophrenic patients who are candidates for psychotherapy are in the rule relatively young. Our own age limits for accepting patients for treatment are 18 and 35 years. This means that most patients still live with their parents or are in close contact with them. In addition, both in the case of hospitalized patients and in that of those who make contact with an out-patient unit it is not uncommon that the initiative to seek psychiatric care has been prompted by some close relative. Contact with the most involved relative must therefore be made already at the time of initial interviews. As noted above, there is evidence that the emotional climate of the environment in which the patient lives is of great importance for the course of schizophrenic syndromes. Thus the immediate environment of the patient must always be taken into account to lessen the risk that therapy will be doomed to failure from the very beginning.

In this respect there is a difference between in- and out-patients. With the former there is the advantage that the patient, at least for a certain time, is away from his habitual milieu; thus, the risk of very early negative influences is less pronounced. Here contact with relatives can be deferred for a short time while priority is given to establishing the therapeutic relationship. The situation is obviously very different in the case of out-patients who continue living in their usual milieu. In this case contact with a significant relative must be established at the time of initial interviews. The patient must be clearly informed of both the fact of the contact and its rationale.

Such a session can be divided into two parts: the first with the significant relative alone and the second with both the patient and the relative. This procedure entails both advantages and disadvantages. One advantage is that it is possible to collect a thorough history concerning the patient without confronting him in an untimely way with details of his own past which could be highly anxiety-provoking.

Another is that it is possible through appropriately provocative questions to make a preliminary assessment of the relative's attitude towards the patient. The major disadvantage is that a suspicious patient may feel excluded from information that concerns himself and suspect that some particular agreement has been reached with the relative from which he is excluded. In the joint session, therefore, one should begin with a short recapitulation of what the relative has reported and then ask the patient for comments. Depending upon the patient's present state some provocative material provided by the relative can be used during the joint session to observe what kind of reaction it elicits. It is very important here that attention be paid to clues derivable from non-verbal communication.

Attitudes have varied in the psychoanalytic literature regarding the evaluation of the patient's report of his early experiences with significant persons, especially his mother. The position of Arieti (1955, 1968a) offers an example: in his early writings he wholeheartly subscribed to the concept of the "schizophrenogenic mother" that had been recently introduced in the literature, whereas he later maintained (1968b) that at a rough estimate only 25% of the mothers of his patients fitted into the stereotyped image. However, the conclusion he draws from this is remarkable: that psychoanalysts had believed what their patients had told them, thus making a mistake similar to the one made by Freud when he came to believe that neurotic patients had been assaulted sexually by their parents (p. 369). In his view the schizophrenic's report of distressing influences from parents may be only the product of his fantasy. Alanen (1958), on the other hand, carried out a careful personal study of the mothers of 100 schizophrenics and found that 84% of them were themselves suffering from serious personality disorders. In particular his analysis of the mother-child relationship revealed the frequent occurrence (85%) of "a type of mother characterized by a dominating and understanding attitude toward her child" (pp. 208–209). Recently Kohut (1977) has considered this subject in discussing the treatment of patients with narcissistic disorders. He stressed the importance of actually meeting the parents of patients accepted for treatment to be able to make an evaluation. His opinion seems to be the contrary of the later view by Arieti; his experience has shown that the opportunity of a direct evaluation probably reveals many more disturbed parents than the patients themselves would report. A very recent study of the mothers of 72 schizophrenic patients undergoing psychoanalytic psychotherapy in Munich has been reported by Roeder (1986): only a few ($n = 16$) of the mothers could be described as overprotective, but a much larger proportion could be classified as emotionally cold and withdrawn.

Unfortunately we have not yet been able to observe patients who have grown up and lived in a conflict-free environment. On the contrary, in almost all our patients a mutually pathological relationship of long standing with at least one significant relative, usually but by no means always, the mother, is clearly manifest. Obviously there are differences in nuances in the descriptions of the mothers of schizophrenic patients. Arieti, for example, mentions attributes of the type described as a "monstrous human being" (1968a,b: p. 68); Rosen (1962) spoke of a perverted sense of motherhood; and Kilpatrick, a Horneyian analyst quoted by Rubins (1969, pp. 138–139), defined this mother-child relationship as lacking empathy and characterized by the substitution of mechanical relations for human tenderness or rejection. Our experience is too limited and unsystematic to permit an adequate evaluation, but our impressionistic view is that the mothers of our patients fit Alanen's description as this emerges from the detailed case reports in his monograph. Recently Sass et al. (1984) found that parents of patients with severe formal thought disorders showed pronounced communication deviance. Our preliminary impression is consistent with this finding.

Regardless however of percentages and degrees of disturbance a sizeable risk remains that the relationship of a patient to a significant relative may be highly dysfunctional. An ideal solution to the problem would be that the most involved relative also receive the opportunity to participate in some psychotherapeutic work. The simultaneous treatment of a non-psychotic member of the family can entail long-range advantages. Szalita-Pemow (1951), in fact, maintained that the mother (or mother substitute) of the schizophrenic is so, "because she rejects and disapproves of herself rather than of the baby" (p. 296). Our own preference, however, is to work with single patients, recommending that motivated significant relatives get in touch with another therapist.

If the patient is to be treated at home some outline of the treatment plan must be discussed with a relative at the joint session. Unfortunately, such discussion by no means precludes negative reactions when the patient (hopefully as a consequence of the treatment) starts to behave in a new way. It is also advisable that repeated contacts be taken up with the significant relative during the course of treatment. This should, perhaps, be done in a joint session with the patient.

Frequency and Structure of Sessions

Also in regard to frequency and structure of sessions there is a difference between in- and out-patients. In-patients live in a therapeutic milieu which is an important part of their "secure base" (Perris 1985b). Here the patient finds easy access to an assistant therapist, and the building of the therapeutic relationship is highly facilitated. Therapy sessions can therefore be held less frequently than with out-patients. Whenever feasible, daily sessions should be planned with out-patients, at least during the early phases of treatment and until a stable therapeutic relationship has developed. Since most schizophrenic patients have no regular work, there is no risk that daily sessions will have a disruptive effect on the patient's ordinary life. Later, when treatment approaches its end, sessions can become more spaced so as to facilitate termination. However, an alternative should be considered in the case of patients in remission, who are able to attend to their work on a normal schedule.

It is also important to plan follow-up sessions to occur at some distance in time from the termination of therapy. In our practice we plan that one such session will take place 3–4 months after the end of treatment.

In principle the structure of the therapy session need not differ from that described by Beck et al. (1979) and others who work cognitively. Stipulating the agenda, reviewing homework, reviewing the previous session and summing up the present session at the end are all elements which can easily be included in therapy with schizophrenic patients. However, a difference may be necessary in the length of the session: shorter sessions (30 min) may occasionally be appropriate, if the patient is manifestly unable to sustain attention for a longer time, as may longer sessions (1.5–2.0 h) if the discussion of some important issue is at stake. Also the use of customary therapeutic techniques need not differ from usual cognitive-therapy routine. These techniques will be described in following sections with particular regard to their use with schizophrenic patients (The order of their discussion here does not imply the order in which they should necessarily follow in practice.)

Distancing and Dysfunctional Cognitions

Most patients entering treatment do not question the validity of their beliefs and conclusions but equate their inferences with reality. This is particularly true of schizophrenic patients, independently of delusional and hallucinatory phenomena. One may include among these beliefs the patient's identification with his disorder. He experiences most of his symptoms as an integral part of himself and is unwilling to rid himself of them at risk of losing his mental integrity. This is especially true with certain hallucinatory experiences (as will be dealt with below). Thus, one early intervention aims at assisting the patient in challenging the belief that he is thoroughly crazy and in making him aware of his potential resources, i.e. in distancing himself as a person from his disorder. This does not mean, of course, that the patient will gain full psychological insight about his condition, but rather that the attention of the patient is diverted from his symptoms and deficits to problems, and that he becomes engaged in their solution.

Most of the cognitive errors identified by Beck in depressed patients (e.g. arbitrary inference, selective abstraction, magnification and minimization, overgeneralizing, self-reference, dichotomous thinking) may also occur, as already reported by Greenwood (1983), in schizophrenic patients. This should not be surprising; dysfunctional thoughts of the type described in depressives have been repeatedly reported also in patients suffering from several other types of mental disorder (e.g. anxiety and phobias, Beck and Emery 1985; Guidano and Liotti 1983; loneliness, Young 1981; eating disorders, Guidano and Liotti 1983; Garner and Bemis 1985). If our previous reasoning concerning the development of individual vulnerability is accepted, one would expect that some dysfunctional cognitions of the type discussed here should be present in most patients suffering from mental disorders, independently of diagnostic categories. Thus, not only is it unlikely that they are specifically related to a given disorder, but it is also reasonable to assume that the occurrence of many such cognitive errors is common to a lesser extent in the general population. It has been maintained, for instance, that people often have erroneous intuitions about the laws of chance (Tversky and Kahneman, 1971), and that intuitive predictions follow a subjective and heuristic representativeness. In making predictions and judgments under uncertainty people show great confidence in their judgment and have difficulty searching for disconfirming information to test hypotheses (Einhorn and Hogarth 1978). Apparently, in practice people commonly rely on a limited number of heuristic bases which sometimes yield reasonable judgments but sometimes also lead to severe and systematic errors (Kahneman and Tversky 1973). Probably that which distinguishes the ill is the fact that several types of cognitive errors occur together in clusters and at a significantly higher frequency than in the heathly. In addition, it could be assumed that attempts to correct bias through feedback mechanisms would not be likely to succeed because of even more dysfunctional basic schemata.

Since the characteristics of cognitive errors have been clearly described in the literature, their identification in schizophrenic patients should not present particular problems. However, there are other cognitive distortions which are characteristic specifically of patients suffering from schizophrenic syndromes and that have not yet been systematically described in the cognitive-therapy literature. These include: predicative identification, precipitate attribution of meaning, egocentric overinclusiveness, failure to distinguish between meanings and causes in arriving at certainty and desymbolization and concretization of concepts. Since identification and correction of cognitive disturbances are particularly relevant for the treatment of schizophrenic patients we will consider these in some detail.

Predicative Identification. Arieti (1948, 1955, 1974a) has reported frequent occurrence of predicative identification; this type of cognitive error has been thoroughly investigated by Matte-Blanco (1965). This type of thinking Arieti has called "paleologic". It can best be understood with reference to von Domarus' principle (von Domarus 1944): whereas the normal person accepts identity only upon the basis of identical subjects (i.e. following Aristotelian logic), the schizophrenic may accept identity based upon identical predicates (i.e. he follows a primordial form of logic). For example, a schizophrenic patient may conclude from the statements, "Björn Borg is a tennis player" and "I am a tennis player" that "I am Björn Borg". Important to note is that the predicate may refer not only to a quality inherent in the objects which are identified, but also to spatial and temporal contiguity. For example, a patient who believes in the presence of God in a church may conclude that, being in a church, he is God. Interestingly, the concept of predicative identification has been used by Mallinger (1974) in a cognitive-therapeutic reformulation of the psychoanalytic concept of transference.

Precipitate Attribution of Meaning. It is generally known from the psychiatric literature that schizophrenic patients are intolerant of ambiguity. As a consequence they are prone to attribute meanings to incoming stimuli before they have been able to distinguish them clearly, with resulting perceptive distortions. Probably such a cognitive distortion, when combined with arbitrary inference, is one of the factors that contributes to the building of delusional experiences, especially those of reference.

Egocentric Overinclusiveness. The concept of overinclusion refers to the tendency to respond to a larger number of objects than properly belong to the given set (Rabin et al. 1979). Lidz (1974) aptly pointed out that the schizophrenic's overinclusiveness is primarily "egocentric"; this refers to the Piagetian conception of egocentrism and aims at emphasizing, according to Lidz, the regressive characteristics of schizophrenic overinclusiveness. Lidz states that, "The schizophrenic patient typically believes that what others do or say centers on him, as in delusions of reference or persecutory delusional systems; or he believes that his thoughts influence others and even the inanimate universe" (p. 95). The use of the term egocentrism therefore seems particularly appropriate; in fact, all egocentrism relies on the presumed omnipotence of thought. Thus, the psychoanalytic concept of the child's "feeling of omnipotence" could easily be understood in cognitive-therapeutic terms. However, rather than speaking of regression it seems appropriate to regard the egocentrism of the schizophrenic patient as the result of his failure completely to decenter cognitively; this would persist throughout his life unless specifically dealt with in treatment.

Confusion of Meanings and Causes. The failure to distinguish between meanings and causes has been described by Jacobs (1982); to a certain extent it can be regarded as related to the concept of "personalizing" as used by Beck et al. (1979). The substitution of meanings for causes occurs in one's urgency to answer the "why?" questions that one poses oneself when confronted with external events. For example, a male patient who is refused a dance may perceive the refusal on the basis of his subjective belief of being unattractive rather than considering that the girl may simply have been tired or was already engaged for that particular dance.

Desymbolization. Searles (1962) introduced the concept of desymbolization to refer to a process which, according to the psychiatric literature, is common among schizophrenic patients. Once-obtained metaphorical meanings become "desymbolized", and the individual reacts to them as though they were literal meanings. For example, a patient who hears one member of the staff telling another:" Patient X tried to make me believe that he had carried out his homework, but I saw through him", may conclude that this member of the staff is really able to "see through" people. On the other hand, desymbolization does not necessarily imply, as Searles seems to believe, the loss of early-acquired metaphorical concepts or the loss of understanding of early-learned proverbs. In fact, inconsistent findings have been reported in the literature in this respect (Rabin et al. 1979). This type of cognitive error must always be noticed, for its presence can negatively influence therapeutic work; cognitive psychotherapy, after all, frequently relies on the use of metaphors.

Concretization and Perceptualization. The type of cognitive error referred to as concretization and perceptualization of the concept has also been described by Arieti (1959), who regarded it as regressive. This refers to the schizophrenic's reluctance to remain at the level of abstract concepts and his tendency to translate concepts into percepts. This process is similar to that occurring in dreams which, according to Arieti, are predominantly visual translations of paleologic thoughts. Arieti believes that in the schizophrenic "Thinking may regress to the level of perception and result in hallucinatory experiences" (p. 544). That which Arieti describes is probably nothing but the psychopathological phenomenon, well-known since the beginning of this century in the German literature under the term *Gedankenlautwerden* ("hearing one's own thoughts aloud"). This concept must be clearly distinguished from true auditory hallucinations.

An alternative interpretation to that advanced by Arieti would conceive this cognitive error in terms of "private speech", in the sense given to this concept by Piaget (1932) and especially by Vygotsky (1934/1962). Piaget took into account as private speech the instance of children talking aloud to themselves; he maintained that this completely disappears by the time of formal operational thought, probably as a consequence of the internalization of social norms and without having been replaced by silent self-directed speech. Vygotsky, on the other hand, maintained that private speech becomes increasingly internalized as children grow to school years and remains so into and throughout adulthood. If we consider that the cognitive-emotive development of the schizophrenic patient may have been hampered by unfavourable environmental circumstances, it seems reasonable to assume that he has had to rely on his "internal dialogue" more than on abstract thoughts as a coping mechanism in periods of more intense distress. Vygotsky (1960/1974) maintains that the relationships among higher psychic functions have been in the past relations among people (p. 197). The suggestion made by Fuson (1979) that private speech serves emotional-expressive as well as self-regulatory and fantasy/role-playing functions is also compatible with the hypothesis advanced here. And the common observation that the experience of this phenomenon becomes even more vivid when the patient is in a stressful situation is not inconsistent with our hypothesis.

There is no difficulty in training patients to identify the most common cognitive distortions and eventually to correct them, but this training should focus first on those faulty cognitions that are less closely related to more severe psychopathological symptoms. For example, if one wants to make the patient aware that he is making selective abstractions and drawing arbitrary inferences, a patient with delusional ideas of reference should first be trained to recognize these errors in fields not directly related to his own delusional ideas.

Primary and Secondary Processes

According to a common view in the psychoanalytic literature the disordered cognitive processes of the schizophrenic patient are regarded as the expression of a regression to (primitive and irrational) primary-process thinking. It is our view, however, that both the concept of regression and that of primary process (and even more so those of "primitive" and "irrational") are inappropriate here. Regarded within the framework of developmental and information-processing theories both concepts, as they are understood in classical psychoanalysis, appear obsolete and can be dispensed with. Two modern psychoanalysts, Noy and Peterfreund, have also incorporated information-processing concepts into their framework. Although these authors diverge in many respects, access to their writings has been of a great help for the development of the ideas developed in this chapter.

Freud's description of primary and secondary thought processes (1895, 1900) is regarded in psychoanalytic circles as one of his major discoveries. (cf. Arlow 1958). Jones (1953) maintained that the discovery of the primary process represents "Freud's chief claim to fame: even his discovery of the unconscious is subordinated to it" (p. 213). Other authors, including Hilgard (1962), point out instead that the distinction between the illogical and impulsive in thought, on the one hand, and the logical and rational, on the other, is a very old one and is not original with Freud. From the point of view of their formal aspects, Freud characterized the primary process as operating by three mechanisms – condensation, displacement and symbolism – while the secondary process follows the precepts and rules of logic. Understandably, the primary process was originally formulated within the framework of economic theory. However, even when Freud (1923) developed his new structural theory, he did not revise these concepts. Despite much debate (especially in the 1950s) no universally accepted revision of this view has emerged (cf. Arlow 1958, for a report of a panel; Noy 1969, 1979), and the issue of the development of the primary process has been remarkably neglected. It has been assumed that these processes are anchored constitutionally and remain forever in their original form. Noy (1969) comments, ironically, that the primary processes are unique in that "they are assumed to develop from nothing and to progress toward nothing" (p. 158). More recent criticism has been focussed on developmental aspects. Holt (1967), for example, maintained that primary processes cannot be present at the beginning of life but must be developed by the growth of the same structures that produce the secondary process. A similar point of view is endorsed by Noy (1969, 1979) who maintains that the course of development of these processes is "determined by the same intrinsic maturational factors" (1979, p. 177).

Both Klein (1976) and Noy have made use of the concepts of information processing and feedback to conceptualize secondary-process thought. Noy expanded Klein's conceptions and proposed that feedback could be regarded as a criterion to conceptualize primary and secondary processes. Accordingly, the latter are defined as monitored and dependent on constant feedback information (that is, "on the consequences of self-generated activity", Klein, p. 244). The primary processes, on the other hand, are all the functions that are not dependent on such feedback (Noy 1969, p. 162). Peterfreund (1971) endorses a quite similar opinion in discussing the major differences in information processing between sleep and waking. He points out that "during sleep there is apparently a diminution of inputs from the outer world of 'reality' " (p. 246).

Noy's main thesis is that primary-process thinking does not recede altogether with the emergence of secondary-process thought, but that these processes develop side by side and are both present throughout an individual's life, although their level of organization and functioning changes. A similar opinion had been expressed much earlier by Burstein (1959), and Rapaport (1967) maintained that, "not even our ordered thinking is free of primary processes" (p. 843).

In fact, instances of "magical thinking" can be found at any age in ordinary people. Also the concept of regression would hardly do justice to the expression of primary processes in artistic manifestations (see also Arieti 1974b). In such cases, the concept of "regression in the service of the ego" (Kris 1952) and that of "tertiary processes" consisting of a particular combination of primary and secondary processes in art and creativity (Arieti 1966, 1974b) have been used to cope with the difficulties deriving from a conception of the primary processes as regressive, primitive and non-developed. If the primary process is regarded, as with Holt (1967), as a special system of processing information in the service of a synthetic necessity, its main characteristics (condensation, displacement, symbolization, etc.), present at a time when complex cognitive structures are not yet fully developed, become easier to understand. Peterfreund (1971) has discussed these concepts at some length in reference to dreams, maintaining that these are easily explainable within an information-processing framework.

Noy (1969) proposes dispensing with any discussion of "primitiveness" concerning the primary process. He suggests, rather, that the development of primary and secondary processes is different because their goals and functions are different. Primary processes can be thought of as developing towards the ability to deal effectively with the self and all experiences which must be assimilated into it, while secondary processes develop towards the ability to deal effectively with reality. In particular, Noy's thesis is that "according to primary process mode, objects, events, and phenomena are organized as experience, and according to the secondary process mode, as knowledge" (1979, p. 180). An important corollary derived by Noy from his assumption about the parallel development of primary and secondary thought processes makes inappropriate use of the concept of regression. In fact, it would be more proper to speak of a "shift" from one process to another and not to consider this shift as one of a regression.

Ryle (1978) aptly pointed out the interest in various forms of thinking among cognitive psychologists. He refers in particular to Bartlett's (1954) distinction between thinking in terms of images and thinking in terms of words and points out that a defining characteristic of images is that they are combined on the basis of common emotions and interests and not by juxtaposition in space and time.

What application can this have in regard to conceptualizing the clinical manifestations of the schizophrenic patient? We have interpreted secondary-process thinking as dependent on feedback from reality. Obviously for such a feedback to operate correctly, it is necessary that decentering (in a Piagetian sense) occur, and that reality be accurately preceived. However there is enough evidence to assume that most of the schizophrenic patients' appraisals of the environment are egocentric, and that they are prone to a great number of cognitive distortions. If so, the corrective feedback necessary for secondary-process thinking becomes markedly reduced, at the same time as "egocentric feedback" might facilitate both the activation of and the shift towards primary-process thinking. This hypothesis is not incompatible with the suggestion by Noy (1979, p. 181) that in patients suffering from schizophrenic syndromes the primary-process mode dominates cognition, owing to a disturbance of the secondary mode in the course of development.

Delusions and Hallucinations

Delusional and hallucinatory experiences belong to the most frequently encountered, albeit not necessarily always present, clinical manifestations of schizophrenic syndromes. Traditionally, both these experiences are understood as characterized by the fact that they are felt with an extraordinary conviction, that they are impervious to compelling counter-argument, and that their content is usually impossible. If this characterization is accepted, it is important to discuss the extent to which delusional and hallucinatory experiences are accessible to cognitive-psychotherapeutic interventions.

Delusional Experiences

A few studies of the application of cognitive psychotherapy in delusional patients suggest that even long-term delusional experiences may prove modifiable (Beck 1952; Hole et al. 1979; Adams et al. 1981). The results reported by these authors are consistent with the opinion maintained by Arieti (1962) and by Jacobs (1980), who used a cognitive approach within a psychoanalytic framework in the treatment of delusional patients. However, before commenting on these studies it is necessary to introduce more general considerations concerning delusional experiences, especially because some of these can, in our view, be generalized to hallucinatory phenomena.

First, as pointed out by Hole et al. (1979) and by Kendler et al. (1983) delusional beliefs can be regarded in reference to various characteristic dimensions. The most important of these are:

1. *Conviction*: the degree to which the patient is certain of the validity of his delusion
2. *Extension*: the degree to which delusional beliefs involve various areas of the patient's life
3. *Pervasiveness or pressure*: the extent to which the patient is occupied by ruminations about his delusional concerns; this includes the patient's seeking delusional goals and interpreting his experiences with reference to his delusional beliefs
4. *Disorganization*: the degree to which delusional beliefs are internally consistent and systematized
5. *Bizarreness*: the extent to which delusional contents deviate from culturally determined, consensual reality

Besides these dimensional aspects, other basic cognitive processes relevant to delusions should be taken into account. Among these processes Jacobs (1980) considers: thinking, knowing, meta-thinking and generating erroneous controlling assumptions (i.e. what we would call basic dysfunctional assumptions or core dysfunctional schemata). Jacobs refers to the work of the neo-Kantian philosopher Arendt (1978) to underline the distinction between thinking and knowing. He points out that thinking normally precedes knowing in that thinking correlates meanings to what we perceive. In the (primary) delusional experience, however, the reverse is true: knowing precedes thinking. Meta-thinking refers to the process of thinking about one's own thinking and may be conceived as consisting of various subprocesses. Important among these are: ability to select and direct the content of one's thoughts and to avoid selective inattention; ability to sustain a continuous cognitive horizon of alternative explanations; ability easily to shift between the concrete and the abstract and to differentiate between causal and meaningful connections (see "Dysfunctional Cognitions", above). According to Jacobs, the ability for meta-thinking is grossly impaired in the delusional schizophrenic.

The last cognitive process, taken into account by Jacobs, refers to the forming of basic, erroneous controlling assumptions that he assumes to be acquired early in life and to predispose one to later delusions (p. 559). Jacobs tends to relate the concept of basic dysfunctional assumptions to Klein's conception of "peremptory ideation" (Klein 1970), that is, to ideas experientially described as imperious, demanding, allowing no denial or refusal (see also Peterfreund and Franceschini 1973, p. 235, n. 13 for a critical discussion of this concept). If the concept of peremptory phenomena is regarded as devoid from the assumptions concerning "psychic energy" that Rapaport (1960) used to explain their occurrence, peremptory ideas appear closely related to the concept of "automatic thoughts" used in cognitive psychotherapy.

Although Jacobs has not been explicit on this point, we can, perhaps, interpret his emphasis on erroneous controlling assumptions and his equating them with Klein's peremptory ideation as implying that they characterize the process of "knowing" in the schizophrenic patient. In support of this view the definition of peremptory ideas given by Klein (1970, p. 359) may be relevant. According to his definition this type of ideation precludes all doubt or question. If this is the case, we can understand why knowing is assumed to precede thinking in these patients. Jacobs is eager to point out that the mere presence of basic controlling assumptions is not sufficient to determine the origin and persistence of delusions. Other factors are obviously also required. Among these Jacobs mentions that, "A person raised in a family that indoctrinates him in controlling assumptions, will never develop the cognitive autonomy of meta-thinking" (p. 560).

In 1952 Beck reported one of the first cases of chronic delusion in a schizophrenic patient treated with cognitive techniques. In addition to some reconstruction of the possible childhood antecedents to the patient's belief Beck encouraged him in carrying out reality testing in order to challenge the belief's validity. According to this report, the patient greatly improved and toward the end of the treatment was almost able to exclude any idea about persecution. Another such case study has been reported by Adams et al. (1981). These authors used a multi-faceted treatment programme consisting of nine sessions aimed at emphasizing the process of attending to appropriate internal and external stimuli. Neither at termination nor at a 6-month follow-up did the patient report evidence of thought disorders.

Hole et al. (1979) have investigated the extent to which the use of cognitive techniques (i.e. focussing, questioning, reality testing) could influence various dimensions of delusional experience (conviction, pervasiveness, accommodation) in eight delusional in-patients. Each patient participated in 7 1-h sessions at the end of which one half did not show any significant clinical change. Of the four who improved all showed reduced pervasiveness while two also showed a decreased conviction in their delusional beliefs. It should be noted that this study was conceived as an attempt to test the prevalent assumption on the inaccessibility of delusional beliefs to corrective information rather than being part of a specific therapeutic attempt.

Jacobs (1980) does not report case illustrations, however he does suggest a cognitive therapeutic strategy for approaching the delusional patient. This strategy consists of helping the patient become aware of his deficiencies concerning the various components of meta-thinking in order to develop them. Later, as his meta-thinking improves, the patient is helped to recognize and eventually correct the specific controlling assumptions that underlie his deficit.

Arieti (1962b) has also reported four cognitive therapeutic strategies for dealing with delusional patients. These consist of helping the patient to learn that he is in a "referential attitude", making him aware of his "concretizing attitude", making him recognize that to sustain his delusional beliefs he must resort to paleologic, and helping him acquire awareness of the "punctiform insight". By "referential attitude" Arieti means that before the delusions are fully manifest, the patient "is searching, looking for references which will corroborate the pre-existing mood" (p 55). In other words, he could be said to commit many of the errors in perception and processing of environmental stimuli described above. According to Arieti, the patient must be helped to recapture the mood and attitude that he had prior to his cognitive distortions. We would add that the patient must also learn to recognize his cognitive errors and how to correct them. By "punctiform insight" Arieti refers to the fact that some schizophrenic patients may, when in distress, intuitively correctly interpret environmental stimuli, although this insight is sustained by paleologic thinking and concretization. As an example, Arieti reports the case of a female patient, who delusionally interpreted apparently trivial events, but whose delusions revealed an insightful evaluation of reality based on the use of predicative identification and concretization.

In one patient of our own attempts to influence the conviction in a delusional belief of reference by the technique of reality testing did not succeed during an early phase of treatment in bringing about significant result. However a change in strategy meant that we focussed on other, more reality-related aspects of the patient's disability (in particular, his having left his job), at the same time that we also focussed on attempts at enhancing his feeling of self-worth. When an enhancement of the patient's self-esteem was achieved, and the patient had experienced in a trial of sheltered work that he was, indeed, able to work, the patient proved able to apply by himself the cognitive techniques that he had meanwhile learned to challenge and correct his original delusional experiences. At a follow-up 6 months later he reported that whenever a proneness to commit cognitive distortions occurred, he was able to mobilize the knowledge acquired in treatment and to stop them.

Another patient of ours, a 27-year-old with a history of delusional experiences over several years, had the conviction of being both God and the Devil and thus of being able to influence others, both positively and destructively. When the latter was at its peak, he became overwhelmed by anxiety and highly destructive. With him our therapeutic achievement consisted in a marked reduction of the pervasiveness of his delusions and in a marked reduction of his conviction of being able to damage others by means of some supernatural power. Anxiety appeared to be reduced, and the destructive behaviour did not recur. However his basic delusion of being both God and the Devil (understandable with reference to the patient's circumstances during infancy and at the present) was not influenced by treatment.

Hallucinatory Experiences

A dearth characterizes the literature concerning the possibility of influencing hallucinatory experiences with cognitive therapeutic interventions. However, as mentioned above, some dimensions relevant for a correct evaluation of delusional experiences can probably be generalized to hallucinatory experiences as well, in particular, the concepts of conviction, pervasiveness, extension and bizarreness. Thus, therapeutic interventions can be conceptualized in terms of attempts at influencing any of these dimensions.

Arieti (1962a,b, 1974a) maintains that with the exception of patients at a very advanced stage of illness, hallucinatory experiences occur when the patient expects them to occur. Since he uses auditory hallucinations as an example, he speaks of a "listening attitude", broadly corresponding to the "referential attitude" described above, Arieti emphasizes that the patient, after a condition of relatedness has been achieved, is able first to recognize when he puts himself into the listening attitude and then to recognize that he puts himself into such attitude when he is in a particular situation or in a particular mood, for example, when, "he perceives hostility almost in the air" (1962b, p. 53). According to Arieti, once the patient learns to recognize the relationship between his mood and putting himself into the listening attitude, a great step has been accomplished, and the patient becomes accessible to further interventions.

We have been able to verify Arieti's assumption in two young female patients of our own. Both reported that auditory hallucinations with a deprecatory referential content typically occurred when they were tense and alone and disappeared when they engaged in social interactions or in some absorbing task. Both patients learned to control the occurrence of their hallucinatory phenomena, but their "voices" never completely disappeared.

It should be pointed out that, although Arieti maintains that an attitude similar to the listening one applies to other modalities of hallucinatory phenomena, we do not have any experience with visual, tactile or olfactory hallucinations to verify this assumption. In addition, we are not sure whether the auditory hallucinations reported by our patients should be regarded as instances of *Gedankenlautwerden* or true hallucinations, or whether the patients' identification of the voices they heard with their own thoughts formulated aloud in the head was an expression of the original psychopathological disturbance or already a result of our therapeutic work with the patients.

Misattributions

The term misattribution refers to the patient's proneness severely to underestimate or overestimate the extent to which he can control his behaviour (Beck et al. 1979; Bedrosian and Beck 1980; Greenwood 1983). It is theoretically derived from Rotter's seminal conception of generalized expectancies for internal versus external control of reinforcement (Rotter 1966) – in short, from the theory on locus of control (LOC). LOC refers to the predisposition to perceive one's reinforcement as contingent on one's own behaviour ("internals") or as determined by extrinsic factors such as chance, fate or powerful others ("externals").

There is support for the assumption that an individual's perception of LOC is dependent on parental antecedents (Davis and Phares 1969; MacDonald 1971; Levenson 1973; Austrin and Aubuchon 1979; Rohner et al. 1980). In particular, the studies reported by these authors suggest that subjects who experienced their parents as showing less rejection, hostile control and withdrawl of relations are more likely to become internals. Internality appeared also to be related with the perception of parental acceptance and with the subjects' level of trust in parents.

In contrast, subjects who report that their parents were more inclined to use deprivation of privileges, punitive behaviour and rigid control seem more likely to become externals.

In studies of psychiatric patients it has been found that those suffering from schizophrenic syndromes are, on average, more external than those with other diagnoses. (Harrow and Ferrante 1969; Levenson 1973; see also Lefcourt 1976 for review). Greenwood (1983) points out that both internality and externality can be evident in schizophrenic patients. Because they assume both their not having any control over their thoughts or behaviour (these being determined by external influences), and believe themselves able to let happen whatever they wish. The patient of our own, discussed above, illustrates this: on the one hand, he believed to be completely controlled by God and by an evil power, but, on the other, he was fully convinced of being able to influence others.

It may be noted that the results of the investigations carried out in schizophrenic patients, considered against the background of reports concerning the possible relationship to parental rearing attitudes, are consistent with our general conception of vulnerability. In addition, these results suggest the hypothesis that the schizophrenics' perception of LOC is egocentric.

One particular type of misattribution, labelled by Beck as personalizing, has been found repeatedly in depressed patients. This consists of the patient's proneness to attribute to his own deficiencies any adverse events, even those beyond his control (cf., also the revised theory of learned helplessness by Abramson et al. 1978). As mentioned above, this process is at the base of the faulty cognition described by Jacobs (1982) as the "failure to distinguish between causes and meanings in arriving at certainty", frequently present in schizophrenic patients.

Misattributions of the latter type are accessible to the various reattribution techniques described by Beck and co-workers (1979) to be used with depressed patients. The goal of such techniques is to identify the many factors which contribute to a negative experience rather than absolving the patient of all responsibility. Since many schizophrenic patients believe themselves to be unworthy, unlovable or total failures, reattribution should be sought by challenging and eventually modifying this dysfunctional self-perception. An example above referred to a patient who attributed to his own unattractiveness a girl's refusal to dance with him. To correct such a misattribution the approach would be, first, to assess whether the patient has the skill appropriate to invite a girl to dance, and, if not, to help him in acquiring it. Secondly, one must review relevant alternatives to the patient's interpretation of the event in an attempt to assign responsibility in a logical fashion. However, it is obvious that the efficacy of this strategy depends substantially on a well-developed therapeutic relationship, since the patient is asked to question a deeply rooted belief, and since a correlation has been shown between the development of internality and trust in others (Austrin and Aubuchon 1979).

On the other hand, as Greenwood (1983) has pointed out, it is more difficult to correct faulty attributions which are central characteristics of the patient's pathological thought and to show a delusional quality. In our experience, any attempt to influence delusional misattributions should be postponed to a later phase of treatment when the patient and the therapist have etablished a stable, trusting relationship and when the patient has become aware of his ability to change dysfunctional beliefs of a more peripheral nature.

Decentering

Frequent reference has been made here to the Piagetian concept of egocentrism and its relevance for an understanding of various psychopathological manifestations by the schizophrenic patient. Egocentrism (taken only in its epistemological sense and without any implication of narcissism or selfishness) refers to the child's inability during the pre-operational phase of development (ages 2–7) to put himself in the place of another person. Indeed, the child in this period believes that everyone feels and thinks as he does. For example, if asked to describe the view of an object from a position different from his own, the child at the pre-operational level is unable to do so. The egocentric thinker may be said to assimilate experiences from the world at large into schemata derived from his own immediate world, seeing everything in relation to himself. Consequently, he attributes life and feeling to all objects; he believes that objects can be influenced by his wishes or by action at a distance, and he presumes that his thoughts are immediately accessible to other people. The child assumes that since everyone thinks exactly as he does, there is no need for explanations. The similarity between the characteristics of egocentric thinking and primary-process thought is evident.

Elkind (1970/1985) suggests that there is a relationship between the child's egocentrism and his assumptions concerning a positive view of his parents. Although such an assumption may be perfectly valid in most cases, egocentrism also contributes to a misinterpretation of its validity when it is contradicted by factual evidence. According to Elkind, such misinterpretations can be regarded as instances of denial. However, he points out that denial is merely persisting in maintaining an assumption despite any contrary evidence. In other words, assimilation has ascendancy over accommodation, and the child is unable to accommodate his schemata to contradictory evidence.

Only with the onset of the phase of operational thought does the child become independent of what is phenomenologically possible and can perform activities in his mind that are impossible in reality. "Decentering" refers precisely to this enlargement of perspective, and, accordingly, to a successive loss of egocentrism. The child, at age 7 or 8 begins to be able to shift rapidly between his own views and the views of others; he becomes "able to step back from one aspect of what is perceptually given and to consider other aspects" (Sollod and Wachtel 1980). However, egocentrism does not recede for ever; in fact (as discussed below), it increases again at successive critical phases, especially in adolescence.

Several authors have attempted to reconceptualize schizophrenic functioning, applying Piaget's ideas (Freeman and McGhie 1957; Feffer 1967; Kilburg and Siegel 1973; Blatt and Wild 1976). Feffer, for example, has discussed various aspects of schizophrenic symptomatology, especially ideas of reference and other delusional patterns, in terms of an underlying egocentrism. Similarly, Freeman and McGhie have attempted a description of schizophrenic thought according to Piaget's levels of cognitive development. In particular, Freeman et al. (1966) have suggested that the degree and nature of cognitive disturbance may be associated with the extent of disruption of human relationships. A related conception has been expressed by Lidz (1973) who emphasized that many types of disturbed families actively encourage egocentric thinking in adolescents and suggested that this process is particularly evident in the families of young schizophrenics. Lidz (1974) has also pointed out that egocentrism increases each time the developmental process brings the child into a new field of cognitive action, to recede slowly when the child masters the new field. Of particular relevance to schizophrenic states is the egocentricity arising early in adolescence and attributed by Elkind (1967, 1978) to the emergence of abstract thinking. Adolescents who meet difficulties in moving through this sensitive phase fail to decenter cognitively and preserve a belief in the unlimited power of their own thought (Piaget and Inhelder 1969). Recently Rishovd et al. (1986) have reported results of an investigation which suggest that egocentrism is a prominent characteristic of the communication of non-paranoid schizophrenics' parents. Kilburg and Siegel (1973) hypothesized that schizophrenic patients are characterized by less complex and advanced cognitive structures than non-schizophrenics. The results of a study testing the formal operation of adult thought, carried out in a patient population, proved compatible with their hypothesis. Blatt and Wild (1976), referring to the opinion maintained by Freeman et al., propose that "in psychosis there are important relationships between the degree and type of disruptions of various cognitive-perceptual functions, the level of definition of self and others, and the level and nature of interpersonal relationships" (p. 7). In a similar vein Sollod and Wachtel (1980) suggest that a withdrawn person can be viewed "as having an inadequately developed construction of social reality with many egocentric and childlike features present" (p. 15). Very recently Baron (1986) in a study of 157 adolescents found a modest but significant correlation between the scores on a measure of egocentrism and those on a measure of dysfunctional attitudes.

A cognitive distortion which has evidently not yet been discussed in terms of egocentrism, but whose characteristics fit egocentric thinking, is the schizophrenic's lack of awareness of asymmetry in human relations (described by Jacobs 1982). Schizophrenics enter any close interpersonal relationship with the expectation of perfect symmetry. Jacobs suggests that this expectation derives from the following underlying assumptions: "If I love you, then you and I are identical in perceptions, feelings, thoughts, responses, and conduct".

From the discussion hitherto it should be evident that some level of egocentrism is frequently present in schizophrenic patients, and that egocentrism is the likely basis of several cognitive distortions observable in these patients.

Research findings which point to a relationship between egocentrism and parental attitudes and those which lend support to a positive relationship between egocentrism and dysfunctional assumptions are consistent with our general theoretical framework focussed on vulnerability. Since egocentrism is present in schizophrenic patients, interventions aimed at promoting decentering represents a very important component of the therapeutic process. The importance of these has been stressed repeatedly in the cognitive-therapy literature with regard to depressive (Beck 1976), obsessive-compulsive (Guidano and Liotti 1983) and anxiety syndromes (Beck and Emery 1985). In practice, therapeutic strategies aim at having the patient challenge the assumption that he is the focal point of all events and at helping him be able to shift between his own views and the views of others in order to facilitate interpersonal communication. Although several common cognitive-behavioural techniques may prove effective in this respect, it should be kept in mind that decentering is a very slow process and one that requires time and patience from the therapist. In particular, more peripheral distortions should always be challenged first. Sollod and Wachtel (1980) summarize this process by maintaining that the therapist's task is to draw the patient's attention to facts which cannot so easily be assimilated into his extant schemata and by so doing encourage accommodation of extant cognitive structures to these facts (p. 17).

Basic Dysfunctional Assumptions

Virtually our entire discussion to this point presupposes the occurrence of some more basic dysfunctional assumption, against which the patient evaluates reality. Such basic cognitive structures could also be labelled basic schemata or, to use Bowlby's terminology, "working models" (Bowlby 1973). In defining this concept Bowlby maintains that "each individual builds working models of the world and of himself in it, with the aid of which he perceives events, forecasts the future, and constructs his plans" (p. 236). Peterfreund (1983), who has adopted Bowlby's terminology, aptly points out that the term "working model" implies something more than a static map or representation. In using such concepts as schemata, cognitive structure, and basic ("silent") assumption one should not presume their static nature. In his characterization of working models Peterfreund (1983) points out that they are changed by the very information received, and that "they must be constantly updated, adapted, readapted checked and rechecked for consistency" (p. 83). We should emphasize, however, that dysfunctional working models which have been developed early, especially those referring to the self, may be relatively enduring; this point of view can be traced as far as back as to James (1890). One characteristic of "schemata", pointed out by Neisser (1967), is that they "systematically distort new constructions" (pp. 286–288). Thus, it could be assumed that cognitive distortions contribute in counteracting the corrective effect of environmental feedback. Goldfried and Robins (1983), who have reviewed the concept of self-schema at some length, point to the tendency to ignore information that is contradictory to one's view of oneself (p. 48). A similar conception has been maintained by Swann and Read (1981) who provided some evidence that people attach greater value to feedback that confirms their self-conceptions.

Little has been written on faulty basic assumptions in patients suffering from schizophrenic syndromes. Jacobs (1980) uses the term "erroneous controlling assumptions" as corresponding to that of cognitive schemata and enumerates a number of these that he regards as "delusiogenic". Examples include the following: "Everything can and must be explained as to its causation"; "Growth leads to catastrophy"; "If you are not responsible for something negative, I am"; "To leave you, means I will cease to exist"; "If I need you, you cannot live without me". Jacobs emphasizes that these assumptions have been assimilated in children growing up in a dysfunctional family environment, and that some of them reflect an impaired individuation-separation (Mahler et al. 1975).

Besides the possible occurrence of dysfunctional schemata of the type described by Jacobs, it should be pointed out that working models of schizophrenic patients related to the self may be of the type expressed in statements such as: "I am unlovable"; "I am unworthy"; "I have to be careful, people want to destroy me". These may be accessible to the patient's awareness because they are obviously reflected in his behaviour. This observation is in a sense consistent with the psychoanalytic opinion that the content of the unconscious of the schizophrenic patient does not need to be discovered since it has become conscious in the psychosis. Young (1986) in a recent comment on the basic dysfunctional assumptions of patients with severe personality disorders, pointed out that these assumptions are "unconditional". This accurate observation probably applies to the dysfunctional schemata of schizophrenic patients as well. This should not be surprising in view of the discussion of primary processes above. In fact, primary-process thinking has among its characteristics the absence of negatives, conditionals or other qualifying conjunctions (Peterfreund 1971, p. 268). Also, primary-process cognition entails a tendency to replace whole perception with partial perception, a confusion of similarity with identity and that which Arieti (1968a,b) calls "primary class formation", for instance, certain characteristics of the mother generalized to all women.

Undoubtedly, a modification of the core structures as discussed above would imply a thoroughly restructuring therapeutic effect. Admittedly, very little is known so far as concerns to the extent to which such a restructuration can be achieved.

Other Therapeutic Strategies

In view of the composite nature of the disability of the schizophrenic patient other therapeutic techniques, besides those reviewed so far, may also contribute in bringing about an improvement in the patient's condition. A few of them will be discussed here.

Correction of Social-Skills Deficits. We have repeatedly underlined here that pronounced social-skills deficits occur in most patients suffering from schizophrenic syndromes and have pointed out that the occurrence of such deficits may contribute to cognitive distortions (e.g. misattributions). Very often disturbances occur in the patient's ability correctly to interpret the complex pattern of communication in interpersonal relations. In particular, uncertainties are often evidenced in our patients as concerns the correct interpretation of non-verbal communication. We believe that the occurrence of such disturbances could easily be predicted from our conception of vulnerability, which takes into account dysfunctional patterns of communication in the childhood family of patients. We therefore maintain that any attempt at correcting these must, to be long-lasting, be preceded by a careful assessment of underlying dysfunctional beliefs and by their modification.

Training in Problem Solving. In a sense, all psychotherapeutic work could be regarded as training the patient in problem solving, as it concerns the solution of either conflictual problems, consequences of psychopathological symptoms or practical problems in daily life. A general problem-solving approach is a major characteristic of cognitive psychotherapy. Problem-solving strategies, however, have been used mainly in the treatment of chronic patients in an attempt to improve their general social competence (Coché and Flick 1975; Siegel and Spivak 1976). In general, this approach focusses on four major variables: (a) ability to recognize problems, (b) ability to define problems, (c) ability to think of alternative solutions and (d) ability to decide which solution is best. In the training of problem-solving the therapist must obviously also be attentive to the occurrence of faulty cognitions by the patient in order to make him aware of their interfering effects and to help him in correcting them. One advantage of this therapeutic strategy is that, when used with in-patients, it can be employed in a group context.

Self-Instructional Training. According to Luria (1976) the development of behavioural control in children is characterized by three phases: in the first, the child receives instructions from persons in his environment; during the second, the child repeats aloud instructions to himself when performing a task; and in the third, he gives himself instructions in the form of an internal dialogue. Meichenbaum (Meichenbaum and Cameron 1973; Meichenbaum 1977) started from the assumption that everyone entertains in varying degrees task-irrelevant thoughts, images and feelings. They hypothesized that this could happen in schizophrenic patients as well, however, schizophrenic patients, in contrast to healthy people, would also be unable to edit or inhibit these task-irrelevant cognitions. Meichenbaum and Cameron carried out a feasibility study to test whether schizophrenic patients could be trained to identify when they were engaged in "schizophrenic behaviours" and by means of a set of self-instructions to modify such behaviours. The results of this self-instructional training programme showed that significant behavioural modification could, indeed, be achieved. However, since this was only a feasibility study, it lasted for only a short time, and no long-term follow up was carried out. Meyers et al. (1976) have applied a similar strategy with a 47-year-old chronic schizophrenic patient in an attempt to influence his pathologic speech. After 15 training sessions the patient was apparently able to control his speech, and continued improvement was evident at a 6-month follow-up. A similar result was obtained in a chronic female patient, reported elsewhere (Perris 1986a, p. 139) by the present author. This patient, upon follow-up at 6 years after discharge from hospital, was still able to control her speech. However minor relapses into a high-pitched, stereotypical speech intermingled with affectless outbursts of laughter still occurred when she felt particularly upset. On the other hand, she was able to correct her speech by herself.

Apparently, both Meichenbaum (1977, Meichenbaum and Cameron 1973) and Meyers et al. (1976) used this therapeutic strategy with chronic patients, as was the case with the patient in Perris (1986). Only relatively circumscribed pathological behaviours have been the target for this technique in schizophrenic patients. Any possible generalization to less chronic patients and to more complex disturbances must therefore await further verification.

A few Comments on the Therapeutic Process

Since the present author has elsewhere examined variables involved in the therapeutic process with in-patients (Perris 1985b, 1988) the following will focus on aspects of the therapeutic process in the individual treatment.

Sequences. The characteristic sequence in the therapeutic process comprises several phases (Fig. 3). The first, or "expectancy phase", is that during the growth of the therapeutic relationship. During this phase the patient oscillates between trust and mistrust and shows approach/avoidance behaviour. Not uncommonly the patient, especially if he had been treated previously in a more conventional way, questions the new approach and asks repeatedly about the purpose of psychotherapy. He seems to be caught in a hope/fear dilemma: he would like to believe in what the therapist tells him, but at the same time he is afraid he will be disappointed if he tries to assert himself. He tests the therapist provocatively, either by making increasing demands to discover what the limits will be or by clearly manifesting his pathological behaviour. This is one of the most delicate phases of treatment. On no other occasion more than this, must the therapist mobilize his empathy, because any unappropriate intervention would lead to a drop out.

The second phase can be referred to as that of "unrealistic optimism". Here the patient has developed a sense of trust in the honesty of the therapist, but he also assumes that all his problems will be solved in a short time and without any particular effort from his side. Such a "honeymoon" phase is well-known in psychotherapeutic practice. This phase is particularly suitable for socialization of the patient to the guiding principles of cognitive psychoterapy and for the training of some of the more difficult therapeutic techniques.

The third phase is mainly one of "hope and constructive effort". This phase is the longest and comprises the therapeutic work, proper, in an atmosphere of collaborative empiricism. It is preceded by transitional disappointment, but this disappointment is as a rule of short duration since a stable relationship has already developed. Obviously, the progress of this phase can be consistent, however, short periods of disequilibrium frequently occur, especially when therapeutic work

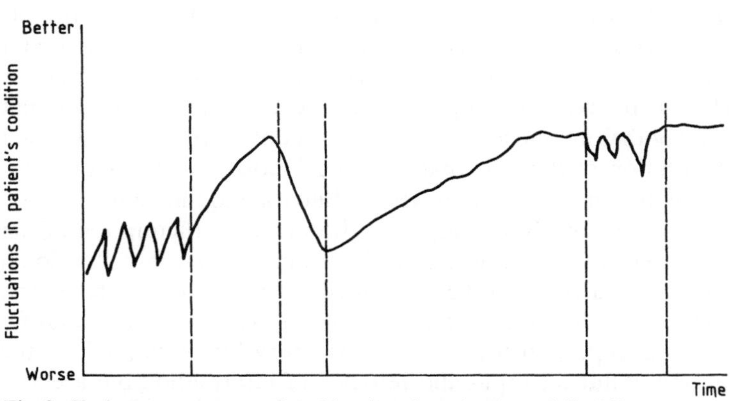

Fig. 3. Various components of a schizophrenic patient's total disability

challenges more basic dysfunctional schemata. Once again, the risk of drop-out increases on such occasions. Such periods of oscillation, however, should not necessarily be viewed as negative.

Finally, when termination approaches, there is often a transitional phase of relapse into the original symptomatology, almost as if nothing had happened since the beginning of therapy. However, if the therapist has sufficiently assumed the role of the "good enough mother", the patient will emerge very soon from this phase at the level he had attained before its beginning – or even at a slightly higher one. Also the characteristics of this fourth phase have long been known, also with regard to the psychotherapy of schizophrenic patients. A symptomatological relapse near termination of therapy has generally been regarded as the expression of resistance or dependency and conceptualized in terms of separation anxiety. Nonetheless, the therapist should never fail to make a realistic appraisal of the patient's social situation, nor should he neglect ensuring that any worsening of the patient is not due to environmental influences.

Challenging and Modifying Dysfunctional Cognitions. This aspect of the therapeutic process involves the modification of cognitive distortions that counteract corrective feedback from the environment and confirm the more basic dysfunctional assumptions. This process is not particularly difficult once a relationship of basic trust has developed. The more realistic appraisal of environmental events resulting from this modification eventually contributes strongly to restructuring of more basic schemata as well.

Recurrent Oscillations in the Therapeutic Process. Recurrent disequilibria in the course of the therapeutic process do not always indicate a worsening of the patient's condition. Borrowing the concept of dissipative structures, introduced by Prigogine (1980), Mahoney (1985) has aptly pointed out that disequilibrium, when it reaches a critical criterion, helps to encourage an open system in the direction of restructuring its ordering processes ("order through fluctuations"). Thus, it could be assumed that disequilibria in the course of therapy occur mainly when fundamental restructuring processes in the patient's working models are in progress.

Modification of Basic Schemata and the Issue of Resistance. Obviously, the ultimate goal of therapy should be a radical modification of the more fundamental dysfunctional schemata or "core structures". To refer to this transformation Mahoney (1980) has borrowed the concept of "scientific revolution", as elaborated by Kuhn (1962), and both Guidano and Liotti (1983) and Perris (1986c) have used the concept of dissolution of the "dogmatic nucleus" borrowed from Lakatos' (1970) conception of the growth of knowledge. Such a modification of basic dysfunctional working models always implies a thorough restructuration of the patient's view of himself, of the world and of his future – that is, a "personal revolution". However to achieve such change is not an easy task. There are several reasons for this, some of which would be considered in the psychoanalytic literature under the umbrella concept of resistance. Confirmatory biases implicit in the self-schemata not only influence input and retrieval of information but are also likely to make one more resistant to counterschematic information (Markus 1977;

Swann and Read 1981; Turk and Salovey 1985). In practice, the modification of early-developed dysfunctional self-schemata implies the change of one's own identity, and no such significant change will ever occur without sacrifice and suffering. Liotti (1987, in press) has recently made a thoughtful comparison of how the concept of resistance is dealt with in psychoanalytic and in cognitive-psychotherapy theoretical frameworks. His conclusions are consistent with the opinion expressed above. There are also other sources of resistance which should always be considered, one of which is resistance due to secondary gain; another is resistance due to negative influences in the patient's environment.

Is there, then, no possibility of promoting such a radical restructuring? The guarded answer of several cognitive psychotherapists is that this possibility does, indeed, exist. However, for a radical change to occur, certain subgoals must first be achieved. The patient must learn new behaviours which enable him to verify his newly acquired autonomy. He must succeed in correcting peripheral cognitive distortions which negatively influence corrective feedback. He must learn to discriminate between past and present (Goldfried and Robins 1983). He must become aware of his dysfunctional working models. And he must become able to perceive the availability of an alternative belief system. Thus, for a personal revolution to occur, the patient must find access to a continuous corrective feedback from reality. Heider's (1958) concept of "balance of cognitive structures" may be relevant to explain this process. When an imbalance is introduced (that is, environmental stimuli are dissonant with the present working models), a tendency to resolve the imbalance will result. The patient can follow one of two ways to accomplish this resolution: either move away from the source of imbalance (that is, drop out of treatment) or effect a change in the cognitive structure.

The Issue of "Insight". The term "insight" has become so abused that one wonders whether it is still useful for indicating the occurrence of a radical change in the condition of a patient. For example, there has been much debate over the distinction between emotional and intellectual insight (see Schonbar 1965, for review), but it is uncertain whether such a distinction is valid and useful. This is based, in fact, on an untenable dualism between emotions and cognitions. Richfield (1963) has emphasized that both are forms of cognition. Moreover, Ludwig (1966) has aptly pointed out that whereas "intellectualizers" have been much discussed, no corresponding discussion has occurred concerning "emotionalizers"; underlines that although the emotionalizer's words may appear loaded with meaning, the meaning often turns out to be more sham than real (p. 310). According to Ludwig, insight should be tested with regard to consistency, continuity and personal and social consequences in order to be regarded as therapeutic. Ellis and Sagarin (1964) divided insight in three stages: (a) when the patient becomes aware that the origins of his present disturbances must be traced back to the past; (b) when the patient acknowledges that he is still influenced by early-acquired dysfunctional beliefs; and (c) when he accepts that the only way out of his present predicament is to be attentive to his dysfunctional thoughts, to challenge them and to work towards modifying his basic assumptions. We should accept attainment of the third stage as evidence that something of importance has, indeed, occurred in the patient.

Concluding Remarks

This chapter contains only an idiosyncratic selection of the manifold aspects of cognitive psychotherapy with patients suffering from schizophrenic syndromes. Examples have had to be omitted of several techniques, e.g. role-play, cognitive rehearsal, modelling, monitoring of task-interfering thoughts. However, all these techniques are thoroughly described in several works on cognitive psychotherapy, and these are easily accessible. Also, no attention has been given here to the feasibility of cognitive group therapy with this type of patient, but a recent presentation of cognitive therapy in a group format for schizophrenic patients has been given by Greenwood (1983). Nor have we dealt with the feasibility of a cognitive approach to family therapy; preliminary accounts on cognitive family therapy are available in the literature (Epstein 1983; Waring 1981). Nevertheless, the advantages of integrating the systematic and the cognitive approaches into the treatment of families of schizophrenic patients have, in all probability, not yet been fully exploited. We have also omitted discussion of the possible advantages of this type of therapy in comparison with other types. An objective analysis of the results obtained by various authors with psychoanalysis or other sorts of psychotherapy is a hopeless task, due both to the imprecision of most reports and to the presence of so many confounding variables. Results of the most recent and ambitious comparison of psychoanalytically oriented dynamic psychotherapy and supportive (also dynamically oriented) psychotherapy (Gunderson et al. 1984) suggest that the effects obtained are comparable, possibly with some advantage for the latter type. No comparative studies of schizophrenic patients in which cognitive psychotherapy was included have been reported so far.

It is to be hoped that other therapists will derive from the reading of this chapter an encouragement to use cognitive therapy with the type of patients examined here – and that they find its use as rewarding as we have.

Acknowledgement. Paul Matussek, MD, PhD, Professor of psychotherapy at the University of Munich has kindly commented on an early draft of this chapter.

References

Abramsom LY, Seligman MEP, Teasdale JD (1978) Learned helplessness in humans: critique and reformulation. J Abnorm Psychol 87:49–74

Adams HE, Malatesta V, Brantley PJ, Turkat ID (1981) Modification of cognitive processes: a case study of schizophrenia. J Consult Clin Psychol 49:460–464

Ainsworth MDS (1972) Attachment and dependency: a comparison. In: Gewirtz J (ed) Attachment and Dependency. Winston, Washington DC

Alanen Y (1958) The mothers of schizophrenic patients. Acta Psychiat Neurol Scand 33: [Suppl 124]

Arendt H (1978) Thinking. Harcourt Brace, New York

Arieti S (1948) Special logic of schizophrenic and other types of autistic thought. Psychiatry 11:325–338

Arieti S (1955) Interpretation of Schizophrenia. Brunner, New York

Arieti S (1959) Schizophrenic thought. Am J Psychother 13:537–552

Arieti S (1962a) Psychotherapy of schizophrenia. Arch Gen Psychiatry 6:112–122

Arieti S (1962b) Hallucinations, delusions, and ideas of reference treated with psychotherapy. Am J Psychother 16:52–60

Arieti S (1966) Discussion. Am J Psychoanal 26:198–200
Arieti S (1968a) The psychodynamics of schizophrenia: a reconsideration. Am J Psychother 22:366–381
Arieti S (1968b) New views on the psychodynamics of schizophrenia. Am J Psychiatry 124:453–458
Arieti S (1974a) Individual psychotherapy of schizophrenia. In: Arieti S (ed) American handbook of psychiatry, vol 3, 2nd edn. Basic Books, New York, p 627
Arieti S (1974b) The cognitive-volitional school. In: Arieti S (ed) American handbook of psychiatry, vol 1, 2nd edn. Basic Books, New York, p 877
Arieti S, Lorraine S (1972) The therapeutic assistant in treating the psychotic. Int J Psychiatry 10:7–22
Arlow JA (1958) Panel: the psychoanalytic theory of thinking. J Am Psychoanal Assoc 6:143–153
Arnkoff DB (1981) Flexibility in practicing cognitive therapy. In: Emery G, Hollon SD, Bedrosian RC (eds) New directions in cognitive therapy. Guilford, New York, p 203
Austrin HR, Aubuchon DJ (1979) Locus of control and trust in parents: a preliminary study. J Clin Psychol 35:304–305
Azima H (1963) Object-relations therapy of schizophrenic states: technique and theory. Psychiat Res Rep No 17. Am Psychiat Assoc., Washington DC
Azima H, Wittkower ED, la Tendresse J (1958) Object relations therapy in schizophrenic states. Am J Psychiatry 115:60–62
Baron P (1986) The relation between egocentrism and dysfunctional attitudes in adolescents. Br J Cog Psychother 4:71–77
Barrowclough C, Tarrier N (1984) Psychosocial interventions with families and their effects on the course of schizophrenia: a review. Psychol Med 14:629–642
Bartlett FC (1954) Remembering. A study in experimental and social psychology. Cambridge University Press, Cambridge
Beck AT (1952) Successful outpatient psychotherapy of a chronic schizophrenic with a delusion of borrowed guilt. Psychiatry 15:305–312
Beck AT (1970) Cognitive therapy: nature and relation to behavior therapy. Behav Ther 1:184–200
Beck AT (1976) Cognitive therapy and the emotional disorders. International Universities Press, New York
Beck AT (1985) Cognitive therapy, behavior therapy, psychoanalysis, and pharmacotherapy: a cognitive continuum. In: Mahoney MJ, Freeman A (eds) Cognition and psychotherapy. Plenum, New York, p 325
Beck AT, Emery G (1985) Anxiety disorders and phobias. Basic Books, New York
Beck AT, Rush AJ, Shaw BF, Emery G (1979) Cognitive therapy of depression. Guilford, New York
Bedrosian RC, Beck AT (1980) Principles of cognitive therapy. In: Mahoney MJ (ed) Psychotherapy process. Plenum, New York, p 127
Beitman BD, Klerman GL (1984) Combining psychotherapy and drug therapy in clinical practice. Spectrum, New York
Bell SM (1970) The development of the concept of object as related to infant-mother attachment. Child Dev 41:291–311
Bellak AS, Hersen M (1979) Research and practice in social skills training. Plenum, New York
Beres D, Arlow J (1974) Fantasy and identification in empathy. Psychoanal Q 43:26–50
Biller HB (1974) Paternal deprivation. Lexington Books, Lexington
Bing E (1963) Effect of childrearing practices on development of differential cognitive abilities. Child Dev 34:631–648
Blatt SJ, Wild CM (1976) Schizophrenia: a developmental analysis. Academic, New York
Bowlby J (1969–1980) Attachment and loss, vols 1–3. Basic Books, New York
Bowlby J (1973) Self-reliance and some conditions that promote it. In: Bowlby J: The making and breaking of affectional bonds, Tavistock, London, p 103
Bowlby J (1981) Sul possedere nozioni che non si supponeva di possedere e sul provare emozioni che non era permesso provare. In: VF Guidano, MA Reda (eds) Cognitivismo e psicoterapia. Angeli, Milano, pp 123–131
Brody EB (1981) Can mother-infant interaction produce vulnerability to schizophrenia? J Nerv Ment Dis 169:72–81
Brown GW, Monck EM, Carstairs GH, Wing JK (1962) The influence of family life on the course of schizophrenic illness. Br J Prev Soc Med 16:55–72
Brown GW, Birley JLT, Wing JK (1972) Influence of family life and the course of schizophrenic disorders. A replication. Br J Psychiatry 121:241–258
Buber M (1954) Die Schriften über das dialogische Prinzip. Schneider, Heidelberg

Burstein A (1959) Primary process in children as a function of age. J Abnorm Soc Psychol 59:284–286
Busse TV (1969) Child-rearing antecedents of flexible thinking. Dev Psychol 1:585–591
Cancro R (1975) Genetic considerations in the etiology and prevention of schizophrenia. In: Usdin G (ed) Schizophrenia: biological and psychological perspectives. Brunner/Mazel, New York
Cancro R (1979) The genetic studies of the schizophrenic syndrome. In: Bellak L (ed) Disorders of the schizophrenic syndrome. Basic Books, New York, p 136
Cheek FE (1965) The father of the schizophrenic. Arch Gen Psychiatry 13:336–345
Ciompi L (1985) Aging and the schizophrenic psychosis. Acta Psychiatr Scand 71 [suppl 319]:93–105
Coché E, Flick A (1975) Problem-solving training groups for hospitalized psychiatric patients. J Psychol 91:19–29
Crumley FE, Blumenthal RS (1973) Children's reaction to temporary loss of the father. Am J Psychiatry 130:778–782
Davis WL, Phares EJ (1969) Parental antecedents of internal-external control of reinforcement. Psychol Reports 24:427–436
Day M, Semrad EV (1978) Schizophrenic reactions. In: Nicholi AM (ed) The Harvard guide to modern psychiatry. Belknap, Cambridge, p 199
Docherty JP, Marder SR, van Kammen DP, Siris SG (1977) Psychotherapy and pharmacotherapy: conceptual issues. Am J Psychiatry 134:529–533
Dow MG, Craighead WE (1984) Cognitions and social inadequacy: relevance in clinical populations. In: Trower P (ed) Radical approaches to social skills training. Croom Helm, London, p 227
Dryden W (1984) Social skills assessment from a rational-emotive perspective. In: Trower P (ed) Radical approaches to social skills training. Croom Helm, London, p 286, 314
Einhorn HJ, Hogarth RM (1978) Confidence in judgment: persistence of the illusion of validity. Psychol Rev 85:395–416
Eisemann M (1985) Psychosocial aspects of depressive disorders. Medical dissertation, Umeå University, Umeå
Eissler K (1943) Limitations to the psychotherapy of schizophrenia. Psychiatry 6:381–391
Elkind D (1967) Egocentrism in adolescence. Child Dev 38:1025–1034
Elkind D (1970) Children and adolescents: interpretive essays on Jean Piaget. Oxford University Press, Oxford
Elkind D (1978) Understanding the young adolescent. Adolescence 13:127–134
Ellis A, Sagarin E (1964) Nymphomania. Inst for Rational Living, New York
Epstein N (1983) Cognitive therapy with couples. In: Freeman A (ed) Cognitive therapy with couples and groups. Plenum, New York, p 107
Erikson HE (1953) Growth and crises of the healthy personality. In: Kluckhon C, Murray HA (eds) Personality in nature, society, and culture. 2nd edn. Knops, New York, p 50
Erlenmeyer-Kimling L (1979) Advantages of a behavior-genetic approach to investigating stress in the depressive disorders. In: Depue RA (ed) The psychobiology of depressive disorders. Academic, New York, p 391
Federn P (1952) Ego psychology and the psychoses. Basic Books, New York
Feffer M (1967) Symptom expression as a form of primitive decentering. Psychol Rev 74:16–28
Feinsilver DB, Yates BT (1984) Combined use of psychotherapy and drugs in chronic, treatment-resistant schizophrenic patients. J Nerv Ment Dis 172:133–139
Field T (1978) Interaction behaviors of primary vs secondary caretaker fathers. Dev Psychol 14:183–184
Field T (1985) Attachment as psychobiological attunement: being on the same wavelength. In: Reite M, Field T (eds) The Psychobiology of attachment and separation. Academic, New York, p 415
Forrest T (1967) The paternal roots of male character development. Psychoanal Rev 54:81–99
Fox NA (1985) Behavioral and autonomic antecedents of attachment on high-risk infants. In: Reite M, Field T (eds) The psychobiology of attachment and separation. Academic, New York, p 389
Frank GH (1965) The role of the family in the development of psychopathology. Psychol Bull 64:191–205
Frank J (1985) Therapeutic components shared by all therapies. In: Mahoney MJ, Freeman A (eds) Cognition and psychotherapy. Plenum, New York, p 49
Frank J, Hoehn-Saric R, Imber SD, Liberman BL, Stone AR (1978) Effective ingredients of successful psychotherapy. Brunner/Mazel, New York
Freeman A (1983) Cognitive therapy with couples and groups. Plenum, New York
Freeman A, Greenwood V (1986) Cognitive therapy. Applications in psychiatric and medical settings. Human Sciences Press, London

Freeman T, McGhie A (1957) The relevance of genetic psychology for the psychopathology of schizophrenia. Br J Med Psychol 30:176–187
Freeman T, Cameron JL, McGhie A (1966) Studies on psychosis. International Universities Press, New York
Freud A (1951) The ego and mechanism of defence. Hogarth, London
Freud A, Dann S (1951) An experiment in group upbringing. Psychoanal Study Child 6:127–168
Freud S (1895) Project for a scientific psychology. In: Strachey J (ed) The standard edition of the complete psychological works of Sigmund Freud, vol 1. Hogarth, London, 1953
Freud S (1900) The interpretation of dreams. In: Strachey J (ed) The Standard edition of the complete psychological works of Sigmund Freud, vols 4, 5. Hogarth, London
Freud S (1905) Three essays on the theory of sexuality. In: Strachey J (ed) The Standard edition of the complete psychological works of Sigmund Freud, vol 7. Hogarth, London
Freud S (1915) Instincts and their vicissitudes. In: Strachey J (ed) Standard edition. Hogarth, London
Freud S (1923) The ego and the id. In: Strachey J (ed) Standard edition of the complete psychological works of Sigmund Freud, vol 19. Hogarth, London
Freud S (1924) On psychotherapy. Collected papers, vol 1. Hogarth, London
Fromm-Reichmann F (1948) Notes on the development of treatment of schizophrenics by psychoanalytic psychotherapy. Psychiatry 11:263–273
Fromm-Reichmann F (1950) Principles of intensive psychotherapy. University of Chicago Press, Chicago
Fromm-Reichmann F (1954) Psychotherapy of schizophrenia. Am J Psychiatry 111:410–419
Fromm-Reichmann F (1955) Clinical significance of intuitive processes of the analyst. J Am Psychoanal Assoc 3:83–88
Fromm-Reichmann F (1958) Basic Problems in the psychotherapy of schizophrenia. Psychiatry 21:1–6
Fuson KC (1979) The development of self-regulating aspects of speech: a review. In: Zivin G (ed) The development of self-regulation through private speech. Wiley, New York
Garmezy N, Clarke AR, Stockner C (1961) Child rearing attitudes of mothers and fathers as reported by schizophrenic and normal patients. J Abnorm Soc Psychol 63:176–182
Garner DM, Bemis KM (1985) Cognitive therapy for anorexia nervosa. In: Garner DM, Grafinkel PE (eds) Handbook of psychotherapy for anorexia nervosa and bulimia. Guilford, New York, p 107
George L, Neufeld RWJ (1985) Cognition and symptomatology in schizophrenia. Schizophr Bull 11:264–285
Goldfried MR, Robins C (1983) Self-schema, cognitive bias and the processing of therapeutic experience. In: Kendall PC (ed) Advances in cognitive-behavioural research and therapy, vol 2. Academic, New York, p 35
Greenson RR (1967) The technique and practice of psychoanalysis. International Universities Press, New York
Greenwood VB (1983) Cognitive therapy with the young adult chronic patient. In: Freeman A (ed) Cognitive therapy with couples and groups. Plenum, New York, p 183
Guidano VF, Liotti G (1983) Cognitive processes and emotional disorders. Guilford, New York
Gunderson J (1979) Individual Psychotherapy. In: Bellak L (ed) Disorders of the schizophrenic syndroma. Basic Books, New York, p 364
Gunderson J, Frank AF, Katz HM, Vannicelli ML, Frosch JP, Knapp PH (1984) Effects of psychotherapy in schizophrenia. II. Comparative outcomes of two forms of treatment. Schizophr Bull 10:564–598
Harrow M, Ferrante A (1969) Locus of control in psychiatric patients. J Consult Clin Psychol 33:582–589
Havens LL (1963) Problems with the use of drugs in the psychotherapy of psychotic patients. Psychiatry 26:289–296
Heider F (1958) The psychology of interpersonal relations. Wiley, New York
Heilbrun AB (1960) Perception of maternal child rearing attitudes in schizophrenics. J Consult Psychol 24:169–173
Hetherington EM (1972) Effect of father absence on personality development in adolescent daughters. Dev Psychol 7:313–326
Hilgard ER (1962) Impulsive versus realistic thinking. Psychol Bull 59:477–488
Hirsch SR, Leff JP (1975) Abnormalities in parents of schizophrenics. Oxford University Press, London
Hole RW, Rush AJ, Beck AT (1979) A cognitive investigation of schizophrenic delusions. Psychiatry 42:312–319

Holt RR (1967) Motives and thought. International Universities Press, New York
Hymowitz P, Spohn H (1980) The effects of antipsychotic medication on the linguistic ability of schizophrenics. J Nerv Ment Dis 168:287–296
Jacobs L (1980) A cognitive approach to persistent delusions. Am J Psychother 34:556–563
Jacobs L (1982) Cognitive therapy for schizophrenia in remission. Curr Psychiatr Ther 21:93–100
James W (1890) The principles of psychology. Holt, New York
Jansson L (1986) Handbook i kognitiv terapi vid depression. Natur och Kultur, Stockholm
Jaspers K (1913) Allgemeine Psychopathologie. Springer, Berlin. Eng transl by Hoening J, Hamilton MW: General Psychopathology. University of Manchester Press, Manchester, 1963
Jolly A (1972) The evolution of primate behavior. Macmillan, New York
Jones E (1953) The life and work of Sigmund Freud, vol 1. Basic Books, New York
Kahneman D, Tversky A (1973) On the psychology of prediction. Psychol Rev 80:237–251
Karasu TB (1982) Psychotherapy and pharmacotherapy: toward an integrative model. Am J Psychiatry 139:1102–1113
Kelly G (1955) The psychology of personal constructs. Norton, New York
Kendler KS, Glazer WM, Morgenstern H (1983) Dimensions of delusional experience. Am J Psychiatry 140:466–469
Kilburg R, Siegel A (1973) Formal operations in reactive and process schizophrenics. J Consult Clin Psychol 40:371–376
Klein GS (1970) Perception, motives, and personality. Knopf, New York
Klein GS (1976) Psychoanalytic Theory. An exploration of essentials. International Universities Press, New York
Kohut H (1959) Introspection, empathy, and psychoanalysis. In: Ornstein P (ed) The search for the self. International Universities Press, New York, p 205
Kohut H (1977) The restoration of the self. International Universities Press, New York
Kris E (1952) Psychoanalytic explorations in art. International Universities Press, New York
Kuhn TS (1962) The structure of scientific revolutions. University of Chicago Press, Chicago
Lakatos I (1970) Falsification and the methodology of scientific research programmes. In: Lakatos I, Musgrave A (eds) Criticism and the growth of knowledge. Cambridge University Press, Cambridge, p 91
Lane RC, Singer JL (1959) Familial attitudes in paranoid schizophrenics and normals from two socio-economic classes. J Abnorm Soc Psychol 59:328–339
Larsson UB (1986) The creation of pictures as a part of a treatment with a cognitive approach. Proc 2nd Int Congr Cognitice Psychotherapy, Umeå, Sweden, 18–20 September 1986
Lefcourt HM (1976) Locus of control. Current trends in theory and research. Erlbaum, Hillsdale, NJ
Leff JP, Vaughn C (1981) The role of maintenance therapy and relatives expressed emotions in relapse of schizophrenia: a two year follow up. Br J Psychiatry 139:102–104
Leff JP, Kuipers L, Berkowitz R, Eberlein-Vries R, Sturgeon D (1982) A controlled trial of social intervention in the families of schizophrenic patients. Br J Psychiatry 141:121–134
Levenson H (1973) Perceived parental antecedents of internal, powerful others, and chance of locus of control orientations. Dev Psychol 9:260–265
Lidz TH (1973) The origins and treatment of schizophrenic disorders. Basic Books, New York
Lidz TH (1974) Schizophrenic thinking. J Youth Adolesc 3:95–98
Liem JM (1980) Family studies of schizophrenia: an update and commentary. Schizophr Bull 6:429–455
Liotti G (1986) Structural Cognitive Therapy. In: Dryden W, Golden W (eds) Cognitive-behavioural approaches to psychotherapy. Harper and Row, London, p 92
Liotti G (1987) The resistance to change of cognitive structures: a counterproposal to psychoanalytic metapsychology. Int J Cog Psychother 1:87–104
Lu YC (1961) Mother-child role relations in schizophrenia. Psychiatry 24:133–142
Ludwig AM (1966) The formal characteristics of therapeutic insight. Am J Psychother 20:305–318
Luria AR (1976) Cognitive development: its cultural and social foundations. Harvard University Press, Cambridge, Mass
MacDonald AP (1971) Internal-external locus of control: parental antecedents. J Consult Clin Psychol 37:141–147
Mahler MS, Pine F, Bergman A (1975) The psychological birth of the human infant. Basic Books, New York

Mahoney MJ (1980) Psychotherapy and the structure of personal revolutions. In: Mahoney MJ (ed) Psychotherapy process. Plenum, New York, p 157
Mahoney MJ (1985) Psychotherapy and human change processes. In: Mahoney MJ, Freeman A (eds) Cognition and psychotherapy. Plenum, New York, p 3
Mallinger A (1974) Transference: a cognitive approach. Am J Psychoanal 34:51-62
Markus H (1977) Self-schemata and processing information about the self. Personality Soc Psychol 35:63-78
Matte-Blanco I (1965) A study of schizophrenic thinking: its expression in terms of symbolic logic and its representation in terms of multidimensional space. Int J Psychiatry 1:91-95
Matussek P (1976) Psychotherapie schizophrener Psychosen. Hoffmann und Campe, Hamburg
Matussek P (1981) The situation of the schizophrenic: the starting point of psychotherapy. Hexagon 'Roche' 2:18-24
Matussek P, Triebel A (1974) Die Wirksamkeit der Psychotherapie bei 44 Schizophrenen. Nervenarzt 45:569-575
Meichenbaum D (1977) Cognitive-behavior modification. Plenum, New York
Meichenbaum D, Cameron R (1973) Training schizophrenics to talk to themselves: a means of developing attentional controls. Behav Ther 4:515-534
Meyers A, Mercatoris M, Sirota A (1976) Use of covert self-instruction for the elimination of psychotic speech. J Consult Clin Psychol 44:480-483
Neisser U (1967) Cognitive psychology. Meredith, New York
Nicholi AM (1978) The therapist-patient relationship. In: Nicholi AM (ed) The Harvard guide to modern psychiatry. Belknap, Cambridge, p 3
Noy P (1969) A revision of the psychoanalytic theory of the primary process. Int J Psychoanal 50:155-178
Noy P (1979) The psychoanalytic theory of cognitive development. Psychoanal Study Child 34:169-216
Nuechterlein KH, Dawson ME (1984a) A heuristic vulnerability/stress model of schizophrenic episodes. Schizophr Bull 10:300-312
Nuechterlein KH, Dawson ME (1984b) Information processing and attentional functioning in the developmental course of schizophrenic disorders. Schizophr Bull 10:160-203
Ollinen K (1986) Dysfunktionella tankemönster och upplevelse av uppfostran i en normalgrupp. Umea Univ, Institute of Applied Psychology, Umeå, Sweden
O'Reilly J (1977) The interplay between mothers and their children: a construct theory viewpoint. In: Bannister D (ed) New perspectives in personal construct theory. Academic, New York, p 195
Palm A (1985) Cognitive changes in schizophrenic patients in relation to a cognitive therapy programme. Proc XIII Int Congr Psychotherapy, Opatija, Yugoslavia, 6-12 October 1985
Palm U (1985) A cognitive treatment programme for schizophrenia. Proc XIII Int Congr Psychotherapy, Opatija, Yugoslavia, 6-12 October 1985
Parker G (1983) Parental overprotection. Grune and Stratton, New York
Parloff MB, Kelman HC, Frank JD (1954) Comfort, effectiveness, and self-awareness as criteria of improvement in psychotherapy. Am J Psychiatry 111:343-352
Perris C (1981) Recent developments and current issues in the study of depression. Idegyógyászati Szemle 34:481-490
Perris C (1985a) An integrative, interactionistic approach to the study of depression. Proc WPA Symp on "Affective Disorders", Athens, 13-17 October 1985
Perris C (1985b) Milieu-therapeutic processes and cognitive therapy. Proc III Int Congr Psychotherapy, Opatija, Yugoslavia, 6-12 October 1985
Perris C (1986a) Kognitiv terapi vid behandling av psykotiska och postpsykotiska tillstand. En översikt. Lákartidningen 83:1488-1491
Perris C (1986b) Cognitive psychotherapy with patients suffering from schizophrenic syndromes. Ideggyógyászati Szemle
Perris C (1986c) Kognitiv terapi i teori och praktik. Natur och Kultur, Stockholm
Perris C (1986d) En terapeuts (ledares) manual för gruppträning av sociala färdigheter för patienter med kontaktsvarigheter. Rep Dept Psychiat Umea Univ, new series
Perris C (1988) Cognitive psychotherapy and milieutherapeutic processes in psychiatric inpatient units. Int J Cog Psychother 2:35-50
Perris C, Perris H (1985) A biological, psychological, and social approach to the study of depression and its implications for treatment. Neurol Psichiatr Sci Umane 5 [Suppl]:67-93

Perris C, Rodhe K, Palm A, Hällgren S, Lilja C, Söderman H (1985) Fully integrated in- and out-patient services in a psychiatric sector. Soc Psychiatry 20:60–69
Perris C, Perris H, Eisemann M (1987) Perceived parental rearing practices, parental affective disorders, and age at onset in depressed patients. Int J Family Psychiatry 8:183–200
Perris H (1982) A multifactorial study of life events in depressed patients. Medical dissertation, University of Umeå, Umeå
Peterfreund E (1971) Information, systems, and psychoanalysis. Academic, New York
Peterfreund E (1983) The process of psychoanalytic therapy. Academic, New York
Peterfreund E, Franceschini E (1973) On information, motivation, and meaning. In: Rubinstein BB (ed) Psychoanalysis and contemporary science, vol 2. International Universities Press, New York, p 220
Piaget J (1932) The language and thought of the child. Routledge and Kegan Paul, London
Piaget J, Inhelder B (1969) The psychology of the child. Routledge and Kegan Paul, London
Piety KR (1967) Patterns of parent perceptions among neuropsychiatric patients. J Clin Psychol 23:428–433
Prigogine I (1980) Time, structure, and fluctuations. Science 201:777–785
Rabin AI, Doneson SL, Jentons RL (1979) Studies of psychological functions in schizophrenia. In: Bellak L (ed) Disorders of the schizophrenic syndrome. Basic Books, New York, p 181
Racamier PC (1959) Psychoanalytic therapy of psychoses. In: Nacht S (ed) Psychoanalysis of today. Grune and Stratton, New York
Rapaport D (1960) Motivation of thinking. In: Jones MR (ed) Nebraska symposium on motivation. University of Nebraska Press, Lincoln, Nebraska
Rapaport D (1967) Psychoanalysis as a developmental psychology. In: Collected Papers of D Rapaport. Basic Books, New York
Reda MA (1986) Sistemi cognitivi complessi e psicoterapia. La Nuova Italia Scientifica, Roma
Reite M, Capitanio JP (1985) On the nature of social separation and social attachment. In: Reite M, Field T (eds) The psychobiology of attachment and separation. Academic, New York, p 389
Reite M, Field T (1985) The psychobiology of attachment and separation. Academic, Orlando
Richfield J (1963) An analysis of the concept of insight. In: Paul L (ed) Psychoanalytic clinical interpretation. Free Press of Glencoe, New York, p 93
Rishovd Rund B, Blakar RM (1986) Schizophrenic patients and their parents. Acta Psychiatr Scand 74:396–408
Roeder H (1986) Mothers of schizophrenic patients. In: Matussek P (ed) Symposium on schizophrenia, Ringberg Castle, West Germany
Rohner EC, Chaille C, Rohner RR (1980) Perceived parental acceptance-rejection and the development of children's locus of control. J Psychol 104:83–86
Rosen JN (1947) The treatment of schizophrenic psychosis by direct analytic therapy. Psychiatr Q 21:3–17, 117–119
Rosen JN (1962) Direct psychoanalytic psychiatry. Grune and Stratton, New York
Rosenfeld HA (1965) Psychotic states: a psychoanalytic approach. International Universities Press, New York
Rotter J (1966) Generalized expectancies for internal versus external control of reinforcement. Psychol Monogr 80: No 609
Rubins JL (1969) A holistic (Horney) approach to the psychoses: the schizophrenias. Am J Psychoanal 29:131–146
Rubins JL (1972) A holistic (Horney) approach to the schizophrenies. III. The therapeutic process. Am J Psychoanal 32:16–44
Rubins JL, Rucker MS (1974) On evaluating the effectiveness of psychoanalytic therapy for the acute schizophrenias. Am J Psychoanal 34:241–256
Rutter M (1985) Resilience in the face of adversity. Br J Psychiatry 147:598–611
Ryle A (1978) A common language for the psychotherapies? Br J Psychiatry 132:585–594
Salmon P (1970) A psychology of personal growth. In: Bannister D (ed) Perspectives in personal construct theory. Academic, New York, p 197
Santrock JW (1972) Relation of type and onset of father-absence to cognitive development. Child Dev 43:455–469
Sass LA, Gunderson JG, Thaler Singer M, Wynne LC (1984) Parental communication deviance and forms of thinking in male schizophrenic offspring. J Nerv Ment Dis 172:513–520
Schafer R (1959) Generative empathy in the treatment situation. Psychoanal Q 28:342–373

Schonbar RA (1965) Interpretation and insight in psychotherapy. Psychother Theory Res Practice 2:78–83
Searles H (1958) The schizophrenic vulnerability to the therapist's unconscious processes. J Nerv Ment Dis 127:247–262
Searles H (1962) The differentiation between concrete and metaphorical thinking in the recovering schizophrenic patient. J Am Psychoanal Assoc 10:22–49
Sechehaye M (1951) Symbolic realization. International Universities Press, New York
Shepherd G (1984) Assessment of cognitions in social skills training. In: Trower P (ed) Radical approaches to social skills training. Croom Helm, London, p 261
Shotter J (1970) Man, the man-makers: George Kelly and the psychology of personal constructs. In: Bannister D (ed) Perspectives in personal constructs theory. Academic, New York, p 223
Shulman BH (1968) Essays in schizophrenia. Williams and Wilkins, Baltimore
Siegel JM, Spivak G (1976) Problem-solving therapy: the description of a new program for chronic psychiatric patients. Psychother Theory Res Practice 13:368–373
Singer W (1986) The brain as a self-organizing system. Eur Arch Psychiatry Neurol Sci 236:4–9
Sloane R, Cristal A, Pepernick M, Staples F (1970) Role preparation and expectancy of improvement in psychotherapy. J Nerv Ment Dis 150:18–26
Sollod RN, Wachtel PL (1980) A structural and transactional approach to cognitions in clinical problems. In: Mahoney MJ (ed) Psychotherapy process. Plenum, New York, p 1
Sroufe LA, Waters E (1977) Attachment as an organizational construct. Child Dev 48:1184–1199
Sullivan HS (1931) The modified psychoanalytic treatment of schizophrenia. Am J Psychiat 11:519–536
Sullivan HS (1954) The psychiatric interview. Norton, New York
Swann WB, Read SJ (1981) Self-verification processes: how we sustain our self-conceptions. J Exp Soc Psychol 17:351–372
Szalita-Pemow A (1951) Remarks on pathogenesis and treatment of schizophrenia. Psychiatry 14:295–300
Trower P (1984) Radical approaches to social skills training. Croom Helm, London
Turk DC, Salovey P (1985) Cognitive structures, cognitive processes, and cognitive-behavior modification. Cog Ther Res 9:1–17
Tversky A, Kahneman D (1971) Belief in the law of small numbers. Psychol Bull 76:105–110
von Domarus E (1944) The specific laws of logic in schizophrenia. In: Kasanin JS (ed) Language and thought in schizophrenia. University of California Press, Berkeley, p 104
Vygotsky LS (1934) Storia dello sviluppo delle funzioni psichiche superiori. Giunti-Barbera, Bari
Vygotsky LS (1960) Il Processo Cognitivo. Boringhieri, Torino
Wallace (1984) Community and interpersonal functioning in the course of schizophrenic disorders. Schizophr Bull 10:233–257
Waring EM (1981) Cognitive family therapy in the treatment of schizophrenia. Psychiatry J Univ Ottawa 6:229–233
Watson G (1957) Some personality differences in children related to strict or permissive parental discipline. J Psychol 44:227–249
Weissman AN (1980) Assessing depressogenic attitudes: a validation study. Proc 51st annual meeting eastern psychol assoc, Hartford, Connecticut
Weissman AN, Beck AT (1978) Development and validation of the Dysfunctional Attitude Scale. Presented at the annual meeting of the Am Educat Res Assoc, Toronto, Canada
Wexler M (1951) The structural problem in schizophrenia: therapeutic implications. Int J Psychoanal 32:157–166
Will DA (1975) Schizophrenia. Psychosocial treatment. In: Freedman AM, Kaplan HI, Sadock BJ (eds) Comprehensive textbook of psychiatry, vol 1, 2nd edn. Williams and Wilkins, Baltimore, p 939
Willenson D (1960) Relationship of adult personality characteristics to perceived parental behavior. Diss Abstr 20:3393–3394
Wing JK (1974) Principles of evaluation. In: Wing JK, Hailey AM (eds) Evaluating a community psychiatric service. Oxford University Press, London, p 11
Winnicott DW (1965) The maturational process and the facilitating environment. International Universities Press, New York
Young JE (1981) Cognitive therapy and loneliness. In: Emery G, Hollon SD, Bedrosian RC (eds) New directions in cognitive therapy. Guilford, New York, p 139
Young JE (1986) Treatment of personality disorders. Proc 2nd Int congr cognitive psychotherapy, Umeå, Sweden, 18–20 September 1986

Cognitive Therapy of Obsessive-Compulsive Disorder*

P.M. SALKOVSKIS[1] and H.M.C. WARWICK[2]

Introduction

Few would dispute that distressing and intrusive cognitions of an unacceptable nature are the fundamental feature of obsessional problems. This simple observation makes it all the more surprising that cognitive therapy has made no significant impression upon the treatment of obsessions. The use of formal cognitive therapy procedures has very seldom been reported. On the other hand, behaviour therapy has been widely employed with outstandingly good outcome in a disorder previously regarded as intractible.

In this chapter we will examine the issue of cognitive therapy for obsessional disorders from a variety of perspectives. Firstly, we will describe a cognitive formulation of obsessions and will then go on to examine cognitive aspects of treatment. In particular we will highlight the extent to which the skills of the good behaviour therapist working with obsessional patients can usefully involve the employment of *ad hoc* cognitive strategies to enable and facilitate the operation of principles of exposure. We will also consider ways in which behavioural treatment may be enhanced by a more explicit cognitive component. We also suggest ways in which cognitive procedures can be used with patients who are otherwise impervious to behaviour therapy.

Cognitive Therapy and Behaviour Therapy: Synthesis, not Antithesis

Much of the detail of what we discuss in this chapter involves the close coordination of cognitive therapy and behaviour therapy techniques. This is quite intentional, because, contrary to views sometimes expressed in this area, we can find no conflict between cognitive and behavioural approaches at a theoretical or a practical level. The emphasis differs somewhat between the two approaches, but to a large degree these differences are complementary rather than contradictory. The general relationship between cognitive therapy and behaviour therapy has been described elsewhere (Salkovskis 1986). At a theoretical level it may eventually be possible to progress towards a deeper analysis of the processes involved in effective treatments (Salkovskis 1987), but at present the evidence suggests that interactions between cognitive and behavioural elements are involved. The

*Paul Salkovskis is grateful to the Medical Research Council of the United Kingdom for their support
[1]Department of Psychiatry, University of Oxford, Warneford Hospital Oxford OX37JX, United Kingdom
[2]The Maudsley Hospital Denmark Hill, London SE5 8AF, Unite Kingdom

elimination of behavioural components from cognitive interventions and *vice versa* is likely to be damaging to the further development of effective clinical strategies and would be extremely short-sighted given the present state of knowledge. Pure cognitive therapy methods would have to better median improvement rates of 75% (e.g. Foa and Goldstein 1978).

Nevertheless, there is room for further advances – within the 75% improvement behavioural treatment is often lengthy, distressing to patients (and sometimes therapists!) and is at times difficult to implement. The 25% of patients who are intractable to behaviour therapy include patients who fail to comply with treatment, those with severe concurrent depression, those having a firm belief in the truth of their obsessions and patients suffering from obsessional thoughts in the absence of overt ritualistic behaviour (ruminators). Not included in these figures are the patients (up to 25%) regarded as suitable for behaviour therapy but who refuse once it is described to them and those (up to 12%) who drop out during treatment (see Foa et al. 1983). This could mean that as many as 50% of patients asking for treatment and regarded as suitable for behaviour therapy do not resolve their problems. Relapse is a further problem; estimates suggest a relapse rate of 20% over a follow-up period of 3 months to 5 years (see Espie 1986). Reasons for this await investigation.

A Cognitive Model of Obsessions

Formal cognitive treatments are usually based on an analysis of the nature of the psychopathology of the disorder concerned and the particular way in which it manifests in the patient being treated. This has proven to be something of a problem in obsessional disorders because until recently there has been no clearly defined cognitive formulation of obsessions. Paradoxically, one of the principal problems in reaching such a formulation has been the cognitive nature of obsessions. In depression and anxiety the way in which events are responded to by particular types of negative thoughts and produce distinct mood states and clinical syndromes has been clearly elucidated and experimentally tested (Blackburn, this volume). In obsessions the primary phenomenon is a cognitive one; obsessions are associated both with anxiety and depression, and environmental influences have proven hard to define. Obsessions therefore require either a totally different cognitive approach (e.g. that of Beech 1974) or redefinition within the context of a general cognitive model of the emotional disorders, such as that of Beck (1976). We have proposed that the cognitive component of obsessions is more extensive than had previously been considered (Salkovskis 1985; Salkovskis and Warwick 1985), going well beyond intrusive thoughts.

Beck's (1976) cognitive approach to emotional disorders depends on the general idea that the emotional response to particular stimuli (thoughts, situations or events) occurs as a result of negative automatic thoughts (NATs). The content of these NATs determines the type of emotional response; that is, thoughts of danger are associated with anxiety, and thoughts of loss are associated with depression (see Blackburn, this volume; Rush, this volume). If obsessions are regarded as conditioned stimuli (Rachman 1971, 1976), it would follow that the

Table 1. Comparison of obsessional thoughts (Rachman and Hodgson 1980) and automatic thoughts described by Beck (1976)

Characteristic	Obsessional thoughts	Negative automatic thoughts
Relationship to "stream of consciousness"	Intrude into	Run parallel to
Accesibility	Very easy	Can be difficult even with training
Perceived intrusiveness (irrelevance of interruption)	High	Low
Perceived rationality	Irrational	Rational
Relation to belief system	Inconsistent (ego dystonic)	Consistent (ego syntonic)
Relationship to external stimuli	Partial	Partial
Attributed source	Internal	Internal
Modalities affected	Linguistic, images, impulses	Linguistic, images
Content	Idiosyncratic	Idiosyncratic

Reproduced with permission of Pergamon Press from Salkovskis (1985)

emotional response is likely to be associated with NATs occurring immediately *after* the obsessional thought. Such NATs should differ from obsessional thoughts in a number of respects, as listed in Table 1.

This still leaves the question of what might distinguish the *content* of NATs associated with obsessional thoughts from those associated with anxiety and depression. Examination of published experimental and clinical literature suggests that thoughts about being responsible for harm coming to self or others could account for the characteristic features of obsessional disorders. Analysis of the thoughts reported by a series of obsessional patients provides further support for such a view (Salkovskis 1985). The hypothesis is that intrusive thoughts are a common occurrence in the general population, reported by up to 90% of normal individuals (Rachman and de Silva 1978; Salkovskis and Harrison 1984; P.M. Salkovskis and H.R. Dent 1987, unpublished observations). These thoughts are usually dismissed easily, except when individuals believe they could be responsible for harm unless they take preventative action by making themselves carry out a particular action or think a particular thought (neutralising). Such neutralising can become an acknowledgment of responsibility and is often accompanied by a sense of relief because it results in a reduction in perceived responsibility. Furthermore, when neutralising takes place, individuals may believe that the harm *would* have resulted had they not acted as they did. These factors will all combine to reinforce the original dysfunctional belief and increase the likelihood of subsequent neutralising behaviours.

Figure 1 shows how these factors interact to produce the clinical features of obsessive-compulsive disorder. As in depression and anxiety, previous experience contributes to a variety of dysfunctional assumptions which remain "silent" unless

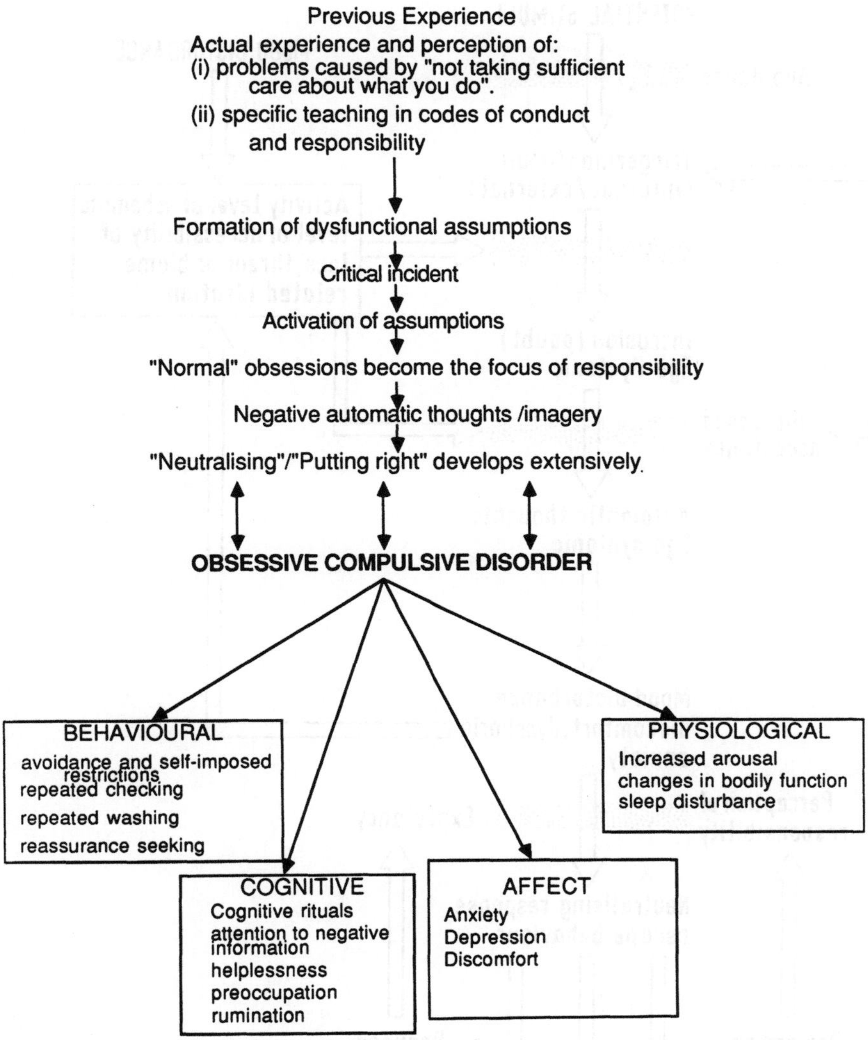

Fig. 1. Cognitive model of the development of obsessive-compulsive disorder (Thanks to Melanie Fennell for allowing our use of the diagram format which she developed)

activated by critical incidents. For obsessionals such critical incidents usually involve increased responsibility, trigger NATs and thereby increase the degree to which neutralising occurs. Once this is set into motion the whole process becomes autonomous, as shown in Fig. 2. This figure also illustrates the considerable impact which mood disturbance, particularly depression, can have on the occurrence of intrusions, NATs and neutralising by changing accessibility of negative information. When obsessions persist, patients learn to avoid situations which provoke intrusions. Avoidance serves a similar function in obsessional patients to that

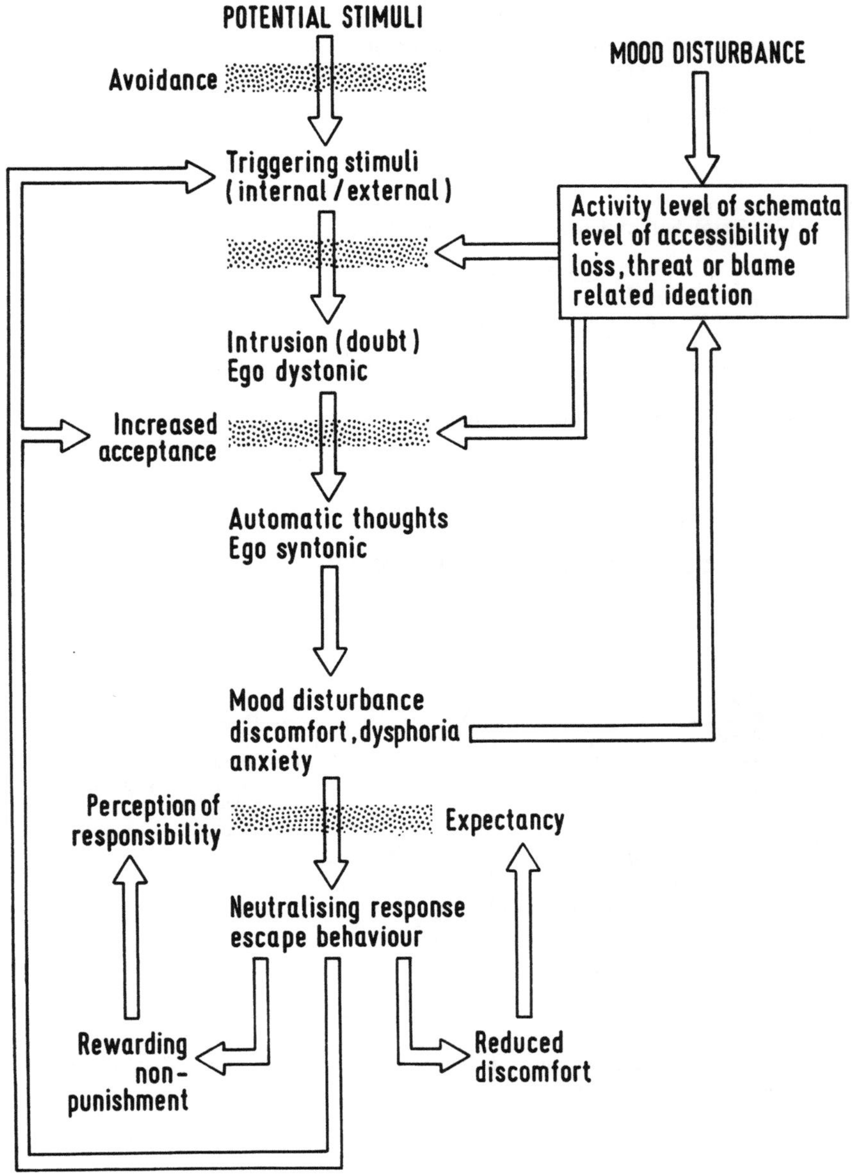

Fig. 2 Mechanisms and modulating influences in the acute expression of obsessional thoughts and behaviour (reproduced by permission from Salkovskis 1985)

observed in phobic disorders (Cottraux, this volume); the behaviour of such patients sometimes comes to resemble that of severe agoraphobics.

The implications of this cognitive formulation of obsessions are described in detail elsewhere (Salkovskis 1985). Central to the model is the way in which NATs concerning responsibility cause the patient to experience anxiety/discomfort about future harm and neutralise to terminate exposure (and reduce responsibility). In turn, neutralising reduces anxiety/discomfort and itself has the effect of maintaining the obsessional thoughts and beliefs about being responsible for harm. Experimental investigation in "normal" obsessions has provided support for the importance of these variables (Salkovskis 1988): there is evidence of an association between beliefs about responsibility and neutralising and between neutralising and amount of disturbance associated with intrusive thoughts (P.M. Salkovskis and H.R. Dent 1987, unpublished observations). Other major implications concern the way in which assessment and treatment are carried out; these are described in detail below.

Assessment

Assessment is intended to provide the basis for a psychological formulation of the patient's problems in terms of predisposing factors, precipitants and current maintaining factors. As described in detail elsewhere (Salkovskis and Kirk 1988), this information is derived from a variety of sources and the nature of the information collected is directed by the psychological model of obsessions. At its simplest, this states that avoidance prevents and neutralising terminates exposure; both prevent habituation and reappraisal taking place. As described above, one of the objects of psychological treatment is to help patients discover the true extent of their responsibility, and that the things which they fear will not actually happen, or that if they do, they are not as disastrous as they seem. From a behavioural perspective this process takes place as part of *exposure* leading to *habituation* (reduction) of anxiety, whilst from a cognitive perspective an additional factor is that *confronting* fears results in *reappraisal.* During assessment and on the basis of subsequent self-monitoring, behaviour tests and report of relatives, the therapist gathers information about the way the problem is affecting the patient. This should include factors which prevent reappraisal or habituation, such as avoidance of things or thoughts which the patient fears and neutralisers which cut short exposure. Such assessment should emphasise *both* overt and covert behaviours.

The form of obsessional thoughts is examined. Remember that obsessional thoughts are, by definition, thoughts which come into the mind unbidden, are unwanted, cause discomfort and are often unacceptable or repugnant to the person experiencing them; they are also experienced as senseless (Rachman and Hodgson 1980). The content of the obsessional thought will be idiosyncratic and may include images (mental pictures) and impulses (urges) as well as thoughts. Close attention should be given to content concerning responsibility and harm coming to self or others.

In contrast to this, neutralising (which can be either behaviours or thoughts) is *voluntary activity* which the patient chooses to engage in as a consequence of upsetting thoughts or, in some more chronic cases, as a way of preventing the thoughts occurring in the first place. Avoidance (overt or covert) is intended to prevent upsetting thoughts being triggered in the first instance. Avoidance and neutralising are usually easy to identify; when difficulty is encountered, useful questions are, "Are there any things you do or thoughts you try to think which would not occur if you did not have your problem?" and "Are there any things

Table 2. Examples of intrusive and negative automatic thoughts (NAT) and of associated avoidance and ritualising

Intrusion	NAT	Avoidance	Ritual
I've not locked the office	It will be burgled and I'm responsible	Being last at work	Repeatedly checking office keys are in handbag
I've not switched kettle off	The office will burn down and it will be my fault	Using kettle etc.	Takes impression on paper of switch in 'off' position, to look at in evening
My family may get ill	I should prevent this	Never says she feels well	Turns kitchen utensils to face the hospital
I might get AIDS through a cut	I will cause my wife and child to die	D.I.Y. so no cuts on hands	Checking in mirror for signs of weight loss
A ghost might come into the house	If I do things when I Have such thoughts, then this is more likely	Going through doors; things to do with ghosts	Pictures an angel as actions are repeated
God is dead	I won't be forgiven	Churches	Thinks a prayer
My hands are dirty	I will make my child unwell	Touching food etc. from outside	Repeated cleaning of hands, kitchen etc.

which you cannot do or think because you have the problem?" Table 2 shows examples of thoughts, avoidance behaviour and neutralising derived from our experience of such patients.

A detailed account of NATs associated with responsibility can be derived through questioning, self-monitoring and behavioural experiments. The procedures closely resemble those used in anxiety and depression (Blackburn, this volume). Once a particular NAT is derived, it is helpful to obtain a belief rating and to use this to decide on the extent to which the NAT accounts for the distress experienced by patients and their urges to engage in neutralising behaviour. A useful rule of thumb is for therapists to decide whether, if they had the same belief to the same extent, they would expect to experience similar degrees of discomfort to those reported by the patient. For example, a nurse had difficulty discarding things, and repeatedly checked:

P: When I walked past a wastepaper basket yesterday in the hospital I thought I might have accidentally dropped a pill into it. I got very upset and had to look through it until I was absolutely sure there was no pill there. It took nearly an hour.
T: How certain are you that you have dropped a pill into the wastebasket?
P: I didn't really believe I had; but I had to be sure.
T: On a rating of 0 to 100, where 0 is "don't believe it at all" and 100 is "completely convinced", how certain were you that you'd dropped a pill.
P: Less than 5 out of 100; I'm always very careful with the tablets, count them, make sure I'm not carrying them.
T: So when you had the thought that you might have dropped a pill, did you have any other thoughts right then?
P: I thought I had to check, or... (pause)

T: Did you have any thoughts about what would happen if you didn't check?
P: Well, if I was wrong, a child might find the pill and eat it.
T: How certain were you that that would happen?
P: The same – less than 5.
T: Did you have any other thoughts?
P: I thought that if I didn't check, and there really was one, I'd never forgive myself; checking is quite easy compared to someone having to suffer their child dying because I was selfish.
T: How much did you believe that your selfishness might kill a child?
P: More; if I don't take proper care and always be vigilant, eventually it probably will happen, and it definitely would be my fault.
T: What rating would you give that thought?
P: Eventually, about 60 or maybe more; I can't be sure. I might do it on purpose because I'm not on guard.

Applications of Cognitive Therapy

Facilitation of Exposure and Response Prevention

As described in the introduction, a proportion of patients either refuse or drop out of exposure treatment, and many others find it extremely unpleasant. The nature of behavioural treatment, which requires the patient to undertake procedures which will be anxiety provoking, may provide an explanation. Often such anxiety is not experienced as an incidental effect but is erroneously perceived as the main focus of treatment. The therapist explains how treatment sessions involve high levels of exposure, and the patient is also told that his usual methods of escape from such anxiety cannot be permitted. Some patients may be unable to envisage coping with the anxiety and distress which they believe that such treatment would provoke. The cognitive techniques described in this section aim to improve acceptability of and compliance with exposure in patients who feel unable to accept or complete exposure treatment. We also suggest and illustrate cognitive strategies which may extend the scope of exposure in cases in which it is not currently effective. These interventions are based on the model outlined above.

Preventing Drop-outs from Treatment

The first example illustrates how the use of cognitive strategies facilitated exposure treatment and prevented a drop-out from therapy.

A patient with a 2-year history of obsessive-compulsive disorder, was taking 1 mg lorazepam daily. She checked lights, taps and switches excessively and was also handicapped by excessive handwashing, especially when doing housework and preparing food. She made some progress with exposure and response prevention, and the checking rituals greatly improved. Despite these gains she refused to touch unwrapped food, e.g. fruit. She arrived at the fourth treatment session having failed to do the homework tasks set – to visit a shop daily and spend some time picking up fruit and to go to the hairdressers, picking up the style book. Although she accepted that habituation had occurred when she had previously tried out behaviours which alarmed her, she refused to carry out within-session exposure to touching fruit, despite reiteration of the exposure principle and therapist modelling. At this point she wished to drop out of treatment because she could not envisage completing homework tasks. This difficulty occurred because she experienced intrusive thoughts concerning the idea that her hands may have lorazepam on

Table 3. Example of the use of vertical arrow technique to deal with high anxiety levels which were preventing exposure

Distressing thought (Anxiety rating = 100)	Probability of this thought being true (0 = no chance, 100 = certain)
" I couldn't ever visit a hairdressers'."	100
↓	↓
(*What is the problem about going to the hairdressers?*)	
↓	↓
" I couldn't ever touch the style book."	100
↓	↓
(*What is the problem about touching the style book?*)	
↓	↓
" My hands would not be perfectly clean."	100
↓	↓
(*If that were true, what would that mean?*)	
↓	↓
" Something might drop from my hands onto the book."	80
↓	↓
(*What would be so bad about that?*)	
↓	↓
" Someone might pick up the book and what I've dropped onto it."	65
↓	↓
(*What would be so bad about that?*)	
↓	↓
" They might get some Ativan, that I hadn't washed off, on their hands."	50
↓	↓
(*If that were to happen, what would it mean?*)	
↓	↓
" They might put their hand to their mouth and swallow the Ativan."	20
↓	↓
(*So what?*)	
↓	↓
" They would get ill and it would be my fault." (Anxiety rating = 35)	4

them (although she realised this was senseless) and she believed that if this was so, she would be to blame for the contamination of others. A cognitive exercise based on the "vertical arrow" (Burns 1980) was utilised to identify the intrusive and automatic thoughts which were interfering with exposure (see Table 3).

The evidence was challenged using cognitive techniques; reviewing the evidence, e.g. normal dosage of lorazepam, considering alternatives, e.g. reasons for someone getting ill in the hairdressers, and generating rational responses. This exercise decreased her degree of belief in the probability of her being responsible for harm, reduced the patient's anxiety from 100 to 35 and enabled her to carry out an exposure session – handling a lorazepam tablet and then a book. She then allowed the therapist to handle the book and eat some fruit without handwashing. She subsequently completed homework between sessions and made a full recovery.

Broadening the Scope of Treatment

In some instances patients may be able to achieve narrowly defined behavioural targets, only to reveal other problems considerably less amenable to behavioural treatment. Relatively rapid resolution of such problems can be brought about by the combination of behavioural and cognitive techniques (see also the section on ruminations, below).

A patient descibed intrusive thoughts of her husband contracting leukaemia. She exhibited extensive rituals, over 100 per day, usually repeating household activities and asked her husband and family for reassurance about his condition many times each day. She avoided doing any activities without his permission and felt that all neutralisation was necessary to prevent harm coming to him. The intrusive thoughts were fragmentary, e.g. "John dying", "John leukaemia", "I hope"; discomfort was associated with the occurrence of NATs, such as "If I carry on I will prove I don't care, and he will get leukaemia." Exposure treatment resulted in reduction of rituals and reassurance seeking but not of avoidance behaviour. She could not consider exposure treatment for this as she found the prospect too distressing. A session using the cognitive techniques summarized in Table 4 was used. The advantages and disadvantages of being obsessional were discussed using the double column technique. She was asked to review the evidence for obsessional behaviour being a sign of concern for her husband.

Table 4. Example of the use of reviewing the evidence and double-column technique to deal with high anxiety levels which were preventing exposure

Advantages of being obsessional	Disadvantages of being obsessional
1. Makes me worry less when I am at my worst.	1. Worries always come back. 2. Stops me feeling good about myself. 3. Keeps the problem going. 4. Stops our marriage being good. 5. Make J. angry. 6. Makes J. think I'm stupid. 7. Stops me doing what I want to do. 8. Stops me getting dinner if J. is starving.

Reviewing the evidence

Intrusive thoughts e.g. "J. dying", "J. leukaemia", "I hope"

↓

Automatic thoughts e.g. "If I carry on or don't check up, then I will prove I don't care about him; he might get leukaemia."

(Belief = 90, anxiety = 80)

How can I prove to my husband that I care?

1. By being a normal housewife.
2. By not being obsessional.
3. By being the same girl he married.

Being obsessional does not show I care. (Belief = 75; anxiety = 45)

After examining her NATs in this way she generated the alternative suggestion that she could best prove her concern for her husband by ceasing to be obsessional. Her anxiety about the prospect of exposure to the avoided situations fell within the treatment session from 80 to 45. Throughout the sessions she clearly understood the rationale for behaviour therapy but when faced with the avoided situations at home found that her level of anxiety interfered with her ability to carry out exposure. She described knowing what she should do and knowing that habituation would occur but felt "too anxious". The results of the cognitive session were therefore summarised on a flashcard, which she then took home and periodically reread. The associated drop in anxiety and reiteration of her belief that she should show concern by not being obsessional meant that she was then able to work through the situations she avoided. Note that this information had been generated by the patient in the cognitive session and therefore did not constitute inappropriate reassurance.

Using highly specific outcome measures this case would have been discharged as improved, having made the necessary 3-point decrease on a 9-point scale of problem severity. Clearly, such patients will continue to have difficulties and will be discharged while distressing problems remain. Comprehensive cognitive behavioural assessment and treatment is indispensable. There is probably a link between unresolved obsessions and future relapse.

Exposure in Patients with Overvalued Ideation

Patients with overvalued ideation either refuse exposure or fail to benefit from it (probably because of between-session neutralising; Foa 1979). We are not only asking these patients to tolerate discomfort but to undergo a procedure which they feel is likely to increase the probability of feared future harm. Rachman (1983) suggests that faulty emotional processing occurs in such patients. The persistence of the false belief revives the fear or compulsive activity at intervals. He points out that therapeutic techniques which modify such false beliefs must therefore be considered.

A patient presented with fears of contamination from cosmetics and ultraviolet light, in case they should give her cancer. She initially responded well to exposure and response prevention but subsequently developed a severe depressive illness with associated relapse of her obsessive-compulsive symptomatology. She commenced treatment with amitriptyline and her mood made a lasting improvement. However, when exposure was attempted during this time, no within-session habituation occurred and her subsequent refusal to take part in further sessions could be interpreted as a failure of between-session habituation. A cognitive intervention was performed (see Table 5); her belief in the thought that she had given herself cancer fell from 98 to 40, and instantaneous ratings of depression fell from 80 to 40.

As she had reappraised the likelihood of the feared consequence, she agreed to make a further attempt at exposure and at the end of 10 days of combined cognitive and behavioural treatment the discomfort elicited during exposure sessions had disappeared. There was a marked drop in the degree of belief in the fears from 98% to 30%–70%, although she never again considered the problem to be senseless. (For a more detailed description of this case, see Salkovskis and Warwick 1985.)

Most of the standard cognitive techniques utilised in the treatment of depression and anxiety (Beck 1976; Beck et al. 1985) can similarly be used to identify and

Table 5. Use of cognitive techniques in a case of overlvalued ideation

Initial depression rating = 80
"I have used cosmetics which have been exposed to UV and have given myself cancer"

Evidence *for* the thought:	Belief	Evidence *against* the thought:	Belief
Initial	98	Initial	5
1. UV is related to skin cancer.	100	1. In beauty salons UV is often along with cosmetics; no problems reported.	50
2. I know that I will get skin cancer from exposure.	98	2. If people own sunbeds, they frequently have them in same room as cosmetics; no problems reported.	60
		3. Sunlight has shone on my handbag continuously in the past.	70
		4. UV shone on babies with jaundice.	65
		5. Psoriasis is treated with UV.	70
		6. UV is used in crime. prevention.	40
		7. UV used in building societies.	50
		8. Disco lights used for years.	70
Final	40	Final	50
Final depression rating	40		

Reprinted with permission of Academic Press from Salkovskis and Warwick (1985, p 248).

modify the automatic thoughts which follow obsessional intrusions. Examples are normalising, identifying and challenging automatic thoughts, decatastrophising, reattribution, identifying and challenging assumptions, behavioural experiments and two-column technique. For a description of these procedures and their use in obsessive-compulsive disorder, see Salkovskis and Westbrook (1987). It is particularly important to use socratic questioning so that all new information is generated by the patients themselves. Provision of such information by a therapist could inadvertently provide reassurance and be interpreted by the patient as sharing the responsibility for their actions.

Facilitation of Reappraisal During Exposure

As described above, one of the main effects of exposure can be regarded as allowing patients to confront previously avoided fears and thereby to reappraise their situation in a more realistic way than they had previously done. Note that the particular concern felt by such patients is often that the consequences of *not* neutralising a particular obsessional thought are that some future harm may come to themselves or to others. This makes them responsible for preventing (through neutralising) such harm. Exposure and response prevention allows patients to discover that despite their worries neutralising is *not* serving any protective function, and that their responsibility is considerably more limited than they had realised.

This process of reappraisal can be directly facilitated by a combination of strategies which are added to exposure with response prevention. Information about the nature of intrusive thoughts is provided, and exposure assignments are presented wherever possible as behavioural experiments. This is done at the point in treatment at which the rationale for treatment is discussed with the patient. The therapist's formulation of the maintenance factors involved is summarised for the patient, and the exposure/habituation/reappraisal rationale is discussed. Prior to exposure sessions in the early stages of treatment the patient's beliefs about possible negative and positive outcomes of the exposure and response prevention task are elicited and then reviewed on completion of the assignment. For example, an assignment could involved not checking doors and then subsequently noting whether or not the car had been stolen. Once exposure is completed, careful attention is paid to what could be learned from the experience. Often with obsessional patients the reappraisal value of exposure sessions can be lost because of factors they use to discount the outcome of the exposure. For example, when one patient deliberately formed a violent thought repeatedly to test whether he would lose control and attack the subject of his violent thoughts, he decided that his failure to lose control may have been due to the presence of the therapist. It is crucial that such views are not argued with, but that the therapist agrees that the patient *might* be correct, and that it would be very useful to discover this by doing the thing that they are afraid of and evaluating the outcome. In this instance the therapist agreed with the patient that one possibility was that the presence of the therapist had made him less likely to lose control. The patient is then asked how he could check this out, which leads naturally and collaboratively on to the next stage of exposure, again carried out as a behavioural experiment.

Cognitive Treatment of Mood Problems Associated with Obsessions

The link between dysphoric mood states and obsessive-compulsive disorder is explicitly defined in the cognitive-behavioural model. The importance of this link cannot be overstressed. Severe concurrent depression has been suggested as a cause of treatment failure. If a severe primary depression is present, treatment of the depression should lead to improvement in obsessive-compulsive symptoms (Gittleson 1966). In other cases however, the obsessional phenomena are primary, as indicated by order of onset, but are exacerbated by deterioration in mood. Anti-depressant medication is certainly not indicated in such cases, while cognitive techniques may be of benefit, especially when the mood changes are predictable and recurrent.

An ambulance driver presented with a 10-year history of severe obsessive-compulsive disorder. He was not clinically depressed and responded to behavioural treatment. He described regular exacerbations of his obsessional difficulties associated with negative thoughts about his work performance. Assessment revealed automatic thoughts concerning his capabilities in comparison with his colleagues.
Stressful events at work activated dysfunctional assumptions, for example, "I can never get any enjoyment from anything I do", and led to NATs. Examples of these cognitions were: "I am a weak

person", "I always back down and let other people walk over me", "I can never express myself properly; I will always get tongue-tied", "I always mess everything up". He would become preoccupied with these thoughts leading to feelings of inferiority, depression and anxiety, which would persist throughout his shift. In accordance with the cognitive-behavioural model, such events led to an increase in his obsessional thoughts and behaviours. He found that the dysphoric symptoms and anxiety made the implementation of exposure and response prevention more difficult.

Cognitive treatment for depression was therefore commenced, as described by Beck (1976). This began with a description of the link between thoughts, feelings and mood and with further emphasis of the link between dysphoria and obsessions. He was taught to monitor negative thoughts and assumptions and to challenge these ideas. Formation of rational responses enabled him to control the dysphoric feelings, and he no longer complained of exacerbations of his obsessional behaviour.

Table 6. Example of the use of dysfunctional thought record to deal with mood changes triggering obsessional thoughts and behaviour

Initial emotion	Automatic thought	Rational response
Sad	"I'm no good as an ambulance man." (belief 85 → 40 after session)	"Yes I am, I have intubated an old lady who they said was very difficult".
Anxious (Works outing)	"I will be sea-sick and show myself up." (belief 70 → 15)	"Why should I be? Others might be if I am. So what if I am?"
Sad	"I always say the wrong thing and I keep doing it once I start." (belief 98 → 40)	"I don't always say the wrong things. I had a good conversation with a colleague today."

The results of this case support the prediction that dysphoric mood changes exacerbate obsessional difficulties. Such mood changes are not central to the model proposed but interact with it at several levels (see Salkovskis 1985). Depression may widen the range of stimuli which provoke intrusions and the range of intrusions which lead to NATs and thus increase the activity level of pre-existing dysfunctional assumptions. Depression is associated with an increased probability of negative thinking, while an increase in anxiety can result in more frequent intrusions. The use of cognitive strategies to deal with such mood changes should reverse these effects; in the above example belief in NATs decreased while alternative rational responses became more accessible. In this way exacerbation of the obsessions was less likely.

It is clear that the presence and importance of mood changes must be evaluated in all cases of obsessive-compulsive disorder and appropriate interventions instigated. Cognitive techniques are likely to be of importance in the management of primary depression with obsessional features as well as in primary obsessional problems where dysphoria is a maintaining factor.

Dealing with Avoidance of Responsibility and Reassurance Seeking

As described above, a key issue in the formulation of obsessive-compulsive disorder is the concept of responsibility. Neutralisation can therefore be understood in this context as an attempt to put things right and to avert the possibility of being blamed for harm. For exposure and response prevention to be successful, all neutralisation must be prevented. Overt neutralisation, in the form of rituals, is easily recognisable and commonly dealt with. However, cognitive neutralisation is often neglected, especially if overt rituals are present. The persistent seeking of reassurance, particularly from those in authority, displayed by many obsessionals is clearly a way of spreading responsibility. Hence, reassurance seeking, like cognitive avoidance and cognitive rituals, is a form of neutralising behaviour which serves the same function as an overt ritual in obsessive-compulsive disorder, i.e. it leads to a short term decrease in fear but a longer term increase and reinforcement of the obsessional behaviour. Exposure and reassurance prevention will enable the patient to habituate to and reappraise the likelihood of being responsible for harm. Despite emphasis on the importance of this type of behaviour (Marks 1981; Warwick and Salkovskis 1985) its assessment is often not included in the behavioural analysis and is therefore not considered in treatment. The importance of instructing relatives in how to deal with such requests is regularly stressed, but it is vitally important also to be vigilant for subtle requests for reassurance during treatment sessions. If the therapist knows of the patient's actions, he may be then perceived by the patient as sharing the responsibility involved. Some subtle requests may not even be recognised by the therapist (or the patient) as reassurance seeking. Active reassurance may therefore be inadvertently (or at worst, actively) given as a way of decreasing discomfort and improving compliance – with potential detrimental effects (Warwick and Salkovskis 1985).

Therapist-aided exposure sessions, modelling and homework instructions can themselves function as reassurance; the patient can interpret them as "permission" from the therapist to perform the necessary exposure without response prevention, thereby absolving the patient from personal responsibility. In such circumstances tasks can be completed with relative ease, but further difficulties will obviously be encountered on discharge. A useful strategy is therefore to direct patients to carry out self-directed homework without disclosing to anyone (including the therapist) the specific actions concerned. This is a difficult exercise for patients to grasp and careful explanation is required, along with regular discussion of records of discomfort. This is best envisaged as "exposure to and reappraisal of responsibility", but it is a particularly difficult concept for patients to understand. Instructions for the exercise may be: "I want you to plan and carry out homework like we have done up to now, but with an important difference. This time, you'll set things up so that you become uncomfortable; don't check, record how uncomfortable you got immediately afterwards, but *don't* tell (or even hint to) anyone at all about what you've done. We'll discuss how you felt next session, but you and only you will be responsible for the task. So, without telling me any details of what you will leave unchecked, can you describe what you have to do for homework this week?"

The following transcript illustrates the recognition and management of reassurance seeking.

T: You managed not to wash at all over the last two days? That's really good.
P: Yes, but I've been very worried about it.
T: Can you tell me a bit about how you coped in that time, I mean, how you dealt with the discomfort over that time?
P: Well, sometimes it hasn't been too bad, but sometimes it's just been impossible, and my family hasn't been too helpful.
T: Your family? What came up there?
P: Well I keep asking for some kind of support, and they won't give it to me.
T: Have your family found it difficult to actually help you think about other things or carry on when you're feeling uncomfortable, like we discussed with them last week?
P: Well, I just can't get rid of this worry that I'll get something awful if I don't wash.
T: Is that the sort of thing you've been trying to talk about with your family?
P: Well, I just feel sure that I'll get something, cancer or something.

[At this point is starts to become apparent from his answers that the patient is not directly responding to the content of questioning but is obliquely seeking reassurance from the therapist in an obsessional fashion; his answers appear to be attempts to describe *details* of his *intrusive thoughts,* whilst the therapist is still attempting to elicit details of his *behaviour*. This is one of the most frequently encountered (and subtle) forms of reassurance seeking within session. It also provides an ideal opportunity to tackle this particular patient's problems "in vivo".]

T: I may be wrong, but by saying these things right now and going over the cancer thing, are you maybe worried that I don't know everything? Are you hoping that I might respond to what you're saying? Perhaps you feel that I'd respond if there was something dangerous?
P: Yes, yes, I suppose so. I mean, I just need to know it's not going to happen. I mean, this treatment gets the anxiety down a bit, but I still might get it. I don't see what's wrong with finding out whether it is going to happen.
T: I think I understand. In the last couple of sessions, we discussed the way that washing your hands can actually continue the problem with feeling contaminated, and the connection is easy to see. I guess with the questions it's harder to see the connection, is that right?
P: Well, yes, the discomfort of not washing has come down, and that's OK, but my mind is still full of worries that need dealing with.
T: So we ought to look more closely at this right now. At the moment I think you're actually quite keen to ask me about things, for me to put your mind at rest about this?
P: Well, I feel that you would know about it, so why don't you tell me?
T: Obviously I should if it's going to make you feel much better, get rid of the problem. Okay, so, how many times would I have to reassure you now for it to last you for the rest of the week?
P: To last for the rest of the week?
T: Yes, I've got the rest of this morning set aside because we were going to do a session with washing. This seems more important right now because you are managing the washing so well. So I've got several hours in which I could reassure you, go over things as many times as you like really. So, how many times would I need to do it to last for the rest of the week?
P: Well, it doesn't work like that.
T: Oh . . . well . . . how do you mean?
P: I mean if you say it lots of times, it doesn't . . . sort of build up a stock that will last for the rest of the week.
T: Ah, I see. So if I actually try my hardest to put your mind at rest right now, how long would it last then?
P: Probably until the next time I touch something "dangerous".
T: You mean like the wanting to wash? It could be as little as ten, or even five minutes? Is that right?
P: Yes, I suppose so.
T: So is it like the washing?
P: Sort of.
T: What are the main differences, then?
P: It might be different because I need to know whether I'm going to catch something.
T: So the difference is that you need to ask, and you don't feel like you need to wash?
P: No, they're similar in that way.
T: Can you think of any other differences?
P: I need other people to ask.

T: Do you need anything else for washing?
P: Well, I need soap and water. If you put it like that, it's not so terribly different.
T: Are you sure you can't think of any other differences?
P: Well, I suppose the only other difference is, asking about it makes my family even crosser.
T: Right, let's check I've got this right, we'll write this down as we go through it, and maybe we can work out a plan to deal with this.
P: Right.

Ruminations

Against the background of the outstanding success of behavioural treatment of obsessive-compulsive disorder, the treatment of obsessional ruminations would seem to be a very simple enterprise. Ruminators appear to have a variant of obsessional disorder without the overt compulsive component, meaning that such patients should show *less* overall disturbance of functioning. Furthermore, ruminations should be particularly amenable to treatment because compulsive behaviour is hypothesised to be one of the principal factors maintaining the obsessions. That this is not so is easily confirmed by the briefest examination of the literature; Rachman (1983) reached the conclusion that "the main obstacle to the successful treatment of obsessions is the absence of effective techniques". This conclusion is based on the observation that both habituation training (exposure) and thought stopping (dismissal training) have not been shown to be effective. Given the sound empirical basis for the effectiveness of exposure and reappraisal therapies in all other anxiety disorders *including* obsessive-compulsive disorder, why should this be so? It could be that ruminations are not related to obsessional-compulsive disorder at all, and that they represent a distinct clinical entity. This seems implausible on *a priori* grounds; as far as can be judged on the basis of present knowledge, the phenomenology of obsessions occurring in the context of obsessive-compulsive disorder and of ruminations is almost identical, although we are currently conducting a study to examine this point more thoroughly

An attractive alternative view is that neutralising behaviours *do* occur in ruminations, but at a cognitive rather than an overt behavioural level. As can be seen from Table 2 above, it is not uncommon for obsessional patients to report engaging in covert neutralising (such as picturing an angel in order to "put right" thoughts believed to be "evil"). When treatment for ritualisers was developed in the early 1970's, there was a strong emphasis on overt behaviour, which may be why covert neutralising was not identified. More recently, a number of reports have considered the possibility of covert neutralising, and suggest that response prevention of covert neutralising might be indicated (P.M. Salkovskis, D. Westbrook 1987, unpublished observations). Note that covert neutralising can often be carried out more frequently than overt (and hence have more impact on the maintenance of the obsession) because it is more "portable" in the sense that the action taken only involves thoughts rather than doors, water, soap and so on. Clinical experience suggests that many ritualisers develop covert neutralising as a way of extending or postponing their rituals to times when they would otherwise be unable to carry them out. Amongst normal subjects "putting the thoughts right" was most commonly observed at a cognitive level. In a sample of 243 subjects 77% of those experiencing intrusions reported cognitive neutralising "sometimes" or more frequently (P.M. Salkovskis and H.R. Dent 1987, unpublished observations). Subjects who frequently neutralise differ from those not doing so in the amount of discomfort associated with their intrusions, how difficult it was to dismiss their thoughts, avoidance of situations provoking their thoughts and scores on the Maudsley Obsessive Compulsive Inventory; in all respects measured, normal subjects who neutralised were more like a clinically disturbed group.

Ruminators can be regarded as patients in whom neutralising (and avoidance) behaviour occurs almost entirely cognitively. If this is true, it is possible that previous treatments have failed because they have not taken account of this by implementing response prevention. This means that exposure will have been prematurely terminated and effective reappraisal prevented. Further factors involved in the failure of previous treatments include the relative difficulty of reliably evoking the feared stimulus (thought). As described above, obsessional thoughts are followed (and therefore reinforced) by the occurrence of NATs which evoke discomfort, making extinction less likely.

Reconstructing the Treatment of Ruminations

Treatment invariably starts with a detailed discussion between the patient and therapist of the preliminary formulation, combined with the provision of information about the nature and meaning of obsessions. Usually the formulation emphasises the idea that people sometimes become upset by normal intrusive thoughts, leading them to neutralise by deliberately performing actions or thinking thoughts; the way in which neutralising maintains and increases the problem by terminating exposure is described and explained. In particular, the patient's attention is drawn to the way in which avoidance and any effort (behaviours or thoughts) directed at "putting things right" or resisting the intrusive thoughts prevent them from confronting their anxiety.

To overcome this problem it is necessary to experience the thoughts again and again, so that habituation of anxiety takes place, and it can be discovered that nothing harmful happens as a result of the unneutralised thought. The way in which unpredictability of obsessional thoughts interferes with anxiety reduction should also be outlined. This explanation and the accompanying discussion forms the rationale for habituation training with response prevention. Understanding and acceptance of this rationale will both improve compliance *and* form the basis of subsequent reappraisal. Patients can thus come to recognise that obsessional thoughts do not have any significance beyond the fact that intrusive thoughts tend to occur about things which worry them. The discussion focuses on ways of helping the natural process of "getting used to the upsetting thoughts without doing anything about them" to take place. It is explained to the patient that the best way to get used to the thoughts is to have them happen in a more predictable way; this can be done by recording the patient speaking their intrusive thought onto a loop cassette tape (see Salkovskis 1983; Headland and McDonald 1987; P.M. Salkovskis, D. Westbrook 1987, unpublished observations).

Once a tape has been recorded (usually using a 30- or 60-s loop), the patient is instructed to listen as closely as he or she can to the tape while it is played a number of times. After each presentation the patient indicates how much discomfort is evoked. Urges to neutralise or avoid which occurred during the audiotaped presentation are then discussed in detail; if neutralising or avoidance did take place in any form during or after the tape presentation, ways of preventing this are explored, then tried out with the tape again until an unneutralised (or even better, unneutralisable) presentation is managed. The aim is to have the patient listen to the tape right through at least once *without neutralising* during this session. As homework the patient is asked to listen to the tape every day and with the same provisions for response prevention. At the same time, he or she is asked to response-prevent any neutralising which occurs day to day, recording the results.

Audiotaped habituation and response prevention is repeated with a range of other thoughts. Careful attention is given to the degree of generalisation to everyday activities, and the programme modified to encompass the most commonly occurring intrusive thoughts. Once extensive and rapid habituation has been obtained with the tape, ways of directly bringing about generalisation are explored. These include (a) having the patient listen to the tape in his or her most problematic situation, possibly using a personal stereo. For example, patients having thoughts about harming people in the street listen to the tape while they walk down the street. (b) Getting the patient to listen to the tape in stressful circumstances. Examples may be either naturally occurring stressful situations (e.g. going to the dentist, capitalising on naturally occurring mood fluctuations) or contrived situations (e.g. getting the patient to engage in stressful imagery or using mood-induction procedures).

Deliberate variations in the taped habituation procedures are introduced to enable habituation to less predictable stimuli; for example, recording a range of intrusive thoughts on an ordinary cassette tape, varying the intensity, content and intervals between thoughts. Finally, habituation to deliberately provoked thoughts without a tape is added. The general structure of treatment regarding reassurance seeking and making the patient increasingly responsible for his or her own treatment and homework sessions apply as in exposure with response prevention. The patient is asked deliberately to provoke the thought (without neutralising) in a variety of situations. (Note that considerations of exposure to responsibility/ reassurance seeking apply as in the section on exposure with response prevention, above; the procedures described in this section relate to the special problems of dealing with the covert nature of ruminations.)

Conclusions and Future Directions

The work described in this chapter highlights the need for new, effective treatment strategies for obsessive-compulsive disorder, particularly in cases in which current treatments are ineffective. As we have tried to make clear, new strategies do not replace behavioural treatment, but supplement and extend existing approaches. Further single case experiments should indicate the potential scope of cognitive approaches; larger scale controlled studies are a later requirement. The urgent need is for further research into cognitive treatment applied to the (up to 50% of all) patients suitable for but not benefiting from behavioural treatments.

References

Beech HR (1974) Obsessional states. Methuen, London

Beck AT (1976) Cognitive therapy and the emotional disorders. International University Press, New York

Beck AT, Emery G, Greenberg RL (1985) Anxiety disorders and phobias: a cognitive perspective. Basic Books, New York

Burns DD (1980) Feeling good: the new mood therapy. New American Library, New York

Espie CA (1986) The group treatment of obsessive-compulsive ritualisers: behavioural management of identified patterns of relapse. Behav Psychother 14:21–33

Foa EB (1979) Failures in treating obsessive-compulsives. Behav Res Ther 17:169–176

Foa EB, Goldstein A (1978) Continuous exposure and complete response prevention in the treatment of obsessive-compulsive neurosis. Behav Ther 9:821–829

Foa EB, Steketee G, Grayson JB, Doppelt HG (1983) Treatment of obsessive-compulsives: when do we fail? In: Foa EB, Emmelkamp PMG (eds) Failures in behaviour therapy. Wiley, New York, pp 10–34

Gittleson N (1966) The fate of obsessions in depressive psychosis. Br J Psychiatry 112:705–708

Headland KSE, McDonald R (1987) Rapid audio-tape treatment of obsessional ruminations. A case report. Behav Psychother 15:188–192

Marks IM (1981) Cure and care of neurosis. Wiley, New York

Rachman SJ (1971) Obsessional ruminations. Behav Res Ther 9:229–235

Rachman SJ (1976) The modification of obsessions: a new formulation. Behav Res Ther 14:437–444

Rachman SJ (1983) Obstacles to the successful treatment of obsessions. In: Foa EB, Emmelkamp PMG (eds) Failures in behaviour therapy. Wiley, New York, pp 35–57

Rachman SJ, de Silva P (1978) Abnormal and normal obsessions. Behav Res Ther 16:233–248

Rachman SJ, Hodgson RJ (1980) Obsessions and compulsions. Prentice Hall, Englewood Cliffs, NJ

Salkovskis PM (1983) Treatment of an obsessional patient using habituation to audiotaped ruminations. Br J Clin Psychol 22:311–313

Salkovskis PM (1985) Obsessional-compulsive problems: a cognitive-behavioural analysis. Behav Res Ther 23:571–583

Salkovskis PM (1986) The cognitive revolution: new way forward, backward somersault or full circle? Behav Psychother 14:278–282

Salkovskis PM (1987) Cognitive therapy: is it always cognitive, is it always therapy? In: Dent HR (ed) Clinical psychology: research and development. Croom Helm, London

Salkovskis PM (1988) Intrusive thoughts and obsessional disorder. In: Glasgow D, Eisenberg N (eds) Current issues in clinical psychology, vol 5 Gower, London

Salkovskis PM, Harrison J (1984) Abnormal and normal obsessions: a replication. Behav Res Ther 22:549–552

Salkovskis PM, Kirk J (1989) Obsessional disorders. In: Hawton K, Salkovskis PM, Kirk J, Clark DM (eds) Cognitive behavioural treatments: a practical guide. Oxford University Press, Oxford (to be published, 1989)

Salkovskis PM, Warwick HMC (1985) Cognitive therapy of obsessive-compulsive disorder: treating treatment failures. Behav Psychother 13:243–255

Salkovskis PM, Westbrook D (1987) Obsessive-compulsive disorder: clinical strategies for improving behavioural treatments. In: Dent HR (ed) Clinical psychology: research and development. Croom Helm, London

Warwick HMC, Salkovskis PM (1985) Reassurance. Br Med J 290:1028

Cognitive Therapy with Depressed Adolescents

T.C.R. WILKES

Introduction

Adolescence is a period in individual development of rapid neurological, psychological and biological change. This period is often delimited by the teenage years, although some consider adolescence to continue until the age of 25. During this highly complex period of personality development dramatic changes take place in the adolescent's expectations, in the values and beliefs of his family and in his outside world. This results in an individual with increased reliance upon peer groups rather than the family of origin and one who is capable of a separate existence in the world.

Adolescents frequently come to the attention of the family because of their frequent misbehaviour and apparent unhappiness. Suicide in this age group has shown an alarming increase over the past two decades (Maris 1985), and many adult affective disorders first present themselves during the adolescent period. (Perris 1966; Winokur 1969) Half the indictable crimes in North America and the United Kingdom are, in fact, committed by those under 21 years of age. Indeed, society, with all its varied legal restrictions regarding drinking, driving, and possession of firearms, goes to great lengths to protect itself from the ravages of adolescent turmoil. Despite these precautions violence is the leading cause of death in adolescents, and even accidents or "accident proneness" may reflect suicidal tendencies (Holinger 1979).

Psychiatric disorders occurring in adolescence, such as major depression, are affected by maturational processes and by transient disturbances that are closely associated with adolescent developmental changes. Thus the disturbed adolescent must be viewed in the context of family, home, peer group, school and neighbourhood. Cognitive therapy is traditionally seen as an effective treatment for depressive disorders in adults, and there are several controlled, methodologically sound outcome trials which confirm this impression (Blackburn et al. 1981; Beck et al. 1985). Adolescents are subject to many episodes of mood disturbance, and this chapter attempts to address the problem of adapting traditional cognitive therapy to the depressed or disturbed adolescent.

Consultant Psychiatrist for Child, Adolescent and Family Services, Mental Health Services, 200- 5 Avenue South, Lethbridge, Alberta Canada T1J 4C7

Diagnosis

Depressive disorders are recognized among the mood and behaviour disturbances of adulthood, but it has only recently been accepted that depressive disorders also manifest themselves in childhood and adolescence. This is in part due to the difficulties of classification in child psychiatry – where one man's fact is another man's fantasy, given the plethora of theoretical orientations that exist to account for emotional disturbances.

Systematic study of psychiatry in general has been hampered by low validity and reliability of diagnostic categories. This problem was partly overcome by the introduction of criteria for psychiatric diagnosis such as those found in the Research Diagnostic Criteria (Spitzer et al. 1978), the DSM III criteria (American Psychiatric Association 1980) and, specifically for childhood depression, the Weinberg criteria (1973).

Much controversy continues about the choice of diagnostic criteria, but there is now a growing acceptance that the DSM III criteria for major depressive disorders offers those of greatest clinical value. The essential features of depression are the same for infants, children and adolescents as they are for adults. However, there may also be age-specific features, such as separation anxiety in pre-school children and school phobia and conduct disorders in older children and adolescents.

Clinical diagnosis of depression may require two to four interviews to assess both the patient and his family. The descriptive diagnosis of depression must be established with such specific criteria as those mentioned above. The severity of symptoms should be measured as well (e.g. Bellevue Inventory for Depression, Petti 1978). Obtaining a family history to ascertain the presence of affective disorders, hyperactivity, learning disorders, sociopathy, alcoholism, etc. in first, second and third degree relatives is important to place the depression in context.

Once the diagnosis is rendered, it should be communicated to both the parents and the patient. The therapist explains that genetic, biochemical and situational factors can contribute to depression. Lowered self-esteem is seen as a symptom of depression that often causes increased sensitivity to criticism and a heightened need for peer support. This explanation helps reframe disobedient rebellious behaviour as a symptom of depression, requiring treatment, and sets the stage for a neutral, non-judgemental, problem-solving alliance between therapist, parents and patient.

During the evaluation ascertaining each family member's perception of the problem is important. A review of the methods already tried and the results, reveals interpersonal disputes as well as familial and individual beliefs about the problem(s). As part of this psychological assessment coping skills and present social supports are revealed. This evaluation naturally leads the therapist to interview the adolescent alone to determine his/her view of these problems and symptoms.

Learning Disorders and Depression

Poor school performance may be a simple correlate of a depressive episode or may point to a primary learning disability exacerbated by depression. Some depressed children have impaired right-cerebral function e.g. decreased performance IQ on the Weschler Intelligence Scale for Children, Revised (WISC-R), leading to learning difficulties that resolve with remission of depressive symptoms (Brumback et al. 1980). Also, learning disabilities may be independent of and antedate depressive symptoms. Therefore it is necessary to assess learning disabilities thoroughly.

The symbol language battery (Weinberg 1982, Weinberg and McLean 1986) requires only 15–20 min to evaluate an adolescent's lexical skills in reading, spelling, arithmetic, printing and writing. These symbolic skills entail specific properties – nominal recall, sequential ordering and orientation. Additionally, verbal and writing communicative skills are assessed; this includes listening to and understanding the spoken word as well as the recall of phonemes. Phasic verbal expression involves recalling and using with appropriate prosody and emotionality common nouns and verbs in speaking.

Phasic writing expression is assessed by observing how the adolescent formulates answers questions and deals with essay writing. Finally, the symbol language battery assists in assessing the individual's symbolization skills. Symbolization is the process whereby words are associated with pictures and pictures with words. Correct association of words and pictures results in correct actions. A symbolic or underlying symbolization deficit is present when neither pictures nor words elicit correct actions; pictures and words that remain unassociated or incorrectly associated result in illogical actions.

Adolescents with specific developmental learning disorders not only have difficulty with school curricula but frequently have difficulty resolving social and interpersonal problems that arise in day-to-day living. Effective interpersonal social problem solving and emotional adjustment are dependent upon the neurological substate of the individual. The symbol language battery test allows an assessment of this substate without implying any covert emotional conflicts.

The Therapeutic Alliance

Teenage negative ambivalence is one of the most difficult issues in treating adolescents, making the traditional collaborative alliance at times impossible. The adolescent, like the toddler, has a greater desire to emphasize separateness from, than agreement with, authority figures. This is reflected in the age-appropriate task of the adolescent to achieve cognitive, emotional and behavioural independence from the family of origin. Agreement with parents and/or the therapist may therefore be perceived as emotional surrender and threaten a loss of identity.

Adolescents are frequently aggravating and oppositional and seldom seek therapy on their own; they are urged or forced to do so by their parents. To facilitate the therapeutic alliance the therapist should acknowledge their reluctance to attend therapy and collaboratively explore such preceptions as "I don't have a problem" and "It's everyone else". The therapist must establish neutrality both by words and behaviour and clarify the role that he/she will play. Early on the therapist should directly address myths commonly held by the adolescent, such as "Therapy is a punishment" or "The therapist knows what I think and feel without me saying it". An accurate assessment of the problem and the development of a plan for its possible solutions are the objects of treatment, and these cannot be achieved without patient cooperation.

The patient is appealed to as a critical collaborator in problem solving, but at the same time one must accept the adolescent's negative ambivalence about therapy; he may, for instance, manifest non-compliance with appointments. Adolescents who fail to keep scheduled appointments often appear later at unscheduled times. When this erratic compliance occurs, the therapist explores the patient's perception of the therapist and the appointment as a vehicle to elucidate the cognitive model of emotional disorders. For example, a 16-year-old who missed his second appointment was brought to the following session by his father. Table 1 presents the triple-column analysis then drawn up by patient and therapist about the missed session.

Table 1. Example of triple-column analysis

Emotion	Automatic thought	Rational response
Fear	"If I go to see the doctor, he might put me back in the hospital."	"I'm coming here to learn how I can be happier at home and school." "I would only return to the hospital if I became so depressed that my life was in danger."

This example shows how non-compliance often reflects the patient's thoughts or fears about the therapist, and how cognitive techniques can identify and counter them. This procedure may be repeated several times to convince the patient that he selectively attends to observations which confirm his distorted beliefs about the world in which he lives. The patient in this example began to enjoy coming to therapy and began to work very hard on homework.

A close liaison between the therapist and the patient's family is vital to overcome counter-therapeutic parental beliefs and expectations and to model problem-solving behaviour for the patient. This liaison reduces possible rivalry between therapist and parent(s). The liaison can be strengthened by frequently exchanging feedback with the parents as well as with the patient during the course of therapy.

However, if despite these parental-therapist transactions a destructive, envious rivalry does develop, this should be welcomed as an opportunity to examine the family's rules, expectations and beliefs of two- and three-person relationships. How does the family deal with the young boy competing with his father or the daughter with her mother? Is there accommodation, understanding and renegotiation along age-appropriate lines? Or is there hostile, demeaning, authoritarian suppression with subsequent interpersonal disputes?

For the structural family therapist this approach would be labelled as an isomorphic dysfunctional transaction (Minuchin 1974), i.e. the family structure is manifested in a variety of transactions that obey the same system rules and that are therefore equivalent. In other words, what is happening with the therapist and parents may be a reflection of what is happening between adolescent and parents.

Analysing Modes of Communication

Adolescents often communicate deep feelings or beliefs in non-verbal ways. Envy can appear in the therapeutic relationship and is common with delinquent adolescents. This can be expressed by a failure to do homework or in a devaluing of any therapeutic help. A defense against envy is the denial of any value in others. Understanding this can assist the therapist when dealing with an aggressive, depressed adolescent who misses appointments and appears at war with the world.

Cognitions such as "Everyone is having a good time but me" or "If only I had money/boyfriend/car . . ." are typical of such an adolescent. Once the emotions and cognitions are acknowledged, a problem-solving technique can be introduced to achieve in a collaborative manner those goals that are realistic, reasonable, suitable and helpful.

The therapist must identify how each patient optimally communicates. For example, a 16-year-old boy continually "forgot" the triple-column assignment (Beck et al. 1979) but evidenced no learning disability. His parents complained that he often wrote poems and drew pictures rather than doing school homework. With this knowledge the therapist discontinued the triple-column technique and requested drawings or poems; the therapist was subsequently bombarded with these. Recurrent themes here of boys being lost or persecuted by an impersonal and frightening world became obvious. These data helped the therapist and the patient make explicit the patient's perception of himself, his world and his future. Just as in play therapy (Klein 1963), the adolescent may communicate in metaphors over the course of several sessions. Here hypothesis testing with logical analysis was used to gradually revise these views of himself and his parents. Ultimately, the boy came to see himself as an individual with a talent for poetry and drawing who was valued by his, albeit strict, parents. As this more realistic perspective developed, new expectations were targeted for future sessions.

Spontaneous verbalizations during the sessions are often direct expressions of the negative cognitive triad of dysfunctional beliefs. As such, they can be used in lieu of written homework to elicit automatic thoughts. A 13-year-old with violent anger and outbursts responded to the therapist:

T: "You look angry, J."

J: "I didn't want to talk to you. All I do is talk. I am here because my parents and that other doctor says I should be here. I want to get out of here as soon as possible. People think that you are mentally sick if you are here – that you are dangerous. People are afraid of us. That's why we are locked up in here like a prison. We don't even get presents here, not like the rest of the wards."

This outburst contains a host of multiple negative automatic thoughts about himself, his future and his environment. This patient saw himself as different, sick, neglected and subject to irrational adult coercions. These strongly held notions must be expressed by the patient and acknowledged by the therapist before discussion with logical analysis or homework experiments can be attempted. Premature confrontation of these ideas risks disruption of the therapeutic alliance.

Once automatic thoughts are elicited, they are evaluated and tested as in adults. However, adolescents, especially younger adolescents, have difficulty with the notion of logical errors, and they often have a lower capacity for empathy, fewer interpersonal skills and difficulty with understanding the consequences of thinking (Kendall et al. 1981). It is often more useful simply to consider alternative ways of perceiving events rather than trying to teach patients how to identify logical errors and to correct them, which requires formal thinking skills. Many adolescents use pre-operational or concrete operational cognitive skills as described by Piaget (1977, 1979). Thus, the patient's level of cognitive development dictates which cognitive techniques are optimal. The more a patient displays a capacity for consequential thinking or an ability to generate alternative views, the less modification of adult cognitive techniques is needed.

Children with learning difficulties can use cognitive-behavioural methods if their optional mode of communication is used. To illustrate this, one can consider the adult therapeutic technique of "point-counterpoint" (Burns 1984, Chap. 10). A 13-year-old, mildly dyslexic boy who was particularly enthusiastic about acting complained about failing to win the school prize. The therapist offered to role-play an antagonistic school friend while the patient was to use answers and arguments just rehearsed.

T: "You're no good J."
J: "What do you mean?"
T: "You didn't win a prize".
J: "Not everybody can win a prize. Besides, I came in second."
T: "That's no good, you've been second before. It's no good unless you win."
J: "I still enjoy being with my friends, and a teacher has to award people's effort as well. Just because you don't win, does not mean that you are no good."
T: "Okay, you have convinced me."

While poorly attentive to written information because of dyslexia, he role-played easily and used verbal memory. In this case the triple-column technique was ineffective.

Dichotomous and Exaggerated Thinking

Persecutory anxiety in adolescents is common. A traditional Kleinian view would suggest that the individual here is unable to tolerate ambivalence and therefore splits and projects. Such adolescents frequently think and say things in an exaggerated manner which they then often regret. They are, of course, struggling with the question of how the world *should* be in "utopia" rather than how it *is* in reality. This overly simplistic, black-and-white thinking can be modified by teaching patients to think along a continuum. To illustrate this, a 13-year-old boy came to his first session after just 1 week back at school following hospitalization. He said that everything was "going terribly". To clarify the meaning of this, the therapist drew a line representing a continuum – from the "best" to the "worst" school situations. With the patient the therapist defined the worst possible scenario as his being tearful and depressed, arguing with everybody, being punished at school, trying hard and not passing any tests, not participating in extra-curricular activities and being kicked out of elective subjects, while his parents were trying to help him all the time. The best scenario included getting most homework done in class without parental help, getting consistently good marks, participating in all extra-curricular activities, being moved out of remedial class and spending more time with school friends. The patient used a pencil to indicate where he felt himself on this continuum at the time of hospitalization; he chose a point very near the worst scenario. He then marked his location for the past week – at about mid-point. During this exercise the patient's mood markedly improved, and at the end he spontaneously noted that things "aren't all that bad".

To provide practice exercises for challenging his dichotomous thinking outside therapy the therapist and the patient developed a vocabulary of moods. This consisted of a scale ranging 0–10 with the following impressionistic callibration: 0, "the pits"; 2.5, "fair"; 5.0, "O.K."; 7.5, "good"; and 10.0, "great". This grading schema he applied to various situations. With this approach to school difficulties the patient reframed his difficulties regarding his attitude expressed in the statement "I really don't like the teachers". With the specific target of "how to deal with difficult teachers", therapeutic progress was facilitated.

Adolescents often wrestle with the problem of omnipotence. One 16-year-old remarked that he "felt invulnerable", stating "I can do anything". On the day before, he had consumed a pint of whiskey, boasting that he could "handle anything"; he became intoxicated and was sent home from school. He then became very despondent and considered himself "weak" because he could not drink that amount of alcohol and remain sober. This dichotomous thinking was challenged through the use of the a continuum (Fig. 1) for measuring his intoxication and his feelings about it. A brief educational discussion then ensued with this patient about alcohol levels in the blood and about liver metabolism as factors relevant to alcohol tolerance which were unrelated to the idea of "toughness". This discussion indirectly confronted his idea of omnipotence in a non-judgemental fashion.

Fig. 1. Example of a continuum for associating physical condition and feelings (here, due to intoxication)

0				10
No effect	Tipsy happy	Laughing, poor coordination	Slurred speech, nausea	Coma

Suicidal Thinking

Depressed children may become preoccupied with death or suicide attempts. Maris (1985) in a review found that the leading cause of death in adolescence is suicide, emphasizing that symptoms indicating a tendency to this should be taken seriously and not dismissed as a passing phase or fad. This is especially important in young females aged 10–14 years and young males aged 15–19 years, as these groups have undergone, since 1960, one of the largest increases in suicide rates. Young suicides are typically more revenge-motivated and impulsive and have more negative interpersonal relations than other suicides. They are also associated with more suicide and divorce in their families of origin.

Adolescents usually do not fully comprehend the meaning of suicide. One 16-year-old, for instance, mentioned that he wanted to commit suicide to "look tough" and gain respect from his peers. He did not recognize that his friends might not regard suicide as a sign of "being tough", and that even if they did, he would neither see their reactions nor experience their praise. The "downward-arrow" technique (Burns 1980, Chap. 7) was used to operationalize the meaning of "being tough". To this patient, "being tough" meant "You're a winner", "You have a lot of friends". Therapy focussed on other ways to achieve these desires; behavioural goals, e.g. playing basketball, running and lifting weights, were identified as more likely to succeed than being dead for achieving these objectives. Note that in the therapy the idea of suicide was initially "accepted" but was rejected ultimately as being both unrealistic and ineffective in pursuit of his actual goal.

A later session focussed on his desire to run away. In this session the "pro-and-con" technique was used (Beck et al. 1979). "Con's" included: "I don't want to be a nuisance to my parents"; "I don't want to lose all my friends"; and "I'd have no support or place to stay". "Pro's" included: "Getting away from church" and "I'd have freedom and be away from my old self". Thereafter the patient still wanted to run away, but the therapist and he agreed that he would not do anything of this sort until he had reviewed his plans in the next session. As homework, he was to determine how much money he would need, and where he would stay. This assignment led him to develop an alternative plan: to stay at home because he wanted a college education, and because leaving home would interrupt his educational ambitions. Therapy then focussed on coping with specific family rules that he found uncomfortable or inconvenient, for he obviously had to accept some rules to achieve this desire and the expected family support. The timing of this discussion was crucial in this case. Guided discovery can facilitate the acceptance of the idea, but conclusions cannot be forced on unwilling, stubborn adolescents.

Parental Beliefs and Family Dynamics

Perceived Responsibility

Parental perceptions and beliefs can either facilitate or obstruct therapy; this is illustrated by the following case. J., a 13-year-old boy, was referred by his family doctor due to depression. Chronic parental discord with a recent parental separation was noted; the father saw him on alternate weekends. After such visits J. became very upset and despondent upon returning home, and this infuriated the mother, for she saw this as indicating that J. was more attached to his father than to her. J. complained that his father's telephone calls were intermittent and unpredictable. Furthermore, when his father said that he would phone, he often did not, which caused J. to plummet into depression. His mother frequently telephoned the father to urge him to telephone J., who was still upset after his father's visit. This operant system rewarded the undesired behaviour – being upset after returning from his father.

The therapist helped identify automatic thoughts that preceded increased sadness and anger when his father failed to call. Logical analysis was used to counter these thoughts, with some improvement. The problem was not resolved, however, until the therapist engaged the family in disrupting the above reward system. To accomplish this the therapist discussed the matter with the parents and corrected expectations of each that the other was responsible for helping J. adjust to the separation. In addition, conflict that J. had with his mother was the focus of a joint session. A series of questions about her anger toward J. enabled her to say that she saw J. as dominating her life. When he became sad, he was often irritable and uncooperative, not helping with any chores. She perceived this behaviour as being "just like his dad", and this view reduced her effectiveness as a parent, as it led to her struggling not to "give in to" J.'s bad behaviour, fearing that he otherwise would end up just like his father. J. reciprocated with thoughts of "She never asks me to do things, she just expects me to know". He felt helpless and angry. During this emotional session, J. shouted "She is my problem".

The therapist encouraged this exchange in order to point out the dangers of presumed mind reading. Each wanted to do the right thing for the other but without clarifying what the other was thinking, feeling and expecting of him, and an argument often ensued. The therapist used a behavioural task to facilitate direct communication and specific expectations. He asked the mother to list chores that she wanted J. to help with and asked J. to do one chore each day. This task helped her see that her expectations had to be made clear, and it helped J. feel important and contributory. The joint interview revealed hidden expectations and beliefs that would only less likely have surfaced during individual sessions.

Family Dynamics

Depressed adolescents often have an enmeshed family pattern (Minuchin 1974); the patient and at least one parent tie their moods and behaviour to the others' internal state. To intervene in this pattern, we developed the Dyadic Mood Monitor Technique. Consider J., the 13-year-old whose visits with his father were associated with dysphoria. He reported, "I can't go out and enjoy myself if she (the mother) doesn't." To test this notion he was asked to complete an activity sheet according to a colour code. This is used traditionally with retarded depressed patients, allowing them to record the "mastery" (M) and "pleasure" (P) which they have experienced throughout the week. However, instead of rating M and P during the day, the mother and son were asked to colour in the compartments according to their *moods*: yellow for good, green for neutral, and red for being unhappy. Both mother and son completed these forms over one weekend and compared them during the next session. The patient had had a good time visiting his father, while the mother, however, was unhappy. In the joint session exaggeration of the cognitive distortion with humour (Beck et al. 1979, Chap. 4) was used to increase objectivity on both parts about their interaction.

The Dyadic Mood Monitor Technique can also be used with families of children with learning disorders (e.g. dyslexia). For example, a 13-year-old boy with depression and dyslexia had an overly involved 40-year-old mother with emotional lability that she tied to his behaviour. Both mother and patient monitored their own moods for 1 week. Results revealed that even when the mother was sad or preoccupied with the welfare of her son, he was, in fact, quite happy and cheerful, watching television or doing homework. These data helped distance her from her son and to become more objective and effective in applying sanctions to his undesirable behaviours.

This homework also facilitated a discussion of assumptions and expectations about child-rearing with her husband during the session. Her beliefs included "My role is emotional nurturance" and "My husband can't do it". She viewed her husband as quite uninvolved with child rearing, which further supported her hypertrophied sense of responsibility to assist her son whenever he was upset. The therapist tried to elicit evidence that she alone was responsible for her son's moods, but without success. Further discussion revealed that although the father worked many hours, when he was home, he often assisted his son in many ways when the son was upset and angry. The father's interventions were, in fact, rather effective. Reviewing these reports with the mother began to challenge her erroneous belief and to reduce her sense of total responsibility.

The homework assignment that followed was to divide overtly and equally between parents the task of emotional support for their son. A regular time when father and son were to talk over concerns was prescribed. The mother subsequently became more assertive as a disciplinarian and confident enough to take a week's holiday away from the family. As the patient improved, the marital discord became more overt. The parents eventually requested joint therapy. Issues of parental roles and meeting each other's expectations became targets of therapy. Cognitive couples therapy was conducted along previously described lines (Rush et al. 1980).

Discussion

Normal adolescence may sometimes threaten the very fabric of society with the newfound sexuality, physical strength and independence of young people. Coercive methods used with 6 year-olds are inappropriate with 16-year-olds. Adolescence must thus become the age of negotiation, but it can rapidly transform to one of nihilism if the negative ambivalence of adolescence is compounded by a depressive syndrome.

Cognitive therapy with adolescents is not a mere simplification of the techniques used with adults. Emphasis is placed more upon cognitive deficits than cognitive distortions, in contrast to adult therapy. Teaching adaptive, alternative problem-solving strategies may take time, and intervals between therapy can be longer than that with adults. This is partly because parents can act as co-therapists; in addition, specific life events such as school games, plays and vacations can provide useful homework tasks with which to judge and pace the course of therapy. These and other differences are illustrated in Table 2.

Table 2. Cognitive therapy for depressed adolescents

1. Diagnosis
   - 1.1 Evaluation of family members for depression.
   - 1.2 A brief cognitive evaluation is an important part of the initial assessment to aid the matching of intervention with symptoms.
2. Therapeutic alliance
   - 2.1 Cooperation with homework may be an insult to the adolescent's self-esteem.
   - 2.2 Non-compliance is more frequently of a cognitive nature.
   - 2.3 Premature identification of automatic thoughts can disrupt the therapeutic alliance.
   - 2.4 Emphasis is initially on cognitive deficits and not cognitive distortions.
3. Modes of communication
   - 3.1 Cognitive processes may be more visual or kinaesthetic.
   - 3.2 Role playing is more often needed for children with lexical-skill problems to teach empathy.
   - 3.3 Teaching vocabulary to decrease dichotomous thinking in adolescents is achieved by using a cognitive continuum.
   - 3.4 Adolescents may find communication at a metaphorical level easier than that at the traditional realistic, cognitive level when considering consequential and alternative thinking pattern.
4. Parental beliefs and perceptions
   - 4.1 Parents often feel guilty, which is cognitively reframed as concern to establish an alliance.
   - 4.2 The therapist may be perceived as a rival parent.
   - 4.3 Family beliefs must be defined empirically during sessions.
   - 4.4 A mood monitor can be used to decrease enmeshment.
5. Eliciting and countering automatic thoughts
   - 5.1 Examining of thoughts is felt as personal criticism.
   - 5.2 More time must be spent monitoring automatic thoughts before challenging them.
   - 5.3 Omnipotence needs to be confronted empirically.
   - 5.4 Outbursts of anger are opportunities to obtain automatic thoughts and dysfunctional beliefs.
   - 5.5 Parents are important as informational checks on reality (e.g. regarding the feeling that "I am no good").
   - 5.6 Establish the reinforcement patterns in the family and associated automatic thoughts in parents, patient and siblings.
   - 5.7 Concrete examples in therapy are often more effective than abstract ones.

Clinically, the sensitivity of the individual adolescent to emotional cues is an important prerequisite for his own recognition of the fact that there is a "problem". This illustrates the value of an assessment tool such as the symbol language battery (Weinberg and McLean 1986), which takes into account receptive and expressive prosody (Ross and Mesulain 1979; Ross 1981). However, whether this procedure is an essential guide to therapy is clearly speculative. Nevertheless training in the identification of emotions such as joy, sadness and anger is often the first major step with adolescents in helping them to develop empathy. They can then consider the consequences of their actions and, finally, alternative problem-solving skills can be cultivated. This ability to step outside one's egocentric perception may be age-dependent and confined to adolescents who have attained the Piagetian level of formal operations. Finally, the family context of the problem and operant reinforcement for the problem-solving behaviour must not be overlooked, as we have illustrated by the case vignettes.

Cognitive therapy with adolescents clearly has implications for the training of therapists. Not only should the therapist be competent and knowledgeable in cognitive therapy but also possess an intimate knowledge of normal human development, neuropsychology and family therapy. In particular, experience in "systems" thinking and circular causality as opposed to linear causality is fundamental to family therapy (Minuchin 1974; Haley 1971) As the family unit is often the setting for the adolescent's depression, initial assessment and therapy must involve the family. Therapists therefore need to be comfortable working in the family context and to be aware of the powerful coercive effects which they can exert.

Future research in this demanding area needs to be directed towards the accumulation of more data-based evaluations. The merits of its interventions have yet to be empirically validated, and the trend towards a generalization of cognitive therapy to depressed adolescents must therefore be tempered with caution. However, cognitive-behavioral strategies have already been used for developing impulse-control skills with pre-adolescent children. (Kendall and Braswell 1984), and a variety of social-skills training programmes incorporating cognitive techniques have produced beneficial results with older maladjusted children and adolescents (Sarason and Ganzer 1973; Spivak and Shure 1974). There are also anecdotal reports of cognitive therapy for mood disturbance in adolescents (McAdam 1986; Bedrosian 1981). However, future research into the neuropsychological substrate of depression is essential to guide the selection of the appropriate treatment intervention. Indeed, the very question of depression in adolescents still entails a degree of polemics (Cantwell 1983), and the presence of left-sided motor deficits and impaired performance IQ as described by workers such as Brumback and Stanton (1982), Weinberg and Emslie (1987), need to be confirmed by others. Children and adolescents are not only different from adults, they are also different from one another. They are continually developing neuropsychologically, and the symbol language battery demonstrates the individual idiosyncrasy of age-determined lexical skills. Developmental information on age-appropriate tasks can provide a meaningful guide for determining the interventions that are most suited to adolescent patients.

Despite all these reservations the empirical nature of cognitive therapy is very helpful in confronting the adolescent's hopelessness, suicidal ideation, narcisistic injury and omnipotence. The collaborative emphasis of cognitive therapy, with its heavy reliance on Socratic dialogue, encourages the parents to act as co-therapists, thus reducing their feelings of helplessness. In addition it encourages the family to examine its functioning at a behavioural, cognitive and emotional level. This facilities identification of dysfunctional family beliefs, expectations and attitudes that may inhibit the adolescent's striving for autonomy and identity.

References

American Psychiatric Association (1980) Diagnostic and statistical manual of mental disorders (DSM-III), 3rd edn. American Psychiatric Association, Washington, DC

Beck AT, Rush AJ, Shaw BF, Emery G (1979) Cognitive therapy for depression. Guilford, New York

Beck AT, Hollon SD, Young JE, Bedrosian RC, Budenz D (1985) Treatment of depression with cognitive therapy and amitriptyline. Arch Gen Psychiatry 42:142–148

Bedrosian RC (1981) The application of cognitive therapy techniques with adolescents. In: Emery G, Hollon SD, Bedrosian RC (eds) New directions in cognitive therapy. A casebook. Guilford, New York

Blackburn IM, Bishop S, Glen AIM, Whalley LJ, Christie JE (1981) The efficacy of cognitive therapy and pharmacotherapy, each alone and in combination. Br J Psychiatry 139:181–189

Brumback RA, Stanton RD (1982) A hypothesis regarding the commonality of right-hemisphere involvement in learning disability, attentional disorder, and childhood major depression. Percept Mot Skills 55:1091–1097

Brumback RA, Stanton RD, Wilson H (1980) Neuropsychological study of children during and after remission of an endogenous depressive episode. Percept Mot Skills 50:1163–1167

Burns DD (1980) Feeling good. Morrow, New York

Cantwell D (1983) Depression in children: clinical picture and diagnostic criteria. In: Cantwell D, Carlson GA (eds) Affective disorders in childhood and adolescents: an update. Spectrum, New York

Haley J (1971) Family therapy: a radical change: changing families. Grune and Stratton, New York

Holinger PC (1979) Violent deaths among the young. Recent trends in suicide, homicide, and accidents. Am J Psychiatry 136:1144–1164

Kendall PC, Braswell L (1984) Cognitive behavioral therapy for impulsive children. Guilford, New York

Kendall PC, Pelligrina D, Urbain ES (1981) In assessment strategies for cognitive-behavioural interventions. Academic, New York

Klein M (1963) The psycho-analysis of children. Institute for psychoanalysis. Hogarth, London

Maris R (1985) The adolescent suicide problem. Suicide Life Threat Behav 15:91–109

Minuchin S (1974) Families and family therapy. Harvard University Press, Cambridge

McAdam KE (1986) CBT and its application with adolescents. J Adolesc 9:1–15

Perris CA (1966) Study of bipolar (manic-depressive) and unipolar recurrent depressive psychoses. Acta Psychiatr Scand [Suppl] 42:149–189

Petti TA (1978) Depression in hospitalized child psychiatry patients: Approaches to measuring depression. Journal of the Am Acad Child Psychiatry 17:49–59

Piaget J (1977) The origin of intelligence in the child. Penguin, London

Piaget J (1979) Piaget's theory. In: Mussen PH (ed) Carmichael's manual of child psychology, vol 1. Wiley, New York

Ross ED (1981) The aprosodias. Arch Neurol 38:561–569

Ross ED, Mesulain MM (1979) Dominant language functions of the right hemisphere. Arch Neurol 36:144–148

Rush AJ, Shaw BF, Khatami M (1980) Cognitive therapy of depression. Utilizing the couples system. Cog Ther Res 4:103–113

Sarason IG, Ganzer VJ (1973) Modeling and group discussion in the rehabilitation of juvenile delinquents. J Consul Psychol 20:442–449

Spitzer RL, Endicott J, Robins E, (1978) Research diagnostic critera. Rationale reliability. Arch Gen Psychiatry 5:773–782

Spivak G, Shure MB (1974) Social adjustment of young children: a cognitive approach to solving real life problems. Jossey-Bass, San Francisco.

Weinberg WA (1982) Delayed symbol language skills and its relationship to school performance. Diagnosis and management. In: Swaiman FK, Wright FS (eds) The practice of pediatric neurology. Mosby, St Louis, pp 1098–1120

Weinberg WA, Emslie G (1987) Attention deficit disorder: a form of childhood depression or other disorders of the brain. International Pediatrics 2:135–145

Weinberg WA, McLean A (1986) A diagnostic approach to developmental specific learning disorders. J Child Neurol 1:158–171

Weinberg WA, Rutman J, Sullivan L, Penick EC, Dietz SG (1973) Depression in children referred to an educational diagnostic centre: diagnosis and treatment. J Pediatr 83:1065–1073
Winokur G, Clayton PJ, Reich T (1969) Manic depressive illness. Mosby, St Louis

Author Index

Abend, S.M. 224
Abraham, S.F. 306, 311
Abramson, L.Y. 49, 53, 103, 109, 111, 112, 124, 128, 210, 359
Adams, H.E. 324, 355, 356
Adler, A. 5, 6, 8, 10, 15, 16, 223, 227
Adler, D. 185
Adler, K, 223
Afonso, H. 290
Agrax, W.S. 309, 315, 317
Aimez, P. 307
Ainsworth, M.D.S. 67–72, 339
Aitken, R.C.B. 166
Alagaratnam, W.J. 105
Alanen, Y. 347
Alexander, F. 26, 49
Alibhai, N. 309
Altshuler, K.Z. 24
Anaximander, 3
Anderson, C.A. 44, 49, 53
Andrews, G. 264
Anbacher, H. 227
Anbacher, R. 227
Arendt, H. 6, 355
Arieti, S. 9, 25, 122, 330, 331, 335, 342, 347, 350, 351, 353, 355–358, 363
Aristoteles 4, 296
Arlow, J. 343, 352, 353
Arnkoff, D. 160, 277, 280, 285, 332
Arrianus 2
Asarnow, J. 12, 160
Ashworth, C.M. 108
Aubuchon, D.J. 358, 359
Aurelius, M. 2, 3, 5
Austin, N. 290
Austrin, H.R. 358, 359
Authier, J. 143
Axline, V.M. 291
Azima, H. 331

Bach, G.R. 290
Bacon, F. 4
Baddeley, A.D. 82
Bak, J.S. 114
Balint, M. 26, 144
Bancom, D.H. 124
Bandura, A. 33, 34, 49, 51, 175, 184, 280
Barlow, C.H. 192, 253–256, 261, 263–265
Baron, P. 71, 361
Barraclough, C. 326
Bartlett, F.C. 354
Bates, B.C. 69
Bateson, G. 47
Baudoin, C. 276
Baumgart, E.P. 109
Beales, S. 310
Beaumont, P.J.V. 306, 308, 311
Beck, A.T. 1, 2, 7, 9, 12, 14–17, 23, 24, 30, 31, 34, 37, 44, 48, 50, 58, 80, 86, 90–92, 99–102, 104–108, 108, 110, 111, 120–124, 126–131, 135, 144–146, 149, 150, 160–162, 165, 167, 168, 171, 173, 179, 182, 183, 187, 193, 198, 203, 206, 224, 226, 227, 229, 230, 250, 253, 256–268, 277, 278, 288, 310, 313, 315, 316, 324, 332, 333, 335, 337, 338, 341, 343, 348, 349, 351, 355, 356, 558, 359, 362, 377, 378, 386, 389, 396, 400, 403, 405
Beck, R.W. 104
Becker, R. 9
Bedrosian, R.C. 343, 358, 407
Beech, H.R. 377
Beitman, B.D. 326
Bell, S.M. 340
Bellack, A.S. 332
Bemis, K.M. 145, 309, 310, 315, 349
Bemporad, J. 122
Benedikt, 254
Beres, D. 343
Bergin, A.E. 147
Berman, J.S. 265
Bernstein, D.A. 288, 297
Bertanlaffy, L. 46
Bieber, I. 9, 25
Biller, H.B. 339, 341
Billings, A.G. 126, 128
Bing, E. 341
Biran, M. 194, 265
Birdwhistell, R. 276
Birk, L. 35
Bishop, S. 124, 164, 174
Bizarro, L. 290
Blackburn, I.M. 17, 101, 103–107, 109, 124, 125, 133, 145, 161–165, 171–174, 377, 382, 396
Blanchard, F.A. 314
Blaney, P.H. 107, 112, 123
Blatt, S.J. 110, 128, 134, 360, 361
Bleuler, M. 93
Blight, J.G. 19
Block, J.H. 286
Bloom, B.S. 286
Blumenthal, R.S. 339
Bonge, D. 114
Bonn, J. 193
Booraem, C.D. 202
Borkovec, T.D. 184, 288, 297
Boskind-Lodahl, M. 306
Bower, G.H. 44, 53, 82, 83, 123, 135
Bowlby, J. 11, 12, 14, 18, 21, 27, 63, 64, 66, 67, 69–74, 76, 130, 184, 338, 339, 340, 343, 362
Bowskill 312
Boyd, J.H. 170
Brady, J.P. 22
Braswell, L. 236, 407
Breger, A. 33, 34, 179
Breggin, P.R. 256
Breitenbach, R. 294
Breiter, H.J. 100, 109
Brenver, D. 310
Bretherton, I. 64, 66, 67, 70
Breuer, J. 10
Brewin, C.R. 113
Brinkley-Birk, A.W. 35
Brody, E. 326

Brown, G.W. 73, 76, 126, 326, 341
Brown, L.B. 310
Brown, R.A. 115
Bruch, H. 20, 38
Bruner, J.S. 46
Brumback, R.A. 398, 407
Buber, M. 330
Bumberry, W. 134
Burns, D.D. 402, 403
Burns, L.E. 184
Burrows, G.D. 255
Burstein, A. 353
Busse, T.V. 341
Butcher, P. 21
Butler, G. 260
Byrne, D. 223

Cacioppo, J.T. 99
Cameron, R. 324, 364
Campbell, D.T. 271
Campbell, E.A. 113, 124
Cancro, R. 327, 328, 338
Cane, D.B. 109
Cantwell, D. 407
Capitanio, J.P. 339
Carroll, L. 24
Cartwright, R.D. 81
Cash, T.F. 114, 125, 132, 133
Cautela, J.R. 33
Cerny, J.A. 264
Chamberlain, K. 104
Chambless, D.J. 101, 180
Champion, L.A. 122
Charney, D.S. 255
Chatham, P.M. 224
Cheek, F.E. 340
Chess, S. 73
Chomsky, N. 48
Ciarlo, J.A. 143
Cicchetti, D. 63
Cicero, 2, 3
Ciompi, L. 328
Clark, D. 190, 191, 193, 255, 257, 259, 261–263, 266, 268
Clement, P.F. 312, 314
Clements, C. 291
Coché, E. 364
Cohen, J. 144
Cohen, R. 202
Colby, K.M. 24, 37
Conte, H.R. 165
Cooley, C.H. 293
Cooper, P.J. 307–310, 312, 314
Cordle, C.J. 316, 317
Corsini, R. 199, 223
Coryell, W. 110
Cottraux, J. 188, 380
Coué, E. 189, 276
Covi, L. 164, 198, 203, 221
Coyne, J.C. 112, 120, 124, 260
Craighead, W.E. 332
Craik, K.J.W. 48, 84
Cramer, B. 47
Crandell, C.J. 101, 114
Craske, M.G. 254, 255
Crowe, R. 255
Crowley, R.M. 25
Crowne, D. 104
Crowther, J.H. 310
Crumley, F.E. 339
Cullari, S. 307, 311

Danker-Brown, P. 124
Dann, S. 339
Dark, V.J. 82
Davanloo, H. 25, 26, 30
Davies, D.R. 82
Davies, E. 310
Davis, W.L. 358
Davison, G.C. 9, 34, 35, 268, 315
Dawson, M.E. 329, 338
Day, M. 330
Debs, 310
Dember, W.N. 1
Dempsey, P. 166
Dent, H.R. 378, 381, 393
Dent, J. 122, 123, 125, 127, 132, 133
Depue, R.A. 136
Derry, P.A. 127, 132
Deutsch, H. 29
Dewald, P.A. 29, 35
Dobson, K.S. 100, 109, 122, 124, 127, 154
Docherty, J.P. 326
Dollard, J. 10, 34
Domarus, E. von, 350
Donchin, E. 86
Dow, M.G. 332
Dryden, W. 62, 63, 332
Duncan-Johnson, C.C. 84, 86
Dunn, R.J. 168, 169
D'Zurilla, T. 283, 284

Eagle, M. 19, 20
Eastman, C. 184
Eaves, G. 100, 110, 112, 124, 132
Eccles, J.C. 58
Edelman, B. 306
Edwards, A.L. 103
Ehrlichman, H. 87
Eich, J.E. 82
Einhorn, H.J. 349
Eisemann, M. 93, 325
Eisler, R.M. 185
Eissler, K. 331
Elkin, I. 149
Elkind, D. 360, 361
Ellis, A. 2, 3, 6, 8, 9, 23, 31, 34, 69, 99, 104, 113, 114, 160, 186, 187, 192, 194, 277, 278, 282, 286, 316, 367,
Emde, R.N. 64
Emery, G. 7, 16, 145, 160, 167, 179, 182, 183, 187, 193, 257–259, 262–264, 268, 324, 333, 337, 349, 362
Emmelkamp, P. 185, 186, 191, 192, 256, 265
Emslie, G. 407
Epictetus, 2, 3
Epstein, N. 368
Erikson, H.E. 63, 330
Erlenmeyer-Kimling, L. 326
Espie, C.A. 377
Estes, W.K. 83
Eunson, K.M. 107
Evans, D.R. 143
Eysenck, H.J. 33, 34, 114, 132
Eysenck, S.B.G. 132

Fairbairn, W.R. 37
Fairburn, C.G. 306–309, 312–317, 319
Fairweather, G.W. 202
Farber, L.H. 38
Farkas, G.M. 34, 37, 38
Fast, J. 276
Faust, M.S. 309
Fazio, A.F. 168, 169
Feather, B.W. 35
Federn, P. 330, 331
Feffer, M. 360
Feighner, J.P. 161, 168
Feinsilver, D.B. 326
Fennel, M.J. 113, 124, 174
Ferrante, A. 359
Field, T. 64, 338, 339
Fishman, C. 291
Flavell, J.H. 47
Flax, J. 19, 23
Fleiss, J.L. 170
Flick, A. 364
Flowers, J.V. 202
Foa, E.B. 377, 386
Ford, D.H. 8–10, 14, 15, 141
Foreyt, J.P. 160
Forrest, T. 339
Fox, N.A. 339
Fox, S. 160
Fradique, F. 286–289
Franceschini, E. 18–20, 21, 355

Frank, G.H. 340, 341
Frank, J. 13, 14, 22, 34, 55, 140, 144, 343
Frankl, V. 58
Franks, C. 31
Freeman, A. 27, 224, 227, 229, 324
Freeman, C. 311, 317
Freeman, T. 360, 361
French, T. 26, 49
Freud, A. 29, 277, 330, 339
Freud, S. 2, 8, 10, 19, 21–23, 29, 49, 50, 63, 73, 130, 223, 277, 327, 328, 330, 347, 352, 353
Friedman, A. 164
Fromm, E. 10
Fromm-Reichmann, F. 330, 331, 339, 342
Frost, R.O. 314
Frye, N. 10
Fuchs, C.Z. 168, 169, 204
Furnham, A. 309, 310
Fuson, K.C. 352

Gagné, R.M. 281
Gallagher, D.E. 168
Gallimore, R.G. 54
Ganzer, V.J. 407
Garamoni, G.L. 185, 186
Gardner, H. 63
Garfield, S.L. 22, 140, 144
Garfinkel, P.E. 306, 308, 310, 314
Garmezy, N. 340
Garner, D.M. 145, 306, 309–311, 313–315, 349
Garssen, B. 190
Gelder, M. 191
Genest, M. 99, 160
George, L. 329
Gershman, H. 23
Gibbons, D.E. 298
Gibson, J.J. 68
Giles, D.E. 17, 90
Gill, M.M. 46
Gilligan, S.G. 82
Gittleson, N. 388
Glen, A.I.M. 170, 173
Goisman, R.M. 25, 35, 36
Goldberg, D. 175
Golden, W. 62, 63
Goldfried, M. 9, 22, 31, 34, 35, 37, 68, 268, 280, 283, 284, 315, 362, 367
Goldiamond, 33
Goldstein, A. 377
Goldstein, A.T. 180
Goldstein, W. 224
Golin, S. 112, 124
Gong-Guy, E. 201
Goodenough, D.R. 81
Gorman, J. 190, 254
Götestam, K-G. 12, 17, 122, 125, 130–133
Gottlib, I.H. 112, 120, 124, 134, 260
Gray, J. 183
Greenberg, L.S. 67, 68
Greenberg, R.L. 206, 267
Greene, S.M. 102
Greenson, R. 29
Greenson, R.R. 343
Greenwood, V. 324, 342, 344, 349, 358, 359, 368
Grieger, R. 186, 192
Griez, E. 190, 255, 256, 261
Griffiths, R.A. 316
Grimm, L.G. 205
Grinker, R.R. 166
Grossberg, J.M. 34
Grünbaum, A. 18–20, 22, 37
Guidano, V.F. 7, 11, 63, 74–77, 182, 277, 283, 285, 338, 339, 349, 362, 366
Gunderson, J. 224, 326, 330, 331, 368

Habermas, J. 19
Hager, W. 82
Hakstian, A.R. 160, 168, 169
Haley, J. 291, 407
Hall, C. 223
Halmi, K.A. 307, 310
Hamilton, E.W. 103, 109, 112, 124
Hamilton, M. 103, 161
Hammen, C. 106, 110, 112, 122, 123, 125–130, 133, 134, 201
Hand, I. 202
Harlow, H.F. 65
Harmon, R.J. 64
Harrell, T.H. 100
Harris, J.C. 228
Harris, T. 73, 76, 126
Harrison, J. 378
Harrow, M. 359
Hartman, H. 19, 29
Harvey, D. 112
Hathaway, S.R. 100
Havens, L.L. 331
Hawkins, R.C. 312, 314
Hayek, F. 280
Headland, K.S.E. 393
Hebb, D.O. 82
Heider, F. 367
Heilbrun, A.B. 340
Hemsley, D.R. 261
Heraklitus, 46
Herink, R. 140
Herman, C.P. 311, 312, 314
Hersen, M. 332
Hetherington, E.M. 339
Hewstone, M. 108
Hibbert, G.A. 182, 183, 261
Hilgard, E.R. 352
Hillyard, S.A. 84, 86
Himle, D.P. 114
Hinde, R.A. 65, 69
Hinsdale, G. 310
Hirsch, B.J. 73
Hirsch, S.R. 340
Hjelle, 223
Hodgson, R.J. 378, 381
Hogarth, R.M. 349
Hole, R.W. 324, 355, 356
Holinger, P.C. 396
Hollender, M. 36
Hollon, S.D. 17, 99, 100, 109, 130, 132, 134, 145, 160, 163, 181
Holroyd, K.A. 160
Holt, R.R. 18, 20, 353
Homme, L.E. 33
Horney, K. 8, 10, 12, 15, 326
Horowitz, M.J. 21, 25, 26, 130, 224
Hout, A. van den, 190, 255, 256, 261
Hoyt, M.F. 30
Huenemann, R.L. 310
Hume, D. 4, 5, 32
Hunt, R. 286
Huon, G.F. 307, 310
Hymowitz, P. 331

Ingham, J.G. 71
Inhelder, B. 56, 66, 68, 71, 276, 283, 284, 361
Ingram, R.E. 135
Ivey, A.E. 143, 280, 281
Ivison, D.J. 308, 309

Jacobs, L. 324, 351, 355, 356, 359, 361, 362
Jacobson, E. 20
James, W. 276, 362
Janis, I. 281
Janoff-Bulman, R. 49
Jansson, L. 343
Jarrett, R.B. 264, 266
Jaspers, K. 327
Jaynes, J. 62
Jerremalm, A. 193
Johnson, C. 307, 312, 314
Johnson, D. 292
Johnston, W.A. 82
Jolly, A. 339
Jones, E. 352
Jones, R.B. 264

Jones, R.G. 114
Joyce-Moniz, L. 280, 281, 286–288, 290
Judd, F.K. 255
Jung, C.G. 8, 281

Kahnemann, D. 94, 182, 349
Kamiya, J. 87
Kandel, E. 183
Kanfer, F.H. 114, 205
Kant, I. 5,6
Kaplan, A.S. 308
Karasu, T.B. 36, 326
Katerndahl, D.A. 254
Katz, J.L. 308
Katzman, M.A. 306, 307, 310
Kazdin, A.E. 276
Kegan, R. 301
Keller, M.B. 170
Kelley, K. 223
Kelly, G. 11, 15, 44, 46, 108, 281, 291, 310, 340, 344
Kemali, D. 82, 93
Kendall, P.C. 17, 99, 107, 109, 115, 130, 134, 160, 236, 401, 407
Kendler, K.S. 355
Kernberg, O. 37, 224
Kiesler, D.J. 141
Kihlström, J.F. 122
Kilburg, R. 360, 361
Kilpatrick, 347
Kimper, T.P. 285
King, P. 301
Kirk, J. 381
Kirkley, B.G. 309, 317
Kirschenbaum, D.S. 317
Kitchener, K. 301
Klein, D.F. 140, 184, 253, 263
Klein, G. 13, 19, 20, 353, 355, 356
Klein, M. 37, 63, 330, 400
Klüwer, H. 46
Knorring, L. von, 82, 93
Kogerski, G.P. 99, 107, 115
Kohlberg, L. 290, 301, 302
Kohut, H. 10, 19, 49, 343, 347
Konorsky, J. 83
Kornblith, S.H. 167–169, 204
Koukkou, M. 80, 82, 83, 86–90
Kovacs, M. 90, 99, 102, 120, 121, 164, 171, 173
Kovel, J. 24
Krantz, S. 106, 201
Krasner, L. 33, 34, 36
Kris, E. 353
Kriss, M.R. 181
Kuhlo, W. 87
Kuhn, T.S. 37, 366
Kuiper, N. 127, 132
Kutas, M. 84, 86

Ladouceur, R. 194
Lakatos, I, 11, 12, 45, 366
Lambert, M.J. 147
Landau, M. 62
Landy, R. 292, 294
Lane, R.C. 340
Lang, P.J. 264
Langer, E.J. 115
La Pointe, K.A. 114
Larson, R. 312
Larsson, U.B. 336
Lashley, K.S. 46
Last, C. 185, 262
Lazarus, A.A. 31, 35, 187, 291
Lazarus, R.S. 66
Lee, 317
Lefcourt, H.M. 359
Leff, J. 74, 326, 340, 341
Lehmann, D. 80, 82, 86–90,
Leibniz, 280
Leitenberg, H. 312, 316
Leon, G.R. 307
Levenson, H. 358, 359
Leventhal, H. 67, 82, 83
Lewidge, B. 31, 175
Lewin, K. 50
Lewinsohn, P.M. 115, 122, 125, 126, 128, 133, 141, 166, 167, 203
Ley, R. 191
Lidz, T. 350, 361
Liebowitz, M.R. 193, 254
Liem, J.M. 340
Lindzey, G. 223
Lineham, M.M. 103
Lion, J.R. 224
Liotti, G. 1, 2, 7, 10–12, 29, 37, 62–64, 74–77, 182, 277, 283, 285, 335, 338, 339, 349, 362, 366, 367,
Lipman, R.S. 198, 221
Loftus, E.F. 56
Lohr, J.M. 114
Long, C.G. 316, 317
Lorentz, K. 65
Lorraine, S. 330, 331
Loveless, N. 86
Lu, Y.C. 340
Ludwig, A.M. 367
Lum, L.C. 191, 262
Lundh, L-g. 11, 44, 54, 57, 67
Lunghi, M.E. 260
Lungwitz, H. 9
Luria, A. 189, 273, 364
Lynn, R. 90

Mac Donald, A.P. 358
Mac Hovec, F.J. 3, 4
Mac Lean, P.D. 65, 69, 144, 160, 168, 169
Machleidt, W. 87
Mack, D. 314
Macnamara, J. 47
Mahler, M. 363
Mahoney, K. 201, 276, 279, 281, 316, 317
Mahoney, M.J. 1, 3, 7, 9, 13, 21, 31, 32, 34, 37, 160, 201, 260, 276, 277, 279–281, 283, 285, 316, 317, 366
Main, M. 69, 70, 75
Malan, D. 26, 144
Mallinger, A. 27, 350
Manly, P.C. 124
Mann, J. 26, 30
Mannuzza, S. 255
Manske, W. 88
Marcus, M.D. 306
Marcus, N. 27
Margraf, J. 180
Maris, R. 396, 403
Marks, I. 179, 192, 390
Markus, H. 127, 366
Marlatt, G.A. 314, 315
Marlow, D. 104
Marshall, W.L. 166
Martin, A.R. 24
Martin, M. 132. 133
Marzillier, J.S. 184
Masterson, J.F. 223, 224
Matarazzo, R.G. 143, 144, 147
Mathews, A. 260
Matte-Blanco, I. 350
Matussek, P. 330, 331
Maudler, G. 44, 58, 83
Mavissakalian, M. 192
Mayer, J.D. 83
Mc Adam, K.E. 407
Mc Clure, M.N. 255
Mc Crea, C.W. 314
Mc Donald, R. 393
Mc Dougall, W. 50
Mc Gaugh, J.L. 33. 34. 179
Mc Ghie, A. 360, 361
Mc Kinley, J.C. 100
Mc Kinney, J. 281
Mc Lean, A. 398, 406
Mc Nair, D.M. 107, 264
Mead, G.H. 291
Mecklenbraucher, S. 82
Meichenbaum, D. 5, 9, 12, 31, 160, 189, 191, 192,

194, 236, 263, 264, 276, 279, 281, 283, 285, 299, 324, 364
Merikangas, K.R. 254
Merluzzi, T.V. 17
Mersch, P. 192, 256, 265
Mesulain, M.M. 406
Messer, S.B. 10, 35
Messick, S. 314
Metalsky, G.J. 124
Meyers, A. 364
Michant, S. 307
Michelson, P.D. 264
Miller, N.E. 10, 34
Millon, T. 224
Mindham, R.H.S. 170, 173
Minkoff, K. 102, 104
Minuchin, S. 291, 400, 404, 407
Molen, G.M. van der, 180
Mollard, E. 188
Monbreun, D.G. de, 285
Mongrain, M. 125, 128–130, 133
Monroe, R.A. 276
Monti, P.R. 185
Moos, R.H. 126, 128
Mora, G. 3
Moreno, J. 291, 297
Morin, C.M. 318
Morita, S. 8
Morris, L.A. 55, 163
Murphy, G.E. 162, 164, 165, 172, 174
Murray, E.J. 10

Nardo, P.A. di, 255
Nasby, W. 122
Neisser, U. 44, 82, 84, 85, 91, 362
Nekauda-Trepka, C.J.S. 103
Nelson, K. 47
Nelson, R.E. 114
Neu, J. 4
Neufeld, R.W.J. 329
Neumann, O. 83, 84
Nevid, J.S. 103, 104
Newman, F.L. 143
Newmark, C.S. 114
Nezu, A. 284
Nielsen, S.L. 103
Nisbett, R.E. 115
Norcross, J.C. 147
Norman, D.A. 83, 84
Norman, W.H. 107, 260
Norton, G.R. 255
Novaco, R. 160, 236, 276, 282
Noy, P. 353, 354
Noyes, R. 255, 256
Nuechterlein, K.H. 329, 338

Offenkrantz, W. 25, 26, 30
O'Hara M.W. 112
Öhman, A. 86–87, 88
Olinger, L.J. 125, 129, 130, 133
Oliver, J.M. 109
Ollinen, K. 341
Ordman, A.M. 317
O'Reilly, J. 340
Orne, M.T. 140, 141
Overton, D.A. 81

Padawer, W. 22
Palm, A. 324
Palm, U. 324
Palmer, R.L. 306
Papsdorf, J.D. 114
Parasuraman, R. 82
Parker, G. 340, 341
Parkes, C. 64, 67
Parloff, M.B. 140, 335
Paul, G.L. 140
Pavlov, 46, 47
Paykel, E. 126, 128
Peale, N.V. 276
Penfield, W. 58
Perls, F. 291
Perris, C. 1, 12, 27, 37, 82, 93, 136, 227, 324, 325, 327, 328, 333, 334, 338, 341, 343, 348, 364, 365, 396
Perris, H. 325, 327
Persons, J.B. 112, 125, 127, 133
Peterfreund, E. 10, 13, 14, 17, 19–21, 23, 37, 328, 338–340, 353, 355, 362, 363
Peterson, C. 111–112, 124, 128
Petrie, K. 104
Petti, T.A. 397
Petty, R.E. 99
Phares, E.J. 358
Phelps, S. 290
Piaget, J. 11, 44, 46, 50, 56, 182, 276, 278, 280, 281, 283, 284, 290, 351, 360, 361, 401
Piety, K.R. 340
Pine, F. 12
Pitts, F.N. 255
Plato, 2, 3
Pokorny, A.D. 102
Poliby, J. 311, 312
Pope, H.G. 307, 309
Popper, K. 19, 58
Posner, M.I. 44, 57, 84
Power, M.J. 122
Price, J. 185

Prichep, L.S. 93
Prien, R.F. 173
Prigogine, I. 366
Primakoff, L. 146, 221
Prioleau, L. 55
Prochaska, J.O. 147
Proktor, E.K. 143
Pure, D.L. 314
Pyle, R. 309, 311

Rabin, A.I. 350, 351
Rabkin, J.G. 140
Racamier, P.C. 330
Rachman, S.J. 33, 183, 377, 378, 381, 386, 392
Raimy, V. 23
Rank, O. 8, 10, 13, 14
Rao, P.A. 112, 125, 127, 133
Rapaport, D. 18, 82, 277, 353, 356
Rapee, R.M. 261, 263
Rappoport, A. 192, 256, 265
Raps, C.S. 112
Raskin, A. 169
Rathjen, D.P. 160
Ray, J.B. 114
Read, S.J. 362, 367
Reda, M. 1, 2, 11, 110, 338
Redman, W.K. 307, 309, 311
Rehm, L.P. 99, 114, 160, 168, 169, 202, 204
Reid, W.H. 224
Reische, T.M. 73
Reite, M. 64, 338, 339
Rendon, M. 25
Reus, V.I. 82
Reynolds, D.K. 8
Rhoads, J.M. 35
Rholes, W.S. 122–125, 131, 133, 134
Richfield, J. 367
Ricoeur, P. 19
Riegel, K. 280
Rishovd Rund, B. 361
Riskind, J.H. 122, 123
Robbins, M. 37
Robins, C. 68, 280, 362, 367
Roeder, H. 347
Rogers, C. 8, 10, 14
Rohner, E.C. 358
Rohrbaugh, J.W. 86, 88, 90
Rose, S.D. 202
Rosen, A. 143
Rosen, J.C. 312, 316
Rosen, J.N. 331, 347
Rosenbaum, M. 114, 174
Rosenberg, B. 199
Rosenfeld, H.A. 331
Ross, E.D. 406
Rossiter, E.M. 318, 319
Roth, D.M. 201, 203, 221

Rotter, J. 115, 184
Roy, A. 136
Rubeis, R.J. de, 163
Rubins, J.L. 326, 330, 331, 347
Rubinstein, B.B. 20
Rucker, M.S. 331
Rush, A.J. 17, 24, 90, 100, 105, 110, 112, 124, 132, 145, 161–165, 170, 171, 198, 256, 317, 377, 405
Russell, B. 67
Russell, G. 306–308
Rutter, M. 63, 326
Rychlak, J.F. 5, 6
Ryle, A. 2, 21, 24, 30, 354
Ryon, N.B. 100

Sacco, W.P. 134
Safran, J.D. 67, 68
Sagarin, E. 367
Saletu, B. 82
Salkovskis, P.M. 193, 263, 376–378, 380, 381, 386, 387, 389, 390, 392, 393
Salmon, P. 340
Salovey, P. 367
Sambrailo, F. 316, 317
Sandler, J. 29
Santrock, J.W. 339
Sarason, I.G. 129, 407
Sass, L.A. 348
Saul, L.J. 224
Schafer, R. 10, 343
Schatzman, M. 73
Scheff, T.J. 291, 297
Schleimer, K. 310
Schneider, J.A. 315, 317
Schneider, W. 44, 54, 57, 58, 83–85
Schonbar, R.A. 367
Schultz, J. H. 297
Schultz, O. 223
Schwartz, R.M. 9, 32, 34, 185, 186
Searless, H. 330, 342, 351
Sechehaye, M. 331
Segal, Z.V. 146, 260
Seligman, M.E.P. 53, 99, 111, 201
Selman, R. 300
Semrad, E.V. 330
Seneca, 2, 3
Shapiro, A.K. 55, 140, 163
Shapiro, D. 265
Shapiro, D.A. 265
Shaw, B.F. 122, 124, 127, 141, 142, 144, 146, 147, 154, 155, 156, 166, 198, 202, 260
Sheehan, D.V. 180, 255
Sheehan, K. 180
Shepherd, G. 332
Sherman, M. 223
Shiffrin, R.M. 44, 54, 57, 58, 83–85
Shipley, C.R. 168, 169
Shorkey, C.T. 114
Shotter, J. 340
Shulman, B.H. 25, 330
Shure, M.B. 407
Siegel, A. 360, 361
Siegel, J.M. 364
Sifneos, P.E. 25, 26, 144
Silva, P. de, 378
Silverman, J.S. 120, 124
Silverman, L.H. 35
Simon, K.M. 229
Simons, A.D. 95, 101, 109, 115, 124, 132, 145, 147, 164, 171, 172, 174
Singer, J.L. 115, 340
Singer, W. 338
Skimer, B.F. 32, 46, 50
Slade, P. 309, 310
Sloane, R. 343
Smith, M.L. 140
Smyth, P. 124, 125, 133
Snaith, R.P. 103
Snyder, M. 54
Socrates, 3
Sokolov, E.N. 48, 87
Sollod, R.N. 360–362
Solomon, J. 69
Speers, M. 277
Spielberger, C.D. 100, 264
Spinoza, B. 4, 5
Spitzer, R.L. 100, 103, 161, 164, 255, 397
Spivak, G. 364, 407
Spohn, H. 331
Sroufe, 63, 340
Stanley, J.C. 271
Stanton, R.D. 407
Stefanek, M.E. 185
Stekel, W. 16
Stern, D. 47
Steuer, J.L. 168
Stevenson-Hinde, J. 64
Stiles, T.C. 12, 17, 122, 125, 130–133
Stravynski, A. 193
Strien, T. van, 314
Strupp, H.H. 22, 23, 140, 144
Stunkard, A.J. 306, 314
Sullivan, H.S. 8, 10, 12, 13, 16, 17, 63, 330, 340
Swann, W.B. 54, 362, 367
Szalita-Pemow, A. 330, 348

Taylor, C.B. 264
Taylor, F.G. 165
Tarrier, N. 326
Teasdale, J.D. 55, 120, 122, 123, 125, 127, 132, 135, 161–165, 174
Thomson, L.W. 168
Thorndike, E.L. 32
Thorpe, R.E. 184
Thyer, B.A. 114, 184
Timmermans, P. 184
Tissot, R. 182
Tobin, A. 25, 26, 30
Tolman, E.C. 48
Tomarken, A.J. 82, 83
Torgersen, S. 136
Touyz, S.W. 308, 309
Tower, R.B. 115
Triebel, A. 331
Trower, P. 332
Tulving, E. 56
Turk, D.C. 99, 160, 263, 364, 277, 367
Turner, J.L. 54
Tversky, A. 182, 349
Tyrer, P. 253

Ullmann, L.P. 33, 34
Urban, H.B. 8–10, 14, 15, 141
Ursin, H. 94

Vaihinger, H. 6
Vallis, I.M. 142, 146, 147, 150, 155
Vaughn, J.P. 74, 326, 341
Vygotsky, L.S. 276. 351, 352

Wachtel, P.L. 34, 36, 360–362
Waddell, M.T. 263
Wallace, C.J. 331
Wardle, J. 306, 309–314
Waring, E.M. 368
Warner, S. 224
Warwick, H.M.C. 377, 386, 387, 390
Waskow, I.E. 141
Waters, E. 64, 340
Watkins, J.T. 105, 162, 163, 165
Watson, G. 341
Watson, J. 32, 276
Watts, A.W. 58
Webb, W.B. 81
Wegman, C. 21
Weimer, W.B. 280
Weinberg, W.A. 397, 398, 406, 407
Weiner, B. 111
Weintraub, M. 105

Weiss, L. 312
Wessler, R.A. 6, 62, 63, 66
Wessler, R.L. 6, 62, 63
Weissman, A.E. 108, 124, 129, 167, 341
Weissman, M.M. 161, 170, 254, 255
Westbrook, D. 387, 392, 393
Wetzel, R.D. 102
Wexler, M. 331
Whitehead, A. 161, 164
Whitehouse, A.M. 311
Whiteman, V.L. 114
Whitt, J.K. 114
Wiener, M.S. 87
Wild, C.M. 360, 361
Wilkins, W. 140
Wilkinson, I.M. 104–106
Will, O. 330
Willenson, D. 341
Williams, J.B.W. 255
Williams, J.M.G. 161, 164, 192
Williams, S.L. 256, 265
Wilson, G.T. 1, 31, 194, 315, 316, 318, 319
Wilson, P.H. 166, 167
Wilson, T.D. 115
Wing, J. 174, 331
Winnicott, D.W. 16, 331
Winokur, G. 396
Winokur, M. 10, 35
Wolberg, I.L. 26, 29, 30
Wolchik, S.A. 310
Wolf, E.M. 310
Wolfe, B.E. 253, 255, 265
Wolley, O.W. 309, 310
Wolley, S.C. 309, 310
Wolpe, J. 8, 10, 30, 31, 179, 260, 264, 291
Woodward, R. 264
Wundt, W. 276

Yalom, I.D. 199, 202, 212
Yates, A.J. 316, 317
Yates, B.T. 326
Yeap, S.S. 307, 309
Yesavage, J.A. 6
Young, J. 146, 150, 349, 363

Zajonc, R.B. 66, 183
Zautra, A.J. 112
Zeiss, A.M. 166, 167
Zeno 3
Ziegler, 223
Zimmerman, M. 110
Zuckerman, M. 111
Zung, W.W.K. 169, 264
Zuroff, D.C. 112, 125, 128–130, 133

Subject Index

ABC-model 86
Accident proneness 396
Accomodation 182
Acting out 298
Agoraphobia 76, 180, 182, 183, 186, 191, 192, 255
Alcohol dependency 160
Amitriptyline 163, 169, 171
Anorexia nervosa 308–310, 315, 319
Anxiety 54, 55, 87, 181, 182, 187, 190, 191, 208, 224, 229, 257, 258, 264, 268–270, 277, 299, 308, 312, 313, 377, 378, 380, 382, 393
  anticipatory 183
  generalized 182, 192, 253, 259, 264, 265, 267, 271
  persecutory 401
  separation 397
  social 193
  speech 193
  test 193
Arbitrary inference 107, 182, 258, 349
Arousal
  autonomic 266
  physiological 257, 259
As if 6, 295, 296, 299
ASQ, see Attributional Style Questionnaire
Assimilation 182
Assistant therapist 330, 331
Association
  principle of 4
Assumptions
  basic, dysfunctional 7, 26, 35, 64, 121, 187, 201, 206, 258, 259, 262, 269, 332, 337, 355, 362, 363
  depressogenic 48
  silent 12, 362, 378
ATQ, see Automatic Thoughts Questionnaire
Attachment 12, 67, 338, 339
  anxious 67, 69, 72, 75
  avoidant 67, 69, 71
  disorganized-disoriented 69, 71, 72
  father-child 339
  resistant 69, 71, 72, 75
  secure 67, 69, 70
  system 66, 68, 72, 73
  theory 64, 65, 338, 339
Attention
  regulation 328, 338
  selective 57, 258
Attitude(s)
  concretizing 356
  dysfunctional 91, 121, 130
  exploratory 70
  listening 358
  parental overprotective 74
    rearing 340
  referential 356, 358
Attributional style 53, 201
Attributional Style Questionaire 111–113, 115, 125, 128
Automatic Thoughts Questionaire 99–101, 109, 125, 130–132
Avoidance 379, 381, 393
  cognitive 390

Basic trust 330, 333
BDI, see Beck Depression Inventory
Beck Depression Inventory 100–102, 106–109, 111, 112, 114, 125, 128, 129, 131, 134, 161, 162, 166, 167, 169, 171, 172, 174, 207, 244, 288
Behaviourism
  methodological 32
  redical 32
Biofeedback 193
Body image 310, 314
Booster session(s) 9, 17, 30

Catastrophic thinking 186
Categorization 46
Catharsis 199
CBQ, see Cognitive Bias Questionnaire
Childhood amnesia 81
  memories 81
Claustrophobia 52
Clocks
  internal 89
Clomipramine 163
Cognitions
  automatic 201, 206
  intrusive 376
  Questionnaire 113
Cognitive
  appraisal 121
  Bias Questionnaire 106–108
  distortions 77, 121, 277, 310, 363
  errors 349

Cognitive
map(s) 48, 339
psychoanalysis 9
Response Test 105
restructuring 62, 188, 189, 192, 193, 264, 265, 268, 315, 317, 318
strategies, depressogenic 93–95
structures 45, 123, 343
Style Test 104–106
Therapy Scale 146–149, 151–153, 155, 156
-volitional school 9
Collaborative empiricism 14–16, 27, 333
Common sense 5
Compensation by exploration of possibilities 283, 285
identity 283, 284, 288
inversion 281, 283, 284, 288
reciprocity 281, 284
Concretization 351
Conditioning
covert 33
interoceptive 256
operant 32–34
Pavlovian 32
Cotherapist team 203
Countertransference 26, 27, 234, 242
Crandell Cognitions inventory 101
Creative painting 336
CST, see Cognitive Style Test
CTS, see Cognitive Therapy Scale

DAS, see Dysfunctional Attitude Scale
Decatastrophising 315, 387
Decentering 292, 294, 315, 360
Defensive exclusion 340
Delusional
beliefs 355
dimensions of 355, 356
experiences 354
phenomena 349
Demoralization 13, 22, 55
Depression 54, 55, 76, 90–92, 94, 99, 101, 102, 120, 124, 160, 205, 208, 213, 224, 229, 255, 257, 264, 308, 312, 313, 377, 378, 379, 382, 388, 389, 397, 398
about depression 55
bipolar 164
dependent 301
endogenous 100, 110
non-endogenous 100, 110
self-evaluative 302
-sacrificing 301
unipolar
Depressive Experience Questionnaire 110, 128
DEQ, see Depressive Experience Questionnaire
Desymbolization 351
Determinism
external 32
internal 32
reciprocal 33
Developmental
constructivism 281
-structural perspective 67
Dialogue
internal 185, 189, 276, 352, 364
Socratic 3, 187, 188, 266, 387, 407
Dichotomous
reasoning 311
thinking 6, 313, 349, 402
Dietary restraint 311, 313
Differential Activation Hypothesis 123, 133
Disequilibrium 366
Distancing 349
Distraction
cognitive 236
behavioral 238
Double-bind 47
Dysfunctional Attitude Scale 101, 108, 124, 125, 129, 130, 141

Eating disorders 76, 160, 307, 349
Egocentric feedback 354
Egoncentrism 4, 5, 71, 77, 360, 361
Empathy 3, 16, 205, 330, 343, 347, 401, 406
Equifinality 46
Equilibration 281
Ergänzungsreihe 327
Erkenntnistherapie 9
Event-related brain potential(s) 86
Experimental neurosis 47
Exposure 179, 182, 187, 191, 238, 265, 315, 316, 381, 382, 386–388, 390
Expressed Emotion (EE) 74
Extension 45, 48, 53, 59, 67

Facilitating environment 331
Fictionalism 6
Fictions 6
Flooding 192

Gedankenlautwerden 351, 358

Hallucinations
hypnagogic 87
Hallucinatory
experiences 354, 357
phenomena 349
Hermeneutics 19
Homework, assignment of 3, 9, 15, 17, 27–29, 1246, 186–188, 193, 207, 209, 217, 337, 345, 348, 390, 403, 405
Hopelessness Scale 101–104, 131
HS, see Hopelessness Scale
Hyperventilation 190, 191, 255, 262
Hysteria 182

Idols 4
Imipramine 164, 253
Information processing
state-dependent 80, 82
theory 21
Insight 367

Intension 45, 46, 48, 59, 67
Internality-externality 185, 359
Intuition, mutual 30
Irrational belief systems 185, 186, 192, 277, 282
Irrational Beliefs Test 114

Life events 55, 123, 129, 130, 326, 329
Locus ceruleus 190
Locus of control 184, 358
Logical errors 121, 257–259, 401

Magnification/minimization 258, 349
Majeutics, see Socratic dialogue
Master & Pleasure 207, 237, 404
Maternal rejection 71
Meaning 21
  cognitive-dialectical development of 281
  dimensions 45
  idiosyncratic 235
  information-processing theory 21
  precipitate attribution of 350
  private 258, 267, 268
  structure(s) 12, 44–46, 48, 50, 52, 53, 55–57, 59, 64, 67, 70
    activation of 53, 57
  systems, tacit 277
Memory
  -driven brain mechanisms 80
  episodic 56, 74, 77
  long-term 81
  semantic 56, 74, 77
  short-term 53
  storages (depressogenic) 81, 94
  structures 44
Mental state 54, 55, 59
Metathinking 355
Micro-training model 143
Misattribution 2, 358, 359, 363
Modeling
  cognitive 279, 283
  covert 316
  participant 188, 194
Moments of experience 12
Mood state-dependent retrieval 82
Mood-induction 132, 133
Mother permanence 340
Mothering 331
  good enough 16
Motor equivelence 46

Nortriptyline 165
Noumena 6

Obesity 201, 279, 319
Object
  permanence 340
  -relations 16, 18, 224
Orienting response 87, 88
Overgeneralization 107, 183, 258, 349
Overinclusiveness, egocentric 350

Paleologic 350
Panic
  attacks 182, 184, 192, 253–255, 261
  disorder 252, 254, 259
  epidemiology 254
Paradigm 37, 38
Paradoxical intention 187, 192
Partial reciprocity 282
Patient-therapist matching 144
Perceptualization 351
Peremptory ideation 355
Perfectionism 51, 52, 314
Personal constructs 44, 340
Personality 45, 223, 313
  disorders, treatment 8
    antisocial 224, 227, 241
    avoidant 227, 246
    borderline 224, 227, 242
    dependent 225, 227, 247
    histrionic 244
    narcissistic 227, 245
    obsessive-compulsive 248
    paranoid 239
    passive-aggressive
    schizoid 227, 240
    schizotypal 241
  multiple 76
Personalization 2, 107, 183, 258
"Phenomena" 6
Phobia
  simple 181, 182, 194
  social 51, 180
Placebo effect 22, 54, 55
Predicative identification 350
Primary process 20, 352–354, 360, 363
Private sense 5
Problem-solving 283, 364, 399, 400, 406
Processing
  automatic 84–87, 261
  control 84, 86
Prophylactic effect 170

Questioning, deductive 28

Rational Behavior Inventory 114
Rational Emotive Therapy 23, 187, 195, 278, 282, 288
Reality-testing 55, 278, 288
Reasoning errors 313
Reattribution 235, 287
Regression 354
Relapse prevention
  bulimia 314, 315
  depression 95, 172
Relatedness 330, 343
Relationship, therapist-patient 9, 15, 26, 36, 63, 188, 332, 333, 341, 398, 400
Repertory Grid Technique 108
Replacement imagery 235
Research plan(s) 12
Resistance 29, 36, 37, 231, 234

Retrieval, mood state-dependent 82
state-dependent 90
Role playing 238

Satori 4
Scaling 235
Schema(ta) 12, 14, 56, 66, 67, 91, 92, 94, 121, 135, 145, 182, 228, 233, 234, 250, 258, 259, 262, 350, 355, 362, 366
activation of 259
active 227
agoraphobic patients 76
antisocial personality disorder 241
apperceptive 6
avoidant personality disorder 246
borderline personality disorder 242
danger 181, 182, 184
delusiogenic 362
dependent personality disorder 247
depressogenic 92, 122, 134, 135
dormant 227
emotional 67
event vulnerability hypothesis 122, 123, 131, 133
histrionic personality disorder 244
narcissistic personality disorder 245
obsessive-compulsive personality disorder 248
paranoid personality disorder 249
schizoid personality disorder 240
schizotypal personality disorder 241
therapy 230
unconditional 363
vulnerability hypothesis 122, 133, 135
Schematic modification 231, 251
reinterpretation 231, 251
restructuring 231, 250, 251
Schizophrenogenic mother 339, 347
Secondary
gain 232
process 20, 352–354
Secure base 27, 343, 348
Selective
abstraction 107, 311, 313, 349
inattention 340
Self-
blame
concept 49, 145, 314
control 58, 168, 310
Schedule 114
efficacy 49, 51, 175, 184, 277
esteem 22, 49, 51, 62, 164, 311, 313, 315, 341, 345, 397
image 51, 335
instruction(s) 280, 281
schema 68, 75–77, 127, 132, 277, 362
statement(s) 285
worth 48
Semantic networks 44

Sociotropy-Autonomy Scale 110
Stimulus generalization 46
Strange-situation 69
Streaming 295
Structures
pre-operational 280
sensory-motor 280
Suggestion 22, 23
Suicidal
attempt(s) 102, 403
behaviour 103
Intent Scale 102, 104
Suicide 73, 104, 219, 396, 403
Superstitious thinking 311
Systematic desensitization 264

Therapeutic session(s), structure of 27, 36, 305, 208
Therapy Preference Scale 149
Thought(s)
automatic negative 55, 58, 131, 181, 257, 259, 356, 377, 387, 389, 400, 401, 404
dysfunctional 315
intrusive 377, 378, 388
listing 185
negative, anxiety-producing 263
obsessional 378
sampling 107
stopping 392
Training
assertiveness 185, 238, 277
autogenic 297
creativity 279
dramatic expression 278
reality 283
relaxation 194, 238, 288
self-instruction 194, 195, 277, 283, 284, 286, 290, 364
social skills 193, 332, 407
stress-inoculation 279
Transference 5, 26, 27, 35, 46
positive 330
Transmuting internalization 49

Unconscious 7, 11, 12

Value 45, 50, 51, 59, 67
Vicarious learning 34
Vomiting, self-induced 306, 307, 309, 312, 317, 318
Vulnerability 101, 120, 122, 124, 126, 127, 133, 229, 257, 262, 268, 270, 325–329, 338, 349, 359, 363

Working
memory 88, 93

Yanas 3

MIX
Papier aus verantwortungsvollen Quellen
Paper from responsible sources
FSC® C105338

If you have any concerns about our products,
you can contact us on
ProductSafety@springernature.com

In case Publisher is established outside the EU,
the EU authorized representative is:
Springer Nature Customer Service Center GmbH
Europaplatz 3, 69115 Heidelberg, Germany

Printed by Libri Plureos GmbH
in Hamburg, Germany